The
BOOKER T. WASHINGTON
Papers

The

BOOKER T. WASHINGTON

Papers

VOLUME 3
1889-95

Louis R. Harlan
EDITOR

Stuart B. Kaufman
ASSISTANT EDITOR

Raymond W. Smock
ASSISTANT EDITOR

University of Illinois Press
URBANA · CHICAGO · LONDON

© 1974 BY THE BOARD OF TRUSTEES OF THE UNIVERSITY OF ILLINOIS
MANUFACTURED IN THE UNITED STATES OF AMERICA
LIBRARY OF CONGRESS CATALOG CARD NO. 75-186345
ISBN 0-252-00410-8

To the Memory of
Margaret James Murray Washington

CONTENTS

Contents

CONTENTS

xi

CONTENTS

Contents

CONTENTS

ADDENDUM

xviii

ILLUSTRATIONS

INTRODUCTION

THE THIRD VOLUME OF *The Booker T. Washington Papers* traces Washington's career from the end of May 1889 until September 18, 1895, when Washington delivered what is often called the Atlanta Compromise address at the Cotton States and International Exposition in Atlanta, Georgia. The volume reveals Washington's gradual rise to prominence as an educator, race leader, and shrewd political broker. All of the characteristics of Washington's racial leadership after 1895 are foreshadowed in his years of relative obscurity before 1895.

Much of the volume relates to Washington's role as principal of Tuskegee Institute. In building his institution, he was also building a powerful base of operations for his growing influence with white philanthropists in the North. At the same time, Washington furthered his involvement with white southern politicians and community leaders in the interest of his school. He also inaugurated the Tuskegee Negro Conferences to extend his influence with black citizens of Macon County and other Black Belt counties of Alabama. Washington found outlet for his protean energy in overseeing all aspects of his school.

This volume also shows Washington's development as a racial spokesman. The Atlanta Compromise address influenced American race relations for decades. Yet the policies of gradualism, economic striving, and accommodation to existing social and political conditions that launched Washington into national prominence were present much earlier as thoughts in Washington's mind. For better or probably worse in American race relations, in 1895 Washington's accommodationism was an idea whose time had come. Whether it anticipated or arose out of conditions is a fine point. The great Reconstruction leader and civil rights advocate Frederick Douglass was dead. Washington, the Negro of the hour, emerged from the wings to bid for a place as the leader of his race.

Continuing an editorial policy established in Volume 2, the editors include much incoming correspondence. In the earlier volume this was necessary primarily to compensate for gaps in the documentary record and to give greater dimension to Washington's life and times. In this volume, however, the main reason for including incoming letters is to reveal the rich social history they contain. Incoming letters from members of Washington's family, including his sweetheart and third wife Margaret James Murray Washington, his daughter Portia Marshall Washington, his sister-in-law Mary A. Elliott, and others, provide additional insight into Washington's personal life. Letters from former Tuskegee students to their mentor also add depth to the papers. Letters of northern philanthropists and foundation agents, who supported Washington and his school regularly for years, often illustrate important friendships with Washington. Many of the donors to Tuskegee were women, often descendants of abolitionist families. Their role in reform movements and philanthropy deserves not to be overshadowed by that of the industrial millionaires such as Rockefeller and Carnegie, important though they also were.

The editors will not hereafter cite sources of quotations or literary allusions in Washington's speeches, except where their importance warrants mention. Many of the quoted passages appear in *Bartlett's Familiar Quotations*. Errors in annotation or attribution will be corrected in the next mention after discovery. Any textual errors will be cited in an Errata section in the introduction of the subsequent volume. Documents that involve conduct or allegations of a scandalous nature are included only if they substantially contribute to understanding Washington and his milieu. These references range from idle gossip to criminal conduct. Inclusion of a document does not mean a judgment of the validity of the statements it contains. Although the editors believe that the omission of names would be a disservice to history, in some cases they have avoided full identification of the persons involved, on the ground that the event itself and Washington's response to it are more important than the persons.

A number of documents cited in Volumes 2 and 3 from the Tuskegee Institute Archives were photocopied by our staff in 1968 and 1969. Subsequently the originals in Containers 1 through 19 were inadvertently destroyed by fire. In this and future volumes wherever reference is made to these documents the citation will include the words "original destroyed."

In this and subsequent volumes, letters from W. E. B. Du Bois are published with the permission of Mrs. Shirley Graham Du Bois and the University of Massachusetts Press, publishers of *The Correspondence of W. E. B. Du Bois* (Vol. I, 1973). No further publication of these letters is authorized without their consent.

The editors are pleased to announce the addition of two new members to the board of editors. Fritz J. Malval, director of the Hampton Institute Archives, has continued to help the editors in locating material in Hampton's rich holdings. Walter Rundell, Jr., chairman of the history department at the University of Maryland, has given the project valuable assistance not only in his departmental role, but in advice and support stemming from his familiarity with the field of historical editing.

In addition to those whose help was acknowledged in Volume 2, the editors would like to express their appreciation to the following:

John McDonough of the Library of Congress and Malcolm Thomas of the Library of the Religious Society of Friends, London, for bringing documents to our attention.

Dennis A. Burton of the National Archives and John D. Crerar, Jr., for their help in indexing the first two volumes and for designing a program for a computerized cumulative index.

John W. Blassingame and Pete Daniel, former assistant editors, for their continued interest and help.

M. A. Harris, president of Negro History Associates, for allowing the editors to reproduce an early Washington letter in his possession.

John D. Macoll, of the National Historical Publications Commission, and John S. Borden, Simone Reager, and David J. Wallace of the National Endowment for the Humanities, for their encouragement and suggestions.

The editors could not have done their work without the imaginative and painstaking work of the other members of the staff. They are Barry A. Crouch, the National Historical Publications Commission fellow in editing, Sadie M. Harlan, Janet Hearne, Nancy Hornick, Barbara S. Kraft, John Lenihan, Carolyn McCreesh, Virginia V. Molvar, Steven T. Neiditch, Hannah Schoenbach, Elaine Smith, and Dorothy J. Warren.

Students in the University of Maryland history department's graduate seminar in historical editing have helped in the annotation process. These are: Jay D. Allen, Bruce F. Ashkenas, Stephen P. Carlson, Elsie Freivogel, Spencer H. Gelband, James M. Hobbins, Donald A. Ritchie, Martha J. Ross, Eugene M. Sprague, and Thomas E. Weir, Jr.

The editors wish to thank the University of Maryland, sponsor of the project, and the various administrative officers and staff members who continue to provide valuable financial and institutional support. We wish to express our gratitude also to the National Endowment for the Humanities and the National Historical Publications Commission for their continued financial assistance.

The editors thank Richard L. Wentworth and Elizabeth Dulany of the University of Illinois Press for their unusual care and fostering interest in the launching and continuation of this series. They allowed extensive illustration through photographs, which are themselves documents of a kind, and provided an attractive design for the volumes.

ERRATA

VOLUME 1, Introduction, pp. xv-xl, are improperly indexed. Page references found in the index are consistently short by two pages. For example, an index entry showing p. xiv will be found on p. xvi. This error applies only to the Introduction; the text of the volume is not affected.

VOLUME 2, p. 411, Roscoe Conkling Bruce graduated from Harvard, not Howard University.

VOLUME 2, p. 483, the letter to Mrs. G. A. Rumbley is incorrectly dated. The correct date is "September 14th [188]8."

CHRONOLOGY

1890   May 3: Margaret James Murray appointed Lady Principal of Tuskegee Institute.

      Aug. 14: Publication of criticism of Negro clergy.

1892   Feb. 23: First Tuskegee Negro Conference.

      May 26: Frederick Douglass speaks at Tuskegee's commencement.

      Oct. 12: Marriage to Margaret James Murray.

1893   Jan. 11: Opening of Phelps Hall Bible School.

      Feb. 18: Samuel Chapman Armstrong visits Tuskegee Institute.

      May 11: Death of Samuel Chapman Armstrong.

      Nov. 15: Speech before the Christian Workers' Convention, Atlanta, Ga.

      November: Criticism of Bishop Henry M. Turner and the idea of black emigration.

1894   Ca. May 15: Lobbying effort before Congress for the Atlanta Cotton States and International Exposition.

1895   June 8: Thomas A. Harris episode.

      Sept. 18: Address before the Atlanta Cotton States and International Exposition, Atlanta, Ga.

SYMBOLS AND ABBREVIATIONS

STANDARD ABBREVIATIONS for dates, months, and states are used by the editors only in footnotes and endnotes; textual abbreviations are reproduced as found.

DOCUMENT SYMBOLS

1. A — autograph; written in author's hand
    H — handwritten by other than signator
    P — printed
    T — typed

2. C — postcard
    D — document
    E — endorsement
    L — letter
    M — manuscript
    W — wire (telegram)

3. c — carbon
    d — draft
    f — fragment
    p — letterpress
    t — transcript or copy made at much later date

4. I — initialed by author
    r — representation; signed or initialed in author's name
    S — signed by author

Among the more common endnote abbreviations are: ALS — autograph letter, signed by author; TLpI — typed letter, letterpress copy, initialed by author.

REPOSITORY SYMBOLS

Symbols used for repositories are the standard ones used in *Symbols of American Libraries Used in the National Union Catalog of the Library of Congress,* 10th ed. (Washington, D.C., 1969).

ATT	Tuskegee Institute, Tuskegee, Ala.
DLC	Library of Congress, Washington, D.C.
DNA	National Archives, Washington, D.C.
GAGTh	Gammon Theological Seminary, Atlanta, Ga.
LNHT	Tulane University, New Orleans, La.
MB	Boston Public Library, Boston, Mass.
MWiW	Williams College, Williamstown, Mass.
MeB	Bowdoin College, Brunswick, Me.
NIC	Cornell University, Ithaca, N.Y.
NN-Sc	Schomburg Collection, New York Public Library, NYC
OFH	Rutherford B. Hayes Library, Fremont, Ohio
ViHaI	Hampton Institute, Hampton, Va.
WHi	State Historical Society of Wisconsin, Madison, Wis.

OTHER ABBREVIATIONS

BTW	Booker T. Washington
Con.	Container
RG	Record Group

Documents, 1889-95

From Margaret James Murray

Fisk University   Nashville Tenn. 5-21-'89

Dear Sir; You asked sometime ago for a recommendation from President Cravath and also from Mr. Jenkins. Mr. Jenkins wrote you[1] and I had our President write the recommendation, but about that time, I heard of Mrs. Washington's illness and so have retained the recommendation until now. Enclosed you will find one from President Cravath[2] and one also from Miss Ballantine[3] the Lady Principal of Jubilee Hall.

I shall be very glad if you can give me work. Very Respectfully,

Maggie J. Murray

ALS   Con. 2   BTW Papers   ATT.   Original destroyed.

[1] On June 3, 1889, William Jenkins wrote that "Miss Murray has already been asked to go to Prarie View Texas. I have had a talk with her and she says that she would much prefer to go to Tuskegee, even if she is offered less than she would receive at Prarie View." Jenkins included Margaret Murray among Fisk's best students. (Con. 2, BTW Papers, ATT. Original destroyed.)

[2] Erastus Milo Cravath wrote BTW on Apr. 16, 1889, characterizing Margaret Murray as "an excellent scholar, a good disciplinarian," and a student possessing "more than an ordinary degree of energy and executive ability." (Con. 2, BTW Papers, ATT. Original destroyed.)

[3] Anna Thankful Ballantine was born in Virginia and graduated from Glendale College in Ohio. She went to Fisk University as principal of young women and held this position for twenty years. On Apr. 11, 1889, she wrote to BTW that she considered Margaret Murray "of good mind, of conscientious religious convictions, of unusual power in gaining influence over those younger than herself, and of ability to direct them." (Con. 2, BTW Papers, ATT. Original destroyed.)

To Oliver Otis Howard

New York. May 26. 89

Dear Sir: You will be glad to know that Mr. C. P. Huntington gave $1000 to Tuskegee this morning.[1] This with your help puts us in pretty good shape. Gen. Ketchum[2] gave ½ a scholarship and Mr. Barbour[3] is going to send a donation very soon.

3

I can never forget your kindness. Tomorrow I return South. Yours truly

Booker T. Washington

ALS   Oliver Otis Howard Papers   MeB.

[1] BTW had spoken to Huntington on Tuskegee's behalf, eliciting the $1,000 gift. He wrote Samuel Chapman Armstrong that Huntington "talked at length on the Southern question and said he expects to do more for Tuskegee." (BTW to Armstrong, May 26, 1889, Armstrong Papers, MWiW.)

[2] Probably Alexander Phoenix Ketchum, born in 1839, who served during the Civil War on the staffs first of General Rufus Saxton and later of General O. O. Howard. Ketchum resigned from the Army in 1867 to resume law practice in New York City. He was prominent in YMCA and Presbyterian Union work.

[3] Thomas Seymour Barbour (1853-1915) was pastor of a Baptist church in Fall River, Mass. A graduate of Brown University and Rochester Theological Seminary, Barbour was the foreign secretary of the American Baptist Foreign Missionary Society from 1899 to 1912. Barbour chaired the American branch of the Congo Reform Association beginning in 1904. This group, which included BTW as a board member and Robert E. Park as executive secretary, was composed of British and American missionary and philanthropic groups which came together to protest the atrocities resulting from a forced labor system that affected millions of Congolese people. Barbour and others, including Alabama senator John Tyler Morgan, lobbied for several years in Congress on behalf of the Congolese. Among the association's publicity pieces against the Belgian ruler was Mark Twain, *King Leopold's Soliloquy: A Defence of His Congo Rule* (1907).

To Samuel Chapman Armstrong

North Conway, N.H. Aug. 13. 89

Dear Gen. Armstrong: I have tried every way possible to keep from borrowing any money this summer, but I am to the place where I *can not* get on with out it, and I therefore write to ask you to lend the school $300 till Oct 15 or Nov. 1. The two months that I was compelled to spend at my wife's bed side at a time when I was usually collecting money has made this request necessary. I know no one else to apply to. The amount can be returned promptly at the time named.

The singers are doing well and I hoped to get all that we would need through them, but see I can not.

My address for the next 4 days will be Bethlehem N.H. Yours truly

Booker T. Washington

ALS   BTW Folder   ViHaI.

To Samuel Chapman Armstrong

Fabyans [Fabyan] N.H. Aug. 19. '89

Dear Gen. Armstrong: Your check for $300 is rec'd and I am very thankful for it and shall see that it is returned at the time promised.

We get before audiences of 50 to 300 every night and I am often surprised to find how much haranguing on the Southern Question they will stand. I am sure we reach people in this way that we would not otherwise. We always speak for Hampton, too. Yours faithfully

Booker T. Washington

ALS   BTW Folder   ViHaI.

From George Washington Cable

Northampton, Mass., Aug [30]th 1889

My dear Mr Washington: Before asking another favor of you, I must first thank you very heartily for your kindness in answering my inquiries concerning an exodus of colored people from Alabama.

In the present instance I ask your help in securing reliable information concerning the crop-lien laws in Alabama.

It would be of great value to the good cause in which I secured your cooperation before, to have an account of the intention, operation and effects of these laws. Could you give this matter the benefit of your own careful attention? If it is impossible for you to do so, can you tell me of some other person who could give me such a statement of the case as would stand before an intelligent or an unintelligent public. The statements must be so made to carry their own authentication with them. Yours truly

G. W. Cable

ALS   Con. 92   BTW Papers   DLC.

From David Lee Johnston

Pratt Mines Ala. 9-25-'89

Dear Prof. I guess you have heard from all the class since school closed but me. I would have written to you sooner but I knew you were away during summer and did not know just when you returned. I had a letter from Prof. Logan a few days since and I was very glad to hear that so many new students were coming in. I hope you will have a full school this term. Some of the boys up here are not coming at all this term. I have tried to persuade them to come but they think it best to remain out. I thought once of teaching this winter but I have decided not to do so as I have a very good job that pays me from $45.00 to $50.00 per month and I think it best to keep it through the winter. I think of giving the school to Goins,[1] but I had much rather some of the girls have it, I find it a hard matter to hear from the girls is why I havent offered it to some of them. It is a very good school and in a very good community. I am sure most any of them would like it. And too I think it will engage two teachers. I will meet the parents to-night, and if I cannot posibly satisfy them by recomending others I will fill one of the positions my self. Love to all the Teachers. Whenever I can I speak a good word for Tuskegee.

Hoping an early reply I am   Very Truly yours

David L. Johnston

P.S. A longer letter next time.

ALS   Con. 92   BTW Papers   DLC.

[1] Howell L. Goins of Tuscaloosa, Ala., was a classmate of Johnston at Tuskegee from 1885 to 1889. After graduation he taught in various towns in Alabama.

From George Leonard Chaney

Leominster. Mass. Sept. 25. '89

Dear Mr. Washington. I enclose the copies of the "Acts" which you sent me.[1] There is no mistaking their language. The control of the

School is with the State. Two of the best lawyers I know agree in this opinion.

Have your advisory Board by all means. And if you ever do anything to change the charter — do it slowly and quietly. I start for Atlanta this noon and shall preach there next Sunday. I rejoice with you on the good start you have made. Yours sincerely

Geo. L. Chaney

ALS Con. 94 BTW Papers DLC.

[1] On Aug. 16, 1889, Chaney wrote BTW thanking him for copies of the Tuskegee Institute acts of incorporation. At BTW's request, Chaney had a lawyer examine the acts to determine precisely where legal control of the school rested. Chaney warned that, though the trustees controlled the property, the state could control the administration. "So long as the State treats the Institution fairly, as it has done thus far, all will be well." (Con. 2, BTW Papers, ATT. Original destroyed.)

To George Washington Cable

Tuskegee, Ala., Oct 8 1889

Dear Mr. Cable: I am very sorry to be so late answering your letter regarding the operation of the crop lien law in Alabama, but every minute of my time has seemingly been employed since receiving your letter. I am glad you are going to give the subject attention and trust that my information is not too late for use.

Of course when the war ended the colored people had nothing on which to live while the first crop was being made. Thus, in addition to renting the land on which to make the first crop they had to get the local merchant or some one else to supply the food for the family to eat while the first crop was being made. For every dollars worth of provisions so advanced the local merchant charged from 12 to 30 per cent interest. In order to be sure that he secured his principal and interest a mortgage or lien was taken on the crop, in most cases not then planted. Of course the farmers could pay no such interest and the end of the first year found them in debt. The 2nd year they tried again, but there was the old debt and the new interest to pay, and in this way the "mortgage system" has gotten a hold on every thing that

7

it seems impossible to shake off. Its evils have grown instead of decreasing until it is safe to say that 5/6 of the colored farmers mortgage their crops every year. Not only their crops before, in many cases they are actually planted, but their wives sign a release from the homestead law and in most every case mules, cows, wagons, plows and often all household furniture is covered by the lien. At a glance one is not likely to get the full force of the figuers representing the amount of interest charged. Example, if a man makes a mortgage with a merchant for $200 on which to "run" during the year the farmer is likely to get about $50 of this amount in Feb. or March, $50 May, 50 in June or July and the remainder in Aug or Sept. By the middle of Sept the farmer begins returning the money in cotton and by the last of Oct whatever he can pay the farmer has paid, but the merchant charges as much for the money gotten in July or Aug. as for that gotten in Feb. The farmer is charged interest on all for one year of 12 months. And as the "advance" is made in most cases in provisions rather than cash, the farmer, in addition to paying the interest mentioned, is charged more for the same good[s] than one buying for cash. If a farmer have 6 in a family say wife and 4 children, the merchant has it in his power to feed only those who work and some times he says to the farmer if he sends his children to school no rations can be drawn for them while they are attending school.

After a merchant has "run" a farmer for 5 or 6 years and he does not "pay out" or decides to try mortgaging with another merchant the first merchant in such cases usually "cleans up" the farmer that is takes every thing, mules, cows, plows, chickens fodder — every thing except wife and children.

It is not very often that the merchant furnishing the supplies owns the land. This in most cases is rented from a different party. So you see that the 2 parties, farmer and merchant, who have the most contact with the land, have no interest in it except to get all they can out of it.

The result of all this is seen in the "general run down" condition of 4/5 of the farms in Alabama — houses unpainted — fences tumbling down, animals poorly cared for, and the land growing poorer every year. Many of the colored farmers have almost given up hope and do just enough work to secure their "advances." One of the strongest things that can be said in favor of the colored people is, that in almost every community there are one or two who have shaken off this yoke of slavery and have bought farms of their own and are making money — and there are a *few* who rent land and "mortgage" and still do something.

The practices that I have referred to are in most cases sanctioned by the laws of the legislature or are not prohibited by law. A few years ago the Ala. legislature passed a law abolishing the crop lien law but it had no beneficial effect and the next session of the legislature reenacted the old law.[1] I feel safe in sawing [saying] that all classes — merchants, landowners and farmers are fast becoming thoroughly sick of the practice.

Enclosed I send you a statement made by Prof. Newton[2] one which I consider the nearest to the truth that has been made by any Southern white man. Then I called your attention specially to what the Montgomery Advertiser says under the caption: "The Mortgage Night Mare."[3]

For the good of the work to which I am devoting my life I prefer that my name should not be used in any printed matter.

If I can help at any time in the good cause I shall be only too glad to do so. Yours truly

Booker T. Washington

Please return the "Southern Letters" as they are the only copies I have.

ALS   George W. Cable Collection   LNHT.

[1] Sections 3286-88 of the Alabama Code of 1876 provided that persons advancing money, provisions, implements, or livestock to enable others to produce crops could have a lien on the crop to the value of the advance. Such liens had preference over all others except those for rental of the land on which the crops were produced. The lien had to be recorded in the office of the county probate judge. In February 1885 the legislature repealed these sections for fifteen counties, including Macon, but in December 1886 and February 1887 the sections were reenacted for the same counties.

[2] Charles A. Newton (1836-1900) was born in Vermont. He went to Alabama in 1857 and taught in several schools. He fought in the Confederate Army and later became principal of Belleville Academy in Conecuh County, Ala. From 1874 to 1894 he served as Conecuh County superintendent of schools. He operated a mercantile firm and also dealt in livestock.

[3] A search through issues of August, September, and October 1889 failed to locate the item BTW referred to.

To Samuel Chapman Armstrong

Tuskegee, Ala., Oct 24 1889

Dear Gen. Armstrong: Will it make any difference with you if the return of that $300 is delayed till Nov. 12 instead of Nov 1 as promised? We could better spare it on the 12 though if it will disappoint or inconvenience you we can arrange it for the 1st.

Please address me at 25 Beacon St Boston. I start there this week. Shall speak at the National Unitarian Conference Phila.[1]

Please send a General letter of recommendation at the same time to Boston.

Matters are going well with us. We are full of students. Yours Sincerely

Booker T. Washington

ALS   BTW Folder   ViHaI.

[1] No copy of the speech has been found. The Philadelphia *Inquirer* (Nov. 1, 1889, 2) characterized BTW's remarks as "an interesting address of the work of the church among the colored people in the South." The *Unitarian Review* praised BTW's optimism. (*Unitarian Review*, 32 [Dec. 1889], 542.)

A Recommendation from Samuel Chapman Armstrong

Hampton, Va., October 26th 1889

This to express my cordial and entire confidence in Mr Booker T. Washington Principal of Tuskegee School, Alabama.

A graduate of this School (with some additional study) — working his way to all the education that he has — he has, by his single handed push & energy, built up the best educational work for the colored people of the South under Negro management. It is worthy to be compared with any, and I earnestly commend Mr. Washington to all as a practical level-headed Christian man and gentleman.

The tone of this purely Negro Tuskegee School is high; the devotion of all its officers and students to their duties is all that could be asked.

Its business affairs are well managed and will bear investigation.

It has won the respect and confidence of all classes; no complaints come from there, while its officers have not always had the kindest treatment.

I beg an interest in and a hearing for Mr Washington.

S. C. Armstrong
Principal

ALS Con. 16 BTW Papers DLC.

From George Washington Lovejoy

Portsmouth Virginia. October 27th 1889

My Dear Mr. Washington: This leaves me getting on nicely in every respect.

Mr. Reid[1] promises me to answer your question as to how long I will have to remain here. I am doing my best at my studies.

You will please over look my bad writing. You know I never was a good writer, and now, I have to do physical labor, which very much unstrings my nervs for writing.

I am working in the U.S. Navey Yard every day. I make $1.52 every day I work. I was very glad to hear of my Brother[2] being in school and having passed such a good examination. I know my brother has fine mental powers. I hope he may remain in school and do well.

I am sticking as clost to my books every night and morning as I ever did in school. I make it a point to loose no time.

I have never seen people wors confused in my life, than they are here, over the arrest of the Baptist Minister,[3] yesterday evening.

Bail was refused and he is now locked up. The charge against him is seduction. He is quite a prominent man, has the confidence of both white, and colored and a strong hold on his church.

Rev. Armstead has done much good here.

Below you will read the law.

"Any person who shall, under promise of marriage, seduce and have illicit connection with any unmarried female of previous chaste character, or any married man who shall seduce and have illicit connection with any unmarried female of previous chaste character, shall be guilty

11

of a felony, and, upon conviction thereof, shall be punished by confinement in the penitentiary not less than two nor more than ten years: provided that the subsequent marriage of the parties may be pleaded in bar of a conviction."

Rev. Armstead is a married man.

It is generally said that the woman is, nor was not, of shaste character.

We hope the best results.

Politicks here is red hot. Both parties claiming they will gain the victory.

I hope to write better some day. Respectfully yours,

G. W. Lovejoy

ALS Con. 92 BTW Papers DLC.

[1] William M. Reid.

[2] Alonzo Lovejoy.

[3] John M. Armistead was pastor of the Zion Baptist Church in Portsmouth, Va., and a member of the Portsmouth City Council. He was the first signer of the so-called Mahone Manifesto, urging blacks to vote for the Readjuster gubernatorial candidate, William Mahone, and protesting the Democratic party's campaign theme of "Negro domination." On Oct. 26, the day of voter registration, racial tensions ran high. Hundreds of extra police and soldiers were put on duty in Negro sections of the state capital at Richmond. No major disturbances occurred, but thousands of blacks were kept from registering by means of "a process known as purging," where registrars rejected blacks on grounds of false residency, and kept others waiting in long lines until after registration desks had closed. The Democrats won by a wide margin.

In the midst of the voter registration tension, Armistead was arrested, charged with seduction of a Portsmouth girl — a felony — and jailed without bond. He was released three days later, and a jury found him innocent after only ten minutes of deliberation.

From Samuel Chapman Armstrong

Hampton, Va., Oct 28 1889

My dear Washington   I enclose letter which I hope will be satisfactory.

I find that I shall need what I loaned you by Monday A.M. Nov 11th. I leave that day for four weeks at the West. Don't fail to have the money here by that morning. I wish I were able to wait longer but cannot.

Hoping that you will make a "strike" at Philadelphia with the Unitarians & glad that Tuskegee is doing so well   I am   Yours sincerely

S. C. Armstrong

ALS   Con. 92   BTW Papers   DLC.

From Moses Pierce

Norwich [Conn.] Novr 1/89

My dear Sir   Yrs of 25th ult was duly recd. I note what you say about needing $400 to complete yr barn, you say that your students have done the work, but certain material supplys & superintendance we are compelld to pay cash for. I know not the size or the Material of yr barn, (whether wood which it should be), or brick which I should think extravagant if it increased the cost. The best barns in New England are wood, for which I supposed you could furnish the frame & covering from your own land & by yr own machinery. I believe in having good building plain & substantial built with economey which you have done, I hope. For a barn, Carpenters or blacksmith shop I do not believe you need brick buildings, wood answers in our climate why not in yours. These buildings should be placed so far apart as to protect them in case of fire. I do not say this to criticise what you have done, for I do not know. But I do know, that some other schools have wasted money in putting up expensive buildings where cheap wood buildings would have answerd every purpose as well. All waste destroys confidence of those who contribute. In regard to my ability to assist you at this time, I have to say that I have retired from active business & disposed of my interest in my former business after near 60 years of service in it. I have given up a large Salery which has curtaild my means of giving. I find I must give up for the present contributing to many objects that I feel an interest in, (among them Tuskegee) untill I can arrange my affairs so as to know what is prudent for me to do. While it is a great pleasure to help those who are laboring for the good of others, I find I must limit what I do to my means which I hope ere long will enable me to do something if not as much as formerly.

With my best wishes for health and prosperity in the good work you are doing believe me. Sincerely Yours

M Pierce

ALS Con. 93 BTW Papers DLC.

From Albert G. Davis[1]

Laudadale. Coosa Co. Ala   Nov. 1st 1889

Dear Prof., You must excuse me for delaying in writing to you about the school I am going to teach. I am laboring under a great many difficulties; the patrons of my school seem to be pleased with me as a teacher, but they are so obstinate, about supplementing the school. The government only appropriates $50.00 to run the school three months. That only allows me $16.66⅔ per months for my services. The patrons have promised to make my salary $25.00 per month, and that will not pay me for my work, as I am told that I will have at least eighty students when the people get through picking their cotton. After the government money expires, I will have to rely wholly upon the people for my salary. The people are not united. They are given to petty quarrels; one whats the school located in this place near his house, and because he cant get it where he wants it, he declares that he will not pay the teacher for his services.

I am sorry to say that both the County and Township Supts. are given to bribing teachers out of their salaries. The Township Supt. want me to pay him to contract with him. I told him, that I would not pay him a cent to save his life, so he hasn't opened his mouth to me about pay since.

When I see you again I can tell you how the affairs are here better than I can write. I intend to write to you regularly. I also intend to do my duty here among the people, and let my pay take care of itself. Yours truly,

Albert Davis

P.S. Please dont publish any of my letters.

A. G. Davis

ALS Con. 96 BTW Papers DLC.

[1] Albert G. Davis of Montgomery entered Tuskegee Institute in the night school in 1886. He graduated in 1889. From 1891 to 1895 he worked out of Selma, Ala., as a railway mail agent on the Mobile and Ohio Railroad. He married Sylvia Robertson Howard, an 1891 graduate of Tuskegee. The Tuskegee catalog in 1898-99 reported that he resided in Birmingham, "present employment unknown." In 1904 he asked BTW to use his influence in behalf of his right to teach, as Isaac W. Hill, state superintendent of education, had accused Davis of speculating in teachers' certificates and threatened to revoke his own. Davis vowed that he was innocent, but BTW replied that he would give Davis no public endorsement. Davis then threatened to expose Washington through a story to the Boston *Guardian* as a man unconcerned about the welfare of his graduates. It is probable that at some time Davis served a jail term, for in 1907 BTW wrote to Joseph O. Thompson, the U.S. internal revenue collector in Birmingham, enclosing a letter from Davis. BTW said: "Without using my name, I thought I would say in this connection, that Mr. [Belton] Gilreath has informed me that he is thinking of using some such case as this as a test to find out if persons can be incarcerated for long terms, after serving out their sentence to cover costs, etc. at the same time." (Davis to BTW, Sept. 22, 1904, BTW to Davis, Sept. 27, 1904, Davis to BTW, Oct. 6, 1904, all in Con. 287, BTW to Joseph O. Thompson, Oct. 7, 1907, Con. 362, BTW Papers, DLC.)

From Mary Elizabeth Preston Stearns

College Hill, [Mass.] Nov 8th 89

Dear Mr Washington, Your kind note found me in bed, from which I am now sitting up in a wrapper trying *hard* to be alive. You are good to think of me with so much sympathy. I want [to] ask you to come to see me, but am not strong enough yet.

The shirts did not reach you last Spring owing to forgetfulness on the part of the messenger. I will send them tomorrow if happily you have not flown. On that case they will be brought back & this note can be forwarded.

You sent me a beautiful Photo of dear Olivia. *Sweet Saint Olivia.* Most dear, and *near* to God, and His Angels. May she strengthen us all! And *forever* inspire your heart, hands, and mind.

Kiss the little darlings She left behind. I am glad they are well — and wish I could give Tuskegee $100.00. I could, but for R R losses.

Too tired for another word. Always your friend

M. E. S.

ALI Con. 97 BTW Papers DLC. Enclosed in Stearns to BTW, Nov. 17, 1889, *ibid.*

From Nathalie Lord

Boston, Nov. 14th 1889

Dear Mr Washington; Our Directors wish me to extend to you their thanks for the service, which you have so kindly rendered us the last few years, in having an oversight of our schools in the Black Belt of Alabama. They wish me also to assure you of their permanent interest in the school, of which you are the Principal. Very Sincerely

(Miss) Nathalie Lord

ALS Con. 92 BTW Papers DLC. Signed as Home Secretary of the Woman's Home Missionary Association.

An Article in *Unity*

Tuskegee, Alabama. [Nov. 16, 1889]

THE TUSKEGEE NORMAL INSTITUTE

There are, I believe, many more churches, Sunday-schools, auxiliary societies, and individuals who, if they knew how much real good could be done by the payment of $50 a year for the education of some worthy young man or woman at the Tuskegee Normal and Industrial Institute, (Tuskegee, Alabama) would be glad to contribute such a sum, or a portion of it. The Tuskegee school has 400 young men and women, who by hard struggle pay their own board by working out about half and paying the remainder in cash; but they are *absolutely* unable to pay *anything* for their tuition, which amounts to $50 a year for each one. Societies and friends must pay this $50 or the students leave school. How can $50 be made to do more good? It provides a *chance* for a student to remain in school a year, working out what he cannot pay, and at the same time learning some useful industry, developing the highest form of *self help*. Thus fitting them to go out into one of the dark places of the South and do what a girl now in mind did two years ago. After graduating, this girl went to teach where there was a large settlement of colored people. She found five-sixths of them renting land and in debt. Their school-house was the wreck of an old log cabin, and the school had never been in session longer than three months in the year. The people were discouraged, took little interest in their school, and had seemingly given up hope of ever bettering their condition. This girl began her work by calling the people together in regular meetings. At these meetings she told them how they could save their money instead of spending it for whisky and snuff, how they could begin buying homes, and by each one paying a little could soon build a neat, comfortable little school-house, and extend the school term to five or six months instead of letting it close at the expiration of the usual three months public term.

One going into that community now could see hope and encouragement beaming from every eye; could see a neat little school-house, which the girl showed the men how to build, she herself painting the blackboards; would find the school term lasting six months; would see neater houses and better farms, in short, the people feeling that they have something to live for. After two years work here is secured a foundation for moral and religious work on which one can build with safety. Not all our graduates have done as well, but they work in this line. The $50 scholarships are our most urgent need, but we can make new or second hand clothing for wear or bed use go a long way toward providing a chance for the students to finish the four years' course.

Booker T. Washington

Unity, 24 (Nov. 16, 1889), 83. The editor, Jenkin Lloyd Jones, introduced the article with these remarks: "Prof. Washington is well known to the Unitarian workers of the country, and enjoys their confidence. We hope his appeal will not fall on dull ears."

From Margaret James Murray

Tuskegee, Ala., 11-17-'89

Mr. Washington: Your letter came to me last week. I have written to Miss Nolen[1] and had gotten a letter from her in which she expressed a willingness to come here. You will do well to secure her for she is a fine young woman. Her address is Miss L. L. Nolen, Fisk University. She can give the lessons in cooking of which you spoke. We are doing well. I enjoy unpacking the barrels. I received two barrels last week but they were filled mostly with books and magazines. There were in one of them a dozen or more creton[ne] handkerchief bags and last night, I gathered a lot of the Annex girls and we had a sewing circle. After the bags were made and the handkerchiefs which were in them were hemmed, I gave each girl a bag and a handkerchief. This morning they invited me to see their rooms and the first thing I saw was the bag. I felt tired last night but after seeing the girls so delighted with the bags I was rested. Mr. Washington[2] gave me permission to sell a pair or two of mens' shoes. I did so and sent to Nashville for some S. S.[3] cards with simple Bible verses on them. I shall give them to my little class. I also send to Phil. for "The Picture World." It is a pretty paper with good and simple stories. The class has grown to seventeen now. Our Clubs[4] are getting on nicely. I am keeping up. All I hope is that I may be strong — strong for the Master's service. Very Respectfully

Maggie Murray

Many thanks for the little pamphlet.

ALS Con. 91 BTW Papers DLC.

[1] Lettie Louise Nolen Calloway, an 1890 graduate of Fisk University, became matron and was in charge of the health department at Tuskegee during the 1890-91 school year. She taught mathematics the following year, and then married Thomas J. Calloway and moved to Washington, D.C. Returning with her husband to Tuskegee, she served as librarian from 1896 to 1898.

[2] John Henry Washington.

[3] Probably Sunday school.

[4] Probably the Tuskegee "Literary Societies," where students met weekly to speak extemporaneously and learn parliamentary procedure.

From Timothy Thomas Fortune

New York, Nov 19 1889

Friend Washington: Your letter of the 18th inst was received. I regret to learn that you have lost your stenographer. Glad to learn however that he gave you such satisfaction. I have in mind a young man I think will fill the bill, and will see him in short and let you know later concerning him.

Nothing would give me greater pleasure than to visit your school. But as there has been expressed such general dissatisfaction at the call of the meeting of the Leagues[1] at Nashville, I have submitted the matter of place to a vote of 14 editors in as many States. So far the replies are nip and tuck for Chicago and Cincinnati.[2] My preference is to meet in the South, but the object[ions] of many to the discomforts of travel, the lack of hotel accommodations, and most important of all a hostile press which virtually controls the matter sent by the Associated Press to the country, may all compel us to change the place of meeting to Cincinnati or Chicago.

If it shall finally be decided to hold the League in the South, in accordance with my original purpose and desire, it will give me great pleasure to deliver two lectures for you, one on "What is a Tariff?" the other, "Benefits of Industrial Education."

Do you want to help me with a small check in the great expense I am in getting the Leagues in shape? All such matters will be reported to the National League. Yours truly,

T Thos Fortune

ALS Con. 92 BTW Papers DLC.

[1] Afro-American League.
[2] In January 1890, the Afro-American League met in Chicago.

From Warren Logan

Tuskegee, Ala., Nov. 22d 1889

Dear Mr. Washington, I think it will be a wise thing to secure the services of Mr Adams[1] if it is the purpose of the school to open the shops he would be expected [to] take charge of. But before we add other shops it will be the part of wisdom, it seems to me, to perfect those already in operation. The Carpenter Shop has never been what it shld be and now it is in a state of chaos — this as far as *teaching* is concerned. The Industrial Room is not up to the Standard of other schools right here in Ala.

Expansion is not, necessar[i]ly, growth. The industries Mr. Adams understands are important and, I think, he will teach them well. Your brother coincides with my views. Yours Sincerely but hastily

Warren Logan

ALS Con. 92 BTW Papers DLC.

¹ Lewis Adams.

From David Davidson Sanderson

Eutaw Ala. Dec 11/89

Dear Sir. A col'd man, claiming the name of H. L. Goins, came to my office this morning, & exhibited a Diploma of Graduation from your Institution, bearing your name, & that of others of the faculty. As I had an examination of teachers yesterday, some of the question papers were lying on my table, & I concluded I would make a slight test of his scholarship. I handed him the 3rd grade paper[1] on Grammar, & requested him to parse the sentence, "John killed a rabbit." John, he said, was a noun of the 2nd person — then 1st person — & finally the 3rd. It was in the *objective* case. I then told him to parse *rabbit*. After a good deal of hesitation, he said it was in the objective case. I reminded him that he had said *John* was in the objective case. He concluded then that John must be in the Nom. case. I asked what it was nom. to? He replied, to the word killed. What part of speech is killed? I asked. An *adjective,* he replied. When I told him he was wrong, he said, It is an *adverb,* then! And so on, to the end of the chapter. I then made a brief examination on Hygiene — which was not much more satisfactory than on Grammar. Arithmetic d[itt]o.

I need not say that I was more than surprised. Your Institution has some reputation, I understand: but how it could issue a Diploma to a student so utterly incompetent to teach the elementary studies of the 3rd grade in the public schools in the State, seems very strange.

It places the Co. Supts in a dilemma. The law requires them to give a permanent license to those holding Diplomas — & yet, as this case proves, they may not be equal to an examination for 3rd grade license. I was compelled to deny licenses to several parties yesterday, who were better qualified than Goins. Of course no faculty can give a pupil brains — but it certainly has an option as to the conferring of Diplomas.

I thought I would say this much, in behalf of myself & other Co. Supts, as well as for the good name of your Institution. It seems to me that its reputation is bound to suffer from such cases as the above. The education of the col'd people is a matter of no personal concern to me more than to any other Christian man, & well wishers of the race; but I have a legal & consciencious Duty to discharge, & I do not wish to be compelled to fill our schools with incompetent teachers, because they hold Diplomas. Resp'y

D. D. Sanderson

Co. Supt. Ed. Greene Co.

ALS   Con. 97   BTW Papers   DLC.

[1] Refers to examination for a third grade of teaching certificate. Alabama public schools were not graded at that time.

To Samuel Chapman Armstrong

Tuskegee, Ala., Dec. 13 1889

Dear Genl Armstrong: What do you think of the wisdom of our trying a singing tour, say from the middle of March to middle or 10 of April? I am very anxious to make *new* friends to get *new blood*. We feel the need of this. The people listen well in the summer and appear to enjoy the meetings, but I fear the impression is not as helpful as it would be, should we find them at their homes. My idea is to take a quartette including Hamilton[1] have one of the students besides myself speak and let the other speaking be done by some prominent local personage. I should not go to Boston or very near it as I have been there once this year, but have in mind going into Ct. N.Y. Western Mass. & Rhode Island. Nothing definite has been done, and I shall take no step before hearing from you.

It would be quite a new venture for me and do not know that I could succeed. I feel sure that I should have to depend on you for much advice and help. The meetings I suppose would have to be held entirely in the churches. Yours truly

Booker T. Washington

ALS BTW Folder ViHaI.

¹ Robert Hannibal Hamilton.

From James B. Washington

Fayetteville W Va. Dec. 22nd 1889

Dear Brother: I rec'd your much welcomed letter which found all very well. It was some what a surprise to me. In reply to your desire of my coming to Alabama, if you can advance me some money I can come in two weeks. I only like 8 days of finishing my month, and would be compelled to teach that 8 days. I certainly want to come, and if you will, or can wait on me that length of time I will come. I only hope that you will hold the place that you have for me that long.

Write to me at once please so that I will know what arrangements to make about coming. Hettie¹ has been to Charleston and for that reason makes my pocket short at present. Let me know all particulars at once. Hopeing to hear from you soon I am   Your Brother

Jas. B. Washington

ALS Con. 86 BTW Papers DLC.

¹ Hattie (Hettie) Virginia Calloway Washington.

From James B. Washington

Beckwith P.O. [W.Va.] Dec 31, 1889

Dear Bro. Will start for Tuskegee Thursday morning on 1,53 o'clock train. I havent rec'd money yet. Your Bro

Jas. B. Washington

ACS Con. 93 BTW Papers DLC.

To Emily Howland[1]

Tuskegee, Ala., Jan. 15, 1890

Dear Madam; The box of magazines you so kindly sent us has been received. These are of much service to us. Our Library has not very much Classical Literature and the reading matter contained in these magazines are of double interest to us. The young men of the Rhetorical Classes were very much delighted to get the Forum.[2] I hope that you will accept our most grateful thanks for your interest in us and your kindness toward us. We have had a great many books given us this year and we feel grateful to all of the friends who have contributed to our Library. Yours Truly

B. T. Washington
Per M.

HLSr Emily Howland Papers NN-Sc. Miss Howland had written to BTW about the shipment of magazines. BTW turned the matter over to Margaret Murray, writing: "Miss Murray: Please attend this and write her after box comes." (Howland to BTW, Dec. 4, 1889, Con. 95, BTW Papers, DLC.)

[1] Emily Howland (1827-1929) was born in Sherwood, N.Y., of Quaker parents. Her father, Slocum Howland, was a farmer and wool merchant who was a Garrisonian abolitionist. Emily Howland never married and devoted her long life to a variety of causes, including abolitionism, women's rights, black education, temperance, civil liberties, and prevention of cruelty to animals. Before the Civil War her home was a station on the Underground Railroad. She was active in the Women's Christian Temperance Union and was a longtime co-worker with Susan B. Anthony for women's rights. She taught black girls in Washington, D.C., before the Civil War (1857-59), and during the war she directed a large refugee camp for freedmen in the District of Columbia. A model of the kind of white philanthropist who sought to make Reconstruction workable, she helped several black families settle on some of her father's land in Westmoreland County, Va. There she founded and supported a school for many years. She was also active in business and served as the first woman director of the National Bank of Aurora, N.Y., for more than thirty years. She was a regular contributor to Tuskegee for many years, usually donating $500 annually and often supplementing this amount with scholarships. She was a warm supporter of BTW until his death in 1915. At the time of his Atlanta address in 1895 she wrote BTW expressing her belief that it was of major significance and was "the true word fitly spoken." She believed that the World's Columbian Exposition of 1892-93 was a turning point in the women's rights struggle and that the Atlanta Exposition also marked a change for the better for blacks in America. (Howland to BTW, Sept. 26, 1895, below.)

[2] *The Forum*, a monthly journal published from 1886 to 1950, presented various sides of controversial issues in a symposium format.

From Eliza Davidson[1]

Columbus Ohio   Jan 16th 1890

Dear Son   I Recived you Chrismas Flower and was glad to know that they came form you and oblige   I was in hopes you had sent Me the Childrens pichturs   But I was decived   I wont you to sened them to Me some time so I can see them   you can have them taken some time and sened them By Mail to Me   I am in hopes that you and the childrn is will and doing well and have in Joyed your selves this new year   I dont know as I will ever B able to come to see you all   But I live in hopes of seeing them in this world

I have Bine Reciveing the Tuskegee Student and I see Olivies Name in it and it gives Me a gate deal of plesurer to know that she was not forgoten   now May God Bless you and your little flamly   you must soon   Yours truly

Elize Davidson

when I Recived your letter it was not sealed and it only had the Christmas Card and flower

ALS   Con. 861   BTW Papers   DLC.

[1] See above, 2:314. She died in 1907. (BTW to Mary A. Elliott, Feb. 23, 1907, Con. 348, BTW Papers, DLC.)

An Excerpt from a Speech in Montgomery

[Montgomery, Ala., Jan. 17, 1890]

You may talk of our disadvantages because of our color, because of race prejudice, because of friction in enjoying civil and political rights, may advise emigration to the West or the Congo, but I am free to say to you as young people preparing for life, that I had rather take my chances for an opportunity to lead a positive, helpful and independent life, right here in Alabama as a black man — and I would not change my color if I could — than in any other section of the Union or anywhere in the world.

Montgomery *Advertiser,* Jan. 18, 1890, 2. This is all of the speech that is known to be extant. The *Advertiser* reported that BTW spoke before "a large audience of colored students and citizens." (*Ibid.*) The excerpt also appeared in *Southern Workman,* 19 (Mar. 1890), 25. The speech, entitled "A Helpful Life," was delivered at the chapel of the Alabama State Normal School.

A Speech Delivered before the Women's New England Club[1]

Boston   Jan. 27th 1889 [1890]

What is the actual condition of the 6,500,000 Negroes who inhabit the Southern States, and who for 250 years through no fault of their own and by the expressed or implied consent of all people, were deprived of the fruits of their labors and kept in abject ignorance, is a question that should often touch the heart of every American citizen? Starting 25 years ago, without a foot of land, without a hoe, without a horse, and unused to self-guidance and habits of economy, his mind befogged with ignorance and superstition, could you have expected him to have travelled very far in the direction of intelligence, wealth and independence? And yet he has made progress, says Dr. Haygood, that has been unequalled by that of any other people on the face of the globe in the same length of time and our progress should [be judged?] not so much by the heights to which we have arri[ved] as by the depths from which we have come. While there has been this almost marvelous progress, I fear we too often overlook the magnitude of the work to be done for this people. I say magnitude because of the immense number of people to be reached, because of their extreme poverty and ignorance and the disadvantage of an acquired race prejudice. With this in view, I wish to spend a few minutes in speaking to you about my people, as I have actually seen their condition in the heart of the South during the last eight years. I know that you want facts whether they are encouraging or discouraging.

Good authorities put the number of Colored people now in the South alone at 6,000,000. In many of the counties of Alabama, and other Southern states they outnumber the Whites six to one, and if you would find the masses and know their real condition, you must leave the town and railroads and go into the interior, on the large cotton plantations. In most cases the whites have left the country and moved into town, leaving the masses of colored people to themselves. Five-sixths of these people live on rented land and mortgage their crops and stock for the food on which to live from day to day, and upon the money value of food, is charged an average of 25 per cent interest. Four-fifths of these are to day in debt because of their own ignorance, their lack of economy, and they are being forced to go into debt for the food on which to keep their bodies alive during the first year of freedom. Starting in debt, being charged an interest on the value of food which was and is still impossible for them to pay, this indebtedness in many cases has overlapped and increased from year to year, until it has fastened its iron claws upon the business and moral life of the people to an extent that is appalling, and the worst of it is, that in many cases the people have lost hope of bettering their condition, and consequently do only enough work to keep body and soul together. As a result of this system, with few exceptions, we find land poorly cultivated, houses and fences going to wreck, live stock poorly cared for, and a "tumble down" air generally. Understand, my remarks apply mainly to rural districts. The moral lessons of such a life are the worst. During slavery the Colored man reasoned this way: my body belongs to master, and taking master's chickens to feed master's body is not stealing. The practice thus started has to some extent been handed to this generation, and when pressed and cramped on every side by this horrible mortgage system, even to get food to keep life in his children, you must not be surprised if he breaks the command– "Thou shalt not steal." Four-fifths of the families live in small, one roomed cabins. Can you wonder that the morals of a people, whose mother, father, brothers, sisters, kindred, strangers, young and old, numbering sometimes ten or twelve, eat, cook, and sleep in the same room, are not all that they should be?

In the country districts the public schools are kept open on an average of $3\frac{1}{2}$ months in the year. The state is able to build no schoolhouses, and as the people themselves are unable to build them, the school is usually taught in the wreck of a log-cabin, or under a bush arbor. The average country teacher is often unable to write his own name correctly and it not unfrequently occurs that there are scholars that know more than their teachers and often too those teachers are as weak morally, as mentally. For moral, religious, and intellectual life, these masses are dependent for guidance on their teachers and preachers, and the number of preachers is legion. These are even more unfitted for their work than the teachers. One church near Tuskegee has a total membership of 200, and 18 are preachers. The character of many of them is represented by one of whom it is said that while he was at work in the Cotton field in the middle of July, he suddenly stopped, looked up to Heaven and said, "Lord, de work is so hard, de cotton is so grassy, and de Sun am so hot, dat I believe dis darky am called to preach." In name these people are certainly religious but its manifestation consists largely in emotion, and they are dreadfully wanting in real practical Christianity. In fact it is hard for a hungry man to be a good Christian. The denominational prejudice is so strong that it works a great injury to the schools and the moral life generally. It is often more important for one to be a Methodist or Baptist than to be a helpful follower of Christ. It is worth attention to note that while a very large proportion of the colored people are church members, Christians in name, being about equally divided between Baptist and Methodist denominations; the mere fact of such membership is misleading, and is no evidence that a large proportion of these people are not just as far from real Christian truth as taught by Christ as any people found in Japan or Africa. In other words a large number of my people without knowing it are Christian heathen and demand as much missionary's effort as the heathen of foreign fields, but to return to education, Each colored child in Alabama will receive for its education this year 81¢ from the state, Each child in Massachusetts about $15.00. Sixty per cent of the colored children in the South attended no school last year, 2,000,000 voters of the South can not read the ballots they have the right to cast. Of the total negro population South of Mason and Dixon's line, one-fourth can perhaps read in a way, but I do not hesitate to say that the number who have enough education to make it of potential effect in shaping and strengthening their moral and religious life, in order to withstand temptation and stand on their own feet as helpful forces in American life is not 10 per cent of the whole population.

Now as to the wrongs growing out of prejudice. You see in the newspapers that the negro is murdered often without a cause, that is true; that he is cheated, that is true; that he is often deprived of political franchise, that is true, that on public highways he is often made to pay for first class accommodations, then forced to accept second class fare, that is true; But this question of race prejudice is rather an uncertain quantity. Let Negro students enter a Southern white school, if the negro remains, the school will break up. Let a negro mechanic enter a northern factory as a laborer, and if the negro remains, the factory will break up. As stubborn and unreasonable as this race prejudice is, no one can keep his eyes open without noticing from year to year a gratifying improvement. The fact is that a large proportion of the American people have for so long a time almost unconsciously associated the Negro with slavery, subjugation, poverty, filth and ignorance that it is hard to separate him in our minds from these conditions, and we find Pat as he comes from Ireland, even before he learns the name of the president of the United States, or before he has had time to change his shirt, begins to speak of "dirty Negroes." Trying as this question is, it is by no means the principal or most weighty part of the problem. Human nature, I find much the same the world over. The poor Irishman or Jew is discriminated against till he gets property, intelligence and moral backbone and then he ceases to be an Irishman or a Jew, and becomes a full-fledged American citizen. It is interesting to note in what form this prejudice exhibits itself, and to what extent it is disappearing. It is rather hard to understand why Southern white people do not object to sitting by the side of a colored person in a street car, and yet if these same persons change from a horse car to a steam car the white person objects to being in the same coach with the negro even though they are thirty feet apart. Notwithstanding the eloquence of the late Mr Grady and newspaper misstatements, the facts are, that in every one of the Gulf states, the Negro is forced to ride in Railroad coaches that are inferior in every way to those given the whites, and they are made to pay the same fare that the whites pay. In many cases, the colored people are compelled to ride in the smoking car, and when this is not the case, one half of the smoking car is portioned off for the colored people, & even in this case the door leading from one room to the other is about as often open as shut. And here I would add that it is not the separation that we complain of, but the unequality of the accommodations. But even in this matter of public accommodation, there is an encouraging change. Ten years ago the same unjust discrimination was made in Virginia, W. Va, and North Carolina, but at present such discrimination is almost unknown in these states and the reformation is gradually working its way farther south. The situation was forcibly explained a short time ago, when I myself was riding through Georgia in a first class car and one of the passengers asked why a negro was permitted in that car. The conductor replied that he got into the coaches in North Carolina and it was hard to get him out after crossing the Georgia line. So far as concerns the Gulf states, the Negro is completely at the mercy of the white man in the state courts. The eloquent Mr Grady disposes of this whole subject in this well sounded sentence: "And in every court," says he "the negro criminal strikes the colored juror from the panel that the white man may judge his case." It would have been the simple truth, if Mr Grady had said that in the whole of Georgia & Alabama, and other Southern states not a negro juror is allowed to sit in the jury box in state courts. And while on that subject Mr Grady might have added even at the risk of spoiling his rhetoric, the information that since freedom there have been at least ten thousand colored men in the South, murdered by white men, and yet with perhaps a single exception, the record at no court shows that a single white man has ever been hanged for these murders. These are but a few examples of his eloquence versus the facts. If time would admit an analysis of Mr Grady's speech I would reveal other equally untrue statements. The practice of lynching colored people is one of the curses of the south. This is usually resorted to when there is a charge of rape. In the midst of excitement when there is no time or disposition to inquire into the facts, some poor Negro is swung up to a tree and made to suffer for a crime which in five cases out of ten was committed, if committed at all, by some one else. Then if the friends of this unfortunate Negro, in their excitement show any sign of indignation and anger and gather in knots to discuss the matter it is telegraphed all over the country that the negroes are rising and troops must be sent to suppress them. A more docile, gentle, law-abiding people, I do not believe are to be found in the world. But even this barbarious mode of attempting to administer justice is being more and more condemned by the southern press, and we are sure that a healthy change in public sentiment is being wrought.

What I shall say regarding the political condition of the Negro, I shall confine to the Gulf states. In the first place, the Southern people in private conversation do not attempt to hide the fact that they regularly and systematically resort to means to nul[l]ify the colored vote — that they are resolved in every case where the colored vote is large enough to have a controlling influence in an election, to see that the colored vote is not counted. Force in the form of shotguns, Klu-Klux-Klans is now rarely resorted to, but the vote is quietly and persistently thrown from the ballot-box or is not counted. This practice has been so effectually used for so long a time, that it is safe to say that not more than one-fifth of the colored voters even attempt to vote in the state, and national elections. So discouraged have they become. But if you ask is not each political party required by law to be represented at the ballot-box by a judge. In answer, it should be remembered that the whole election machinery is in the hands of the whites, and it is very convenient to fulfill that part of the law, by appointing as a judge to represent the republican party, some colored man who can neither read nor write. In the districts where the colored people outnumber the whites there the colored people have the least chance for expressing themselves politically.

. . . . .

can, by virtue of his superior knowledge of the chemistry of the soil, knowledge of improved tools and best breeds of stock, can raise 50 bushels of corn to the acre, while his white neighbor raises only thirty, and the white man will come to the black man to learn. Further they will sit down on the same seat and talk about it (the value of trades).

The negro will not be respected as a man until his business side as well as the moral and religious side is developed, and here comes in the value of industrial training. Trades Union[s] at the north exclude colored mechanics. These Unions are gradually working their way south. Heretofore the negro has had a monopoly of the trades. In building a million dollar City Hall in Richmond Va recently, not a negro was permitted to lay brick. Before the war a large number of colored boys were apprenticed by their masters to learn trades. The apprentice system is dying out, and the negro as a mechanic, as he will go to the wall. The industrial schools meet this demand, and furnish at the same time, the best moral training. At the Tuskegee Normal School, we have 400 students, half of them young men, and the demand to learn trades along with the 4 years literary course is much greater than we can supply. We have recently completed a three and a half story building. The bricks for the building were made by our students, several of whom get enough knowledge of brick masonry to enable them to go into any town or city in Alabama and make an independent living as brick makers. The sawing of the lumber was by the students, and more than one has learned to handle a steam saw. The brick laying, plastering and painting and carpentry were done also by the students. This building cost $6000 and in its construction we taught enough students trades to average 6 mechanics for each $1000 entering into the cost of the building. This gain in addition to the permanent use of the building for a dormitory. We are needing another building just as badly as we did this one, and can make six thousand dollars do the same amount of good again. While the boys did this work, the girls made and laundried their clothes and in that way were taught sewing and Laundrying. This illustrates in some degree, the plan and scope of the industrial work at Tuskegee. Nothing tends more to develop moral back-bone than Industrial training. During its 8 years existence the Tuskegee school has sent out many class room and mechanical teachers. Yes more than 100 young men and women. The moral and uplifting influence exerted by each of these teachers, in the communities where they labor is almost beyond calculation. I wish you could go, as I have gone, into one of these cotton districts, where all is discouragement and demoralization resulting from debt, mort- gaging, renting, and lack of school advantages, and then go there two or three years later, and see the change that I have seen, wrought by one of these teachers. I have in mind one of our girls who went three years ago into a community where every thing was just as dark and discouraging as any thing I have mentioned. She began her work by calling the people together in weekly meetings. In these meetings she told them how to stop renting and mortgaging and begin the buying houses. She told them how they could save their money and build a school house, and prolong the school term. If you were to go there to day you would see hope and encouragement beaming from every eye; you would find them buying little farms and instead of the wreck of a log cabin, a neat comfortable framed school-house, and the school term lasting 7 months instead of three. All this they have done without a dollar's out-side aid — only they have had some- one to show them *how to help themselves.* And herein lies the solution of this vexed Southern problem. Some one to lead.[2] This is bringing a race from darkness into light and putting it on its feet. I do not believe that there is any missionary work in the world that gives such satisfactory results in so short a time for the money spent. We do not ask direct helps for the masses but help to enable such institution[s] as Tuskegee to send teachers as leaders and guides into every com- munity. $50 scholarship.[3] The one good thing that the negro got out of slavery was the power of hard work. He works now, but he does not know how to use the results of his labor. The Tuskegee School under no denominational control, with its 640 acres of land, 12 industries, $100,000 in property, with 27 teachers, is trying to prepare 400 young men and women to go out [and] do the same kind of work that I have attempted to describe.

HDf Con. 955 BTW Papers DLC. A 16-page draft with occasional minor corrections in BTW's hand. Page 12 of the original is missing.

[1] BTW apparently hoped to speak off the record. In a letter a month prior to this speech, the club's secretary wrote BTW: "The rules of the Club strictly forbid reporting & we endeavor to have this particular rule thoroughly enforced. I think therefore that you will be able to speak freely; but, of course, the members of the Club are likely to repeat to outsiders anything they may hear. They will refrain from this however, if you request them to, I presume." (L. M. Peabody to BTW, Dec. 17, 1889, Con. 1, BTW Papers, ATT. Original destroyed.) This assurance of privacy apparently led BTW to make statements that were bolder than his customary public utterances. It was, for example, uncharacteristic of BTW to attack Henry W. Grady, champion of the New South. But Grady's death shortly before this speech, the privacy of the occasion, and the northern audience caused BTW to be more critical than usual.

[2] This phrase was added, possibly as a heading, in BTW's hand.

[3] Another addition in BTW's hand.

From Portia Marshall Washington

Tuskegee, Ala. Feb. 11, 90

Dear Papa, I have all your letters and postal cards. We were all very sorry to hear that you were so sick, and we are glad to know that you are well again, and will be with us so soon.

Baker and Davidson are as good as two little boys can be and they and I have been well ever since you went away. But Sapphira[1] has been very sick with pneumonia. She was taken sick Monday, and Wednesday Uncle John received the despatch that you were sick. She was in bed all that week. We sent for her mother, and she came and stayed until Saturday morning. Sapphira does not feel real well and strong yet, but you know she will go to school as long as she can walk.

Davidson was a real good little boy on his birth day. We put his tray on the table in the morning, and it has been there ever since. It was too cold that morning for him to go to breakfast, and he was asleep at dinner time, so he did not go to dinner but did go to supper, and he seemed to like his tray very much, for he looked at the pictures and put his hands on them, and laughed. Aunt Susie[2] has named the baby Gertrude.

The pig that you sent Mr. Greene[3] was dead when it got here, and the calf did not come at all. Miss Murray says that five barrels and some boxes have come since you went away, but she does not open them over here when you are away so I have not seen any of them. I have not broken either of my big dolls, but Lily was very sick Saturday when she was out of the trunk, but she is better now. A week ago today I received a beautiful letter from Mrs. Baker. I have not answered it yet, but shall do so soon. I cannot think of anything more to write except, good bye, and come home soon to your loving little

Portia

HLSr Con. 17 BTW Papers DLC. Dora S. King drafted this letter for 6½-year-old Portia.

[1] Listed both as Sophira and Sophia Lavinia Warren in the Tuskegee school catalogs. She entered Tuskegee as a junior in 1889 and graduated in 1894. From Notasulga, Macon County, Ala., she taught in the county after graduation.
[2] Susie Miller (Mrs. John Henry) Washington.
[3] Charles W. Greene.

From Catherine Impey[1]

Street, Somerset, England   March 5/90[2]

Dear Mr. Washington   I forget if I have ever written you before — I feel as if I had known you for years — having so long & often heard of you & your successful work. Years ago someone sent me a little parcel of the *Southern Letter* & it at once opened my eyes to the possibility of an Anti-Caste. For years I had tried to get a good paper set on foot on this question but supposed the risk of expense & the tax on my time made it impossible I should myself attempt it & yet no one else was saying what I wanted said — or not saying it to the people I felt I might reach. Your paper was an inspiration to me. I found the cost of printing would be very inconsiderable — I tried to get my English printers to make mine just like yours in shape & style. All I can say is Anti-Caste became a living reality. It is most encouraging to find how far it reaches. It stirs up newspaper correspondence — brings letters from your Gen. Armstrong — from the democratic press &c into our English papers. May God bless it to the good of your people & mine. yours very respectfully

C. Impey

P.S. am sending this to my white friends in America those of them who as yet have made no response to the repeated sending of the little paper.

C. I.

ALS Con. 95 BTW Papers DLC.

[1] Catherine Impey (1847-1923) of Street, Somerset, England, was a Quaker and a vegetarian. She was active in several temperance societies in England and also did social and humanitarian work among the poor. Her strong racial liberalism led her to publish *Anti-Caste,* patterned, in physical makeup at least, after BTW's *Southern Letter.* The masthead described *Anti-Caste* as "Devoted to the Interests of the Coloured Races." In several trips to the United States beginning in 1878, she managed to acquaint herself with the outstanding black leaders of the late nineteenth century, including Frederick Douglass, Joseph C. Price, T. Thomas Fortune, Benjamin T. Tanner, Daniel A. Payne, John C. Dancy, T. McCants Stewart, William Still, and Ida B. Wells. *Anti-Caste* stressed the brotherhood of man regardless of race and concentrated on racial conditions in America, but also included items related to Australia, India, and British colonies in Africa. Miss Impey published *Anti-Caste* from March 1888 until July 1895, except for a time in 1893-94 when it apparently did not appear. The April-May issue of 1895 was a memorial issue to Frederick Douglass, and the final number carried a reference to Tuskegee Institute and the Tuskegee Farmers' Conference, "both due to the wonderful organising talent of a negro gentleman, Mr. Booker T. Washington." (*Anti-Caste,* 1 [Mar. 1888], 1; *ibid.,* 7 [June-July 1895], 8.)

[2] Miss Impey's personal note to BTW was written on the back of a circular letter dated February 1890. In the circular she wrote that *Anti-Caste* was designed to argue against racial discrimination and segregation. She believed that treatment of persons "based merely on physical characteristics, surely involve[s] a degree of wrong and injury to individuals. . . ." She denied that one race was inherently superior to another and thought racial differences were due to "*advantages* of education, wealth, influence, &c." which whites monopolized in a manner "purely tyrannical and unjust — altogether inconsistent with civilization and dishonouring to religion." She admitted that "the coloured people, taken as a whole, are in an inferior *condition*," but she denied that this was due to "natural inferiority." She believed her newsletter, circulated in Europe as well as America, would help allay racial misunderstanding.

From John Henry Washington

Tuskegee, Ala., Mch. 9-1890

My Dear Brother: Yours of the 7th inst to hand. The plans of the house were received Mch. 2nd and given to Mr. Carter[1] to make out the bill of lumber.

I have tried to push him on the bill of framing and he told me that I could get it Wednesday 12th which will not give a chance to do much, if anything by the meeting of the association[2] as, perhaps all the lumber will have to be sawed.

I am sure it is a mistake to give the seniors the privilege of taking any of the girls to church or even taking any.[3] They have not attend prayers the last two Sunday nights and last night they were all strung out a great distance from each other. Besides it was half past ten or near eleven o'clock when some of them got to Ala. Hall.

We will have to be more careful about matters here.

Only last night Mary White[4] slip out of Ala. Hall and ran away. Some of the girls saw her leave and notified Mrs. Pindle[5] but she got away. I took several of the best students and serched the place but she could not be found and we have not heard from her at this hour 3 o'cl'k P.M.

We got hold of two letters of Jettie Simpson[6] which some fellow has written her to meet him at a certain place tonight. Not any name was signed to it. Matters are going well otherwise. The children are all well. Have gotten in some work students and will be out the most or all of next week. Shall write tomorrow. Hastily

J. H. Washington

ALS   Con. 98   BTW Papers   DLC.

[1] John W. Carter of Scottsville, Va., graduated from Hampton Institute in 1889 and joined the Tuskegee faculty in January 1890 as head of the carpentry division of the industrial department. He left Tuskegee in 1900 or 1901.

[2] The Colored State Teachers' Association meeting at Tuskegee Institute on Apr. 9, 1890.

[3] Warren Logan also wrote to BTW warning him that the policy of allowing senior boys to escort girls to Sunday evening church services was a mistake. "For the past two Sunday nights," Logan wrote, "the Seniors as a body have been absent from the Chapel service — also the young women whom they chose to carry out." Logan questioned BTW: "Do you think the parents of girls would approve of their daughters being out at night until eleven with young men —

and no teacher with them?" (Logan to BTW, Mar. 10, 1890, Con. 96, BTW Papers, DLC.)

⁴ Mary White of Fitzpatrick Station, Montgomery County, Ala., attended the B preparatory class of Tuskegee in 1889-90.

⁵ Eliza A. Pindle.

⁶ Jettie Simpson of Notasulga, Macon County, Ala., attended the B preparatory class in 1889-90.

From Alfred Haynes Porter

Brooklyn, N.Y. Mch 10. 1890

Dr Sir. I was present with my wife last evening at Plymouth Church and heard your address. We thought the singing very fine, and the one student who spoke did exceedingly well; but what I want most to say is, that we were charmed with your address. I will tell you frankly that I said to my Wife before going, "Washington has a little hesitancy in speaking, is a little slow," and I do not expect very much in the way of an address. I will say, we were both very agreeably surprised! I have heard many of the Speakers from the Institutions at the south, but I have never listened to an address or appeal for this cause, that to my mind was as effective or as well delivered as your address of last evening. It should do good for your cause and I hope and trust this will be the result. Yours Truly,

A. H. Porter

ALS Con. 3 BTW Papers ATT. Original destroyed.

To Samuel Chapman Armstrong

New Haven, Conn. Mar. 15 1890

Dear Gen. Armstrong: Replying to your kind favor of recent date regarding Anderson bird,[1] I have to say that I was compelled to ask him for his resignation for the reason that his *extreme sensitiveness* made him offensive to most every one. On several occasions he was *very* rude even at the table to the lady teachers. I was greatly disappointed in him. Aside from this I am sure it would be against

Tuskegee for him to take Mr. Cayton's[2] place. Mr. Cayton and I have always helped each other in many ways that you do not know of. Bird would be in a position to do us harm.

Our meetings so far have been successful beyond my expectations. All have been well attended. At Dr. Ludlow's[3] church in East Orange we secured 6 scholarships. Yours truly

Booker T. Washington

ALS BTW Folder ViHaI. Written on stationery of the Aldrich House.

[1] Edmond Anderson Bird taught natural science and rhetoric at Tuskegee during the 1889-90 school year.

[2] Thomas A. Cayton was born in Hampton, Va., graduated from Hampton Institute in 1873, and also attended school in Norwich, Conn. He held positions as principal of a black school in Charlottesville, Va., and with the U.S. Revenue Service in Newport News. He served Hampton as an agent for the *Southern Workman* and traveled as agent with the Virginia Colored Concert Company, which toured England, South Africa, and Australia.

[3] James Meeker Ludlow (b. 1841) was a graduate of Princeton (1861) and Princeton Theological Seminary (1864). He held pastorates in Albany, N.Y., New York City, and Brooklyn before he became pastor of the First Presbyterian Church in East Orange, N.J., in 1886. Under his direction the East Orange church grew in size, wealth, and prominence among Presbyterian churches of the area. Ludlow wrote several books, including a sentimental work *Along the Friendly Way: Reminiscences and Impressions* (1919).

From Mary A. Elliott

Athens [Ohio] March 16th 1890

Dear Brother We are all as well as usal, I myself have had rather poor health this winter but am feeling a great deal better for the past month. I hope this may find you and the children well, and doing well. I hear from your School quite often through the little papers and am glad to hear of the great progress being made in every thing pertaining to the school. I expect as soon as I can in the future to give somthing to Olivis Memoril Scholarship Fund. Booker my reason for writing to you to day is, that I wish to say to you that we are going to make a change. I hope for the better, But am not sure. I am going to move to Columbus and go into the same business ondly add dressmaking to it. Have rented my house out here have to pay high rent in Columbus, But not so much as I would in the main part of City. I am going out

37

on West Broad St 468. I should think a bout one half mile east of Mother's[1] house toward the Capitol, am going to start tomorrow if nothing prevents. Dock[2] can get some buisness there to do which will help me a good deal, and I will be close to Hiram[3] and Mother and if you and the children can ever come we can all see them. Kelly[4] took it very hard a bout Olivia's death. Emma[5] she is married again married a man by the name of Newton, getting a long better then usal I think Mother feels proud to think that you dont for get her and write to her some times. She wants to see the children. Tell my little girl Portia, that Aunt Mary has not forgotten her, and, when I get fixed up a little shall write to her soon. Give Uncle John and Aunt Susie, and little cousins my love and kiss the children for me, and write when you can and dont feel toward me as if you were a stranger, but feel and talk to me as if I were your Sister I feel as if you were my own brother. I am a poor writer and dont write as often as I should, have done, but look over it as I have a good deal to weerry my mind in my buisness but am going to have a wman help me. You are haveing good success with your school work and am in hopes will be in couraged to still go forward.

M. A. Elliott

ALS Con. 17 BTW Papers DLC.

[1] Eliza A. Davidson.
[2] Noah A. Elliott.
[3] Hiram R. Davidson.
[4] Possibly William K. Davidson, reported in the 1870 census in the household of Eliza Davidson in Albany, Ohio, as a mulatto farm laborer, nineteen years old, born in Virginia.
[5] Emma Davidson Newton? (See above, 2:314.)

From Russell Lant Carpenter

Bridport, [England] March 19, 1890

Dear Mr Washington, I inclose a draft for £10, made payable to your Treasurer, Mr. W. Logan. Mrs. Carpenter joins with me, in this donation. Please therefore to enter it as from

Rev. and Mrs. Russell L. Carpenter } £10
    Bridport, England.

I write to *you,* as I am accustomed to do; [as?] I might have written to your "chaplain," Revd J. W. Whittaker, who has written me a note, *for which please to thank him.* You have a Bridgeport, I think, in the U.S., and he has directed to me Bridgport. Please to notice that I live at Bridport (without the g) — the *Port* of the *Brid,* or Brit, a little stream that flows into the British Channel.

We send our donation for the general purposes of your Institute, to be used as you think best. Mr. Whittaker informs us, that our last donation was given to aid a student, Miss Charlotte Singleton,[1] who has written a pleasant little letter to acknowledge it. She informs us that she is now earning part of her maintenance as a waitress. That occupation with us is — a person who waits at table, or possibly, you so describe those who also attend to general housework, which seems a more improving occupation. I take for granted that she is preparing to be a teacher. You have waiters, in plenty, among your people! I am very glad that you are preparing your pupils to be useful in many ways. The industrial department in your school is one of the best features. Mrs. Carpenter was pleased with C. Singleton's note, and has written one to her, which I inclose.

During the last year, we have heard more than we had done for a long time, of the alienation between the two races. It has made us very sad. It is a great comfort to me, to have from you reports that your School is favourably viewed by your neighbours. The more the "coloured people" are trained to useful occupations, and receive an education which will help them to be truly independent, and to rise above the contempt and oppression which befall the ignorant, the sooner will come that true equality, and mutual kindness and esteem, which we so much desire.

At one time, I thought it a pity that you should spend any of your scanty funds in sending me your monthly Letter; but it no doubt helps to keep up my interest in your School. I am often much pleased with the letters of your former scholars. Now and then I regret that there are some errors of the press, which might easily have been corrected.

Last year you informed us of your most sad bereavement. I hope that you, and your family, are now in your usual health. I am most thankful to say that Mrs. Carpenter is considerably better than she was a year ago. She is still infirm, but I hope that, before the summer closes, she may have regained her former strength.

We have heard from our old friend, Mr. Douglass,[2] since his settlement in Hayti. He seemed full of work, but he reported himself and Mrs Douglass as in fair health. Mr. Douglass was my guest when he first came to England, in 1840, and our friendship has by no means diminished. We are about the same age. He has visited us three times since my marriage.

When you next write — to acknowledge receipt — would you tell me whether you regularly receive the Band of Hope Chronicle,[3] and whether you wish it continued. Do you see any periodical recommending kindness to animals?

Who was the English friend who sent you 100$, last year. I wonder whether he is an acquaintance of mine. Believe me, yours faithfully

Russell Lant Carpenter

I have been lately reading, and reviewing, the last two volumes of the Life and Times of W. Lloyd Garrison.[4] The last volume, with the portraiture of his character, was especially interesting. I was never what was called "a Garrisonian," as regards his disunion views.

ALS   Con. 104   BTW Papers   DLC.

¹ Charlotte Leslie Singleton of Blossburg, Jefferson County, Ala., entered Tuskegee in 1889 and graduated in 1894. She taught in Jefferson County after graduation. She married B. F. Proctor, but continued to teach.

² Frederick Douglass was minister to Haiti from 1889 to 1891.

³ Apparently an organ of the Band of Hope, a youth organization opposed to liquor, tobacco, and profanity.

⁴ Wendell P. and Francis J. Garrison, *William Lloyd Garrison, 1805-1879: The Story of His Life Told by His Children,* 4 vols. (New York, 1885-89).

From George Washington Cable

Northampton, Mass. March 21, '90

Dear Sir: I hold the invitation of Mr A. K. Smiley,[1] proprietor of the Lake Mohonk Mountain House, Ulster County, N.Y., to attend a large and important conference of educators of the Negro race, similar to the I believe very successful Indian Conference lately closed at that place. This Negro Conference[2] is projected for June 4, 5, 6, 1890. Ex-President Hayes is expected to preside and such men as Generals Armstrong, Eaton,[3] Fisk,[4] and Whittlesea,[5] Ex-Governors

Chamberlain[6] and Bullock,[7] Ex-Justice Strong,[8] Presidents Mitchell,[9] Woodworth,[10] DeForrest,[11] Cravath,[12] Drs Strieby,[13] Hartzell,[14] Haygood[15] and Roy,[16] Lyman Abbott,[17] William Loyd Garrison[18] and many others named as members.

In answer I am today mailing the letter a copy of which please find enclosed. Is it too much for me to hope that in case Mr Smiley should extend his invitation to you, you will accept it. Hoping to hear from you early, I beg to remain, Yours truly

G. W. Cable

TLS Con. 94 BTW Papers DLC. The enclosure was George Washington Cable to Albert K. Smiley, Mar. 21, 1890. Cable advised Smiley to invite three or four black educators to the Negro conference and suggested BTW, William S. Scarborough of Wilberforce University, and J. W. Cromwell. He supposed that the absence of any Indians at the Mohonk Indian Conference "was owing to the fact that the Indian race does not yet furnish such notable representatives." Cable also suggested that if the presence of black delegates would cause embarrassment because of lodging and entertainment of black guests, he believed the men he mentioned "will accom[m]odate themselves to any honorable arrangement to avoid embarrassment."

[1] Albert Keith Smiley (1828-1912) was born in Vassalboro, Me., of Quaker parents. He graduated, along with his twin brother Alfred H., from Haverford College. After teaching for many years, in 1869 Smiley purchased land at Lake Mohonk in Ulster County, N.Y., and established a successful inn and vacation spot. Smiley's brother also purchased land at nearby Lake Minnewaska. In 1879 President Rutherford B. Hayes appointed Smiley to the Board of Indian Commissioners, and he headed an investigating committee to purge the commission of corrupt officials. Because of his interest in Indian welfare, he called the Lake Mohonk Indian Conference in 1884, held at his resort, that brought together leading white men to discuss Indian affairs. The conference met annually until 1916, and Smiley played an active role in its affairs for more than twenty-five years. The Mohonk Indian Conferences had an important impact on federal Indian policy. Indians were not invited to attend the conferences until after 1890, when a few Indian representatives did attend. Smiley was also host of two conferences on the Negro in 1890 and 1891 and a conference on international arbitration in 1895. (Burgess, "We'll Discuss It at Mohonk," 14-28.)

[2] The Mohonk Negro Conference of 1890 was originally suggested by Rutherford B. Hayes, who spoke at the 1889 Indian conference and expressed the hope that the Indian work could be expanded to include blacks as well. Albert K. Smiley responded immediately with the announcement that a Negro conference would be held the following June at his Lake Mohonk resort. About 100 persons, all white, attended the first conference. In late May and early June of 1891 the second conference on the Negro, attended by 150 persons, met and adopted a platform that supported industrial education and land ownership for blacks. The conference did not include political questions and avoided controversial issues of race relations.

[3] John Eaton (1829-1906) graduated from Dartmouth in 1854 and went to Ohio, where he was a school principal in Cleveland and later superintendent of

schools at Toledo. After attending Andover Theological Seminary he entered the Union Army as a chaplain. In 1862 General Grant selected him to take care of the displaced Negroes who were streaming into the army camps. Later in the war he was a colonel in a Negro regiment. During 1865 Eaton was an assistant commissioner in the Freedmen's Bureau for the District of Columbia. He then moved to Tennessee, where he edited the Memphis *Post,* advocating free public schools. He served as state superintendent of schools for two years and then as U.S. Commissioner of Education (1870-86). In his later years he was president of Marietta College in Ohio (1886-91), and then of Sheldon Jackson College in Salt Lake City, Utah (1895-99). Eaton was briefly superintendent of schools for Puerto Rico in 1899. He was the author of *Grant, Lincoln and the Freedmen: Reminiscences of the Civil War with Special Reference to the Work for the Contrabands and Freedmen of the Mississippi Valley* (1907).

4 Clinton Bowen Fisk (1828-90) was reared in Michigan Territory, where he lived in abolitionist homes and helped to conduct slaves along the Underground Railroad. After various business ventures, he joined the U.S. Army at the outbreak of the Civil War. After the war he became assistant commissioner in the Freedmen's Bureau for Kentucky and Tennessee. In 1866 he opened a school for Negroes in Nashville which became Fisk University (1867). In 1874 he was appointed to the Board of Indian Commissioners and was its president from 1881 until 1890. A Republican who was also an ardent prohibitionist, Fisk ran on the Prohibition ticket for governor of New Jersey in 1886 and for president in 1888.

5 Eliphalet Whittlesey (1821-1909), after graduating from Yale, taught in Alabama and then became a pastor in Maine and a member of the Bowdoin College faculty. After service in the Civil War, he became an assistant commissioner of the Freedmen's Bureau for North Carolina. In 1866 he was transferred to bureau headquarters as adjutant general. In this capacity he visited many Negro schools in the South. He aided in establishing Howard University and was on its faculty from 1867 until 1874, when he was appointed secretary of the Board of Indian Commissioners by President Grant. He was a member of the board from 1882 to 1900. Whittlesey often attended the Mohonk Indian Conferences. He was active for years on the American Board of Commissioners for Foreign Missions.

6 Daniel Henry Chamberlain (1835-1907) graduated from Yale in 1862 and attended Harvard Law School, but dropped out and received a commission in the predominantly Negro Fifth Massachusetts Regiment. After the war he settled in South Carolina and was elected to the 1867 constitutional convention, where he joined the black delegates in insisting on racially integrated public schools. The effort failed, however, and the University of South Carolina was the only public school in the state to be integrated. From 1868 to 1872 he was state attorney general. In 1874 he was elected governor of South Carolina, and ran again in 1876. Results of this election were disputed, and when President Hayes withdrew federal troops, Wade Hampton become governor. Chamberlain later practiced law and served on the faculty of Cornell University.

7 Rufus Brown Bullock (1834-1907) was born in Bethlehem, N.Y. He became a leading expert in telegraphy and organized a telegraph business in Augusta, Ga. (1859). He used his telegraph skills in the Confederate Army, rising to the rank of lieutenant colonel. After the war Bullock continued his business and expanded into other fields, organizing a bank and becoming president of the Macon and Augusta Railroad (1867). He was a Republican member of the Georgia constitutional convention and was elected governor in 1868, serving until 1871. He

stood trial in 1876 for embezzlement of public funds and was acquitted. He continued an active business life in his later years as president of the Atlanta Cotton Mills, president of the Atlanta Chamber of Commerce, and director of the Union Pacific Railroad. As one of the commissioners of the Atlanta Exposition in 1895, he was instrumental in persuading the other white commissioners to invite BTW to speak at the opening exercises. After BTW had delivered his Atlanta Compromise address, Bullock rushed to the center of the platform to shake his hand in a symbolic gesture of New South unity.

[8] William Strong (1808-95) was an associate justice of the Supreme Court from 1870 to 1880. His views on federal civil-rights legislation were conservative.

[9] Edward Cushing Mitchell (1829-1900), a Baptist minister and educator, graduated from Waterville (later Colby) College and Newton Theological Seminary. After serving briefly as editor of the Chicago *Present Age,* he was acting president of Roger Williams University in Nashville, an institution for Negroes, during 1884-85. From 1887 to 1900 he was president of Leland University in New Orleans, a black Baptist school.

[10] Frank G. Woodworth, president of Tougaloo College in Mississippi, a black school sponsored by the American Missionary Association.

[11] John William De Forest (1826-1906) was born in Connecticut. In 1851 he wrote a *History of the Indians of Connecticut.* He served in the Union Army and then became a Freedmen's Bureau agent at Greenville, S.C. He was mustered out of service in 1868. Moving to New Haven, he wrote several novels.

[12] Erastus Milo Cravath.

[13] Michael E. Strieby.

[14] Joseph Crane Hartzell (1842-1928), a leading promoter of Methodist educational and mission work, was educated at Illinois Wesleyan University and Garrett Biblical Institute, Evanston, Ill. As presiding elder of the Methodist church of New Orleans from 1873 to 1882, he established schools and a hospital for blacks. He also founded and edited the *Southwestern Christian Advocate* to promote northern Methodist work among the blacks. In 1883 he became assistant corresponding secretary of the Methodist Freedmen's Aid and Southern Education Society (Cincinnati), and from 1889 to 1896 was corresponding secretary of this society. From 1896 until his retirement in 1916 he was an energetic missionary bishop in Africa.

[15] Atticus Greene Haygood.

[16] Joseph Edwin Roy (1827-1908) graduated from Knox College and Union Theological Seminary and served as a pastor in Illinois for five years. He became involved in antislavery activities and was an ardent defender of John Brown. When he visited "Bleeding Kansas" in 1858, a leading free-stater tagged him "the fighting preacher." After serving one year as the American Missionary Association district secretary at Chicago, Roy served with the Home Missionary Society for eighteen years beginning in 1861. In 1878 he became field superintendent for the A.M.A. and during his seven-year tenure oversaw the organization of some fifty churches. In 1885 the A.M.A. reappointed him district secretary at Chicago, and he held that position until 1903.

[17] Lyman Abbott (1835-1922), pastor of the Plymouth Congregational Church in Brooklyn, had published BTW's article castigating the Negro clergy. (See below, Aug. 14, 1890.) Abbott was one of the leading American clergymen of his day. He had been active in Reconstruction social work as secretary of the American Freedmen's Union Commission (1865-69). In the early 1870s he began book re-

viewing in *Harper's Magazine,* and his connection with Harper & Brothers led to a second career as editor and publisher. From 1870 to 1876 he was editor of the *Illustrated Christian Weekly.* In 1876 he became associated with Henry Ward Beecher in the editorship of the *Christian Union.* In 1881 Beecher withdrew, and Abbott assumed the role of editor-in-chief and continued in this capacity until his death in 1922. In 1893 the *Christian Union* became the *Outlook,* one of the most influential journals of the period. When Beecher died in 1887, Abbott succeeded him as pastor of the Plymouth Church until 1899. Abbott's success and affluence, and perhaps his age, made him more conservative in his later years on racial and social issues. In matters of theology, however, his liberalism is indicated by his *Theology of an Evolutionist* (1897).

BTW's autobiography *Up from Slavery* originally appeared serially in the *Outlook,* and Abbott gave BTW much valuable advice on its writing and organization. (See above, 1:xxiii, xxvi-xxix.) The two men remained close throughout BTW's life, both in ideology and literary partnership. BTW published many of his articles in the *Outlook,* and sent Abbott much of the material for his editorials on southern and racial affairs. Abbott was active in the Ogden Movement, which reflected BTW's outlook on race relations.

18 William Lloyd Garrison, Jr. (1838-1909), a son of the great abolitionist, was a wool merchant in Boston from 1866 to 1883 and an investment banker there from 1883 to 1902. He carried on the family tradition of reformism, supporting free trade, Chinese immigration, woman suffrage, and the Henry George single tax. Like other members of his family, he aided Tuskegee and industrial education but balanced this with support also of black higher education.

From Amanda Ferguson Johnston

Malden West Va   April the 4 1890

My Dear Bro   all well & Hope this may find you the same Bro.   Ben[1] Has Bin up the River nearley 3 months & Haster pay so much Bord i think id Better rent out & go up there   We are trying all we Can to get the monney   We want to know what you Say about it   times is so Dull that the pelople is moveing a way from Here   tomas Rolling   John Wiley   Charley Ross   6 yong men left for pennsylvania With ther famieleys   Hope to Here What you say a Bout it soon. tell me What you think of it   from Sister

Amanda Johnson

ALS   Con. 861   BTW Papers   DLC.

1 Benjamin Johnston, her husband.

To George Washington Cable

Tuskegee, Ala., April 7, 1890

Dear sir: Your very kind favor regarding the Mohonk Conference I found awaiting me on my return from the North. Were it possible for any action of yours to increase my respect and love for you[,] your position in this matter would certainly do so many fold. I have delayed an answer some days thinking that an invitation might reach me or that I might hear of one of the other gentlemen suggested by you receiving one. As yet I have heard of none. I have known for some time that this conference was to be held, and confess that I thought it a little strange that no invitation came to me. Still I supposed all along that other colored men had been invited. I do not think I can be called a sensitive man, but the disposition on the part of many of our friends to consult *about* the Negro instead of *with* — to work for him instead of *with* him is rather trying and perplexing at times. The action of the movers in this conference I confess I can not understand and can not see but that the exclusion of colored men will in a large degree cripple the influence of any deliverance the Conference may make.

It may interest you to read a marked article in the "Cleveland Gazette" which I send by this mail. Should an invitation come later I shall inform you. Yours truly

Booker T. Washington

ALS   George W. Cable Collection   LNHT.

To Margaret James Murray

[Tuskegee, Ala.] April 7 90

Miss Maggie J. Murray: This is to inform you that you are hereby appointed Lady Principal of this institution[1] to take effect at the close of the present session. In due time a notice of your appointment will be made known to teachers and students.

There will be an increase in your salary, said increase to be made in Sept '90 and you will be informed later of the exact amount of the increase.

B. T. Washington

ALpS   Con. 106   BTW Papers   DLC.

¹ BTW wrote to Rosa Mason on the same date, accepting her resignation as Lady Principal and praising her work. (BTW to Mason, Apr. 7, 1890, Con. 106, BTW Papers, DLC.)

From William S. Scarborough[1]

Wilberforce Univ. Wilberforce O. April 17— 1890

My dear Sir: Yours is at hand. In reply I have to say that I have not received, as yet, an invitation to attend the "Mohonk Negro Conference." So far as I am aware no Negro has, up to date, been invited to be present.

A card, just received from Mr. Cable leads me to infer that an invitation will be sent to some one or two of us and perhaps more — to whom I know not. With best wishes I am, Yours very truly —

W. S. Scarborough

ALS   Con. 97   BTW Papers   DLC.

¹ William S. Scarborough was born a slave in Macon, Ga., in 1852. His father, securing his freedom, encouraged his son to attend school. Scarborough graduated from Oberlin College in 1875. He became a noted linguist and a teacher at Wilberforce University. His textbook, *First Lessons in Greek*, was published in 1881. In 1883 he married Sarah C. Bierce, a writer and normal-school principal at Wilberforce. He was president of Wilberforce from 1908 to 1920.

Scarborough was occasionally more outspoken than BTW on racial matters in the 1880s and 1890s, but he moved to a more conservative position. By 1900 he was endorsing the Hampton-Tuskegee goals of industrial education and accommodation to southern white demands. By 1909 he had moved toward a position more critical of Washington, becoming a member of the Committee of Forty set up by the National Negro Conference.

In *Arena* magazine in 1890 Scarborough stated publicly and more forcefully what BTW had said privately to George Washington Cable (see BTW to Cable, Apr. 7, 1890, above): "... the recent Mohonk Conference called to consider the moral, intellectual and social condition of the negro, with the negro *in persona* left out, convinces me that there is a great deal of insincerity on the part of many so-called advocates of the race...." Scarborough thought it was absurd that the black man's view of the race question was presented by a white man. "Why not give the negro a hearing," he wrote; "let him plead his own cause and give his own views relative to these issues. . . ." Scarborough also noted that the "improperly styled 'Negro problem,' is in reality the white man's question." (*Arena*, 2 [Oct. 1890], 560-67.)

From Amanda Ferguson Johnston

Malden West Va   Apri the 18. 1890

my Dear Bro   yours letter was Delay jus Come all Well Hope all well with yu Bro yur advise was gud i thought i would on acount of Ben haveing such high Bord to pay   We Have Had so much Bad luck i Know i Cant Have the money i Cant Rent to enney one that would take Care of it i am all Clean fix as well as Could B   expecte with what i Had   iv Bougt nothing new since. i Hated to Break up Ben Dont want me to move But trying to get the money. He gets 1.25 per day & pays 11.00 for Board & keeps us at Home   So yu Know & He Has joust work three months   We are going to do the Best By the 29 of July   i want to Know if we Can get what we like fom yu   i mus look out for some one now so i Can Depend on them   i will Be gud if yu will — & Be Here if nothing Hapens us   Bro i started to pay a det yesterday & lost 10.00   i found it soone & it got out so some one tried to Break in at night i alarme Help Came so they tried the[y] thried i shout the[y] left

Hope to Here Soone   from Sister

Amanda Johnson

ALS   Con. 17   BTW Papers   DLC.

From Ednah Dow Littlehale Cheney[1]

Jamaica Plain [Mass.] April 22d 1890

Dear Mr. Washington, I rec'd a letter from Lula D. Fant[2] this morning which makes me question whether a little caution is not necessary to those pupils who correspond with donors to the school. In both letters she asks for money or something. Now it is quite natural that the pupils should feel as if their Northern friends could and would

47

grant their little requests — but is it not most important to break up this facility of begging and inculcate the feeling of self reliance which will elevate them to true self respect? I have the same thought about Italians and think the new Government has done most wisely to prohibit fees and begging as far as possible. I should not feel justified in lending money to a young girl of whom I know so little. It is quite natural that she should like to have a pretty graduation dress — but the desire for such things is the stimulus to effort to work — or it is a dangerous taste. I say this because I do not want a custom to become general which might offend your Northern friends. I cannot well spare time to write to Lula today or often but I will answer her letter at some future time. Yours with earnest interest

Ednah D. Cheney

ALS Con. 94 BTW Papers DLC.

¹ Ednah Dow Littlehale Cheney (1824-1904), born in Boston, was a prominent "bluestocking" intellectual, women's rights advocate, and educational philanthropist. Lacking in formal education, she secured her prodigious learning through close contact with people such as Ralph Waldo Emerson, Margaret Fuller, Theodore Parker, and other transcendentalists. Interested in reform movements from an early age, she joined the crusade against slavery in the 1840s and 1850s, writing a number of articles for antislavery newspapers under her maiden name, Ednah Littlehale. In 1853 she married the artist Seth Wells Cheney, who died three years later.

During the Civil War she served on a commission to aid black soldiers and was secretary of the Freedmen's Aid Society for ten years, certifying and encouraging teachers to take up the cause of Negro education in the South. After the Civil War Mrs. Cheney toured the South on numerous occasions on behalf of both black and white education. She aided financially both Hampton and Tuskegee, but most of her philanthropy was directed toward Atlanta University, since she believed in an education grounded in philosophy and the humanities.

Mrs. Cheney was a leader of the women's rights movement. She helped found the New England Women's Club and the Association for Advancement of Women. She was a backer of the New England Hospital for Women and Children, where women physicians could receive practical training. She pressed for wider educational and professional opportunity for women, and was especially active in the fight for woman suffrage. An active lecturer and writer, Mrs. Cheney was the first woman to speak in the Divinity Chapel at Harvard, over the opposition of many faculty members. She gave annual lectures at the Concord School of Philosophy. Among her more than fifteen published works were several collections of juvenile stories, art criticism, a guide to social games, a biography of Louisa May Alcott and a collection of her letters, a sequel to Ibsen's *The Doll's House* called *Nora's Return,* and an autobiography (1902).

² Lula Dona Fant, of Margerum, Colbert County, Ala., entered the B preparatory class of Tuskegee in 1888 and was in the junior class during 1891-92. She did not graduate.

From the Members of the School Band

Normal School, Tuskegee, Ala., April 25, 1890

Dear Principal: We, the members of the T. N. S. Brass Band, submit the following: We do not feel as though we have been rightly treated. We have done all in our power to make the band a success, and, on the face of that, we have not received any encouragement.

These are some of the remarks, made by Col. J. H. Washington:
1st   We have disgraced the School.
2nd   He wants us to distinctly understand that Foster[1] has taken too much liberty upon himself as a student. It was our understanding that Foster and Daniels[2] were to be leaders of the band, to take out unsuitable ones and put in suitable ones. He, also, refused to let us have a drum major.

We have bought a new drum and are expected to pay for it by the fifteenth of May. In our first effort to raise the money, we went to town Saturday, and we are very sorry to know that we were ridiculed on coming back, by being called monkeys and such reflecting on the school.

We are in need of music sacks; and, on asking for them, were told to gather them up and bring them to the office, and there would be some possible chance of our getting them; which is impossible to do, from the fact that they are all torn up — save a few.

As the above statement is grievous to us, after putting forth all our efforts to bring the band out, we would like to know, 1st wherein we have reflected on the school, in the manner of which he has spoken. 2nd who do you mean to rule the band?

We would like to have a decided answer from this, between this and Tuesday morning. Very respectfully,

Members of the Band

Foster }
Daniels } Leaders

ALS   Con. 94   BTW Papers   DLC.

[1] Samuel Berkeley Foster, of Gainesville, Ala., was in the A middle class in 1889-90 and in the senior class the next year. He apparently did not graduate.

[2] Marshall Gaston Daniels, of Milton, Fla., entered the Tuskegee night school in 1889. One of Tuskegee's most popular and energetic students, Daniels was known as an excellent singer and musician and an outstanding orator. He worked

in the printing office until graduation in 1894 and then became editor of the *Tuskegee Student* and director of the band and orchestra. He also taught arithmetic at Tuskegee. After one year on the Tuskegee staff, he resigned to further his education at Berea College, where he died suddenly on Mar. 30, 1896. At his funeral in Berea his cornet, covered with white flowers and ribbons, was placed on his casket.

From John Henry Washington

Tuskegee, Ala. Apr. 26-1890

I recommend that A. R. Lewis[1] be given a warning for disorderly conduck and carring pistols.

He has had three this term.

He also breakes beds and chairs in his room and dances in it till he has caused nearly all the plastering in the room below him to fall.

I recommend that Wm Perkins[2] have a warning for continually smoking in his room.

He has been spoken to several times by lady teachers about it and I have marked him but he continues to do so. Very Respectfully

J. H. Washington

[*In BTW's hand:*]

Caldwell[3] — smoking.

ALS Con. 98 BTW Papers DLC.

[1] Alonzo R. Lewis of Montgomery, Ala., entered the B preparatory class for the 1889-90 school term. He remained only one year longer, as a junior.

[2] William Perkins, of Pensacola, Fla., was a member of the B preparatory class for the single year 1889-90.

[3] Charles Columbus Caldwell, a junior from Pensacola, Fla., entered Tuskegee in 1888 and was last listed in the B middle class in 1890-91.

To Ednah Dow Littlehale Cheney

Tuskegee, Ala., April 29 1890

Dear Mrs Cheney: I thank you for your letter regarding Lula Fant. We do not encourage our students to ask for help but tell them that help must not be asked from Northern friends. We feel that it is far better to throw the students on their own responsibility with regard to personal expenses and that securing some friend to pay the tuition is enough help except in a few exceptional cases and Lula Fant is not one of these cases for her parents do provide reasonably well for her expenses though they can not give her what *she* thinks she need[s]. We have found too that the students most ready to ask for such help are not the most deserving of it.

Your letter gives me an opportunity to speak to our students as [a] whole on the subject of begging. Yours truly

Booker T. Washington

ALS   Ednah Dow Cheney Papers   MB.

From Samuel May[1]

Leicester, Mass. Apr. 29/90

Dear Mr Washington, Yrs. of 21st came duly. We were just then engaged in raising the money for the A. U. A.[2] — which has now been sent in. Of this, $25. (twenty five dollars) are for Tuskegee — this amt. is the contribution of 2 persons, in addition to what they do for the Assocn. otherwise, including the Montana (Indian) School.

There is a vast deal to be done to keep our country from drifting into "the bad," espec. with the demons fighting us of *ignorance and appetite* (and the accursed temptations of alcohol & tobacco), and we must *keep at it*. You do right to *stir up* all of us, so far as you can, and help *to arm* as many young men & women as you can with "the whole armor," that they may "withstand," both for themselves & others, the powers of evil. Truly Yrs.

Saml May

ALS   Con. 96   BTW Papers   DLC.

[1] See above, 2:176.
[2] American Unitarian Association.

To Edgar James Penney[1]

[Tuskegee, Ala.] April 30th 90

Dear Sir: You may be a little surprised at this letter. I confess that my visit to Selma resulted in my making up my mind to secure if possible your services for the coming school year beginning Sept 1st for the reasons that we need you and that you might not be available at the end of another year.

Of course you understand that the Bible Training School is not assured as yet, is only in prospect — but I think it will come, but I think it will take at least one or two years to get it on foot.

If you can decide to come to us next school year we should want you to take for your special work the "Chair of Mathematics" which would mean six recitations a day in the following subjects: Senior's Geometry, A Middler's Algebra, B Middler's Arithmetic, 2 divisions of Juniors in Arithmetic, 1 division of Preparatories. Of course the work outside of the Class Room that you would feel like doing and would do, I need not mention the opportunities for religious work exist on every hand.

If you come Sept. 1st of course you would be on hand for the Bible Training School in case we can get it on foot in the future.

Now as to the salary — we can offer nothing tempting; but can only offer you the same for the first year as that paid Rev. Whittaker[2] the first year viz, $600. for the nine months work. While I would not promise it, it is probable that work for two months of the Summer would be given you either in holding County institutes or working in the North, that would add to your year's income.

Regarding the house for you to live in, I think I told you in my letter, that there was no suitable one on the school grounds that could be given you, so early as the 1st of Sept., and that it is against our rule for the school to pay rent for Teacher's houses on the outside, but in case you decide to accept my proposition, I shall become personally responsible for the rent of the house for as long a time as it may be found necessary to rent one on the outside.

I have in mind two houses one of which I am sure can be secured for you provided that will suit. One is about a quarter of a mile from school in the direction to Town. It has under one roof four rooms two of which are quite large and a very large hall running through the house. The family who has just moved out of the house used the back part of this hall as a Dining Room having a screen in front. There is a kitchen and one other room detached from the main part of the house perhaps 20 or 30 ft. distant. These two rooms I do not think are in very good condition but I think the landlord would improve them. This house presents a very pretty appearance and I think you would like its surroundings. There are at least two acres of land belonging to it divided into three parts one of which is used as a cow pasture, a garden and the other which is partly covered with trees makes a pretty grove. It is one of the most picturesque and pretty places in Town and I think you and Mrs Penney would fall in love with it.

Of course it would be very much better if you could be nearer the school. There is a house that you may remember which has a number of large trees in front of it just opposite the school grounds, which has four rooms under one roof and two rooms 12 or 15 ft. distant from the main house. This house I think you would like perhaps better as it is practically on the school grounds, but I am not quite sure that the present tenant could be gotten out of it [by] Sept. 1st.

I trust I have made myself clear in all matters, and if I have not, I shall be glad to give you any other information in my power.

I remember you mentioning my call being formal and definite so that you can use it with the A. M. A.[3] In case you are inclined to think favorably of what I offer, I shall be glad to put the proposition in a more formal and definite shape.

Please be kind enough to remember me to the children and Mrs Penney, Yours truly,

B. T. Washington

HLpS Con. 106 BTW Papers DLC.

[1] Edgar James Penney (1852-1935) was born in Oxford, Ga. He graduated in the first class of Atlanta University (1876). He was ordained a Congregationalist minister at the Andover Theological Seminary in 1880. From 1891 to 1907 he served as chaplain of Tuskegee Institute and dean of the Phelps Hall Bible School. After leaving Tuskegee, Penney was connected with a small industrial school for blacks in Braxton, Miss., and served as pastor of a white church in Mason City, Iowa (1911-13). In 1916 he was living in Oklahoma.

[2] John W. Whittaker.

[3] American Missionary Association.

From Mary Fletcher Mackie

Hampton, Va., May 2 1890

Dear Mr. Washington— Gen. A. has returned to Hampton. He is better but far from well and has to be very careful not to over-work, the least bit knocks him all up. Directly after Commencement he goes North to rest. He is to spend the month of June in the Adirondacks with his friend Dr. Denison[1] and hopes to be much benefitted by the camp life. Dont worry about him and yet we all feel a little anxious all the time. Hastily but Sincerely yours

M. F. Mackie

ALS Con. 96 BTW Papers DLC.

[1] John Henry Denison (1841-1924), a Williams College classmate of Samuel Chapman Armstrong, was a Congregational minister. In 1869 he married a daughter of the Williams College president Mark Hopkins. He became chaplain of Hampton Institute in 1878 and later served six years as pastor of the Williams College church, retiring in 1889.

To Margaret James Murray

[Tuskegee, Ala.] May 3 [189]0

Miss M. J. Murray: Your salary for the coming school year beginning Sept 1, while acting as Lady Principal, will be ($500) Five Hundred Dollars and board for the sessions' work. I very much wish that it could be made more but see no way to do so at present. I trust this will be satisfactory.

B. T. Washington

ALpS Con. 106 BTW Papers DLC.

From John Henry Washington

Tuskegee, Ala., May 5/1890

Mr. B. T. Washington: Referring to the complaint made by Foster[1] and Daniels[2]: The matter of disgracing themselves was reported by

R. W. Taylor,[3] Gloss Germany[4] and Robt. Pindle[5] who came in the office and asked that the band not be allowed to go out anymore as the way they acted was a disgrace to the school. I refer to the time that attended Anderson school.

I did tell Foster he had taken to much libety in going to the carpenter shop ordering pole for drum major.

As to what was said about them going to town I do not know as I was in bed sick. They have said nothing to me about music sacks. I think they saw Mr. Logan about that.

J. H. Washington

ALS Con. 98 BTW Papers DLC.

[1] Samuel Berkeley Foster.

[2] Marshall Gaston Daniels.

[3] Robert Wesley Taylor, of Pensacola, Fla., entered Tuskegee in 1887. After graduating in 1890 he taught for a few years in his home town and then joined the faculty of Tuskegee Institute in 1893 as northern agent and instructor in mathematics. When in the North, Taylor was an effective platform speaker who gave lectures on "Booker T. Washington: The Inspirer of Negro Youths" and "Folks in Dixie." The proceeds of his lectures went to Tuskegee. (Circular, ca. 1901, Con. 276, BTW Papers, DLC.) When Taylor left the employ of Tuskegee in 1906, it was apparently at the suggestion of BTW, who believed Taylor had so much ability that he should engage in a business career more rewarding than his work as northern agent. He told Taylor what he said he had told many people, "that you are the only person who has ever helped me raise any money . . . worth counting, and that your place could not be filled." (BTW to Taylor, Jan. 10, 1906, Con. 34, BTW Papers, DLC.) Apparently Taylor's business venture was unsuccessful, for in 1907 he returned to the employ of Tuskegee. (BTW to United Merchants Improvement Co., July 1, 1907, Con. 362, BTW Papers, DLC.)

[4] Gloss Lorenzo Germany, Jr., of Union Springs, Ala., was a member of Tuskegee's class of 1891. After his four years at Tuskegee he taught for two years in Birmingham and then in Bullock County, Ala., schools.

[5] Robert Alexander Pindle, of Columbia, S.C., attended Tuskegee from 1888 to 1891. After graduation he was a teacher and tailor in Sumter, S.C.

To Atticus Greene Haygood

[Tuskegee, Ala.] May 10 [189]0

Dear Sir: While fully appreciating the help received from the Slater Fund in the past and being deeply grateful not only to the Board but to yourself for this help, I write to know if it is not possible for this school to receive an increase during the coming year.

With almost no help beyond the labor of the students we have built what is considered one of the best barns in the state and are now building a brick laundry in the same way. But this is the main ground on which I ask for an increase: A short time ago we saw an opportunity to get an excellent colored mechanic[1] who understands and can teach *tinning, harness-making* and *shoemaking* and fearing that another such opportunity would not offer we employed him at a salary of $100 per month and he is now teaching in all these much needed industries. Can you not help us out on this? Yours truly

B. T. Washington

ALpS   Con. 106   BTW Papers   DLC.

[1] Lewis Adams.

From Atticus Greene Haygood

Sheffield, Ala. May 10/90

Dear Mr W: The Board[1] adds for next year $200. making $1200 next year. The added $200. may help get y'r new department harness (?) established. What is y'r view of its use? Yrs etc.

A. G. Haygood

ACS   Con. 95   BTW Papers   DLC.

[1] Slater Fund board of trustees.

From George Washington Lovejoy

Portsmouth Virginia, May 12th, 1890

My Dear Mr. Washington: I shall in writing this letter, attempt as near as I can, to explain to you, my presant condition and future outlook as I see it.

I have studied very hard since I have been here, I have not allowed any thing to come between me and my studies. I feel that I have been greatly benefited, and now the time has come for me to prepair to make an other step.

I shall have to do some kind of work a year or two before beginding to practice. I need not here attempt to detail to you the necessities to an attorney's success, that you know better than my self. But I will name some of the things.

I must have books. You know I cannot succeed without them.

I must necessarily have some furniture in my office, I must have clothes with which to begin, and money to pay my board and other expenses, for a while.

I cannot expect to make enough in the beginding to meet my expenses. So you see it is necessary for me to begin prepaired.

I think I have made a surficient inroad on the law, or will have, by the first of Sept., to stand on my own legs. Mr. Reid[1] thinks I can make it by my self after a little.

Viewing the situation as I have: I here ask you if you don't think it best for me to look for some work for next Fall and Winter? I will use the money I make to buy books and keep studing at the same time; but I must say to you, I do not see a single thing around here to do.

There are so many people around here and such a little work; there are four or five candidates for the cleaning of every spittoon.

I hope you will not think I am lording my self, when I tell you I think I have done well to study, as I have and kept up my bills at the same time. I have worked at the U.S. Hospital, on the whalfs loading ships and in the U.S. Navyyard.

There has been as much pregidist here exhibited against me on the part of the laborers as you would expect to see, shown towards men who had gone to take strikers places.

Please write soon and let me know what you have to suggest. Respectfully yours,

G. W. Lovejoy

P.S. I will go to Hampton to the Commencement.

ALS   Con. 96   BTW Papers   DLC.

[1] William M. Reid.

From Maria A. Benson

Nashville Tenn., 5-20-'90

Dear Mr. Washington: Nothing could have been a more pleasant surprise to me than your letter of the 8th inst. I meant to answer sooner but the thief Procrastination prevented me.

I am feeling much better now than when I left, but I am still far from well. I think Mr. Washington, and I hope you will pardon my presumption and plain speaking, that you make a great mistake in keeping yourself so aloof from those who work for you. I'll venture to say that there are not more than two or three of your teachers who sympathize with you as they would if you were a little more sociable. There are not more than two there I think, who are not conscientiously doing their duty but I think all would be more willing to work if they felt that you had an interest in them beyond their drudgery in the schoolroom. Granted that there is an enormous strain upon you in your arduous and noble work, still if you would at times come out of yourself and enter in to the lives of those about you, you would find that you had gained strength.

I know that the seeming disinterestedness of your teachers is a cause of grief and annoyance to you. Shall I tell you why? Because they have not your confidence and, as they think esteem, and as a consequence, they do not respect and esteem you as they should. I love the work at Tuskegee, I love the people and only regret that my health caused me to leave. I had hoped to stay there and make my department as good as any of its kind in the country. I have wanted to say to you what I have said in this letter many times but the opportunity never offerred itself until you wrote me that letter. It was a perfect revelation to me and showed me how I, with hosts of others, misjudged you. Again begging your pardon for my plain speaking and hoping that you will believe that I said all this in good will and friendship. I am yours sincerely,

Maria A. Benson

ALS   Con. 861   BTW Papers   DLC.

To James Dickens McCall[1]

[Tuskegee, Ala.] May 26th, [189]0

Dear Sir: I am in receipt of your letter of a recent date applying for the position as Teacher of Science in this Institution for the coming scholastic year. In reply I would say that the position is still unfilled and as you have been recommended to me by Miss Murray and others, I should be pleased to have you take the position.

I am very desirous that the person filling this position shall come with the intention of filling the position permanently, that is, so long as the salary and his relation to the institution continue satisfactory.

I am very anxious to make Science a strong and prominent feature in this institution. This institution is peculiarly a Missionary one being supported almost entirely by charity and it is very important that those connected with it in the capacity of Teachers be of a strong, earnest, Christian character.

In the way of salary we can pay you for the work $38. and board — the board including washing, room, etc.

Should you take hold of the Department and build it up, this salary would perhaps be increased later.

Our school year begins the first Monday in September and it will be well for you to be on hand one or two days before that time.

Please let me have an early and definite answer. Yours truly,

B. T. Washington

TLpS Con. 106 BTW Papers DLC.

[1] James Dickens McCall, of Rome, Tenn., graduated from Fisk University in 1890. He taught science at Tuskegee from 1890 to 1906. From 1897 to 1902 he also assumed the duties of head of the academic department.

From Cornelius Nathaniel Dorsette

Montgomery Ala   May 31st 1890

Prof B. T. Washington   Col Jones[1] nominated on first Ballot. Hurah.

Dr. Dorsette

HWSr Con. 95 BTW Papers DLC.

[1] Thomas Goode Jones (1844-1914) was educated in Montgomery, Ala., schools and in Virginia. At the outbreak of the Civil War he was a cadet at Virginia Military Institute. He joined the Confederate Army, rising to the rank of major. He was present at the surrender of Lee at Appomattox and was bearer of a flag of truce. After the war he practiced law, farmed, became active in local government in Montgomery, and served several terms in the Alabama legislature. He was a colonel of Alabama state troops from 1880 to 1890 and was elected governor in 1890, serving two terms. Jones called out the militia and Pinkertons to crush the 1894 Alabama strikes and later was attorney for the Louisville and Nashville Railroad. It is possible that BTW played a role in Jones's reelection in 1892. Jones had a history of supporting Negro rights that BTW could not overlook. In 1883 as an officer of Alabama state troops Jones saved a black man from a lynch mob in Birmingham, and as governor he protected the Negro school funds from being undermined by white supremacists. According to one account, written five years after Jones's reelection, BTW actually campaigned for Jones among black citizens. More likely he may have toured the Black Belt, privately urging blacks to support the Democratic governor. C. N. Dorsette, BTW's close friend and confidant, openly campaigned for Jones. BTW's growing political influence with Theodore Roosevelt made it possible for the Tuskegean to secure Jones's appointment to a federal district judgeship in 1901. While on the bench Jones played an important role in the Alabama peonage cases. He ruled against the Negro plaintiffs in two suffrage cases in 1903-4, however, and used his court to protect mining companies against strikers, and to block state regulation of railroads. (See Daniel, *Shadow of Slavery*, 43-81, and Harlan, *BTW*, 255-56, 308-10.)

From Helen Wilhelmina Ludlow

Hampton Va. June 2, '90

Dear Mr Washington   I return with thanks, Mr Cable's interesting letters. The General and Mr Frissell have also read them with interest. The one to Mr Smiley I had seen in some colored journal from which I took the extract for the Workman.[1] The General was away when I wrote the editorial but he saw and approved it before it went to press. You may be sure it expresses his sentiments.

He has gone now to the meeting.[2] Let us hope it will have good results in spite of what we must consider a mistake — and one of these a change of plan for the next meeting in accordance with Mr Cable's sensible suggestions so courteously expressed.

Miss Nichols[3] has returned quite enthusiastic — of course — over

Tuskegee. I hope her letters were satisfactory to you and will prove useful.

Miss Folsom[4] declares she is quite jealous of her. She was North however, and got back after Miss Nichols had said she would go. Miss F. is a *very* good writer, with more experience than Miss Nichols and it may be well to remember her as a possible reporter for you another year.

I am glad to hear that you had so successful an Anniversary.

With hearty congratulations thereon and good wishes and greetings for you all   Ever cordially,

Helen W. Ludlow

P.S. Have you heard of the General's engagement? Congratulations are in order. He is to marry, early in September, Miss Ford,[5] a teacher here for the last two or three years, an attractive, interesting woman — about half the General's age — a great favorite with her pupils in her department of natural history.

We all trust that the marriage will give the General that home happiness and rest that will crown the life he has so long lavished on his work for humanity, and at the same time give him new strength for it and prolong his days.

I knew you would be interested to hear about it if you have not already heard.

H. W. L.

ALS   Con. 96   BTW Papers   DLC.

[1] Miss Ludlow wrote for the *Southern Workman:* "We hope for good things from the new Mohonk Conference in June, to which Mr. A. K. Smiley, with characteristic hospitality and broad humanity has invited a large number of the friends of Negro education and progress. That it is limited to white people will no doubt be felt — and by none more than Mr. Smiley himself — as a serious limitation on its effectiveness, both in moral influence and in the full understanding of the subject, to which such men as Dr. Price of Livingstone College, Mr. Washington of Tuskegee, and others, could contribute valuable practical experience and personal demonstration." The editorial went on to praise G. W. Cable for stating publicly that blacks should be included. (*Southern Workman,* 29 [May 1890], 49.) When Samuel Chapman Armstrong returned from the conference he took a more conservative view of Smiley's motivation. "In order to be sure and get the Southern white men to come, he [Smiley] decided not to invite any colored people. He has been criticized for that, as you know. He is a warm friend of the colored

race. His whole object was their benefit. But he thought it best to do one thing at a time." (*Southern Workman,* 29 [July 1890], 77.)

2 The Lake Mohonk Negro Conference.

3 Alice May Nichols Townsend taught in the Hampton night school and also wrote for the *Southern Workman.* In October 1890 she married and moved to Philadelphia.

4 Cora M. Folsom.

5 Mary Alice Ford Armstrong.

From Jacob Tileston Brown[1]

Lincoln University Pa. June 3rd 1890

Prof Booker Washington   Accept congratulations. Lincoln University gave you honorary AM today.

J. Tileston Brown

HWSr   Con. 861   BTW Papers   DLC.

1 Jacob Tileston Brown (b. 1863) graduated from Hampton in 1888 and Lincoln University Seminary in 1891. He served as principal and later as president of Florida Baptist Seminary in Jacksonville from 1892 to 1896. He was the pastor of the Dexter Avenue Baptist Church in Montgomery, Ala., from 1896 to 1898. Brown also held several church positions in Texas and was founder of Boyd's Academy in Oakwood, Tex. (1904-5).

To Samuel Chapman Armstrong

Tuskegee, Ala., June 7 1890

Dear Gen. Armstrong: Please be kind enough to send me a new letter of recommendation to 25 Beacon St. Boston.

I want to ask you if it is not asking too much for a letter of recommendation for Rev. John W. Whittaker, our chaplain. He is an Atlanta graduate, a thorough earnest gentleman and perfectly loyal. He has been with me two years and I feel that I *know* him and can *trust* him. He has helped me in the North and is going to do so this summer again. He has gone into new fields. He is a graduate of the Hartford

Theological Seminary. If you send one for him, both can be sent to 25 Beacon St. Yours truly

Booker T. Washington

ALS   BTW Folder   ViHaI.

From Blanche Kelso Bruce

Washington, D.C. June 11 1890

My dear Prof. Washington: I am highly gratified to receive your valued favor of the 5th inst. and the accompanying newspapers containing reports of my humble effort on May 29th.

The Boston Traveller could not have given a more flattering notice than did the Montgomery Advertiser and the other Ala. papers. Grateful as I am for the good things said, I am not so vain as to think that my remarks alone inspired them. They spring in large part from a frank recognition of your high standing in the community and the great work that you are doing for the upbuilding of the people. I am under obligations also for your kindly reference to my address in the last issue of the Cleveland Gazette.[1]

Remember me kindly to your brother & family and also to your co-workers whose acquaintance I made during my pleasant stay with you. Sincerely yours,

B. K. Bruce

ALS   Con. 94   BTW Papers   DLC.

[1] A report of the Tuskegee commencement, perhaps written by BTW, appeared in the Cleveland *Gazette,* June 7, 1890, 2. It said in part: "Mr. Bruce's subject was the 'Race Problem,' and he spoke right out as to the rights of the Negro — not mincing matters, but saying what he would have said in Boston or New York. But notwithstanding his straight-forward speech, as soon as Mr. Bruce was through, the most prominent whites in the audience — all life-long Democrats — crowded around him and congratulated him in a most hearty manner. The Montgomery *Advertiser* reported that 7,000 persons attended the commencement and characterized Bruce as the "grandest representative of his race, the best informed, the best orator, and the man best calculated to give good advice to the colored race. . . ." (May 31, 1890, 4.)

From Hiram R. Davidson

Insane Asylum   Columbus Ohio   June 13— 1890

Dear Brother. Your favor of May 31st inst. is at hand. it reached me too late, to be of any service to them. they got here on friday, and I did not get the letter until monday. am very sorry, on Mrs King's[1] account, as she had conciderable trouble to find us. however, they got here all right, and they are I presume, in Boston ere this. they left here on wednesday morning.

I congratulate you on your choice of a nurse. I do not think you could have made a better one. Mrs King, is certainly a moddle, booth morally and Intellectually. I hope you can arrange to keep your children under her charge for a while, so that they may have the benefit of a correct training.

hopeing that you are well, I am yours as ever,

H. R. Davidson

ALS   Con. 17   BTW Papers   DLC.

[1] Dora S. King.

To Warren Logan

New York. June 14, 90

Please keep an eye on the "student" and let nothing be published that will give trouble in the way that Lovejoy did.[1]

It is my plan to go to Boston tomorrow or Monday.

B. T. W.

Send out those circulars as fast as possible.

ACI   Con. 3   BTW Papers   ATT.   Original destroyed.

[1] On the Lovejoy incident in 1887, see above, 2:367-68.

To Samuel Chapman Armstrong

Stevens House   New York, June 28 1890

Dear Gen. Armstrong: This morning I had a very pleasant call on Mr. C. P. Huntington at his summer residence in Westchester. He spoke about his intention to visit Hampton within a few days and that he is planing to give a sum of money for the enlargement and support of the saw mill &c.

He gives Tuskegee $1000. Yours truly

Booker T. Washington
25 Beacon St., Boston

ALS BTW Folder ViHaI. BTW wrote on the stationery of the Stevens House but gave the Boston mailing address.

From William D. Floyd

Opelika, Ala., July 14th 1890

My dear teacher: With much regret I write you relative to something I heard Rev. McEwen,[1] of Mont'y., say about some remarks made in your address at the closing exercises at Nashvill, Tenn. at Fisk University. Some pastor, Baptist I think, per surname Jackson of Nashvill wrote him. Said that you remarked, out of four hundred (400) Colored Baptist Churches in Alabama only about fifteen intelligent pastors could be found to carry the gospel. He remarked, (McEwen) that "I am going to refute it all." Again, he (Mc.) said that if you didn't put half (½) Baptist teachers in your School that he was going to raise his voice against the School. He proposed to split the School. Furthermore, stated that you were only a Normal School Graduate and the only way you could raise money North was telling the people that the Colored people in the South were very illiterate. He said that within a very short while he would be heard from through the Baptist Leader. His remarks were very offensive to me on this line. I simple do this as a matter of duty, to inform you of what is going on without a cause, I believe.

I would like, if you should see proper to mention the fact to Rev. Mc. to keep my name out of the matter. I inform you of this because I feel duty bound so to act toward you. With the proper means you can or may ascertain whether he has made any assertions relative to what I've said above. Don't mention my name unless an absolute necessity then I don't care.

By reading the Baptist Leader you'll know whether he has anything against you or not. I know you will. I simple mention this fact because this will increase your interest in the matter.

I have resigned Troy School for reasons, I think justifiable. I think it for the better.

My mother is quite ill and has been for a month or probably more. She doesn't improve any it seems. Temporary relief at times. Respectfully,

William D. Floyd

ALS Con. 95 BTW Papers DLC.

¹ A. N. McEwen.

From George Washington Campbell

Tuskegee, Ala., July 16 1890

My Dear Sir: Your letter of 12th Inst to hand.

Permit me to congratulate you on the position you have taken on the question we have been discussing in our correspondence,[1] and I hope the politicians of the north will not succeed in keeping themselves in power by passing any bill that will humiliate and degrade either the whites or blacks of the south, *class* legislation ought not to be tolerated either north or south, such legislation is not necessary. *Just let us alone,* and there is no question but what the whites and blacks will harmonize, and each class will be benefitted by being left to *work* out its own destiny.

I never shall forget the impression made on my mind the day the Hon Mr. Bruce[2] delivered his address on the occasion of the closing exercises of your school. I occupied a seat that enabled me to see the faces of 2000 or 3000 col[']d people that composed the audience and I can say that I never saw *Satisfaction* and *Contentment* more indelibly impressed on the countenances of any audience than on that occasion. I wish that some of the "howling" politicians of the north could have witnessed that scene.

We are having very dry weather our crop prospects are still good but it will be necessary to have some rain soon.

Some sickness in town and Country, caused by extreme hot weather. Hope you are well and that you may gather in the *shekels*. Yours very Truly

G W Campbell

ALS   Con. 94   BTW Papers   DLC.

[1] BTW apparently opposed the federal elections bill of 1890, the so-called Force Bill, that would have caused states denying blacks the vote to lose representatives in Congress, as provided for in the Fourteenth Amendment.
[2] Blanche Kelso Bruce.

From Harriet S. Tolman[1]

"Green Lodge"   Wianno, Cape Cod, Mass. July 17th, 1890

Dear Sir, You may remember the name of my mother — Mrs. James Tolman[2] — as one of your correspondents last Winter. We have just heard from our friend Rev. Charles Lombard[3] — of your intended visit to his parish in Plymouth, & have thought that possibly you might like to come here while in this vicinity. Unfortunately it is not at all convenient to come here directly from Plymouth although we are in the same region. But if you can give us another Sunday, we will do our best to make it both pleasant & profitable for you. We have a good deal of the old anti-slavery tradition in our community of Summer residents, as we include Mr. William Lloyd Garrison, & Mrs. E. B. Chace[4] whose father[5] was the first president of the American Anti-Slavery Society. She would be happy to have you address a company in her large parlor — a place where we often have gatherings on Sunday evenings. And my Mother & I would be pleased to have you our guest for two or three days — say from a Friday until a Monday or Tuesday, & would also be happy to provide your ticket to & from

Boston so that the journey should be no expense to you. We have long felt a desire to know more about your work, & have wished that we could do more than simply subscribe for a scholarship — as Mother did last Winter. We hope that if you can address a company here some amount might be raised towards a scholarship, but of course cannot promise definitely.[6] A Sunday would be the only time favorable for an address, as it is then only that the gentlemen are here. If you find that you can accept our invitation, I will suggest a time for coming. We will then send you particulars of the journey. Yours with good wishes —

(Miss) H. S. Tolman

ALS Con. 97 BTW Papers DLC.

[1] Harriet S. Tolman was probably the "Miss Tolman" who was among the first to build a home in the Wianno area of Cape Cod. (See Trayser, *Barnstable,* 438.)

[2] Mary (Mrs. James T.) Tolman of Newton, Mass.?

[3] Charles Parker Lombard (1845-1913) was pastor of the First Church in Plymouth, Mass.

[4] Elizabeth Buffum Chace (1806-99), a longtime activist in woman suffrage and anti-slavery causes. Her summer home at Wianno was a gathering place for reformers.

[5] Arnold Buffum (1782-1859) was first president of the New England Anti-Slavery Society, beginning in 1832, and was a founder of the American Anti-Slavery Society in 1833.

[6] On Sept. 2, 1890, Harriet S. Tolman wrote BTW that his visit to the Wianno colony had resulted in raising $100 for Tuskegee, $50 of which was a "Wianno Scholarship." (Con. 700, BTW Papers, DLC.)

From Augustus Field Beard[1]

New York, July 19, 1890

My dear Brother: Is it your wish that we should appoint Miss Anna C. Hawley teacher of the A.M.A. at your school for the coming year? and if so, will you kindly tell me what salary she receives; how much per calendar month, and whether her traveling expenses to and from her home are additional? or would you prefer that we should nominate some other teacher to this position? Your early attention to this will greatly oblige me.

And now will you kindly do me a great favor? I was greatly gratified with your after dinner speech at Fisk University at the Alumni meeting. Would you be willing to put what you said respecting the religious condition of affairs in writing, so that I could use it if I wished to, in our endeavor to build up our Theological work? You will remember that you spoke very cordially and kindly of our purpose to have a Theological Seminary at Fisk, and that you exhorted the students to think definitely of Christian work and of the Christian ministry, and you made some statements then relative to the impurity both of the Methodist and Baptist denominations, that is, the impurity of the ministers in the Methodist and Baptist denominations, contrasting the relative purity of our Congregational pastors with what you knew about the pastors in the Black Belt.

If you would give this to me in writing, it would be a most valuable testimony coming from you, and would be highly appreciated by us in behalf of those whom we are trying to bring out of just this condition which you described.

Thanking you in advance for your courtesy I am, Yours sincerely,

A. F. Beard

TLS Con. 94 BTW Papers DLC.

[1] Augustus Field Beard (1833-1934), a Congregational minister who graduated from Yale University and served as pastor of the American Church in Paris for a number of years before, in 1884, becoming a secretary of the American Missionary Association. In 1886 he became corresponding secretary of the A.M.A. and from 1903 to 1928 was editor of the association's magazine, the *American Missionary*. He wrote *A Crusade for Brotherhood: A History of the American Missionary Association* (1909).

From Timothy Thomas Fortune

New York, July 23 1890

Dear Mr. Washington: Your note of the 22nd inst was received. Glad to have a word from you.

Shall make note of the item of news and information you furnish me concerning Cable and the Mohonk Conference Pharisees.[1] Cable appears to be a square man. Yours truly,

T. Thos. Fortune

ALS   Con. 95   BTW Papers   DLC.

[1] Fortune was outraged that the white sponsors of the Mohonk Conference on Negroes did not invite any blacks to attend. When Lyman Abbott, a member of the conference, was asked why no blacks were invited, he replied: "A patient is not invited to the consultation of the doctors on his case." Fortune believed, using Abbott's analogy, that the real reason was that the white doctors did not want to come in contact with black doctors. Fortune wrote that if blacks were denied access to such conferences, "the scalpel will be constantly gliding into the wrong portion of the patient's anatomy, to the squandering of vast sums of money and the retardation of the patient's progress." The *Age* estimated that there were 20,000 black teachers, 20 bishops, and 100 editors who had more knowledge of the status of Negroes than the white members of the Mohonk Conference. (New York *Age*, June 21, 1890, 2.) At BTW's suggestion, Fortune reported that George W. Cable had boycotted the Mohonk Conference because no blacks were invited to attend. "Let Dr LYMAN ABBOTT bite upon that fact," Fortune wrote. (New York *Age*, Aug. 2, 1890, 2.)

From Six Students to Warren Logan and Washington

Tuskegee, Ala., July 26 1890

Sirs: We, in behalf of our brother workman and school-mate Wm Connowley,[1] do hereby acknowlege our sorrow for him in his great trouble — that of being suspended from this Institution for the period of one month. Our grief is so great that we are prompted to ask, that if any punishment save that of suspension can be inflicted, it will greatly alleviate the trouble with him, and to some extent, put an end to our sorrow.

We are confident that you as officers of this school have discharged your duty in full view of the fact that Connover's many acts of disobeisance have culminated into one too large to be passed over in silence, and that you in the discharge of that duty have acted with equity. But please consider also that he has been turned out without even a penny with which to buy bread. If food he gets, which he certainly must, and a couch upon which to rest his body, it will be through the kindness of Tuskegee's people and not that his financial condition will enable him to purchase such. Sir, all these things stare us in the face, at the same time remembering the cause of his being placed thus, and have evoked from us this plea for a reconsideration of the punishment you have inflicted, in so much that he may be allowed to be with us again but under some other punishment if possible. Your obt. Servants:

> M. G. Daniels
> H. R. Wyman[2]
> T. A. Brocks[3]
> Amanda Crum[4]
> Lizzie Wright[5]
> Anna Terrell[6]

ALS Con. 95 BTW Papers DLC.

[1] William Wadsworth Connover, of Hartford, Conn., attended Tuskegee's night school from 1889 to 1891.

[2] Henry Russell Wyman of Montgomery attended Tuskegee's night school from 1887 to 1891, when he was a member of the B middle class.

[3] Thomas A. Brocks, a night-school student from Ft. Deposit, Lowndes County, Ala., attended Tuskegee in 1889-90.

[4] Amanda E. or H. Crum, as her middle initial was variously represented in the Tuskegee catalogs, was from Furman, Wilcox County, Ala. She attended Tuskegee in the junior and B middle classes from 1888 to 1890.

[5] Elizabeth Evaline (or Evelyn) Wright of Talbotton, Ga., entered the Tuskegee A preparatory class in 1888 and graduated in 1894. She then taught in various parts of South Carolina before founding Voorhees Normal and Industrial School, Denmark, S.C., serving as principal. In 1906 she married Martin A. Menafee, one of her teachers. She died on Dec. 14, 1906.

[6] Annie M. Terrell of Raleigh, N.C., attended Tuskegee as a junior in 1889-90.

An Article in the *Christian Union*

Tuskegee, Ala. [Aug. 14, 1890]

THE COLORED MINISTRY
ITS DEFECTS AND NEEDS

By Booker T. Washington

Principal of the Tuskegee Normal School

What is the actual condition of the colored ministry in the South, is a question that should interest every one. As a part answer to this question I give the following extracts taken from the leading editorial of the Alabama "Baptist Leader," the organ of the colored Baptists of Alabama, edited by the Rev. A. N. McEwen, of Montgomery, a well-informed and reliable minister: "The greatest object of over two-thirds of the Baptist ministers of Alabama is to collect their salaries. They care no more for the moral and intellectual training of the people than they care for the snap of their finger. They care no more for schools, for public enterprises, than if there were no such things. . . . In some parts of the country where our missionaries travel, they find preachers who do not take a paper of any sort, nor read the Bible; in fact, they cannot read, and yet they are attempting to lead the people." So far as it goes, the foregoing extract tells the truth; but in order to grasp the situation it is well to bear in mind that there are in the fifteen Southern States, including the District of Columbia, at least 7,000,000 colored people to be reached with the Gospel. In their religious opinion these people are almost equally divided between the Baptist and Methodist denominations. This is about the numerical force: Colored Baptists, 1,120,000 church members, 10,000 churches, and 7,000 ordained ministers; Methodists (divided into the African, Zion, Wesleyan, Northern, and Colored Methodist branches), with about the same numerical strength as the Baptists, making a total of 2,240,000 church members in these two denominations. In Alabama there are 21 Congregational churches, with a combined membership of 1,326 persons, and an examination will show that the average colored Congregational members in each State will fall below 1,000, the average membership for each church being about 50. Outside of the two leading denominations — Methodists and Baptists — the combined membership of all other denominations, Presbyterians, Episcopalians, etc., in the South will not equal more than half of the numerical strength of the Congregationalists, so that it is safe to say that the total membership of all other denominations, exclusive of Methodists and Baptists, is about 22,500. About 2,264,500 of the 7,000,000 are church members. But what is the character of the preaching that these masses receive, whether church members or not, and what does belonging to the Church mean to them? The ministers representing the Congregational, Presbyterian, and Episcopalian Churches are, as a rule, intelligent and earnest, yet they are so cramped by denominational lines that they reach and influence but a small number.

Now as to the intelligence, morality, and religious earnestness. After coming into direct contact with the colored ministers for eight years in the heart of the South, I have no hesitancy in asserting that three-fourths of the Baptist ministers and two-thirds of the Methodists are unfit, either mentally or morally, or both, to preach the Gospel to any one or to attempt to lead any one. The Baptists claim ten thousand churches and seven thousand ordained ministers; but it is perfectly safe to say that each church contains an average of four persons licensed to preach, and the same is true of the Methodists. One Baptist church near Tuskegee has a total membership of two hundred, and eighteen of them are preachers; but the character of many of these preachers can be judged by one, of whom it is said that, while he was at work in a cotton field in the middle of July, he suddenly stopped, looked upward, and said, "O Lord, de work is so hard, de cotton is so grassy, and de sun am *so* hot, I bleave dis darkey am called to preach." With few exceptions, the preaching of the colored ministry is emotional in the highest degree, and the minister considers himself successful in proportion as he is able to set the people in all parts of the congregation to groaning, uttering wild screams, and jumping, finally going into a trance. One of the principal ends sought by most of these ministers is their salary, and to this everything else is made subservient. Most of the church service seems to resolve itself into an effort to get money. Not one in twenty has the business standing in the communities where they reside, and those who know them best mistrust them most in matters of finance and general morality.

With such spiritual leaders, the mere fact that so large a proportion of the seven million colored people in the South are church members is misleading, and is no evidence that a large proportion of these church members are not just as ignorant of true Christianity, as taught by Christ, as any people in Africa or Japan, and just as much in need of missionary efforts as those in foreign lands.

What is the difficulty in the present mode of supply, and how can it be supplemented and enlarged? At present each denomination doing missionary work in the South has one or more theological seminaries. Those seminaries, as a rule, shape their courses of study after the model of Andover, Hartford, or Union Theological Seminaries. The consequence is that a *very* small proportion of the young colored men entering the Southern theological seminaries are mentally fitted to pursue with profit such courses. The smattering of Greek and Hebrew and other difficult branches they are dragged through merely serves to muddle many, and they leave the seminary in a muddle, knowing nothing well. But this is not so bad as the fact that a discouragingly small number enter these seminaries, and a very small proportion of those entering graduate. To illustrate: I hold in my hand the catalogues of the principal and, in some cases, the only theological schools in the South, of the Congregational, Presbyterian, and Baptist denominations. In one case the whole number to graduate this year in theology is two, and in the next six are in the graduating class; but the middle class is empty and none will graduate next year. The Baptists have concentrated their theological work upon one seminary, and while the Baptists have ten thousand churches to be kept supplied with intelligent ministers, only five ministers finish the course of study this year in their seminary. In the cases cited the courses of study occupy three and four years. Granting that those who finish courses of study are masters of what they have gone over, is it not plain that, after due allowance is made for the few qualified colored ministers educated in Northern seminaries, and for those educated at normal schools and colleges who enter the ministry without special training, the need for a helpful ministry in this country, to say nothing of Africa, is not being met even in a small degree?

It should be borne in mind that the masses of the colored people, and those most in need of help, live in the country, and that at least four-fifths of the educated colored ministers go into the cities and towns. In fact, during my eight years' residence and traveling in the country districts, I have not come into contact with a single educated minister preaching in the country, and I repeat, for emphasis, that, outside of the Baptist and Methodist denominations, the educated ministers do not reach in their own congregations an average of over fifty persons, though they do do much general work for the uplifting of the people, and give them examples of what a church should be. I have no unfriendly word for the theological work now being done, nor should I ask that the standard of scholarship be lowered, for we need broad and deep theologians; but it is painfully evident that something needs to be done to give the masses trained and helpful ministers — to supplement the present ministerial training. I am thoroughly convinced that if a school, to be known as a Bible Seminary or Bible Training School, were established at some central point in the South, on a thoroughly Christian but *strictly* undenominational basis, with a one or two years' course covering such branches as would fit a student to get a comprehensive idea of the Bible, to teach him how to prepare a sermon, how to read a hymn, how to study, and, most important, how to reach and help the people outside of the pulpit in an unselfish Christian way, it would be a great power for good. To begin with, one teacher could do the work that I have suggested for forty or fifty students, and I am sure that such a seminary would be crowded with students from the beginning. When the school grew to the point where two or three teachers were demanded (and it would be well to have, as early as possible, the leading denominations represented in the force of teachers) $1,500 or $2,500 would supply the teaching force, and at the same time thirty or forty men could be sent out each year with a training that would enable them to go into the country and elsewhere among the masses of the people and help them in a most effectual way. As such a seminary would be non-sectarian, all denominations would enter it, and it would send forth every year a stream of young men who would fill Baptist and all other pulpits. In other words, they would reach the masses. In the present seminaries the tuition alone of ten or a dozen sometimes costs $3,000 or $4,000. With the proposed Bible seminary this sum could be made to educate many times this number.

Christian Union, 42 (Aug. 14, 1890), 199-200. BTW gave a speech on this subject at the Fisk commencement in June 1890.

From Dora S. King

Hanover Mass. Aug. 19/90

Mr. Washington, The children are all well, even Davidson, who is just now struggling with five teeth. That little front one has not come through the gum yet, and now he has four large ones starting. They are the ones we thought he was cutting just before he left Tuskegee, that is, his eye and stomach teeth. He has had a little disturbance of the system, but only a little. I scald all his milk, just as we did when he was younger, and he has medicine before each meal, and just before retiring at night, to keep his system in order. He sleeps a great deal, (which is very good for him just at this time) and comes to be "cuddled" which he never thinks of doing when he is well. I had hoped he would have four or six weeks rest between the two little front teeth and the next set, but he did not even wait to finish the front ones. If he gets through with these all right, I shall be very thankful, as the next four are not critical ones, and will complete his first set, and he will have no more until he is six years old. The other children are well, and Portia is waiting patiently for her letter.

My salary was due yesterday, the 18th. You will please remember my request for the September salary in connection with that for August, making fifty dollars all together. Mrs. Winslow's[1] money for the board is due Thursday Aug. 21st, so if you care to send both amounts at one time it will perhaps save you trouble. The whole amount will be,

for Mrs. Winslow	$30.00
" myself	$50.00
	$80.00

Send by check or money order, which ever will give you the least trouble.

Dora S. King

ALS Con. 17 BTW Papers DLC.

[1] Possibly Harriet Howard Winslow (1804-99) of Hanover, Mass.

From James Robert Williams[1]

Mobile Ala. Augst 29. 1890

Kind princible I cannt exspress my sorrow and sadnus I feels as a sheep lost from it flock I would be under ten thousand obligations if I could get my sentence remitted I am shore that such will never be the case again how sad I feels to-night knowing that they are students leaveing for School and I cannt go if you will give me another triel I will be true in ever scence of the word Kind sir you know our greates men makes mistakes but I hope this will last me all my life I hope you will look in to this to and think surpose it was you asking for forgivenus I can only ask forgivenus sadnus has approach my heart and tears have approch my cheeks this night While writeing thou I am under ten thousand obliga[tions] any how and I am only two sorrow that I hasent been able to do what I wanted to do for the school. sicknus stop me Mrs. Josephen Mathews has a good quiet boy[2] 16 years old she wishes to put him in the Wheel right Shop or in any trade deparment most but she perfers the former trade spoken of I wish you write to her your self address N.E. Cor. Congrus & Kenady St Mobile in Cf henry Hamilton

Nothing more pleas exscuse mistakes and bad writeing and write soon address N.W. Cor. Jackson & Konx st.

James R. Williams

ALS Con. 98 BTW Papers DLC. BTW wrote in the margin: "Mr. J. H. W.: What do you think of this B.T.W." John H. Washington replied in the margin: "I think he might [be] allowed to return to work again. J.H.W."

¹ James Robert Williams, a night-school student from Mobile, attended Tuskegee from 1889 to 1891.

² Possibly Walter Mathews of Mobile, who attended the Tuskegee night school from 1891 to 1893.

To William Hooper Councill

[Tuskegee, Ala.] Aug 30 [189]0

Dear sir: You are of course aware of the appropriation by congress to help agricultural schools &c.

I propose (and Prof. Patterson¹ has agreed to it,) for us 3 to have a meeting in Montgomery early in Sept and decide 1st on the prop[os]ition to ask the legislature to give to the colored people, 2nd on an equitable division of the fund² among the 3 schools. If you agree to this name a day when you can meet us in Montgomery.

This plan I think preferable to a "squabble." Yours truly

B. T. Washington

ALpS Con. 106 BTW Papers DLC.

¹ William Burns Paterson (1850-1915), born in Tullibody, Clackmannanshire, Scotland, immigrated to the United States in 1869. After working as a common laborer in the Midwest, he worked on railroad construction near Selma, Ala. In 1870 he began a school for blacks, Tullibody Academy, moving it to Marion in 1879. About 1885 he was appointed president of the Lincoln Normal University, with about 300 students. It was moved to Montgomery in 1887 as the Alabama State Normal School. (See above, 2:320.) The Slater Fund made an annual contribution to its industrial courses, and many of its industrial teachers were graduates

of Tuskegee. Like BTW, Paterson took pride in the number of his graduates who became teachers and artisans. (Dabney, *Universal Education in the South,* 2:439-43.)

[2] The Morrill Act of 1890 provided subsidies to states for agricultural college education. This was often confused at the time with the Hatch Act of 1887, which provided federal funds for state agricultural experiment stations.

From Robert Charles Bedford

Montgomery Ala   Sep 2 1890

Dear Prof   Your kind letter came this morning. I wrote a card yesterday as Mrs Bedford had told me of Mr Garner's[1] statement that you were sick. I am glad to know that you are up. Many of the best members of the church still think it wrong for me to leave them. A meeting is called for Monday night Sep 8 to consider the matter but the discussion over the coming of a colored minister not only greatly unsettles things and impairs my usefulness but makes my work unpleasant and hard. The AMA wish me to continue in their service which I have agreed to do provided a suitable arrangement can be made between us. In the present great and growing needs of the South in every direction I cannot feel that it is right that I should give up my 8 years of experience. I certainly do not want to and I confidently expect the right path will open for me and my hand and voice will still be permitted to labor where my heart so truly is. Personally I am greatly attached to this church but my conviction is very strong that there will be no real peace till they have tried a colored minister. Mr Jackson[2] is at Selma well qualified having graduated from Talladega and Oberlin and has had nothing to do since leaving school. I expect he will be sent here. Many of the people are acquainted with him and like him.

I greatly sympathize with you in your constantly increasing responsibilities and for your sake alone, were it not for the suffering of the church I would not think of leaving here. Strange as it may seem and unwilling as I am to believe it yet I fear it is true that the severest charge brought against me and that by colored people who claim great "race pride" is the kindly spirit I have so innocently borne to Tuskegee, Mt Meigs, and all other schools and churches outside of the city that have asked my help while I have not had less of the same feeling for all the churches and schools in the city. I do not want

to have the church divided by an agitation of these matters and therefore I feel that the less said the better now and perhaps when I am
gone these things will all be understood. I will write you as soon as I
hear from New York. I trust the school opened well and that every
thing looks promising. With kind regards to all. Your bro

R. C. Bedford

ALS Con. 94 BTW Papers DLC.

[1] Mitchell Dorsette Garner entered Tuskegee in 1890 and graduated in 1896.
He taught carpentry in the Kowaliga, Ala., Industrial School and in 1898 became
a member of the Tuskegee faculty in carpentry. He was still a member of the
faculty at BTW's death.

[2] Joseph Samuel Jackson, born in Mansfield, La., in 1862, received a B.D. de-
gree from Talladega College in 1889 and a B.D. degree from Oberlin in 1890.
He was probably Bedford's successor, for the 1892-93 catalog of Talladega re-
ported him as a pastor in Montgomery. Later he served churches in Cleveland,
Steubenville, Columbus, and Cincinnati, Ohio. He received a D.D. degree from
Wilberforce University in 1915.

From Dora S. King

Hanover Mass. Sept. 5/90

Mr. Washington, Yours of the 26th containing check for $30.00 came
safely to hand. You will perhaps remember that when the children had
been here two weeks Mrs. Winslow wished for their board money for
that length of time, and I wrote you that the two weeks would be up
on the 20th of June, as we came here the 12th. I also stated that after
that time she would like the money once in *four* weeks, and unless I
am greatly mistaken I stated that the next four weeks would close
Thursday July 24th. I also told you when you were with us, at what
date the money was due in July, and that Hanover is now a money
order office. I wrote you about it that first time particularly so that
there should be no misunderstanding. The third payment was due
Thursday August 21st and the next one will be due Thursday September 18th the same date at which my salary is due. She never takes
boarders by the month, but always by the week. I think I once told
you that I pay for my children's board by the week and receive my
salary by the month, so that at the end of three months or thirteen
weeks I pay out sixty-five dollars for their board and receive only

seventy-five, giving me only a surplus of ten dollars for clothing, shoes and so forth, for the children and myself. That was why when we were making arrangements for the summer, I asked you to pay my children's fare from Boston to Tuskegee, and let me repay you when we are settled at the latter place. I told you at the time, that if I had the care of your children during the summer, my salary would not enable me to pay their fare. If you have forgotten that conversation, we will be obliged to make new arrangements.

With regard to the children calling each other brother and sister, I will do the best I can. The custom is distinctively southern, and one with which I have had no personal contact. As I understand it, the eldest girl is called sister and the eldest boy brother, not only by the family, but by outsiders as well. Do you wish Portia and Baker to call Davidson brother? You may or may not know that Baker seriously objects to being called brother. I have often heard him tell the teachers at Tuskegee that his name was not brother but Baker.

I shall not be able to go to Nantucket tomorrow, as I had intended, on account of Davidson's teeth, and shall not go until after you come this way again. That little front tooth cut through the gum Saturday Aug. 30th, and now the left eye tooth is nearly through. The children are all well, and Portia begins to show the benefit of her summer's visit. She put on a dress, the other day, that she has not worn for four or five weeks, and she laughed to find that it had grown both tight and short. She shows as great a change in temperament as in physique, she is so much more cheerful and childlike than she was. She sleeps well and as a child should, and has an excellent appetite. We are still having very warm weather, yesterday was decidedly uncomfortable, but today is not as warm.

D. S. King

ALS   Con. 17   BTW Papers   DLC.

From Portia Marshall Washington

Hanover Mass. Sept. 5/90

Dear Papa, I have been going to school four days now. The first day I was homesick, but I am not now, I am having a good time every day, and I am getting real fat. I eat a great deal more than I did when I came here, and I like my food.

Lilla Taylor was here last week. She came Monday and stayed until Saturday. Her grandma came for her and took her home. She was dreadfully homesick and cried nearly all the time she was here, and we didn't have a good time with her at all. Baker and Davidson are good little boys and are as well as they can be. Please give my love to Golda and the rest of the children. Your loving little

Portia

HLSr Con. 17 BTW Papers DLC. Dora S. King wrote the letter for seven-year-old Portia.

From Margaret James Murray

[Tuskegee, Ala.] Sept. 16–90

Mr. Washington   I have found out all I can of the fight in the Laundry. Dora Taylor[1] and Minnie Jones[2] should be treated very severely. I think Dora should be sent away not only because she is worse than the other one but we need this for a warning to the other rough girls in the Laundry.

M. J. M.

ALI Con. 96 BTW Papers DLC.

[1] Dora Taylor, whose name was variously recorded in the Tuskegee records as Dora Mary Low Taylor and Mary Dora Taylor, was a night-school student from Montgomery. She attended Tuskegee from 1890 to 1893.

[2] Minnie Carrie Jones of Marietta, Ga., was a member of the Tuskegee preparatory class from 1890 to 1892.

To Warren Logan

Atlanta   Sept 18th 90

Some time during my absence I think it would be well to devote one or two Sunday evenings to hearing the "summer experiences."

That encourages them to do well during the summer.

B. T. W.

ACI   Con. 2   BTW Papers   ATT.   Original destroyed.

From Julia Crudine Allen[1]

Tuskegee Ala. Sept 18th 1890

When I left Tuskegee last June 13th I went to Lowndesboro, Lowndes County Ala. There I began an Independent school, which I taught for two months. I found my work to be very hard the first two weeks, but afterwards I got a long nicely.

It was very hard work for me to get up a summer-school as they had never had one before. After I had work so faithfully among the people they became some what interested and sent their children to school regularly. I had a very good school for six weeks.

I attended Sunday-school every Sunday. The prospect for liveing among the coloreds are very good about one fifth of them own homes very few of them have good houses. They have not as yet realized the importance of saveing their money. The land in Lowndes county is the richest I ever saw in my life. They have not enough interest in education. Morals are medium. As far as I have been their churches are in good circumstances. They did not have any school house I had to teach in church. I advised them to build a school house, so they have the lumber and was prepareing to build a house 30 x 40. The people are able to have good schools and nice houses if they would only sacrifice the money. They also need a person with a great deal of influence to work among them.

They make money but dont save it. The people out in the country do a great deal of mortgageing they pay very heavy percentage from one year in to another.

How a wealthy colored man got his start in Lowndes

It would be amuseing to any one to hear just how this gentleman got his start. He is now worth $3000. He says that he would take the meat that was fried for supper and save it for breakfast; and the greece he would eat for supper he worked that way untill he saved enough money to buy him a home and by saveing what he made he has become a rich man. Respectfully

Julia Allen

ALS Con. 94 BTW Papers DLC.

[1] Julia Crudine Allen May (d. 1895) was first listed in the Tuskegee catalogs in 1886 as a junior from Columbus, Ga. She may have been the same person as the Julia Allen listed in the junior class in 1885, from Lee County, Ala. She graduated in 1892, married, and taught for one year in Lowndesboro, Ala.

From Olivia Egleston Phelps Stokes[1]

[New York] September 20th 1890

Dear Sir, I received your letter with the printed statement of the work done by the school, and enclose $2,000 which I give to help in the education of colored men of good moral character, particularly those who have the ministry in view.

This amount is to be invested in good, safe securities, and the interest used for the purpose indicated. I would be glad to have care taken in selecting young men of ability and character to be aided by this fund. I remain   sincerely yours

Olivia E. P. Stokes

ALS Con. 95 BTW Papers DLC.

[1] Olivia Egleston Phelps Stokes (1847-1927) and her sister Caroline Phelps Stokes (1854-1909) were daughters of a wealthy banker and real-estate owner and of an heiress of the Phelps family. They were devoted to each other and, as neither married, were seldom separated. They traveled together all over the world, wrote several books, and made innumerable gifts to religious, educational, and other public institutions in the United States and abroad. Among their principal gifts to Tuskegee Institute were Phelps Hall in 1891 and Dorothy Hall in 1901. The sisters had a particular interest in the welfare of blacks, and the residuary estate of Caroline and much of Olivia's wealth went into the Phelps-Stokes Fund, established in 1910 to promote the education of Negroes in the United States and Africa.

From Henry F. Downing[1]

New York, Sep. 27th, 1890

Sir: Herewith please find clippings from the New York World of the 27th inst., being a speech delivered by Isaiah T. Montgomery[2] in the Mississippi Constitutional Convention on September 17th.

His address cannot but have an influence upon the minds and actions of blacks and whites alike, not only in the state of Mississippi but all over the country as well. His surrender of the rights of 123,000 Negroes upon the altar of expediency is an act unprecedented either for its heroism or for its audacity. Which? How do the Negroes of the United States view this question, do they agree with Mr. Montgomery, or do they condemn his utterances. It is necessary that an expression of Negro sentiment should be had in this connection. If they do not wish to endorse his words they cannot afford to be silent. If they believe with him, it is necessary that he should be supported.

This being the view which intelligence recognizes in this matter, we have issued this circular letter, inviting brief expression of opinions for publication, from prominent Negroes all over the country. We are sure that none would have greater weight nor be read with more general interest than yours.

Trusting the importance of the matter will earn us a speedy reply, We are, Yours respectfully,

Henry F. Downing

TLS Con. 99 BTW Papers DLC.

[1] Henry F. Downing was president and manager of the United States African News Company in New York, of which T. Thomas Fortune was secretary. This news service handled items for many of the black leaders of the period, and it listed as contributors Blanche K. Bruce, Frederick Douglass, John Mercer Langston, John R. Lynch, Joseph C. Price, William S. Scarborough, T. McCants Stewart, Ida B. Wells, BTW, and others.

[2] Isaiah T. Montgomery was born a slave in 1847 on the Mississippi cotton plantation of Joseph E. Davis, brother of Jefferson Davis. His father, Benjamin T. Montgomery, who had been a driver on the Davis plantation, leased the plantation and operated it after freedom until 1878. Isaiah Montgomery first experienced freedom in 1863 when Admiral David D. Porter's Union forces ran past the Vicksburg batteries and claimed territory along the Mississippi River. Montgomery became Porter's cabin boy for several months. After the war he assisted his father until the latter's death in 1878. He then took charge of the plantation until 1883,

when recurring floods forced him to abandon it. In 1887, with the cooperation of the Illinois Central Railroad, he founded the all-black town of Mound Bayou in Bolivar County, Miss. His long life as patriarch of the Mound Bayou community was interrupted by a brief and unsatisfactory experience as a federal officeholder. He was a receiver of public monies in Jackson in 1901-3, but BTW, his sponsor, persuaded him to resign before he was removed for mixing public and private funds. He subsequently repaid the $4,700 his accounts were short and was never prosecuted for embezzlement. Montgomery frequently supplied BTW with information on race matters in Mississippi.

Montgomery was the only black delegate at the Mississippi constitutional convention in 1890. In the speech referred to, Montgomery in a frankly accommodating manner advocated reduction of the black vote by literacy and property qualifications. This brought charges that he was a "traitor," a "Judas." As T. Thomas Fortune remarked, "No flippant fool could have inflicted such a wound upon our cause as Mr. Montgomery has done in this address." (Quoted in Meier, *Negro Thought in America*, 38.)

The historian Vernon L. Wharton found it "hard to believe that Montgomery, regarded by whites and blacks alike as honorable and sincere, deliberately betrayed his race and his county merely to retain his seat in the convention, an empty honor at best." Perhaps, like BTW in many of his compromises with southern whites, Montgomery hoped that race relations would be improved, in an era of unprecedented lynchings and other violence, by reducing the black vote to a total considerably below that of white voters, and thus ending the threat of black supremacy. Perhaps Montgomery thought that the better educated and more affluent blacks could reenter the political mainstream in a subsequent era of greater racial harmony. Yet Montgomery's reasoning for what seems a race betrayal remains a mystery. (Wharton, *Negro in Mississippi*, 211-12.)

From James Fowle Baldwin Marshall

Weston [Mass.] Oct 1, 1890

Dear Booker, Your note is just received. I congratulate you on this first contribution to your Endowment Fund. No better investment for your school could probably be made than toward the purchase of the farm you speak of, and which it would be greatly for the interest of the School to own. But it would be in accordance with the wish & intention of Miss Stokes to have the money used in this way unless the farm could be bought clear of all other incumbrance so that her donation would be in the nature of a first and only mortgage upon it. If you have no instructions from her as to method of investment, I should either see her, or ask the advice of some good business man like Mr Peabody[1] of the Banking firm of Spencer Trask and Co of New York, R C Ogden of Phila or William Endicott Jr[2] of C. F. Hovey & Co Summer St. as to the best and safest investment. The rate of interest is so low on all safe investments, that it seems a pity that this money could not be used toward the purchase of a farm that will be so much more profitable to the School. Perhaps Miss Stokes would consent to have her gift used in this way, though she would wish to be assured that the rest of the purchase money would be forthcoming, and that her donation would not be swallowed up by a forced sale of the land at a sacrifice. Have you no business friend in N.Y. who knows Miss Stokes and could see her and set forth the advantages of the investment. But it is of *the first importance* that the wishes of the donor of this first contribution to your Endowment, should be sacredly fulfilled. Yours faithfully

J. F. B. Marshall

ALS   Con. 94   BTW Papers   DLC.

[1] George Foster Peabody (1852-1938), born in Columbus, Ga., moved with his impoverished parents to Brooklyn, N.Y., after the Civil War. There, forced to leave school and become an errand boy, he eventually amassed a fortune in banking and investments, particularly western and Mexican mines and railroads. He was a leading Gold Democrat in the Bryan era and was Democratic national treasurer in 1904. One of his chief interests was education. He had a paternal interest in both white and black southerners, and gave large sums to white colleges and black industrial institutes. He became a charter member of the Southern Education Board in 1901, and for years was treasurer of the General Education Board. His connection with Hampton Institute, on whose board of trustees he served, probably first brought him into contact with BTW. Approving of BTW's emphasis on industrial education, he became a benefactor of Tuskegee Institute. As early as 1889 he donated $75 to the school, and he served on its board of trustees from 1900 to 1911. He was a friend and adviser of Woodrow Wilson and of Franklin D. Roosevelt, whom he interested in the development of Warm Springs, Ga. Peabody married Katrina Trask, widow of his banking partner, after a courtship of decades. They made her home, Yaddo, on Lake George, a summer resort for artists.

[2] William Endicott, Jr. (1826-1914) was after 1850 a partner in the dry-goods firm of Charles Fox Hovey. He also had banking and railroad interests. Though never a political officeholder, he took a strong interest in politics, first as a member of the Free Soil party and later as a delegate to the first Republican convention, in 1856. In the 1880s he became a Mugwump. Among the objects of his philanthropy were Massachusetts Institute of Technology, the Boston Museum of Fine Arts, and the Perkins Institute for the Blind. As treasurer of the Perkins Institute, he became a personal friend of Helen Keller.

To William LeRoy Broun[1]

[Tuskegee, Ala.] October 15th. [189]o

Dear Sir: Replying to your favor of recent date, requesting information regarding this institution. I beg leave to say that as to the legal title, the legislature in establishing it simply designated it as a "Normal School for the Education of colored teachers," but it is usually styled "the Tuskegee Normal and Industrial Institute."

The property is deeded to a board of twelve trustees who hold it in trust for the benefit of the school. The control of the operations of the school is vested in a board of three State Commissioners originally appointed by the State Legislature. The twelve trustees who hold the property include the names of the three State commissioners.

The institution had its origin in 1881 in an appropriation of $2000 annually from the State. Six years ago this appropriation was increased to $3000, which amount is now annually received from the State.

The real property consists of 680 acres of land mostly of. . . .[2] modius and are used for school room and dormitory purposes. The other buildings are smaller and are used for teachers' residences, work shops, etc., and the whole is valued at $100,000.

Mental Work

No students under 14 are admitted to the institution, and the course of study occupies four years and includes Reading, Spelling, Grammar, Rhetoric, American and English Literature, Arithmetic, Algebra, Geometry, History ancient and modern, Constitution and School laws of Alabama, Botany, Physical Geography, Physiology, Civil Government, Political Economy, Mental Philosophy, Mental and Moral Science, Book-keeping, Penmanship, Freehand Drawing, Methods of Teaching, Vocal and Instrumental Music.

Agricultural and Mechanical Work

In all cases the actual work is done by students in all the industrial departments. The following shows the scope and extent of our agricultural work for the present year:

Acres in turnips	3
" " beets	1½

"	"	tomatoes	2
"	"	onions	1½
Acres	in	beans	1
"	"	squash	2
"	"	Pumpkins	1
"	"	Cucumbers	1
"	"	radishes	1½
"	"	water-melons	3
"	"	musk-melons	1
"	"	kale	½
"	"	asparagus	¼
"	"	okra	⅛
"	"	strawberries	½
"	"	parsnips	⅙
"	"	spinach	⅙
"	"	cauliflower	1/16

STOCK

the number of stock is as follows:

horses	7
colts	3
mules	4
oxen	15
cows	11
calves	7
hogs	80
sheep	8
barnyard fowls	125
total	260

FRUIT TREES

Number	of	Apple Trees	60
"	"	cherry "	15
"	"	pear "	80
"	"	peach "	250
"	"	plum "	8
"	"	apricot "	4
"	"	chestnut "	6

88

"   "   Jap. persimon   4
"   "   ornamental   "   275

Care of stock and fruit culture receive special attention.

We have recently completed a new barn at a cost of $4000. which will house sixty head of stock and has all the convenience for caring for and making manure. Enclosed you will find a picture of this barn which is wholly the work of students.

Industries in Operation

These industries besides farming are in constant operation: brick-making, plastering, painting, carpentry, black-smithing, wheel-wright-ing, saw-mill work, printing (outfit costing $15,000), tinsmithing, shoe-making, harness-making, sewing, laundering, and cooking.

Number of students, officers, teachers, etc.

Students enrolled last session	447
Resident Students	47
Non- " "	400
Average age	18½
Officers and teachers	28
Counties represented	50
States "	15

Past Financial Year

SOURCES OF INCOME

State Annual Appropriation	$3000
"John F. Slater" Fund	$1000
Peabody Education Fund	$500
Donations	$25,327
Total from all sources	$29,827

Conclusion

In all the agricultural and mechanical work the idea of teaching the best methods of work is kept uppermost.

We seek to accomplis[h] three things through the industrial work, (a) To enable the student to pay a portion of his board expenses in labor,

(b) To teach the student *how* to work — giving him a trade when possible,

(c) To teach the *dignity* of labor.

Our nine years experience lead us to feel that these objects are being accomplished in a marked degree.

If there is other information needed, I shall be glad to furnish it. Yours respectfully,

TLp   Con. 106   BTW Papers   DLC.

¹ William LeRoy Broun (1827-1902), born in Virginia and educated at Green Academy and the University of Virginia (M.A. 1850), became an outstanding educator in the South. He taught physics and chemistry at Oakland College, Miss. (1854-56), and organized Bloomfield Academy near the University of Virginia (1856-61). He served in the Confederate Army as commandant of the Richmond Arsenal. After the war he taught at the University of Georgia (1866-75) and then at Vanderbilt (1875-82). He was professor of mathematics and chairman of the faculty at the University of Texas at Austin (1884), and president of Alabama Polytechnic Institute in Auburn (1884-1902).

² One line of the press copy is missing.

From Mary A. Elliott

487 West Broad. Columbus O. [Oct. 23, 1890]

My Dear Brother   It has been quite a while since I have heard from you and the children. I suppose that they have returned home, to the south I mean, before this time. Mrs King written to me some time a go from her home in Mass. saying that the children were getting a long nicely, said little Baker was looking well. I was glad to hear it, he looked delicate, so did Portia. I dont think she spoke of her individualy. I hope she is looking well. Davidson was looking well as any child could look he has so much force a bout him, he is born to *rule* you mind what I say he will make himself felt in this world if he has a chance and lives to grow. he has got great *will* power. if he is little you can see it in him. Booker I was glad to see you when you stoped off, but it appears more like a dream sandwiched between two days, because your stay was so short, yet we appreciated your visit so much be assured of that. Mother's heart warmed to ward you more than ever when she saw and talked with you. She hardly got acquainted with you when she saw you the first time. We are glad to hear of the great success, your School is meeting with   May the Lord bless you all the way along, is my prayer; I do so much wish that I could come and make you and the children a visit, and see your little Kingdom as dear Sister Olivia use to call it to me, when she wanted me to come   when I say I would like to come, dose not express half what I feel. I could get to see her grave. But I will not say things to make you feel sad   I get so filled with emotion I can hardly write but I know that you are brave and will make your way if you live, to honer and fame, if you swerve not frome the path you have been pursueing. I see our folks quite often they all would of been glad to have seen you when you was here. There are three families Hiram's Mack's and William's Davidson's   Mack Davidson is our full cousin   His Father and Olivia's and my Father were twin brothers. Hiram and Mack send love to you and the children. I have bought a lot here in Columbus and am building a house on the back part of it mostly for mother to live in at present. The place that I live in is not comfortable for to live in, she is still able to weave but she has been rather frale noticeable so, since early in the Spring she had a hard spell of LaGripe she has never been the same. Still she goes, most all the time dose her work and weaves carpet. So you see that is one of the things that keeps me from the South. I want to finish the house if I can be fore it gets too cold and we have rather large rent to pay. and it keeps us moveing to make ends meet yet I hope we will get through if Dock and I both stay well. Mother sends her love to you and the children so dose uncle Dock. Please to give Mrs King, best regards, with much love to you and children. I remain your sister

Mary

ALS   Con. 17   BTW Papers   DLC.   Postmarked Oct. 23, 1890.

A Sunday Evening Talk

[Tuskegee, Ala.] Oct. 26th, 1890

READING A MEANS OF GROWTH

As I stated to you the other Sunday evening, I am trying to indicate as far as possible some means of growth, and to-night I want to speak to you on reading as a means of growth, and we cannot ask ourselves too often where is its real importance. It is man's duty to grow; he cannot stand still. It is true not only of man but of all nature, everything either grows or decays, and this is specially true of students. The student either goes forward or backward, he grows better or worse, he grows stronger or weaker. Each of you should ask yourselves whether or not "I am growing and improving," and you should find out as far as possible all the means of improvement and growth.

Goethe once said of Schiller, if he missed seeing him for two weeks, that he was always surprised to find how much he had grown. He meant to emphasize the fact that Schiller was a man continually growing; there was no standing still with him. So as students we want to be continually growing. Now I have spoken several times of opportunities of doing good, of benefitting somebody else, by giving your lives for some one whose condition is not so fortunate as ours, and persons cannot accomplish any thing in this direction unless he has something to give out. You will find out that you cannot do any good unless you are continually filling yourselves as fast as you give out and replenishing yourselves with just such things as are helpful to yourselves, and to others. So I want to emphasize the importance of reading, of constantly filling your mind with all that is good. Lord Bacon said "reading makes a full man." Take the persons who are in political life, they are narrow because they do not look beyond their duty. Take the Northern man in his prejudice against the South, and the Southern man in his prejudice against the North, you will find that they are not the persons who have read well and have breadth of thought. Take the persons who are most prejudiced on the race lines. Take the colored man, he does not read such things as will broaden him out. The same thing is true of the white man, of church members, of the Methodist who hates the Baptist and of the Baptist who hates the Methodist. You will find that they are persons who do not read. Even in business there is always a temptation to confine one's self to business to the detriment of his improvement, but the person who does this, who does not look beyond and strive to enlarge himself, does not win the success at which he is striving. Such a person must read. The world is always looking for persons who have something to say and who have knowledge and culture, and in proportion as you get culture and knowledge, your society will be in demand. The world likes to get into the society of those who have something to give out, something that is going to benefit somebody and you cannot give out, unless you are continually filling yourselves. Books, you will find, will not only do this, but books will keep you in good company. You get acquainted with friends and you are deserted and disappointed by them, but it is not so with books, when you make a book your friend, it is loyal to you; it is comforting to you. When you get tired you put it down and take it up again and it is the same to you. There is nothing that helps to tone up the mental and moral fibre so well as books. Take the persons who are continually reading good, elevating books, they are not the persons who yield to temptations. You will find by pursuing this course, that your desire to enter into temptation, to do that which is low and degrading and that which is beneath you will be lessened.

Now what should we read? Take the daily papers. Every person should keep up with the daily news. But there is opportunity for mistakes. A person should keep up with the news, and get hold of the nucleus of events, but not with everything that is in the usual daily papers. First look at the head lines and pass over what is not worth reading. Do not follow the criminal news and other scandals which can only whet the appetites of the vulgar. If you cannot get hold of a good daily paper, get hold of a good weekly paper. You will find all the bad left out and all the good left in.

There are the religious papers, nearly every large religious denomination has its weekly paper which contains not only its religious literature but other reading matter put in the most compact and readable form, so that a person can take up one of these papers and post himself on whatever is going on in the world.

Then, get acquainted with the monthly magazines which come here regularly. You will never have such an opportunity again. If you have not time to read an article through, get acquainted with the tone and scope of it. As a rule a person should get into the habit of reading his Bible. You never read in history of any great man whose influence has been lasting, who has not been a reader of the Bible. Take Abraham Lincoln and Gladstone. Their lives show that they have been readers of the Bible. If you wish to properly direct your mind and necessarily your lives, begin by reading the book of all books. Read your Bibles every day, and you will find how healthily you will grow.

Do not make the mistake of reading books that are too high. Read history, biography, and other good matter. A person should have a regular time for reading, you are not so busy that you cannot devote some time to reading.

You owe it to yourselves, you owe it to your parents, who are supporting you here in this institution to get into the habit of growing, and especially we should not suffer a Sunday to go by without reading some helpful book. We never feel so miserably as at the end of a Sunday that is idly spent, or frittered away in some trifling conversation. Get into the habit of saying "I am going to put in my Sabbaths to the best advantage and gain something through the medium of some good book."

Start a library. You can get hold of one. You can get the nucleus of a good library now. It does not require a great number of books.

Persons who have been well read through the medium of books; they have read them well, have looked up all the references, all the characters, all the cities mentioned, and the person therefore who reads one book thoroughly will become educated, indeed he is an educated person.

Books, therefore, should be treated kindly. Their leaves ought not to be turned down nor any disfiguring writing made in them. There is to my mind a kind of sacredness in books, and I want you all to feel and to appreciate this. I speak to you thus because these things are at the bottom of your education. In a few days Mr. Hamilton and myself will go North to interest people in you, and if we tell them that we have a body of young men and young women here who are putting forth efforts to develop themselves, you do not know how much courage and strength we shall have in speaking of you, whom we have left behind putting in every minute of your lives, using every opportunity that is offered for making yourselves stronger and more useful for the battle of life. If we have such students we are going to succeed and you will therefore see that the success of this work depends on you, but if you neglect the opportunities here presented to you, this work will fail and we shall be without the aid and sympathy of those who are now interested in us.

Tuskegee Student, 2 (Oct. 31, 1890), 1-2. M. Arnold Morin recorded this talk "phonographically."

From William Burns Paterson

Montgomery, Ala., Oct 30, 1890

Dear Sir: A reply to your favor of the 17th was delayed as I expected a visit from the President of our Board on Monday of this week. He was sick and could not come, and I have just returned from a visit to him. Your interpretation of the act[1] is correct, but I am sure we can arrange it so as to carry out as nearly as possible our original agreement. I too think that our original proposal was the best thing to be done.

I now suggest that you set a time that suits you to come here before you go North, notify Council[2] to come here, and we can talk the matter over. The matter ought to be so arranged as best to subserve the interests of the Colored race.

Confidentially, the Auburn Trustees were very indignant at the plan to divide with the Colored. They are to have a meeting next Monday. I am working with Palmer[3] & Seay[4] to get a favorable recommendation in their reports. But Seay is a candidate you know, and must go slow. Palmer is going out, and his mind is wrapped up in his new undertaking.

Hoping that we can meet soon, I am, Yours very sincerely

Wm. B. Paterson

ALS   Con. 96   BTW Papers   DLC.

[1] Probably the Morrill Act of 1890.
[2] William Hooper Councill.
[3] Solomon Palmer.
[4] Thomas Seay.

To Rutherford Birchard Hayes[1]

Tuskegee, Ala., Oct. 31 1890

Dear Sir: I want to thank you with all of my heart for your picture. It will always be a priceless treasure with me. Yours truly

B. T. Washington

ALS OFH. On the letter Hayes wrote: "Perhaps the ablest and most useful Colored man in the Country — Certainly a most worthy man. H."

¹ Rutherford Birchard Hayes (1822-93), former president of the United States, spent his last years working for various humanitarian causes. He was president of the National Prison Association (1883-93), the first president of the board of trustees of the John F. Slater Fund (1882-93), and a member of the board of the Peabody Education Fund.

From Theophile Tarence Allain[1]

Soulouque P.O., La., Nov. 2nd 1890

My Dear Friend: Enclosed, please find a letter from my good old friend Prof. W. D. Godman, of Gilbert Seminary La. who wishes me to send my son Theophile[2] back to his Seminary. But, I have selected you and your school for many reasons.

1st I believe that my present work in building 1000 and hundreds of thousands cubic yards of Levees on the banks of the Mississippi River, in this day and time — will compare favorably with the record of any colored man in the Republic — and therefore I propose to leave a business record behind my boys, if, and I do hope that they will have brains enough to appreciate that fact.

Now, I would like for you to get the *credit* of training my son Theophile.

If he has in him any of the qualities of his mother, you will be able to do some thing with — as to myself, I have not been a good and virtuous man all of my life.

Accept for yourself and all at the normal school my perfect consideration.

Theophile T. Allain

ALS Con. 94 BTW Papers DLC.

¹ Theophile Tarence Allain, Sr., was born in west Baton Rouge Parish, La., in 1846. He was educated in Somerset County, N.J., but returned to Louisiana as a sugar planter in Iberville Parish. In 1870 he owned a 790-acre sugar plantation valued at $15,000, employed thirty-five laborers, and produced 7,000 hogsheads of sugar, 4,000 gallons of molasses, and other farm produce valued at $14,400. (Census of 1870, Productions of Agriculture, Iberville Parish, La., RG29, DNA.) Allain was not only a large-scale businessman but a leader in Louisiana politics. He served in the Louisiana House in 1873-74 and the Louisiana Senate from

1874 until 1882. He also represented Iberville Parish in the state constitutional convention in 1879, where he led in the founding of Southern University for blacks, the first state-supported black institution for higher education in Louisiana. For many years Allain supplemented the income from Soulouque Plantation by contracting for construction and repair of the Mississippi River levees in his area. About 1900 he moved to Chicago, where he continued his interest in politics. He became an itinerant Republican political orator among black voters in election years.

[2] Theophile Tarence Allain, Jr., attended Tuskegee from 1890 to 1892. He did not graduate.

From Daniel Alexander Payne

Wilberforce, O., Nov. 3, 1890

Dear Sir: I had seen the various animadversions from North, South, East and West, against your sentiments with reference to the colored ministry South; but I wished to read for myself what you had said to incense the grumblers, knowing that one can be so misrepresented through animadversions. Therefore, I wrote, asking that you send me a copy of the original article. Having read it, I must hasten to support you.

For nine winters my residence has been in the South, and this has given me ample opportunity for observing the great defects that your eight years have afforded you. In 1865 I organized the Southern work of the A.M.E. Church, having with me three well educated men, one being an Elder[1] and two Deacons — James H. A. Johnson[2] and T. G. Steward.[3] From that period until this, some twenty-five years, I have been operating more or less in Southern fields, beginning with the Baltimore Conference on the Atlantic sea-board and running down the Gulf.

During the Governorship of Andrew Johnson, and under military protection of the Secretary of War, I opened the work of the A.M.E. Church in Nashville, Tenn., which has since spread to New Orleans, that city having been previously embraced in the connection. As long as I could lead here, there and elsewhere, the demand was for well educated Christian ministers. But other leaders demanded numbers regardless of education. They called for quantity and not for quality, forgetting the historic fact that twelve well qualified men were sufficient to overturn the heathen Roman Empire into a Christian one. The A.M.E. leaders called for numbers and not for qualifications.

Scores of cases like that you illustrated by the story of the cotton field hand who thought the sun too hot for him to remain at such work, have come to my notice, and I have had occasion to tell such unqualified men that I believe they left the cotton patch and corn field and entered the ministry because they thought it would be an easier way to get a living.

In regard to the moral qualifications of the Methodist and Baptist ministers, so far as I have seen and known them by personal contact, I believe that you have not overstated, but rather understated the facts. I say emphatically, in the presence of the great Head of the Church, that not more than one-third of the ministers, Baptist and Methodist, in the South are morally and intellectually qualified. I will stand by this statement, and can demonstrate the truthfulness and shameful and painful facts, with regard to name, times and places. Doubtless I shall be assailed like yourself for speaking truth and recording facts. Denominational bias and influence will not cause me to suppress the truth nor to hide facts when it is necessary to speak out with the spirit of Christian reform. I am a Methodist of the Methodists, head, heart and soul; and while I love Methodism sincerely, I love Christianity better. Therefore, in behalf of Christianity, I speak what I believe and know to be true with reference to our people South. I commenced forty-seven years ago to labor for a well educated and thoroughly Christian ministry. The Apostles and Prophets were all condemned for speaking out against the corruption of the chief priests and the Churches. But a power from above compelled them to cry out.

Your relation to the South as an educator entitles you to a respectful hearing. Fraternally yours,

Daniel A. Payne

Indianapolis *Freeman,* Nov. 29, 1890, 4. Published with BTW's letter to the editor of the Indianapolis *Freeman,* Nov. 22, 1890.

[1] James A. Handy (b. 1826), who began his career as a preacher in Baltimore, spent many years in missionary work in the South, establishing A.M.E. churches in North and South Carolina and Alabama. He was a powerful speaker and a skillful diplomat with southern whites.

[2] James Henry Andrew Johnson, born in Baltimore, entered the Baltimore Conference of the A.M.E. Church in 1865, but was almost immediately sent to the South at the end of the Civil War as a missionary. He helped to organize the South Carolina Conference and some churches on the eastern shore of Virginia.

In 1870 he returned to the Baltimore Conference, of which he became presiding elder in 1882.

[3] Theophilus Gould Steward (1843-1925) was a prominent A.M.E. minister and author of many works on theology and black history. After several years as an A.M.E. missionary in the South at the end of the Civil War, Steward established churches in Haiti, New York, Pennsylvania, and Delaware. Joining the U.S. Army as chaplain of the Negro Twenty-fifth Infantry, he served during the Spanish-American War and the Philippine insurrection. In 1907 he became professor of history, logic, and French at Wilberforce University.

From Warren Logan

Tuskegee, Ala., Nov. 19 1890

Dear Mr. Washington: Your several favors with checks enclosed have been received and are most welcome.

Patterson is doing everything in his power to secure the Congressional fund.[1] He is now claiming that his school is the Agricultural and Mechanical College for the colored people and was established as an offset to Auburn. I saw him in Montgomery last Saturday, and he told me that he was certain of receiving the part of the fund that is to go to the colored people. The only thing he is in doubt about is the amount that he will receive. He has had a circular printed, copy of which I enclose, which he has circulated among the legislators.[2] As an offset to this, I have had your report to the State Commissioner with some additions printed, and Mr. Campbell is going to carry them down to Montgomery to-morrow and see that they are put in the hands of the members of the legislature. I have thought that it would be well to have extracts from the speeches of Senators Morgan[3] and Pugh[4] printed and put in the hands of the legislators that they may see that it was the intention of our Senators in favoring the measure that the money should come here. We are preparing to make a bold fight for the fund. When I told Patterson that he had no agricultural department connected with the school and therefore was not entitled to any part of the appropriation, he said that he meant to establish an agricultural department with this money, and the reason that he had not already established one was that he had no funds with which to do it. Yours truly,

Warren Logan

HLS   Con. 2   BTW Papers   ATT.   Original destroyed.

¹ The Morrill Act of 1890.

² According to M. Arnold Morin, Paterson had "published a pamphlet showing the merits of his school, which he says was built up without Northern aid and influence." (Morin to BTW, Nov. 19, 1890, Con. 2, BTW Papers, ATT.) Six days later John H. Washington wrote to Warren Logan: "Every advantage possible is being taken by Mr. Patterson. He has said that we waste our money and that each dept. is deeply in debt." (J. H. Washington to Logan, Nov. 25, 1890, Con. 2, BTW Papers, ATT.)

³ John Tyler Morgan (1824-1907) practiced law in Tuskegee for ten years before moving to Selma in 1855. He fought in the Confederate Army, achieving the rank of general, and resumed his law practice after the war. During Reconstruction he championed ideas of white supremacy and states' rights. He was elected to the U.S. Senate in 1876 and served until his death. An advocate of African colonization of American blacks, he had a longtime interest in development of the Congo and in 1904 was active in the Congo Reform Association.

⁴ James Lawrence Pugh (1819-1907) practiced law in Eufaula, Ala., for almost forty years. He served in the Confederate Army and also was a member of the Confederate Congress. He served in Congress as a Democrat from 1880 until 1897.

From Robert Charles Bedford

Beloit Wis   Nov 20 1890

Dear Prof Washington   I regret so much that you have to be away from the school so long. The interests there are so great that I feel your presence is needed constantly. The cry every where is that the Negro can not manage any thing. I find in the North thus far a great many colored churches quarreling among themselves and eating each other up. I hope notwithstanding you have to be absent so much you will be able to keep everything well in hand.

Fearing you may not have seen the Gov's¹ message I inclose that part of it relating to the grant of Congress. You see how clearly it is his purpose to divide it between two institutions one colored and one white. What I have already sent you from the report of Dr Otts² clearly indicates to me that it is the full purpose of the Dr and Prof Paterson in case it is so divided to get it for Montgomery. You note the proposed purchase of 50 acres of land for agricultural purposes proposed by Dr Otts for Montgomery. I think Prof P. will live fully up to his agreement with you but if the division is made between 2 schools only do you not imagine he will feel it is duty to get it for himself? Are the interests of Tuskegee sufficiently guarded on this point?

The argt that the state should give so little to Tuskegee because it gets so much from the North is anything but appreciative of [and?] should it receive the U S grant it would serve greatly to draw attention to it.

Dr Chaney's[3] position seemed to be some like my own. He had a young man who he thought could take the ch[urch] and his course as to the future was quite unsettled. He seemed to think it quite probable he should live hereafter at the North.

How about the Charter to the school? It has occurred to me that if the act with reference to the Trustees could be amended so that they could perform the duties usually devolving on Trustees Viz try and sell both personal and real property soon and he could see the case would be met.

Please introduce me all you can to parties whom I meet and with whom you are acquainted. I want to get an acquaintance with the field so that I can reduce the expense of travel by making the most possible of each trip.

Let me hear from you often. All send regards. Your friend

R. C. Bedford

ALS   Con. 3   BTW Papers   ATT.   Original destroyed.

[1] Thomas Seay.
[2] John Martin Phillips Otts.
[3] George Leonard Chaney.

To the Editor of the Indianapolis *Freeman*

Tuskegee, Ala., Nov. 22, 1890

Prof. B. T. Washington's Defense of His Attack on the Colored Ministry

Special to The Freeman. Let this be understood in regard to what they have said or shall say regarding the colored ministry, that no resolutions or actions or words of individuals or organizations will have the least effect in preventing my saying just what I consider to be in the interest of the race and truth. The day for scaring men into silence is gone, and the world loves and honors the man who speaks his convictions, and who does not think one thing in his heart and speak another with his tongue. But why this hue and cry? What Bishop Payne and I have said can hurt no pure, upright, capable man. It is the fraction that is not right that we condemn — that we seek to arouse public sentiment against, not the fraction that is gratified. If a man is righteous let him be righteous still. Why should any one seek to defend the immoral and incompetent? Those who are pure and strong will stand out with all the more brilliancy and prominence because of their purity and strength, and this discussion cannot hurt, but will help this class; and it does not seem possible that any one will want to defend the corrupt. We divide the ministers into two classes, the upright and the immoral, the weak and the strong; but some would seem to say by their argument, "Don't do this; keep us all together."

I make no attack on any denomination or individuals, but it is corruption that I seek to help destroy.

There come times in the history of races as well as individuals when as much good can be done by a plain statement of faults as a laudation of virtues; and every one who knows that in this matter Bishop Payne and I are only saying in print what thousands of others are saying in private. Who is the better friend to the ministry — to the race, the one who speaks out plainly, or the one who is constantly stabbing in private?

There is no use of our mincing matters; every Bishop, every presiding elder, every leading man who comes into contact with the ministry knows exactly what we are talking about; knows that a large proportion of the ministry is wholly unfit to attempt to lead any one. Whether Bishop Payne or I have put the fraction of the unqualified a little too high or a little too low has small bearing on the main question — which is that far too large a proportion of those who are attempting to preach the gospel are unfit; and in our attempt to draw attention to this fact, we shall have the support of every one who loves the race.

But when it is considered that in my former article I included (and I think that Bishop Payne does the same) in my proportion of incompetent ministers not only pastors of churches, but that large class who get authority in some way to stand in the pulpit as local preachers, I cannot see how any one can say the proportion of the unfit has been put too high.

Our friends all over the country in all denominations stood ready to help us to a qualified ministry; but it is in this as in other matters; in order that help may come, they must know the bottom facts, and in order to give these it becomes often necessary to state unpalatable truths. Our friends will honor the race far more for being ready to expose corruption than for covering it up.

What I have said regarding the colored ministry in the Southern States is not based on theory, statistics or hearsay, but on what I have seen and have come in contact with in the heart of the South.

Whether the ministry knows it or not, the masses of the people are on our side in this discussion, (but if I stood alone my conscience would be enough support), and the means are demanding as they have never done before that there is a chance in the character of a large proportion of the ministers who stand in their pulpits.

But some seem to think that my experience is not broad enough, that I have not come enough into contact with the rank and file of the ministers to justify me in speaking as I have. To this I answer, let one whose name is not only national but international, and whose name is a synonym for learning, courage, purity and the truth speak. Will any one say that Right Rev. Daniel A. Payne, D.D., L.L.D., senior Bishop of the A.M.E. Church, does not know whereof he speaks? Below I append his letter. Yours for the race,

Booker T. Washington

Indianapolis *Freeman*, Nov. 29, 1890, 4. BTW sent Bishop Daniel A. Payne's letter of Nov. 3, 1890 (above), to the *Freeman* along with his own statement. The *Freeman* published them together.

From Margaret James Murray

Tuskegee, Ala., Nov. 22, 1890

Dear Mr. Washington, Your letter came one day this week and I can not tell you how much I felt what you said of your Christian life — not that I think you an unchristian person but I have had always such strange thoughts of you in this connection. I have lately felt that perhaps you are right and I am not, still I do cling so to my old way and feeling.

It is a bright and lovely afternoon and all human souls ought to be perfectly happy but I wonder if I am. I am sure that I myself am not right or I could not have this strange feeling which has come over me lately and which keeps me so distant from my Savior. My very nature seems to be one of constant rebellion. I do not pray nor read with the same delight that I once had in these things.

You were likely surprised at the letter I sent you in regard to Miss Walker.[1] I am very sorry that I sent it. You have enough to do and to bear. I feel that we who are here should be more patient for your sake but I was indignant at the time. I think I have never in my life been so angry as I was when I wrote that letter. This is no excuse for the letter.

Miss Walker and your brother both said that you had told them that I had nothing to do with her place, at least your brother said this and she said that she had not been told that I had any thing to do with her in her work. Your brother feels that I have been instrumental in the change which he claims has come over you. I was bitter toward him and told him the same.

I am not sorry at all that he told me this for I can now better steer from him but I detest anything which is false or which seems spiteful. I do not wish you to write Mr. Logan nor your brother concerning this unless you desire but I do think that I ask no more than what is right when I ask you to say in Miss Walkers presence — to her when you return that as far as the girls are concerned in her Department, I am not trespassing when I interfere. I shall say no more on this subject for I dare not trust my self to day.

Mr Whittaker[2] preached an excellent sermon this morning. Him that is weak in the faith, receive ye, but not to doubtful disputations. I felt drawn upwards for a while.

Thursday we shall hail with delight. Mr Whittaker doesn't want the stand put up until after the sermon but the actors say that it must go up before. Mr W. says if it does he will not preach so here we go.

The students are very much interested now in outside work. Some of the boys walk five miles to do Sunday School work. The Baptist Sunday School which Mr Calloway,[3] Miss H[4] & Miss B.[5] attend has increased from twelve to forty three. Do you not think this is good for Baptists? I want to get Silvia and Kitie to take work about three miles from here. They are strong and can stand the walk.

I do not like to have the students so free to spend their money for pleasure as they seem inclined. I understand that one club wants to solicit .50 cts from its members for an entertainment. I shall speak to the girls of this tomorrow and try to pursuade them that this is too extravagant. This is a fault with all students.

I got the games yesterday and I enclose $5.00 for them. They are all just as interesting as they can be. Accept our thanks for your trouble and remember that Miss Nolen[6] and I will do all that we can to entertain you with them. We had an interesting prayer meeting last night. I am so glad that Mr. Whittaker is here and above all I am glad that I learned at the first to trust in you and in him — if this were not true, I should certainly drift very far.

I think that we do not get as many barrels as we did last year. We have had two from a new place.

I think that Mrs. Calloway[7] will give up her work in the Sales Room. I can not blame her even though she asked for it. It is not pleasant to work with Miss Walker and those two places might just as well be separate. You would be surprised to see how well Mr. Mann[8] does work. He is settling down so too.

Mrs. J. B. Washington will not be here very much longer. I feel real sorry for them. They are so young and so little able to care for themselves. I am very much troubled about Ida Thompson[9] — she is so weak. I should hate to give her up. I wish that she might be cared for by friends. I wonder if I tire you. I thought I should not wait until after the Teachers' meeting to write. Miss Nolen says that she is still improving. She is anxious for the clock and says she will send her thanks when she gets it. Miss Lee[10] and the girls moved yesterday. They are happy as they can be. We have no more now with more than five in it. O my! how glad I shall be when only three are in these rooms. If I am not here I shall come on a visit for this purpose. If I do not stop I shall tire you. Yours Respectfully,

M. J. Murray

ALS Con. 17 BTW Papers DLC. Written on letterhead stationery of "Miss M. J. Murray, Lady Principal."

[1] Norma E. Walker Carter.

[2] John W. Whittaker.

[3] James Nathan Calloway received an A.B. degree at Fisk University in 1890, the year of BTW's graduation speech there castigating the Negro clergy. Calloway was inspired by BTW to go to Tuskegee and use his advanced training and considerable talent in uplifting the rural black masses. He taught mathematics at Tuskegee from 1890 to 1893, then was business agent from 1893 until 1897, serving part of 1896 as a lobbyist for Tuskegee in Washington, manager of Marshall Farm at Tuskegee 1897-1900, teacher in charge of the Tuskegee cotton-

raising experiment station in the German West African colony of Togo 1900-1901, and teacher of agriculture at Tuskegee at least until 1930.

4 Sylvia Robertson Howard Davis, of Mt. Meigs (Montgomery County) and Richmond (Dallas County), Ala., entered Tuskegee's preparatory class in 1885. She graduated from Tuskegee in 1891 and attended a school for nurses. Marrying Albert G. Davis (class of 1889), she settled in Birmingham, where she kept house and worked as a nurse.

5 Katherine (Kitty) Juanita Baskins Barr graduated from Tuskegee in 1891, and took charge of the laundry at Tuskegee for the school year 1891-92. She graduated from the Provident Hospital Training School for Nurses in Chicago, married Elmer E. Barr, and lived in Los Angeles, where she worked as a trained nurse.

6 Lettie Louise Nolen Calloway.

7 Nannie S. Calloway was in charge of the sales room in 1890-91.

8 Thomas L. Mann was in charge of the printing department at Tuskegee from 1890 to 1895.

9 Ida Belle Thompson McCall of Birmingham, Ala., night-class student in 1887-88, graduated in 1892. She was an instructor of geography and history at Tuskegee until 1901. She married James Dickens McCall, also a member of the faculty.

10 Eliza A. Lee taught drawing and writing at Tuskegee from 1888 until 1892. In 1891-92 she was also matron of Armstrong Hall.

From Warren Logan

Tuskegee, Ala., Nov. 29 1890

Dear Mr Washington: Your letters of the 22 and 25 inst. have been received. All is being done than can be done to get the Federal money. Mr. Campbell went to Montgomery and made a statement before the Committee on Education. Waddy Thompson also appeared before the committee and made a strong speech in our behalf. Patterson is resorting to some very low methods to defeat us. It is doubtful whether he will succeed. Council has appeared upon the scene and entered his claim to the appropriation. Next to his own school he favors Tuskegee. I think the whole matter is going to be put off till after the recess which comes the 10th of December and lasts until the 20th of January.

The buying is still being done in the town wherever we can get goods. It has taken all of the money that I can get hold of to pay outstanding notes and bills that could not be put off, so that I have not been able to pay anything on account of Hobbie and Teague as yet. We owe them something over $900.

Mr. Washington has had Menefee[1] looking after his work while he was in Montgomery. He has been gone only two or three days at a time, so that there is no very great interruption in his work.

Matters are going smoothly at the school. Thanksgiving passed off very pleasantly, the students having enjoyed the day. Yours truly,

Warren Logan

HLS Con. 2 BTW Papers ATT. Original destroyed.

[1] Crawford Daniel Menafee was a junior at Tuskegee Institute in 1888-89 and 1889-90 and a member of the B middle class in 1890-91. He apparently did not graduate, according to the Tuskegee catalogs, but for a number of years after 1895 he was a Tuskegee instructor of horticulture and in charge of buildings and grounds.

From John Robert Clifford[1]

Martinsburg, W.Va., Nov. 30th 1890

My dear sir: After reading your able article in the *Plaindealer*,[2] I feel it my duty, though some distance from you, to step under, & assist in holding up your hands, in defense of right. As you say, thousands condemn in silence what you do openly, & then defend openly, what they condemned in silence or *"private."*

Not only have you the backing of all good people, but God's soft whisper — *"Well done good & faithful servant."* I send yo[u] a copy of my paper, which a month or more ago, sanctioned your first assertions, & is itchingly waiting to espouse every thing you may say on the same line of thought. Very truly yours,

J. R. Clifford

ALS Con. 4 BTW Papers ATT. Original destroyed.

[1] John Robert Clifford (b. 1849) was born in Grant County, W.Va. He graduated from Storer College, Harpers Ferry, W.Va., in 1878. A lawyer, an active Republican, he was for ten years principal of the black schools of Martinsburg, W.Va. Clifford founded the Martinsburg *Pioneer Press* in 1883. As its editor and publisher, he increased its circulation from 100 to more than 1,000. Buying a larger press in 1888, he used it to print his "neat, 4-page paper" and for job printing. He resigned his position as principal to give full time to editing and printing. His paper was described in 1888 as a Republican paper commanding "considerable influence among both races." During the Cleveland years, he was

president of a Negro Mugwump group, the National Independent Political League. He was a member of Alexander Crummell's American Negro Academy. (Aler, *History of Martinsburg,* 387-88.)

[2] Probably a reprint of BTW's letter to the editor of the Indianapolis *Freeman,* Nov. 22, 1890, above.

From Ida B. Wells[1]

Memphis Tenn. Nov. 30, 90

Personal.

Prof. B. T. Washington: I am so impressed with the reply to your critics in the current issue of the Plaindealer, that I at last do, what I have been intending, ever since I read your manly criticism of our corrupt and ignorant ministry — write to one who is a stranger to me in every respect save that of reputation.

I have long since seen that some one of the name & standing of yourself, *among ourselves,* must call a halt and be the Martin Luther of our times in condemning the practices of our ministers, and I know no one more fitted for the task than yourself.

In my numerous scribbling, I long ago took the same ground, and by accompanying copies of my paper, you will see that we are continuing the good work.

To a man whose conscience is his guide, words of encouragement and sustenance are not necessary, yet I cannot refrain from adding my mite to the approbation your utterances and work have received from the rank & file of our people. Respectfully

Ida B. Wells

ALS   Con. 4   BTW Papers   ATT.   Original destroyed.

[1] Ida B. Wells-Barnett (1862-1931) was born in slavery in Holly Springs, Miss. She attended a local Negro school and also went to Rust College in Holly Springs. In a yellow fever epidemic in 1878 she lost her parents and a brother and she was left to care for the remaining children in the family. Moving to Memphis in the early 1880s, she taught in the schools in Shelby County, Tenn. In 1884, she sued the Chesapeake and Ohio Railroad for putting her in the Jim Crow car. She won the case in local court but in 1887 the decision was reversed in the Tennessee Supreme Court. From 1884 to 1891 she taught school in Memphis. Beginning in 1887 she also wrote a column for a church paper which started her on a career in journalism. She purchased part ownership in the Memphis *Free Speech and Headlight* (shortened to *Free Speech* in 1892) and did some local muckraking regarding the segregated schools of Memphis that resulted in the loss of her job as

teacher. In 1892, when three black businessmen were lynched in Memphis, she boldly criticized the white people of Memphis for condoning the violence. Her press was destroyed by an angry mob in retaliation for her editorials. She continued to speak out on lynching through the pages of T. Thomas Fortune's New York *Age* and also on the lecture circuit. In 1893 she lectured in England, Scotland, and Wales. She became the leading crusading journalist in the fight for black civil rights and in the anti-lynching campaign. In 1895 she published *A Red Record: Tabulated Statistics and Alleged Causes of Lynching in the United States 1892-1893-1894,* which was also a history of lynching since the Civil War.

In 1895 Miss Wells married the lawyer Ferdinand Lee Barnett, founder of Chicago's first black newspaper, *The Conservator,* and became active in Chicago civic affairs and women's club work. In 1910 she founded the Negro Fellowship League to aid black migrants to the city. She continued to play an active role in the anti-lynching crusade, often holding mass meetings of protest and personally investigating cases for her newspaper articles. She was one of the founders of the NAACP in 1909-10. In 1899 she sharply criticized BTW for failing to denounce lynching in clear-cut terms. After the turn of the century she and her husband were leaders of anti-Washington sentiment in Chicago.

From Robert Charles Bedford

Beloit Wis   Dec 4 1890

Dear Prof   Yours with petition inclosed is just recd. I do not see how it can be refused unless it is the purpose of the Legislature to make merchandise of the grant and sell it to the highest bidder. A clearer case of justice than the giving of the whole to Tuskegee never existed.

I find myself restless at the North and shall never be at ease till I am back South again. My heart is there and I feel that I am needed there and my whole life is wrapped up in Ala. I feel that great good will result from my work here to the South or I could not stay for a moment. As it is I hope you will keep an eye out and whenever an opportunity offers where I can have a reasonable home for my family and be near enough to you so that I can continue my old connection with the school and preach as a basis for the largest possible public good be sure and let me know at once. I love the North and am welcomed heartily and my labors seem to be acceptable but I do not feel that I am needed here but most of all my whole heart is with the whole South. Now my dear Brother you know more about this than any other human being and I trust you will give it most serious consideration. I have read with great interest of the new steps being taken both in Georgia and Ala to unite the 2 Congl bodies. There may be hope here for something. I trust a right spirit is at the bottom of it. Your bro

R. C. Bedford

I have just recd a very kind letter from Rev Dr Crawford of Sparta Wis. I preach for him Dec 16th. At Tomah my mother's home Dec 7.

R. C. B.

ALS Con. 3 BTW Papers ATT. Original destroyed.

From Ellen Collins[1]

New York. Dec 6. 1890

Sir, We have a good double-faced gold watch which was carried by my Father[2] for several years. It is too good and valuable to be given to a very young person, and we have been thinking to whom it could be given. My Father was greatly interested for the people of your race, and would I think be pleased if one of them should wear it. It has occurred to us that perhaps you would like it for yourself.[3] You may already have one, but if not, and this would be acceptable to you, just say so, and we will have it put in order and sent to you. Perhaps it would be in time to reach you as a holiday present.

I hope school matters move along well. Respectfully

Ellen Collins

ALS Con. 861 BTW Papers DLC.

[1] Ellen Collins (1828-1912) was born and reared in New York City. In 1861 she was active in war relief work as chairman of the committee on supplies for the Woman's Central Association of Relief, a branch of the U.S. Sanitary Commission. From 1865 to 1870 she worked for the New York Freedmen's Relief Association encouraging New York women to support Negro education. During the 1870s she was active in New York charities work investigating public institutions such as hospitals, almshouses, and asylums. In 1880 she invested more than $20,000 of her own money in the restoration of several tenement houses in New York, which she rented to the poor as part of an experiment in model tenements. She conducted the tenements successfully for twenty-three years. Of Quaker ancestry, she formally joined the Society of Friends in 1899.

Miss Collins was an enthusiastic supporter of BTW and his school, frequently giving both money and advice to BTW. Her correspondence also reveals a friendly personal relationship between her and BTW. In 1892 she wrote BTW that she sometimes questioned the value of charitable work, since ultimately "a man's fortunes be very much in his own hands." She said she had sympathy for those who "persist in coming short of what they were meant to be and do" but she believed they were often injured by aid from others. She confessed: "My reputation is therefore not a good one for helping the depressed, people say or think I am too severe, perhaps so, only do let people use their own powers bodily and mental." (Collins to BTW, Sept. 7, 1892, Con. 5, BTW Papers, ATT. Original destroyed.) When Ellen Collins died in 1912 her estate of more than $200,000 went to various charities, including large gifts to Negro education and to the New York Society of Friends.

[2] Joseph B. Collins, president of the Mutual Life Insurance Company and the United States Life Insurance Company, and one of the founders of the Association for Improving the Condition of the Poor.

[3] BTW accepted the watch for his own use. Miss Collins had it repaired at Tiffany's, and the firm apparently forwarded it to Tuskegee about Jan. 20, 1891. (Collins to BTW, Jan. 19, 1891, Con. 861, BTW Papers, DLC.)

From Warren Logan

Tuskegee, Ala., Dec 6 1880 [1890]

Dear Mr. Washington: I have received $50. from a Mr. Hamilton[1] at Fond-du-Lac, Wis, as a result of Mr. Bedford's work. This is the only amount that has been sent to me. Mr. Bedford has collected a number of small amounts which he has kept for his expenses.

I am glad to hear that you are having large & enthusiastic meetings and hope they will pan out well for our work.

The Montgomery matter is progressing satisfactorily. Waddy Thompson says we are sure to get the Federal money, but we cannot be sure of this until we really get it. Patterson is doing everything that he can do to get the money. Waddy Thompson tells me that he had a three hours debate with State Auditor Hogue[2] on the matter before the committee on Education of the House. The point that the opposition is making is that our school is not a state school, that is, that the property does not belong to the State but to individuals. It is very likely that a committee will visit the school just after the adjournment for the recess next week. This is the best thing that could happen for us, and they will then be able to see for themselves what we are doing and compare our work with that of the Montgomery school.

Miss Mason[3] has not yet sent in her contribution, and I shall use the

Endowment money to pay the teachers, and shall hope to replace it with Miss Mason's gift. Yours truly

Warren Logan

HLS Con. 2 BTW Papers ATT. Original destroyed.

¹ Probably Woodman Clarke Hamilton (b. 1834), who owned a successful lumber business and was director of the Milwaukee Harvester Co. He was a member of the board of education in Fond-du-Lac and active in Congregational church work.

² Cyrus Dunlap Hogue (1848-92) attended Howard College and the University of Alabama, and graduated from Washington and Lee University. He practiced law in Perry County, Ala., and was elected to the state legislature in 1882, serving several terms. He served two terms as Alabama state auditor (1888-92).

³ Ellen Frances or Ida Means Mason.

From M. Arnold Morin

Tuskegee, Ala., Dec. 8 1890

Dear Mr Washington: I suppose you have got my letter telling you that I have sent two cuts to Dr. Coppin.¹ He wrote anxiously for them and I immediately sent two. Have attended to what you ask about the colored papers this way. The Phil. Christian Recorder has quite a sarcastic article on your reply. You will note carefully a marked article in the Southern Chris. Recorder.

I am sure you will not be told of the dissatisfaction of the students in regard to the cooking of their food. On several occasions they have been to Miss Murray to complain of what they had to eat. The cook thinks that because they are colored, they must be satisfied with the uncooked and burnt food. On Sunday evening the bread was served up and it was found to contain weavels and other insects. They took some of the bread to Mr Logan's that very evening and some to Miss Murray. Of course she told them to be patient and no doubt it would not occur again. They would have murmured more if they were not good students in this respects, but just at this very moment such a thing should not occur as many will write home and tell how they are treated. The same sort of bad flour was given to the teachers, but no one touched the biscuits. I think your brother is leaving too much of the com.[2] work to Menafee who has not intelligence enough to see the harm such a thing can do the school. Yours truly,

M. A. Morin

ALS Con. 2 BTW Papers ATT. Original destroyed.

[1] Levi Jenkins Coppin (1848-1924) was born in Maryland of free parents and received his schooling in Delaware, where he then taught school for a while. He was ordained as a minister of the A.M.E. Church in 1879 and quickly rose in the ranks. In 1887 he graduated from the Philadelphia Episcopal Divinity School and then became editor of the *A.M.E. Church Review* (1888-96). In 1900 Coppin was elected bishop and served in South Africa (1900-1904). Returning to the United States, he held posts in South Carolina, Maryland, Virginia, and North Carolina.

[2] Commissary.

To Warren Logan

25 Beacon St. Boston, Dec. 11 1890

Dear Mr. Logan: Both of your letters of Dec. 6 are received. The statement you sent showing how money has been spent was not necessary as I have been sure all along that you were using the money in your judgement to the best advantage, but I feared you did not see the urgency of the Hobbie & Teague case as strongly as I did. I take note of the other matter mentioned in your letter. I hope by this time that you are a little relieved financially. There is one comfort we are not the only people hard pressed. Money is very tight here and business men feel it, though the situation is constantly growing better.

I hope you will hear from Miss Mason soon.

I hope to start South on the 22.

I am glad to hear about the Federal money and am anxious to know what the Committee did and said.

Do not go into the dirt with Patterson even if we lose the money.[1]

Has that "Club" money been sent?

I am glad to hear that matters are going smoothly there, and hope that those notes will soon be paid if you have not already been able to do so. The enclosed ck for $20 I cut by mistake but suppose you can use it.

Mr. Hamilton will send something tomorrow.

We have many promises in the way of scholarships after Jan 1.

My baby is much better. Yours truly

B. T. Washington

Just as soon as any money can be spared pay H. & T. more and begin buying there.

B. T. W.

Wherever you think it wise, get parties to extend notes. Business men all over the country are doing this.

B. T. W.

ALS   Con. 95   BTW Papers   DLC.

[1] BTW wrote Logan two days later: "I would enter into no 'mud slinging' with Patterson no matter how low he descends." (BTW to Logan, Dec. 13, 1890, Con. 3, BTW Papers, ATT. Original destroyed.)

From Francis J. Grimké

Washington, D.C. Dec 12th 1890

Dear Prof. Washington: Your letter reached me yesterday and gave me much pleasure to hear from you, and of the good work which Tuskegee is continuing to do. God grant that your life may be long spared, and that the work may continue to increase each year.

So far, as I see now, I think it will be possible for me to accept your kind invitation to visit Tuskegee some time in the latter part of Feb. or the first of March. If I find that it will be impossible for me to do so I will write. If you do not hear from me to the contrary you may expect me. I need not say it is always a great pleasure for me to be with you, and the teachers and pupils of your school.

I read with a great deal of interest your article on "The Colored Ministry." Every word that you say is true. No one, who is at all acquainted with the facts in the case will call in question the truth of what you say. The condition of the colored Ministry in the Baptists and Methodist churches in the South is unquestionably a deplorable one. And in my judgment is to day the most serious obstacle in the way of our elevation as a people. These churches have the masses of our people, and through them the people will be largely reached. Hence the importance of having in their pulpits particularly the right kind of men. I sincerely hope that your article will result in some good.

Please remember me kindly to the teachers and friends at the School. Mrs. Grimké joins me in kindest regards to yourself. With best wishes. As ever   Your Sincere friend

Francis J. Grimké

ALS   Con. 4   BTW Papers   ATT.   Original destroyed.

From M. Arnold Morin

Tuskegee, Ala., Dec 13 1890

Dear Mr. Washington: I suppose you would like to hear something about the visit of the Committee.[1] They came on Thursday morning, the number being 6, exclusive of Mr Campbell and the two Thompsons. The school was fully prepared for them. They went into several of the recitation rooms and listened to the students and it happened at the time of their visits that the brightest students were on their legs reciting. After visit to class rooms they went to the indus. depts. and to the barn. They saw the students at work in all. They went to the brick yard and saw the newly burnt kiln of bricks. They saw the students at dinner. They went to their dinner at noon, returning at 3 o'clock. The students assembled in the chapel and sang some selections, then Mr Davis spoke, account of which I have written for Advertiser.

They were strongly impressed with the scope of the work and were agreeably surprised at what he [they?] saw. The boys drilled in their presence, attended by the band.

One of them remarked that there is as much difference between this school and the one at Montgy as between the New Orleans Exposition and a small dry goods store.

I would like you to send me approving word so that Mr Logan will pay me for the Student work. I charge $5. per month for work on four issues, and I did work on eight issues, making $10. Yours truly

M. Morin

The enclosed clipping is from the Advertiser of today. (Dec 13). You will see it is a better account that [than] the Students. I have ordered 50 copies.

ALS Con. 2 BTW Papers ATT. Original destroyed.

1 The Montgomery *Advertiser* reported five members of the committee were on the tour of inspection. They were John M. Davis, chairman, of Fayette County, E. B. Langley of Tallapoosa County, E. C. Jackson of Lee County, W. C. Hufham of Bullock County, and J. R. Simmons of Macon County. Also on the tour were George W. Campbell, a trustee of Tuskegee, Tuskegee's mayor W. P. Thompson, and Waddy Thompson, editor of the Tuskegee *News*. Chairman Davis spoke to a school assembly in glowing terms: "To-day, in this school, in this island of civilization, I have seen the most wonderful sight I could ever have seen." While praising the students he also cautioned them that "There are people looking upon you, upon this school here," urging them to set a good example "and you will be a blessing to yourselves and to the race." Davis praised BTW, who was away from the school during the inspection, as "one of the best men in the United States." (Montgomery *Advertiser,* Dec. 13, 1890, 7.)

To Ednah Dow Littlehale Cheney

25 Beacon St. Boston. Dec. 21 1890

Dear Mrs. Cheney: I hope you will not misunderstand the liberty I take in doing so but I write to know if there are any persons to whom you could give me an introduction that might prove helpful. I find money hard to get but our expenses at Tuskegee do not stop.

I thank you very much for the donations from the fair which I have gotten from the Unitarian rooms. Yours truly

Booker T. Washington

ALS Ednah Dow Cheney Papers MB. Written on Tuskegee Institute letter-head.

From John Robert Clifford

Martinsburg, W.Va., Dec 28th 1890

My dear sir: Replying to yours, of the 25th inst., just rec'd, will say, You have nothing to fear; you are right, & it is a great pity, that thousands of our young men, who know as well as you do, of the existing state of affairs, have not the moral courage to boldly sustain you. I would to God, that we had scores of Washingtons & Paynes. God will bless you & future generations honor you. Why, my dear sir! for the past 12 years, I have been boldly opposing & exposing the rottenness of Negro preachers. One time, about 6 years ago, they combined & came to my house with clubs, declaring they would kill me, for having published an article headed Sentimental Religion, which had no direct reference to them. But the fact that they took it to heart, plainly showed that it most forcibly applied to them. I had them arrested & convicted. No longer than yesterday, the people of the F. B. Church, called on me through their representative & begged that I should stop publishing Kirk's bad deeds, from the fact that it was hurting the church &c. How absurd for men of common sense to make such confessions. Well, you may rest assured, that a war vs. him shall be kept up until his departure from this place. If our lamented Wilson were living he could & would tell you of many battles I have fought, & he was always with me. When I last saw him, he told me of the very facts you're so manly exposing. Every thing I have seen vs. yours, is, indeed, muscles of thought minus bones or the frame, hence they tumble up in a fluffy shape.

Before closing, allow me to sincerely congratulate you on the best work of the South educationally, carried on by our own people. God bless you & give you long life & plenty to do, as you do what you do with your whole heart & that right. I like your kind of work, & think of starting a Normal School in the near future. I like the newspaper business & also law, but the old preacher class, supported by their many worshippers, have been fighting me so long, that I find it next to impossible to do more, than fairly live.

You may look for an able article in your defense, by Prof. Geo. T. Jones. Have written him to do so. Following him, Prof. F. L. Cardozo[1] will sustain you. Let us keep up the war, until the enemy succumb.

Hoping you will excuse the entirely too long response, I am, Very truly yours

J. R. Clifford

ALS   Con. 4   BTW Papers   ATT.   Original destroyed.

[1] Francis L. Cardozo (1837-1903), or Cardoza, was born of free parents in Charleston, S.C. After some education in a Negro school, he was apprenticed at age twelve to a carpenter for five years, and also worked four years as a journey-

man. In 1858 he entered the University of Glasgow, and completed his education at Presbyterian theological seminaries in Edinburgh and London. Returning to the United States in 1864, he was a pastor in New Haven for a year. In 1865 he returned to Charleston and founded Avery Normal Institute, with American Missionary Association help, and was its principal for three years. In 1868 he served in the state constitutional convention, and later in the same year was elected secretary of state. In 1871-72 he was a Latin instructor at Howard University. In 1872 and again in 1876 he was elected state treasurer. When the Conservatives gained control of the state government in an era of political recriminations, Cardozo was convicted of mishandling state funds, but Governor W. D. Simpson later pardoned him. All through Reconstruction Cardozo retained his interest in education. He promoted public schools, served on the board of trustees of the University of South Carolina, and received a law degree there. After 1877 Cardozo resided in Washington, D.C., where he worked in the auditing office of the Post Office Department and was for six years a clerk in the Treasury Department. From 1884 until his death he was principal of a black public high school in Washington. (Sweat, "Francis L. Cardoza — Profile of Integrity in Reconstruction Politics," 217-32.)

To Margaret James Murray

[Tuskegee, Ala.] Jan 1 91

Miss Murray: As soon as possible I wish you in connection with Mr. Whittaker to draw up a complete set of rules for the guidance of teachers in all their relations to the school. Wherever you think it necessary for definite rules to be tabulated to guide teachers in their dealings with students I wish you to make such rules. In doing this it is most important that you bear in mind our peculiar condition, in the class of teachers required for combining mental and industrial work, the scattered condition of some of the teachers, and also the fact that a number live family lives and a larger proportion are apt to be in their own houses in the future.

In this connection I wish you to give me the names of any teachers who in your judgement have not so far complied with the requirements mentioned in the enclosed pamphlet. Respectfully

B. T. Washington

ALpS Con. 106 BTW Papers DLC.

To Margaret James Murray

[Tuskegee, Ala.] Jan 1 [189]1

Miss Murray: This is to authorize you to make what ever changes and improvements you wish to regarding any matters pertaining to the conduct of the girls. In the matter of the girls passing from one building to another and matters like this, if you feel that the "watching" now done by teachers is not conducive to the best and highest development of the girls, make what ever changes you think best.

B. T. Washington

ALpS Con. 106 BTW Papers DLC.

From Frank C. Blundon[1]

Baton Rouge, La., Jany 8 1891

My Dear Bro: Allow me to play Hur to Bishop Payne's Aaron and your Moses. Have often thought to write you a congratulation for honesty and backbone. Am sorry the would-be wise one's who sit in their libraries hundreds of miles from the scene, and those whom brief authority or "much learning" hath blinded, do not see fit to acknowledge what every or any sensible man or woman who is working in the field or who is at all posted in the matter knows to be very largely true. We are white but our whole life is given to helping the colored people up the heights of knowledge and just such opposition as is thrown against you now is the great retarding obstacle to the progress the race needs. What astonishes me is the fiery opposition of such men as Albert,[2] of the S. W. Christ Advocate, etc. A very peculiar thing about their opposition is that whereas yourself and Bishop Payne offer proof they offer nothing but wind. I am very sorry to notice the acrimonious statements made by some of the good brethren. Let us hope that out of all of it may come a new determination on the part of all friends of the race to enlarge the opportunities for doing better as they have opportunity. Surely all this fair Southland needs a brighter intellectual sunlight, or rather specific rays on some subjects. We are with you heart and hand in the cause of christian education and hope to see [the] day when the lamentable condition may not exist among the leaders of the people.

I write this as an encouragement to you to go on frankly telling the people of their errors, kindly persuading them to reach after better things. This is a personal letter, and not written for publication. This statement is rendered necessary because I have "got left" if you will pardon the expression, by writing to some of the public men in New Orleans.

Hoping your school is in a prosperous condition I am   In His name,

Frank C. Blundon

The bull dozing in the eastern part of this Parish has injured our school considerably though our enrollment for last year was 192.

ALS Con. 4 BTW Papers ATT. Original destroyed.

[1] Frank C. Blundon and Ada C. Pollock-Blundon were principals of the Live Oak Preparatory School, a coeducational black school in Baton Rouge. The school's letterhead proclaimed: "We aim to teach Self Respect, Self Control, and Luke, X, 27."

[2] Aristide E. P. Albert was editor of the *Southwestern Christian Advocate,* a New Orleans–based paper that was the official organ of the Methodist Episcopal Church in its work among the freedmen. Begun in 1872, the *Advocate* became a leading black religious paper and included among its early editors Hiram R. Revels.

To George Washington Cable

Tuskegee, Ala., January 9th. 1891

Dear Mr. Cable: I have yours of December 29th and reply as far as I can. You may not know that the State of Alabama has so far provided no school houses for the public schools. That is left to the people, and the result is that the schools among the colored people especially are usually taught in church houses. In some of the larger towns and cities the local authorities have made provision for the building of school houses. I have looked carefully over the State Superintendent's report and find that he gives no estimate of the value of school property owned by the State, but I am sure I will be inside of the truth when I say that the property owned by the State and used for the benefit of the colored people is valued at less than $200,000. I am sorry that I cannot give you a more satisfactory answer. Yours truly,

Booker T. Washington

TLS   George W. Cable Collection   LNHT.

From Edward Augustus Johnson[1]

Raleigh, N.C., Jan. 12/'91

Dear Sir: I mail you to-day a copy of my history — School History of the Negro Race in Am. Probably you have heard of the work. I send it that you may look over the work; and if it meets your approval, I trust you will give it a place in you[r] course of study. It has been adopted by several of the schools in this state already, the first school to adopt it being Shaw University, one of the leading schools of the country for colored students. You will find that it contains information that every colored child should know. I have spent several years in preparing the book and sincerely hope that such leading educators as yourself will feel justified in endorsing it. I do not claim for it per-fection, but it is my small contribution to the race's interest. It is not a profitable undertaking. The object is not so much to make money as to get the facts of history into the hands of the race. We have been grossly neglected by most all historians, and if you teach some of the text books that we use in N.C., the pupils will learn from them that they belong to the most inferior race on the earth and also fail to learn one single great thing done by a negro.

Please let me hear from you. If you should decide to place the book in the hands of your pupils — the price would be 80¢ per copy. Yours respectfully,

E. A. Johnson

ALS   Con. 4   BTW Papers   ATT.   Original destroyed.

[1] Edward Augustus Johnson (1860-1944) was born in slavery in Raleigh, N.C. He acquired his education in night school and eventually attended Atlanta Univer-sity. He was principal of a Negro school in Raleigh and also served as alderman

in Raleigh. He wrote *A School History of the Negro Race in America from 1619 to 1890, with a Short Introduction as to the Origins of the Race; also a Short Sketch of Liberia* (Raleigh: Edwards and Broughton, Printers and Binders, 1890). The book viewed black history largely in religious and biblical terms. For example, Johnson saw the historical condition of African peoples as the result of the fall of the Egyptian empire, which was in accord with biblical prophecy. Johnson wrote several other works of a historical or anthropological nature, including *History of Negro Soldiers in the Spanish-American War* (1899), *Light Ahead for the Negro* (1904), and *Adam vs. Apeman and Ethiopia* (1931). Johnson studied law at Shaw University and eventually became a dean and trustee of the school. In 1907 he moved to New York City to practice law and became a member of the Harlem Board of Trade and Commerce and active in YMCA and church work. In 1917 he became the first Negro elected to the New York legislature.

From Warren Logan

Montgomery Ala., Jan'y 19th 1891

Dear Mr Washington   I find that the legislative committee is at Huntsville to-day. They will come here to-night or to-morrow.

McIver[1] tells me that the Advertiser has made no change of front on the question of what school should receive the Hatch fund. It is still strongly in favor of Tuskegee. The article[2] that appeared in an issue of last week in which mention was made of Patterson's school, McIver says, means nothing whatever.

Patterson is however preparing a circular in which he will incorporate the article in regard to the refusal of Secretary Noble[3] to approve the division of the fund made by the Ga. legislature and the Advertiser's article on the same subject.

I enclose the matter of another circular that he is going to get out. Everything is very quiet here — and I can tell very little about the situation until the legislators reach the city and I can see some of them. Patterson has got to be watched constantly and his movements counteracted. Yours Sincerely

Warren Logan

ALS Con. 4 BTW Papers ATT. Original destroyed.

[1] D. W. McIver, who worked for the Montgomery *Advertiser,* told BTW in a letter of Sept. 16, 1889: "If I can be of service to you at any time, by way of any notice through the columns of the Advertiser or if you have any special for publication, you will only have to inform me. The Advertiser is the friend of your School, & is always ready to aid you...." (Con. 92, BTW Papers, DLC.)

2 The Montgomery *Advertiser* of Jan. 16, 1891, p. 4, commented in part: "It is evident from the rulings at Washington that there can not be a division of the fund among a half dozen institutions. It must go to one white and one colored upon the basis of population. This would about divide the fund into two parts. Auburn will, under this ruling, unquestionably get the part intended for the white college. The Colored University here is a State institution and more directly under State management than any others of that class applying for a portion of the fund. The Legislature will have to settle the matter at an early date after re-assembling. When that is done the $15,000 will be paid over to the State."

3 John Willock Noble (1831-1912) was Secretary of the Interior under President Benjamin Harrison from 1889 to 1893.

A Circular to Hampton Graduates

Tuskegee Normal School, Tuskegee, Alabama, January 20, '91

As a Hampton graduate, I take the liberty of addressing you on a subject, in which I think both of us feel a deep interest. You probably know that after twenty years of work at Hampton, Miss Mary F. Mackie resigns her position at the close of the present session. What Miss Mackie's work and influence have done for every Hampton student, I need not mention to you, what these twenty years of work have done and are doing for thousands of communities in the South through the medium of Hampton graduates and ex-students, is known to us all.

The question I wish to put to you is this; should not these years of unselfish labor for our race, receive some special recognition from us as Hampton graduates? If you agree with me in this, will you send me on receipt of this letter 50 cts. (or more if you can) to be used by the graduates residing at Hampton; in selecting and presenting to Miss Mackie a suitable testimonial in recognition of her services?[1]

As soon as the money is collected, it will be turned over to the treasurer of the Alumni Association, and Miss Mackie will be given the name of each donor. Please do not put this off, but reply at once. Money can be sent by postal note, registered letter or in postage stamps. Yours fraternally,

Booker T. Washington

[*Handwritten:*]

May we not depend on you for more than 50¢ as many will send nothing? B. T. W.

PLSr Con. 861 BTW Papers DLC.

¹ The Hampton alumni presented Mary Mackie with $180 in nine twenty-dollar gold pieces, enclosed with the cards of 225 contributors, in a box made at Hampton. Lined with crimson velvet, the box had a top of carved holly wood and sides of hard oak from the ribs of the *Merrimack*.

From Elizabeth P. Jones

[Dorchester, Mass., ca. Jan. 20, 1891]

Dear Mr. Washington: Through the kindness of Mr. Hardwick,¹ the executor of Mrs. Baker's² will, I am allowed to quote the following article:

"64th. I give to Booker T. Washington, of Tuskegee, Alabama three thousand dollars, with the expectation that he will use the same for his children, but I do not wish hereby to create any trust for which he shall be legally accountable in any Court."

You may be assured of my hearty congratulations in the gift that dear Mrs. Baker made you. Sincerely your friend

Elizabeth P. Jones

For the present, I have the care of things here at the house.

ALS Con. 17 BTW Papers DLC. Written on the back of M. L. Williams to BTW, Jan. 20, 1891. Williams advised BTW of Mrs. Baker's "last days upon earth," and briefly described her funeral.

¹ Benjamin Cutler Hardwick (1833-1912) was a longtime friend and neighbor of Eleanor Baker and a Dorchester, Mass., businessman. He was a contributor to Hampton and Tuskegee institutes.
² Eleanor Jameson Williams Baker.

To Warren Logan

Tuskegee, Ala., January 22nd. [23] 1891

Dear Mr. Logan: I think the article in the Advertiser this morning helps matters considerably.¹ I find that Mr. J. H. Washington is not able to go down to Montgomery this week. He is not better but improves slowly. I take it for granted that you will come home Saturday night or Sunday morning, and we will arrange for some body to go back first of next week. I have just received a Boston paper containing the last of Mrs Baker's public bequests, and she leaves Tuskegee $4000. This is almost as much as she has left to any educational institution, Hampton getting $6000. She also leaves me personally $3000. in addition to this. Matters at the school are going on well. Yours truly,

B. T. Washington

TLS   Con. 2   BTW Papers   ATT.   Original destroyed.

[1] On Jan. 23, 1891, a letter from "Citizen" to the editor appeared in the Montgomery *Advertiser*, p. 7. It was probably submitted to the *Advertiser* by Logan or a white friend of Tuskegee. The letter warned the Alabama legislature of the difficulty the Georgia legislature had had with federal authorities because of its refusal to share with black schools the funds appropriated to the state under the Morrill Act of 1890. If the money did not go to Tuskegee, said "Citizen," under the Secretary of the Interior's ruling "Alabama will have to wait till an agricultural department is established in some colored school and actually put into operation before the State can secure its first payment of $15,000. Where is the money coming from to purchase land and equip such a department?"

To Dora S. King

Tuskegee, Ala., Jan. 23 1891

Mrs. King: Since you have decided not to remain I may find it necessary to fill your place before the time mentioned by you arrives for the reasons that it is important that [I] get some one *used* to my children and *settled* before I leave again, and it may be that I may be able to secure a person soon and could not do so later on.

B. T. Washington

ALS Copy   Con. 17   BTW Papers   DLC.

To Warren Logan

Tuskegee, Ala., Jan. 26 1891

Dear Mr. Logan: Your telegram rec'd. Thompson[1] is still sick. You better prepare brief for Senator Handley.[2]

If McAlpine[3] speaks I think it will be well for you to suggest to the committees that if it is their purpose to begin hearing outsiders we can begin that game too and thus all of their time will be taken hearing outsiders. I want to be there if possible at the joint meeting and I wish you would telegraph me as far ahead as possible. I fear Thompson is dangerously sick and I do not think we can depend on him further. Telegraph or write me every thing of importance. Matters go well here. Yours &c.

B. T. Washington

ALS Con. 2 BTW Papers ATT. Original destroyed.

[1] Waddy Thompson.
[2] William Anderson Handley (1834-1909) represented Chambers and Randolph counties in the Alabama Senate. He was a member of the conference committee for the omnibus liquor bills.
[3] Probably W. H. McAlpine.

To Samuel Chapman Armstrong

Tuskegee, Ala., Jan. 27 1891

Dear Gen.: Your letter with Mrs. Bullard's[1] enclosed is received. Mr. J. M. Davis, Chairman of the House Committee on Education is a good man and knows you. He says he was your classmate in College. I think he will do any thing he can for you.

Whatever is done, must be done soon as the Leg[i]slature adjourns soon. The Gov. is Thos. G. Jones.

I am going to Montgomery to morrow and may be able to get more information when I shall write you again. Shall do all I can. Yours Sincerely

B. T. Washington

An expenditure of $15. to some Montgomery lawyer would ensure its passage as the matter will have to [be] *pushed* in order to not be too late.

B. T. W.

ALS BTW Folder ViHaI.

[1] Elizabeth L. (Mrs. Stephen H.) Bullard (d. 1895) was a sister of Harvard's president Charles W. Eliot and also a sister of Mrs. Henry W. Foote, wife of a Hampton trustee. She was a close friend of Mary Tileston Hemenway (see above,

2:150), with whom she worked on behalf of Indians. Mrs. Bullard was president of the Massachusetts Indian Association from 1886 to 1895 and was especially interested in the Indians at Mt. Vernon Barracks, Ala., some of whom were sent to Hampton.

To Samuel Chapman Armstrong

Tuskegee, Ala., Jan. 29 1891

Dear Gen. Armstrong: I was in Montgomery yesterday and I think I can get that bill through as it is late in the session. I shall have to pay about $15 to have it "watched."

Enclosed I send a map showing where Tuskegee graduates are teaching. I hope it is satisfactory to you.

In addition to the $4000 left the school by Mrs. Baker she left me personally $3000 for the benefit of my children. This is a great relief to me and will enable me to devote myself more fully to the cause.

I am preparing to send a copy of the enclosed circular to each one of the Hampton graduates. All here wish to be remembered to you. Yours truly

Booker T. Washington

P.S. I have having the bill drawn so as to prevent whiskey being sold within 3 miles of the reservation. Will this suit?

B. T. W.

ALS   BTW   Folder   ViHaI.

From Elizabeth L. Bullard

Boston Mass. Feb. 4th [1891]

Dear Sir, I have just rec'd Gen. Armstrong's note enclosing your two about the Apache Bill in the Alabama legislature.

I do not know how to express my gratitude to you for your efforts. This School for the Apache children has been kept for about two years & the progress of the Pupils is all that we could ask. They are both docile & intelligent, also fond of their Teachers.

The Parents show a most creditable desire that their Children should be taught, & many of the men, under the kind & wise super-vision of Lieut. Wotherspoon[1] specially detailed by the Sec. of War, are forming habits of industry & civilization. I am in constant correspon-dence with one of the Teachers, & think I know the truth of the situation.

Any one is at liberty to visit the School, though no Indian child can ever be "shown off" in the presence of a stranger.

You can judge how anxious I am to have this terrible temptation of liquor removed from their immediate neighborhood. It is unreasonable to expect them to resist it, (altho' some of them have done so) & of what use is it, to teach the Children reading & writing, if they are to be dragged down by examples of intoxication!

Assuring you again that what you have done for these poor prisoners will be highly appreciated by the Mass. Indian Assn,[2] I am Yours, with many thanks,

Elizabeth L. Bullard

I enclose my ch'k to save time & hope you will find no difficulty in cashing it.

ALS   Con. 3   BTW Papers   ATT.   Original destroyed.

[1] William Wallace Wotherspoon (1850-1921), an army officer who commanded a company of troops at Mt. Vernon Barracks, Ala., from 1889 to 1894. He was in charge of 500 Apache prisoners of war, including Geronimo. Wotherspoon served with the Twelfth Infantry in the Philippines for more than three years beginning in 1899 and eventually attained the rank of major general.

[2] The Massachusetts Indian Association, organized in 1883, had 1,150 members in 1891. Its special work was an Apache school at Mt. Vernon Barracks, Ala. Established in 1890, it reported at the end of the first year that the Indian boys had requested haircuts. "The amount of barbarism cut off with those elf-locks can hardly be over-estimated. The love of savage decoration, the warrior's grasp of the scalp-lock, the wild unkempt scorn of civilization, all fell before those scissors, and a new vista of progress is unveiled." (Women's National Indian Association, *Annual Report, 1891,* 11-12.)

To the Editor of the Montgomery *Advertiser*

Tuskegee, Ala., Feb. 5, 1891

Editor Advertiser: The report in your Wednesday's paper was calcu-lated to do me injustice regarding the speech I made before the colored convention. My whole life since I have been in the State, as an educator, has been given to showing that education will cement the friendship of the two races, not alienate them. So far from denouncing anybody as being bitter, I should have been willing for the whole Legislature or all the citizens in Tuskegee to have heard all that I said.

I can refer any one who wants to know my character and standing, as to matters that concern the white and colored people to the citizens of Tuskegee, in whose midst I have lived and worked for nine years, and among whom I expect to pass the remainder of my life.

B. T. Washington

Montgomery *Advertiser,* Feb. 6, 1891, 7.

A Sunday Evening Talk

Tuskegee, Ala. [Feb. 8?, 1891]

SELF DENIAL

I want to impress upon you, what I have attempted several times before, the duty and utility of trying to live a life of unselfishness, a life of self-denial, a life devoted to the good of others. The more experience one has in the world and the more he studies and comes in contact with those about him the more he learns that the people who live the happiest lives in the world are those who are continually striving, whether seen or unseen, to make the world happy or better by the opportunity given them for having lived in it.

Indeed the experience of the world teaches that the people who are the most unhappy, who have the most cloudy days, are those whose lives are devoted to themselves, who are seeking continually their own happiness. Take the life of Lord Byron who had education, wealth and influential friends. Near the close of his life he said that he could not count in the whole course of his life eleven happy days, and he doubted much if he lived on he could have counted one round dozen. People who live for themselves are the most miserable persons you know. You will find that persons who are continually striving to get this world's goods, and heaping up for themselves, never get satisfied, they are always miserable. Even those who have splendid fortunes and are

129

seeking after an education as you are doing here, are not happy, they are miserable, miserable because they have a wrong end in view, they are living not to make the world better but living for their own pleasure, for their happiness, for their own selfish ends; who seek after their own glory, who think themselves better educated than others, who like to have their names sounded around that they are scholars. These persons are never happy because they are not using their education for the benefit of the world and making those about them happy. It is alright to get money, but the getting of money is not the highest aim in the world. Go to some of the persons who possess the largest fortunes in the world, and you will find that instead of enjoying a life of happiness they are leading a life of misery from morning till night, they do not enjoy a single moment of happiness while they are striving to get money.

Take the life of William E. Dodge. He amassed a considerable fortune, but every dollar he got hold of he consecrated to the use of the Lord, to bringing about the Kingdom of Christ upon earth. There are thousands who are rich — and to become rich is not a sin — who make a wise use of their money, but if you make the mistake of trying to get this world's goods with a view to gratify yourselves, you will find that your life will be miserable, because it will not answer the purpose for which God puts us in the world. Persons who deny themselves for the benefit of others, put down self always, have an element of strength in their character, in their self-denial. Why is it that the young man who is raised up in the country, is so often much stronger than the city boy whose opportunities are so much larger? Because that boy has learned to practise self-denial, to deny himself of privileges, and so when he comes into contact with the city, he has learned that lesson so well that he gains greater strength than the city boy whose advantages are larger. The same thing is true of those in school. It is not those who have got a plenty of money, whose mothers and fathers send them all they want, that are the best scholars, but it is the boy whose poverty is evident to him, who does not want to get into the company of his fellows, because of his torn garments or old shoes, that is going to make a real man of himself by this self-denial. This is the secret of Abraham Lincoln's success in life, that great man, the "first American," as he is called, sleeping on a bed of leaves without any covering in a log cabin. He practised this self-denial, and it gave him an element of strength which won for him the name of the "first American."

I mentioned to you before the story of Sir Philip Sidney who was lying on the battle field wounded and suffering. A cup of cold water was brought to him but seeing the suffering of his wounded comrade beside him, he gave the soldier the water, telling him that he needed it more than he. He learned this self-denial not then on the battle field, but before, all through his life so you will find after all that this lesson of self-denial, this living for others, is the only real living in the world, the only worthy end of life. Let us all strive to do this: The life worth living is giving one's life for the good of others, to forget ourselves and do something for others.

It is related that when the battle of Fredericksburg was still raging and when no truce had been declared, a soldier heard the cries and moaning of the wounded, and getting to the point where he could no longer stand these cries, he went to the commanding officer and said; "I cannot stand this any longer I want to go and relieve the sufferings of my comrades." "You do not know what you are asking" replied the officer "To attempt to go out and relieve those who are suffering." The soldier said he would rather go, and with the consent of his officer, he went amid all the cannonading, and at his appearance the roar of the battle ceased, and the form of the soldier was seen moving among his comrades ministering to them, and when he came back from the battle field, he came back as a hero and was worshipped. Instead of taking the best seat, let us see that those about us are made comfortable; instead of laughing at the new scholar take him in hand and make it pleasant for him; instead of yielding to our appetites, to sins that will degrade us and bring us to shame and sorrow, let us put down self that will enable us to accomplish the best end in life and enable us to grow stronger. When you go out to work, stop where the people need your help most, where you can accomplish the most good, go not in the place where you are to be most pleasantly located, find that corner that is the darkest where the people have the least help and see how bright and cheerful you can make them, and when you have done all that you can look back on your life with pleasure because you did not live for yourselves. If we can send out of this institution such characters, you do not know how much you contribute to its success, how much good your life will be and how much people will miss you when you are gone.

Tuskegee Student, 3 (Feb. 13, 1891), 1. Stenographically reported by M. Arnold Morin. The preceding Sunday was Feb. 8, but there may have been a longer time between delivery and publication.

To Warren Logan, Margaret James Murray, and James Nathan Calloway

[Tuskegee, Ala.] Feb. 12 [189]1

To Mr. Logan:
  Miss Murray,
    Mr. Calloway,
  You are hereby appointed a committee to decide on the text books to be used.

B. T. Washington

ALpS Con. 106 BTW Papers DLC.

To Margaret James Murray, Warren Logan, and Anna C. Hawley

[Tuskegee, Ala.] Feb. 12 [189]1

You are hereby appointed a committee to revise the Course of study for next year.

B. T. Washington

ALpS Con. 106 BTW Papers DLC.

From Elizabeth L. Bullard

Boston Mass. Feb. 15th [1891]

Dear Sir, At the last meeting of the Executive Committee of the Mass. Indian Assn. it was voted that "The thanks of the Exec. Committee of the M. I. A. be presented to Mr. Boker T. Washington for his valuable & efficient services in pushing the bill now before the Alabama Legislature for abolishing the liquor traffic around the Mt. Vernon military Reservation."

E. L. Bullard

Sec. pro tem.

The ladies quite understand that the Bill has not yet passed, & also that perhaps it never will, but nevertheless they feel & express their gratitude for your efforts.

Some of them have worked hard, & some have paid liberally for the School for the children of the Apache Captives, & feel much grieved that their work should be rendered almost worthless by the terrible temptation of strong drink.

If the Bill should pass, you will have done much to save the tribe.

I hope you rec'd the check for $15. wh. I mailed to you immediately on the receipt of your letter to Gen. Armstrong — about 10 days ago. Yours truly

E. L. Bullard

ALS   Con. 3   BTW Papers   ATT.   Original destroyed.

From Ellen Collins

New York. Feby 28/91

Sir, The enclosed is cut from the Evening Post of this date. Probably you know that the Editor[1] is greatly opposed to the Blair Bill, and the Force Bill, and all such measures, which he esteems crippling to our colored brethren. But here the Editors of the two papers quoted seem to take the most advanced position on this question. I am heartily at one with the opinion that "we can never teach any one to do for himself by doing it for him," but I cannot help entertaining a question as to whether your people are as yet able to provide for themselves in matters of education. Certainly they do not yet see their power or their privilege and one cannot wonder. While therefore I can heartily applaud all such editorial statements as educating in themselves, I do not see why Atlanta University and Tuskegee School should not have gifts just as Harvard University has. But I would not make them as from White people to Colored people, but as from intelligent citizens who desire to promote learning — and yet there is one other sentiment. For two hundred years we wrongfully cut off your chance, in so far as that goes, we owe you a heavy debt; the way to pay it as honest men would wish to, is to set an open door before you, and at the same stimulate you to put forth your best efforts to make use of this opening. I do rejoice over the defeat of the bills. Some day when you can, let me know what you believe as the result of your personal efforts. Respectfully

Ellen Collins

ALS   Con. 4   BTW Papers   ATT.   Original destroyed.

¹ Edwin Lawrence Godkin (1831-1902). He edited *The Nation* after 1865 and was editor-in-chief of the New York *Evening Post* from 1883 to 1900. His opposition to the Blair and Force bills was couched in terms of principles of nineteenth-century liberalism and fear of governmental power.

From Emily Howland

Washington D.C. March 5th, 1891

Dear Sir   A lady from Boston and myself wish to take a trip South as far as Tuskegee, to visit your school and other institutions for colored youth as opportunity offers. This lady, Miss Mary L. Eastman, was a race teacher for years, and is now one of the best public speakers that we have. She is interested in the cause of education and also, deeply in the welfare of the colored people.

We should like to go in the course of two or three weeks, and I take the liberty of writing to ask you if this be a good season for visiting your country, and if it be malarial now or ever; also what the route thither should be. Could we take Hampton by the way or Richmond? I dislike to trouble you with these questions and would not but that I think that Miss Eastman's visit to your institution will be of value in many ways. I have just rec.d a letter from one of your students (Mitchell Garner) which interests me perhaps he or some other pupil could write the answers to my questions and relieve you of the task. The letter may be addressed to me as follows

112 M. St., N.W.

Washington, D.C.

Respectfully

Emily Howland

ALS   Con. 3   BTW Papers   ATT.   Original destroyed.

From Julia Strudwick Tutwiler[1]

[Livingston, Ala.] March 7, 1891

Dear Sir: I wish to write to you on a subject concerning the colored youth of Alabama which has occupied much of my thoughts for the past few years: You are aware that the Legislature of Alabama has now for the third time refused to give an annual appropriation of ten thousand dollars to establish a Reformatory. There are more than two hundred colored boys under the age of seventeen now in training for the lives of professional criminals; those called "county convicts" are at the mining-camps. Those called "state convicts" are at the penitentiary, where up to this time they have had no teacher and no training that would fit them for a better life than that of animals.

Now these boys are to be hired out with the other convicts to the highest bidder, who furnishes at the same time the guarantees required by the state as to treatment etc.

Now in your catalogue I see that you have a farm of 800 acres three miles from the Normal College. You have every facility for erecting buildings, you have great executive ability and enthusiasm for the uplifting of the colored race; why should you not hire these two hundred colored boys and establish an Industrial Reform school? Some of your teachers would doub[t]les[s] give their services free of charge at night to these poor outcasts. Philanthropic friends at the North will assist you in an effort so Christ-like, with money, with clothing with counsel. You can afford to pay the same hire for them that any one else would pay, and might state in your bid that you will do this, and

135

will also give the boys the advantages of a Reformatory-Industrial Education and at night the elements of an English Education. You could say that it would be still a Prison but a "Children's Prison," adapted to the age of those within its walls. The cultivation of fruits and vegetables, canning and evaporating them would serve to pay most if not all of their expenses.

I wish you could erect two buildings at a distance from each other and from your college — one for the boys and one for the *women,* of whom there are now more than a hundred at the Penitentiary and in County-prisons. I am very sure that they could earn their living by gardening and laundry-work.

I believe that if these people can be helped it is by their own race, who understand them who sympathize with them, and who are willing to make sacrifices for them.

You may use this letter in any way you please, but not my name. If you will write to the Governor and Inspectors on the subject I will enclose the letter in one from myself.

J. S. Tutwiler

ALS Con. 4 BTW Papers ATT. Original destroyed.

¹ Julia Strudwick Tutwiler (1841-1916) was born and reared in the South. She became a prominent educator and prison reformer in Alabama. In 1881 she was appointed co-principal of Livingston Female Academy and spent almost thirty years at the institution which became Livingston Normal College. In 1891 she was elected president of the elementary education department of the National Education Association. She lobbied in the Alabama legislature for better educational opportunities for women, winning admission of women to the University of Alabama.

Active in prison reform from 1879, Miss Tutwiler worked to improve conditions in Alabama prisons and to promote religious instruction as part of a program to rehabilitate prisoners. She opposed the convict-lease system but found it too entrenched to abolish. Her poem "Alabama," written in the 1870s, was adopted as the Alabama state song.

To Halle Tanner Dillon¹

[Tuskegee, Ala.] April 16th [189]1

Dear Madam: I am in receipt of yours of April 9th and in reply would say that we expect to have in the future a resident physician at this institution and prefer a lady. It is my intention to pass through

Philadelphia either in May or June and at one of which times I shall like to see you, provided you think it well to consider our proposition. I will not make our offer binding until I have seen you. In the meantime I write the facts in reference to the position so that you will let me know whether or not you are inclined to consider the offer favorably.

We will pay a salary of $600. a year with board for twelve months' work, including one month for vacation. This is with the understanding that you would teach two classes a day, if necessary, and take full charge of the health department. We should expect you to compound your own medicine as far as possible. We are making our purchase of drugs at wholesale rates. Our greatest out-lay at present is for medicine. We are compelled to buy in small quantities at the local drug stores.

The State of Alabama has a law requiring all persons who practise in the state to pass either a local or state examination. You can take either of these as you prefer. I do not think you would find any prejudice shown in the examination on account of your color. I should want you to begin work 1st of September 91.

Tuskegee is a town of about 3000 inhabitants, one-half colored. In addition to the salary named I may add that we have in connection with the institution 30 officers and teachers, seven or eight of these have families. This work of course would have nothing to do with your school work and the compensation would be extra. We have constantly on the school ground not far from 450 students. We have never had a resident phys[i]cian. I think you would like the work here as it is entirely in the hands of colored people. We are a little colony within our [town?]. I desire to say that while the salary is not very great we have in view those who are willing to come for the good they can do. This institution is largely supported by charity and we are always glad to have workers of a broad missionary spirit.

If you wish for any other information I shall be very glad to furnish it. Yours truly,

B. T. Washington

It is probable that while I cannot speak definitely regarding this you will get the greater part of the practice of these teachers and families.

TLpS Con. 106 BTW Papers DLC.

[1] Halle Tanner Dillon Johnson (b. 1863) was the daughter of the distinguished

A.M.E. Church leader Bishop Benjamin Tucker Tanner, and the sister of the painter Henry Ossawa Tanner. Growing up in Philadelphia, she studied medicine at the Woman's Medical College in that city, graduating in 1891. BTW wrote to the dean of the college inviting a black graduate to apply for a position at Tuskegee, and Halle Dillon wrote indicating her interest in the post. (Halle Tanner Dillon to BTW, Apr. 11, 1891, Con. 99, BTW Papers, DLC.) In 1891 she became the first woman to pass the Alabama medical examination. (See An Address at a Mass Meeting in Washington, D.C., Nov. 20, 1891, below.) Dr. Dillon was resident physician at Tuskegee from 1891 to 1894. In 1894 she married Rev. John Quincy Johnson, who taught mathematics at Tuskegee in 1893-94.

From Warren Logan

Tuskegee, Ala., April 16th 1891

The committee appointed by you to investigate the charge against Emma Parker[1] of using tobacco has finished its labors and makes the following report: Emma Parker is guilty, both as to the offense of night before last and of using tobacco right along since the first charge was preferred against her. The committee recommends as a punishment that the honor of speaking at Commencement be taken from her and that her diploma be withheld for at least one year.

Mr. Calloway[2] wishes to [be] reported as dissenting from the punishment as far as withholding the diploma goes.

Warren Logan
Chairman

ALS   Con. 3   BTW Papers   ATT.   Original destroyed.

[1] Emma Jennie Parker of Livingston, Ala., entered as a junior at Tuskegee in 1887 and graduated in 1891. She taught at Livingston and elsewhere in Alabama, and later in the Birmingham city schools.

[2] James Nathan Calloway.

A Sunday Evening Talk

Tuskegee, Ala., April 19, 1891

SOWING AND REAPING

"Sowing and Reaping" is the subject that I wish for a few minutes to call your attention to. All classes and conditions of men have a most implicit and abiding faith in the laws that govern the material universe. In other words, they believe that certain causes will always produce certain effects. Thus, scientists learned long ago that water cooled to 32 degrees Fahrenheit becomes frozen, and when heated to 212 degrees Far. would produce steam. By observation and experience men have learned to have the most complete confidence in these laws. They have learned the fact that water freezing under certain given conditions and evaporating at other certain given conditions, is not a mere matter of chance, but knew that back of it there is law and order. Furthermore they have learned that such changes could not take place with such precision without an intelligent and All-wise Being to direct. So much faith have men in the natural law just mentioned that in the Northern part of the United States, especially in Maine, we find them investing millions of dollars in the ice industry. Why are they willing to risk their all in this business? It is their faith in the unchangeableness of this natural law. If they found that during one year that the freezing point was reached and water did not freeze, and the next year when the freezing point was reached that the water boiled instead of freezing, would they be willing to invest money? They are willing to invest because they are sure that these natural laws can be depended upon — that certain causes will always produce certain effects — that cooling the water to a certain temperature under natural conditions, will always produce ice. There is no may-be or guess work about it. There is absolute certainty. Even greater faith is exercised in the opposite law which causes water to evaporate at a certain temperature. Pinning their faith to this law men not only invest money but are ready at any time to risk their lives. Every year corporations put millions into the building of new railroads, on the strength of their faith in this law. If they thought there was even one chance in ten after the railroad was built and the locomotive constructed and put on the track, and heat applied, that the water on being heated would fail to generate steam, there would be much hesitation if not failure to invest. On the strength of our faith in this law we risk our lives. Every one who travels on a rail road or in a steamship does so because he believes that the water will continue to evaporate and furnish the power necessary for controlling the movements of the car or vessel. There are instances when man's faith in the laws that govern the material universe becomes almost sublime. In one part of the Bible we are told if we have faith even so small as a grain of mustard seed we can say to yonder mountain be thou removed and planted into the sea and it shall be done. On a cursory examination this seems impossible. It is hard for us to realize that man can attain to such faith, yet a little thought convinces us that man's faith has done even more than this.

One of the first and interesting objects that the visitor to New York City sees is the vast structure — the Brooklyn Bridge — that spans the Hudson and binds the cities of New York and Brooklyn together. Analyze this structure and we find it composed of iron, stone, earth and wood. Analyze the mountain and we find it composed largely of the same material. This, then, is an instance where man's faith in the laws of gravitation, of cohesion and chemical affinity, has not only enabled him to pluck up the mountain and transport it to the sea, but by his faith he has suspended the mountain in the form of iron, clay, stone and wood, in mid-air between heaven and earth, where it will remain for ages a monument to man's faith in the natural laws of God. So it seems to me that there is no need of further argument to show that man has the most implicit faith in the immutable laws that govern whatever is tangible in the outward world. Now if we believe that God in his providence has so arranged that certain laws shall govern the outward world, that certain effects shall always follow certain causes, is it reasonable to suppose that our Creator has not been even more careful to place our own

BODIES

under law? Here, as in the outer world, nothing is left to chance. And this is as it should be, for the body is the home and foundation of our mental, moral and spiritual nature. The condition for a sound mind is a sound body. "A sound mind in a sound body," the Latin proverb has it. In reference to the body, as we sow so shall we reap. A few of the plain laws which nature has laid down for the government of the body are: temperance, regularity in eating and drinking, sufficient and regular sleep, proper exercise and cleanliness and care as to dress.

In ninety-nine cases out of one hundred you find a person who eats regularly, is not given to strong drink, has regular hours for sleep and exercise, keeps the body clean and obeys all the common laws of health, and you find one who is almost perfect in health. Nothing is more true than the Bible injunction: He that soweth to the flesh shall of the flesh reap corruption. The man or woman who sows to the lusts of the flesh, by indulging in alcoholic drinks, or giving way to the sexual appetites, is breaking a natural law; and just so sure as there comes a time for reaping the corn put into the earth, so sure there will come a time of reaping for those who break the laws that pertain to the body. Each one of you can call up before you this morning instances, perhaps, of some near and dear friends, who started out in life with a sound, robust body with which to fight life's battle. But they ran for a while and began tampering with nature's laws. First, perhaps, an unnatural appetite for strong drink was created, and the body, like any delicate and complicated machinery, has all its parts affected when one part is in an abnormal condition. When this appetite for strong drink got its hold on our friends, then there followed in quick succession a breaking of all the laws relating to health — irregularity in eating and sleeping, carelessness in dress, a gross neglect of the body and surroundings and a yielding to all the lower appetites, and then come weakness of mind, a diseased body and, perhaps, months or years of bodily pain and disease, and finally an unnatural death. These are some of the results that are just as sure to follow the breaking of nature's laws regarding the body as the tender flower is to be killed or withered when exposed to the frost of winter. There is no escape from it. On the other hand, he who keeps nature's laws in this regard, reaps his reward in a sound, robust body — a body that can endure and stand the test when an emergency comes.

Besides, there is a sort of animal happiness (if we may call it this) that arises as the result of a healthy body, that counts for much in the battle of life.

We have now seen that the natural world and our bodily organism are under law, and going another step we shall find that the same is true of our

MENTAL SIDE.

"Had I the height to reach the pole,
    To reach the ocean with a span,
I'll still be measured by my soul,
    The mind's the measure of the man."

So important a part of our nature our Father would not leave to chance for its government. Here, too, as we sow we shall reap. If the mind is employed during youth as it should be in getting knowledge, and in strengthening the faculties there will follow in manhood, old age a harvest of mental happiness.

141

Let the students in this institution refer to the week when they have enjoyed the highest degree of mental happiness, and they will find that the preceding week was one of earnest study — of hard work. The students who stand at the head of their classes and are head and shoulder above their fellows are reaping the reward of mental industry — mental application of some past period. Industry — application to study, research — persistency — will bring satisfaction, growth, strength, power, position. This is the law. We can no more change it than we can the law of gravitation that makes the apple come to the ground. Each of you know of a student perhaps one of your class mates, who to day is sowing in idleness — shirking his studies — dodging this duty and that one, spending his study hours to no purpose — copying this lesson and falsifying another one. In short his whole mental effort is a sham, a lie *from the beginning of the year till its end.* That student is now sowing, but the time of reaping will come. There is no power in existence that can change this law. The mental reaping will follow the mental sowing just as certainly as decay comes to the body when the heart ceases to beat. You know some who are already reaping fruits of days and months that have been thrown away. The misery, the disappointments, the failures in business, the want of ability to cope with their fellows, have already begun to dawn upon them. Two men started in the same school, in the same class with equal opportunities, equal natural abilities. The one who sowed in earnest, hard study may be seen today in actual life reaping. He holds positions of honor and trust. His advice and influence are sought after on all occasions. Instead of being compelled to seek positions, positions are constantly seeking him. He is surrounded by a happy family whom he is able to support in comfort. Let us imbibe this truth into every fiber of our nature: industry — application to duty — brings happiness and prosperity.

The one who sowed in idleness may also be seen reaping in actual life. Being without that high degree of mental development which carries with it mental grasp — mental equipoise — decision of character — mental control — enabling one to comprehend and systematize a large and complicated business, he finds it hard to secure employment. He fails in every line of business he undertakes. Instead of positions seeking him, he is constantly seeking positions. Each day he endures the anguish of seeing the one who started out in life when he did, going up step by step while he is conscious that his course is ever tending downward. Failure follows failure, disappointment follows disappointment till he finally settles down to a useless hand to mouth existence, without influence, without position, without satisfaction that his life has been of an iota of value to the world — his life a blank — a failure, and he can only add:

"Of all sad words of tongue or pen
The saddest are these it *might* have been."

In this connection, let us recall Horace Mann's impressive admonition:

"Lost, yesterday, somewhere between sun rise and sun-set, two golden hours, each set with sixty diamond minutes. No reward is offered for they are gone forever."

Keep in mind our fundamental laws — cause and effect — idleness the cause — failure, misery the effect. But this law goes further running not only through the material world, our physical nature, the world of mind, but it is just as prominent and immutable in

MORALS AND RELIGION.

"Be not deceived, God is not mocked. Whatsoever a man soweth, that shall he also reap," are the words of the Bible, and the truth of this injunction has been verified by observation and experience since the world began, and since this is true, how can we expect to escape the consequence of breaking it? If we were to find one who believed that the heating of water would cause it to turn to ice, we should say that such an one had lost his reason. Why? Because of our faith in the durability of this law. The wonder is to find why people have so much faith in one natural law and its consequences and are utterly regardless of another, when both have the same Being for their author, and both are equally sure of being enforced. And especially are we perplexed to find persons who have the light of education to guide them, hoping to escape the consequences of breaking nature's laws, whether they relate to the physical or metaphysical. In our relation to our fellow-men, nature teaches us, and nature is supplemented and strengthened by the experience of men and the teachings of the Bible, that he who steals, defrauds, lies, deceives, commits adultery and fornication, will be punished not alone in the great beyond, but in this life. The law of God and nature is that every person shall tell the truth, not steal, and live in sexual purity. No person can ever lie or steal or commit adultery without receiving punishment in this life. The punishment is often delayed and we cannot count upon it with the same precision as the material world, but sooner or later the punishment comes with inexorable certainty. If one steals or lies, the punishment comes first from a wronged conscience, comes in the form of remorse — that worm that dieth not nor alloweth its fire to be quenched. Milton carries this idea of remorse or pain still further when he says:

> "Regions of sorrow, doleful
> Shades, where peace
> And rest can never dwell: hope
> Never comes, that comes to all:
> But torture without end still
> Urges, and a fiery deluge, fed
> With ever burning sulphur
> Unconsumed; Such place eternal
> Justice had prepared for those
> Rebellious; here their prison
> Ordained in utter darkness, and
> Their portion set so far
> Removed from God and
> Light of Heaven, as from the
> Center thrice to the utmost pole.
> O, how unlike the place from
> Whence they fell."

Punishment comes again in the loss of the respect and confidence of our fellow students and fellow men. When the body is defiled by drink or adulterous habits, we have added to this remorse of conscience, loss of standing in society, a wrecked and diseased body and mind. With body wrecked, mind impaired, and character gone, we have reached the acme of human misery. But those who obey laws which God has given us for the guidance of our moral conduct are not left without their reward. Show me a man who is prosperous and happy through a long series of years in his business life — one who is held in high esteem in the community and I will show you one who is truthful, honest and virtuous.

He who lives for himself alone, sows to himself, makes his own comfort, his own gain the first and last consideration, will not reap happiness, but wretchedness and uneasiness instead. On the other hand one who gives himself to others, bears their burdens, reaps a reward in [the] form of happiness that is beyond the comprehension of the selfish. We have a most beautiful example of the results of this unselfish living in the life of the late Mrs. Walter Baker. Her whole life was one of unselfish sowing among the poor people of her own city, among colleges in the West, among the Japanese in Japan, the Hindoos in India, among our own people in the South. Her heart took in the world, and as a result she was continually reaping the results of her benevolence and broad interest, and it is doubtful if during the closing years of her life she ever spent a day that was not filled with the most intense happiness.

What is true of morality is true of religion. Draw nigh unto Me and I will draw nigh unto you, says Christ. This is the law and it runs all through religion. When we find ourselves drifting away from Christ, growing cold, indifferent, luke-warm, it is the effect of not living up to the standard laid down by Christ — it is the effect of neglecting our private devotions and the reading of our Bible.

Let me leave this thought, if we would live happily — live honored and useful lives — lives modeled after that of our perfect leader — Christ, we must conform to law — learn that there is no possible escape from the punishment that follows the breaking of law. Growth in this direction cannot be completed in a day, but let us make one supreme effort to begin growing in the direction of conformity to God's laws. We must not become discouraged if we do not see ourselves growing. As Prof. Drummond says, "All great things grow noiselessly. All thorough work is slow. All true development is by minute, slight and insensible degrees. The higher the being the slower is the process of growth."[1] Biologists tell us that the smallest form of animal life reaches maturity in an hour; the next higher in a day and those still higher require weeks and months, but man at the top requires years for his development. What we want to be sure of is that there is constant growth each day we live — growth out of self into the lives of others; growth out of our lower nature into a higher; growth out of our animal nature into the rational; growth out of sloth and indifference into industry and application; growth out of sensuality into purity; growth out of a luke-warm life into the true warmth of

Christian living; growth *into faithful serving and joyous reaping;* growth towards

"One God, one law, one element,
And far off divine event
To which the whole creations move."

Tuskegee Student, 3 (May 1, 1891), 1, 3; *ibid.* (May 8, 1891), 1.

[1] "All thorough work is slow; all true development by minute, slight, and insensible metamorphoses. The higher the structure, moreover, the slower the progress." (Henry Drummond, *The Changed Life* [Philadelphia, 1898], 74-75.) Drummond's address was first published in 1891.

Charles E. Davidson[1] to
Olivia A. Davidson Washington

[Cannon City, Colo.] Aprail 20th. 91

Dear Sister   it is with grate pleasure that i write these few lines   i am well and when these few reaches you they may find you injoing good health

Olie you know every sence we left the South we have not seen one another but i hope to god we will see each other before long   Olie i am an onest man and now through the low and black acts of a jelous woman i am in trouble   Olie i have spent over five hundred dollars on this Case and i have no more and am behind the bars now   Olie a little more money will get me out of hear dont be afraid to help me please for i can repay you double

Olie i hate to tell you but i have to do so   i have got five years to serve behind the Bars and for god sake help me   i am under a world of respect for you one of the hiest members of the famlie but god knows i cant help it   it will take $150 to take my case to the D.C. Supream Court and Gage Whiley will write to you   Olie my wife will soon be a mother and for god sake save me   dont forget Mrs. C. E. D.[2] let me know soon so i will close   may you neve be unforchine enough to know this   goodby from your Brother

Frank E. Crawford

Direct Frank Crawford Cannon, City. Colo in care of William Smith

do not let none of the famlie know this please

ALS Con. 17 BTW Papers DLC.

[1] Charles E. Davidson, Olivia Davidson Washington's younger brother, listed in the 1870 census as a nine-year-old mulatto in the household of Eliza Davidson. The internal evidence of this letter and Mary A. Elliott's reference to "Charley" indicate that Frank E. Crawford was his alias. (See Elliott to BTW, Aug. 24, 1891, below.) He addressed his letter to Olivia, unaware that she had died two years earlier.

[2] Mrs. Charles E. Davidson.

To George J. Davis

[Tuskegee, Ala.] April 27th [189]1

Dear Mr. Davis: Enclosed I send you a New York draft for $146.20, and this plus $25. — Mr. McAdoo's[1] contribution — which Mr. Banks[2] will hand you makes $171.20 which (minus the expenses) the Hampton graduates have sent me to be used by the resident graduates in purchasing a suitable testimonial for Miss Mary F. Mackie, to be presented to her at the close of the present school year, as a token of the love and esteem in which the Hampton graduates hold her for her twenty years of faithful service to our beloved Alma Mater and the race. The total sum collected was $195.65, and the endorsed itemized account will show that the expenses were $24.45.

I wish to assure you that the work of collecting this money has been one of most loving service. What Miss Mackie has been to me personally it would be impossible for me to express in words.

I have sent by express to the address of Mr. Banks the name and amount contributed by each graduate as well as each letter received in answer to the appeal. When Miss Mackie has time I believe that it will be a most pleasing task for her to read this large number of letters — some two hundred and fifteen in all. In them she will get an idea how much the graduates love her. I join my prayer to hun-

147

dreds of others that she may be spared to spend many happy and beautiful days. Yours truly,

[Booker T. Washington]

TLp   Con. 106   BTW Papers   DLC.

¹ Orpheus McAdoo, a graduate of Hampton in 1876 who taught in Virginia schools before returning to teach at Hampton. In 1881 he took BTW's place in charge of the Indian boys' dormitory. In 1886 he joined a group of Negro singers who toured Europe, Australia, and New Zealand. He formed his own company of singers in 1890, composed mostly of Hampton graduates, that toured Europe and South Africa.

² Frank D. Banks.

Washington's Household Expenditures

[Tuskegee, Ala., April 1891]

Household.
April.

15th	1 pr. vases	1.00
	1 vase	.50
	2 cans pineapple	.60
	Cream pitcher	.10
	Baking powder	.50
	Cuticura soap	.25
	Shoes for Davidson	1.00
	1 doz. bars soap	.50
	Butter	.50
	Eggs	.45
	Hat for Baker	.25
	" " Davidson	.25
	lemons	.30
	Hamburg & buttons	1.00
18–	Washing	1.25
	Ammonia	.10
	Glycerine	.20
	Vaseline	.25
	Box toilet soap	.50

25th	Washing	1.25
30th	10 yds. narrow lace for Davidson.	.50
"	6 " hamburg " Portia	.45
"	" " " " Baker	.54
"	Embroidery for Davidson & "	.60
		12.84

Wilson & Wilborn.[1]

Apr. 16	Flour	6.50
" 28	"	7.00
"	ham	1.75
"	2 brooms	.75
4	Fish	.70
18	"	.70
25	"	.80
		$18.20

Salesroom.
April.

1st	12 spools cotton	.60
"	3 yds. gingham	.30
"	3 " table linen.	1.45
8	2 papers pins.	.10
17	slate pencils	.05
"	lead "	.05
"	10 yds. nainsook	1.10
"	25 " cotton cloth	3.13
"	1 tooth brush	.15
27	9 spools cotton	.45
"	2 cards buttons	.20
	tooth brush.	.15
		$7.73

Commissary Acct. Apr.

1	3 qts. syrup.	.37
"	3 doz. eggs.	.36
"	2 lbs. butter.	.40

2	3 cans corn.	.45
"	" " tomatoes.	.33
"	3 " peaches.	.75
"	3½ lbs. lard.	.28
"	2 " butter.	.40
4	13 " ham.	1.62
"	3 doz. eggs.	.36
5	3½ lbs. lard.	.28
"	2 " sugar.	.14
"	2 doz. eggs.	.24
"	2 lbs. rice.	.14
7	½ gal. syrup.	.25
"	6 lbs. lard.	.48
"	5½ " fish.	.28
11	6 cans peaches.	1.50
"	" " corn.	.90
"	" " tomatoes.	.66
"	12 lbs. ham.	1.44
"	3 doz. eggs.	.36
"	4 lbs. lard.	.32
13	8 " "	.64
"	1¼ " butter.	.25
14	3 " coffee.	.72
		$13.92

	Am't. bro't. forward.	$13.92
14	2 cans tomatoes.	.22
"	4¾ lbs. lard.	.46
"	3 doz. eggs.	.36
17	bottle catchup.	.20
"	½ gal syrup.	.25
"	13 lbs. ham.	1.62
18	6 bars soap.	.25
"	4½ lbs. lard.	.36
20	3¾ " "	.28
21	4 " fish.	.32
"	2 cans peaches.	.50
"	4 lbs. ham.	.48

23	4	"	lard.		.32
27	3	"	butter.		.60
"	4	"	meal.		.32
Beef 17 lbs.					1.09
8 gals. oil.					1.20
25th	3 doz. eggs.				.36
					$23.11

Household.

	12.84
Apr. 30th Baking powder	.50
" lemons	.30
	13.64
By cash for April.	7.36
Sewing " Mch.	4.05
	$25.05
Commissary	23.11
Wilson & Wilborn	18.20
Salesroom	7.73
Total for April 1891.	$74.09

HD   Con. 861   BTW Papers   DLC.

[1] Wilson and Wilborn was a Tuskegee grocery firm. Andrew Jackson Wilborn, one of the partners, was an 1888 Tuskegee graduate who also worked as a shoemaker. He was a state commissioner on the board of trustees of Tuskegee beginning in 1905.

To Samuel Chapman Armstrong

Tuskegee, Ala. May 2 1891

Dear Gen. Armstrong: Our Lady Principal, Miss M. J. Murray is arranging to spend 3 weeks during June at the State Normal School at New Britain Conn. observing methods &c. I am also expecting to spend a few days there. Will you drop Mr. C. F. Carroll,[1] the Principal a line about this school so that we will have his interest and help? Yours faithfully

Booker T. Washington

ALS BTW Folder ViHaI.

[1] Clarence F. Carroll was principal of the New Britain Normal School from 1881 to 1893. A Yale graduate, Carroll made his school noted particularly for the thoroughness of its practice-teaching program. Considering teaching an art, he opposed teaching by a set method and urged giving teachers the maximum of freedom.

From Amanda Ferguson Johnston

malden, West Va   may the 6 1891

my Der Bro   dont think Hard of me for not writeing the Day i re-cived alberts[1] phortagraf   i was Clening House for a laddy & lifting a hevy peice Hurt my Back & am jus getting over it   Hope all well i want johns & james picture   i would not known albert if i Had Seen Him   He is jus like Clara[2] now   i will Be glad to get the things enny time yu send them   Bro i never Can forget yu   yu Have Bin mor than a Bro   i Can never tell what i think of yu   Bro yu ask me How i was getting a long   i will tell yu jus as it is   Ben yu know Has all ways provied for His famiely Best as He Could   He Cant get work Here   He is up the rver & Bording withe Cousin Salle[3]   i try every month to save & looks as if i did not   i'll pay my intrus this month   i work all i Can   i Have a nice garden Clara & i put in   Bro yur Haus makes me proud to think of it & think How it is kept in side   But are no prowder than i am if i Can get mine paid for   i'll Do all i Can this year   i all ways forget to speak of the little papers   alls ways send them   i love to rad them so much   love to emma & jhns & james famiely   Write sune as father[4] is faling fast   old man bill truslow & snyder is dead   Write sune   Sister

Amanda Johnson

Richard Watson is Building By gilbert lovely[5]

ALS Con. 17 BTW Papers DLC.

[1] George Washington Albert Johnston.

[2] Clara Jane or Clara Juanetta Johnston, as her name is variously listed in the

Tuskegee catalogs. The daughter of Amanda Johnston, she was born about 1879. She entered Tuskegee in 1893 and was awarded a certificate in agriculture in 1901. (See above, 2:7.)

[3] Sallie Agee Poe.

[4] Washington Ferguson.

[5] Gilbert Lovely, a black coal miner in Malden, born about 1845. He was a near neighbor and a lifelong friend of the Fergusons and Washingtons.

From Timothy Thomas Fortune

New York, May 15 1891

Dear Sir: It is very generally understood that the Hon. Frederick Douglass will resign the post of Minister Resident and Consul General to the Republic of Hayti sometime during the ensuing summer. In the event that he does resign, I desire to succeed him.[1] If you favor my desire in this respect, I will thank you to have the kindness to secure for me the signatures of three to five of the leading Republicans at your point on one of the two blanks here enclosed, and all the Ministers of the race in your city if possible, upon the other, and return the two to me by June 1st. Yours very respectfully,

T. Thos. Fortune

Be glad to have you sign this with the male members of your faculty.

F.

TLS Con. 4 BTW Papers ATT. Original destroyed. The postscript was handwritten.

[1] Douglass resigned on Aug. 11, 1891, but Fortune was unsuccessful in his effort to succeed him.

From Timothy Thomas Fortune

New York, May 26 1891

My dear Friend: Your favor of the 22nd inst., with endorsements to the petition, was received. I thank you sincerely for your interest in the matter and appreciate your offer to aid me in any way you can. General Armstrong has given me a strong endorsement and says he will get others to do so. Everything is working smoothly. Lack of ready money to push matters as I have planned is the only damper, but this will be perhaps be overcome.

I thank you again, and the friends. Yours truly,

T. Thos. Fortune

ALS Con. 4 BTW Papers ATT. Original destroyed.

A Commencement Address to the Class of 1891

[Tuskegee, Ala., May 28, 1891]

Ladies and Gentlemen of the Graduating Class: It is said of Ralph Waldo Emerson, the great philosopher, that at one time one of his friends, noticed him standing near a window seemingly intently gazing at something in the distance. When the question was asked "what are [you] looking for Mr. Emerson?" The answer came, "I am trying to find Ralph Waldo Emerson." Ladies and gentlemen on this the most interesting and eventful day of your life, I would remind you to remember Emerson's reply. Find yourselves as often as possible. Today you take your places in the busy ranks of the world as men and women. You go forth where the struggle for existence is often great and perplexing, where temptations will allure and entice you on every hand, where success will often prove as disastrous as failure. In the midst of these new conditions my last word to you is, to stop, weigh anchor and find yourselves as often as possible. As your teachers and your friends during the years that you have spent here, we have tried in our humble way, to help you to acquire that power — that mastery over self — that would enable you to find yourselves — that is all any teacher can do for you — that is all education can do, nothing more. Hence forth you must find your way almost wholly without our aid. You must be your own checks, your own spurs, your own props, your own guides, you must furnish your own inspiration, your own enthusiasm. However much we wish it were possible for us to be near to help, to advise, to strengthen, to encourage in your hour of gloom, trial and disappointments, we can not be, but we have rendered you a greater service if we have made you masters of your own minds, your own appetites, your own bodies.

While I have councilled you to find yourselves, to measure your heights, and your depths, your strength and your weakness, your failure and your success, your growth and your decline as often and as accurately as possible, I would further admonish you to let *us* find you as often as possible. Let us find you as I believe you leave us today. You leave us with good names, worthy ambitions, a spirit of self sacrifice, and a purpose to give your lives unselfishly to the highest interest of humanity. Will you let us find you in the years that are to come, the same Emma,[1] the same, Kittie,[2] the same Silvia,[3] and the same Smith,[4] the same Williams,[5] the same Dillard[6] — only made stronger and brighter and more consecrated by use and service? Will you let us find you with no stain attached to your character, no charge of failure to perform duty however humble? And now my dear friends with the giving of these diplomas, in the name of the officers and teachers I bid you good bye, and need I add that we shall always carry you in our hearts, shall always pray for you. No parent ever sent forth his child into the world with more loving tender interest than that with which we shall follow you.

"Our hearts, our hopes are all with you." God bless you. Good bye.

AM   Con. 955   BTW Papers   DLC.

[1] The only Emma in the 1891 class was Emma Jennie Parker. (See Warren Logan to BTW, Apr. 16, 1891, above.)

[2] Katherine Juanita Baskins Barr.

[3] Sylvia Robertson Howard Davis.

[4] Charles (or Clarence) Vincent Smith, an 1891 graduate of Tuskegee, went on to graduate from Meharry Medical College and became a physician in Pensacola, Fla.

[5] Robert Craig Williams also went to Meharry Medical College and graduated as a pharmacist in 1893. He later returned to Meharry and graduated as a physician in 1898, settling in Augusta, Ga.

[6] Burton Harrison Dillard settled in Lopez, Ala., after graduation, taught school, and worked as a carpenter.

From Theophile Tarence Allain

Soulouque P.O. La., June 1st 1891

My Dear Friend: Your very kind favor came to me after my returned from our county seat, Plaquemine La., where I went to attend the lectures of the "White Normal Institute," colored teachers were seated on one side and the white teachers on the other.

Well, your boys and girls came very near getting in to trouble, coming between Chihaw[1] and Montgomery Ala., there were too many for the colored cars, and the conductor put a large number of your boys and girls in the white cars — and, it seemed for a while as if war would take place at any time. Knife and Pistols were seen in the hands of bad white men, and I was of the opinion that the train would not be allowed to go in to Montgomery with the colored boys and girls in the white cars.

I am glad that my address is being asked for, because I made the address to build up your school, and it will do more in that way than any thing that has taken place in the South. I will send my son and 3 other boys[2] in Sept.

If the address is re-produced send me copies. Remember me to Mrs. King;[3] Mrs John Washington, and kiss Logan for me. Your friend —

Theophile T. Allain

ALS   Con. 4   BTW Papers   ATT.   Original destroyed.

[1] Chehaw, Ala.

[2] Possibly Anitole Emile Martin, who graduated in 1897 and became a tailor in the U.S. Army and at Tuskegee; Lewis Felix Breaux, who attended Tuskegee from 1893 to 1895; and Joseph Holmes Breaux, who attended Tuskegee from 1894 to 1896. All were from Plaquemine, La.

[3] Dora S. King.

To Edgar James Penney

Boston, Mass   June 13, 91

Dear Mr. Penney: You have perhaps heard that Rev. Mr. Whittaker has given up his work at Tuskegee and has taken a church in New Orleans. This leaves us without a pastor, and while it is not the exact work you had planned to come to Tuskegee for, I write to know if matters can be arranged satisfactorily, if you will be willing to take his place. I shall not before hearing from you go into details as to salary, duties, etc.

A few days ago I had a talk with my friend in Brooklyn who had the other project in hand, and they are still quietly pushing it. In case we are successful in getting that on foot you would be at Tuskegee ready to take hold of it, and by that time we might be able to to secure some one else for the pastorate.

I hope for a very early reply, Yours truly,

[Booker T. Washington]

P.S. I should add I have been in correspondence with one other person, and have not yet received his final reply, but I feel pretty sure that he will not take the place. I wish that you and Mrs Penney would go to Tuskegee and rest for a while this summer. Address me here.

[Booker T. Washington]

TLc Con. 861 BTW Papers DLC.

To Edgar James Penney

Boston, Mass, June 23, 1891

Dear Mr. Penney: Yours of the 17th is received and I am very glad to know that there is a prospect of our securing your services[1] at Tuskegee where I am sure you will find unlimited opportunities for doing good — opportunities for helping hundreds of young men and women who will in turn help thousands of others. Such an opportunity does not often come to one. I think I understand you thoroughly as regard[s] the kind of work you want to do. It is pastoral and religious work that we wish you to engage in principally. We should not ask you to teach more than two classes a day and I hope it will not be so many for a good part of the year. I shall however want you to make one or two short trips to the North during each year. To teach the students as individuals of course requires time and this is the kind of work we want at Tuskegee. I think we will have no trouble in agreeing on the minor details of your work as I know your heart is right. Mrs Penney, I am quite sure, would be made very happy in having an opportunity to influence and help our girls. It would be a great lift-up to have her on the grounds.

We should want you to come with the idea of remaining permanently connected with the school. Now as to salary we cannot offer you anything very tempting as we are not rich as the American Missionary Association. We should pay you for the first year $800 including a house. This is more than Mr. Whittaker got at first. This would mean for eleven months' work, giving you either one month or six weeks and perhaps more if you desired it for a vacation. This you see would give you an opportunity to spend one month or more in working for the school in the North each summer.

We were just on the eve of beginning the erection of a house for Mr. Whittaker when he decided to change his work. After we found that he was not going to remain, the preparations for the house were stopped. If you came to Tuskegee we would want you the first of September if possible. The house Mr. Whittaker used, as you perhaps remember, had but four rooms. This is still empty but I am sure it is too small for you. Our plan is to put up, a house containing seven rooms, to be used as a pastor's residence. Would this be large enough for you? We cannot promise to get this done by September first, but in case you decide to come to Tuskegee I shall have them begin on this house at once and push it as fast as possible. In the mean time you will have to leave your family in Selma or occupy the house formerly used by Mr. Whittaker, or it might be that we can get you a larger house in town that you might [use?] temporarily.

I might add by way of precaution that you might as well prepare yourself for a battle with the American Missionary Association. They will do everything possible to prevent your going to Tuskegee as they are sensitive regarding our work but they always treat us well and I am sure that Tuskegee has their highest respect and good wishes.

Your friend in Malden, Mass, was very kind to me when I was there.

If I have not made myself clear please write me again. Yours truly,

B. T. Washington

Write as early as possible.

TLcSr   Con. 861   BTW Papers   DLC.

[1] Penney accepted the position. Tuskegee paid his moving expenses and provided tuition funds for his children. (BTW to Penney, July 3, 1891, Con. 861, BTW Papers, DLC.)

From John Gideon Harris[1]

Montgomery, Ala. June 27– 1891

Dear Sir: Since promoting the funds — sent me by the Peabody fund — to be used for Institute work, Dr Curry, for good and sufficient reason has change[d] the direction of a part of the original donation, which necessitates a re-apportionment. From the Program you send me — I see you hold five institutes of three days each aggregating fifteen days — or say three weeks — for this service — I will pay you, one hundred dollars — which will amount to six dollars pr. day actually engaged. You know that this money is not to pay salaries, but actual expenses. It gives you a fine chance to electioneer for your school, at no expense to you.

As soon as you have closed at Hayneville, send in your report — in detail — and I will give you a cheque for the money. Yours Truly,

Jno. G. Harris

ALS Con. 99 BTW Papers DLC.

[1] John Gideon Harris (1834-1908) was Alabama superintendent of education from 1890 to 1894. An 1858 graduate of Cumberland University's law school, he practiced law, served as a major in the Confederate Army, and ran unsuccessfully for Congress in 1870. In 1873 he was appointed to the board of commissioners of the Alabama State University for Colored Students in Marion, Ala. As superintendent of education he vigorously promoted education rallies and summer teachers' institutes. When he retired from office, in June 1894, the Colored State Teachers' Association passed resolutions endorsing Harris's administration and commending "his deep and active interest in the education of the colored race." They called him "a friend who has stood by us." BTW signed the resolutions as president of the association. The Alabama Education Association of white teachers passed similar resolutions of commendation. (*Biennial Report, Superintendent of Education, State of Alabama, Sept. 30, 1894*, 168.)

From James W. Austin

Boston, July 23 1891

Dear Sir, By the Will of the late Gen. James F. B. Marshall a Legacy of One Thousand dollars was bequeathed to "The Tuskegee Normal School."

Under the laws of Massachusetts I am allowed two years to settle the estate, but I will pay the legacies as soon as practicable. Yours truly,

James W. Austin
Executor

ALS   Con. 99   BTW Papers   DLC.

From Margaret James Murray

Tuskegee, Ala., July 24, 1891

My Dear Mr. Washington, I am here at home. It is not too warm and I am trying to rest for my work. Yesterday, I was very sick all day but I am up to day. You are well I hope. I wish that you were here and yet I do not. I want some one to talk with and yet I am afraid to tell you all that in my heart is. You never grow angry with me and for this reason I sometimes let you see that I am really unhappy. I called you Booker because I knew that it would make you happier but I could not do so this morning. I am with Mrs. Morin and she is very kind to me. I think that her mother will stay with you if you write her. If you wish my help after writing her I shall be glad to give it. You have been so good to me that I can never repay you. I wrote Miss Lischy.[1] Perhaps it is just as well that you have Mrs. Ferguson. I never like to see any thing done hurriedly. Miss Sprague is quite young. Miss Peake[2] and your brother have hard times together. It is strange that he is so kind to his own wife and so much the other way to other women. I get thoroughly disgusted with these rough hewn stones down here. I have lots to tell you when I see you. Barrett[3] is dead. Poor fellow! I did not get to see him until he had died.

The pictures are good. I am glad that you like them. Where are the others? Yes, you may give Miss Lord[4] one and one for your sister. Bring the others with you. I had a letter from Mr. L. the day I got yours. I shall write him Sunday or some time soon. He asked for one of my pictures — perhaps, I shall give him one. I shall have the room fixed for Mrs. Dr. Dillion.[5] Is there any. Your room will be cleaned for you. Mr. Washington. I think that Tom is honest but no one can tell when temptation will come to a young man. It is all risk you know.

Still if you are going to trust any one you may trust him. How did you and Mr. Wheelock[6] make it? Would you mind getting me a string of beads plated gold. Do not pay more than $1.00. I am or shall be greatly in your debt but then I shall get out soon. I wrote my mother and sent her a photo. The shoes fit the children except Davidson's — they are too small. Mrs. Morin and I sleep in Mrs. King's room and you can imagine how early I awake for Baker and Davidson begin their conversation with the dawn. I shall go to the Hall soon for I think I shall feel better over there. I feel just as if I could sit down by you and have a good cry this morning. Mrs. Morin's mother is here. She is such a nice old lady.

I hope to hear from you soon.

Take lots of love for your self.

Maggie

ALS   Con. 861   BTW Papers   DLC.

[1] Olive J. Lischey, teacher in the Tuskegee training school during the 1891-92 school year.

[2] Sarah F. Peake Greene graduated from Hampton in 1885 and taught for nine years in the academic department at Tuskegee. She married James Matthew Greene, a Tuskegee instructor of brick masonry.

[3] Perhaps Frank Burgoyne Barnett, a junior in 1891-92.

[4] Nathalie Lord.

[5] Halle Tanner Dillon.

[6] Fred D. Wheelock, librarian and night-school teacher.

From Hollis Burke Frissell

Hampton, Va., July 24th 1891

Private

Dear Mr Washington: I wish you would let me know about Miss Dillinghams scheme for work in Alabama.[1] She is pushing ahead in her usual enthusiastic way & I dont want to throw cold water upon her plans. If she is acting under your direction with your knowledge of the country &c I think it is all right, but she must have some one who will look at things more coolly than she is likely to do. I am very fond of Miss Dillingham & believe thoroughly in her devotion but she moves quickly from one thing to another. Patient endurance needs to be cultivated by her. If this scheme is one that she can start & that others can take up & that you can direct being down there all right. I have asked Mr Gilman[2] who is at Jamaica Plains to confer with you about it. Cordially Yours

H. B. Frissell

ALS Con. 99 BTW Papers DLC.

[1] Mabel Wilhelmina Dillingham and Charlotte R. Thorn, who had previously taught at Hampton Institute, founded Calhoun Colored School at Calhoun, Lowndes County, Ala., in October 1892, with six teachers and some 300 pupils. They were co-principals until Miss Dillingham's death in 1894. Her father, the Rev. Pitt Dillingham, served as co-principal from 1894 to 1909. From 1909 until 1921 Miss Thorn was sole principal. Modeled after Hampton and Tuskegee, Calhoun was a community elementary and industrial school. BTW served for many years on its board of trustees, as did Hollis Burke Frissell. (See An Address at the Funeral of Mabel W. Dillingham, ca. Oct. 17, 1894, below.)

[2] Frederick N. Gilman (d. 1892) came to Hampton in 1881 from Boston, where he had worked for an importing and mercantile firm. His health had failed, and he undertook light tasks, such as the charge of the knitting department at the school, until his recovery from a prolonged illness. For a time he was business manager of the *Southern Workman*. In 1889 he succeeded General J. F. B. Marshall as treasurer. His ill health continued, however, and he died in 1892, of pulmonary tuberculosis.

From Mary Elizabeth Preston Stearns

Tufts College P.O. Masstts. August 11th 1891

Dear Friend. In memory of a noble life on Earth,[1] "without haste and without rest," securing immortality with the angels of God — beyond our vision — never beyond our love, and reverence, I extend to you, who can "never *forget*" the enclosed

Washington, Davidson Scholarship for 1891.

This day opens anew the cruel wound her departure has made in your heart and all the years to come, until the summons comes to call you to her side again. I cannot doubt that she is with you, not on this hallowed day, but on all the days of toil, and labor, in the work she loved so well, and *died,* that *it* might live. And *it will live!* Holy is her dust, as any Martyr of the Christian Church. Radiant evermore, the crown she has won.

The years as they hasten by only add lustre to her spotless, heroic memory.

To me, she shines like a star: too far for my poor deservings to reach, but, beckoning with its light to strive on, and on, forever. May her exalted character and life be an hourly stimulus, in your mighty work — never doubting that her inspiration will be sufficient for all its perplexities, and often dreary toil.

Give to each of the dear Children, an extra kiss, telling them, that it is love for the angel Mama, who will never forget them.

With thoughts, and sympathies, beyond words — believe me, your steadfast, and her loyal friend.

Mary E. Stearns

I hope my memory has not blundered, as to *the day!*

ALS   Con. 100   BTW Papers   DLC.

[1] Olivia A. Davidson Washington, who died May 9, 1889.

To Mabel Wilhelmina Dillingham

[Tuskegee, Ala.] August 15th [189]1

Dear Miss Dillingham: I have not answered your letter of July 30th[1] earlier because I wanted to visit Calhoun before doing so. I went there the day before yesterday and spent the whole of yesterday inspecting the prospects for the school. I am glad to say that I found the out-look even more promising than I had dared hope for. I was disappointed only in one respect: The people are more than anxious for the school. I wrote to Rev. Mr. Jones some days before going there that I wanted the matter kept quiet as I wanted to look around quietly without attracting attention, but in spite of this precaution it was interesting to see that the news had spread through the settlement, and all day long people were arriving some on mules, some in buggies and some in ox carts. All were eager to know what the prospects of "their school" were.

Mr. J. Bell, the principal white man in the community, who gave the land, was the one I went to see. I wanted him to understand that the school was to be conducted by Northern white ladies and something of its character, so that he could not say later on that he did not understand about matters. After I had explained everything to him I found him still firm in his determination to give 10 acres of land for the school. He showed me the land that he would give. I think it is well located. He says that he is ready to make the deed just as soon as the trustees are selected. I feel reasonably sure that there will be not far from one hundred and fifty scholars the first year, and you can depend on them to pay 50 cents per month for tuition. I am also quite sure that the people will give $500 in cash towards the new building.

I was disappointed as to the price of the land which you wish to buy privately. Land in that section is a good deal higher than I supposed it was, much more than it is near Tuskegee. Mr. Bell says that it is because it is near the railroad. I find that he is willing to sell you 10 or 20 acres adjoining the school land, but he will not let it go for less than $25 per acre. He says that he has been asking other people much more than this, but for the purpose of getting the school started he will let you have it for $25 per acre. Before going further about the private land I shall await to hear from you.

Very near the site for the school there is a large grove composed of oak trees. I tried very hard to make Mr. Bell agree to let this grove be included in the part that he would sell to you, but I could not bring him to this point. Perhaps you can get it from him after you go to Calhoun.

I am decided that Rev. Silas Jones, Mr. Wilson H. Harris and Mr. David Marsh will be suitable persons for trustees, the two latter living at Calhoun. Yours truly,

Booker T. Washington

TLpS Con. 106 BTW Papers DLC.

1 Mabel Dillingham authorized BTW to purchase up to 20 acres of land at $10 per acre for the Calhoun school site. She also left in BTW's hands the matter of choosing two trustees from Calhoun. (Dillingham to BTW, July 30, 1891, Con. 4, BTW Papers, ATT. Original destroyed.)

From Halle Tanner Dillon

[Montgomery, Ala.] 8-20-91   1.30 P.M.

Dear Sir, Have just come in to my dinner & find your note. Am glad to know you are all interested in my success. It certainly is pleasant to me when far from home to find friends, such as I have been fortunate to make since my stay here.[1] I am getting along *well*. Try to keep before [myself] the possibility of failing but unless some harder and more complex than anything they have given me yet I feel that I can not, but, if they mark me fairly[,] get thro. Mr Brassell[2] is very kind & pleasant & seems to think I am doing *well*. The pie[,] Doctor[,] is finished and gone. I will not, I am afraid get thro by Saturday, the day before my last branch will drop you a card.

Yesterday evening a man in the Capitol stopped me & demanded in rough voice "what my business was at the Capitol every day." I told [him] to "ask Dr Cochran[3] Supervisor & he would tell him," just now I met the same man on the corner of Union & Washington Sts he glared at me, I dont suppose it amts to any thing but confess it sort of bothers me.[4]

I am really trying to do the best that I can in my studies & hope to succeed.

Again thanking you all for thinking occasionally of me   I remain Sincerely

Halle T. Dillon

Hope you will be able to decipher this hurrededly written note.

H. T. D.

ALS   Con. 99   BTW Papers   DLC.

[1] Halle Dillon stayed in Montgomery, Ala., while studying for her medical examinations. BTW's friend, C. N. Dorsette, helped her prepare for the examinations by drilling her on medical questions. (Dorsette to BTW, July 26, 1891, Con. 99, BTW Papers, DLC.)

[2] Walter R. Brassell was a clerk of the Alabama State Board of Health.

[3] Jerome Cochran (1831-96 or -97) was a physician who founded the Alabama Medical Association and the state health office. He was Alabama state health officer until his death.

[4] The man who questioned Dr. Dillon was a capitol grounds policeman named O'Brien. (See Dillon to BTW, Aug. 23, 1891, below.)

From Benjamin Tucker Tanner[1]

[Philadelphia, Pa.] Aug. 20 1891

My dear Mr President: Booker T. Washington   Your letter of Monday Aug. 17 came to hand. It was a most pleasant surprise. Accept thanks for your thoughtful consideration. Of course, we are all anxious about the Doctor.² Not that we have any misgiving as to her ability to pass any reasonable and just examination. But we know that both her sex and her color will be against. For the consideration you took accept my grateful remembrance; and be kind enough to convey to Dr. Dorsette, whom I have not the pleasure of knowing, the same. Will you not write to me again? Fraternally,

Benj. Tucker Tanner

P.S. Love to our daughter.

ALS Con. 100 BTW Papers DLC.

¹ Benjamin Tucker Tanner (1835-1923) of Philadelphia was a prominent bishop of the A.M.E. Church. Born of free parents in Pittsburgh, Tanner attended Avery College and Western Theological Seminary, working his way through school as a barber. During the Civil War he was a minister in the District of Columbia. In Baltimore after the war he was editor of the *Christian Recorder* from 1868 to 1884. From 1884 to 1888 he edited the *A.M.E. Church Review*. He served as bishop from 1888 until his retirement in 1908. Tanner urged blacks to advance along economic lines, and emphasized racial solidarity and self-help. He generally sided with BTW in issues of racial philosophy; he also advocated efforts to secure civil rights, but he could never be called an agitator.

² Halle Tanner Dillon, Tanner's daughter.

From Halle Tanner Dillon

[Montgomery, Ala.] 8-23-91

Dear Sir Yours of the 21st inst rec'd. I finished up Surgery and half of Obstetrics. I will not according to present indications get thro before Tuesday evening. The surgery was quite hard. Still I think I have made enough to pass me.

Dr Dorsette is very anxious that I should remain in Montgomery at least a week, will he says take me around with him on proffessional visits to his patients. Of course if he will do this, I know it would be of benefit to me from a medical stand point but really I am so tired at present that I feel when [I] finish my last branch I shall have will power enough to enable me to get back to Tuskegee and that will be about all until I have gotten over to some degree the strain which this examination has made upon me both mentally and physically.

Dr Cochran, has been up to the Capitol to see me, he certainly treated me very pleasantly indeed. You know he examines my Chemistry & Physical Diagnosis. Mr Bressell[1] the clerk told me that I had gotten a good mark in Chemistry. I shall if nothing happens ask him about the other branch to morrow.

A Reporter from the "Montgomery Advertiser" called at the Capitol and wanted to make note of my taking the Examination but both Mr Bressell & myself strenuously objected to any such thing until after I have received my report from the Board.

Received a visit from Prof Calloway yesterday morning.

The man who accosted me so uncermonously the other day is named OBrien, and is employed on the Capitol grounds as police. I do not think it is neccesary to have any one accompany me. I really think now, that I am in a calmer frame of mind that is was only curiosity on his part.

I think now that unless some thing occurs which I know not off that I will leave here Wednesday morning for Tuskegee on the 8.10 train.

Now Professor, there is just one thing which I would like you to attend to for me, and I hope you will believe me when I say that I hate to annoy you with such trival affairs. But can you see the House-Keepers of Alabama Hall and have them put a double bedstead in my room? The one I occupied during my stay there was *simply* awful so far as comfort was concerned. I really trust you will not think I am finding fault: but the prospects of sleeping again upon *that couch* are *overwhelming* and force me to speak against my own personal in-clinations.

I trust you will pardon me if I have wearied your patience with this long letter, and offer as an excuse that [it] is a dull day, I am lonesome, and feel in the humor for talking even at the distance of forty miles. Respectfully

Halle T. Dillon

ALS Con. 99 BTW Papers DLC.

[1] Walter R. Brassell.

To William Addison Benedict[1]

[Tuskegee, Ala.] Aug 24 [189]1

Dear Mr. Benedict: It has now been decided that this institution will employ you for a year to raise money in the North for it at a salary of $1500 a year — you to begin work Sept 1 1891.

We have the greatest faith in your ability to succeed and believe that practical help will come to the school as result of your work.

Any help y[ou ca]n secure during Sept and October will be twice blessed as these are going to be *very hard* months with us. There is almost a financial panic in this section now — four banks in Montgomery have failed this summer. This will lessen or hold back cash from our students and those with whom we do business in the South.

You can use your own good judgement about where to begin, only keeping in mind that I will see those whose names appear in the financial report I sent you.

Episcopalians as individuals help us much.

I shall be absent a part of Oct. but want to plan to be here when you are. How would the middle of Oct suit you? I think I can be here about that time. I *think* I shall be in Boston near the 15 of Sept.

By today's mail I send you some more literature.

Call on me for any help I can render.

I mean to be present at the Unitarian National Conference Sept 24-26 and shall speak. We shall be compelled to refuse admission to many students for want of room. Yours truly

Booker T. Washington

ALpS Con. 106 BTW Papers DLC. Brackets indicate editorial insertion of obliterated letters.

[1] William Addison Benedict (b. 1822) attended Harvard and Amherst and served as a Congregational minister in Sutton, Mass. From 1884 until 1891 he was a field worker for the American Missionary Association in Orange Park, Fla. He was nearly seventy when he undertook to work as a fund raiser in New England for Tuskegee, "thankful that I am free from the trammels the A.M.A. throws around its workers, and have an open field." (Benedict to BTW, Sept. 24, 1891, Con. 4, BTW Papers, ATT. Original destroyed.) His age may have been a reason for his unsatisfactory service. (See BTW to Benedict, Feb. 8, 1892, May 11, 1892, Jan. 28, 1893, below.)

From Mary A. Elliott

Columbus   Aug 24th 1891

My Dear Brother   I was thinking yesterday sabbath how well I would like to be with you all a while, or see and talk with you at least.

I hope this may find you and the little ones well and happy. I suppose that you are getting a long by what I read or hear through the Student very near every week. We get to hear from the school which gives us great satisfaction to think what great progress the school has and is makeing. The knowledge that we get through the Student makes us feel near to you all, and gives us a desire for the up building of the school aside from other Closter ties. I think you did a good thing when you got some one in Mrs King's place. I am so *glad* for I dident think that she had the right kind of feeling for the children and all the love that the children could ever have for her would be through fear. I dident want to make you unhappy by telling you what I thought. So I hope that you have got a good woman in her place. I am sure that the change will not be for the worse. Tell me if the children are well, and if they grow. I suppose the hot weather is hard on them and if you are well? I do hope Dear brother that you will stop for a moment and think; for your children's as well as your own happiness you should rest more then you do. The future wellfare of the school also demands it. You work hard most of the time through vacation. I hope that you have taken some rest this summer. I have had a nervous prostration for several weeks by working hard at my trade and being over heated by the warm weather. I never experienced any thing of the kind before. I have not been capable of writing my hand and armes have almost been useless for several weeks past. But thanks to the Lord I am getting so much better again that I feel incouraged greatly. Mother is living in her new house she has moderatly good health   she still weaves. She sais tell little Baker that may the Lord bless his little heart for praying for her. She sais she prays for him every night too. She sais kiss them for her. Tell them Aunt Mary and Grandma[1] both prays for them. Tell them to be good children. I know that Davidson's temper will be his greatest cross, poor little dear I wish

I could take him in my armes this minuet and love him. I hope Portia is good little girl. I will write to her soon.

Well Booker it was a great surprise [to] us to hear of Charley's[2] condition. You have heard Dear Olivia speak of him he was wild, and if ever any body tried to make any thing out of a nother she did in his case. That is why he feels her death so much. We thought he must be dead for the past two years. I sent the letter to Kelly.[3] Charley has written to us he got our address from you. He sais he got the picturs you sent to him and I think he values them more highly then any thing he ever got in his life. I am glad that you was so kind to him, for this is a world of sorrow. All send love to you.

Good by Dear brother and write when you can. Your sister

M. A. Elliott

ALS Con. 17 BTW Papers DLC.

[1] Eliza Davidson.
[2] Charles E. Davidson.
[3] William K. Davidson.

To John Henry Washington

[Tuskegee, Ala.] Aug 31 [1891]

Mr. J. H. Washington, Supt Industries: As to the Barn I notice that the plows, wagons &c under the barn are not kept in an orderly systematic manner. They are thrown here and there much as one would see them on an ordinary country farm. This should not be so.

———

Provide a small boy to be kept on the girls' side under the charge of the matron, to clean around the buildings regularly.

———

There is one stove in Annex and two laundry that need to come out.

———

See me about fixing Dr. Dillon's office at annex.

B. T. Washington

ALpS Con. 106 BTW Papers DLC.

From Emily Howland

Sherwood N.Y. Sept. 7th 1891

Dear Sir   Your letter of the 2nd is just rec.d. I have had you in mind for weeks, but knowing that the school was not now in session I thought you might be absent from the institution. I thought that this year I would make the $50.00 $100.00. Since seeing is believing, my visit to Tuskegee has certainly more than doubled my interest in it.

I should like this sum to be applied for the benefit of a lady student, because women are handicapped & generally discriminated against, in the race of life. For this reason they should remember each other.

I am sure that the visits to Tuskegee of two persons so well known & well esteemed, (of eloquent tongue & pen) as Miss Eastman[1] & Mr. Barrows,[2] bodes good to your grand school. I hope that they share my faith that in importance it ranks first, among the institutions of learning for col.d people in the South, by reason of location & it must always hold a position of great importance in solving the problem which both white & col.d Americans are given to work out in this period of their history.

My visit to your institution was a memorable one to me in many ways, though I had been in the South a good deal I found I had never been before where Slavery had done its perfect work. Whenever I think of your school it seems like a brilliant star rising out of great darkness.

I should like to be remembered to Mrs. Logan, Miss Murray and all the teachers who may be with you, of whom I retain grateful memories for kindnesses received. Cordially

Emily Howland

I have not rec.d a "Southern Letter" lately, is it discontinued during the summer?

I send my check because I can do it at once, for a draft I must send a distance to the Bank. If the check prove troublesome or you have to pay for collection return it & I will get a draft instead.

ALS   Con. 4   BTW Papers   ATT.   Original destroyed.

[1] Mary L. Eastman.

[2] Samuel June Barrows (1845-1909) was a State Department employee after the Civil War, serving for a time as secretary to William H. Seward, Secretary of

State (1867). In 1875 he graduated from Harvard Divinity School and a year later became pastor of the First Unitarian Church in Boston. He was editor of the *Christian Register* for sixteen years and from 1897 to 1899 he served one term as a Republican congressman from Massachusetts. He was also a well-known New York journalist and a leading expert on prison reform. From 1900 to 1909 he was corresponding secretary of the New York Prison Commission.

From Timothy Thomas Fortune

New York, Sept 11, 1891

Personal

My dear Professor: Circumstances I could not control have placed me in an embarrassing position, and if possible I would like you to help me out of it. I have got to meet a note of $200 October 1, and I cannot do it. I want you to advance me $200 on note, with interest, for six months, if you can possibly do so. You can hardly have a doubt that the note would be taken up promptly at maturity. You would render me a greater service by the accommodation than I can hope to render you.

The League and Press conventions and the Haytian Mission contest have knocked my finances higher than Gilderoy's kite, and I must have time to recover or suffer seriously in credit and otherwise. I know of no friend that I can approach with more confidence than yourself in this emergency.

I would like to spend two or three weeks at Tuskegee this winter, and shall give you a week if I get my affairs straight and decide to go to Florida.

With kind regards, and hoping to hear from you soon, Yours truly,

T. Thomas Fortune

ALS Con. 1 BTW Papers DLC.

From Amanda Ferguson Johnston

malden West Va Sept the 15 1891

Der Bro   i waited to Here when yu was comeing But recived no word so i am compell to write   Hope this may find all well & Doing the same   i wanted to see yu so i[']ll Do the Best i Can in writeing   we are Doing verry well in liveing But can['t] save much money   so Bro yu Have Done more than a Bro   But i see i cant make it so i ask yu. Joseph is going to get married & the girl wants this House   Mr Coleman herd & told Ben   Bro if yu will pay it i never will ask yu for a nother cent   i know it is Hard for me to ask for it. Had rather ask than for the people to know the talk is out   that is a Big ask if i Had it & yu wanted it yu could get it to keep yur Home   So Bro if yu will send it By the 29th of this month   send a check so no one will know enny thing about it   plese Dont say know But send if you plese the Done all i could to save it & see i cant   plese Dont think Ben is not trying to save.

i would not Have the people to Here that for nothin if yu send the princible i[']ll Have intrus reddy   one Hundred & fifty Dollars. let me Here at once

sister

Dont tell John

ALS   Con. 17   BTW Papers   DLC.

From Timothy Thomas Fortune

New York, Sept 21, 1891

My dear Prof Washington: Your favor of the 16th inst was received. I am sure I appreciate the position in which you find yourself, financially, and regret it on your account as well as on mine. It is the most uncomfortable situation in which I ever found myself and I have been am very much cut up by it, as I have found that it is easier to get into such a pickle than to get out of it. I am sure that if you could you would, and there is much satisfaction in that fact. With kind regards, Yours truly,

T. Thos. Fortune

ALS   Con. 1   BTW Papers   DLC.

A Recommendation from
Samuel Chapman Armstrong

Hampton, Va., Oct 26, 189[1]

This is to introduce Mr. Booker T. Washington the head of the Tuskegee Alabama, Colored Normal and Industrial School.

It is a noble, notable work; the best product of Negro enterprise of the century.

I make this statement advisedly.

I beg a hearing for Mr. Washington. He is a true "Moses."

As much as any man in the land, he is securing to the whole country the moral results which the Civil War meant to produce.

Tuskegee is the bright spot in the black belt of the South.

It is a proof that the Negro can raise the Negro.

S. C. Armstrong

ALS   Con. 99   BTW Papers   DLC.

From Margaret James Murray

Tuskegee, Ala., Oct. 26. 1891

My Dear Booker— It is Monday night and I am just faged out. Got up at seven — ate no break fast — called the roll at 8:30 — came over and visited the sick till 10 — went to the faculty meeting till five minutes of eleven — taught a class the last hour before noon. Took dinner with Mrs Logan and came pretty nearly being late — kept Mr Hamilton's classes the three periods after dinner. Met the girls at 4:30 and finally ended by stopping by to see how Miss Lischy[1] is getting on — and now I am in study with the girls but I am glad of this fact because I should imagine that I was too tired to write you if I had nothing to do. I miss you my dear I really do. It is rather strange to say a thing like this but then it is true.

Sunday was another blue day for me. Ida[2] was taken sick Saturday night and I did not get any sleep and this put me in a bad humor and I am awful when my temper gets the best of me. I hear you say Amen. Davidson has been real sick but he is much better and will soon be alright. I saw Bacon this after noon and he is bright enough. Mr Washington you do not have much sympathy with me because I feel as I do in regard to little folks — I get annoyed at myself but the feeling is here just the same. I am glad that you got Mrs. Washington to see after the childrens' clothes. She has made Baker a very pretty little suit and is now doing sewing for Davidson. Miss Lischy does not like Emma at all and I think it is better to send another girl over there. Emma boards at least a half dozen girls from there and never says a word to Miss Lischy. She goes off without permission and gives as an excuse that she is not a student here. Another girl will do more and better work although she may not be so good a cook. I think unless you object I shall make the change Saturday Nov 1st. I shall take Jennie away when Miss Moore[3] gets here. Has she written you any more love letters? Her letters are more like love letters than are mine? You would laugh if I were to tell you that I am jealous of her. I hope that you will not work too hard. Do not stay away longer than is absolutely necessary! Mr. Carter has not yet returned but I suppose that he will be here soon. Mr. J. H. planted a tree in your yard Saturday — a mulberry tree. It would have been better if it had been an oak. Miss Peak[4] came over Sunday and cried an hour or so — poor woman she is such a strange mixture.

Miss Lischy has the organ over there. I guess Mr. H will be angry enough. I got her to attend to the music scholars and they are delighted with the idea. Mr. Penny is here cranky as ever. Mrs. Penny was over to see me Sunday. She is a pleasant refined woman. We have no serious cases of sickness now and things are moving on nicely I think. Do come as soon as you can. Take lots of love for your self and think of me often. Yours.

Maggie

ALS Con. 17 BTW Papers DLC.

[1] Olive J. Lischey.
[2] Ida Belle Thompson.
[3] Mary C. Moore.
[4] Sarah F. Peake Greene.

From Thomas Junius Calloway[1]

Washington, D.C. October 31, 1891

My dear Sir: There exists in this city as you may know the Bethel Literary and Historical Association. It is the custom of this society to hold in Metropolitan Church every Tuesday evening public meetings and to be addressed by some speaker. Prof. James Storum the President who knows you quite well heartily indorsed the idea and urged a prompt invitation from me to you to deliver an address before the citizens of Washington under the auspices of the Bethel Literary. The evenings before mentioned by you fall on Thursday and Friday nights. The purpose of this letter is to inquire if you could not remain over or else make it a point to be hear on the Tuesday following which I believe is the 24th of Nov. You could only reach Tuskegee of course on the morning of Thanksgiving but there are so many meetings held in Metropolitan Church that the Society is always restricted to its special evening.

My plan is in case you can accept this proposition to have a luncheon, or banquet following to which I propose to have twenty-five or thirty of the prominent men of Washington. Everything is working admirably and should you not be able to change your date I shall arrange for a smaller reception in Dr. Grimpke's[2] church and the banquet following elsewhere. Should you find it convenient to appear before Bethel I would like your subject as early as possible. The average length of papers is forty five or fifty minutes. It is the custom in this society to discuss papers in five and ten minutes speeches by any one in the audience and often some one will take pleasure in denying facts presented. I would suggest therefore that you use only such arguments and figures as are no where questioned by best thinkers. I do not mean by this to humor any pet theories or cower under the fear of criticism but to show you in what manner it is best to fortify yourself. I trust you will give them some bombs to set them to thinking, and I am sure you can do great good.

Miss Nolen[3] spent two days here very pleasantly for her friends and herself I think. Prof Spence[4] & family leave Monday for Fisk. Very truly,

Thos. J. Calloway

ALS Con. 861 BTW Papers DLC.

[1] Thomas Junius Calloway was born in 1866 in Cleveland, Tenn., and graduated from Fisk University in 1889. He served as assistant principal of a high school in Evansville, Ind., and as clerk in the War Department in Washington, D.C., before becoming president of Alcorn A & M College for a brief tenure in 1895. From 1896 to 1898 Calloway was a northern agent of Tuskegee Institute. He was the managing editor of the Washington *Colored American* in 1898. He then served a year as principal of Helena (Ark.) Normal School and was U.S. special commissioner to the Paris Exposition (1899-1901). At Paris he was in charge of the extensive exhibit of photographs of Hampton Institute that was designed to promote industrial education for blacks along the Hampton-Tuskegee model. Calloway returned to Washington, D.C., and for five years worked as a War Department clerk. During this period he also attended Howard University's law school, receiving an LL.B. degree in 1904. He was manager of the Negro Department of the Jamestown Exposition of 1907. He then became a real-estate dealer and lawyer in Washington, D.C. Residing in Maryland, he was appointed secretary of the Maryland Inter-Racial Commission. Calloway was a staunch supporter of BTW and was a leader in what became known as the "Bookerite" faction in Washington, D.C.

[2] Francis J. Grimké, pastor of the Fifteenth Street Presbyterian Church in Washington.

[3] Lettie Louise Nolen Calloway.

[4] Adam Knight Spence (1831-1900), born near Aberdeen, Scotland, moved at about three years of age to southern Michigan. He attended Oberlin College but was forced to leave after his father's death. He graduated from the University of Michigan in 1857 and taught there for twelve years. He went to Fisk University in 1870 as instructor in Greek and French and had a lasting influence on many of its students. He later became dean of the faculty. Perhaps his most enduring accomplishment was helping George L. White to train the first company of the famous Fisk Jubilee Singers in 1870-71. He encouraged the experiment of sending them on a tour of the North.

From Margaret James Murray

Tuskegee, Ala., Oct.-Nov 1st 1891

My Dear Booker, Your little note came to me this week and need I tell you that I was glad to get even a note from you. I wish very much that I might be of some help to you in your hard duty but I *never can be*. I think of you often — I really believe that I have been blue this week.

I suppose that you wish first to hear of the children. Davidson is much better — almost well. He comes often to see me and Baker is doing nicely. To day, he recited this verse "I am the true vine and the husbandman is my papa" which was fun to the children.

Mr. Washington, you have no idea how I feel because I can not feel toward Portia as I should. And I somehow dread being thrown with her for a life time. I sometimes make up my mind that I will not let any talk to me of the child and then I forget. She kinder understands it too and I hate it. I wonder Mr. Washington if it is a wise and Christian thing for me to love you feeling as I do? Still I shall be absolutely honest with you and if you feel that you prefer giving me up I should find no fault with you. Dont be angry or annoyed.

We have had some trouble this week but nothing that will seriously affect us. Parker[1] was suspended for the rest of this year. I feel that Albert[2] is going the wrong road now. He is so easily influenced. Perhaps you might help him by writing him. He was in the trouble and received by vote of the Faculty two warnings.

Is Albert to saw your wood? or is old man to do it? I can not see why Albert can not do so.

Emma was so unpleasant to Miss Lischy that I took her away. I hope that I did the best thing. I was afraid that Miss Lischy would come away and I knew that you would be miserable.

Have you written Miss Moore. Do not make a mistake by not being explicit to her or with her. Mrs. J. H. Washington is getting their winter clothing for them — the children I mean.

Mrs. Logan brought me some ice cream Friday night.

Mr. Penny preached a very practical sermon this morning. I was not there. I lost my key and had nothing to wear.

Miss Peak[3] sent me over something nice to eat to day.

Miss Hawley[4] and Brown[5] are still here, mean as ever.

I am very much pleased with my class teachers. I think that they are doing good work except your protegee and I expect nothing of her.

Miss Lischy is carrying on the Instrumental Music and she does it well. The students are now in the Annex dining room and seem quite happy. I do not like the place at all still I have nothing to say. I am going to send and get some nice curtains for your books in the Library. Do you not think that I am good.

I am going to have a new office boy tomorrow for which thing I am so glad. Robt. Glover[6] is still here.

Miss Cropper[7] is now in Night School in Mr. Mann's[8] place. I bought a pair of shoes for Sophira[9] and Emma. You owe me $4.00. Do you not think that you do too much for Sophira? She ought to be made to feel that she has herself to look out for. I get sick of her dependence. No Mr Logan has paid me nothing. He owes $2.50 and this week he gave me $20. I hope that you will say nothing to him of it because I do not like to dun him but I need money sorely for the folks at home.

The woods are now just lovely. The leaves are decked in red and yellow.

The Laundry is doing better now.

My sister is coming to see me before Xmas.

When will Mr. Hamilton return? Yours

Maggie

ALS Con. 17 BTW Papers DLC. Apparently the date is Nov. 1 and the mention of Oct. was a slip of the pen.

[1] Perhaps James Parker of Montgomery, a B middle student in the night school in 1890-91. He was not listed in the 1891-92 catalog.

[2] George Washington Albert Johnston.

[3] Sarah F. Peake Greene.

[4] Anna C. Hawley.

[5] Ellen M. Brown.

[6] Robert William Glover of Mobile entered Tuskegee in 1891. He spent three years in the night school and two in the day school, but did not graduate.

[7] Lula M. Cropper, a graduate of Tuskegee in 1889, taught in the training school from 1891 to 1901.

[8] Thomas L. Mann.

[9] Sophira (Sophia) Lavinia Warren.

From Halle Tanner Dillon

Tuskegee, Ala. 11-2-91

Dear Sir: Davidson is still much improved.

As his nervous condition responded so nicely to treatment I have not done any thing about the operation I spoke to you about. The condition exists and sooner or later will have to be attended to, as it will interfere with his proper developement; But as long as he keep[s] as well as he is now I think it would be well to wait until he was some thing stronger. Will you kindly some time before long send me word as to how much the expenses of Miss Nolen & S. Sadie[?] were?

Trusting you are well   I remain   Respectfully

H. T. Dillon

ALS Con. 99 BTW Papers DLC.

From Olivia Egleston Phelps Stokes

[New York] November 5/91

Dear Sir, Your letter of November 4th has been forwarded to me. I am glad to know that the scholarship is doing good. I am particularly interested in the preparation of colored young men for the ministry. As in listening to colored preachers I have felt their lack of Bible knowledge in their sermons, and of definate practical Christian instruction. I should be glad to know whether your experience has shown you the same need, and if so, how and where can young colored men be best prepared for the Christian ministry. I would like to have you communicate with me on this subject, and a letter addressed to 37 Madison Avenue will reach me. Should you remain in New York until the end of next week, I would also be pleased to have you call and talk over this subject with you.

You could let me know of your plans for remaining in town, and believe me   Yours truly

O. E. P. Stokes

ALS   Con. 100   BTW Papers   DLC.

To Warren Logan

Crawford House   Boston, Nov. 12 1891

Dear Mr Logan: Since telegraphing you I enclose another $100. With what the Misses Collins[1] will send I hope you will be some what relieved.

Since writing you today I have considered the matter fully and decide that since we charge our students so little for board and do so much for them, that I wish you to give written orders to each person in charge of student laborers, to reduce their wages one $\frac{1}{5}$ let this be done whether they work by the hour, day or month. I do not wish this to apply to night students. Let this be done rather than reduce the amount of labor. Hastily yours

B. T. Washington

ALS   Con. 100   BTW Papers   DLC.   The fraction ⅕ was originally written ¼, then crossed out.

[1] Ellen and Mary Collins.

From George F. Richings[1]

Harrisburgh Pa   Nov 12th 1891

Dear Sir   I wrote you sometime ago asking for one of your photographs and a sketch of your life, at that time you were away. I meet a few days ago at Wilberforce Ohio an old friend of mine in the person of Bishop D A Payne, he urged me to write again and by all means secure your photo.

Now bro Washington I think I can be of some help to your work as I am before both white and colored audiences in all parts of the country.

I should like if it could be had a picture of some of your industrial work. I am now showing up some of that kind of work from quite a number of the M E Schools.

Try and give me all points of interest in connection with your work. Hoping to hear from you at an early date I am   Yours truly

G. F. Richings

ALS   Con. 103   BTW Papers   DLC.

[1] George F. Richings was for many years an itinerant white lecturer before black church groups and other audiences. His lecture "The Negro before and since the War" was accompanied by stereopticon slides. From 1904 to 1907 BTW secretly paid him a monthly salary to conclude his lecture and slides with a paean of praise for Tuskegee and panoramic view of Tuskegee's campus. "Of course the minute people get the idea that you are an agent of Tuskegee," BTW warned, "that minute in a very large degree your influence would be modified." (BTW to Richings, Jan. 25, 1905 [1904], Con. 23, BTW Papers, DLC. See Harlan, "The Secret Life of Booker T. Washington," 409-10.)

From Thomas Junius Calloway

Washington, D.C. November 16, 1891

My dear Sir: As I had previously written you I was expecting to have you lodge with me as I have quite comfortable lodgings now. But as I shall not be able to be away from my office work there will be very little to be gained so that if you prefer the Hotel alright. Although I assure you your stay with us would be very welcome.

Fred. Douglas[1] will be present on Friday night to meeting and to the banquet or luncheon at my house.[2] I have made no engagement for you for Thursday evening. Respectfully yours,

Thos. J. Calloway

ALS Con. 861 BTW Papers DLC.

[1] Frederick Douglass.

[2] Calloway invited twenty leading black citizens, including Douglass, to his home at 1735 12th Street, N.W., to coincide with BTW's speaking engagement in Washington, D.C., on Nov. 20. Douglass was too ill to attend. (See Douglass to BTW, Nov. 20, 1891, below.)

From Timothy Thomas Fortune

New York, November 18, 1891

Dear Sir: Referring to your favor of the 13th inst., permit me to say that as we constitute the labor force of the South and can only maintain our predominance in that respect, which is the basis of all prosperity everywhere, by thorough technical education in the skilled trades, the necessity for industrial education must therefore take the highest rank. In the present stage of our development it is of more importance than collegiate and professional training. The work that your School is doing in this respect will be more generally and generously appreciated ten years hence than now. Very respectfully,

T. Thomas Fortune

ALS Con. 99 BTW Papers DLC.

From Alfred Haynes Porter

Brooklyn   Nov 19. 1891

My dear Mr Washington. Your favor of 18th to hand. I am much pleased that Miss Stokes takes such interest in the plan we have talked so much about. I regret that I have not felt able to furnish all the funds to carry out the plan myself, as I am sure it would be a great satisfaction to any one in years to come to have started this much needed branch of the work. If you please you can say to Miss Stokes that Dr Cuyler[1] will answer for my interest and for some practical knowledge of work for Freedmen, and that I am convinced that Tuskegee is the place and Mr Washington the man to inaugurate this plan of educating and training the colored ministers. If I rightly understand your plans and what is needed to carry them out, I should say if Miss Stokes would set apart say $2,000 a year for 3 years, giving you the opportunity to show her and others what could be done in this line, it would be better than furnishing a new building; still if she comes up so nobly to help this work on she must be left to do it in her own way! Keep me advised as to what you do as I stand ready to help so far as in my power, both in giving and finding others to join. I envy Miss Stokes, for though our Bkln City Miss[io]n with its 25 to 30 Missionaries takes much of my interest as Pres't, still I believe this plan promises the greatest reward in future results. Yours truly

Alfred H. Porter

ALS   Con. 3   BTW Papers   ATT.   Original destroyed.

[1] Theodore Ledyard Cuyler (1822-1909), from 1860 until his retirement in 1890 pastor of the Lafayette Avenue Presbyterian Church in Brooklyn.

From Frederick Douglass

Cedar Hill, Anacostia D.C. Nov. 20, 1891

Dear Mr. Washington: I fully intended to hear your lecture and should do so but for the state of my health. You have my best wishes for your lecture and your vocation. Truly yours

Frederick Douglass

This will be handed you by Miss Hattie Sprague[1] my grand Daughter.

ALS Con. 16 BTW Papers DLC.

[1] Harriette (Hattie) Sprague was one of the seven children of Frederick Douglass's daughter Rosetta and Charles Sprague.

An Address at a Mass Meeting in Washington, D.C.

[Washington, D.C.] Nov. 20 '91

THE SOUTH AS AN OPENING FOR A BUSINESS CAREER

So far in our quarter of a century and more of freedom I think few will deny that the questions of politics, civil rights, education, and religion, have occupied the greater part of our time and energy, and this has been well; and I doubt if it is true of any other problem on which so much has been said, that so much has been said that was true and helpful and so little that was false and hurtful. The general discussion of these subjects whether in the North or the South, by black men or white men, by friend or foe, has tended on the whole to put the race on a higher plane and in a better position before the world. But while this is true I wish to call your attention to another subject, one that has too long been neglected and that in a large and potent sense constitutes the condition on which our political and civil problems are to be solved, and I think I might add educational and religious. When we disarm ourselves of all partisan feeling and take a calm disinterested view of our political status we must conclude that there has been little if any political progress in the heart of the South among the masses and I think when we attempt still further to divest ourselves of partisan feeling and consider the good of the race alone, we must reach the conclusion that we shall not be able much longer to say that this lack of political progress is due to this or that party being in power. I must confess that during my ten years residence in the black belt of Alabama I have observed little if any change in the political condition of the masses by reason of the one party being in and the other being out. While there has been most commendable progress along the line of securing our civil rights we must acknowledge that that question is far from being settled as we would wish it.

Now is it not a fact that in seeking a solution of these questions that we have too largely overlooked business development as a factor, in the settlement and the South

As an Opening for a
Business Career?

I do not say that it is a panacea, but I do give it as my opinion as the result of ten years of contact with all classes and conditions in the South that business development is the entering wedge to the solution of many of these problems. While surrounded by so much that is wrong and exasperating in politics, in courts of law and public accommodations, I am constantly surprised to find an almost entire absence of prejudice against the Negro in all matters that pertain to business, and even the most prejudiced and bitter white man likes to comment with local pride on the business success of a colored man in his locality. When the business standing of a black and a white man are equally good there are few if any banks in the South that draw any color line in discounting their paper or extending any business courtesy. These race problems to my mind will be solved in proportion as the black man gets hold of something that the white man *wants* or *respects,* and we must confess that this is not very different from human nature the world over; usually when two persons associate together and the one is careful to accord the other all his just rights it is because one has something that the other wants or the one is obligated to the other. It is either money or social position, or political influence, or culture, or perhaps a daughter or something that the one wants to get from the other. Often one of the surest and quickest ways to reach a man's heart is through his pocket or his eyes or something tangible. When I went into the town of Tuskegee, Alabama, ten years ago to start the Tuskegee Normal and Industrial Institute, there were some white people who always made it convenient to turn their heads the other way when we met in the streets. Among the first industries that we started in connection with our educational work was a brick yard, we manufactured the best bricks in that vicinity and those same white people after a while wanted bricks and they came to us for bricks. We started our wheelwrighting and blacksmithing departments and they wanted wagons and buggies made and repaired, and they came to us for this work; and then came the printing office. They wanted printing done and they came to us to get that done, and our young men now set up and print for a white man one of the county democratic papers, and the same patronage has been given to all of our industries. This came about by our having something that they wanted. By reason of this we became acquainted with each other, our interests in that community became mutual, instead of all the dependence being on one side, the black man dependent on the white for everything, there was an interdependence, an interlocking of our business interests. We wanted their trade, they wanted ours, we owed them, they owed us, and thus gradually the business interests of whites and blacks in that community have become so knit together that I believe that it is just as unlikely that any such race conflicts should take place in that little town, such as often disgrace many Southern communities, as here in the city of Washington. During the first few years that we were engaged in the establishment of the Tuskegee Institute, every once in a while when something displeased them we could hear murmurs of complaint from a certain class and threats about getting rid of the school. As soon as possible we erected near the public road in full view a large three story building, and then this was followed by another large four story brick building, and then another large building, and so on with large and small buildings till we have in all fifteen buildings, and all the talk about driving that institution from that town has ceased months ago. About two years ago in Montgomery, Ala., the feeling of the whites against the colored suddenly grew to fever heat because of some expressions reflecting on the South that Dr. C. N. Dorsette, perhaps the most successful colored physician in the Gulf States, was reported to have made. There were signs and threats of lynching and mob violence on every hand and no one knew what the next hour would bring. In the midst of this excitement, thinking that I might be of some service to the doctor I went to Montgomery. My first question was, "What are you going to do, doctor?" Says he, "Washington, I am going to do this, I am going to open a drugstore"; and he did open a drug store on one of the corners of the principal thoroughfare in that city and now has a large three story brick building owned by himself and employs three clerks and is locted only a few rods from where Jefferson Davis in delivering his inaugural address said that he would found a government whose chief corner stone would be slavery. Since the establishment of this drug store the threats against Dr. Dorsette have completely hushed. (Webster and Choate.)

While our efforts at Tuskegee are largely directed toward the Normal and Academic training of our students, it is because we recognize the value of the business element that we push the industrial training along with the mental. As a foundation for our industrial training we have farms of 1480 acres on which are carried on 15 industries, consisting of farming, brickmaking, brick masonry, plastering, painting, blacksmithing, wheelwrighting, carpentry, saw-mill work, harness making, shoemaking, tinning, printing, laundrying, sewing, cooking, and mattress making, and expect soon to add surveying, architecture and other higher branches along the line of technical work. Largely by means of these industries we have built up a property that is easily valued at $125,000 free from encumbrance and the institution is carried on at an annual exp. of over $40,000. It is our object to surround the student with such an air of business and industry during the years that he is with us that it will be next to impossible for him not to make himself felt in active business, or in some other sphere of usefulness; and there is a positive enthusiasm over the opportunity to learn trades, and we cannot begin to supply the demand for trades. Understand I am not one who believes that industrial is the only training that our youths should have; for I believe thoroughly in the value of the highest classical education obtainable. But I think we need both — some the classical and others the industrial and technical. By experience we have found that as we can send out into cities, towns and country districts, young men who can start brick yards, wagon shops, saw-mills, tin and harness shops, printing offices and other industries and thus create something that will not only make them independent but bring them into business relations with and *make* the whites depend *on* them in a business sense, that a change in the relations of the races does take place. Let us go on with this kind of development till a Negro gets to the point, as is already true in some cases, where he can get a mortgage on a white man's house that he can foreclose at will, well that white man will be rather careful about driving that Negro away from the polls when he attempts to vote, and will hesitate about attempting to drive him from a first class car. It is along this line I think we have got to look for the final and safe settlement of many of the race difficulties. It takes no argument to prove that as the race develops in business prosperity it will have a wholesome effect on schools, colleges, and religion, for it is a mighty hard thing to make a good Christian of a hungry man.

But let us for a few minutes take a somewhat different view of the subject and inquire what are the resources and inducements offered by the South as a field for business. Few I think will deny that the most important elements of wealth in any country are iron, wood, land, and climate. We do not I fear fully appreciate the rapidity and character of the material development that is taking place in the South and now is the time for us to strike while this development is in comparative infancy. With all the disadvantages presented by the South we can find our way to the front sooner through *Southern prejudice* than *through Northern competition*. But what of this development? You have perhaps read Grady's description of a burial in Pickens County, Ga., where

"The grave was dug through solid marble, but the marble headstone came from Vermont. It was in a pine wilderness, but the pine coffin came from Cincinnati. An iron mountain overshadowed it, but the coffin nails and screws and the shovels came from Pittsburg. With hard woods and metals abounding, the corpse was hauled on a wagon from South Bend, Indiana. A hickory grove grew near by, but the pick and shovel handles came from New York. The cotton shirt on the dead man came from Cincinnati, the coat and breeches from Chicago, the shoes from Boston; the folded hands were encased in white gloves from New York, and round the poor neck, that had worn all its living days the bondage of lost opportunity, was twisted a cheap cravat from Philadelphia. That country, so rich in undeveloped resources, furnished nothing for the funeral except the corpse and the hole in the ground, and would probably have imported both of those if it could have done so. And as the poor fellow was lowered to his rest, on coffin bands from Lowell, he carried nothing into the next world as a reminder of his home in this, save the halted blood in his veins, the chilled marrow in his bones, and the echo of the dull clods that fell on his coffin lid.

"There are now more than \$3,000,000 invested in marble quarries and machinery around that grave. Its pitiful loneliness is broken with the rumble of ponderous machines, and a strange tumult pervades the wilderness. Twenty miles away, the largest marble-cutting works in the world put to shame in a thousand shapes its modest headstone. Forty miles away four coffin factories, with their exquisite work, tempt the world to die. The iron hills are gashed and swarm with workmen. Forty cotton mills in a near radius weave infinite cloth that neighboring shops make into countless shirts. There are shoe factories, nail factories, shovel and pick factories, and carriage factories, to supply the other wants. And that country can now get up as nice a funeral, native and home-made, as you would wish to have."

The facts drawn out by this picture are not much if any overdone.

The growth of the iron industry within a dozen years has been tremendous. An English expert in iron making recently said the South will not only control the iron market of the North but of Europe. Ex-congressman A. S. Hewlett of New York, who has lately invested in the South says: "Alabama will be a region of coke made iron on a grander scale than has ever been witnessed on the globe," and others capable of judging have added the same opinion concerning Tennessee and Georgia.

But one may suggest that the colored men who are able to begin the manufacture of iron are rather few, but we must note the innumerable collateral industries that this industry fathers. Why, in a little town in Alabama located near this iron region that twenty years ago was seemingly dead and ready for burial, there have sprung up as if by magic these industries:

Rolling stock company.
Railway-car works, employing 1,000 hands.
Charcoal company.
Iron Bridge company.
Car wheel company.
Horse shoe and nail factory employing 60 hands.
Oak extract company.
Steam engine and boiler works.
Sash and door factory.
Street railway.
Cotton compress.
Telephone and electric light companies.
Wheelbarrow works.
Brick yard.
Water works.
Ice factory.
Furniture factory.
Chair works.
Three banks.
One building association.
Bottling works.

Artificial stone works.
Carriage factory.
Two iron furnaces, etc.

A few years ago the Elyton Land Company of Birmingham, Ala., was organized by 12 men with $12,000 paid in capital, and 5,000 acres of land were bought. The $12,000 was changed into $200,000 of stock making 2,000 shares of $100 each. Since this organization on this capital $5,500,000 in cash dividends have been paid, and every dollar invested is now worth $2,500 and was at one time worth $4,000 in open market. This it is true is rather an exceptional case but it indicates what brains and hard work can do.

Take the timber industry as another source of wealth. Leaving out some portions of Canada it is safe to say that the South is the most heavily wooded of any portion of America. For example in Florida. $1\frac{9}{20}$ of the 38,000,000 acres that compose the state are covered with the most valuable timber, such as yellow pine, white oak, live oak, hickory, ash, cedar, cypress and magnolia. Then in Alabama there are over 20,000,000 acres of timber that has been practically untouched, and these lands may be had from $1 to $5 per acre. On such an intelligent company as this is, I need not try to impress the commercial value of this timber land; millions of dollars worth of lumber are now being shipped by water and railroad, not only throughout the United States but to Mexico, and Europe.

You are too well acquainted with cotton and its collateral industries as a source of wealth for me to occupy your time in its discussion, but I would add the Negro and the mule are the only forces so far discovered that can produce cotton, but the trouble is we and the mule do the producing and the white man gets the larger share of the profit. (Story about man from Norfolk.) Of the millions of cotton, Rice, and Sugar that come from the South ⅚ of it is the product of the Negroes sweat and muscle but his ignorance and the greed of others deprive him of the profit. Cotton land and land for general agriculture is now cheaper in the South than it will ever be again and the development in the manufacture of cotton and cotton seed oil is not far behind the material development in other respects. At least $40,000,000 are now invested in the South for the manufacture of cotton seed oil alone. Georgia alone has invested in ten years $2,000,000 in fertilizer factories. This to say nothing of the millions constantly being put into cotton factories.

But what has all this to do with the Negro? He can't start a cotton factory. Perhaps not, but it is well to keep in mind this about the son of Ham, as much as he is abused and condemned, wherever there is any business being done, any money to be earned or spent, the son of Ham is found somewhere near by and he is going to get some of that money and is going to spend some. If a new style of hat, coat or shoe or neck tie appears on Pennsylvania Ave. he may not be up in style the first Sunday they appear, but look out for him the next Sunday.

To come more to the point, this material development has opened up opportunities for business in the South for our race and especially the educated that we little dream of. There is scarcely a town of any size in the South where a wide awake young man could not go and within a few years grow independent in the single industry of brick-making contractors. Then there is the manufacture of wagons and carts. The South that [is] using more farm wagons than any other section imports ⅚ of them from the West, and there are hundreds of smaller industries out of which men have made millions such as the manufacture of lead pencils, clothes pins, cedar buckets, brooms and so on. If none of these industries suit your fancy, start a saw-mill or open a coal mine. The combined capital of a few will start either of these enterprises.

As this development goes on the black man wants somewhere to keep his money and he is not afraid to put it into a colored bank if it is managed on first class business principles, as has been so well proven by the very successful banking and building association in this city, for whose success you deserve the very highest praise, and we have examples of the same truth in the success of the colored banks in Richmond, Chattanooga, and Birmingham. The Capital Savings Bank and Industrial Savings Company on whose invitation I appear before you are business institutions that are an honor to any city or race not only are they helping the citizens of Washington but they are a pillar of fire by night for the ignorant and inexperienced millions in the far South. Ah, gentlemen you little knew when you came together a few years [ago] with doubt and fear, with bated breath and throbbing hearts to form these organizations, that you were kindling a fire that will soon spread into every city of the South and know that institutions of such value to the race will have hearty support of this whole city. There are at least 40 cities in the South that would support first class banks. As the Negro gets money he wants to buy land and the real estate and building and loan association business will pay in most any part of the South; and when he builds his house he wants it insured. There is the fire insurance agency. In all the Southern states I do not know of a single colored fire insurance agent, and yet it is true that the black man keeps millions of dollars worth of property insured. In all branches of mercantile business there is a most encouraging opening for business. Already nearly a half dozen Tuskegee graduates have gone into the grocery business and are without exception succeeding. Two of them opened a grocery store in a little shanty in Tuskegee three years ago and have already bought a corner lot and are doing with one exception the largest grocery business in the town and their customers are about equally divided between white and colored. Another one has lately opened a job printing office on the main street in Montgomery and his office has been crowded with paying work from the beginning. Similar examples could be given of those who are succeeding along other lines. Almost every town in the South of 4,000 inhabitants or more will support a competent colored physician and I might add the same of dentistry and the drug store and every town that size will support a grocery store or dry goods, or millinery business. Not only will the Negroes support physician[s] but in most cases the whites will respect them. Recently Dr. Halle Tanner Dillon passed successfully the Alabama Medical State Board, being not only the first colored woman but the first woman of any race to pass that examination, and is now the resident physician at the Tuskegee Institute. During the ten days that she was occupied in this examination not the slightest treatment did she receive from any member of the board that was not fair and courteous. [A] White man failed. Since she has entered upon her practice the local physicians have answered without hesitation her calls for consultation, showing not the least feeling against color or sex.

For a number of years it has been said by many that the Negro would not patronize his own race in business. In regard to this I cannot answer for the District of Columbia and the more Northern states, but so far as this charge applies to the colored people in the far South it is wholly untrue and unjust. There are to be found no more loyal

race people in the world than are to be found among the hard working masses in the South. Let any colored man enter any avenue of
business and if he is capable, clean in his business methods, true to
the race, not relying on his color for success, but on his superiority in
his business, that man will be stood by and supported. Not only this
but my experience has been that our people take a peculiar delight
in patronizing each other. Some of the most pleasing experiences in
my life have been in seeing the glow of intense happiness that has
shown itself on the face of some old mother or father who had been
taught from childhood that everything must come from the white
man, when for the first time they went to patronize a colored physician,
or drug store, or to place their children in an institution officered by
Negroes. From its opening the Tuskegee Institute has been in competition with scores of institutions officered by white men and its class
rooms and dormitories have been crowded from the first and we cannot find room for more than half who want to come. With 31 officers
and teachers and nearly 600 students — men and women — representing 15 states, during ten years work at the head of that institution,
I have never received anything from parents, teachers or students but
the most deferential respect and cordial and sympathetic support.

The Negro can control labor in the South. Other things being equal,
a colored man can secure laborers just as easily as a white man.

But it is in the South as all over the world; success will only come to
those who win and deserve it. We have got to stick to what we undertake, got to stick through failure and success, through clouds and sun-
shine, and have got to have that faith in our business that will lead
to success when all the world sees failure looking us in the face. When
we begin it will be surprising how many people there are who will be
able to show us how *not* to succeed, to tell us how *not* to do a thing.
Suppose three young men in this city next week organize a company
to go down into Alabama and start a saw-mill. Before 24 hours pass
a dozen men will be able to tell them why the enterprise cannot succeed. But what these young men want is, to be told how to succeed.
It requires little brains or foresight to tell a person how *not* to do a
thing. We never began the erection of a large building at Tuskegee that
there were not a number of persons ready to tell us how not to erect
it, but we were looking for the man who could tell us how it could
be done.

As a race we need just a little more of the "root hog or die and jump overboard — sink or swim" quality. We like pretty well to stay near a stated salary for which some one else is responsible.

Those who have risked most have usually gained most. The Huntingtons, Hopkins, Mackays, Stanford's and Fairs and Algers, but for the fact that they saw that by going early into an undeveloped country, sleeping on boards, living for months in shanties, cooking out of doors, if necessary, was their only road to wealth and influence would never have reached the positions that they have. The coal, iron, lumber and cotton fields of the South offer to-day almost the same opportunity that these men had.

With the exception of preaching the gospel of Christ, there is no work that will contribute more largely to the elevation of the race in the South than first class business enterprises. Aside from the direct good to the individual or individuals, a business success cuts as a two edged sword — bringing from the white man confidence and respect, giving the Negro faith in the fidelity and ability of his own people and creating at the same time an inspiration that will lead to higher mental, moral and material development of the whole race.

Never a mother however ignorant and seemingly unthoughtful, sees the spectacle of a bank presided over by a black man and a Negro at the cashier's desk, that does not go away with new life, new hope, new determination — resolved that if education, moral and religious training will do it, her boy too shall one day be lifted to a position just as honorable and responsible.

TMd Con. 955 BTW Papers DLC. The mass meeting was called by directors of the Capital City Savings Bank and the Industrial Building Savings Company. Several corrections and insertions in BTW's hand are incorporated. Excerpts from this speech appeared in the form of an interview in the Washington *Post,* Nov. 22, 1891, 7.

From Thomas Junius Calloway

Washington. D.C. Nov. 25, 91

My dear Sir: I sent you a number of copies of "Post" and enclose here your manuscript. I was solicited to read it before Bethel Literary last night and consented with some hesitation because I didnt have your consent and for fear I might not be able to put *your feelings* into your expressions. Those who heard it however flattered me with have-ing succeeded quite well. A discussion as is the custom followed and quite a number heartily indorsed the paper in full. Indeed no one found any exception, but Mr. Ricks who announced himself a personal friend of yours asserted that the Normal training in Hampton & Tuskegee was not far enough carried. This several of us answered to the complete satisfaction of all I think.

I am sure your visit here has been fruitful. Very truly yours

T. J. Calloway

ALS   Con. 861   BTW Papers   DLC.

To Warren Logan

25 Beacon St.   Boston, Nov. 26 1891

Dear Mr Logan: I have received your letter and am very sorry that another death has occurred.[1] I am glad the girls mother was there.

I am glad to hear that Miss Moore[2] is at my house.

Gen. A.[3] is still in a bad condition, one side is paralyzed, and the doctor has little hopes for him. This week will decide his case, but all are sure that even if he lives he can never be himself again. He has his mind and talks of every thing but himself. He was taken while speaking Thanksgiving.

Please have a number of those Phillips Brooks circulars printed on *good* paper and send me 150 by the 10 if possible. I shall want them on the 10 and 50 more by the 15. Put students at 511.

I am glad matters are going well.

Shall write again soon. Yours truly

B. T. Washington

ALS   Con. 100   BTW Papers   DLC.

[1] Emma Lee Thomas, of Ansley, Pike County, Ala., a member of the C preparatory class in 1891-92.

[2] Mary C. Moore.

[3] Samuel Chapman Armstrong.

From Francis J. Grimké

Washington D C   Nov 28th 1891

Dear Prof. Washington: Your letter of the 25th inst. reached me yesterday, and I hasten to reply. The establishment of a Bible School at Tuskegee for the better training of our young men for the work of preaching the gospel among our people in the South is in my judgment, a most desirable thing to do. The greatest need of our people, in the South, to day, I believe, is an intelligent ministry, a ministry with a good foundation in English and a thorough knowledge of the English Bible. How to get a sufficient number of men thus trained into the field is a question of the greatest importance, and one in which all true friends of the race ought to be interested. So far you have done a splendid work at Tuskegee. No language can possibly over estimate its importance. The more intimately I have come to know it, the higher it has risen in my estimation. I have followed the history of Tuskegee during the seven years that I have known of it, with the deepest interest, and have rejoiced in the many valuable additions that you have made to it from year to year; but none has given me greater pleasure than the one which you now propose to make. It will, I believe, greatly enlarge its influence and usefulness.

As to the importance of the work, there can hardly be a doubt in the mind of any one who is at all acquainted with the condition of our people in the South, and the character of the preaching that most of them, especially in the rural districts, are compelled to listen to.

As to the desirability of beginning such a work at Tuskegee, the reasons, it seems to me, are equally clear and conclusive. (1) The just splendid history of the school is itself strong presumptive evidence of the wisdom of putting it there. Whatever has been undertaken so far has been a success, and nothing has been undertaken which has not been required by the necessities of the case, in answer to a present and pressing need. (2) The school is already well and widely known. It has already made for itself a reputation, and is as a city set upon a hill. (3) It draws not only a large number of students, but from a very wide area. All these things, together with the excellent management, and the wisdom which has always characterized the work at Tuskegee, make it sure that any money put into such a work there will not fail to accomplish the end desired. I trust that nothing may stand in the way of the speedy realization of your hopes in this respect. With best wishes for your success in the great work in which you are engaged, I am Yours truly

Francis J. Grimké

ALS Con. 4 BTW Papers ATT. Original destroyed.

From Horace Bumstead[1]

Atlanta, Ga. Nov. 29, 1891

My dear Mr. Washington: Your article on "The Colored Ministry: Its Needs and Defects" was read by me with great interest when it first appeared in the Christian Union, and has been read again with renewed interest in the form of the tract which you have sent me. I am very glad to learn that you are planning to carry out its ideas in establishing at Tuskegee a Bible School of the sort that you have described.

I do not yield to anyone, as you well know, in my advocacy of the higher education for as many of the colored people as can get it thoroughly and use it well. And I believe it is a wise thing for as many as possible of the brighter young colored men who go into the ministry to get such a thorough equipment for their work as is offered in the northern theological seminaries.

At the same time, I realize how very limited is the number of those who are able to spend the time and money necessary to get the higher theological education, how much greater is the number of those who could get such a training as you propose to give in your Bible School, and how great a field of usefulness is open to such workers in all the South, and especially in the region where your Institution is located. For all these reasons, I most heartily approve of your plan and wish it the most abundant success. Yours very sincerely,

Horace Bumstead

TLS Con. 99 BTW Papers DLC.

[1] Horace Bumstead (1841-1919), a white man, president of Atlanta University. A graduate of Boston Latin School and Yale, he served as an officer of the Forty-third Massachusetts Regiment of black troops in battles around Richmond and Petersburg. After travel and study in Europe, he became a Congregational minister

in Minneapolis. In 1875 he moved to Atlanta University, where his Yale class-mate, Edmund Asa Ware, was president. Bumstead was an instructor in natural science until 1880, professor of Latin 1880-96, acting president 1886-87, and president 1888-1907. Strongly imbued with a missionary spirit combined with racial egalitarianism, Bumstead sought to give to the "talented tenth" of black college students broad cultural opportunities such as were available in the best white colleges. Thus, in significant respects his racial and educational philosophy differed from BTW's philosophy. A certain coolness in the relationship between the two men was probably one of the reasons BTW turned more often to Fisk than to Atlanta for faculty recruits.

From A. N. McEwen[1]

Mobile, Ala. Nov 30the 1891

Dear Sir   Your favor of the 25the inst is before me and I have read with care its contents, and would say in reply.

That I favor very much your *(the) idea* of establishing a Bible Training School in connection with your work at Tuskegee.

I believe such a School would fill a long felt want in the State, and you can relie on me for any assistance that I may be able to render you in the establishment of such a School.

I believe Tuskegee would be the proper place to locate such a School, because hundreds go there that will not attend or can not attend else where. You have done untold good for the Negroes of the South in the establishing and running of the Normal and Industrial School at Tuskegee, but should you succeed in establishing a Bible Training School at that place I shall regard it as the crowning work of your life.

Say can not you induce some rich friend to help you in such a work, may God bless your effort in such a interprise.

With best wishes that you succeed   I am your very Respectfully

A. N. McEwen

You can publish if you wish.

ALS   Con. 3   BTW Papers   ATT.   Original destroyed.

[1] A. N. McEwen, who had previously edited the *Alabama Baptist Leader* in Montgomery, in the fall of 1891 moved to Mobile as pastor of a Baptist church and editor of the *State Republican*. (McEwen to BTW, Sept. 10, 1891, Con. 100, BTW Papers, DLC.)

A Speech at Old South Meeting House, Boston[1]

Boston   Dec. 15 '91

To a young man just emerging from slavery with all its demoralizing environments, and entering into the pure, strong, active and unselfish influence of General Armstrong's personality as it was my privilege, with hundreds of others, to do, there came as if by miracle all at once, a new meaning to the possibilities and the object of life, that is hard for most in this audience to understand or appreciate. So, aside from our sense of obligation to General Armstrong for his long years of work for our race, there is a deep and tender love in our hearts for the man himself; a nearness to him, and confidence in him that makes those of us who have been his students not only love but worship him. While at work in the far South for the elevation of our race, when we have grown discouraged at the many difficulties by which we were surrounded, it has been the mental picture of Gen. Armstrong, who knew no discouragement, that has given us strength to go on and conquer. When we have grown selfish and disposed to live for ourselves, the vision of General Armstrong, who never seemed to know aught but to live and do for others, has come and made us ashamed of our selfishness, and when we have been inclined to grow indifferent and inactive, the form of General Armstrong who never seemed to rest night or day, winter or summer, has come before us and given new zeal and new activity.

It has been my privilege while a student at Hampton, as well as in later life, to see something of the way in which General Armstrong has actually worn away his life, not in his cause nor Hampton's cause but for the Nation's cause — *your cause*. If time permitted I could tell you how in the early days of Hampton when the Institution was sorely pressed for means I have seen him arrive at home at 4 o'clock in the morning from a long Northern tour, begging for funds, speaking at meetings night after night, and filling his days with going from door to door, from office to office. And how, without even going to his room, I have seen him go to his office and plunge into his work of the day while students and teachers were yet in bed.

Future years will show more clearly than these the value of General Armstrong's work. His central idea has been from the first that the salvation of the negro and of the South was in industrial development and in cementing, not tearing asunder the friendships of the blacks and whites. I can remember how, not many years ago, the wisdom of Gen. Armstrong's plan of industrial education found many doubters at the North and many opposers at the South among the most prominent colored men. But now, as the results begin to manifest themselves, how happily has all this changed? What would have been the result supposing that the education of the negro had gone on without industrial training? Without my words you understand better than I that the effect of mental development is to increase one's wants, & sensitiveness to bring about an unrest. General Armstrong saw that there would be danger to the peace of the whole South unless while his wants were being increased by mental training, industrial training at the same time increased his capacity to supply those increased wants.

He saw too that the negro must be prepared to live side by side of his white brother of the South, and that industrial education would create the desire for ownership in land and the ability to develop industries that would make the negro a producer as well as a consumer — industries that would make the white man dependent on the black man for something instead of all the dependence being on the other side.

He saw as this development went on that it would bring about, as it is doing, an interdependence of the races; that their material and business interests in those Southern communities would become so linked together, so interlaced, that the interests of the two races would be identical, and that instead of strife there would come peace and union.

He also saw that it was through such development, such union, that we must finally look for the solution of the political and social troubles that are so far from being settled in the South; and that industrial education would, in the near future, destroy the idea of labor being degrading that has held back and retarded like a nightmare, the progress of both races in the South, and would soon make them see in labor a privilege and blessing instead of a curse.

From the first, in this matter of education at the South, we have had your help and the struggles of the colored people themselves. We are now gradually gaining one other element of strength, I mean the interest and co-operation of the best class of Southern white people. As Hampton, Tuskegee, and other Institutions have been able year after year to present to Southern white people object lessons showing the value of an educated colored man, letting them see that an educated man was a help instead of a hindrance to the progress of the South, and as they have seen year after year, these educated young men and women revolutionize and regenerate whole communities, giving them ownership in homes instead of the rented one room log cabin, and bank account instead of a debt; and six or eight months school taught in a neat frame schoolhouse instead of three months taught in a wreck of a log cabin; a moral stamina instead of habits of moral crookedness and weakness. As the whites have seen this they are changing their feelings and actions towards the education of the ~~colored man~~ Negro.

A few weeks ago as I sat in the office of the Superintendant of education in the State of Alabama,[2] who but yesterday owned scores of black men and women, he said "Mr. Washington, I have grown to this point, if there is any difference in my heart, in my desire to help in the education of the two races, I do not know where to find it." Legal slavery is dead, but there is a mental, moral, and industrial slavery in the South that is not dead, and will not be for years to come. What was 250 years being done cannot be undone in 25 or 30. It seems to me that the vital question that centres in this meeting is; Shall the work and influence of Hampton go on? Hampton is the heart that is sending a constant stream of life-giving blood into every State and County in the South. Shall it flow on? That the American nation might see the value and power of this work, Gen. Armstrong has practically given his life, and now the question that comes to each of us with renewed emphasis as that grand hero lies prostrated, is: What will we give of our service, of our substance, that his work may be continued and perpetuated?

TMd Con. 955 BTW Papers DLC. An abridged and edited version of this speech appeared in the *Christian Register*, 70 (Dec. 24, 1891), 850-51

[1] Samuel Chapman Armstrong a few days earlier was stricken by a paralytic stroke while on a fund-raising tour of the North. He lay at the Parker House in Boston, where doctors feared that he would not recover. Armstrong's friends in Boston gathered at Old South Church to honor him and to help raise the money he had gone there to secure. Edward Everett Hale, who presided, called the enthusiastic crowd a "Boston town meeting" and urged similar gatherings for Hampton in future years.

[2] John Gideon Harris.

A Statement on the Afro-American Press

[Tuskegee, Ala., 1891]

OPINION OF PROF. B. T. WASHINGTON

Few agencies for the uplifting of the colored people have accomplished more good than the negro newspapers. These papers have served to create race confidence, in that they have taught the colored people that the colored man could manage a business requiring the out-lay of money, brains and push that a newspaper enterprise demands. The colored editors have rendered most valuable service to the cause of education by constantly stimulating and encouraging our people to educate themselves and their children.

The papers have served as educators to the white race, in matters that pertain to the progress of the negro. The white press readily sees our dark side, but is not disposed, as a rule, to go far out of its way to let the world know of the negro's advancement.

The work of the colored newspapers has thus far been one of love and self-sacrifice, few if any of them paying in dollars and cents; but there has been evident growth, both in the make-up of the papers and in the paid circulation, and I apprehend that the day is not far distant when they will bring in an encouraging revenue. Already Mr. B. T. Harvey is publishing in Columbus, Ga., a colored daily, and he seems to be supported in his efforts to an encouraging degree.

I. Garland Penn, *The Afro-American Press and Its Editors* (Springfield, Mass., 1891), 446-48.

From Cornelius Nathaniel Dorsette

Montgomery, Ala., 1/5 1892

Dear Prof Washington I know you think strange of my not writing and I might as well tell you now I am again having trouble with my head & while I say nothing about it to any one its quite a serious thought to me privat[e]ly and outside of medicine I can do but little without bringing on trouble, my business letters I have my private secty do all that now. I *most heartily* endorse the step of that school for preachers you spoke of.

I think it would be well for Dr Dillon to come down & talk with me for a day or so. I can be of help to her. She is very despondant & I know I can help her.

If your matron has any thing in your Barrells that will help Jimmy Taylor[1] in the way of clothing please let him have it.

When are you coming down. Hastily yr

Dorsette

ALS   Con. 4   BTW Papers   ATT.   Original destroyed.

[1] James Henry Taylor of Montgomery, Ala., was a Tuskegee student from 1892 to 1895. He apparently did not graduate.

To James Dickens McCall

[Tuskegee, Ala.] Jan. 9. [189]2

Mr McCall. On going through the various [bran]ches of your work we are glad to say that on the whole it is in good condition.

There are some special points to which we desire to call your attention. The Labratory is not kept in an orderly condition. It would improve matters greatly if more shelves were put in. Send in to me the number of shelves needed and where you wish them placed. Everything in the Labratory is not labelled and kept in its place.

The Museum needs more room. Make out a definite order of what you wish in this regard. The specimens are not orderly kept and many are not labelled. There have not been enough additions to the Museum. To this point we call your especial attention. The addition of new specimens is entirely in your charge.

The Civil Government class seems to be in good condition.

Each member of the Botany class should be made to make a Herbarium each year and this Herbarium put in such form that it can be preserved by the student. Also a specimen Herbarium by each class should be left in the hands of the school each year. We find not a single member of the A Middle class has a complete Herbarium preserved from last year. This should not [be?]

Lectures in Natural History, we think, should be given with as few technical names as possible. Whenever it is possible students should have the [act]ual specimen before them to examine.

The work of the Senior class in Physics we consider to be very satisfactory.

B. T. Washington
For the Faculty

HLpS Con. 106 BTW Papers DLC. The press copy used here is blank on the left margin for two or three letters of the initial word of each line. The editors' reconstruction of the missing letters seemed doubtful in only two instances.

To John A. Roy[1]

[Tuskegee, Ala.] Jan 9th [189]2

Mr. J. A. Roy: Replying to your note of January 7th I would say that it always gives the greatest satisfaction to comply with the wishes of the teachers in any way I possibly can. I am always glad to raise their wages when it is possible to do so. At present I hardly see how you can consistently ask us to increase your wages. I hope you realize that the expense of carrying on the farm has been very great this last year, and in addition to this the crop was a very great failure. I did say that I would increase your salary just as fast as you made your work of value to the institution. The best way to secure an increase is to take hold of the work and make yourself invaluable to the school. The idea in purchasing the farm was to have it supply the school with grain, syrup, potatoes and such other products, and in addition to this the school should get from the farm in the near future hogs, poultry, beef, milk, & butter etc. If you will take hold of the farm and bring it up to the point where we can secure such products from it we shall be very glad to increase your salary. There are few young people who have such an opportunity as yourself and the whole matter is with you. If you will make the farm pay well we will give you more money. If not, we cannot give more. We shall give you just as nearly as possible what you desire in carrying on the farm and hold you responsible for results. If they are good you will share in the profits and if they are bad you will share in the bad results. The more you can look out for the wants of the farm yourself the more valuable you will be to the institution. Take the matter of securing seed sugar cane for another year; if you can show your ability to find them yourself instead of putting the school to the trouble of finding these seeds you will be demonstrating your increased ability to the institution and so in other matters. Yours truly,

B. T. Washington

TLpS   Con. 106   BTW Papers   DLC.

[1] John A. Roy, a graduate of Hampton and manager of its Shellbanks farm, went to Tuskegee in 1889 and managed the Marshall Farm of 800 acres for one or two years beginning in 1893. He married Victoria Perdue, a Tuskegee graduate of 1891, who served as matron of Marshall Farm. He left the employ of the school about 1895.

From Samuel June Barrows

Boston, Jan. 20 1892

My dear Mr. Washington, I enclose herewith two checks of $50.00 each.

One of them is from Mrs. E. Herbert Clapp of Germantown, Pa. I found on my recent visit to that place, that owing to a division that has occurred in their church and, is now of four or five years standing, a very few people have to bear the burden of expenses. There is a good deal of wealth among the seceding members, and now that the pulpit is vacant and they are seeking a new minister I hope the man who comes will succeed in reuniting the society. It did not seem expedient to take a collection, but I feel that there is a good deal of money in Germantown which you ought to have, and I think that a little later it would be a good field for you to work. Mr. Nichols[1] of the Spring Garden Society took up his collection the Sunday I was there and I spoke on "the Problem" at his church in the evening.

Please send an acknowledgement of this check to Mrs. Clapp, and I think it would be well to send her "The Student" and some literature.

The other check has an interesting and romantic history. You will receive in due time, by parcel post, a little box. On opening it you will find a chocolate baby about two inches long. If we had lived in the South we would have swathed him in cotton; living in the North we enswathe him in paper and hope that he will keep warm and will not be injured on his journey. In slavery times negroes used to be boxed and sent to the North; this is the first case I have heard of of their being boxed and sent South. The history of this chocolate baby is simply this.

Since I returned from the South I have been subjected to a great deal of persecution by my friends in the North. I am called a Negrophilist, a Negromaniac, and such terms. Indeed, when I returned from the South, several of my younger friends, thinking that I had become so enamored of the dark race that I did not think much of the white one, blacked their faces to receive me. On my birthday I was presented with a birthday cake and to make the gift acceptable it was decorated with 46 little black licorice figures. They looked like the coal black miners I saw at the Pratt Mines in Alabama where the white miners were just as black as the colored ones, and I could not tell the difference till they were washed. I hope you will sympathize with me in the persecution I have to suffer on behalf of Tuskegee, but, I mean that the institution shall get some good out of it if possible. Among my Christmas gifts was a box from a city in Ohio containing this chocolate baby. The giver is an accomplished young lady[2] in Cleveland. There was nothing to indicate whether it was sent as a compliment or a reproach. I promptly acknowledged the gift, and told this fair young lady that she evidently knew that I was trying to digest the Negro problem; but that I did not mean to swallow the Negro in doing it. I believe in extinguishing the Negro *problem* but not in extinguishing the Negro. The best way to extinguish the problem is to teach the negro how to live. I suggested to this young lady that it would be necessary for her to make some reparation to the colored race. I am not in the habit of making threats, but, I recorded one on this occasion; I declared that I never would eat the chocolate baby till the giver had raised or subscribed $50.00 for a scholarship to Tuskegee. A few days ago I received a check. The young lady had brought forth fruits meet for righteousness; but I do not wish to turn her righteousness into meat, so I have concluded *not* to eat the baby after all. When it first came it was worth only 50 cents, now that it is worth $50.00 it seems too valuable for a meal. I have never had that much paid for a meal of mine in my life. It has seemed to me that the best thing to do with this Christmas present would be to send it down with the check to you, and let it be assigned to some small niche in the institution, while the money which accompanies it shall be used to establish the *"Chocolate Baby Scholarship."* My wish is that it should pay the tuition of some one of your girl students. You need not be particular to find one of just the same color as the baby. Though I am sorry to part with my Christmas gift, I should be willing to send you down a whole regiment of chocolate babies if they were worth $50.00 apiece. The young girl to whom you assign this can send her acknowledgement to me and I will forward it to the lady.

I shall soon begin to work on the plan I proposed. The young lady is now engaged on the matter in comparing your list with our list of churches. Can you not send me some more reports or circulars? That little pamphlet you have just issued with pictures is a very telling thing. Have you any to spare?

If you refer to the "Chocolate Baby Scholarship" in any way, I think it will be well not to mention the name of Miss Southworth in connection with it, for I have not obtained her permission to reveal her identity.

I think it is extremely doubtful about getting up a party to go Tuskegee, but I have not absolutely abandoned the idea. Cordially yours,

S. J. Barrows

HLS   Con. 101   BTW Papers   DLC.

[1] Possibly William W. Nichols, a machinist who resided at 1330 Spring Garden, Philadelphia.

[2] Probably either Mary or Fanny Southworth, daughters of William J. Southworth, a Cleveland wholesale grocer. On Jan. 3, 1894, L. S. Richardson, whose address was the same as the Southworths', wrote to BTW sending a $50 contribution from "Miss Southworth" to the "Chocolate Baby Scholarship." (Con. 6, BTW Papers, ATT. Original destroyed.)

From H. W. Nichols[1]

Lockport N.Y. Jan 22, 1892

Dear Sir   Sometime last fall I saw an article in the New York Witness in which you solicited aid for the Normal and Industrial school at Tuskegee Ala or rather aid for the students studying there which I suppose means the same thing. Not knowing any thing about the school or its management I wrote for information to the Editor of the Witness enquiring if he knew any thing about it. I received his answer the other day which is satisfactory with one or two exceptions. He did not say whether it is a school for colored youth exclusively or whether young people of both races are admitted to its privileges. Now I wish to be informed on this point. I am an old fashioned abolitionist was such before the war I labored and prayed and voted for freedom and have seen no reason since to change my mind about the wickedness of slavery. But I am an old man now and can do but little more being over 83 years of age but believing that the cruelties practiced on the colored people and sufferings by them endured can never be atoned for by any sacrifices we can make for them still I believe we ought to do something to pay the debt owe[d]. And if you will select some young colored man who is anxio[u]s to get an education one who is pious active and intel[l]igent I will give my check for $50. to aid him in securing an education. I wish you to make the selection as you are on the ground and know best on whom to confer the favor and tell him to write and let me know whethe[r] he considers it a favor. And I also wish to know the name of the pe[r]son assisted. Yours for the right

H. W. Nichols

ALS   Con. 103   BTW Papers   DLC.

[1] H. W. Nichols was a farmer near Lockport, N.Y.

From W. H. Harvey[1]

Bessemer, Ala., 1/28/1892

Dear Sir   Yours of some days ago to hand, contents fully noted. I regret that it is necessary to again express my objections to your institution. I am also willing to make any reperation in my power except returning my boy to the school.[2] I do not think I would be discharging my duty to force him to again subsist on the food furnished for students   Fresh meat or poor beef, once a week. The ballance fat meat and peas, half cooked corn bread, very similar indeed to prison fare.

I dont like to express myself in this tone but your letter of prior date, in tone forces me to be more explicit. Very Respt yrs   Obt Svt

W. H. Harvey

ALS   Con. 102   BTW Papers   DLC.

¹ W. H. Harvey was proprietor of the Pioneer Saloon in Bessemer, Ala.

² John Frederick Harvey of Bessemer attended Tuskegee Institute only in 1891-92, in the junior class.

A Circular Announcing the Tuskegee Negro Conference

[Tuskegee, Ala., ca. January 1892]

A NEGRO CONFERENCE

TO BE HELD IN THE

BLACK BELT OF ALABAMA

There will be an interesting and somewhat unique Negro Conference held at Tuskegee, Alabama, under the auspices of the Tuskegee Normal and Industrial Institute of which Booker T. Washington is principal, beginning Feb. 23d, 1892.

The aim of Principal Washington is to bring together for a quiet conference, not the politicians and those usually termed the "leading colored people," but representatives of the masses — the bone and sinew of the race — the common, hard working farmers with a few of the best ministers and teachers.

In the Conference, two ends will be kept in view: First, to find out the actual industrial, moral and educational condition of the masses. Second, to get as much light as possible on what is the most effective way for the young men and women whom the Tuskegee Institute and other institutions are educating to use their education in helping the masses of the colored people to lift themselves up.

In this connection it may be said in general that a very large majority of the colored people in the "black belt" — cotton district are in debt for supplies secured through the "mortgage system," rent the land on which they live and dwell in one room log cabins.

The schools are in session in the country districts not often longer than 3 months and are taught in most cases in churches or log cabins with almost no apparatus or school furniture.

The poverty and ignorance of the Negro which show themselves by his being compelled to "mortgage his crop" — go in debt for the food and clothes on which to live from day to day is not only a terrible draw back to the Negro himself but is a severe drain on the resources of the white man. Say what we will the fact remains that in the presence of the poverty and ignorance of the millions of Negroes in the "black belt" the material, moral and educational interests of both races are making but slow headway.

———

Any information about the conference may be had from Booker T. Washington, Tuskegee Normal and Industrial Institute, Tuskegee, Alabama.

To . . . .
You and your friends are invited to be present.

PD   Con. 861   BTW Papers   DLC.

From Sarah Newlin

Philadelphia, Feb. 5th. [1892?]

Dear Mr. Washington, My sister[1] and I send the enclosed cheques, each for fifty ($50.00) dollars to keep up the scholarships we started last year. I think I mentioned before that I want mine given to a girl who is preparing herself to teach.

I have, or rather we have, received five or six copies of your Report, all but one of which are wasted, as one is enough. There is no "Mrs. Newlin," in the household. I read your Reports & the "Southern Letter" regularly and watch your progress with much interest. I am sorry you do not follow in the footsteps of Hampton as to mentioning pupils with out titles. In the school where I was educated the teachers never spoke of the girls with any title, but simply as Jane or Eliza so & so, and I think such simplicity is more natural and wholesome than your way, young people are indirectly taught by it that they are expected to earn the respect that titles imply, and claiming, and being expected to claim, little for themselves they are apt to deserve the more. Truly yours,

Sarah Newlin

I was rejoiced to read that you "would not change [your] colour if [you] could." Certainly that makes you a better leader for your people and you have a noble work in your hands on which I congratulate you.

P.S. I have just noticed that almost all your contributors are set down in your Report without title, while your pupils are always mentioned as "Mr." and "Miss" So & so. This is curious! It reverses the order of nature.

ALS   Con. 103   BTW Papers   DLC.   Brackets appeared in the original. BTW wrote in the margin: "Mr. Logan   I think it well to give attention to what she says about titles. B.T.W."

[1] Katherine Newlin.

To William Addison Benedict

[Tuskegee, Ala.] February 8th [189]2

My dear Mr. Benedict: I have received yours of Feb. 1st mentioning the bequest of Dr. R. W. Wood.[1] One of the executors, Mr. R. C. Humphreys, had already written me some time ago about this bequest. Dr. Wood began giving small sums to the school when it was first organized and gave every year until his death.

We note up to this time you have not sent in any report for the month of January. I am sorry that your work so far does not fulfill expectations. In my first correspondence with you you will remember we said we had tried several persons in connection with the collection of funds for this institution, and with almost no exception they had not paid their expenses. When we considered your appointment I said to our treasurer and others that I felt quite sure you will prove an exception.

You remember you said in one of your previous letters that you could raise $30,000 per year for the institution and we were led to believe that your experience and acquaintance with people would enable you to secure funds without having to go through the long, "breaking in" process that a man unacquainted with the ways and means would go through, and when you sent your report for December you said the one for January would show quite a different state of things. The time has now come when we must look facts squarely in the face in a business way. So far as the figures before us show you have collected in all $269.21, $25 of this comes from Miss Amelia H. Jones of New Bedford, who for the last six years has given us regularly every year $50, but her last address was put down Boston, so in this way you were misled; but up to the first of February this institution owes you $625, and you have collected of this amount $269, thus leaving the institution in debt to you in the sum of $356. So you see we are poorer by this amount than we were this time last year, and at the same time our salary account is very much enlarged by your being employed, thus making the appropriation of money spent for securing funds very much larger than it should be and throwing us open to the criticism of the public along that line. These are plain facts that we in our relation to the public cannot escape. I hope you will not understand that I mean to speak in an unkindly spirit. I think we will both understand each other by being business-like and frank.

The book on Anatomy and Physiology has been placed in the hands of our resident physician who will use it. Yours truly,

B. T. Washington

TLpS   Con. 106   BTW Papers   DLC.

[1] Robert Williams Wood (1803-92), a graduate of Waterville (later Colby) College and Bowdoin College Medical School. He lived from 1839 until 1866 in the Hawaiian Islands, first in charge of the American Hospital for Seamen in Honolulu and then as a grower and manufacturer of sugar, a crop he is credited with introducing to Hawaii. His acquaintance with Tuskegee Institute may have come through Samuel Chapman Armstrong or James Fowle Baldwin Marshall, both of whom had many ties with Hawaii.

From Elie G. Reese[1]

Normal School   Tuskegee Ala. Feb-11-1892

Dear Sir   it is with much plesure that I wright to you Mr Wisington
I want to do you hear to Student when there have not been treated
right by Teachers. I have not ben treade right. Mr. Roy have not
treat me right he nock me on the head like I was some dog this morning and he told me that when I come back there that he was going to
whip me. he got his whip this morning to whip me but I came up here.
Mr Wishington I do not want to go back down thire I want to be
treated lik I am human but if I go back down thire he will not treat
me right. I have all redy writen to my mother a bout how Mr Roy
done me   he will not bother th large Boy's but he will bother the
litter Boy's.
   ansew this if you plese. forme

Elie G. Reese

ALS   Con. 103   BTW Papers   DLC.

[1] Recorded in the Tuskegee catalog as Ely Reese of Montgomery, in the B
preparatory class in 1891-92.

To Norma E. Walker

[Tuskegee, Ala.] Feb. 13th [189]2

Miss Walker: The Faculty have considered in all of its bearing the
offence of your speaking in the presence of students and teachers in
the dining room sarcastically and in a manner unbecoming a teacher,
of the action of the Faculty in inspecting your department.
   We have been careful to get the evidence of a number of those who
heard the remarks and the tone and spirit in which they were spoken
and are convinced that the indiscretion has been committed. Such
action of a teacher strikes at the heart of the institution and cannot be
tolerated. We have decided to ask you to put in writing what you

have said to us verbally — that is that you meant no disrepect towards the Faculty. We also request you to state in writing that you regret the spirit and character of your language. When this is done we shall consider the matter at an end. Yours truly,

B. T. Washington

TLpS   Con. 106   BTW Papers   DLC.

From Thomas McCants Stewart

New York, February 16, 1892

My Dear Prof. Washington: I have your very kind letter telling me, that the Trustees of your Institute may again want me to deliver the address at your Commencement in May next, and asking me whether I can accept.

At this writing, I don't know what to say. I am afraid I cannot get away from engagements here; but I shall look through my court and general calendar and endeavor to see what is ahead. I shall also enquire as to whether I can come through to Tuskegee on a Pullman Car, and escape both the Separate Car Law and the roughs who, judging from reports, sometimes invade the Pullman and take passengers out, and force them into the "Jim Crow" car.

If I should decide to come down, can I get away from Tuskegee without being subjected to indignities by the Railroad Company, which indignities I do not court, and which I propose to avoid as long as I possibly can, if not for the rest of my natural life? Yours truly,

T. McCants Stewart

P.S. Have just had a call from Dr. Derrick. Perhaps, best not to depend upon me. Some of my time this year will be given to our Gen'l Conf.

TLS   Con. 99   BTW Papers   DLC.   The postscript is in Stewart's hand.

To John Gideon Harris

[Tuskegee, Ala.] February 20th [189]2

Dear Sir: Since you were here I have thought and planned much in regard to the Summer Institute on the plan suggested by you, and am convinced that it will be an improvement on the plan adopted last year. If I correctly understand your plan, it is to have the institute held at some central point for three or four weeks, and get the teachers from a number of the counties to attend. This, I am sure, would accomplish more good than a small institute held for three or four days only in a place.

After giving the matter careful attention I am inclined to think that Union Springs, Bullock County, is the place where such an institute could be made the greatest success, for these reasons:

1st. The County Superintendent[1] takes a deep interest in the colored teachers.

2nd. It is a small place and many of the teachers would be boarded for nothing, and the others would have to pay but little.

3rd. The people, both white and colored, would take pride in seeing the institute made a success.

4th. The teachers would attend from Bullock, Macon, Pike, Russell, Lee, Barbour, Henry, Coffee and Dale Counties.

With $300 or $400 I could secure a number of first class teachers, well up in the latest methods, and who would devote their head and heart to the work.

Now is the time to secure good instructors, and to begin organizing and advertising, and I hope you will hear from Dr. Curry soon. Yours truly,

B. T. Washington

TLpS   Con. 106   BTW Papers   DLC.

[1] W. C. Wilson.

Samuel Chapman Armstrong to the Tuskegee Faculty

Hampton, Va. Feb. 23, 1892

Dear Friends: Many thanks for your most kind and thoughtful letter of Feb. 17th.

It is trying to be confined to one's bed for months but my prospects of ultimate recovery seem bright. All this is a part of life's discipline meant for good by God who sent it with its special lesson of patience and submission which I am trying to learn.

The record of Hampton graduates is the greatest comfort to my life. Tuskegee is perhaps the brightest spot in the South; those who make it so and have made it what it is are an e[a]rnest and noble set of workers in whose records and triumphs I find the greatest satisfaction and comfort.

The hundreds of little candles lit by Hampton and Tuskegee are, I believe in the line of God's special and providential care and will I hope multiply many times in the dark places of this country. It is killing work to get the necessary funds to spread the needed light but I believe that if we do our work well aid and relief will come at the last moment and prevent any disaster to the mother institutions.

God speed you all at Tuskegee. You are a comfort to me and your loyalty to duty and sound ideas make the future of Tuskegee and of your own lives truly great.

While I am dictating this the convention at Tuskegee is doubtless going on. I am extremely sorry that I can not be there and await with the keenest interest Miss Ludlow's report of it all. It is a wise move and will do good. There is nothing like the gospel of common sense and patient self reliance and great hope and faith. These, I believe, you all have. Preach and practice them and all will go well. Long live Tuskegee and her noble army of workers. Faithfully your friend

S. C. Armstrong

HLSr Con. 101 BTW Papers DLC. The salutation reads: "Dictated to the Teachers of the Tuskegee School."

The Declarations of the First Tuskegee Negro Conference[1]

[Tuskegee, Ala., Feb. 23, 1892]

We, some of the representatives of the colored people, living in the Black Belt, the heart of the South, thinking it might prove of interest and value to our friends throughout the country, as well as beneficial to ourselves, have met together in conference to present facts and express opinions as to our Industrial, Moral and Educational condition, and to exchange views as to how our own efforts and the kindly helpfulness of our friends may best contribute to our elevation.

First. Set at liberty with no inheritance but our bodies, without training in self-dependence, and thrown at once into commercial, civil and political relations with our former owners, we consider it a matter of great thankfulness that our condition is as good as it is, and that so large a degree of harmony exists between us and our white neighbors.

Second. Industrially considered, most of our people are dependent upon Agriculture. The majority of them live on rented lands, mortgage their crops for the food on which to live from year to year, and usually at the beginning of each year are more or less in debt for the supplies of the previous year.

Third. Not only is our own material progress hindered by the mortgage system, but also that of our white friends. It is a system that tempts us to buy much that we would do without if cash were required and it tends to lead those who advance the provisions and lend the money, to extravagant prices and ruinous rates of interest.

Fourth. In a moral and religious sense, while we admit there is much laxness in morals and superstition in religion, yet we feel that much progress has been made, that there is a growing public sentiment in favor of purity and that the people are fast coming to make their religion less of superstition and emotion and more of a matter of daily living.

Fifth. As to our educational condition, it is to be noted that our country schools are in session on an average only 3½ months each year, that the Gulf States are as yet unable to provide school houses and as a result the schools are held almost out of doors or at best in such rude quarters as the poverty of the people is able to provide, that the teachers are poorly paid and often very poorly fitted for their work, and as a result of these things, both parents and scholars take but little interest in the schools, often but few children attend and these with great irregularity.

Sixth. That in view of our general condition, we would suggest the following remedies: 1st, That as far as possible, we aim to raise at home our own meat and bread. 2d, That as fast as possible, we buy land, even though a very few acres at a time. 3rd, That a larger number of young people be taught trades and that they be urged to prepare themselves to enter as largely as possible all the various avocations of life. 4th, That we especially try to broaden the field of labor for our women. 5th, That we make every sacrifice and practice every form of economy to purchase land and free ourselves from the burdensome habit of living in debt. 6th, That we urge our ministers and teachers to give more attention to the material condition and home-life of the people. 7th, We urge that our people do not depend entirely upon the State to provide school houses and lengthen the time of the schools, but that they take hold of the matter themselves where the State leaves off, and by supplementing the public funds from their own pockets and by building school houses, bring about the desired results. 8th, We urge patrons to give earnest attention to the mental and moral fitness of those who teach their schools. 9th, That we urge the doing away with all sectarian prejudice in the management of the schools.

Seventh. As the judgment of this conference we would further declare: That we put on record our deep sense of gratitude to the good people of all sections for their assistance and that we are glad to recognize a growing interest on the part of the best white people of the South in the education of the Negro.

Eighth. That we appreciate the spirit of friendliness and fairness shown us by the Southern white people in matters of business in all lines of material development.

Ninth. That we believe our generous friends of the country can best aid in our elevation by continuing to give their help where it will result in producing strong Christian leaders who will live among the masses as object lessons, showing them how to direct their own efforts towards the general uplifting of the people.

Tenth. That we believe we can become prosperous, intelligent, and independent where we are, and we discourage any efforts at wholesale emigration and recognizing that our home is to be in the South, we urge that all strive in every way to cultivate the good feeling and friendship of those about us in all that relates to our mutual elevation.

Southern Workman, 21 (Mar. 1892), 41, 45.

[1] BTW considered the first Tuskegee Negro Conference "a day memorable in the lives and fortunes of the great bulk of the Negro population in the 'Black Belt' of the South. It was a strange and altogether new movement in which the Negro was called upon to participate." He invited about seventy-five "of the common, hard-working farmers, as well as mechanics, ministers and teachers," and was surprised when "nearly 400 men and women of all kinds and conditions came." (See above, 1:135-36; for another account of the early conferences, see BTW, "How I Came to Call the First Negro Conference," *A.M.E. Church Review,* 15 [Apr. 1899], 802-8.)

The actual proceedings of the first conference were recorded and a typescript was made. A search of the BTW Papers has not, however, uncovered the typescript. Subsequent conferences were reported fully in the *Southern Workman* and occasionally in newspapers such as the Montgomery *Advertiser.* BTW was especially cautious regarding coverage of the first conference, and he released only the formal declarations. (See BTW to William Torrey Harris, May 4, 1892, below.)

To Samuel Chapman Armstrong

Tuskegee, Ala., February 26th 1892

Dear Gen. Armstrong: You will, I know, excuse my not writing this letter with my own hand. I am now in a great rush just arranging my affairs to start North in a few days, and I want to send this letter to give you a little idea of the Conference in advance of Miss Ludlow's arrival home. You will be glad to know that the conference was a success beyond anything anyone of us had dared anticipate. There were not far from 500 men present representing 13 counties in the heart of the "Black Belt." They were the hard working farmers, and some teachers & ministers the bone and sinew of the race. I am quite sure it would have rejoiced your heart, could you have been here to witness the sound common sense which they displayed. There was little complaint. They showed clearly and saw and realized their miserable condition, and that they wanted light, and they all realized that education was their only salvation. Although I had sent invitations to the best in each community, in the afternoon when there were 425 present we asked those who owned land free from debt to hold up their hands and only 23 did so. The whole day was spent in receiving facts of the most valuable and encouraging character. The most encouraging thing in my opinion was to see the amount of hard common sense that these people have in spite of their ignorance and poverty and their keen realization of their present condition. There were no long speeches, no cut and dried programme; everyone felt free to tell his condition and that [of his] neighbors; they did this most admirably. The native eloquence, wit, and humor displayed in describing their condition were intensely interesting.

Another thing that interested me, perhaps, as much as any thing else, was the great amount of interest shown by the American Missionary Association. Through Dr. Beard[1] you will be surprised and glad to know that the association sent three of its strongest men here, including Prof. Wright,[2] to take part in the convention and to report the proceedings for the Northern papers. These men were of great help and value. Prof. Wright who naturally takes a gloomy view of things said to me after he spent three days at the school and one in the convention, that in all of his travels and connections with this Southern work he had never seen anything that had given him so much light and encouragement as what he had seen at the Conference and of the influence of this institution in this vicinity. The other two A.M.A. representatives were stronger in their approval and the results of the conference. One of the others said that the day's proceedings were a perfect revelation to him. The proceedings of the Conference were most keenly sought after by Northern papers. There were reporters here from the Independent, Christian Union, Congregationalist, Advance, and the Chicago Inter-Ocean sent a staff correspondent to report the proceedings. Three letters descriptive of the school and the Conference are to appear soon in the Inter-Ocean. Every one present expressed himself as being anxious that these meetings be held every year. I think this will be done.

I have been hoping to call by Hampton to secure some teachers for next year on my trip to the North, but I fear I will not be able to do this before my return South in April.

Miss Stokes[3] who is to give the new building will be here to-morrow to complete the arrangements for the building. The plans for it are being drawn in New York.

We are very anxious to have a full account of the proceedings published in pamphlet form and Commissioner Harris[4] has written that he thinks his department can aid in publishing them. I don't know if it will be of advantage to have the Bureau of Education publish the proceedings or not. Hastily yours,

Booker T. Washington

TLS BTW Folder ViHaI. A few minor changes appear in BTW's hand.

[1] Augustus Field Beard.

[2] Walter Eugene Colburn Wright (1843-1908) graduated from Oberlin College in 1865 and Union Theological Seminary in 1868. A Congregationalist minister, he served as professor of natural science at Berea College from 1882 to 1890. From 1890 to 1892 he was field superintendent for the American Missionary Association, and later was professor at Olivet College in Michigan.

[3] Olivia Egleston Phelps Stokes.

[4] William Torrey Harris (1835-1909), a distinguished Hegelian philosopher, was superintendent of the St. Louis schools (1868-80) and U.S. Commissioner of Education (1889-1906).

From Margaret James Murray

[Tuskegee, Ala.] Feb. 27 92

Mr. Washington   I wish that you would speak to the gentlemen teachers in regard to their actions at Ala. Hall. Almost all at least too many of them stand in the halls [or] on the porch and spend their time talking to the girls. It not only looks badly but it injures the girls and does not benefit. The teachers (ladies) and girls also are speaking of it and they feel as I do. Mr. Green[1] the painter even went so far as to ask for the company of one of the girls. All almost all of them should be spoken to and this conduct should be stopped. A good deal of it is really disgusting and foolish and I am sure that a hint to these men will be sufficient. Respectfully

M. J. Murray

ALS Con. 949 BTW Papers DLC.

[1] John C. Green taught house and carriage painting from 1892 to 1912.

From Mary A. Elliott

Columbus Ohio. March 16th 1892

My Dear Brother. It has been a good while since I have written to you, but my heart felt wishes are with you evry day. I dreamed of being down with you all at the School last night and it is all so fresh in my mind that I thought I would write. I think it was reading the little papers that made me dream of being with you all. It appears to me as though I am and have lived an aimless life. When I read of all that you have done and are still doing, and of the great progress beyond expectation that the School is making it is wonderful, and to look back just a few years and to see where and how you started with a small School, and with what rapid strides it has made in number, and prominence. It almost makes one dizzy. I know that there were many impediments to overcome, and the dark clouds of sorrow have risen over the way, yet through the help of God you have come out triumphant so far and better fited for your life work than ever before. It is hard to say, *Thy will be done.* I have not been able to say it untill a short time ago. All I can say Dear brother it is my prayr that as you are battleing for the right that you may not grow weary and that success may crown your evry effort.

I received the children's pictures and am glad that you was so kind and thoughtful as to send them to me, as this is the first one of little Davidson's that I have ever had of my own. I alwais have to go over to Grandma's to look at him. I think the children all three have grown a great deal. Davidson looks so sweet and cute with his little chuby hands and his hair roached up on his forehead if Aunt Mary could just get a hold she could love him almost to death would squeeze him hard she fears. Kiss them all for me Grandma and Uncle Dock sends love. Grandma sais thanks for the pretty Christmas rememberance you sent to her. I dont see Hiram very often since the weather has been cold. He got religion this winter. The weather is very cold here for the past week moderateing a little today.

We are all as well as usal. Hope this may [find] you and children well. All my love and give your brother J & wife my regards   Good by

M. A. Elliott

ALS   Con. 17   BTW Papers   DLC.

222

From Warren Logan

Tuskegee, Ala., March 22nd 1892

Dear Mr. Washington: I am very glad indeed to hear of the good results of the Hartford meeting. The Misses Collins[1] have sent in their donation for the Water Works and I have acknowledged same. I have also written them that I would take the $500.00 and lend it to Farmers with the understanding that they are to return it the next fall with interest, interest being at a lower rate than they are accustomed to paying. Yours truly,

Warren Logan

TLS   Con. 99   BTW Papers   DLC.

[1] Ellen and Mary Collins.

From Warren Logan

Tuskegee, Ala., Mar 23 1892

Dear Mr Washington   Mr Bedford has just returned from Selma & Montgomery. He says the Ala. Literary at Montgomery have engaged Fred Douglass for $100. to speak in the Opera House in Montgomery on the *night of Commencement*. In order to keep this appointment it will be necessary for him to leave the school at 5 o'clock. I think we should try to prevent Mr Douglass' going to Montgomery on the same day he speaks here and think it can be done if the matter is put before him in the right way. Yours truly

Warren Logan

ALS   Con. 100   BTW Papers   DLC.

To Alex C. Bradford[1]

Tuskegee, Ala., April 29th 1892

My dear Sir: When in Washington day before yesterday I saw Mr. Douglass and learned from him that he himself had written you or had asked Mr. Calloway[2] to do so, telling you that he thought he would have to change his arrangement and speak there on the 25 and here on the 26. This I told Mr. Douglass I could not agree to and he asked me to see you, which I attempted to do when I was in Montgomery last night but you were gone from your place of business, that he would have to re-arrange his plan and speak in Montgomery on the night of the 26th leaving here in the evening to be with you for your meeting. This arrangement he says will be final. If you have not already done so you will receive a letter from him or from Mr. Calloway, his agent, speaking of this matter. He is very sorry, as well as myself, that so many changes have had to be made. I hope you will not misunderstand me in the matter. Having Mr. Douglass come here is a matter of business. It will be hard for you to understand the great amount of expense I have had [to go] through to accomplish this purpose. In addition to getting Mr. Douglass here I have to pay a man to accompany him on this trip, and you see it will not be proper treatment of us for him, after accepting our invitation, to go to another place near by and speak before coming to us. All public lecturers are very careful in a matter of this kind. It has taken me nearly six months to arrange this trip and [I] have had to bring pressure to bear from a very large number of sources in order to get Mr. Douglass to come. I write you these facts early so that you may know what to depend on. In case this arrangement is carried out I shall do all I can to make your meeting in Montgomery a success. I shall see that the exercises here are closed in plenty of time to allow Mr. Douglass to take the train for Montgomery and also make an announcement if you desire it of the meeting. As he will have a different subject there many will be attracted to your meeting from our Commencement. I am perfectly willing to co-operate with you and the Montgomery people in any way I can, but at the same time I must keep in view the interest of this institution, for it is the institution's money that is being spent.

I think you will receive a letter from Mr. Douglass or Mr. Calloway either to-morrow or next day. Yours truly

B. T. Washington

TLpS Con. 106 BTW Papers DLC.

[1] Alex C. Bradford, a black barber in Montgomery. According to the evidence of the 1880 census, he would have been about forty-seven in 1892.

[2] Thomas Junius Calloway?

To Frederick Douglass

[Tuskegee, Ala.] April 29th [189]2

Dear Mr. Douglass: According to promise I have delivered your message to Mr. A. C. Bradford in Montgomery to the effect that you would speak there on the night of the 26th of May, and not on the 25th, leaving here after our Commencement exercises in time to reach Montgomery for the lecture there. This arrangement I find can be made to work, and this arrangement I have said to Mr. Bradford would be final. For you to speak in Montgomery before coming here, would defeat one of the main objects which I have in view in having you at Tuskegee, and I hope you will not consider for a moment any proposition to appear at any meeting in Alabama before coming to Tuskegee. I shall go ahead with our arrangements with the understanding above stated. We shall look for you here on the 24th. Yours truly,

B. T. W.

TLpI   Con. 106   BTW Papers   DLC.

To Eliza Bolling[1]

[Tuskegee, Ala.] May 3rd [189]2

Miss Bolling: The Faculty has decided to ask you to have the girls' rooms given a thorough cleaning this week with a view of trying to get rid of the bed bugs that are to be found in all the buildings.

It is not to the credit of the school and much to its hurt to have the constant report of bed bugs existing in the rooms. The girls not only talk about the matter among themselves but report it to their parents, and it brings disgrace on the institution. The cleanliness of the rooms is in your hands and we hold you responsible for this. Miss Murray says that she has spoken to you about the matter several times and given you a girl to do the work, but it has not been done. I have told Miss Murray to let you have as many girls as you desire. Dr. Dillon will help you in making any mixture to help eradicate the bed bugs. This must be attended to right away. I wish to have the buildings cleaned this week. This cleaning must be done once a week during the remainder of the term so that we can get rid of this pest.

In this connection I wish to say that it will amount to nothing without your remaining constantly with them while they are doing the cleaning. This [we want] you to do until each room is thoroughly cleaned. Any help that Miss Murray or myself or any one else can give you we shall be glad to give, but we shall rely on you personally that the work is thoroughly done.

B. T. Washington

TLpS Con. 106 BTW Papers DLC.

¹ Eliza Bolling was matron of Alabama Hall, the women's dormitory, in 1891-92. Born in Farmville, Va., she was an 1881 graduate of Hampton.

To William Torrey Harris

[Tuskegee, Ala.] May 4th 1892

My dear Sir: I have not yet sent you the proceedings of the Tuskegee Negro Conference for the reason that the more I think over it the more I seem to be convinced that it is not wise to publish the proceedings in full. I fear that if this is done it would tend to restrict discussion in the future and embarrass persons who take part in the meeting. In order that the meetings be valuable they must be free in every sense. We have not yet gotten to the point in the South, I fear, where we can discuss the interests of the race along all the lines with perfect freedom. While I know that there is much in the report that would be of value, still I fear the cause of education would be more hindered than helped by publishing the proceedings. We have them carefully type-written and shall at any rate keep the matter for future reference. I shall be glad to know your opinion on this point. Yours truly,

Booker T. Washington

TLS File 901 Office of Education RG12 DNA.

To William Burns Paterson

[Tuskegee, Ala.] May 4th [189]2

Dear Sir: Yours of May 2nd has been received and is somewhat of a surprise to me. I would say, however, at the outset that it is against my custom to make reply in regard to tales that are floating about in the air. Any man who is at all before the public will have any number of stories put into his ears, and if he permits himself to be influenced by them I find he will impair his usefulness for work, and it has been my rule to neither deny nor affirm such stories. While of course I knew that Mr. Council[1] in speaking before the Legislative Committee used your color to prejudice the members against you I do not know that he used your color in connection with the State Teachers' Association in the same way. If you fear that your continued connection with the State Teachers' Association will be used against you to hurt your work in Montgomery, that of course is a matter that you alone can decide. But granting that what you have heard regarding the conversation had by myself and Mr. Council is true I don't think that would excuse you from not participating in the work of the State Teachers' Association. Mr. Council and myself are but individuals, the association is a public body, we are not the association.

In regard to any conversation had by myself and Mr. Council concerning you I wish to say most emphatically that the report which you say you have heard is entirely false. I have never in public or in private said or intimated that I was against your holding your present position. On the other hand I have always said that I was opposed to drawing the color line in any way. I told Mr. Logan and others who worked for Tuskegee to secure the Federal Grant that if we could not get it without drawing the color line not to fight for it. Further I am opposed to putting any colored man in a position simply because he is colored, or removing a white man from a position where he is doing well simply because of his color. The colored people should be the last people in the world to draw the color line. I have said on more than one occasion that we as a race should not be ungrateful but should show our gratitude to the white people who helped us when we were unable to help ourselves. If I had it in my power to say who should be president of the Montgomery school I should certainly give my vote to you. What I did say perhaps in a conversation with more than one person in Huntsville was that I thought you made a mistake in allowing your feelings towards Mr. Council to prevent your attending the Huntsville meeting and that opinion I still hold. Mr. Council is not the association. The Association met in the town of Huntsville and not in Mr. Council's school, and I still hold that opinion regarding the Birmingham meeting.

Now I suppose the person[2] who told the tale to you regarding the Huntsville conversation will be just as ready when I see him to bring a tale to me that he heard from you. I think you allow yourself to be unduly exercised over efforts which you hear are being made to oust you out of your position. I do not believe there are efforts of the kind being made.

Thanking you for your kind words and wishes for success, I am, Yours truly,

Booker T. Washington

It is my opinion that if you drop out of the State Association it is going to place you in an attitude to be misunderstood and impair your usefulness.

B. T. W.

TLpS   Con. 106   BTW Papers   DLC.   The postscript is in BTW's hand.

[1] William Hooper Councill.
[2] Possibly J. D. Bibb. (See Bibb to BTW, July 5, 1892, below.)

To William Addison Benedict

[Tuskegee, Ala.] May 11th [189]2

Dear Mr. Benedict: I think it must be plain to both of us at this time that it is not possible to make your work in the North succeed in the way we hoped it would, and I don't think it right to have our expense fund swelled to the amount that it is now being done by your salary without its resulting in a very large increased income to the school.

Within a short time we must decide on those to be employed another year, and I can see, I confess, no ground on which to recommend your re-employment, that is if I base my recommendation on what has been accomplished in the past.

You remember what I said to you when we first talked over this matter, that those persons whom we have heretofore employed [as agents] had done little more than paid their expenses, but in [your] case we find ourselves indebted to you in the sum of ... at this time. This you see is not encouraging, and I don't [think, under the circumstances,] that I can recommend your re-employment.

. . . . .

The fall, winter and spring months are the ones that ... years of experience have taught us that the money must be gotten in, and so you see it would hardly be possible for you to do better during the summer than you have done during the past months.

Please be careful not in any way to call on our old givers. Mrs Danielson of Providence, R.I., complained to me not long ago that you had called on her with reference to money for the girls' building. Mrs Danielson had made an extra donation and of course it was not pleasant to be called on a second time within a short time. Yours truly,

Booker T. Washington

TLpS Con. 106 BTW Papers DLC. This is a dim and incompletely reproduced press copy.

An Address to the Graduating Class of Tuskegee Institute

[Tuskegee, Ala., May 26] 1892

To those of us who live in the South, the cotton plant is a very familiar and interesting object. There are none of you that do not understand to what an extent our prosperity depends upon this vegetable. You know with what care and solicitude we prepare the ground, you know how we plant, hoe, and plow and with what anxiety and expense we protect this plant, from every thing that endangers its life or hinders its development. You know how we watch its every stage of growth. When we see the bud we say that is hopeful, when the flower appears we say that is beautiful, but our reward does not come and our anxiety is not relieved till the cotton — the fruit appears in all its beauty and grandeur. Without the fruit, the plowing, the planting, the hoeing would all have been lost — would all have been in vain.

And after the fruit is borne we some times take interest in watching

.   .   .   .

have tried to protect you here and strengthen you there, how we have urged you forward in this and held you back in that. You know how our hands, heads, and hearts have been wrapped up in you by day and by night.

As your teachers with the giving of these diplomas our official work is done. Like the farmer we are now ready to "lay you by." But as with the cotton plant our work will all have been in vain unless the fruit — the cotton comes. Will you bear fruit? The answer is with you. The answer must come not alone in resolves, or words, but in high and earnest deeds for the elevation of your brothers and sisters. For the longer I live the more I am convinced that the only thing worth living for is the lifting up of our fellow man.

The saddest day in the history of any institution is when it hears of the failure of one of its graduates, the happiest, when it hears of one's success.

With all the seeming disadvantage of race, color, & poverty with which you will meet, I believe that no class, ever went out of any institution, black or white, North or South, with a brighter prospect for a useful and successful life than is before you. For it is the history of the world that before a man who is a gentleman in earnest with real worth, color, race, poverty, accident of birth and every other obstacle gives way. God bless you all.

ADf Con. 955 BTW Papers DLC. Page 2 of this 4-page document is missing.

An Account of the Tuskegee Institute Commencement

[Tuskegee, Ala., May 26, 1892]

On May 26th occurred the Eleventh Annual Commencement of the Tuskegee Normal and Industrial School, at Tuskegee, Alabama.

This notable institution does more than send out its annual quota of colored teachers to the field; its very presence is an inspiration and an education to the neighborhood. This is evidenced by the multitudes who assemble to witness its annual Commencement excercises. The sight was a most picturesque one. Early in the morning the visitors began to arrive; in wagons, in carts, in ox-teams, on horse-back, on mule-back and on foot. Gray-headed men and bright-eyed children marched along, eager to see what was being done by the sons and daughters of their people. From miles and miles away they came; and by noon the School grounds were filled almost to overflowing. A moderate estimate places the number of visitors at five thousand. The mule teams and other vehicles lined the road many deep for a quarter of a mile.

After a morning spent in the inspection of classes and in examining products from the School farm and workshops, the vast throng of spectators assembled in the "Pavilion," a rough temporary structure, to listen to the Hon. Frederick Douglass, of Washington, D.C., who delivered the annual address.[1] His subject was "Self made Men," and he spoke, in spite of his three score and fifteen years, with all the eloquence, spirit and humor of youth. The tenor of the speech, so far as it touched upon race questions, was calm and dispassionate. He urged economy, thrift and common sense, and declared that the Negro had no right to live unless he could live honestly, giving a fair equivalent for everything he received. "Let us alone, and give us a fair chance," said he. "But be sure you *do* give us a fair chance. That's very important."

A graduates' reception in the evening concluded the exercises of the day. The Senior Class this year numbers fifteen; six girls and nine boys. It is safe to say that they will do all in their power to help their people in the line of practical progress, and do what they can to leaven that great mass of ignorance and superstition in which their work will be cast.

Southern Workman, 21 (July 1892), 122. Written by E. W. Blake.

[1] Robert C. Bedford, writing for the Montgomery *Advertiser,* reported that Douglass was favorably impressed with the changes in Alabama when compared with the past. "Verily," Douglass said, "it would seem as if John's apocalyptic vision was realized and that he looked on a new heaven and a new earth." (Montgomery *Advertiser,* May 27, 1892, 3.)

To Charles W. Greene

[Tuskegee, Ala.] May 31st [189]2

Mr. Greene: The Superintendent of Industries[1] makes complaint to the faculty about several matters concerning your work. Some of these matters I have spoken to you about before, but there seems to be no change in regard to them. It is but just to you to say that these matters have been complained about so long that they have reached a serious point where we sh[a]ll be comp[e]lled to take action that we do not want to take if it can be avoided, unless there is a change.

Take for example the fence around the brick-yard. The school has paid out a large sum of money for wire fencing, and the fence is practically amounting to nothing, owing to the fact that the rail fence is either left down or the gate to the field left open almost every night. This matter you are in charge of and you are paid to keep these things in order, and I should not have my time taken up when it can be occupied in the interest of the school in other ways, reminding you what your duties are in regard to these matters. There is no reason whatever why the fence cannot be kept up and the gate shut and the brick-yard pasture used to some good.

Notwithstanding all that has been said about the feeding of the stock there is still no system in regard to the feeding. Hay and oats are not cut up as they should be. The Superintendent of Industries reports you for not obeying his orders in regard to letting the cows remain over night in the nut grass field. I am sure that you will find that a large part of this trouble comes from your not giving personal attention, but relying entirely on the students. It will not do to tell students to do any work; personal attention is needed. In this connection I wish to remind you that you are relieved from all out-side work, more so than our former farm managers. Mr. Ferguson[2] has had to superintend the plastering, making bricks and doing other work, and now we have gone to the expense of hiring a man to take charge of the brick-yard, so that you will give more personal attention to the duties of the farm, and still your work is not done satisfactorily. I hope that this will be the last time I shall refer to these matters. I dislike to have to speak in this way, but my duty to the school compels me to.

I wish you would report to me in writing some time this week what your plan is with regard to the disposing of the milk and the making of butter. It would be most important that the milk be made to yield the greatest income in every way possible.

I think that you will find that the injury done to our two horses is due to the want of system in feeding of the horses. To have two of the most valuable horses injured in this way is a very great financial loss to the school.

Mr. Chambliss[3] complains that sand is not supplied regularly at the brick-yard nor mud ground. Please report to me what is necessary in order to remedy this trouble. How much more team is necessary?

In regard to the feed of the stock we have gone to the expense of getting a cutter, but the Superintendent of Industries reports that this cutter is seldom used. It is impossible for me to spend more time in taking up your department in the way that I have, and I ask you most earnestly to make a change in regard to your work.

B. T. Washington

TLpS Con. 106 BTW Papers DLC.

[1] John Henry Washington.
[2] Henry Clay Ferguson.
[3] William Vivian Chambliss.

From L. J. Hall

Colorado State Penitentiary   Cañon City, Colo., June 7th 1892

Dear Sir: In answer to yours of the 2nd inst relative to Frank Crawford, an inmate of this institution I would say that the prisoners are allowed to have good reading, such as magazines weekly papers &c they are not allowed the daily or Sunday edition of daily papers. Papers and stamps for their correspondence are furnished them. Enclosed you will find copy of the rules governing these matters. Books of study are allowed. Very Respectfully

L. J. Hall
Chaplain

HLSr Con. 17 BTW Papers DLC.

An Address before the Alabama State Teachers' Association

[Birmingham, Ala., June 8, 1892]

AIMS AND RESULTS OF TEACHING

Ladies and Gentlemen of the State Teachers' Association: It is well for us as educators, once in a while to pause in the midst of our labors, and ask ourselves what are the ends in view for which we are laboring, what are the results for which we are toiling, what is the type of humanity which education seeks to develop? In the membership of this Association we have represented the teacher whose days are spent in the isolated log cabin, with spelling book and primer as well as the college professor whose hours are occupied with the higher forms of science and literature. No matter how seemingly humble or how exalted may be the position — what is the goal towards which all in common are struggling? In this utilitarian age when hands and minds are so largely occupied with things material — with that which seeks for shelter, food and clothing we are tempted as educators to forget the end and mistake the means for the end to be attained. Some of us seek to make a skilled hand, to give practical knowledge of agriculture, to give a technical and scientific knowledge that will enable one to help supply the immediate wants of the body — that will not only enable one to make himself independent by supplying himself with this world's goods, but will put him in a position to administer to the material necessities of his fellows. All this is well and most praiseworthy, but this is not the end of education — to provide the stomach, to fill the pocket, to shelter the body, but pave the way to that far off and higher purpose. First we teach the child about our knee the word, then the sentence; then the numbers. Soon follow history and the sciences.

If we have not as teachers learned to do so, let us begin to use our curriculum of studies as so many pillars in the pyramid that is to bear our pupils upward. If we choose, let us make reading, grammar, rhetoric, one pillar; geography and history another; science another; ethics and the Bible another, but let it ever be borne in mind that these are but *means* not *ends* — that these studies are but instruments to lead our pupils up, up into that higher atmosphere of truth, virtue, love and unselfishness and higher still till they learn to lose themselves in service for others and it can be said of them as of the great Teacher: "They went about doing good." This, fellow teachers, I consider the true end of all education.

Oh, my co-workers, let us not degrade our calling by considering that our mission is merely to cram the mind with facts or to fit our pupils to pass an examination, to give ability to earn a living or to make them skilled in the tricks of trade. No, ours is a higher, nobler mission than any of these — the formation of a Christ-like character. As compared to this,

> What are "Place, titles, salary or gilded chain?"

*   *   *   *

> "Greatness and Goodness are not means, but ends."

My friends, do any of you feel discouraged, disheartened — do any of you feel that your work is a drudgery — that your school work the past year has been a failure, have any of you had such miserable surroundings that your heart sinks whenever you enter your school house or boarding place? If these things have been true of any of you, let me suggest that you cannot imagine what a change, yes, what a revolution it will make in your feelings and influence, if, instead of going about your task merely to have so much geography or history, or arithmetic, mastered or memorized, you teach with the idea uppermost of training an immortal soul — of forming character in the highest and best sense of changing habits of falsifying into habits of truth, of changing dishonesty into honesty, of changing laziness into thrift, of changing sin into righteousness, of teaching the pupils to:

> Look UP and not DOWN
> To look out and not in,
> To look forward and not back.

My friends, let me urge you as teachers to get near to as many human souls as possible. This getting near some one is a blessed and rare privilege. Let me urge you to enter into the real life of your pupils, make their life your life, carry them in your heart by night and by day.

If we can do no more it is a great and beautiful thing to give an upward turn to even one human soul,

"Forget self in love's service and the debt
Thou canst not pay the angels shall forget,
Heaven's gate is shut to him who comes alone
Save thou a soul and it shall save thy own."

PD Con. 1113 BTW Papers DLC. Alabama State Teachers' Association, *Minutes of the Eleventh Annual Session, Held at Birmingham, Ala., June 8th, 9th, and 10th, 1892* (Tuskegee, 1893).

From Mary A. Elliott

Columbus, O. June 12th 1892

My Dear Brother, I hope this may find you all well. I Recd your kind letter of June 7th and was glad to hear from you. I feel that it is myself that should apologize for my long delay in writeing   I should have told you whither I got home safe or not. I started to write last Tuesday, but I was so crouded with work that I dident finish it. I arived home safe one week ago to day eleven ocloc 11.30 oclock A.M. and I do assure you that I suffered no inconvenience whatever   it was rather early when I started your place for breakfast. I knew that you were tired from over work and dident expect or think it necessary that you should get up. It was ondly five minuits drive   the morning was beatiful and the air braceing   dident get to the car much too soon. But after I got to Cheehaw, I had to wait untill ten 30 min. train was behind time. I got breakfast at the house of a colored woman who gives meals to transient persons so I got along allright. Whilst waiting I got a man to look for me some Magnolia buds, but he could ondly find two, but one was so far developed that it bloomed before I got to Atlanta and the other was two weak to bloom, so I brought Mother nothing but leaves, rather sad. But told her that my mind was so fraught with what I had saw and heard whilst in the South and against I got through telling her that she would be more then compensated for all the flowers that I could have brought. Dock said to

Mother that it would take Mary six months to tell all she saw and heard she laughed and said that she was glad that I went on that account. Yes I can tell something of what I see if I dont have to get up on a floor or a rostrum. But my brother if I was as able mentaly and could talk as well as you do, also others I heard whilst there, I would be willing to devote the rest of my life in the interest of you School.

I thank the Hevenly Father that He permited me to live to see it in so much glory and prosperity well to my trip again I got to Atlanta, I think a bout 2.30 oclock P.M. Emma dident know about my being in Tuskegee. I thought that I would take her on surprise so I got on street car got off at the No on Post street that I alwais wrote to and she had moved they said so I was directed to where Mr Newton her husband had been working and they told me that he had worked most two years but they had shut down. thought they knew where he did work amost two miles frume there in a nother part of the city at a large furnistre store or factory. They telephoned, and found him there, so I got on a Street Car and went by the directions given me. I went to the office and asked if there was a man by Name of E. M. Newton on their pay role and they said yes, and sent for him he was very much surprised to see me and said that Emma and children had went North a bout ten days ago, and that he was going some time next month. So there was nothing for me to do but to go back to depot but he got excused. he said I must have supper it was then 4 oclock he said they quit at 5 any way so we got on Street Car I was tired he took me to where he boarded looked like a nice place he went and dressed and come down stairs. The head lady treated me kindly, we had supper early he told me that Emma had such poor health and that she dident like Atlanta. so they had concluded to go back North, and that she and children was at this time in Cincinnati at one of his sister's on Vine St. and that I must be sure and stop and see them and they would be over joyed to see me, & that Emma had fallen frome a Cable Car just as she was getting off and had hurt herself but not fatally and he pulled a newspaper cliping out of his pocket book and I read it myself Claudine had sent it in a letter she written to him had got it that same day. he wanted me to stop and see her so I felt more lonesome then ever. So sory that I dident know it then I would not have stoped at Atlanta, lost that much time   he said he was in a steady job   he is a grainer and finisher and that he ondly gets twelve dollars a week when he use to get 18 dollar and he thinks that he had better stay untill he is sure of as good or a better one in the North. They wanted me to stay untill next day   I would be rested for my trip   no no I thanked them and that I should go to the Depot. But Mr Newton said that the train that I would have to take wouldent be in untill 10.30 oclock that eve. He tried to make things as pleasant as he could under the circumstances, taken me around and showed me a part of the city, Grady Monument with its dark figures in Bronze   perhaps you have saw it on Marrietta St. it dose not strike you as being artistic   It appears to be composed of grey and whteish granite, large and square but not tall   the squars grow smaller as they go up   I dont think it is over eight or ten feet high. he is standing on top of this pile represented in dark Bronze also two females in dark Bronze sitting one on each side of the monument low down toward the base   one represents liberty and the [other] virtue   all three of the figures are large and as black as night and looked like the foreboding of evil   saw the Goveners Mansion with many other Modern buildings   among the later the Equitable Life Assurance is the prettiest.

Atlanta dose not come up to my expectations in beaty as I have alwais heard it spoken of as a beatiful city. It has a Hit and Miss appearence, the Streets are so iregular, beautiful buildings take up a large space and then tumble down buildings a larger space. So many Colored people grouped on the corners and along streets apparently in idleness   poor people looked like they had no object in life beyond the present moment. Mr Newton went with me to Depot and I bought my ticket for Columbus   Got my bagage checked, he staid with untill I started 10 30. I got to Chattanooga next morning a bout six oclock eat my breakfast, and bought lunch to last me to Cincinnati, and I got into Cinnati a bout half past 5 oclock   think the same evenging I think, found Emma in bed   she still had bruses from the fall she got but she was a great deal better and could walk over the house but had to lay in bed most of time   looks thin and poor   the Cable car people have been to see her and offered to pay her Doctor bill or any expenses that she may have to make dureing her sickness. she appear to be comfortable   they have two rooms to themselves joining his sister   Emma sais her husband sends her money evry week and she is not needing any thing. Claudine is nearly as tall as her mother   she appears to be quiet and not quite as pretty as she use to be   favors her Aunt Olivia some also the rest of us   I felt sorry to leave them so soon but had to. Claudine she remembers little Portia   asked me all about her. Claudine and little Lizie Newton His daughter went to train with me   Emma eat breakfast with us   I left Cincin the next mornig at 7.45 min 7. oclock and 45 m   I got home the same day sunday at 11 oclock 30 min A.M.   found all well. Gald to see me. I do hope that you will forgive me for writeing such a long letter. the most of it too that could not interest you much   one thing I will not expect you to answer it. ondly wanted to tell you a bout my journey.

I can say truthfuly that I enjoyed my stay with you and children more then I can describe and indeed I met so many that were pleasent that my stay with you all sliped away faster then I wished. I hope the time may come again some time in the future that I can come again and visit you all in your pretty home   I am glad that you have been getting a long well since Miss Moore left   I thought that you would get a long better   I think the children will be alright when they have some one that can have a bett[er] influence over them. I am glad that you have made the arangement that you have   I think it will be the best thing you can do and they will be where Miss Murray can see them often   I am glad that the children have taken so kindly to her they appeared to like her when I was there. There is some thing good in her if children loves her. I like her as far as I got acquainted with her and I hope Booker that you may both live happy and understand each other   Clouds will come and almost obscure our pathway but let none come between you and her. you must remember that she will have trials with the children and you must not expect too much of her   I think she will do all she can to make your household what it should be and you will be her protector as well as the children's   May God bless you both with all three of the little children is my prayer. Give Miss Murray my love and kiss the children for me. I thank you for kindness to me   Grandma sends her love to you and children. Your Sister

M. A. Elliott

ALS Con. 128 BTW Papers DLC.

From Edward Lille Pierce[1]

Milton Mass 18 June '92

My dear Sir Yours of 15th is received.
I was greatly pleased to learn that Mrs Baker's legacy to you had been securely invested for the benefit of your family. I am always anxious that persons situated as you are shall have something to fall back upon when the capacity to earn has passed.

No one of your race interests me so much as yourself. Unlike others you *act* instead of *talking*. You work for your people instead of whining about them or seeking some public office for yourself.

Mrs Pierce[2] and myself were at Orangeburgh in April, and were delighted with all we saw.

If you come this way, I shall esteem it a privilege to have a call from you. Yours very truly

Edward L. Pierce

ALS Con. 102 BTW Papers DLC.

[1] Edward Lille Pierce (1829-97), a graduate of Brown University and Harvard Law School, served for a time as the law clerk of Salmon P. Chase, who spoke of his "cool and sound" judgment. A man of strong antislavery convictions, he served under General Benjamin F. Butler at Fortress Monroe as supervisor of the care of the black "contrabands" who escaped into the Union lines. In 1862, when Union forces seized the South Carolina sea islands, Pierce became the superintendent of a large cotton plantation at Port Royal. The experiment of transforming slaves into free laborers was undertaken under his shrewd, moderate policies of "benevolent paternalism." After the Civil War Pierce returned to Port Royal briefly as a cotton factor, in the belief that the experiment needed better trade connections. He later practiced law in Boston, held local public offices, and wrote several books, including an edition of the letters of Charles Sumner. (Rose, *Rehearsal for Reconstruction*, 21-24, 145, 237.)

[2] The second Mrs. Pierce was Maria L. Woodhead of Huddersfield, England, whom Pierce married in 1882.

To James Nathan Calloway

[Tuskegee, Ala.] June 27th [189]2

Mr. J. N. Calloway: If you can find the time, some time this week, I wish you to make a thorough inspection of the farm in charge of

Mr. Greene.[1] The home farm should present a model after which our students and others can take pattern and few things help so much in the conduct of any enterprise as the eyes and opinion of a number of persons. Our farm work should be the *best* that our surroundings will allow, and we must be satisfied with nothing less.

In making the inspection, please keep these things in view: condition of crop, fences, fruit trees, grapes, stock, barn, milking and butter-making.

Also let me have your opinion as to whether or not you find ground that should be in cultivation but is not, and other matters that you think will better the farm. Please report in writing.

If you will show this note to the Superintendent of Industries[2] and the Farm Manager, it will let them know your authority. Yours,

B. T. Washington

Send in your bill for services. B.T.W.

TLpS Con. 106 BTW Papers DLC. The postscript is in BTW's hand.

[1] Charles W. Greene.
[2] John Henry Washington.

From James Nathan Calloway

Tuskegee, Ala., June 30 1892

Dear Sir You probably understand how difficult it is to look over a place like ours and report it in a way that justice be done to all. At any rate I shall report things as they appeared to me. Taking for granted that our home farm is especially a truck, fruit and dairy farm I shall criticise these things most severely.

Truck

The truck as a whole is quite grassy. This however is being killed quite rapidly. The cabbages look best of all. The tomatoes show a great lack of attention. This crop can not make more than half. The sweet potatoes in the new-ground have just been cleaned but have suffered a little from neglect. The peas above reservoir look quite well. The corn and cane are growing nicely but need work.

241

Fences

The fences are good if compared with others of this vicinity but realy they are poor. These will suffice until something is produced that will need protection.

Fruit Trees

I find that about one-third of the fruit trees have been gnawed by the rabbits and are dying. This comes from lack of care during the Spring months.

Grape Vines

The grape vines are a failure. The old ones are scrubby and neglected and the young ones are dying. It is money thrown away to buy them. This can and should be remedied.

Dairy-farming

The cows are so much better than formerly that I can find not fault with them or their condition. One thing, however, might be done which I think will increase their milk and better their condition. That is that they be fed at 5 o'clock in the morning instead of 7 o'clock. Then they can be let out while the morning is cool. Yours truly

J. N. Calloway

ALS   Con. 101   BTW Papers   DLC.

From Joseph D. Bibb[1]

Montgomery Ala   July 5 — 1892

Dear Sir: I am informed that Prof. W. B. Paterson claims to have in his possession a letter written by you concerning the stand I have taken against white teachers in colored public schools,[2] and that the letter condemns my actions as being unnecessary as well as "ungrateful." I have discredited the statement thinking it peculiar to *his shrewdness;* but this spurious letter (as I am compelled to believe it must be if there be any on that line at all) is winning for him a following he could not otherwise induce to support his cause.

While the justice of my side makes me fearless, and I am convinced that my course is honorable and upright, yet I should find sufficient reason for unpleasant reflection if it were true that *you* had put the weight of your judgment, your influence, your position against me in this matter.

Please reply as early as convenient. Very respectfully

J D Bibb

ALS Con. 99 BTW Papers DLC.

[1] Joseph D. Bibb was born in Montgomery, Ala., and attended the Swayne Public School there. He enrolled at Fisk University, but decided that he could learn best from black instructors and moved to Livingstone College, an A.M.E. school with an all-black faculty, of which J. C. Price was founder and president. He received an A.B. degree there in 1886. Bibb taught for one year at W. B. Paterson's state normal school in Montgomery, spent ten years as principal of Swayne School, and served for two years as professor of Hebrew and Bible history at Morris Brown College in Atlanta. He then became an A.M.E. minister in Montgomery.

[2] At the meeting of the Alabama State Teachers' Association in Birmingham, on June 9, 1892, Bibb read a paper on "The Negro Teacher in His Relation to the Negroes' Future." He advocated the employment of black teachers whenever possible. W. B. Paterson lead the discussion. "He said that he felt the paper was a personal attack and asked that he might speak in behalf of himself." Others also spoke, and interest being high and the hour late, BTW as president postponed further discussion until the next morning. After speeches on both sides of the question, Bibb concluded with "very animated" remarks. He said: "I have been accused of being ungrateful, I am accused of ingratitude, because I am fighting for that which makes this audience beautiful. I came not here to fight man, but to fight for principles. If I have erred, it is not of the heart, but of the head, and the error, if any, has been so because of my devotion to my people. If in my death, my people would be elevated, let me die." Resolutions relative to Bibb's paper were offered by several persons, and two of them were adopted. The first was: "*Resolved*, That it is the sense of this Association, that when it is the law of the State, for the races to be separated in schools supported by the State, that where colored teachers, equally competent with whites can be found, the colored teachers should be put in control of the colored school." The second was: "*Resolved:* That the statement as published in the *Birmingham Age-Herald*, that 'The paper read by Prof. J. D. Bibb was a direct blow at the State Normal School of Montgomery,' is a mistake, and that we request the reporter to have this statement corrected." (Alabama State Teachers' Association, *Minutes of the Eleventh Annual Session, 1892*.)

From Margaret James Murray

Tuskegee, Ala., July 10th 1892

My Dearest Booker, It is Sunday again and almost the same time that I talked with you last. I got the telegram and you can not think how glad I was to get it for it seems that you have been gone so long and

I always wait so long for a letter. I hope that a letter from you will come to-day or tomorrow. I wrote last Sunday so that you got my letter not later than Thursday.

We are still having rain so that every thing is so wet and damp and then it retards the out door work. The men have finished the white-washing in Alabama Hall but it is very poorly done. In many of the rooms, the pictures which were pasted upon the wall were not re-moved. I spoke to Mr. Torrents about it and he said that Mr. J. H. Washington told him to hurry over it. Of course I dropped it because Mr. Washington would never say that he had given such an order. The work at the Annex goes on but slowly. I am sure that work should be hurried because it should be ready to be put in order the last of August and it should not be delayed if other things are delayed. I mean to speak to Mr. Logan of this but I do not know that it will do any good for he is like a piece of clay in the hands of another.

I have not been to the brick yard but Mr. Green[1] says that things are moving on nicely. Of course you are obliged to divide this statement by 2 in order to get a correct answer.

Mr. Carter[2] has returned and has gone to work. He spent the first afternoon at the organ. He is so fond of music. As far as a woman can judge the work is doing pretty well. Mr. Penny gets on with the Night School now and I get a little more rest. He is so fond of little things. The other day a large piece of plastering fell down and instead of having it swept out, he laid it aside to get a chance to bring it to the meeting. It will be fun to see Mr. J. H. Washington turn in his chair and perhaps lose his temper. I do not despise little things but I often get so tired when Mr. Penny begins.

I get frightened at you when you get impatient at him for he is an older man and I should be sorry if he noticed your impatience. Mr. Morin claims that Mr. Hamilton steals all of the papers not for any use but just because he is too stingy to let any one else have them to read. He inspects this quite frequently for some purpose. Mrs. J. H. and Mrs. Hamilton[3] come over here at night very often. I suppose you think it strange that I do not go oftener to Mrs. Washington. It is not that I do not like her but she says such uncomfortable things that for days after I have left her, I am miserable and I just refrain from visiting her so often. Sometimes when I am in the most pleasant mood, she just chills my very blood by some slight prophetic remark and I vow that I never will get into her company again. I do not think that I was made for constant contact. I often shudder to note the change which has come over me since I have been engaged in this work and I try too, to influence my self differently.

Dr. Dillon will soon be here, sometime next week. I mean to leave just the night before she gets here. I do not know why it is but I get so nervous whenever she is near me. I do not dislike her but I do not care to be at all intimate with her, and to avoid her I would go a mile. I never think of her without remembering that the bitterest words you have ever spoken to me were on her account, at least, they were the result of a conversation concerning her. I have tried a thousand times to forget this but I know that I can not and so I have ceased trying.

Mr. and Mrs. Calloway[4] left for Demopolis Thursday. I almost fear for their baby, she has grown so thin and weak and they say that it is so low in Demopolis.

Sophira[5] has gone home. She grew dissatisfied after you left and I told Mr. Logan to give her the money for you. As long as she was here Lottie[6] paid no attention to any thing and Sophira felt that since Lottie was being paid, she should at least look after the children. I am very much surprised at Miss Young and yet I do not know that I am right because I never felt that you were doing the right thing in getting her. She has left the house twice for hours at the time and all the doors and windows in use open. One night just before nine I went thro the whole house and found every thing opened. I spoke to her of this and she said that you and Sophira always left the house open still she promised to close it hereafter. She claims that she can not attend her own room and so I send a girl over. Yesterday it rained so hard that the girl did not get over until after noon and Miss Young's bed was still unmade. She has been to town four or five times since you left and every time she has ridden. I am thoroughly disgusted with her. I shall say nothing to you of her care of the children for it will only disturb you and besides I am here and while I am obliged to stand and see much that I do not like they will not really suffer as long as I am here. Yesterday, she left them three hours at Mrs. Penny and before I found it out Davidson had run in the drizzling rain for more than an hour. In this respect, I am not surprised — almost any other young girl would do the same. I made Davidson and Baker each a pretty dress this past week. I am going to make two for Portia Monday and Tuesday and then I think they will have enough for the summer. Portia tells me that her nose bleeds every night and that often her stomach is sick. I thought that I should ask Mrs. Penny to have Dr. Johnson see her? or perhaps wait until Dr. Dillon gets here? You know that I told you that I had a request to make of you? It is this, if I go with you in the fall, will you not get me a bedroom set to match my desk? I do not like dark furniture and the Oak does not cost much more than the other. You might leave out the wardrobe and get three pieces, the dresser, washstand and bed. Mr. Washington I really want to go with you in October. I do not wish to be away from you longer and if we find it necessary to wait longer I shall break the engagement because I do not feel that we have any right to be to each other what we are and still remain from each other. And then too, the longer we wait, the harder it will be for the friends on both sides. I wish that we were together to day. I always like to stay near you on Sunday. Do you miss me to day.

I came across this article this week and knowing that you would like it I send it to you.

You will not read all of this letter but then I feel better when I tell you every thing. Lovingly

Maggie

ALS Con. 17 BTW Papers DLC.

¹ James Matthew Greene taught brickmaking and plastering at Tuskegee from 1892 to 1908.

² John W. Carter taught carpentry at Tuskegee from 1889 to 1901.

³ Altona Lillian (Mrs. Robert Hannibal) Hamilton, wife of the Tuskegee music instructor.

⁴ Probably Mr. and Mrs. James Nathan Calloway.

⁵ Sophira Warren.

⁶ Lottie Virginia Young Greene (1872-1946), a Tuskegee graduate of 1889, who later married Charles W. Greene and taught in the Tuskegee night school.

From Margaret James Murray

Chattanooga, Tenn., July 15, 1892

My Dearest Booker, I am here in Chattanooga with my best girl friend (Mrs. Willis).¹ I came in last night. I was taken sick at three oclock yesterday and when I got here I could not stand upon my feet but this morning I feel much better than I did. This letter I meant to have written you Wednesday night but I just could not. Before I begin I must tell you that I should have written you this letter long before this but I did not wish to disturb you but it is now a question of w[h]ether I shall not disturb you or whether you will be unhappy some time later. It is this. Baker and Davidson are not getting any attention this summer except that which people are inclined to give them. While I was there I did all that I could but you know that I am obliged to be careful. I am circumsribed in all things concerning the children, and had it not been for this fact I should not have left. Mr. Penny came down the night before I left and told me that I should write and then I made up my mind to do it. It has been raining ever since July came in and the children stay out in the rain right along. Often Miss Young goes up to your house and sleeps for two hours and then she will go up stairs at the Pennys and sleep and all of this time, the children play in tubs of water or run in the rain.

They are left at Mrs. Pennys with no one to look after them and but for the kindness of Mrs. Penny Davidson would now be sick. She often brings him and puts her baby's dry clothes upon him. I spoke to Miss Young and she said she kept Davidson in out of the rain whenever she found out that he was in it. As I said I was obliged to go no further. Mr. Penny said that he was going to write a note to her for imposing upon Mrs. P in this way but I do hope that he did not for I am afraid that she will take them and leave them with some of those Colored folks around there or down to Mrs. Washington and this I do not want. I can not tell you how I feel over this and I have tried to keep it from you until it reached this point. I want Davidson because he is so self willed and sweet. Dont you think that you might go home to the children a little sooner? I do not wish them put into the hands of any other woman. Mrs. Penny will board them and you might take Hattie² to care for them. Miss Young thinks that you will not want her longer than the last of this month and I wish you would let her go and let the children be at Mrs. Pennys altogether and there they will get better attention until you get there. I would have stayed there instead of asking you to go, but I could do so little that it kept me unhappy and cross. I did all of the sewing for them before I left and I left money with Miss Young and also with Kittie³ for them. I am making their winter clothes this summer. I am going to get a pritty blue suit for Baker and Davidson here and then when I go with you I shall not have so much to do indeed when I finish the sewing they all will have all that they will need for a [while.] Please write me just [when you] can go and in [the mean]time, write to Mrs. [Penny?] so that she may take [Davidson] and Baker at the close [of the] month. I am tired today [and unfitted] to write you a decent [letter] now since I have [done my] duty in dropping [you] this information in [regard to] the children I shall [wait] for a letter from you. [Please] do as you like about Miss Young.

Maggie

ALS Con. 17 BTW Papers DLC. Part of the last half-page was torn off from top to bottom. Written on letterhead stationery of the Southern Inter-State Exposition, listing among the officers "H. N. Willis State Commissioner."

¹ Martha (Mrs. H. N.) Willis.
² Presumably Hettie (Mrs. James B.) Washington.
³ Katherine Juanita Baskins Barr.

From Margaret James Murray

Chattanooga Tenn. July 17 — 92

My Dearest Booker, I am tired to night. I rode into church this morning and this after noon I took a long drive and since I have been entertaining one of my old flames but not withstanding this I shall not retire without answering your letter which came in last night after I had finished and sealed your letter and then I wanted time to think before sending this letter. Monday. I began this letter last night but I just wanted a letter from you and so I waited until to day but the letter never came. I think that I had better stay at home with the children. It is true that I have too always planned to go away when you go especially on the long tours but I know so little of the care of children, I do not even know how to dress a child properly and I think that it will be too cold too for Davidson. I will learn my lessons alone but all that I learn improperly you may correct when you come back. We have been apart so much that often I just long to stay a long, long time but next summer perhaps we can be with each other. I am as you in regard to having the children left in the charge of anyone else. I utterly detest the way in which Miss Young acts and yet I do not wish to be too harsh on her for she is so foolish and silly and of course her age has much to do with it all.

In regard to the changes we shall want to make, I have thought that we might better settle upon them afterwards indeed I greatly prefer that no changes be made until we are together there in the house. We can see what we want and what we need. Don't you think this is better.

Do you not think that we will be happier in the room upstairs — the one opposite the guest room? Or are you so wedded to the room down next to the Library? I do not like this room and it is so much nicer and cooler up stairs and then it is quieter. What do you say to the change. I want a pretty carpet for the floor, some pretty lace curtains, the Oak set bed *dresser* not bureau washstand and a real pretty washstand set and the chairs for our room. We can rest so much better if every thing is delicate and refined. I hope that you will not think me very extravagant. I am still waiting to see if you are coming by Chattanooga. We can spend the day upon Look Out and *your race* here is doing so nicely that you can['t] help being interested in its doing. I rode almost all over the city this morning. I began at five oclock and we did not get home till twelve and then I was so very hungry. We went down to the river and near the bridge and every where. The morning air was just delightful and I did so wish for you. Would you not have enjoyed being with me. I am having a real nice time. Martha is trying to get me to take lessons in housekeeping from her. She is a splendid housekeeper but I am a dull pupil. I had rather wait and learn those lessons from you. You will not be as impatient with me as other people will be, will you?

In regard to my doing a part of my work, do not give an answer too quickly because we can talk it over when you come and you will understand me better and then if we can not see our way clear, we can do something else but I hope we both will feel the same about it. I had rather give up slowly than to give up all at once.

I am sleepy now and must bid my Booker good night.

Maggie

ALS Con. 17 BTW Papers DLC.

From Halle Tanner Dillon

Tuskegee, Ala., July 18th 1892

Dear Sir: I arrived here Sunday and found that Portia had been, was still, suffering with a mild form of itch and a bil[i]ous attack. She is still quite unwell to day and Mrs Penny according to your request called me in to see her. While I do not think it necessary that you should feel alarmed about her condition yet I thought best to inform you of her sickness. I trust that may be much improved in [a] few days. Will keep you informed, every day as to her condition. Respectfully

Halle T. Dillon

ALS   Con. 101   BTW Papers   DLC.   Addressed to BTW in Boston.

From Margaret James Murray

Chattanooga, Tenn., July 21 1892

My Dearest Booker, I sat for a long time yesterday wondering why I could get no news of you and just as I turned over in the hammock and vowed I would not send you another line until I had a decent letter from you, the man returned from town with your card and you can too truly imagine how mean I felt at the thoughts which I had entertained against you. It seems so hard that I do not hear from you this summer as I have done in other times. I try not to be too silly for your letters for I know that you have so much to do in so short a time and you have to work so hard. I shall be glad when we are together for then I can relieve you of so many hard things at the school if I can be with you in your trips. I think of you so often in your lonely trips while you are away from [me?]. I do hope that you are well now and are getting on nicely with your work. I am glad that you are going home to the children. I did not leave Tuskegee because of my needed rest for after you left and I saw how things with the children were going for your sake I would have remained and should have done so but my actions toward them are so circumscribed that it made me miserable to be around them. Mrs. Washington you know is never out except at night and it is little that she can do and besides she knows as much as a cat about caring for children. Hers live by the goodness of Providence. Several times Mr. and Mrs. Morin spoke to me of writing you but I hated to trouble you and now I wonder if I did the wisest thing in the world when I told you, still my love for your happiness prompted me to do it. Mrs. Penny is a gentle kind woman and she would only hint because she did not want to insult Lottie but Mr. Penny was very much wrought up the night before I left and then I held in no longer. I shall be glad when I know that you are there with them. I wish that Mrs. Penny would take them and keep them until October. Her ideas about the rearing of children more nearly correspond with mine than any other person I know. If you go in early August, your presence will hurry every thing up especially the Annex. I asked you to come by but perhaps you do not wish to do so, since you are so anxious to get home.

I shall not be away longer than the middle of August. I am literally worn out and it has been a long time since Martha and I have been together and we have so much to say to each other. I had a letter from Allie Pierce[1] Wesson Miss asking for a recommendation to teach at her home but I thought it best to have you write it. I shall drop her a card tomorrow and tell her that you will send it immediately. Do not fail to send it (Wesson Miss). Guess how many times I have read your letter? Four times and even now I am not satisfied. I think that I am going to have my hair cut before I return. It has begun to fall out so much. I am going to have some pictures taken and perhaps I will give you one? I have spent the last two days in reading Hawthorne's "Scarlet Letter" and wonder to my self that I have not read it long long ago. It is such a fascinating and yet such a terrible tale of sin misery and woe. The plan is such a natural one and not only natural but a frequent one. Did you ever read it. If you have not and wish to do so or at least wish to know it I will condense it and send it to you. The scene was laid in Mass.

I spent the first of the week reading Irving's "Sketch Book." I liked many of the tales so much. I think that one may get clearer ideas of the German superstitions from this book than any I have read before, indeed you get a great deal of English history. I enjoyed reading "Westminster Abbey" "The Specter Bridegroom" and Stratford on Avon. I was just about concluding with others that Shakespeare was not Shakespeare but now I am undecided. I read a most interesting article in the July Are[n]a concerning Shakespeare and Bacon and I confess, I felt very much as many others do — that [there was] no such person as William Shakespeare. I have tried to read History this summer but I have not done much of it. It tires me so soon to try [to] do any heavy studying. It is night now and long ere this you are fast asleep. I hope that you will get a good nights rest and be fresh for work tomorrow. Do you remember writing to Robt. Mabry[2] of Chattanooga, and telling him that he could return to school? He wrote Mr. Logan saying that you did. He was expelled in your absence and I know that you did not think of this when you wrote him. Perhaps you had better speak to Mr. Logan and then write Robt. I should feel sorry to have this boy permitted to return so soon after his actions there last fall. I am quite sure the others feel as I do about the matter. Do not [be] too harsh a critic upon this letter. I am too sleepy to over look it.

Maggie

ALS Con. 17 BTW Papers DLC.

[1] Allie Lee Pierce of Wesson, Miss., was in the B middle class of Tuskegee in 1890-91. She did not graduate.

[2] Robert Lee Mabry of Birmingham, not Chattanooga, entered Tuskegee in 1890 in the junior class. He spent the school years 1891-92 and 1892-93 in the B middle class. In 1893-94 he was in the A middle class; in 1894-95 in the senior class. He did not graduate.

From Margaret James Murray

[Chattanooga, Tenn.] July 27 1892

My Dearest Booker, I have been trying to write you all day but four of the Chattanooga teachers came out at an early hour this morning and they did not leave until tonight. I do not often write you after night for then I am tired and not fresh and I always feel that I should give you the best part of my time. I can not let the night go by and and not have a little chat with you. It makes me feel so much nearer you when I write. You can never guess how much I have thought of you today. I can not separate any pleasantry from you. I long to have it so that we can be together oftener. I do get so tired of this constant separation. When I first found that I cared for you, I used to picture myself going on all of your trips with you — but I did not sit down to write a love letter nor to give you an idea that I can not willingly give up this idea. You have my letter by this time and understand what I shall do in regard to the children and I know that you agree with me in this matter. Do you not? I received all of your letters and I think that I have now answered all of your questions. Have I not. I had not planned to go home at least I promised Martha to stay here with Martha [a] month but Laura[1] has written for me. Our mother[2] is rather old and not a strong woman and I do not think that I want to go there next summer for I am going with you then unless I change my mind. I want you to write me a good loving letter before you leave for Tuskegee so that I shall get it before I leave for Miss. Will you do this and be sure to send me a telegram when you start for home. I shall feel perfectly satisfied when you are there. Please tell me what you will do with the children and yourself during August September and part of October. I would not open the rooms again because the furniture and every thing is so badly used and I hate badly used household goods. The Pennys have to be careful of all that they do. It would have resulted differently if you had written a letter and not so soon after I sent you the letter. It does not matter now that soon you are to be there. Do not let any one coax you into buying any thing for the children. I got a list of all of their clothes and they have plenty. I am having others made for them but I do not mean to let them have them until I am there with them and they will not be taken care of if I should let them go to them. I only meant to send you a note tonight but I see I have not yet stopped. You get tired of all this. I should be so happy if you were to send me now and then a longer letter. I miss you so much that I often long for these long letters but I do not blame you for you have so little time for writing letters. I am going into the city tomorrow to get my photos taken. Do you wish one? Bye bye,

Maggie

ALS Con. 17 BTW Papers DLC.

[1] Laura Murray Donaldson, Margaret James Murray's sister.
[2] Lucy Murray.

From Margaret James Murray

[Chattanooga, Tenn., ca. July 1892]

. . . . .

I can not tell the exact date dearest and I do not care to do it until I know what time you are to go North. You will go in October as usually but I do not know w[h]ether you are to go the middle or the later part. If you do not object we will marry here at Martha's. She is very anxious to have us do so and it is most convenient for us both. Do you not think so? I should lose only a week if we come here and I do not think it necessary for me to lose more and you need not lose more than two days, whereas if we go else where, both will be obliged to lose more time. Mr. Washington do you think I should go on with the work in the Academic Department? I should so much love to do this and yet I do not wish to be selfish in regard to the cares that come to every wife and that will come to me doubly. I love to work in the class room, and I want to make some money too because I shall need many things for the house and the children that you will not know of. I like a pretty home. Lettie[1] is anxious for me to take her mother for this first year and I have been thinking that perhaps it would be a good thing if I do. I have given her no answer because I did not feel sure that I wanted her and I did not know what you would say to it. However, I shall tell Lettie plainly that if I take her mother, I shall expect her to do all of the house work except the cooking. I hope that you will tell me plainly what you think best for me to do in this matter.

In regard to coming here. Perhaps you had better not try to come because you will be here in October and then it will keep you longer from the children and I really want you to be there. Martha just begged me last night to ask you to come but I had rather you would be at Tuskegee. I shall not be here longer than next Thursday. I shall run down home for a few days and then I shall join you at Tuskegee and we shall be so very happy. Will we not? I will not promise to write Mrs. Eliot.[2] I want to write her and yet I do not want to do so. I love her though.

I wrote you last Sunday. Why did you send those five words? I do hope that you can come home before Xmas. I hear that Mr. Hamilton will be here soon. I do not feel very elated over his coming.

Mrs Logan's mother is here. She has lost her son and seems to feel it deeply.

I hope that you keep up your strength.

I do not write to Chicago often. I have written only once since you left? I had a letter last week. I'll show it to you when you come if you wish to see it.

I am tired to night. Miss Moore will be here next Friday. I have lots of funny things to tell you of her but I shall hold them until you get here. Try not to feel ill toward [her] — perhaps she will get over her ———— for you — any way let us hope that she will.

They tease me a great deal about her but I have no fear. Need I have any?

Lots of love to you.

Your Maggie

ALfS Con. 17 BTW Papers DLC. Probably only the first page of the letter is missing, since the contents seem rather complete.

[1] Lettie E. Nolen Calloway?
[2] Mary A. Elliott.

To Hallie Quinn Brown[1]

[Tuskegee, Ala.] August 10th [189]2

Dear Miss Brown: I write you according to promise.

The duties of Lady Principal are to have control of the girls in all that pertains in their school life — that is their physical, mental, moral and religious training. The Lady Principal is assisted by two matrons regularly and the Lady Principal has authority to demand whatever assistance she thinks best of the ten or a dozen lady teachers connected with the school.

The Lady principal has the control of the class work for both sexes and is responsible for the cleanliness of the class rooms.

In a general way, I think I have outlined all the duties. We have few cast iron rules and you would find yourself at liberty to make many changes. I think you will see that little of the time of the Lady Principal is occupied in dru[d]gery, but we wish her in the main to see that the work of others is done well.

There will be plenty of opportunity to teach elocution. I do hope that you will decide not to go to California, but even if you do not give up your California trip, I hope you can come here for a week in September and come for a permanent stay after you return from California.

The salary will be $60.00 per month and board. Board to include all expenses except travelling — this is something more than our present Lady Principal is being paid.

If there is anything in the plan that I have outlined that you do not like, I hope you will say so. I should not be willing to let the matter of a few dollars stand in the way of your coming.

I can but repeat that I believe there is no place where your life can be given in a way to better lift up those, who in time will lift thousands of others up than at Tuskegee and we shall be slow to take "no" for an answer.

I saw Dr. Dorsette a few days ago and he is enthusiastic over your coming. Yours truly,

Booker T. Washington

TLpS Con. 106 BTW Papers DLC.

[1] Hallie Quinn Brown (1850-1949), noted elocutionist and lecturer, was Lady Principal at Tuskegee in the 1892-93 school year. Born in Pittsburgh, she was the daughter of two former slaves who had secured their freedom before the Civil War. Her father worked as a riverboat steward and express agent and acquired considerable real estate in Pittsburgh. The family moved to Ontario in 1864 but returned to Wilberforce, Ohio, in 1870 so that Hallie and her brother could attend Wilberforce University. She graduated in 1873, taught school in Mississippi and South Carolina, served as dean of Allen University, Columbia, S.C., from 1885 to 1887, and taught in the Dayton, Ohio, public schools from 1887 to 1891, establishing a night school there for adult migrants from the South. She was professor of elocution at Wilberforce (1893-94, 1900-1903), and spent five years in the 1890s in Europe as a traveling lecturer. A leader in the Negro women's clubs, she was president of the Ohio State Federation of Colored Women's Clubs (1905-12). In 1893 she helped found the Colored Women's League of Washington, D.C., forerunner of the National Association of Colored Women, of which she was president from 1920 to 1924. She was also active in the Women's Christian Temperance Union and the woman suffrage movement. In the A.M.E. Church she made an unsuccessful bid to be the first woman to hold an office in its General Conference. Hallie Brown's writings included two books on public speaking and a collection of biographical sketches of black women, *Homespun Heroines and Other Women of Distinction* (1926).

From Mary Elizabeth Preston Stearns

Tufts College P.O. Masstts. August 11th 1892

Booker T. Washington, and the holy Memory of Olivia Davidson Washington!

Dear Friends — for I can not seperate what "God hath joined together["] on this day forever sacred in our hearts.

In the unfathomable silences of God her heroic spirit is living and working in aid of all your best endeavors. "So *near,* —and yet so *far,*" from these mortal eyes, wh[ich] are "holden that they cannot *see.*["] Heaven forever bless you my honored friend, in every task of your mighty work! and be *very sure* her inspiration is always with you; must, and will sustain; strengthen; and hold up your hands.

Around the dear children she gave you, and the world, her loving arms are spread; her loving whatchful eyes are beaming. Give them double the number of kisses *this* day — and add some, for your, hers, and their own friend in all faithfulness; in all devotion to the *cause* which has sanctified our friendship. With tears, that *will* come, for the vanished *form* and smiles for your high, and steadfast endeavors. I am always yours.

Mary E. Stearns

PS. I propose to send your College a Cast of the Bust of John Brown, together with some account of its history — to be preserved as a Memorial of what he did for the "People who sat in great darkness."

ALS Con. 103 BTW Papers DLC.

To Robert Charles Bedford

[Tuskegee, Ala.] August 18th [189]2

Dear Mr. Bedford: We are planning to have in connection with the work to be carried on in Phelps Hall, a Summer school of Theology to be in session the last two weeks in August of each summer, and we hope to be able to have the next session begin next August. It is our plan to bring together for two weeks a large number of the best class of ministers throughout the South, especially those in charge of churches, to hear lectures from the most eminent persons that we can get hold of, and it is the purpose of this letter to ask you to map out a course of lectures for these two weeks. I think that there might be two lectures each day. We hope to get hold of several of the colored bishops and several of the most prominent white teachers in the Southern schools for lectures. Of course you understand that it is very necessary that everything be [s]imple and practical. I hope you will be able to have a course of [lect]ures yourself on some subject as you know better than anyone the condition and needs of the colored ministers. We think that a great deal of good will come from this movement.

The progress on the new building is not what I hoped it would be; still it is being very substantially erected. Yours very truly,

[Booker T. Washington]

TLp Con. 106 BTW Papers DLC. The press copy omitted a corner of the first page.

From Ellen Collins

New York. August 23. '92

Dear Mr. Washington, Thank you for your letter received this morning. I am very sorry to think there is trouble in store for your poor neighbours, I hoped prosperity was coming. But all those things are settled for us in the way really for the best.

I want to ask a favor now. A colored (nearly white) gentleman, a Harvard graduate and lawyer, made the foolish but very serious mistake of seeking a position in Washington. He has lost that and others since, and has a wife & family, and is hard pressed for a living. He has all the ability and education that ought to secure competence, but political influence being against him, has suffered severely. Now is your staff full, or do you need a man, and have you means to pay him? This man has also been a teacher. I understand he looks almost white, his wife also. Your school is not to be in any sense a shelter for unfortunates, or incapable people. I only mention it in case you happen to need more workers, and would like to correspond with him. His name is Greener.[1] He does not know that I ask this of you, as I will of Mr. Frissell; but if you care to hear further, send a letter to me and I will see that it is passed on.

Thank you for sending to Miss Thorne.[2] I am sorry Miss Murray has not been well. Do remember us very cordially to her. I am going to send her now a little parcel of illustrated books, that we have long had, and some of her girls may now like to see.

We thought you were at the North, and hoped you would come in and see us. Have you any special want just now? It is nearly time to drop another slip into your coffers. Truly yours

Ellen Collins

ALS   Con. 5   BTW Papers   ATT.   Original destroyed.

[1] Richard Theodore Greener.
[2] Charlotte R. Thorn.

From A. A. Woodson[1]

Memphis Tenn   Aug 28th 1892

Dear Sir: I received the photograph of Mrs. Washington[2] some time ago and think it very much like her as I remember her. I thank you very much for it and I certainly appreciate it very highly. I don't really know any thing of Mrs Washington's brother's and sister's death.[3] They lived in Miss. near Hernando. Very probably some of the people now living there could tell you some thing of the circumstances attending their death. I hope you and your children are enjoying the best of health. If you are ever in Memphis again, I'll be very glad to see you and talk with you about Mrs. Washington. Please pardon my long delay, but it could not be very well helped. Again thanking your for your kindness   I am   Yours sincerely,

Mrs. A. A. Woodson

ALS   Con. 103   BTW Papers   DLC.

[1] A. A. (Mrs. Benjamin F.) Woodson was the wife of a black lawyer, later undertaker, in Memphis.
[2] Olivia A. Davidson Washington.
[3] Joseph Davidson, and possibly Martha L. Davidson. (See Mary A. Elliott to BTW, Aug. 30, 1892, below.)

From Mary A. Elliott

Columbus Ohio   Aug 30th 1892

My Dear Brother. I Rec both of your last letters and was glad to
hear from you in deed. I have been quite sick myself for the last two
weeks past   nervous prosteration caused from heat and over work
sewing and triming. I felt so much refreshed from my visit south that
I felt as though I could get throug the summer alright but the heat
has been intensely sev[ere] here this summer, more so then in 20 years
past it is said. I am feeling much better now. I was sorry to hear that
little Portia had been sick during your abscence   she must have been
quite sick if she was near having Typhoid fever   I am glad she is
well again   tell her she must write to Aunt Mary, and that she will
answer her letter right a way. tell me all about her self and little
brothers.

I am so glad to hear that the little boys has been well. I suppose
they did as well as if they had of come North. I know that they were
tickled to get out on the ball yard. They are both full of life   I would
like to watch them play. I know that it would be all Davidson could
do to contain himself, poor little fellow.

Aunt Mary will take it all back about him being naughty   he is no
worse then other children of his size   he his not much more then a
baby yet. I can hear him yet going over his sweet baby talk. He acted
too cute for any thing the afternoon that you taken us to se Olivia's
land   he was so happy   said we was going to see *his* house, *his* house,
but finally admited reluctantly however, that it was Baker's too. and
after we got there, and looked around, was ready to start back he took
a contrary spell, and dident want to come back? if you remember,
wanted you to come back go back home and get chairs and other
things and stay there at the new house? So many things he did and
said, leaves lasting inpressions on the mind. Holding his little cup to
his ear when at the table testing the water to find whither it was gen-
uine or not or the same that you were useing   Booker without doubt
he is a wonderful child of his age. His temper will be the hardest to
over come, yet he is full of love and goodness combined with the
greatest force and will power of any child I ever met with. He is a
book unread, but you can read enough on the title page to know that

he is in posession of traits that will make him a born *leader* in what ever he under takes if he lives. The germ of all these things are now visibly plain to be seen in him if you study him with attention as to Baker my sweet little boy, he will be a classical Gentleman, understand judgment and equity, and will do much good in the world I hope.

It looks as though Aunt had started out to read destiny but had not though[t] of such a thing untill this minuit. it is too funny, and I do assure you that I dont lay claim to such knowledge. But as I have said so much about brothers I must say somthing a bout Sister. Portia if she lives will make a fine Scholar and will be able to instruct others in the higher branches of science more notable in Astronomy, if her eyes grows stronger I do hope they will. I dont think that I am wrong. I formed that idea of her when she was quite small when I first made her acquaintance in Athens. she is a dear *little* child She was then. When we all [meet] if we ever do I will tell why I think so. So papa dont get weary of reading this kind of talk for I amagin that I am talking to you and the children face to face. besides I believe all that I have said about them is true. I am glad [to] hear that Dear Miss Murry is better and is back again with the children I feel satisfied that she will [do] what is right by the children I know that the children looks pretty in their suits. I hope that you may be lucky enough to secure the service of Miss Hallie Q. Brown. Dear brother I am glad to think that you all would like to have me come again. it would be more then I could expect to come next year but if I could come in two or three years from now I would feel it I great treat I can truly say that I never spent ten days of my life so pleasent, yet sadness would at times almost over come me. yet Booker I think or did whist I was there on a visit, that the shadows and disappointment had fallen on you more heavly then on my sef, and yet you had not swerved from duty or the principle, that you both started to carry out, and I derived strength from the thoughts of it, and I pray that our Hevenly Father may still give you strength and a desire to go on and do still greater work, and that you may be spa[r]ed to rear your children in the way they should go and that your future may be brigher. I am glad that you had the oppertunity of meeting some of Olivia's friends. she [had] a great many I am some little with the Cassels myself. they nice people. I do so wish that you could of seen Lizzie's[1] & little Joe's[2] graves they lay side by side at Hernando, Miss. Mother and I both hope that it will not be long before we can see you all. perhaps you can come and let the children come, this coming spring or summer. I am building on the same lot that mother lives on. our rent is high where we live now 20 dollars a month and I thought we would try and build if am not able to finish this winter I want to get the store-room done. I know that it is a buisy time now for you, and teachers Pleas remember me kindly to Miss Murry. Kiss the children for me. Dock, with Mother sends their love to you and the children Your Sister

Mary

excuse this long letter and many mistakes

ALS Con. 17 BTW Papers DLC.

¹ Possibly Martha L. Davidson, reported in the 1870 census in the household of Eliza Davidson in Albany, Ohio. She was then thirteen, a mulatto born in Ohio, and at school.

² Joseph Davidson appeared in the household of Eliza Davidson in Albany, Ohio, in the 1870 census as a mulatto, age eight, born in Ohio, at school.

To George Washington Cable

Tuskegee, Ala., Aug. 31st 1892

Dear Sir: Enclosed I send you a copy of the recent law passed by the Alabama legislature for the distribution of the school fund between the races.¹ You will notice that the entire matter is left in the hands of the township superintendents. As our students have not returned from their vacation I cannot send you at this time their testimony as to the working of this law, but it has greatly cut down the appropriations to the colored schools. Yours truly,

Booker T. Washington

TLS George W. Cable Collection LNHT.

¹ The Alabama Constitution of 1875 established a state school fund for the support of common public schools. The constitution prohibited local taxation for school purposes, thus making the state school fund the sole public source of support for schools. State property taxes provided the major source of income for the school fund. The constitution also restricted the amount of money which could be spent

for any school purpose other than the salaries of teachers to only 4 percent of the total fund.

The law regulating the distribution of the school fund instructed the state superintendent to apportion the fund on a strict per capita child population basis. This provision, combined with the constitutional injunction that schools should be provided throughout the state for the equal benefit of all children regardless of race, prohibited state and local officials from practicing racial discrimination in the distribution of the school fund. In other words, all public schools were equally poorly supported.

All through the 1880s agitation for the right to levy local taxes for white schools was coupled with expressions of discontent about sharing equally with black schools. Representatives of the white counties charged that the Black Belt white county superintendents were taking from the state money for black schools and spending it on white schools, thus giving Black Belt whites an advantage over other whites.

The Apportionment Act of 1891 represented a compromise between northern Alabama white county representatives who agreed to give Black Belt counties local control over school apportionment and Black Belt legislators who agreed to increase the total amount of money appropriated for the school fund. Passed in February, it allowed the township trustees to "apportion to each school . . . such an amount . . . as they may deem just and equitable." In giving local officials discretion over the distribution of the school fund, the act gave legal sanction to racial discrimination in the distribution of school funds.

The Apportionment Act of 1891 did not directly affect Tuskegee Institute. Although black normal schools were funded out of the school fund, the state directly controlled the funds appropriated for normal schools. Local officials did not enter into transactions concerning normal schools. BTW's concern probably stemmed from his interest in the welfare of the black community. A detailed discussion of the various pressures leading to the act is in Bond, *Negro Education in Alabama*, 148-63.

From Henry B. Rice

Malden, W.Va., Sept. 15, 1892

Dear Friend, Yours of recent date was received; it was a most agreeable surprise; I regarded it as a treat to receive a letter from one who must turn his attention from pressing duties, if he would find time to write a friend.

It shall be only pleasure for me to do you the service which you requested. Uncle Wash[1] is my janitor; he is well, and, at present, has no need that he can not meet.

Would it not be well for you to write Amanda[2] in regard to Clara's[3] education?

Hoping that God may continue to bless my race through you, I remain forever, Very Respectfully Yours,

H. B. Rice

ALS Con. 103 BTW Papers DLC.

1 Washington Ferguson, BTW's stepfather.
2 Amanda Johnston.
3 Clara Juanita Johnston.

From Isaac Edwin Gates[1]

New York, Sept. 15th 1892

Dear Sir: Mr. Huntington received your letter of the 9th inst just as he was leaving for California and authorized me to say that he will pay the $1000. toward the expenses of your new building,[2] remitting the same say $200. per month as you require funds as the work progresses. Please advise me when you will need the money and I will remit accordingly. Very truly yours

I. E. Gates

ALS Con. 4 BTW Papers ATT. Original destroyed.

1 Isaac Edwin Gates (1832-1916) was brother-in-law and confidential secretary of Collis Potter Huntington. He left the ministry to serve as vice-president of several of Huntington's holding companies. He was also chief executor of Huntington's estate.
2 Ellen Collins also donated $500 for the construction of the building. (Ellen Collins to BTW, Sept. 7, 1892, Con. 5, BTW Papers, ATT. Original destroyed.)

To H[enry] Bell[1]

Tuskegee, Ala., Sept 20 1892

My dear Sir: I thank you very much for your courteous and prompt reply to my letter regarding the graves of my relatives in Mississippi. Perhaps I did not state to you that Miss Olivia Davidson died two or three years ago and she and I were married in 1886 and had two children. By this mail I send you some pamphlets which will give you an idea of this institution. She had more to do with the founding of this institution than any one else. I shall write to Mr. Clark to-day regarding the graves at Hernando. Yours truly,

Booker T. Washington

TLS   Con. 861   BTW Papers   DLC.   Addressed to Bell in care of the YMCA in St. Louis.

¹ H[enry] Bell apparently had been a pupil of Lizzie (Martha L.?) Davidson when she taught in Hernando, Miss. (See Mary A. Elliott to BTW, Oct. 24, 1892, below.) A Henry Bell was reported in Hernando in the 1870 census. He was a black farm laborer, age twenty-seven.

To Emily Howland

Tuskegee, Ala., Sept 29 1892

Dear Miss Howland: I hope you will not misunderstand my note which left here yesterday. Your letter of the 24 with your check for $200 came today and we are so very gateful for your generous gift. Some how Sept usually seems the hardest month for us financially.

This is an exceptionally hard year in the South. There not much over a half of cotton crop made and the price is exceedingly low. The masses are in debt and there will be much suffering this winter.

Notwithstanding this the colored people seem determined to secure an education and our school is more than full.

I thank you very much for your suggestion about putting some thing in the Register.

We shall be glad to use your gift as you direct, and it will do much good. The weather is very pleasant here just now. At some time I hope that you can come to see us again.

It may interest you to know that Miss Murray and I are to be married Oct 12. In this way both [of] us think that we can be more valuable to the cause to which we have dedicated our lives. Sincerely yours

Booker T. Washington

ALS   Emily Howland Papers   NIC.

To Robert Hannibal Hamilton

[Tuskegee, Ala.] October 4 [189]2

Mr. Hamilton: The Faculty desires me to speak to you regarding instrumental music. Our institution is entirely too far behind in this matter, and we shall be compelled to make greater progress in this line. At this present time, you will note that our institution has but three or four students in instrumental music while other institutions have two and three dozens. We are convinced that a part of the difficulty arises from the fact that in some way the individual students are not enthusiastic over their work and there is complaint among several who have taken lessons previously that they do not receive proper attention from you. Of course you can easily see how these complaints spread from one student to the other and prevents others from engaging to take music. We think that it will be a good plan to have you allow some of the more advanced students in instrumental music play the marches in the chapel or some of the familiar hymns. Putting them forward before the public in this way will go a long way toward encouraging them. Silvia Williams[1] is a girl who has considerable musical ability and in time will make a fine player. It will be a good plan to let her play . . . in the chapel. I think it will also be well to write to her mother concerning Sylvia continuing her course in music.

There are many other suggestions I might make but I do not think it necessary to go further into details except to say that we are all in . . . and of the opinion that Celia McDonald[2] who has such a superior voice should be given an opportunity to further cultivate her voice. If we do not take hold of her and bring her voice out some other institution will do so and get the credit for it.

We hope that you will give these matters proper attention.

B. T. Washington

TLpS Con. 106 BTW Papers DLC.

[1] Sylvia Jelean Williams of Montgomery attended Tuskegee Institute from 1890 through 1893, rising from the A preparatory to the B middle class. She did not graduate.

[2] Celia Elvetus McDonald of Montgomery attended Tuskegee Institute in the junior class in 1887-88, the B middle class in 1888-89, and the A middle class from 1889 to 1892. She did not graduate.

An Item in the Boston *Evening Transcript*

[Boston] Oct. 8, 1892

One Millstone of the Negro's

There is perhaps no one thing that is so hindering the progress of the masses of the colored people in the South as the fact that the bulk of them still live in low, dark, miserable, one-roomed huts, writes Mr. Washington, the principal of the Tuskegee (Ala.) Normal Institute. Often have young women teachers from Tuskegee, on going into a new community to teach, had to sleep in the same room with a whole family, including old and young men. Often the old cabin is torn down and an attempt is made to build a better one; but in most instances the last is but a slight improvement on the first one, simply because the people as a whole do not know how to build good houses. This statement applies with equal force to schoolhouses and church buildings. My ten years' experience in this part of the South working for my people convinces me that if drawings (pictures) of neat little cottages with two or three rooms with glass windows to let in God's sunlight, accompanied by simple working plans, can be distributed throughout the South, an immense amount of good will be done. What influences the colored people more than anything else is something in the shape of an object lesson. Give them an ideal to work up to, and thousands of them will find a way to build a good house. If friends of the South will put into the hands of this institution $200, $300, or $500, or any part of these amounts, I will have made, copied and sent throughout the South as many drawings as the money will provide. If money can be secured in time, hundreds of these plans can be distributed among those who will attend the Tuskegee Negro Conference in February, and to thousands of others through the graduates of the various institutions of the South who go out to teach. If I can put 20,000 or more of these lithographs into the hands of 20,000 negroes this winter, a long step in the direction of the solution of this perplexing problem will have been taken.

Boston *Evening Transcript,* Oct. 8, 1892, 9.

The Certificate of Marriage of Washington
and Margaret James Murray

[Tuskegee, Ala., Oct. 12, 1892]

THE STATE OF ALABAMA, MACON COUNTY

To any Licensed Minister of the Gospel in regular communion with the Christian Church or Society of which he is a member, or Judge of the Supreme, Circuit or City Court, or Chancellor within the State, or Judge of Probate, or Justice of the Peace, within their respective Counties — GREETING:

YOU ARE HEREBY AUTHORIZED TO SOLEMNIZE MARRIAGE

between *B. T. Washington* Colored, and *M. J. Murry* Colored, and to join them together in Matrimony, and certify the same in writing to this office as required by law.

Given under my hand this *10* day of *Oct* A.D. *1892*.

W H Hurt
JUDGE OF PROBATE

This Certifies, That I have solemnized Marriage between Mr. *B. T. Washington* Colored, and M *M. J. Murry* Colored, according to law, at *Tuskegee* in said County and State, on the *12* day of *Oct* *1892*.

E J Penny[1] *Chaplain T.N.I.I.*

PDS Probate Court of Macon County, Ala. The italicized portions were handwritten by the judge of probate.

[1] Edgar J. Penney.

From Mary A. Elliott

Columbus Oct 24th 1892

My Dear Brother: In answer to your kind letter or letters   yes my Ancle has caused me some pain   I was a little imprudent and tried to walk too soon which caused me to suffer more pain then I otherwise would   I have been in bed five weeks going on six   But am now

getting on very well   now the pain has left me and I can stand a lone
on my feet but cant walk yet ondly by the aid of my crutches   I cant
sit up long at once   I am now proped up among the pillows writing
with a pencil, for which I hope you will excuse me as I cant handle
ink very well. I will have to give up Dress making this winter but
will try and keep up my Milliner work unless I can sell out my stock
to some one   I hope I can as I wont be able perhaps to walk much
this winter and would have to hire some one to do the triming.

Well! my Dear Brother I hope that you will look over my seemingly
ingratitude in not sending back the letter that you was more then kind
to send to me concerning Dear Lizzie's grave   I got the letter mis-
placed in some way   so many difrent persons puting away things in
my first illness whilst I was not able to see after any thing   it worried
me a great deal, it was found yesterday in a book. Mother feels so
greatful to you to think that you was kind a nough to be so thoughtful
a bout the graves   she shed tears when I read Mr Bell's letter to you.
I hope it is not to late yet to write to him   I have often heard Lizzie
speak of this Mr Bell as being one of her model boys   I am glad to
hear from him and to know that he is trying to do good in the world.
Well! I congratulate you and Mrs Washington in your happiness and
I pray that you may have a long and peaceful life and that the children may love and obey their new mama. I think they will, for whilst
I was there I thought that Davidson and Baker was getting to be
considerable taking with Miss Murry as well as was their papa and
she appeard to be with them. I am glad that little Portia is strong
a gain and is going to school   she will be a fine scholar if she ondly
can have her health. I am sorry that my being ill hindered me from
sending you both some kind of a weding present. Booker I am proud
my dear brother to think that you have been invited to speak or
address the Congress on Africa of the World's Columbian Exposition,
93   I think it quite distinguished and I know that Mrs Washington
feels the same way   tell [her] to write some time when she has some
leisure moments   I have forgoten if I asked her to write when I
answered her letter   I meant to do so. I am glad to read of the great
success the School is having. I know that you all will feel better when
you can be settled in your own home. since I have had to be confined
to my bed I am with you all in mind halfe of the time and I have
dreamed of being with you all and seeing and walking on the grounds

that when I wake it appears to me that I have in reality been with you all in body. Mother sais to tell you that she wishes you much happiness, and the children much love and many kisses   Dock sends love and wishes you much success and happiness in your new life, and we all join in one voice and inviting you and Mrs Washing to visit us early in the future, perhaps as you go to the Exposition. I fear that you cant make out my writing   Good by to all of you my loved ones

Mary

ALS   Con. 17   BTW Papers   DLC.

To Warren Logan

Crawford House   Boston, Nov 11 1892

Dear Mr. Logan: Just as fast as possible get that Perdue matter settled. It is very important.

I have returned the charter to Mr. Bedford with one suggestion.

I did not have time before leaving to speak to you about Mr. Brewer's[1] charges. They are heavy as I knew they would be. If he succeeds he wants $400 if he fails $200. While these are big figures — yet when we consider the importance and nature of the work I think it best to pay this. He argues that it may keep him in Montgomery the whole session and he will lose much practice in Tuskegee by reason of his absence. Out [of] the am't mentioned he pays his own expenses.

Just as soon as you receive money from New England people let me know.

Hope to send you some money soon. Yours truly

Booker T. Washington

ALS   Con. 6   BTW Papers   ATT.   Original destroyed.

[1] BTW wrote S. L. Brewer of Tuskegee on Oct. 12, 1892, asking him to draft and seek passage of an act of incorporation. BTW said: "We prefer paying so much for the effort and a larger amount in case it is passed all right." (Con. 106, BTW Papers, DLC.) Brewer promised BTW: "You may rest assured I shall devise some means to have the bill passed." Brewer actively lobbied for the bill, which became law on Feb. 21, 1893. (Brewer to BTW, Feb. 18, 1893, Con. 6, BTW Papers, ATT, original destroyed; the act, Feb. 21, 1893, below.)

An Announcement of the Opening
of Phelps Hall Bible School

[Tuskegee, Ala., November 1892]

A BIBLE SCHOOL IN CONNECTION WITH
THE NORMAL AND INDUSTRIAL
INSTITUTE AT TUSKEGEE,
ALABAMA

The desire for increased opportunities for those who wish to fit themselves for the ministry or other forms of Christian work in the South, has been long felt. To meet this need, a generous lady in New York has erected at Tuskegee, a large and beautiful three story building, called Phelps Hall, a picture of which is herewith given, containing a chapel, library, reading room, office, four recitation rooms, forty sleeping rooms; to be used as a Bible School. The donor of this building has furnished each room in the most comfortable and convenient manner, making it the most beautiful and desirable building on the School grounds. This new department will open January 11th, '93; and those who wish to attend should write at once for a circular giving the course of study, expenses, etc. Students will be given an opportunity to work out a portion of their expense, and a few can work out all their expenses. Those who desire can board in town. The teaching will be wholly undenominational. It is the aim of this new department to help all denominations, and not to antagonize them. This Bible School is not in opposition to any theological work now being done, but is simply a means of helping. The faculty will be composed of some of the strongest men in the country, Rev. Edgar J. Penney will be in charge of the work and he will be assisted by Mr. J. D. McCall. Right Rev. B. T. Tanner, Rev. C. O. Booth,[1] D.D., Rev. R. R. Morris,[2] D.D., have been engaged to give a regular course of lectures during the term. All who can possibly do so should be present the first day. For further information, Address

B. T. WASHINGTON, Principal,
Tuskegee, Ala.

PDSr   GAGTh.

[1] The Reverend C. O. Boothe, probably a local black clergyman, assisted as a

lecturer in the Phelps Hall Bible School for many years. He was listed, for example, in the 1898-99 Tuskegee catalog in that capacity.

² R. R. Morris was an A.M.E. Zion minister in Montgomery, pastor of the Old Ship Church. In 1891 he worked in support of the State Colored University's claim to a share of the Morrill Act funds.

To Warren Logan

Crawford House   Boston, Dec. 7 1892

Dear Mr. Logan: I have rec'd your telegrams regarding Miss Shaw's death and Miss Mason's¹ gift. It is very sad about Miss Shaw. I hope to attend her funeral in N.Y.

Miss Mason's gift I know is very timely and helpful.

I telegraphed you tonight to reserve one half of it for the land payment. We must take no risks on that. If they want it I wish you would try to pay the *new teachers in full.*

I had a telegram today from Mr. Campbell saying that our bill² had passed the legislature. Yours truly

B. T. Washington

ALS   Con. 6   BTW Papers   ATT.   Original destroyed.

¹ Either Ellen Francis or Ida Means Mason.

² See An Act to Incorporate Tuskegee Normal and Industrial Institute, Dec. 13, 1892, below.

From Mary A. Elliott

Columbus   Dec 9th 1892

My Dear Brother, I am ever so glad to hear from you. I suppose that you was in the east from reading the little Student. Is my wound Well? not entirely, but can say that it is a great deal better and I feel to praise the Heavenly Father for His Great mercies toward me. I can walk around in the house without my cruches, somthing that I dident expect to do this winter   want to visit Mother to day if I can. We are all as well as usal. Dock is not feeling so well this Winter, but still keeps going. I often tell him that we ought not to complain. When I look at Mother and see how she works evry day weaving evry day makes her living independently of her children, so far, in most evry thing. I am so glad to hear that the dear little children have been well and happy since you all began house keeping   a[l]so that Mrs Washington is getting along so nicely and doing all she can for them, for Davidson cant do very well without a mama, it is his nature he is a tender harted little child. They liked their new mama very well I thought and she rather liked them I thought more then she cared to let on dear woman, Maggie you call her; sounds pretty if there is any thing in a name.

Davidson is a little jealous that is what is the mater with him that he reminds his mama that it is not her papa, all three would feel that way untill they got use to the change, for the privilege of sleeping with papa was at a high premium when I was there.

Well I hope dear brother that you are meeting with success in your work and that you may keep your health and reach home in time to spend happy Holidays with the loved ones. I hope that the time will come in the future that I can visit you all again, nothing would give me more joy. If I cant next year I feel that the time will come that I can come. We expect to move soon into our new house   it is on the same lot that Mother lives on. we will finish a nough to move into so we will not have to pay rent as what we are now paying will go in to our home. It is not far from where we live now. In three or four weeks if I keep on improving I can walk as well as ever. I hope.

Is it possible that Hiram [has] written to you. I am glad. Hiram he is to be pitied more then censured poor brother. I am glad that you do write to Frank.[1] he complains and sais his own born brothers are not as kind to him as you are   he writs scorching letters to us some times   I will write to him soon. Kiss the children for me also Mrs Washington   Your Sister

Mary

P.S. Dock and Mother send love to you all. Grandma would like to se[e] the children. she brought pictures over and we were talking a bout them yesterday. she is so glad that I got to go and see you all. Good by

M.

ALS   Con. 17   BTW Papers   DLC.

[1] Charles E. Davidson, alias Frank E. Crawford.

An Act to Incorporate Tuskegee Normal
and Industrial Institute

[Montgomery, Ala.] December 13, 1892

To incorporate the Tuskegee Normal and Industrial Institute and amend an act to amend an act to establish a normal school for colored teachers at Tuskegee, approved Feb. 16, 1883.

Section 1. *Be it enacted by the General Assembly of Alabama,* That an act to amend an act to establish a normal school for colored teachers at Tuskegee, approved February 16th, 1883, be amended so as to read as follows: Section 1. That George W. Campbell, S. Q. Hale,[1] Lewis Adams, Oliver Howard, Henry D. Smith, B. T. Washington, Geo. L. Chaney, R. C. Bedford, Warren Logan, C. N. Dorsett, and such others as they may under this act associate with them, and their successors, be and are hereby constituted a body politic and corporate, by the name of the Trustees of the Tuskegee Normal and Industrial Institute, and shall have perpetual succession, and a common seal, and by the name aforesaid they and their successors shall be capable in law and shall have full power and authority to acquire, hold, possess, purchase, receive and retain to themselves and their successors forever any lands, tenements, rents, goods, chattels or interests of any kind whatever, which may be given or bequeathed to them or by them purchased, or which have already been bequeathed or purchased for the use of said institution; and said trustees may receive any gift or inheritance which may be given as an endowment fund, and they and their successors shall have full power to convey, transfer and dispose of the same in any manner whatsoever they may judge most useful to the interest and legal purpose of said institution, and, by their corporate name, they may sue and implead and be sued and impleaded, may answer and be answered in all courts of law and equity, and said trustees shall have the right to make contracts in behalf of said institution.

Sec. 2. *Be it further enacted,* That the purposes of said Tuskegee Normal and Industrial Institute shall be as follows: For the instruction of colored teachers and youths in the various common academic and collegiate branches, the best methods of teaching the same, and the best methods of theoretical and practical industry, in their applications to agriculture and mechanic arts; and for the carrying out of these purposes, said trustees shall have the power to establish and provide for the support of any departments or schools in said institution, and to control the operations of the same, to grant such diplomas and confer such degrees as are customary in other colleges of like grade, to appoint such officers for presiding over and transacting the business of this body as may be necessary and prescribe their duties and obligations, to appoint the time and place for their meetings, to determine their own tenure of office, and to adopt such rules, regulations and bylaws, not contrary to the laws of this state or the United States, as they may deem necessary for the good government of the said Tuskegee Normal and Industrial Institute. The said institute shall not be begun nor continued with a less number than twenty-five (25), nor be taught for a period less than nine (9) months of each year. Pupils from this state shall be admitted free of tuition, on giving an obligation in writing to teach for two years in the public schools of this state after they become qualified.

Sec. 3. *Be it further enacted,* That when there shall be a vacancy in the board of trustees occasioned by death, resignation, removal or refusal to act, the remaining trustees or a majority of them shall supply the vacancy at the next annual meeting. It shall be lawful for any five of the trustees to call a meeting of the trustees whenever it is deemed by them expedient to do so.

Sec. 4. *Be it further enacted,* That the number of trustees shall never be less than seven nor more than fifteen, the majority of whom shall constitute a quorum.

Sec. 5. *Be it further enacted,* That all property acquired by said Tuskegee Normal and Industrial Institute, or Tuskegee Normal School, or Tuskegee Institute, or by whatever name so called, before the passage of this act, are hereby ratified and confirmed to the trustees of said Tuskegee Normal and Industrial Institute.

Sec. 6. *Be it further enacted,* That there is hereby appropriated, out of the general school revenue set apart for the education of colored children, the sum of three thousand ($3,000) dollars annually for the maintenance and support of said school, and the apportionment of the general fund for colored children shall be made to the several counties of this state, after the deduction of the sum herein appropriated; the said appropriation shall be under the control of the commissioners hereinafter provided for, and shall be applied in such manner as they deem best to carry out the purpose of this act, and said commissioners shall be members of said board of trustees with the same rights and powers as the other trustees.

Sec. 7. *Be it further enacted,* That the school shall be under the direction and control of a board of three (3) commissioners, which shall consist of the following persons, to-wit: George W. Campbell, S. Q. Hale, and Lewis Adams, who shall select one of their members as chairman of the board, and shall have power to fill any vacancy that may occur in the board. In case a majority of the commissioners can not agree upon a person to be chairman, or a person to fill a vacancy in the board, then such disagreement shall be certified to the superintendent of education for the state, and that officer shall forthwith appoint a member of the board to be chairman, or a person to fill the vacancy, as the case may be, and the member of the board so appointed as chairman, and the person so appointed to the vacancy shall have the same power and authority as if he had been selected by the board. The commissioners shall make an annual written report to the superintendent of education of the condition and progress of the school, the teachers that have been employed, the number of pupils that have been in attendance, the manner in which the appropriation has been expended, the branches that have been taught, and such other facts relating to the school that may be of public interest and importance.

Sec. 8. *Be it further enacted,* That the chairman of the board of commissioners shall give bond in double the amount of the appropriation, for the safe keeping and faithful application of the sum appropriated. The bond to be approved by the judge of probate of Macon county and filed in his office, a certified copy of which shall be forwarded to the state superintendent of education and placed on file in his office.

Sec. 9. *Be it further enacted,* That the chairman of the board of commissioners of the Tuskegee Normal and Industrial Institute shall, after the execution, approval and filing of the bond, and the certified copy of the same as provided hereinbefore, present to the state superintendent of education a requisition for the amount herein appropriated, and the superintendent of education shall thereupon certify the amount to the state auditor, who shall draw his warrant for the same on the state treasurer, payable to the chairman of the board of commissioners for the maintenance and support of the said Tuskegee Normal and Industrial Institute, as hereinbefore provided, and a like requisition shall be presented and the sum herein appropriated so drawn each year as the same shall accrue.

Sec. 10. *Be it further enacted,* That so long as the property, real and personal, of said Tuskegee Normal and Industrial Institute is used for the purpose of education, the same shall be exempt from taxation of any kind.

Sec. 11. *Be it further enacted,* That all laws and parts of laws in conflict with any of the provisions of this act be and the same are hereby repealed.

Approved December 13, 1892.

Acts of the General Assembly of Alabama, Passed by the Session of 1892-93 (Montgomery, 1893), 887-90.

[1] Samuel Q. Hale, at one time editor of the Tuskegee *News,* served as mayor of Tuskegee in the 1870s and as postmaster from 1885 to 1891.

To Helen Wilhelmina Ludlow

Tuskegee, Ala., Dec 30th 1892

Dear Miss Ludlow: Some time during this winter or early in the spring I am planning to take a trip through the Sugar plantations of Louisiana and some portion of the Black Belt of Mississippi in order to acquaint myself more accurately of the real condition of the masses of the people and their needs. I am quite sure there is a state of things existing among the colored people of these plantations that the country should be made acquainted with. The point of this letter is to ask you if you would like to have some account of my trip for THE SOUTHERN WORKMAN or if you know of any paper that it would be well to write to. I have written to the editor of the Boston Transcript about the matter, but I do not know whether or not he would care for such letters.

I consulted with Gen. Armstrong about this trip and he was very anxious to go with me. I hope you will speak to him about the matter. Of course I understand that it would be impossible for him to attempt anything of the kind. He may have some suggestions about the trip that would be of value. When I last saw Gen. Armstrong he seemed very anxious to attend the Conference[1] which will be held the latter part of February and he said he meant to do so. If you can do so will you please find out whether it is likely that he will come and let us know as early as possible as we have some plans on foot for his comfort while here, and we would like to know in order to begin now to carry them out. We feel if he comes we can make him comfortable during his stay and it will be a great privilege to us to do so. We hope to see some one from Hampton at the Conference and wish much you can see your way clear to come again. I mention your coming especially because we feel you would have an opportunity to note the changes in the condition of the people from year to year better than a new person.

We are all still full of work. Yours truly,

Booker T. Washington

TLS Miscellaneous MSS MWiW.

[1] Tuskegee Negro Conference.

To Wilbur Patterson Thirkield[1]

Tuskegee, Ala., Dec 30 1892

Dear sir: I am exceedingly sorry that I have not been able to reply earlier to your kind letter of recent date. When your letter came I was absent from home and when I returned I found so many matters claiming my attention that I was compelled to delay longer than I desired, a reply. Now I fear my reply is too late for your purposes.

I have been convinced ever since I have been engaged in work for my people that efforts along all other lines of education for my People would be to a large extent fruitless or greatly hindered unless at the same time we could have an intelligent and consecrated ministry. In bringing about this result — I speak advisedly when I say that nothing to my mind has gone so far in this direction as Gammon Theological Seminary — when I was there some time ago and had the opportunity of looking through your buildings my heart went up in thanks to our Father for that noble work for my race.

A few months ago when I spoke out on the subject of the condition of our ministry I was misunderstood by many, but I was then and am now willing to be misunderstood if I can aid in calling attention to the need of a better ministry.

I watch your efforts with interest. You are right in getting hold of the southern white ministers. We need their help. We must get nearer to each other. I like your unselfish, whole-souled manner.

Thank you for your encouraging words regarding our new department. We dedicate Feb 7 and I now extend you a hearty invitation to be present. Dr. Lyman Abbott delivers the address. Yours Sincerely,

Booker T. Washington

ALS GAGTh.

[1] Wilbur Patterson Thirkield (1854-1938?), a white Methodist clergyman, was the first president of Gammon Theological Seminary (1883-1900). He had graduated from Ohio Wesleyan University and the theology school of Boston University. From 1900 to 1906 Thirkield was in Cincinnati as general secretary of the Freedmen's Aid and Southern Education Society of the Methodist Episcopal Church. He served as president of Howard University from 1906 to 1912. During most of his presidency BTW was a member of the board of trustees of Howard and one of Thirkield's strong supporters. Thirkield left Howard upon his elevation to bishop.

A Speech before the New York Congregational Club

[New York, Jan. 16, 1893]

THE PROGRESS OF THE NEGRO

Gentlemen of the Congregational Club: It is now but little more than 15 years ago since I left the hills of West Virginia with the purpose of reaching in some unknown way the Hampton Institute — an institution founded and still fostered by the American Missionary Association. At length I found myself in the city of Richmond without money, friends or shelter. An opening under a side walk afforded me shelter by night and an outgoing ship loading pig iron furnished me work by day till my purse was sufficiently full to enable me to reach Hampton with a surplus of 50¢, and there I found an institution founded by you which gave me the opportunity to work my way through. After finishing my studies I resolved that I would go into the far South and spend my life in trying to give the poor but worthy young men and women of my race the same opportunity to secure an education by self-help as was afforded me at Hampton.

And now, it is a rare privilege to be permitted to address some of the representatives of that religious body which has done the broadest, deepest, most telling and unselfish work for the elevation of my race. I say unselfish, for I feel that the secretaries of the American Missionary Association will agree with me in the expression that if the value of the work of Congregational churches in the South is to be measured by the number of Congregational churches organized or the number of individuals that has become congregationalists, the work has not been of the most encouraging character. For where you have placed one Congregational minister in a Congregational church, you have placed 20 in a Methodist or Baptist pulpit; where one Congregational teacher you have given a score of Methodists or Baptists education.

(Story — Hard to make a Negro anything but a Methodist or Baptist)

But if we are to judge of the value of your work by the manner in which you have broken through denominational lines by reason of the superior character of your work; placed in every center, at least, one pure Christian church that serves as a light house in its influence and lessons as to what a church should be; educated the Christian leader in all denominations, the teacher, the professional man, the farmer, the mechanic; established the model Christian home and forced a life-giving current into the moral, economic and industrial life of every section of the South — if the value of the work of the American Missionary Association be measured, as it should be, by these standards, I believe it has no parallel in the history of this or any other country.

But, gentlemen, I did not come here to talk in this general manner. Will you forgive me, if for a moment, I take the Tuskegee School in Alabama as an example of the progress of the Negro, and in doing this I use it as an example, not selfishly, but because the work at Tuskegee will represent a similar work being done by a dozen or more of American Missionary Association Schools. Starting a little over ten years ago with one teacher and thirty students in a worn-out church and small shanty, the Tuskegee school has gradually grown during these ten years into 511 students representing every Southern State, the Indian Territory and Africa, and 32 officers and teachers, and so anxious are the masses for education that we have been compelled to refuse this year admission to nearly 500 for want of room and means.

At Tuskegee as in most, if not all, of your schools in connection with the mental and religious training we have industrial work. Through the industrial system three ends are sought: First to give the students an opportunity to work out a portion of their board bills. Very soon after beginning the work at Tuskegee, we found that few of those who came were able to pay in cash the $8. per month charged for board and remain during the 9 months session, so we started the practice of giving them an opportunity to work out about $3 of the $8, and they are able, as a rule, to pay the remainder in cash and remain during the session. Second: The school furnishes labor that is of value to the institution and gives the students an opportunity at the same time to learn something from the labor within itself. We have just completed a three-story brick building. For this building our young men made the bricks at our brick yard, did the brick-masonry, plastering, painting, tinning, carpentry, and the sawing and planing of much of the lumber. While the young men do that kind of work, the girls make and launder their clothing and are thus taught sewing and laundering. In the end the institution has the building for permanent use and the students, the knowledge of the trades connected with the completion of such a building. At the head of each industry there is a competent teacher so that the students not only do the work but get hold of the principles and practice at the same time. On this plan 400 acres of land have been cultivated the past year. This plan runs through all our 14 industries. Then we make the industrial system valuable in teaching and emphasizing the dignity of labor and in giving moral back-bone — in teaching that labor neither hurts nor disgraces anyone to use his hands in any manner found necessary — and I might add in passing that the idea of manual labor being disgraceful is not in any sense original with the colored people down in the South.

(Anxiety for trades — Do not give in full value of taxable property — Heresy trials.)

Thus, during these ten years, there has been built up at Tuskegee, almost wholly by the labor of the students — friends in the North giving the money to buy land and the material which we could not produce, and to pay the teachers — a property that is valued at $170,000, including 1400 acres of land. On this property there are, counting large and small, 18 buildings and all except two have been erected almost wholly by the labor of the students, and there is not a dollar of mortgage about any of this property.

But to accumulate students, industries, buildings and land is far from being the object of these Southern institutions. In everything that is done in the religious teaching, mental work and industrial training, it is constantly kept in mind that it is all being done as a means to an end — the fortifying of the heart, head and hand in a manner to enable these students to go out and reach in the most effective manner that large mass of our people found mainly on those large cotton, rice and sugar plantations. You understand that it is not possible for any except a very small percentage of the masses to pass through our higher institutions. In view of this it is plain that the most effective and economic thing for these higher institutions to do, is to spend their means and energy in preparing a class of strong Christian leaders who will use their education not for selfish ends but who will go out and spend their lives showing the masses how to help themselves.

Just what is the actual condition of the mass of colored people in the "Black Belt" section in the South to-day? Legal slavery is dead, but there is an industrial, mental and moral slavery that is very far from being dead, and it will be years before that kind of slavery is blotted out. Taking Alabama as an example, in the country districts you will find at least ¾ or ⅘ of the people in debt by reason of the mortgage or crop lien system. The first year our people got their freedom they had nothing on which to live while they were raising the first crop. The former masters said: If you will give a mortgage on the crop which you expect to produce this year, I will advance you the money or food on which to live while the crop is being grown. In this way the mortgage system started, and it has grown and overlapped from year to year and fastened itself into the moral and industrial life of not only the colored people but of the white people as well to an extent that it is hard for you to realize. Poor men whether black or white who are compelled to seek assistance through these mortgages are charged an interest that ranges from 25% to 40%, and if you bear in mind that this money is not used in most cases but for 4 or 6 months the interest mounts up beyond 100 per cent.

Four-fifths of these people live in small one-roomed log cabins and as many as that rent the land on which they live.

The schools in Alabama are in session on an average of 3½ months during the year. This is the average for the state and it is very seldom they are in session longer than 60 days in the count[r]y districts. The State has so far been able to give no money for the building of school houses, and the result is the schools are taught in churches, & wrecks of log cabins with nothing in the form of conveniences or apparatus. Last year each colored child received from the public fund for his education 83¢ and the whites but a few cents more, while each child in Massachusetts received not far from $20. This does not mean that the State is not becoming interested in public education. At almost every session of the State legislature a slight increase is made in the appropriation, but the trouble is the children increase faster than the revenue from taxable property.

As to the moral condition of the masses in the country districts. During slavery my people reasoned something like this: My body belongs to my master, and taking master's chickens to feed master's body is not stealing, and they are inclined to apply this same kind of logic to the mortgage system, and it is not hard for you to understand some of the results of that kind of reasoning. And then, too, it is not hard for you [to] understand something of the moral condition of a people where mother, father, children, relatives, strangers, of all sexes to the number of 4, 6 and even 10, eat, cook, sleep, get sick and die in one room. The public statistics represent a very large proportion of our people as being church members. But belonging to the church does not in many cases mean all that is implied and is no reason why the bulk of our people are not just as much in need of Christian teaching as any people to be found in Africa or Japan. To be a little more plain. In the South we find it a pretty hard thing to make a good Christian of a hungry man. No matter how long the people have belonged to the church or how much they get happy and shout in church, the Negroes have after all a good deal of human nature and if they go home from church at night hungry and find nothing to eat they are tempted to find something to eat before morning. This is human nature the world over and is not confined to the Negro. That kind of religion which will help him fill not only his heart, but his stomach, clothe and shelter his body and surround himself with some of the conveniences and comforts of life, is the kind that is best for the Negro as well as the white man.

(Story about give me Jesus.)

In all this I simply mean to emphasize the fact that with all the mental and religious work, there will be no permanent progress unless at the same time we give attention to the material and industrial side.

But there is a brighter side. What is the remedy for this condition? If the Negro got any good out of slavery, it was the habit of hard work — of swallowing bitter pills and chewing hard bones. The most of them as you find them, especially in the country districts work hard to-day. I know you will find a class around the corners of the streets and railroad stations that loaf just as you will find among any people; and we have some black sheep in our flock just as there are in all flocks, but the bulk work hard from year to year. The trouble is they do not know how to use the results of their labor. What they labor hard for gets away from them mainly by reason of the mortgage system, often for whiskey, tobacco snuff and cheap jewelry. I have gone into one-roomed cabins and found clocks for which they have paid on the installment plan $12 or $15 and everything in that cabin aside from that clock would not be worth $15. It was reported some time since by one of our students that it is common for the people at his home at the end of the year, if they save any little money, to spend it in buying buggies for $60 and $70, and at the same time they do not own a horse or a mule to draw the buggy.

About six years ago a young girl[1] finished her course at Tuskegee and went into one of these thickly settled cotton communities to begin her lifework. She found the people in debt, discouraged as I have mentioned — had been in debt ever since the war — living from hand to mouth on rented land in one-roomed cabins. They have never had a school longer than three months and that taught by an inferior teacher, in a wreck of a log cabin. Finding this condition of things this girl took the three months public school provided by the state as a nucleus for her work, but she did not stop with this. She went among the mothers and fathers and got their confidence. She then organized the older people into a society that came together every week. In these meetings she would tell them in a plain, simple, common sense manner how to keep out of debt, how to stop mortgaging; she would keep their accounts for them, tell them what to buy and what not to buy, how to sacrifice — to live on bread and water, if necessary until they could stop mortgaging and begin the buying of a home of their own. The first year this girl was in this community she got a number of these people to stop mortgaging and make contracts for the buying of homes. In addition to this the first year this girl was in this community she so directed the efforts of the people that by their contributions in labor and money they built and furnished with apparatus a neat, comfortable little framed school house to take the place of the log cabin which they had formerly used. The next year these people through the guidance of their teacher added by their own contributions two months to the original three months school. The next year they added another month, and now every year they have an eight months school taught in this comfortable school house. Now, my friends, I wish you could have the privilege of going into this community as I have had, and of looking into the faces of these people and see them beaming with hope and delight, of going into their little homes, through their farms, into their day school, Sunday school and church services and see the complete revolution, yes, regeneration that has been wrought in the industrial, educational and religious life of this whole community by the work of this one girl. Bear in mind that no body gave them a cent of money with which to build that school house or to add any months to the original school term. It all came by having this leader, this guide, in their midst to show them how to direct their own efforts. This is the work that the graduates of Tuskegee, Hampton, Fisk, Talladega, Tougaloo and other institutions are doing, sending out a class of leaders who go among their people as object lessons, as centers of light, and I could point to many other such examples. And if my ten years of experience and observation in the heart of the South are worth anything, I give it as my opinion that it is to this kind of work we have got to look for the solution of this problem in the South. The colored people as a mass do not need charity scattered among them, but they do need to be led, to be guided, to be stimulated until they can get onto their feet. If you were to go among our people as I often do and see them living in the miserable way that they do you would be inclined to grow impatient and say: If these people were worth their freedom they would not be in this condition after 25 or 30 years of freedom. I have felt this way and I have asked an individual here and there: "Why are you content to live here in this manner with nothing present or in prospect for yourself and children?" When I have asked this question I have heard them say: "I want to change. I know that this is not the right way to live, but the truth is I don't know how." When I have gotten this answer and gotten a good look into their worn and haggard face void of mental strength, of mental activity & of will power, I have realized as I never realized before, the terrible curse of slavery upon my people. The greatest injury that slavery did my people was to deprive them of that sense of self-dependence and executive power which are the glory and distinction of the Anglo-Saxon race. For two and a half centuries they were taught to look to some one else for their food, shelter, & clothing and every move they made in life, and what was 250 years going into a race cannot be gotten out in 25 or 30 years unless we at least give them object lessons in the form [of] Christian leaders.

(Tuskegee Conference)

What effect does education have on the civil and political relations existing between the two races? The reports in the daily press of murder, Lynch law, ballot box stuffing and intimidation you are acquainted with, and these reports are generally true, but I have never been inclined to the opinion that I could render the best service to my race by spending my time in a continual recital of the wrongs. It seems to me that as a race we are just now in the position of a sick man and it is more sensible to put our time and energy in finding a way to get well than in bemoaning over how we became sick. As an entering wedge there is an absence of prejudice against the colored man in the South in the matter of business that counts for a great deal. When it comes to business, pure and simple, I believe that the black man has a better chance in the South than in the North, and I believe that he can sooner conquer Southern prejudice than cope with Northern competition.

(Examples of business)

I think we will find that friction between the two races will disappear in proportion as the black man gets hold of something that the white man wants or respects. It happened a few days ago in the town of Tuskegee that two white men met a colored man in the street, and it also happened that the colored man owns some property, has a nice little home, keeps a bank account, has some education and pays his debts. After the two white men had gotten by one was overheard to say to the other: "By Josh, it is all I can do to keep from calling that Negro Mister when I meet him."

When I went into the town of Tuskegee ten years ago to start the

Tuskegee school, there were some people who usually seemed to make it convenient to look the other way when we met in the streets, and this went on until the school started a brick-yard. We manufactured good bricks and these same people came to us for bricks. We started our wheelwrighting shop, and they wanted wagons and buggies made and repaired, and they came to get that kind of work done. We started our Printing Office and the whites came to us with job printing. Our office does the job printing for that entire section — black and white, and for a while one of the County Democratic papers was printed in our office by our students. Now, by reason of our having something that these people wanted, they came to us and we got acquainted with each other. From discussing bricks we discussed education. There came about an interdependence — a dovetailing of our business interests, and our institution has not warmer friends anywhere to-day than are to be found among those white people in that little town. Now, we have found by experience that what is true of that institution is true of an individual, and that is another reason why in addition to sending our teachers to do the work that I have indicated, we push the industrial work of Tuskegee, for we find as we can put, as we do every year, young men and women in those Southern towns who can start Saw-mills, brick yards, harness shops, printing offices — young men who by reason of their skill and intelligence, can produce something that will make the white man dependent on the black man for something instead of all the dependence being on the other side — as we can do this we see that a change for the better does take place in the relations of the races. And you help us to go on with this business development of the Negro till a black man gets to the point — as many of them are already getting — where he can get a mortgage on a white man's house that he can foreclose at will — well, that white man won't drive that Negro away from the polls when he sees him going up to vote and he will be slow about kicking him out of a first class car. Now, my friends, it is a slower and perhaps more roundabout process, but it is right along these lines that we have got to look for the solution of all these problems in the South, and along these lines they are slowly but surely to be solved. With the education, the property, and moral back-bone, the Negro will soon be able to take care of the voting himself.

(Whites Helping)

How can you best help in the righting of all these matters? Most

287

assuredly by giving your money where it will result in producing those Christian leaders to which I have referred.

(Cannot supply demand)

It will surprise and delight you to see how far $50, a $100 or $1000 for tuition or general expenses can be made to go in educating young men and women who, when they get their education, will go into some dark corner and spend their lives in showing the masses how to lift themselves up something [in] the way that I have attempted to indicate.

(Story of Fred. Douglass)

TMd Con. 955 BTW Papers DLC. There are occasional minor editorial corrections in BTW's hand.

[1] Probably Cornelia Bowen. (See above, 2:191.) In 1888 she founded Mt. Meigs Industrial Institute. In 1893-94 she spent a year at Teachers College, Columbia University. She later attended the University of Glasgow.

To Warren Logan

Tuskegee, Ala., Jan. 25th 1893

Mr. Logan: Please see that 50¢ are deducted from Lockett's[1] wages for having breakfast late Sunday morning.

B. T. W.

HLIr Con. 6 BTW Papers ATT. Original destroyed.

[1] There was no Lockett in the Tuskegee catalog that year, but Barnie Hill Lockhart of Columbus, Ga., was a junior and William Henry Lockhart was a night-school student.

To William Addison Benedict

[Tuskegee, Ala.] Jan. 28th [189]3

Dear Sir: I have not replied to your letter of December 31st earlier for the reason that I had to make two trips to the North since receiving this letter, thus my time has been taken up.

I have not as yet presented your report to our Financial Committee, very largely for the reason that I felt ashamed to do so. I told you in the beginning, you will remember, that they would be guided very largely in their actions regarding employing you by my advice. On my advice you were employed and now for you to ask them to take a large sum of money out of our treasury to pay you is rather humiliating. There are two sides to this matter. You will remember that you represented that you felt sure that you could raise $100,000 in three years. Now if there was any shadow of truth in this, is it not reasonable to suppose that you would have raised $3000. for the first year. To all contracts there are two sides. One is that the employed is to do certain things and the employer is to do certain other things. You are inclined, I know, to hold us strictly to account for the fulfilment of one side while you have failed to comply with the other side in a very large and disappointing measure. We are not inclined to be unreasonable in the matter, but I beg of you to think about it and ask yourself whether or not you are doing this institution justice to take this sum out of its depleted treasury to pay you. You remember that I said to you in our conversation last year that the school had been deceived in this matter once before, that we had employed a man that did not cover expenses and that we did not wish to have a similar experience with you.

Mr. Logan calls my attention to the fact that you have not sent in the names of the persons who gave the $70. I hope after you have considered this matter fully you will let us hear from you. Yours truly,

B. T. Washington

TLpS Con. 106 BTW Papers DLC.

From Emily Howland

Philad.a Jan. 31. 93

Esteemed friend   I think that I have never acknowledged your last letter announcing your expected marriage with Miss Murray. I suppose this has already become history. I am sure both of you have my cordial best wishes for yourselves and for your work.

I have not forgotten that you told me also that you feared that there would be much suffering in your part of the South on account of the failure of the cotton crop, and I have had that painful outlook in mind ever since, intending to contribute my mite toward the relief of some of the sufferers. I enclose herewith a postal note for ten dollars to be added to your Relief fund and expended as, those who have it in charge, consider most needed.

The severe weather of two weeks ago has multiplied appeals for help to the poor. I have just come on from Washington. While there I heard much of the efforts made to raise money for the relief of the suffering. The city poor never appeal to my sympathies as do those in the country, because they are often the creators of their own misery, by their vicious and improvident habits, and are so indolent as to prefer to be fed by charity, which ought to be cold, but when people have striven to earn a living and failed thro' no fault of their own I think that they ought to be helped. Thinking that this letter may find you gone I shall address it to yourself & Mr. Logan.

Please remember me to your wife and believe me   Cordially

Emily Howland

ALS   Con. 6   BTW Papers   ATT.   Original destroyed.

From Samuel Chapman Armstrong

Hampton, Va., Feb 14 1893

Dear Mr Washington   Your letters are recd. Thanks for information. Mr Howe[1] is coming here to go with me to Tuskegee. Hope to arrive there next Sat. ev. Will telegraph our start. I am still lame not able to walk well, but get around with a cane with little trouble. Glad bright weather has come again. Hope I will have a fine day next Tuesday the 21st. Delighted if my letter in the "Post" did you any good. Will do all I can with my pen for Tuskegee. I am now doing some heavy work for Hawaiian Annexation for a N.Y. paper. I dictate daily now.

Regards to all   Sincerely yours

S. C. Armstrong

ALS   Con. 6   BTW Papers   ATT.   Original destroyed.

[1] Albert Howe.

1. Margaret James Murray Washington.
Booker T. Washington Papers, Library of Congress

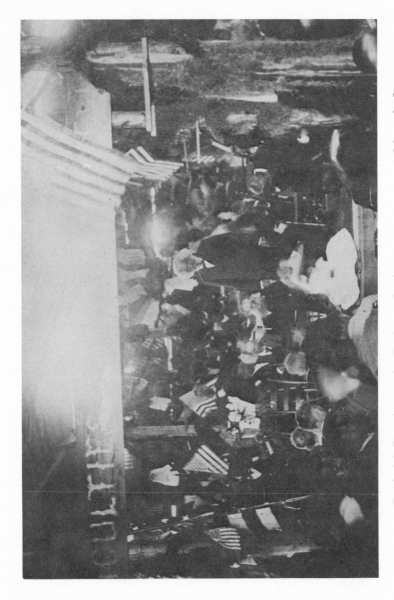

2. Frederick Douglass at the Tuskegee Institute commencement, May 26, 1892.
Booker T. Washington Papers, Library of Congress

3. Frederick Douglass, ca. 1894.
Library of Congress

4. James Fowle Baldwin Marshall, ca. 1889.
Hampton Institute Archives

5. Hollis Burke Frissell, 1893.
Hampton Institute Archives

6. Mary Fletcher Mackie, ca. 1890.
Hampton Institute Archives

8. Edward Wilmot Blyden.

7. Bishop Daniel Augustus Payne.

William J. Simmons, *Men of Mark* (1887)

9. Bishop Henry McNeal Turner.

10. Theophile Tarence Allain.

12. Thomas McCants Stewart.

William J. Simmons, *Men of Mark* (1887)

11. Richard Theodore Greener.

13. William Henry Baldwin, Jr., 1899.
John Graham Brooks, *An American
Citizen* (1910)

14. William Hooper Councill, ca. 1902.
Booker T. Washington Papers,
Library of Congress

15. Timothy Thomas Fortune, 1887.
Simmons, *Men of Mark* (1887)

16. The Negro Building at the Atlanta Exposition, 1895.
Walter G. Cooper, *The Cotton States and International Exposition* (1896)

17. Emily Howland.
Elizabeth Cady Stanton *et al., History of Woman Suffrage* (1902)

18. Irving Garland Penn.
Clement Richardson, ed., *National Cyclopedia of the Colored Race* (1919)

19. Booker T. Washington, 1895.
Harper's Weekly, 39 (Sept. 14, 1895)

From Henry Demarest Lloyd[1]

Chicago, Illinois, February 16th, 1893

Dear Sir; I am very much pleased to know that you intend to accept the invitation to address the Labor Congress.[2]

According to our present plans my wife and I intend leaving Chicago next Sunday, arriving in Montgomery Tuesday morning in time, we hope, to attend your convention. Will you be good enough to have two bed rooms reserved for our accommodation? Very truly yours,

H. D. Lloyd

TLS   Con. 6   BTW Papers   ATT.   Original destroyed.

[1] Henry Demarest Lloyd (1847-1903), a Chicago lawyer and newspaper writer, was a champion of labor and reform causes, including defense of the anarchists convicted after the Haymarket Riot in 1886 and the miners in the anthracite strike in 1902. He was the author of *Wealth against Commonwealth* (1894), a scathing criticism of monopolies, particularly Standard Oil Company. He ran for Congress in 1894 on the People's Party ticket. In the last year of his life he joined the Socialist party.

[2] The Labor Congress was a feature of the World's Columbian Exposition in Chicago in 1893. (See BTW to Lloyd, July 29, 1893, and an account of BTW's speech, Sept. 2, 1893, below.)

An Account of Samuel Chapman Armstrong's Visit to Tuskegee

[Tuskegee, Ala., Feb. 18–ca. Mar. 11, 1893][1]

Gen. Armstrong's welcome to Tuskegee will never be forgotten. When those who witnessed it have passed away it will take its place among the traditions of the School.

As a mark of sympathy and respect to him, Gen. Tyler,[2] of the Western R.R., stopped the New Orleans limited, at Chehaw, and Capt. Wright[3] ran out a special from Tuskegee. Though nearly midnight, the students waited patiently for his coming, and when the courier announced his approach, the whole campus was suddenly wrapped in flames; students, armed with brilliant torches, in open ranks, lined the driveway, and led by the band and waving banners, all formed ranks and followed the party to the Principal's residence, where songs and cheers and tears of gladness showed how deep and hearty was the welcome to one who seemed so like a father to all, and whose self-sacrifice had made Tuskegee possible. The uncovered head, the single word, and the deep emotion with which it was uttered, showed that the welcome was as heartily appreciated as it was gladly tendered.

It was the good fortune of the School to have three weeks of the General's presence. He had not expected to be able to go around much, but his surroundings were a tonic and inspiration to him and he was rarely still. Sunday morning he listened to his old friend, Dr. Harding,[4] of Long Meadow, Mass., and at night he himself occupied the time.

It was his first attempt since his affliction, at addressing a large audience, and when he first began, he would ask, "Do you all hear me; can you understand what I say?" and, as the hearty response of "Yes, yes," came back from all over the house, much of his old spirit and force returned to him and he spoke with great power for more than forty minutes. All were surprised together, and together all gave thanks to God for the restoration to him of that wonderful gift of eloquent speech.

On Tuesday, Feb. 21st, came the Conference. To save his strength as much as possible, Mr. John Washington, Disciplinarian and "Col." of the School battalion, had prepared a Sedan chair, and the young men picked him up and bore him proudly to the Chapel of Porter Hall. He was wholly in his element. The Chapel was crowded with the plain, hardworking farmers of the Black Belt. To him who knew them, their hard lot was written on their faces, and his heart went out towards them. About him were many of his Hampton graduates; Washington, the educator; Dorsette, the physician; Logan, the treasurer; Hamilton, the musician; Greene[5] and Roy,[6] the farmers; Driver, the wheelwright and blacksmith; Carter, the mechanic; Mann,[7] the printer; Miss Burke,[8] the matron and nurse; Miss Peake,[9] the leader in religious work; and "Col." John Washington, the man of business.

Dr. Dorsette introduced the Gen. to the Conference. He spoke standing. Among other things he said: "The world listened to the Conference of last year and was pleased with it and spoke kindly and hopefully of it. I was glad you recognized the Southern white people and what they have done for you. It was a Conference of common sense. It did not burthen the public with grievances, but recognizing good naturedly, the wrongs that existed, it sought to find remedies for them. Think of something besides yourselves. I want to tell you of Prof. Howe, and what he has done in redeeming worn out lands. He will tell you that if cotton is king the cow-pea is queen. I advise you to meet in your various communities and talk over matters of common interest. Provide for raising your own meat and food supplies. Build yourselves homes, churches and schools."

His wise and weighty words will bear fruit. With deep emotion expressed in one of its declarations, the Conference said "We cannot forbear special mention of General S. C. Armstrong, whose life God has so graciously spared and who is permitted to be with us to-day."

The beautiful days, the kind and loving care of all, his deep interest in the work of the School, along with the earnest entreaty of many friends, induced him to remain at Tuskegee till after the dedication of Phelps Hall, on March 9th. What busy days. He wrote accounts of the Conference for the press, conducted a large correspondence, read all the papers and magazines, with Herndon's Life of Lincoln; spoke often to the students; visited every department of the School, and made a trip to Montgomery and Calhoun. He praised the air and water of Tuskegee. Many of the best citizens paid him their respects. Dr. Dillon's remedies increased his strength; Miss Burke's nursing was that of a friend rather than of a nurse; the reading of Miss Peake, and the singing of the students brought him many restful hours, and there was the abounding hospitality of Mrs. Washington.

The dedication of Phelps Hall was an occasion of great interest to him. It gave him much pleasure to meet at the School, the Misses Stokes and their brother Thomas, along with Dr. and Mrs. Abbott, and other New York friends, and even more pleased was he to meet, not only the colored people, but also the leading white people, clergymen and business men from Tuskegee, Montgomery and other portions of the state, sharing together in the brightening hopes foreshadowed by the exercises of the day. Many great themes were crowded into his short address. He told of grave responsibilities and great dangers social, political and moral. "Tuskegee is here because of these things. It tells its own story. Put faith in man as you do in God. Give men and women a fair chance. Poverty must not be made a man's curse." He spoke of the danger of waste, the dignity of work, and the still greater dignity of obedience.

General Armstrong, by this visit, has not only greatly blessed Tuskegee, but his influence will take a wider range and be felt, more and more, throughout the entire gulf South.

Southern Workman, 22 (Apr. 1893), 57. This account was written by Robert Charles Bedford.

[1] Armstrong arrived on Feb. 18 for a three-week visit.

[2] Edmund L. Tyler of Atlanta was general manager and purchasing agent of the Atlanta and West Point Railroad Company, which met the Western of Alabama at West Point, Ga.

[3] W. H. Wright was treasurer and agent of the Tuskegee Railroad until 1902. The railroad traveled 5.5 miles between Tuskegee and Chehaw on narrow-gauge rails. In 1893 the line had two locomotives, one passenger car, six freight cars, and one baggage car. It maintained passenger service until 1942.

[4] John Wheeler Harding.

[5] Charles W. Greene.

[6] John A. Roy.

[7] Thomas L. Mann.

[8] Wilhelmina C. Burke.

[9] Sarah F. Peake Greene.

An Account of the Tuskegee Negro Conference

[Tuskegee, Ala., Feb. 21, 1893]

To the Southern Workman: Tuesday, Feb. 21st, was the day of the Negro Conference at Tuskegee, called by Mr. Booker T. Washington, at his Tuskegee Normal School.

The Conference opened at a quarter of ten, in the large chapel of the school. The room was filled.

The central figure on the platform — the one toward whom all eyes and hearts turned — was dear General Armstrong.

It was fine to hear the singing of the opening hymn, "Am I a soldier of the Cross," by the hundreds of people gathered there.

It was a most touching, as well as encouraging sight, to see those farmers and their wives coming together at the call of Mr. Washington, to find a way out of the debt and other troubles which threaten to swamp them.

A short prayer was offered, then Mr. Washington opened the Conference. He urged the people to stick to the spirit of last year; to lose sight of all small personal grievances; to present the real condition of the people, and find, if possible, a way out of their difficulties.

His speech gave the key note to the meeting.

The reports given as to whether any practical good has resulted from last year's Conference were exceedingly interesting. They seemed to indicate that more are trying to get homes, to buy land, and to do more for the schools than ever before.

One or two men reported unfavorably, saying that the men in their districts do not work long or hard enough to get homes; that because the Bible says, "Work six days and rest one, a heap o' folks work three and rest four days."

One man, who said more stealing had been done this last year than the previous one, was asked if there was a special necessity for this increase; his reply was, "Yes; dar's been more starvin'." In his place, the school was for three months only.

The point of great interest is the fact that in the counties where the schools have seven and eight months' sessions, the people are getting out of debt, are buying land, building homes. From Macon, Tuskegee County, came the report that eighteen families have bought homes during the last two years.

After these reports were given, General Armstrong spoke. He was introduced by Dr. Dorsette, of Montgomery — a Hampton graduate — as "the man who has been both iron and steel — both father and mother to the Negro." A great wave of love and reverence for this man who has given himself for the service of man, seemed to sweep over the whole people.

The General gave such wise, helpful, inspiring thoughts to them! He dwelt especially on the "sanctified common sense," shown by the Negroes at the Conference last year; of the increased respect, all over the country, for men who could meet and discuss so sensibly and so kindly, their difficulties and troubles, without complaint of others.

He showed them how half of their cotton crop goes to pay for Western pork, and imported molasses and coffee, and urged them to raise their own pork, and, instead of planting all cotton, to plant two-thirds of their land in food supplies. He said, "If cotton is King of the South, the cow pea is Queen."

The Declarations were then read, and one by one discussed.

First came the subject of the Mortgage System.

A farmer of Macon county gave his experience, which surely ought to be a lesson to others. In 1873, he raised no corn — all cotton, and, as he put it, "The pain lasted 'till I got into the corn country."

This farmer now owns one hundred acres; raises enough corn to feed his hands and stock, and, for four years, has raised the first bale of cotton in the county, for which he gets a premium. "Big cotton raisers," he said, "are the ones who come to town early to see when the mortgage door will be open."

The rate of interest on mortgages runs from 8 per cent. to 15, 25 and 30 per cent.

The matter of the one-roomed cabins was taken up. One man was reported as living in one room with thirteen in the family. Mr. Washington distributed among the people a plan of a two-roomed cabin which can be built for $300.

The discussion on schools was very interesting.

To one who lives among these people, who sees and knows how desperately poor they are — the amount of money raised by them for schools is astonishing.

This year, at Mt. Meigs, a little country settlement in Montgomery county, the people have raised $540 for the school there; the colored people of Calhoun, Lowndes Co., have raised $594 for its school, and reports were given of various schools that had been extended by the Negroes themselves, from the three months allowed by the county to four and five months.

The discussion in regard to teachers and preachers came next. There is no doubt that the day is near at hand when the illiterate, unprincipled preachers and teachers, who have been such a curse to the Negro, will have to "take to de woods," and have only themselves for company.

Next came the question of the treatment of the colored women by the colored men. The feeling seemed to be that, in this regard there has not been marked improvement. The General spoke again here, and told them that no race can rise whose women are ill-treated.

The discussion on the question: "Is our religion carried into our every day life?" was a practical one. One preacher said he had 1,300 church members, 300 of whom were "real," 600 "dead"; the rest "not accounted for."

Prof. Henderson[1] of Straight University, urged the people to appeal more to public sentiment, in the right way. His word was a very helpful and practical one; through him a resolution was passed approving the recent action of the Governor of Alabama, in regard to lynching.

Mr. Moore,[2] of Washington, who represented the American Missionary Association, spoke of five things necessary to every true man. Quoting from Senator Morgan:[3] 1st, Land; 2d, Law; 3d, Labor; 4th, Education, emphasizing industrial education; 5th, Spirit of love.

The Conference closed at half-past four; the white Presbyterian minister of Tuskegee, pronouncing the benediction.

Every one at the Conference must have got help and encouragement from it.

The spirit throughout was fine. No complaining of oppression; no shifting the cause of present troubles to other shoulders. Each man stood on his own feet; acknowledged his failures and mistakes in a manly way; then all went to work to find a way to better things. The Conference met to build up, not to pull down.

The watchwords for the coming year are to be, "Less cotton, more corn." "Fewer Mortgages, more buying of land." "Better homes"; "Better schools."

Are not these people solving the "Negro Problem," while others talk of solving it?

DECLARATIONS

The interest awakened by the Conference of last year and the practical results accomplished by it, lead us to believe in the wisdom of an annual gathering of the masses of the colored people who shall give to the public their own views as to the condition of the race, suggesting methods of improvement and remedies for existing evils.

As the outcome of our Second Annual Conference, we make the following declarations:

First — In our review of the past year we believe that progress has been made with reference to the vital points put forth by the last Conference especially in the effort to supplant the Mortgage System by the Cash System; in the purchase of property, the supplementing of the school funds by private subscription and the building of better school houses; the greater care in the choice of teachers and preachers; the more considerate treatment of women; the making of religion a matter of daily living and the loosening of the cords of sectarian prejudice.

Second — While we realize how much has been done for our race we are yet appalled by the vastness of the numbers who are still practically untouched by any inspiring or uplifting influences.

Third — The unfortunate condition of the people manifests itself in the utter poverty of their surroundings; their homes are often mere hovels with a single room; their living is coarse and scant; the soil is poor; they are weighted down with accumulated debts; unplanted crops are mortgaged; the school runs for three and a half months; a suitable school house is the exception; the teacher as a rule is poorly fitted for his work; what has been said of the school house and the teacher may as truly be said of the church and the preacher. Under these depressing circumstances immorality takes deep root and shows itself in the form of intemperance, gambling and loose habits generally.

Fourth — As remedies, in part, for this state of things we would reaffirm the nine suggestions in declaration sixth of last year. In addition we would most earnestly urge the doing away with the one room cabin and call no place home that has not at least two rooms in it; we would discourage the indiscriminate use of excursions; we urge the diversifying of crops with the raising of our own meat and poultry; we advise our women to avoid loafing about the streets and other public places; we would discourage the habit of wasting Saturday; we deplore the tendency to leave the country to find a home in the cities; we advise greater care of our girls and boys and an earnest effort to find employment for them at home; we would urge the laying aside of all minor issues and the concentration of our energies upon the securing of property, that we may become taxpayers; upon the getting of an education, that we may intelligently exercise the rights of citizenship; and upon acquiring of correct moral habits, that we may be able to establish a character among our neighbors that shall be above suspicion and compel respect.

Fifth — That we are convinced that our standing among men is to be of our own making and that we shall best aid in the establishment of a correct standard of living by drawing a sharp line between virtue and vice and in visiting upon all wrong doers the full weight of a right public sentiment.

Sixth — We believe if the railroads of the South will treat their colored patrons with fairness, that the increased travel on the part of the colored people will add largely to their revenues.

Seventh — We believe that the many acts of lawlessness and the increased frequency of lynchings are not only injurious to the cause of good morals but that they greatly retard the prosperity of the South by keeping out capital and checking immigration.

Eighth — We renew our gratitude to our friends who have so long and so generously aided us by their sympathy and their means. We cannot forbear special mention of Gen. S. C. Armstrong whose life

God has so graciously spared and who is permitted to be with us to-day; we ask their continued patience and interest, reminding them that great and long continued wrongs cannot be righted at once nor without a large outlay of consecrated service and of treasure.

Ninth — That we express our love of country and our desire to fit ourselves for the best and most helpful citizenship and that we may become able to share in all the burdens as well as the privileges of good government. We regard the South as our home and we urge all to avail themselves of the opportunity now afforded to buy land and other property at exceptionally low rates and share, with those around us, in the development of the country and in the increasing value of our property.

Tenth — In all our journey, thus far, we recognize the good hand of God. We most earnestly ask His blessing upon the declarations we have this day put forth and we trust that, through His help, they may result in our own and the common good.

Southern Workman, 22 (Mar. 1893), 50-51. Mabel W. Dillingham wrote this account from Calhoun, Ala.

[1] George Washington Henderson (b. 1850), a graduate of Yale Divinity School, was professor of theology and university pastor at Straight University, New Orleans. He was later professor and dean at Fisk University (1904-9). In 1909 he joined the Wilberforce University faculty, teaching Latin, Greek, and German.

[2] Lewis B. Moore of Howard University.

[3] John Tyler Morgan.

An Amendment to the Act Incorporating Tuskegee Normal and Industrial Institute

[Montgomery, Ala., Feb. 21, 1893]

An act to amend an act to incorporate the Tuskegee Normal and Industrial Institute, and to amend an act to amend an act to establish a Normal School for colored teachers at Tuskegee, Alabama.

Section 1. *Be it enacted by the General Assembly of Alabama,* That an act to incorporate the Tuskegee Normal and Industrial Institute, and amend an act to amend an act to establish a Normal School for colored teachers at Tuskegee, approved December 19, 1892, be amended so as to read as follows:

Section 1. That George W. Campbell, S. Q. Hale, Louis Adams,[1] Oliver Howard, Henry D. Smith, B. T. Washington, Geo. S. Chaney,[2] R. C. Bedford, Warren Logan, C. N. Dorsette, and such others as they may under this act associate with them, and their successors be, and are hereby constituted a body politic, and corporate, by the name of the Tuskegee Normal and Industrial Institute, and shall have perpetual succession and a common seal, and by the name aforesaid, they and their successors shall be capable in law, and shall have full power and authority, to acquire, hold, possess, purchase, receive and retain to themselves and their successors forever any lands, tenements, rents, goods, chattels, or interest of any kind whatsoever, which may be given or bequeathed to them or by them purchased, or which have already been bequeathed or purchased for the use of the said institution, and said trustees may receive any gift or inheritance which may be given as an endowment fund, and they and their successors shall have full power to convey, transfer and dispose of the same in any manner whatsoever they may judge most useful to the interest and legal purposes of said institution, and by their corporate name they may sue and implead, and be sued and impleaded, answer and be answered, in all courts of law and equity, and said trustees shall have the right to make contracts in behalf of said institution.

Sec. 2. *Be it further enacted,* That the purposes of said Tuskegee Normal and Industrial institution shall be as follows: for the instruction of colored teachers and youth in the various common academic and collegiate branches, the best method of teaching the same, the best method of theoretical and practical industry in their application to agriculture and the mechanic arts, and for the carrying out of these purposes said trustees shall have the power to establish and provide for the support of any department or school in said institution, and to control the operations of the same; to grant such diplomas, and to confer such degrees, as are customary in other colleges of like grade; to appoint such officers for presiding over and transacting the business of their body as may be necessary and prescribe their duties and obligations; to appoint the time and place of their meeting, to determine their own tenure of office, and to adopt such rules, regulation and by laws, not contrary to the laws of this State or the United States as may be necessary for the good government of the said Tuskegee Normal and Industrial Institute. Said institute shall not be begun nor continued with a less number than twenty-five pupils, nor be taught for a period less than nine months of each year. Pupils from this State shall be admitted free of tuition on giving an obligation in writing to teach for two years in the public schools of this State after they have become qualified.

Sec. 3. *Be it further enacted,* That when there shall be a vacancy in the board of trustees occasioned by death, resignation, removal or refusal to act, the remaining trustees or a majority of them shall supply the vacancy at the next annual meeting. It shall be lawful for any five of the trustees to call a meeting of the trustees whenever it is deemed expedient to do so.

Sec. 4. *Be it further enacted,* That the number of trustees shall never be less than seven nor more than fourteen, the majority of whom shall constitute a quorum.

Sec. 5. *Be it further enacted,* That all property acquired by said Tuskegee Normal and Industrial Institute, or Tuskegee Normal school, or Tuskegee Institute, or by whatever name so called before the passage of this act, are hereby ratified and confirmed to the trustees of the Tuskegee Normal and Industrial Institute.

Sec. 6. *Be it further enacted,* That there is hereby appropriated out of the general school revenue the sum of three thousand dollars annually toward the maintenance and support of said school, and the apportionment of the general fund for colored children shall be made to the several counties of this State after the deduction of the sum herein appropriated. The said appropriation shall be under the control of the commissioners herein after provided for, and shall be applied in such manner as they may deem best to carry out the purposes of this act, and said commissioners shall be members of said board of trustees with the same rights and powers as the other trustees.

Sec. 7. *Be it further enacted,* That the appropriation shall be under the direction and control of a board of three commissioners, which shall consist of the following persons, to-wit: George W. Campbell, S. Q. Hale and Louis Adams, who shall elect one of their number as chairman of their board, and shall have power to fill any vacancy that may occur in the board. In case a majority of the commissioners cannot agree upon a person to be chairman, or a person to fill a vacancy in the board; then such disagreement shall be certified to the superintendent of education for the State; that officer shall forthwith appoint a member of the board to be chairman, or a person to fill the vacancy, as the case may be, and the member of the board so appointed as chairman, and the person so appointed to the vacancy, shall have the same power and authority as if he had been selected by the board. The commissioners shall make an annual written report to the superintendent of education of the condition and progress of the school, the teachers that have been employed, the number of pupils that have been in attendance, the manner in which the appropriation has been expended, the branches that have been taught, and such other facts relating to the school as may be of public interest and importance.

Sec. 8. *Be it further enacted,* That the chairman of the board of commissioners shall give bond in double the amount of the appropriation for the safe keeping and faithful application of the sum appropriated; the bond to be approved by the judge of probate of Macon county and filed in his office, a certified copy of which shall be forwarded to the State superintendent of education, to be placed on file in his office.

Sec. 9. *Be it further enacted,* That the chairman of the board of commissioners of the Tuskegee Normal and Industrial Institute shall, after the approval and filing of the bond, and the certified copy of the same as provided hereinbefore, present to the State superintendent of education a requisition for the amount herein appropriated, and the superintendent of education shall thereupon certify the amount to the State auditor, who shall draw his warrant for the same on the State treasurer, payable to the chairman of the board of commissioners, for the maintenance and support of the said Tuskegee Normal and Industrial Institute, as hereinbefore provided, and a like requisition shall be presented, and the sum herein appropriated so drawn each year as the same shall accrue.

Sec. 10. *Be it further enacted,* That so long as the property, real and personal of the said Tuskegee Normal and Industrial Institute is used for the purpose of education, the same shall be exempt from taxation of any kind.

Sec. 11. *Be it further enacted,* That all laws and parts of laws in conflict with any of the provisions of this act be, and the same are, hereby repealed.

Approved February 21, 1893.

Acts of the General Assembly of Alabama, Passed by the Session of 1892-93 (Montgomery, 1893), 887-90.

¹ Lewis Adams.
² George Leonard Chaney.

To the Editor of the *Southern Workman*

[Tuskegee, Ala., Feb. 22, 1893]

Gen. Armstrong arrived here Saturday night Feb. 18, little after mid-night. The train was three hours late. The Tuskegee train made a special trip to Chehaw to meet him. Notwithstanding the lateness of the hour, the students and teachers had a very attractive and fine demonstration in his honour. It was something on the order of a torch-light procession; bon fires and brass band and singing intermixed. Instead of torchlights, we had pine wood knots.

The girls and boys formed a line through which he passed and as the carriage drove through them, each one waved a lighted piece of pine wood, the band playing "Hail to the Chief." The General enjoyed it all immensely and seemed very much overcome.

But I write to you especially to say that Gen. Armstrong surprised us all very much by speaking to our students and teachers in the chapel last night for thirty or forty minutes. I think most every one of us heard every word he said. It is very encouraging to him to know that he can speak to so large an audience.

Southern Workman, 22 (Mar. 1893), 40.

From Sarah Newlin

Philadelphia, Feb. 23rd 1893

Dear Mr. Washington, My interest in Tuskegee has not at all lessened, and I was surprised to get a note from you the other day reminding me that this was "about the season" when my sister and I have sent you scholarships! They were sent in February last year and I think it would have been better to have waited at least until February was past before asking for them. You would have received them, as neither of us had forgotten them. I enclose cheques for both now — $50. each — in all $100. I am truly glad that you can see the good results of your work, though I never doubted that any good, faithful work had such results.

I lent $25. to one of the farmers around you last March and am waiting eagerly to see the result of the experiment. I shall be much pleased if he is ready to pay the debt, principal and interest, promptly. The time for the payment is close at hand. Let me hear from you about it, it was lent through one of your officers, when it is due. If it has been the means of helping one of the struggling ones to really improve his condition in the least degree I shall be delighted. But let me know the exact truth.

I should have liked to be present at your annual Conference, but the journey is much too long. I am sure Gen. Armstrong was a help. Truly yours,

S. Newlin

ALS   Con. 5   BTW Papers   ATT.   Original destroyed.

To John W. Carter

[Tuskegee, Ala.] Mar. 14th [189]3

Mr. Carter: By advice of the Faculty, I make the following statement to you: You must be aware that your work is not satisfactory in the sense that we wish it to be. The frequent reminders that you have had of this fact from this office and the office of Supt. of Industries,[1] must have made you aware of the dissatisfaction before now.

First, at the bottom of the trouble is the fact that you *do not obey orders,* that is, you have obey[ed] orders or not as you like. We never know what to depend on in regard to your carrying out orders of the Superintendent of Industries, or others who have authority to give them. For example, a rule was made sometime ago that the heads of departments must not leave their work and go to town or off the place during work hours without permission from the Superintendent of Industries. You pay no attention to this order.

Second, there is a lack of system running all through your department. Tools are scattered here and there and there is no system as to giving them out. This lack of system is further shown in your Friday class, and in the course of study which you have handed in.

Third, this lack of system exhibits itself in the waste of nails and other material wherever your men are at work or have been at work. The careless way in which the order for the sash for Phelps Hall was carried out, incur[r]ing a loss of more than $40. is an illustration of this point.

Fourth, students in your charge are not pushed forward in *carpentry* work with any degree of satisfaction or system. The result is, students become dissatisfied and take the first opportunity to leave. In plain words, the students feel that they are not being taught carpentry and they feel that they are not permitted to use the tools as they should. The student who mentioned last night that he had been in your department 5 months and had not worked with tools, is a fair example of many others who have been in your department.

The fact that you could have kept an order like the one for the Calhoun desks in your possession without reporting about it one way or the other, shows a lack of reliability and is injurious to the school.

It is felt by all that you have the ability to do work when you want to, and that you do often perform work that will bear inspection; but it is done at too dear a cost on the time, patience and strength of some one else who has to be constantly following up your work. Phelps Hall, as it now stands, is an excellent example of the kind of work that you are able to do.

In view of the facts just stated, it has been decided that unless there is a change in the matters just stated between now and [the] first of June, the school will not employ you for another term; in case there is a change, the school will be only too glad to retain you in its employment. Yours truly,

B. T. Washington

TLpS Con. 106 BTW Papers DLC.

[1] John Henry Washington.

From William Watson Thompson[1]

Tuskegee, Ala., March 14 1893

Dear Sir: I have a warrant for Frank Bell   I got after him out in the country this morning and he out run me. I think that he has gone to the scool he went in that direction and I learn that he has some brothers out there will you please find out if he has been out there and let me know at once, or would I be asking two much to ask you catch him for me if he is out there. I am sure that he has either run there or will be there tonight. Very Respect

W W. Thompson
Shff

ALS   Con. 8   BTW Papers   ATT.   Original destroyed.

¹ William Watson Thompson, born about 1863, was the younger brother of Charles Winston Thompson and the elder brother of Joseph O. Thompson of Tuskegee. As a youth he was a clerk in a store, perhaps that of his father, W. P. Thompson. He was for a time sheriff of Macon County. He owned a large plantation near Tuskegee, and bought and sold farmland in several surrounding counties.

From Warren Logan

Tuskegee, Ala., Apr. 10 1893

Dear Mr Washington   I have received all of yours but have been too busy to write in acknowledgment. Several days ago I sent names of N.Y. people who have given in your absence. Trust you have received the list.

It has turned out that the men charged with rape on Mrs Cox are innocent — and that the guilty ones are Robt Alexander and Pugh's two boys.¹ They have made a confession of the whole matter. The feeling against them is running very high and it is not unlikely that they will be lynched. We rather expected the mob Sat. night and stayed up until late but it did not come.² The sheriff took the boys out of jail and secreted them somewhere Sat. night and Sunday. They will be charged if they are not lynched. It is a terrible affair in all of its aspects. Yours Sincerely

Warren Logan

ALS   Con. 105   BTW Papers   DLC.

¹ The crime took place at Big Hungry, about seven miles west of Tuskegee.

² The threat of mob action apparently lingered over the town for weeks, for on May 3, 1893, "A Colored Citizen" wrote an anonymous letter to the Tuskegee *News:*

"In these days when we hear so many reports of mob law on every hand, it is a relief to know that there is at least one place in which the people stand manfully up for the enforcement of the law, whether it applies to the black man or the white man. I am sure that there is not a sensible and self-respecting colored man in Macon county that does not think more of the white people now than he has ever done in the past; and I am also sure that there is a strong public sentiment growing among the colored people of this county that favors the inflicting of a just punishment however severe on all wrong-doers whether black or white.

"I cannot close this article without adding that the colored people feel that they owe a debt of gratitude to the Sheriff of Macon county and the brave men who have stood by him, which they cannot pay. Had we not had a sheriff who had it in his heart to see justice meted out to the poorest and meanest criminal, our county would have been disgraced and there would not have been today that warmth of feeling toward, and confidence in, the white people on the part of the colored people that now exists and which I think will be more apparent in the future than it has been in the past." (Tuskegee *News,* May 4, 1893, 2.)

From M. Arnold Morin

Tuskegee, Ala., April 10 1893

Dear Mr. Washington: I send you another copy of Inter-Ocean, also S.L. Mr. F. Rudd of 102 Br'dy, New York, writes for the name of the girl referred to in S.L. who worked for a small pay. It is Lula Newton. I sent him her name and address. Mr. Young[1] who recently came from Tuscaloosa says that she is married to a worthless fellow.

Bell has gotten 5 years in the Prison.

The Pugh boy and his accomplices who were in jail for stealing the trunk with clothing of students have made a clean breast of all their villanies. They it was who shot Mr Cox and entered his house, stole and did other things round about. Such being the case, the Harris boy has been given his freedom on the action of the Grand Jury.

I sent you Student. Yours truly,

M. A. Morin

P.S. The enclosed letter you will read. Have written the writer, thanking in your name for his appreciative remarks and regretting that we have not but one copy of the address.[2] The address appeared in the C.U. of the 25 March and he [can] get a copy there.

M.

ALS   Con. 105   BTW Papers   DLC.

[1] Nathan B. Young came to Tuskegee Institute in 1892 as teacher of history

and English. He was head of the academic department and teacher of pedagogy from 1893 to 1897.

² The address given by Lyman Abbott at the dedication of Phelps Hall Bible School. (See *Christian Union,* 47 [Mar. 25, 1893], 567-69.)

To Warren Logan

[New York City] Apr. 15 1893

Dear Mr. Logan: Enclosed I send you $50. The Misses Collins will send you some thing today or tomorrow. Your telegram came last night.¹ At present I see nothing to do but "grin and bear it." I am working as hard as I can night and day. Relief I am sure will come soon from some source. As far as you can you had better get notes extended.

This I wish you would say to the faculty — I am quite convinced that donations from the North in the future are going to be more largely than ever devoted to industrial education. I meet this sentiment on every hand. To hold our own we must put every industry in the best possible condition. I have had a talk with Mr. Morris K. Jesup and from what he says I feel rather sure that another change is coming in the Slater Fund. He favors strongly reducing the number of schools to be helped to two or three. Hampton he says they are sure of. He has asked me to call to see him Sunday at 5 to confer with him [in] regard to Tuskegee. The Board seems to think well of us at present, but we must go upwards or we can not stand the test. I now feel more convinced that ever of the wisdom of relieving just as soon as possible Mr. J. H. Washington from all care except the superintendence and development of the industries. A visit from Dr. Curry may be expected at any time.

I have just rec'd a telegram, asking me to go to Boston to speak at two meetings there in the interest of Hampton — for this reason I shall not reach home before wednesday night. Yours truly

Booker T. Washington

ALS Con. 6 BTW Papers ATT. Original destroyed. Although this letter appears on Tuskegee letterhead, BTW was writing from New York.

¹ It asked, "Matters pressing at Bank what shall I do[?]" (Con. 105, BTW Papers, DLC.)

From Ella Holland

Boston Mass. April 17, 1893

Dear Friend— I guess you will be a little surprised to know that I am not with Mrs. Hardon[1] now. It was my desires to stay with her and I tried to do so. You know I staid with Mrs. Hardon winter months and I ment to have staid with her two months longer but I could not stand her treatment to me any longer. I am now staying with a family in Boston. I would have come direcly home, but my money would not allow me. I was sorry to leave and she did not want me to leave, she wanted me to stay another year, but did not treat me in the right way for me to stay. I told you last fall how she treated us and it was just like we told you, and has been worse since. She thought we belong to her. I know I was under her care and a long ways from home. That's why I think she should have treated us better. Mrs. Hardon, I say is a very kind woman in words and not all together in deed, I mean to her servants. She has spoken many good words of advice to me, which will do me good, as long as I live. She has also done many good things for me. The only objection I have to Mrs Hardon, she treats her servants to much like slaves. So far as her work went with me I did not fret about my part of it. I know I have got to work where ever I go. I am not telling you in what ways she didn't treat me right but will if ever I see you gain. I mean to live and act right just the same, as I did when I was with her. I did not run away from her. I walked away. She will tell you, no doubt when she writes you that I run away. I told her four weeks ago to write you for some more girls, that I was going to leave but she would not, now she say I ran away. I told her I was going and I went. We tried to leave her and come home three months ago but she would not let us. Her family from the oldest down to the baby says that she dosen't treat her girls right that's why she is all ways without girls. Mr. Hardon has told her (so her son says) if she dosen't treat her girls better in the future than she has in the past that he is not going to help and she will have to do the best she can. While I was with [her] I give good honest work I did not try to shirk any of it. She has said before my face and hind my back that I could do as good work as what she called smart girls. I guess she'll go back on all of that now but I can not help it. I just could not stay there any longer.

You need not be uneasy about your money you will get it just the same and monthly not every two and three months but every month. I hope you wont think hard of me. I would not have left before the last of may if Mrs Hardon had [not] hurt my feelings so bad. I staid there four weeks all alone and done my work and Martha too with a little exception, then she did not want to pay me for it but Mr. Hardon, being a good honest man, without her consent paid me extra. That killed all of my feelings for her. Yours respt.

Ella Holland

ALS Con. 104 BTW Papers DLC.

¹ Anna Wallace Wilson Hardon (b. 1836) was the wife of Henry Comfort Hardon (b. 1829), who for thirty-five years was headmaster of the Shurtleff School for Girls in south Boston. BTW was able to supply her with two girls in 1890 and another two in 1891, who earned wages and learned housekeeping work under Mrs. Hardon's direction. Mrs. Hardon was pleased with her influence upon the first two girls. She wrote BTW toward the end of their year term: "Both are in good health and I think you will see a graceful maturity about them that will help them all their lives." (Hardon to BTW, July 27, 1891, Con. 99, BTW Papers, DLC.) But the girls showed a dissatisfaction with Mrs. Hardon's stewardship similar to that of Ella Holland. "We do work that other families hire men to do and Mrs. Hardon tells the neighbors that that is the advantage of having colored girls," they wrote. "There is no pleasure what ever in living in a Northern family not as much as one would find by staying at home. The best place for any girl (and most especially when she is a colored girl) is at home." "The girl of to day," they reasoned, "values her freedom to much. . . ." (Lottie and Mary to BTW, May 15, 1891, Con. 4, BTW Papers, ATT. Original destroyed.)

To Nathan B. Young

Tuskegee, Ala., 4-22nd 189[3]

Mr. Young: If you come into contact with or know of any student or students who are specially lacking in moral earnestness in class work deportment or labor, will you be kind enough to write their names on this paper, indicating their weakness, and return it to me not later than Monday noon?¹

B. T. W.

TLI Con. 105 BTW Papers DLC.

¹ Young replied at the bottom of BTW's letter, listing eight female students he

considered "morally careless in some instances." BTW sent the same memo to several other Tuskegee teachers, who reported a few male students, mostly for bad deportment in class. One teacher, J. D. McCall, replied: "So far as I know all the really bad students are now either expelled or under suspension." (BTW to McCall, to J. H. Washington, and to Mary P. Weaver, all Apr. 22, 1893, Con. 105, BTW Papers, DLC.)

To Charles W. Greene

[Tuskegee, Ala.] April 24th [189]3

Mr. C. W. Greene: You have been spoken to several times about the condition of the barn and especially about the proper care of the stock in regard to feeding and other matters. On going through the barn yesterday at milking time I found neither you nor Mr. Wheelis[1] was there. The whole matter was left in the hands of irresponsible students, and the consequence was the cows and horses were not being properly fed. Notwithstanding the many times about which we have spoken about the mixing of the feed for the horses and mules; notwithstanding the fact that we have recently gone to the expense of purchasing a mill for grinding the corn I found the horses and mules being fed on dry corn. The bran for the cows was being mixed in a small old box entirely unsuited for the purpose and was not being properly done; in short it is evident that there is little if any system of work at the barn. Feed I found sitting here and there in sacks. There is plenty of room at the barn for everything to be arranged in a systematic manner. On the back side of the barn and all around it there is rubbish in the shape of lumber, wagon bodies and things of that kind. Things need to be put in proper condition.

· · · ·

the school but an unwarranted expense. While the barn is being put in proper condition I hope you will concentrate all your attention on the farm and see if you can make it what it should be. I remind you of the fact that you have been relieved of the care of the brick-yard. Thus being relieved I had hoped you would make improvements. On the other hand the school is growing and every man and every department in connection with it must grow, and if this is not the case some one must suffer.

B. T. Washington

This takes effect April 25, 93.

TLpfS Con. 106 BTW Papers DLC. At least one page is missing. The postscript is in BTW's hand.

[1] Franklin Pearson Wheelis, in the A middle class in 1892-93, graduated from Phelps Hall Bible School in 1894 and from Tuskegee Institute in 1895. About 1900 he became presiding elder of the Colored Methodist Episcopal (C.M.E.) Church, Mobile District.

From Cornelius Nathaniel Dorsette

Montgomery, Ala. 4/26th 1893

Dear friend   I have been listening for some time to hear from you relative to The Speaker[1] for this year? Will you go to Hampton? I notice from the papers that Tuskegee will do some hanging soon, cant we arrange to have that a little farther from our Commencement day[?] I will see the Gov. if need be, & try to have it deferred at least one month. Write me.

Mrs Dorsette has been very ill but is now better. Hastily yours

Dorsette

ALS Con. 5 BTW Papers ATT. Original destroyed.

[1] The commencement speaker was Thomas McCants Stewart.

To Samuel Chapman Armstrong

Tuskegee, Ala., April 27 1893

Dear Gen. Armstrong: There is going to be either this or next year a new move on the part of the Slater Fund trustees. From what I have gleaned I think it the desire of some of the trustees is to concentrate on Hampton and one or two other schools or start a new school.

At his request I called to see Mr. M. K. Jesup when in New York and had a long talk with him. He favors strongly *Hampton* and Hampton methods. Will you be kind enough to write him a letter giving your impressions of Tuskegee during your 3 weeks visit here. I think it will help us much.

The Slater Board has already doubled our appropriation for the coming year. Yours truly

Booker T. Washington

ALS BTW Folder ViHaI.

From Robert Charles Bedford

Rockton Ill Apr 28 1893

Dear Prof Yours of Apr 24 just recd. I am glad indeed to learn of the increase from the Slater Fund. Aside from its great help it is a marked testimony to the worth of the school. How would it be to ask Dr Abbott to write a letter to the Slater Trustees?

I have made some investigation with respect to graduates from Auburn and I find out of 253 graduates 22 are farmers 6 of whom are dead. Sixteen living farmers in 32 years! I mean to look further into this matter. Surely the U S funds expended in this way do not afford very much practical encouragement to agriculture. Yrs

R C Bedford

ALS Con. 104 BTW Papers DLC.

To Morris Ketchum Jesup

[Tuskegee, Ala.] April 29 [189]3

Dear Sir: According to your request I write you regarding the plan and scope of the work done by this institution and the use it could make of a larger appropriation from the Slater Fund.

Tuskegee is in a large measure, an extension of Gen. Armstrong's work into the far South — the Black Belt. From the first day that

313

school opened at Tuskegee the industrial education has been made the central and main feature. This is evidenced by the fact that out of a total income of $238,000, during the 11 years that the school has been in existence $167,000 has been spent in securing an industrial plant and in the payment of instructors connected with the industrial departments.

During the last financial year the total expenditures of the institution were $55,000 and $32,000 was spent in the improvement of the industrial plant, purchase of material, and payment of instructors in the industrial departments. Out of the 34 officers and teachers the past year the time of 19 was occupied wholly or in part in the industries.

Through the industrial system we seek to accomplish 3 ends:

(a) To give the students an opportunity to earn all or a portion of their board bill so that they can remain in school the whole year by self-help. Without this opportunity many would attend only a few months.

In the present condition of the masses of our people no institution can do the best work for its students that does not have a boarding department which furnishes the opportunity for systematic and practical training in the common duties of life, viz, bathing, cooking, eating, care of table, manner of dress, laundering, neatness of bed-room, general surroundings &c.

(b) To give the students skill in some industry. To this end the institution has provided labor that is valuable in an economic sense to the institution and at the same time furnishes the opportunity for skilled training. For example: we have just completed a large 3 story brick building in which to house the majority of our industries. The young men who manufactured the bricks, did the brickmasonry, plastering, sawing of lumber, carpentry, iron work, painting, tinning, &c. Three things were accomplished in the erection of this building: 1st, the money given for its erection has been made to benefit the students rather than outsiders, and the students have been enabled to remain in school; (2) it has furnished the opportunity for training in practical skilled industry which is the great need of the South; (3) a building for permanent use has been provided. In this way all of the 19 buildings now on the school grounds except two have been built.

During the last two years by the advice and encouragement of Dr. Curry we have made great progress in giving the students a more intelligent idea of the underlying principles of the industries by means of mechanical, architectural drawing, lectures &c, and we find that this has made the students better prepared for the practical work.

The industries now in operation are the following, and it will be seen that they are those adapted to meet the immediate and pressing needs of the people, for it is a patent fact that for the next 25 or 40 years it will be a matter of "bread and not meat" with the masses of the Negroes: Farming, including fruit culture, Dairying, Stock and Poultry raising, Brickmaking, Brickmasonry, Plastering, Saw-mill work, Carpentry, Painting, Shoe-making, Harness-making, Tin-smithing, Blacksmithing, Wheelwrighting, Printing, Mattress-making, Mechanical drawing, Architectural drawing, Cooking, Common Sewing, Dressmaking, Millinery work, Laundering and General house-keeping.

(c) Our industries are a means of forming character and teaching the dignity of labor. Thus our graduates become leaders in the highest sense.

Aside from the value of the industry in itself, it is far better to have the student receive his literary education through the medium of industrial work than to have the whole cost of his education *given* him. Example — A student builds a wagon. It may cost $50 and sold for for $48. It is far better for the independence, usefulness and manliness of the student to ask a Northern friend to pay the $2. deficit than to give the student the $50 out-right for his education.

The consciousness of the fact that he has the ability to create a *real* wagon, not a toy, is an inestimable influence on the character of the man.

There are several reasons why I believe that if we could get say $10,000 without interest, from the Slater Fund, we could keep it in tact and return it in a reasonable length of time (though do not think that our trustees would give a mortgage to secure such loan) and at the same time make it accomplish Mr. Slater's desire "to aid in lifting up the colored people."

Among the reasons are these: (1) Tuskegee is located in the heart of the Black Belt of the South and has a constituency, and the public sentiment among students and teachers is unanimously in favor of industrial training. Notwithstanding there are over 500 young men and women here, the institution has been compelled to refuse admission to nearly 500 more who wanted to take the industrial work.

(2) It has a plant valued at $180,000 in the way of 1440 acres of land, 19 buildings used for dormitories, industrial shops, class work,

&c. The money would go largely into increasing the teaching power and productive value of the present industries. Many of the industries are now operated at a great disadvantage for want of a capital with which to supply material in large quantities; better machinery and tools, and [in] some cases stronger instructors.

(3) Tuskegee has always steered clear of all denominationalism, hence reaches all classes and spends no time in spreading sectarian doctrines.

(4) It has a boarding department and is in the country away from the influence of city life which often tends to educate the young colored men and women *away* from the masses.

(5) The work that Tuskegee is doing is past the experimental period. Its value is shown by the fact that its graduates are engaged as *leaders* in all lines of industrial work and are in constant demand. One graduate who learned brick-making here superintended last year the manufacture of 600,000 bricks. The people are the practical value of this training. The school has a system of contracts which compels the students to remain at a trade or industry 2 or 3 years.

(6) The literary course of study at Tuskegee is confined to a plain English education — going far enough into the sciences mathematics and general literature to enable the students to understand the principles of the industries and to form the habit and love of study.

(7) The industrial system fully developed here could be made to serve as a great object lesson in the way of industrial education in this part of the South.

The Negro is not yet sure of his own ability. It has been proven that the white man can succeed in what he undertakes. It has been proven that the Negro can be developed under the immediate control of the white man. It remains to be proved how far the Negro can develop under his own direction. Nothing helps and encourages a Negro so much as to see one of his own number succeed. Does not the success of Tuskegee in the past argue well for its success in the future if properly helped on its feet, with a larger sum of money? Success here, wholly under the control of Negro instructors, would give the masses of the colored people a confidence and stimulus, that few other things could by reason of the object lesson furnished. Yours truly,

Booker T. Washington

TLpS   Con. 106   BTW Papers   DLC.

From Thomas McCants Stewart

New York, Tuesday May 23rd, 1893

My Dear Professor: Everything was "OK." I got space in Pullman to New York. So be happy.

Now, what shall I say about my visit? Words are inadequate to cover it. It was a *heavenly* one.

Let me say: (1) Please bring me in June a *framed* picture of yourself and teachers. I want a frame made at Institute; (2) By Fall, I should be house-keeping in Brooklyn. After that, there will always be a *Washington Room* in our house. Yours truly,

T. McCants Stewart

P.S. Have been bilious — too far gone to get out letter for *Age;* so I shall be a week late. I write Mrs. W. in this mail.

ALS   Con. 5   BTW Papers   ATT.   Original destroyed.

A Speech at the Memorial Service for Samuel Chapman Armstrong[1]

Hampton, [Va.] May 25, 1893

A few nights ago while driving in the woods of Alabama I discerned in the distance a large, bright fire. As I came nearer the light I discovered that by its glow several busy hands were at work building a comfortable, tasty, framed-cottage to replace the one room log hovel that had been their abode for a quarter of a century. The fire by which this house was being built was lighted at Hampton by Gen. Armstrong 25 years ago. What matters it that this fire was 25 years in passing through Hampton, through Tuskegee, through the Tuskegee Conference, to this lonely spot in Alabama? It was doing its work nevertheless, surely and effectively — and so it will be through the generations that are to come.

I am asked to perform a serious and embarrassing duty — speak of General Armstrong. It would be comparatively easy for us to speak of him as our teacher, but he was more, to hundreds of us who knew no man that we could call father; he was more and dearer than a

317

father. It would be easy to speak of him as a friend to our race, but he was more, and the term "friend" is cold and barren when applied to him; he was the heart of the race — his great heart held us all so constantly, so strongly, so tenderly, that it gave way at a time when most men begin to live. The power of his personality, his influence over his students, the tenderness, the love, the confidence that existed between them, are, I think, indescribable and unexplainable and so we shall not, I hope, be misunderstood if we seem not only to revere but to worship his memory.[2]

But on this occasion General Armstrong would be the last to wish us to utter mere words of praise. Every atom, every spark of energy in the economy of his great being was consecrated to and concentrated on one purpose — the lifting up of the unfortunate whether black, red or white. In Virginia, North Carolina and the more Northern states you know how and where his life has penetrated and given light for darkness, hope for despair and success for failure, and showed the world that there is a way to save the most degenerate and most despised.

What is the influence of this great life in the far and darker South. (And in referring to this you will excuse me if I refrain from attempting to explain how and why Tuskegee's work is his work, is his soul marching on, and how the fragrance of his life will carry it on in the future; how without his fatherly advice, his unselfishness, at times when we were surrounded by darkness and doubt, for there were acts of his that to me are too sacred and precious for utterance.) The rose which I would place in his grave today is his work at Tuskegee.

Eleven years ago Tuskegee was one of hundreds of similar villages scattered through the Gulf States. Today it is the light-house for that section. Eleven years ago there were 30 students and one teacher; now 600 students and 38 teachers. Then scarcely a dollar and not a foot of land; now 1400 acres of land, 20 buildings, and real and personal property worth $180,000; then one blind horse; now 260 head of live stock. Then the plantation where the Tuskegee Institute stood had known nought but the labor forced by the lash; today there are 19 industries kept in motion by 600 as happy hearts as can be found in America; then some feared that the Negro youth would be ashamed to work for his education, but these students have made and laid into these buildings with their own hands 2,000,000 bricks and of 20 buildings, 17 have been built and furnished by students themselves.

But our great chief taught us that students, land, buildings, horses and industries are of no value except as they contribute to the elevation of man. How has Tuskegee met this test? First, it had to overcome the indifference or hostility of many of the whites. This has been accomplished to such an extent that in Tuskegee the voices and hands of as many whites as colored are ready to be raised in defense of the Tuskegee Institute. While I knew of the respect in which General Armstrong was held by the whites of the South, I did not know until his recent visit of three weeks to Tuskegee how deeply he had won his way into their hearts until it was shown by their warm and cordial welcome.

With my own people the problem was this: Surrounded by a dense, ignorant mass of 30,000 within a radius of 100 miles of Tuskegee, outnumbering the whites in some counties six to one, their schools in session three months, taught as a rule in wrecks of log cabins by teachers of inferior morals and ability. The slavery of the mortgage system like a cancer eating up soul and body, leaving the Negro in debt, landless, homeless and too often with empty stomachs and clotheless body. Their moral and religious condition you can easily understand when it is said the ¾ lived in one roomed cabins and many of their churches served as cloaks to hide the sin and immorality of minister and congregation. How has Tuskegee tried to penetrate this darkness — to remedy this condition? Let a single example answer: Six years ago a young girl[3] educated at Tuskegee went into one of those communities where she found the people much as I have described, groaning under a load of debt, with worn and haggard countenances, without hope for themselves or their children. Finding this condition of things this girl took the three months public school as a nucleus for her work. But she was not content with this: She went among the parents, gave instruction in house-keeping, organized a sewing class, advised here and reprimanded there. Soon she organized the older people into a club that met every week. In these meetings she would tell them in a plain, simple, common sense manner how to save, what to buy and not to buy, how to sacrifice, how to live on bread and water, if need be till they could get out of debt and stop mortgaging. Thus by showing them how to use the results of their labor, how to turn their earnings in the direction of their mental, industrial and moral uplifting, the first year she caused many to stop mortgaging and make contracts for the buying of homes. In addition she showed them how by their own efforts to build and supply with proper apparatus a neat, comfortable school house to replace the wreck of a log cabin. The second year out of their own pockets they added two months to the original three months school; the third year two more months were added, and now every year they have an eight months school, taught in their new school house. Now my friends, I wish you could have the privilege that I have had of going into that community and seeing the complete revolution, yes regeneration, that has been wrought in the mental, industrial and religious life of this community by the efforts of this one girl. Bear in mind that no one gave them a cent of money with which to make any of these changes, they all came about by reason of their having this Christian leader, this object lesson, this guide to show them how to use, to their own profit, the money which had hitherto been scattered to the wind in mortgages, high rents, for whiskey, snuff and cheap jewelry. Gen. Armstrong saw more than 25 years ago that it was to this kind of work — this helping the masses to help themselves — that we must look for the solution of the Negro problem and along this line it is slowly but surely being solved. The greatest injury that slavery did my people was to deprive them of that sense of self-dependence, habit of economy, and executive power which are the glory and distinction of the Anglo-Saxon race and we need not expect what was 250 years going into a race to be gotten out in 25 or 30 years; and Gen. Armstrong early saw that the only way to help these weaknesses was through the teacher educated in head, hand and heart. The work that I have attempted to describe is what he taught Tuskegee to do, and it is the work Tuskegee is doing. To do more or less of the work that I mentioned that young girl is doing, we have had at Tuskegee since the school started over 3000 students, 500 of whom have finished the course or have received enough training to enable them to do good work, and they are now laboring as teachers, ministers, farmers, mechanics, and merchants, and these have taught not far from 30,000 children mainly in Alabama, Mississippi, Georgia, Florida, Louisiana and Texas. Besides Tuskegee has been able to aid in starting those excellent schools at Mt. Meigs and Calhoun and to put in motion the Tuskegee Negro Conference which gives an annual opportunity for six or eight hundred Negro farmers to attend college for one day and fill themselves so full of hope, plans and inspiration, as to methods of growth, that it is bursting out all through the year in the shape of better schools, new homes, better ministers and practical religion.

At first Gen. Armstrong's methods and efforts were opposed by many but now the Armstrong fire is spreading all through the South and all acknowledge that from the first he was right. He, at the beginning, recognized the fact that the first 50 or 75 years would be occupied mainly with matters of bread and meat, and that the South was in need of people who could do something, who could put the fire under the pot. Others may excel in philosophy and theory but the Hampton man is always the one who *can do* something.

And now for what remains. The question still before us especially in the Gulf States — Alabama, Mississippi, Georgia, Louisiana and Florida — is a large and serious one. The work is far from being done, but Gen. Samuel Chapman Armstrong has found the way which those of us who remain are to follow. There are hundreds of thousands, yea millions, in the far South that are unreached. The problem is one largely of morals and industry, but with Gen. Armstrong's faith in God and faith in man it can be solved. Standing now in the midst of the greatest sorrow that this institution has ever known, is it asking too much of you as students and graduates that out of this sorrow, this disappointment at not being permitted to behold here today our great father and savior who loved us and guided us as tenderly as any earthly parent, is it asking too much that out of this loss, there shall come a reconsecration to duty, an intensifying of zeal, an increase in the usefulness and unselfishness of our work that shall bring out of his death a blessing to the cause rather than a loss.

Hampton men, ours is a precious heritage. We have been [re]deemed and made what we are by the life blood and death of the greatest man of modern times. We cannot afford to waste in vain.

TM   Speech Collection   ATT.

¹ Armstrong died on May 11, 1893.

² In an edited version in the *Southern Workman*, 22 (June 1893), spec. supp., v-vi, this paragraph was stripped of many of its poignant and psychologically revealing phrases. In that version it reads: "It is a serious embarrassment to me to speak of General Armstrong. It would be comparatively easy to speak of him as our teacher; but he was more than our teacher. He was the heart of our race, and held us so strongly and tenderly in his great heart that it broke at the time when most men have just begun to live. It would be comparatively easy to speak of him as our friend; but he was more than friend — that word is cold and barren. General Armstrong, and the power of his personality and influence over his students; his tenderness, his love, his confidence in them, was so indescribable that I hope you will not think it irreverent if we not only reverence but almost worship him."

³ Probably Cornelia Bowen. (See A Speech before the New York Congregational Club, Jan. 16, 1893, above.)

Proceedings of the Triennial Reunion
of the Hampton Alumni Association

[Hampton, Va., May 28, 1893]

In accordance with the call issued by General Armstrong several months before his death, the graduates who attended the Triennial Reunion of the Hampton Alumni Association, met on Friday, May 28, with other graduates and ex-students, for a conference upon the needs of their people and the best way to improve their work among them. Also, according to the General's wish, Mr. Booker T. Washington presided at the meetings, which were held morning and afternoon in Whitin Chapel, Virginia Hall.

The meeting was opened with prayer and singing, and then Mr. Washington made the introductory speech, thus announcing the purpose, and touching the key note of the Conference.

"It was the wish of General Armstrong that the graduates of Hampton should meet here to day in a kind of informal conference to report what has been done and is to be done for the people among whom we work, and discuss the best way to improve our work for them.

"In all the sadness that fills our hearts on this occasion, we have cause for congratulation that the ideas General Armstrong originated here so long ago are now being adopted and appreciated throughout the South. There was a time, as you know, when a Hampton man, in some places in the South, was looked on with a little distrust. I am quite sure that feeling has entirely disappeared, and that the people realize as never before that in this all round education General Armstrong has had the right idea, and there is enthusiasm all over the South over the plans and methods adopted by the teachers sent out by this Institution. There is a remarkable change. You remember when Frederick Douglass and Mr. Bruce[1] opposed General Armstrong's idea of education — honestly opposed it, thinking it was wrong. Their opposition has entirely disappeared and General Armstrong's work and methods have now no warmer supporters than Douglass and Bruce and such men, leaders and thinkers, both colored and white, throughout the South. We may congratulate ourselves that we have lived to see this change.

"But we have not met to exchange congratulations, but to discuss the needs of our people and how we can best meet them.

"I will speak first of the needs of the South in Alabama, Mississippi, Georgia and, especially, Louisiana. When I have spoken of the condition of the people as I have seen it there, I have sometimes found people doubt some of my statements, thinking the picture too dark — over-drawn. I confess one is apt to get mistaken ideas by staying only a few days in a place. A few weeks ago I conversed with a Hampton teacher who had spent three or four weeks at Calhoun. I found this woman had gone into the way of life of the people and found out their real condition. She had gone into their homes, their churches, their Sunday schools; had found out the relation between the men and their wives; had gotten the real facts of the condition of the people. You can't get an idea of this from the windows of a palace car — you've got to eat and live among them, see their condition with your own eyes.

"The thought I wish to impress on us as Hampton graduates to whom General Armstrong left this great work — the responsibility of finishing the good work he started here, twenty-five years ago — is this: That the problem is vast and serious; the work is not done; in many sections of the Gulf states the masses of the people have not been touched. One is inclined to be discouraged by the vastness of the work. As to public schools, it is very seldom that you find in Alabama, Georgia and the other Gulf states, more than three months sessions, except in the large cities and towns. These are facts. These are problems that you don't have in Virginia. No move has been made there to appropriate money toward building school houses. The people are left to provide them; and so what schools there are are held in log cabins or bush arbors or under a tree. In many of the counties, when I, or some of our Tuskegee teachers go out, under advice of our State Superintendent, to hold County Institutes, we don't find — after all that Straight and Tougaloo and Talladega and Tuskegee have done to send out graduate teachers, when we call the county teachers together to talk over methods, we often don't find one in sixty, or one in a hundred in any sense capable of the work. We spent the time before we went out in mapping out three or four weeks of Institute work, on methods, object teaching, etc. In one county, we had to throw all our preparation aside, and spend the time in teaching how to write and spell as if they were children. One of the teachers — principal of a school — attended the Institute and went home and beat his wife. That is not an uncommon occurrence. When you go into Louisiana you come into the influence of the Roman Catholic church. The lottery system flourishes there and is most demoralizing.

"I had occasion some time ago to say something about the ministry among the Negroes of the South. I said it not without consideration. Now, after further examination, I have not a thing to take back — the whole truth was not told.

"You find at the bottom of much of the misery, the crop mortgage system. It is hard for you here to understand the extent to which this cause of evil enters into the lives of the people there. Many have become discouraged. True, all do get a little something to live on. I mention these things not to discourage you but to show you the work there is to be done, and I hope that more Hampton graduates will go to the far South, to Georgia, Louisiana, Florida, Texas and the other Gulf states. There is nothing to invite you there but hard work for our people. You will have to build your own school houses in most cases; you will have to make some place decent enough to board in, you will have to secure your salary from the people themselves; often you won't find school officers ready to provide what you need. But I believe that if you go with the Hampton spirit and the ideas and methods General Armstrong has taught us, you can revolutionize the communities where you go. One point is encouraging; the people want light; they are ready to be guided and led; they will live and die for such a teacher. I have never yet seen any of these people, who, when a consecrated young man or woman came to settle down among them to do a life work as teacher, would let them go hungry or naked. I have never seen a community that did not rally to their support, build a school house and sustain them in every way. There is a kind of satisfaction that comes in doing such work in the South that you can get in no other way. I'd rather teach school on a cotton plantation for $10 a month than go to any place of service in New York City for $50 or $100 a month; for every lick there strikes at the heart of things and you see the results. In a few months you see results; the people brightening up; a change taking place in their countenances and in their home life; they dress their children better, save their money, get homes, add to the school term. In so many instances, with such simple, earnest work, have I seen a community made over again. I don't believe any satisfaction to any man or woman equals that in this kind of work.

"Rev. Mr. Harding,[2] whom we many of us knew and loved, and who now, spending his winters in Florida, we think of as not of the North only but of the South, will now give us the pleasure of hearing from him."

Mr. Harding's Speech

"I was in the Episcopal Church in Florida last Sunday evening. It was a very rough building with slab seats. The preacher talked rather incoherently and the service lasted till midnight. In that shanty of a church had been kept a school. There were a few rude benches and a little bit of a blackboard, but, I am happy to say, there had been there for a few months a good teacher from the Avery Institute, a school of the American Missionary Association in Charleston, S.C., a sweet, lovely Christian girl. The people gave her her board. While she stayed she illustrated all that Mr. Washington has said. Things began to change and brighten. But I am sorry to say we can't have her any more. Dr. Baird[3] visited the school and said, 'It seems to me we are spending too much money here for so little result.' I told him that no doubt such a teacher could fill a larger field. So we shall lose her. Now I put it to you, are there not some of you who will come for the Lord's sake to take hold of that work and see such results as Mr. Washington has told you of. The people all are densely ignorant. We want another teacher like Miss Hollis. I have tried to tell them about Hampton and Tuskegee but they don't understand it. They want a teacher."

Mr. Washington said "It seems best that we try to find out, in a conversational manner, the condition and needs of the people. First, we'll get reports on the condition of the schools in regard to teachers.

Is There Need of More Teachers?

"I have heard it said that the schools are well supplied with competent teachers. Is that true? Don't wait; speak quickly, briefly and to the point."

Mr. Geo. W. Brandom, class of '82, who has been engaged in temperance and S.S.[4] work as well as teaching ever since graduating, and is now regularly employed by the Missionary Department of Hampton Institute to visit schools and communities in the State, spoke on this point as follows:

"For the last few months I have been travelling all through southern Virginia visiting our graduates and their schools, and many other teachers also. I find in these counties a great need, at least for better teachers. The best material possible is not used in some places. One reason is on account of politics.

"Last fall in a certain county, every colored male teacher was obliged to sign an agreement to support the Democratic party. Some went off to other counties to avoid it and untrained teachers who would sign it were put in their places. The second reason is that in some counties salaries have been cut down; in one county no colored teacher is paid more than $25 per month, the majority $20 — so many have gone where they can get better pay and do as much or more work."

Mr. Washington — "Is there need of more teachers? That is the point we are to consider."

Mr. Brandom — "There is need of a better class, and therefore of more, because turning out the poor ones will leave vacancies."

Mr. Geo. W. Jackson of '75 — from Halifax Co. said, "I partly sympathize with Mr. Brandom. There is a need of more money."

Mr. Washington — "Stick to the point."

Mr. Brandom — "Yes. In my county, by the School Report, there are 9,000 colored children of school age — between 5 and 21 — out of that population, 3,500 were not in any public school last year. Why? Because there were not enough schools for them. On the school rolls, there were never less than 40 — from 40 to 120 — for one teacher. So nearly half the children have no teacher and no school. But the trouble is there is not money in the treasury to pay for any more."

Mr. Edward M. Canaday of '76, who has taught school and carried on a successful dry-goods and grocery business in Williamsburg since graduating, said, "I have had considerable experience for seventeen years. I have taught 14 years. We have not enough self-sacrificing teachers. We have enough of such as have been described, but we need more devoted to the interests of their people. In my county Hampton graduates always have precedence."

Mr. Wm. F. Grasty, class of '79, principal of a graded school in Danville, Va., where he has taught ever since graduating, said, "We

don't need more teachers, but we need more good teachers, in Pittsyl-
vania Co. Too many come simply for the compensation.

"We have a good Superintendent whose aim is to weed out such and
the schools are progressing. We need not more but better teachers."

Mrs. Rose Ella Lumpkin Brown of Hampton, Va., class of '80, said:
"I have just closed a school which I have taught for three years, in
Hampton. I have taught twelve years in five counties of the State. For
two years I had a school of 125 children, with no assistant.

"We do need more teachers. One reason is, our population is increasing.

"Another reason is, that we need to add to our work industrial
training to use the hands, sewing and cooking classes, etc. Now one
teacher with 125 children has more than enough to do without that.
Of course there are good and bad in every class of people. Hampton
teachers have held their own, and in the five counties where I have
taught have had the preference till last year when in Surry county,
the Supt. gave orders to give the graduates of the Petersburg Normal
Institute schools [preference?] on their diplomas without examination.
But in the next county there are 18 Hampton teachers. We do need
more teachers."

Mr. Godfrey R. Jackson of St. Simon's Mills, Ga., class of '75, who
has taught ever since graduating, in South Carolina and Georgia, said:
"We need more good teachers. I mean we need better teachers; not
who can be good in high salaried places in the cities but good when
placed way out in the dark corners — in a school house in the woods
and swamps, where the people are wild. Let him go out and dig, grub
out palmetto roots and let the light shine through the woods. That's
the kind I call good teachers. We want more of that kind."

Mr. Geo. P. Inge of Charlottesville, Va., class of '79, said: "We
need more teachers and better teachers, but the way to get them is to
pay better wages. A teacher has got to live. If he gets living wages he
can afford to stay in a place. In my section the pay is pretty good and
the teachers stand well, getting first grade and some professional
certificates."

Mr. Washington — "What proportion of them are Hampton graduates?"

Mr. Inge — "There are about 40 colored teachers in the county.
At least a fifth are Hampton graduates, but many are from the city
public schools."

"By whom are the city public schools taught?"

"Three of them by Tonserl, Kelser and myself [Hampton boys] and of the two young lady teachers one is a Hampton graduate."

Mrs. Della Irving Hayden, of '77, who has taught ever since graduating, principal of the graded school in Franklin, Va., has done a great deal of S.S. and temperance work, and is now Lady Principal of the Petersburg Normal Institute, said:

"My county gives preference to Hampton graduates. We do need more teachers. I know of two schools — with 125 children — closed in Southampton Co., and others in Isle of Wight Co. for want of teachers. I tried to send them some from Petersburg but all our graduates were employed. And we need better teachers."

Mr. Washington; "We have heard chiefly from Virginia. Let us hear from some other State."

Miss Julia E. Williams, Class of '89 said, "We do need more colored teachers in New Jersey. The examinations are very hard and we need more that are better prepared. Our Superintendent prefers Hampton graduates, and sends to Hampton when he has a vacancy to fill."

Mr. Daniel Simmons who has been teaching his "year out" in the Calhoun School, Alabama, under Misses Thorn and Dillingham and has now returned to take his Senior year in the Class of '94, said: "My three months' experience in Calhoun has been long enough to convince me that more teachers are needed in Alabama. The first day we opened school we enrolled 350, and had to turn away over 100 clamoring for admission. We have already had to refuse hundreds of applications for next year, because our rolls are over full, though it is four months before school will reopen. There are hundreds all about us who have never had a chance to go to any school. What teachers others have had have been incompetent to teach. One teacher within a mile of our school did not himself know the rudiments of arithmetic. We do need more teachers, and I pray God to rouse some who are throwing away their time and talents in cities for mere money getting, to go South and enter on this work and I desire that the Lord will enable me to spend my life in such work in such a place. When I look at the great life that ebbed out a few days ago, it inspires me to spend my life in just such work."

Mr. Frank T. Trigg, Class of '73 who has taught ever since graduating, been principal of the city colored schools of Lynchburg, Va., and conducted several of the Peabody summer Normal Institutes, and who is now principal of a group of schools in that city, said: "We do need more teachers and more competent teachers. One great thing they need is the element of 'stick-to-it-iveness.' I have taught in Virginia from Washington Co. to Smithfield, been examined by all the superintendents, and have been engaged for seven years in Institute work. At Abingdon I had a ten months school for five years. The secret of success is to stick to it, and more important than knowing much is to know what to do, how to apply your knowledge."

Miss Martha S. Doles, Class of '82 said, "I have taught for eight years in Southampton Co. The great trouble is not in lack of teachers but in want of teachers with backbone. I am thankful to say that we have some in our county who are ready to work and to stick to work. We have two or three very good workers. Then we teachers need to keep on studying all our lives. I found my children were catching up to me and I would have to get out of their way, so I went to Hartshorne College for a year."

Mr. Wm. A. Yancey, Class of '73, who has taught ever since graduating till recently, when he has been employed in Mission S.S. work by the Presbyterian Home Miss'y Soc. said: "I taught for eighteen years, and since then have been engaged in establishing Sunday schools. In one county I haven't met more than one or two well prepared teachers. One is doing very good work. Many of the others are from the old-field schools and some of them don't know the rudiments of arithmetic. We need teachers to take their places; better and self-sacrificing teachers."

Mr. Patrick W. Oliver of '77, who after three years of teaching and farming went into the grocery business and investment in real estate in Roanoke, Va., in both of which he has been very successful, said: "We do need more and better teachers, and also better salaries. I believe in moving from place to place when you can do better for yourself. It is said 'a rolling stone gathers no moss.' It is just as true that 'a setting hen never fattens.' We need money and we need education, and we can't get ahead without both."

Mr. A. B. Roberts, Class of '73 said: "I taught fourteen years in Virginia, West Virginia and Maryland, then I abandoned that work. When I entered Hampton, I signed an agreement to teach three years, I taught fourteen. I often went hungry. I walked hundreds of miles in those years to take examinations and to my school. I had rough times. I was once threatened with violence if I didn't leave the district. I found one door of my school house nailed up. I stayed. I armed myself with a pistol and my boys with razors and taught the term out. There is money enough in the South to support the schools and pay decent salaries, but it goes into politics instead. Mr. Washington said he'd rather teach for $10 a month than work for money at $100, I wouldn't. Mr. Washington is a great man, I am not a great man. I am in the minority perhaps, but if you want me to teach you must show me the money."

Mr. Washington said: "We have given as much time as we can to this subject. It seems conceded that in some places there is need of more teachers and in most places need of more well prepared ones. Let us now inquire into

THE CONDITION OF SCHOOL HOUSES."

Mr. Yancey said: "There is great need of better school houses in many country districts of Virginia. I have travelled over the state; there have been many improvements in twelve years, but many of the schools are still held in log cabins. Some belonging to the districts ought to be torn down. Last winter I saw one with a hole you could pitch a boy through in the side, and holes in the floor."

Mr. Wm. H. Ash of '82, who has taught most of the time since graduating, and who has become a lawyer and been a member of the Virginia Legislature, reported himself from Loudoun Co. and said; "The school houses in my county are in very good condition, but we need more of them.

"In a few years there will be no log cabin school houses. In every community but three or four, there are very fine and comfortable buildings and the school authorities are making their best efforts to this end. In our last teachers' meeting of the county, this subject was under discussion and they reported generally excellent order. I teach in Leesburg, the county-seat. My school house is two stories with four rooms. Others are equally good."

Mr. Thomas C. Walker, Class of '83, who has taught the same school in Gloucester Co. ever since graduating, and is also a very successful lawyer, and a man of excellent influence said: "For two or three years my business has called me to travel much through that and other counties. We need four new school houses for Gloucester

Co. In those communities the schools are now taught in Social Halls, given or rented by the people. In one district where there are 20 children there is no school. An effort is being made by some of the educated colored people to have a school and a teacher there and cover the expense.

"I am glad to say our school authorities are doing what they can. Ten years ago there was no school house in the county. To-day there are twenty-six colored teachers and all but four of them teach in good school houses supplied by the public authorities. King and Queen Co. adjoining, is not so well fitted out, and more and better school houses are needed. In Middlesex Co. they are little and old and need to be replaced. Across the Rappahannock in northern Virginia, in Lancaster there are not as many as are needed; the children are running in the roads. In Richmond Co. there are about enough. In Accomack and Northampton Counties — I went over there winter before last to make a personal examination of this subject. Some in Accomack are good and well fitted up. More and better ones in other places are needed. In Princess Anne Co. they are pretty well, but more and better ones are needed. Eastern Virginia is doing well. A great deal depends on the teacher's influence. In Gloucester Co. I began to teach in a little old school house of one room, with forty children, some larger than I. I called the people together and suggested adding another room. They had no money. I said, We'll make some. Before Christmas, we had another room and an assistant teacher and so we went on. We can build our own school houses when the public authorities fail to."

Mrs. M. C. Taylor (May Cummings, Class of '82) of Cumberland Co. said; "We have only six or seven school houses in the county and only one frame one. All the colored schools are in log houses and in the pine woods. We need more and better ones. I have to live a mile from my school and a great many of the children live a mile and a half from the school. I tried to get another house built among those, but the authorities said they could go to the next county, but they can't cross the water to get there. We need school houses all over the county. There is no probability that we shall get better schools till we can get Hampton teachers there or others interested in the salvation of the race. We now have only two Hampton teachers besides myself, only one of them is a graduate; the authorities prefer to get teachers in the county rather than send away. We need more school houses, more teachers and more Hampton graduates."

Mr. Washington: "What could the people do to build school houses, lengthen terms etc.?"

"We have only five months schools, and the colored teachers are always given only third grade certificates; if any have first grade certificates, they only get third grade pay, $25 or $20. There are grumblings among the people about Hampton Middlers being sent them instead of graduates. A Middler stays her five months and you never see her again. Kate Mosely, a Middler, has two rooms and 100 scholars."

Mrs. Rebecca Wright Short, of Surry Co. (under-graduate of '78) said facetiously, "I've just been waiting for the right time to put a wedge into this discussion and now I've got it. As to better school houses you may argue in vain about the need of them. Let me tell you what to do and how to do it to get better ones. The great trouble all the way through is just politics, that's why we don't have better teachers. I went out as a Middler, but I have worked up my own diploma, and I am going to tell you how to get your better teachers and school houses. To be a good teacher you must be preacher, housekeeper and carpenter and farmer. I let my children see I can do anything that is right for me to do. Come here, son" — Amidst much laughter and applause, a small, bright eyed image of his mother stepped out as if used to obey and stood on the seat where she lifted him, "I have resigned teaching myself because I am a married woman. Some of you have read what General Armstrong told us: 'Do what you can do well, and do it as well as you can.' I have all I can do in being a good mother; now hear how you can build your school house. My husband bought a place in the woods. In 1892 we went there. I told him I'd rather be dead and buried than have no church to go to. I went to the homes within reach and asked the people to send their children to my little house and I would have a school. If you want one, tell your people as I did, to give what they can — eggs or butter, etc., and have a festival and buy lumber and soon you'll get them interested and they'll build their own school house and then the Supt. will send you a teacher and let you pick out such as you want."

Mr. Washington; "We must get now to the next subject to consider."

The Industrial Condition of Our People

"I have seen much discussion of this in the Northern papers lately. What proportion of the colored people do you find owning land? Is it increasing? Does the one-room cabin life increase or decrease? In the Gulf States, the crop-mortgage system is a great evil. To what extent do you find it?"

Mr. Brandom, Mecklenburg Co. Class of '82, wished first to add a word on the previous subject of school houses. "In my fourteen years work I have met many graduate teachers who have built their own school houses on their own land, furnishing money to buy the land. Of sixteen colored schools I know only two have been built by the public officers; there are only three real school houses for colored teachers, the others teach in little halls or churches. School houses are much needed where I have been. Log houses soon fall down, get dangerous, and are too small. In many places only fifty per-cent. or less of the children are enrolled in school.

"As to industrial advancement, I find the people everywhere struggling to get homes, buying land and building more than ever; yet wages are low and many only rent. Where they own their farms and houses they are able to save and to keep their children in school. Great stress ought to be put on the matter of trades. I find few young mechanics, there are a few in the towns. In the country there are generally only the old ones who learned a trade in slavery times. Persons who have buildings to erect employ white mechanics mostly, while the colored people are getting small wages for unskilled labor."

Mr. Washington; "In regard to

The Condition of Education among the Colored People

"Prest. G. Winston[5] of the University of North Carolina says, in the *Christian at Work,* 'The mass of the race is less zealous for education than ten or twenty-five years ago.' How many of you agree to that? Raise your hands." Four hands were raised. "How many disagree?" Many hands were raised. Mr. Patrick Oliver of Roanoke, ('77) remarked "Plenty of white men who work for me can't write their own names."

Mr. Yancey said; "I have been a close observer of this point. Take the condition twenty-five years ago. The school system was not established then. At that time there were night schools of two or three hundred, many of them old people — my mother went; there were young people too; now of course the novelty is gone; the race is long and the people don't seem so anxious as when everything was new. Take it ten years ago, the times are harder now, and many want to make money more than to get an education."

Dr. Strieby[6] said; "The question ought to be narrowed to the last ten years, the comparison is not fairly made between now and twenty-five years ago. Then the people had a vague idea that education would make them just like their masters, and that it was something they could get in a hurry. Even any falling off in ten years has been partly explained; then they had fewer chances to get homes than they have now, but the comparison is fairer."

Rev. Dr. Rice,[7] Sec'y of the American Tract Society,[8] said "I think Mr. Washington said twenty years not twenty-five, but take ten; that is fairer. I am exceedingly anxious to know as to this. If the charge is really just, it is time we were waking up to change it."

Mr. Geo. W. Jackson, of Halifax Co. Class of '75; "We have in our county, Teachers' Institutes. Twelve years ago you would find ten teachers present. Last week forty out of the forty-five were present. I have been a teacher there seven years; my experience is all over the county, and it is that there is no decrease in the general desire for education but a strong desire to go higher.

"In my immediate vicinity, the people have formed a club, taxing themselves ten cents a month each, to extend the public school session by private subscription. If there is any truth in the statement in any section, I believe the fault lies with the teachers in the immediate vicinity."

Mr. Washington; "Those who know of cases where the people pay by private subscription for [a] longer school term, please raise your hands." Thirty-three hands were raised.

Mr. Washington; "I think the fact is simply that there is a decrease in the novelty of education; the just emancipated slaves thought it was something that would make them ladies and gentlemen, let them stand round the streets or sit in the parlor all day doing nothing. Now the people have learned differently. I know there is more intelligent earnestness for education to-day than ever before."

Mr. J. W. Fenderson of Accomack Co. Class of '91, said "I have been for two years teaching in the county. I have been informed by

Dr. Mapp, Supt. of Education in the County and Clerk of the School Board, that the colored people don't show the desire for education that they should; the school I took had fallen off from fifty to eleven under a teacher from a Northern college; but it came up again, and when I left the people begged me to stay and they would extend the term two months."

Mrs. Rose Ella Lumpkin Brown; "I have taught in Elizabeth City Co. Southampton, Surry, Princess Anne and Norfolk Co's, and last in the town of Hampton. I closed my school with 125 pupils, and I talked with the parents and secured places in the North for the mothers to work. Many told me they were willing to leave their children with the grandmothers and go to work to keep them in school. My own mother was a widow and she went to New York to work so her children could go to school, and some of us went to work days and went to night school. I believe the interest in education is not decreasing."

Mr. Washington, "Let us pass to the question of

THE INDUSTRIAL CONDITION, AND SECURING OF HOMES."

Mr. Wm. M. Reid, Class of '77, who after several years of teaching is a successful lawyer, of excellent standing in Portsmouth, Va., and has just been appointed by the Governor to the State Board of Curators of the Hampton School, said, "I have not been a teacher for the last eight years, but have been in the way to get at a good many facts bearing on the case. The people are very largely getting homes and accumulating property. Statistics made three years ago showed a very commendable number of persons owning homes. I have made inquiries also in Greenville, Isle of Wight Co., in Surry Co., Elizabeth City Co., and on the Eastern Shore. The tendency everywhere is to the getting of homes. The mortgage system we don't understand as it is understood in the far South. For the eight years I have been in the way of hearing complaints if any were made, I have never heard any complaints of liens or mortgages. We have deeds of trust which are really mortgages given for a piece of land till it is paid for. It puts the people in the best position, gives them the best motive to improve."

Mr. Washington; "In the cotton States, there is a system of giving mortgages on the cotton crop before it is planted, with a lien on the stock, the household furniture — I even heard of one man — a Baptist preacher — who gave one on his wife! A merchant in the town took one on what were named as two cows, Jane and Sallie, and when he foreclosed he found that one was the man's wife and the other his daughter."

Mr. W. C. Anderson, of Salem, New Jersey, Class of '89 said "I believe that the Negroes in general are more interested in education and in getting homes, than they were ten years ago, but I have been teaching in New Jersey for five years and I suspect that gentleman who made the charge against it in the paper, got his idea from the Negroes in the North. I do believe that they there are less interested than they are [in the South?] in education and in getting homes. Their advantages are greater, the schools in Salem are open ten months in the year, the parents have the opportunity to send their children all the time, but when warm weather comes the attendance falls to maybe six or seven. So I left and took a school in Plainsville which had been kept by an uneducated white man.

"As to property, I don't see much of it among them; most rent; they can't get enough to get started toward owning a home. I know it was not my fault."

Inquiry was made by Mrs. Rose Ella Brown, what chance there is in New Jersey for the colored pupils after they leave school. "Can they get positions as teachers?" Mr. Anderson replied "Yes; there are three grades of certificates they can get."

The Conference now adjourned till after dinner. In response to a request communicated by Mr. Harris Barrett, Mrs. Armstrong presented by him a cordial invitation to all the graduates and ex-students to call at the Mansion House on the General's family and see the little son; a privilege of which all gladly availed themselves.

At 2 P.M. the Conference reassembled for the afternoon session. The subject considered was,

IS THE NEGRO HOLDING HIS OWN IN SKILLED LABOR?

Mr. Yancey said; "The colored people used to do all the carpentering, blacksmithing, plastering and other mechanical work in the South. Very few do so now, the trades are slipping out of our hands. The young men won't learn trades when they have the opportunity. We have got to learn trades and create a demand for our labor."

Mr. Godfrey Jackson of St. Simon's Mills, Ga. Class of '75, said, "The colored laborers are holding their own in Georgia. There has been a boom in building and the greater part of the work has been done by colored mechanics — not the old men trained in slavery, but by men trained since the war. The houses they build are good enough for any man black or white. In Darien many of the old mechanics have died. The young men have learned the trades and are carrying them on. There are three or four colored skilled mechanics to one white. Reference was made to one in the *Darien Gazette*, Mr. Lawrence Gardiner, a painter and builder."

Mr. Patrick Oliver, "A colored boy came into Roanoke carrying a hod. Some of the best buildings in that town have been built by that boy. There are several other leading colored mechanics, carpenters etc."

Mr. Washington, "What effect do the Labor Unions have on Negro skilled labor? Are Negro mechanics admitted to them?"

Rev. John Kirby of Hampton, Va., Class of '80 said; "Labor unions exist to some extent among colored mechanics, because they have not been admitted to white Unions."

Mr. Washington; "Is the color line drawn in the Labor Unions? What do you all say? Yes or No?"

A unanimous "Yes."

Mr. Ash said; "The colored people are holding their own in skilled labor both as to numbers and efficiency. Six in Loudoun are working at the carpenter's trade to-day where five years ago there was one; and their work equals that of white carpenters."

Question — "Are they able to make out estimates of cost, etc.?"

Mr. Ash, "Yes, one is able to take any $5,000 job; to build as fine a house as you can find in any country town of five thousand inhabitants. Last year he built a cottage equal in architecture and beauty to any white man's in town, and we pride ourselves on our homes in Loudoun."

Dr. Strieby said; "I take great interest in this question and should like to get at [it?] in a clear and fair, just way. We often hear it said that the old mechanics trained in slavery are passing away and few are taking their places. I want to know if that is true or false, and what the difference is between this and ten years ago.

"A skilled mechanic must have trained brain as well as trained hands."

Mr. Ash, "Two years ago, a company of men from Massachusetts came to Leesburgh to light the town with electricity. They employed a colored boy in some position. He was smart and rose rapidly and in less than twelve months was capable of managing many things. They said he learned quicker than their other white apprentices. But the prejudice was such that they had to discharge him and take a white boy in his place."

Mr. Washington; "Where did the six carpenters you spoke of learn their trade?"

Mr. Ash, "One came from Alexandria, one from some where else; the other four learned their trades from them. One had a limited education; the other could only read and write a little."

Mr. Patrick Oliver, "In Roanoke, colored men have run the furnaces. In the gas works not a white man is employed. Colored men run the cable cars. The colored boss of the shop gets $1700 a year. In '83 a Southern man put the colored men in; the whites kicked, but he kept them in. In the foundry it is the same. In the boiler department they are employed but not in as high positions. Now as to bricklaying; the three contractors in the town are all colored except one."

Mr. Thos. H. Lockery of '86, who after teaching three years in Virginia has been car porter on different roads from New Jersey to Dakota, thought that "the colored people in the North and West have retrograded as to skilled mechanics in the last ten years, because they are shut out from the Labor Unions."

Mr. Grasty, '79, said that in Danville, Va. his home, a tobacco town, there are few skilled colored mechanics. There are a few carpenters. "My father and Inge's father are carpenters, but they didn't teach us or others their trade. The old mechanics are passing away and there are no young men taking their places; the white carpenters do most of the work. But in bricklaying they are progressing. I know one who is a contractor and has contracts on very large buildings. He has made it a point to seize on young colored men and teach them the trade; though he is not an educated man, he teaches those who are. In painting there are three old men who are skilled but we are not holding our own in that trade as we should."

Mr. Washington, "There is danger of thinking that because there is decrease [in] skilled laborers that means decrease in all prosperity. Don't they go into buying land and accumulate property?" "Yes" (unanimous).

Mr. Trigg — "Our best mechanics are those who have learned in slavery time without pencil or rules — old men who have learned to cut up lumber, but who cut it to waste. The skilled white mechanics can draw plans and we want men who can do that. I saw in the mill here at Hampton, beautiful drawings by a boy of this School, who has just completed his trade. When he goes out, he'll be able to teach apprentices and command a good business. It is too late in the day to learn a smattering of trades. We want more such mechanics as Hampton furnishes — like Sullivan, who worked three years here in the harness shop, and now has his own shop and seven apprentices."

Query — "Are the colored people in general holding their own as to skilled mechanics?"

Mr. Trigg — "No. They are just in a transition stage between the old time and the new."

Mr. Wm. Weaver, of Cappahosic, Gloucester Co., who, leaving Hampton from the Middle class of '75, has taught ever since and has built up an Industrial School on the Hampton plan, doing excellent work, said: "Most of those who learn trades now learn them from the old mechanics, but the really skilled laborers come from the Industrial Schools. They are our only hope."

Mr. Geo. P. Inge of '79 from Charlottesville, Va. said: "In my section colored carpenters are doing very well, taking contracts of from $3,000 to $5,000 buildings. They learn from colored mechanics. A majority of the plasterers are colored men. They get good wages. I think in my section, the colored people are advancing in skilled labor. I know a family of five or six sons who have all learned trades."

Mr. A. J. J. Sykes of Norfolk Co., class of '80, said: "I have never known old mechanics who were able to draw, but they were skilled workmen. I know good ship carpenters, who can do all but draw the plans; those are drawn by white men. I know some young men who are good painters, carpenters, joiners and machinists, getting employment in the Navy Yard and on private jobs. One man has a mill of his own and saws lumber."

A vote was called for on the point as to whether the colored people are holding their own as to skilled mechanics. Twelve voted yes; thirteen, no, but most did not vote, seeming to think the question too hard to be answered by one word, or that they did not feel sure about it.

The next subject considered was the

Moral Progress of the Race.

Mr. Washington said: "This statement is made by some: that the morality of the people of the Negro race is in a very discouraging condition. What are the facts? Let the consideration include many points."

Mrs. Taylor, class of '82 said: "That is a fact where I have lived. I have seen a man, his wife and three children living in a one room cabin; sometimes from eight to twelve or thirteen live so all in one small room. I should say that three-fifths of the people are living in that way. There is no chance of improvement under such a condition."

Mr. Alex. H. McNeil of '77, said: "I hope you will bear in mind that poverty always leads to inferiority in the moral condition. The condition is bad where there is abject poverty and hopeful under other circumstances."

Mr. Washington: "We want to get the facts. What is charged is that it is not from poverty only but because they want to be bad naturally."

Rev. John Kirby of Portsmouth, Va., class of '80, said: "I think the outlook is hopeful; the people are improving. The higher individuals rise, the darker appears that which may seem to be immorality. Over crowding is supposed to always mean immorality; but, while some are very bad, that is not always so. Then, from the reports of police courts, it is concluded that the whole race is hopelessly degraded. But it should be noticed that the same individuals are brought up repeatedly; they are not all new cases. Then, a large proportion of the cases are from a floating population that don't belong really to the community which is credited with them. Then boisterous, rough and coarse manners are often supposed to indicate the worst immorality, and that is not always so. I feel myself exceedingly hopeful from the improvement I see taking place."

Rev. Mr. Harding: "I asked a white man from Georgia what he thought. He spoke kindly of the colored people as I have found most of the Southern white people do, but he said 'The condition is bad, there is much immorality.' He told me of an intelligent colored preacher who was afraid he would have to leave his church because his high moral principles had set the people against him and they preferred a man they had before, a fascinating man but known to be bad. The church had given him papers of recommendation and would like to get him back though they knew his character. Would such a state of things exist in Virginia?"

Mr. Kirby: "No, not when guilt was proved. I don't believe it."

Mr. Geo. W. Jackson of '75, from Halifax Co., Va., said: "Six years ago I was Secretary of our Church Co. Association, and again last year. I had the chance to compare the two reports. There were 50 per cent. less excommunications reported than there were six years ago, in the report covering 36 churches. In my own community I can say morality is on the increase. There is not half as much immorality as there was, and as the light of education increases, morality increases in proportion."

Capt. R. R. Moton,[9] disciplinarian at Hampton Institute, class of '90, said — "Isn't it our tendency to grow more critical of others as our own eyes are opened by education? When I went home last summer I noticed more, but the same things I should have passed without notice ten years ago."

Mr. Harris Barrett, class of '85, resident in Hampton, Va., and for a number of years in a responsible position as bookkeeper, and at times cashier in the treasurer's office, at Hampton Institute, said: "While not a member of any church in Hampton I have been for four or five years in close contact with ministers of this community and can testify that every one of them is a high minded Christian. The Rev. Mr. Shorts, one of them [a graduate of our Pastors' Class] has been making a crusade against unlicensed bar-rooms and other evils, and some of those he had offended tried to burn him out. Statistics, which I have studied carefully [Mr. Barrett is Secretary of the colored Building and Loan Association which he assisted in starting in Hampton greatly to the benefit of the people.] — prove that here the moral condition is rising. The people are living better; the old one room slab hut is getting to be the exception. There is a stratum of the lower class, but there is a better class that looks down on such evil and it must cloak itself from sight. That is our way up. Society must be divided into strata by morality and respectability. Newport News being newly settled by all sorts, has had a bad reputation, but even that is beginning to rise."

Miss Mary A. Tucker of Hampton, Va., class of '84, said: "It is not of Hampton I rise to speak, though what Mr. Barrett has said of it is all true, but I want to speak of Farmville, Va., where I taught for three years. I can testify that the colored ministers there are trying to inculcate morality and that the people are improving. A minister told me 'I will leave no stone unturned to root out immorality, and my people feel the same way.' That is our work for our people."

Mr. Walker of Gloucester, class of '83, said: "Of the 100 churches in the 'Norfolk Association' (Baptist) I have visited two-thirds, and know the pastors. I don't know one who does not rebuke sin wherever he sees it. Last Tuesday I heard a pastor say to one of his deacons, 'There's got to be a change in your conduct or you leave the church!' I don't know one of them who drinks at all."

Mr. A. J. J. Sykes, class of '80, said: "I have taught in Norfolk and Surry Co's and Salem, Va. I have never had any trouble from the preachers. They have helped my work, and I theirs."

Mr. Canaday, of Williamsburg, class of '76, said: "My minister has been pastor of one Baptist church for twenty years. No one is more strong in efforts to uplift the people than he is and his deacons sustain him. It is the same with the other churches. Those who drink or are otherwise immoral are turned out of them. I have known but one exception to co-operation from our ministers in my efforts for the people in fourteen years of teaching."

Rev. John H. Tazewell, class of '74, who has taught for six years, been colporteur for the Am. Tract Society, worked his way through our Pastors' Class, and is now trying to build up a much needed church in Newport News, said: "It is a fact that our people in Newport News have a bad reputation morally in the low element that has collected from other places. They come just to pick up money and are no better after they get there than they were before they left other towns — Hampton for instance." (Laughter, and a sly inquiry "Didn't you go there from Hampton?" which Mr. Tazewell had to acknowledge was the truth. But he might have claimed to be one of the "ten righteous" who would save the city.) "But, with all that, the outlook is encouraging. The place is improving. The hard times are helping us. Since the public works have closed, a great many of the bad set have left the place."

Mrs. Rose Ella Brown said she had "Known the time when the girls who went to teach in Newport News had to board in Hampton to get a respectable home, but now there are quite a number of good Christian families there."

Mr. Major Wright of Newport News, class of '78, said: "I was sent as census enumerator to Newport News in 1880, and I helped the surveyors who laid it out. I have been Commissioner of Revenue of Warwick Co. and have known the town from the beginning. At one time it had a terrible name for immorality. Poverty Row, Hell's Half Acre and such names were appropriately given to some quarters. But it is very different now and improving."

Mr. Henry C. Payne of Hampton's first graduating class, (71) who after teaching a number of years, has made a highly respected position for himself in West Virginia as a successful business man and excellent boat-builder, said: "I taught seven or eight years in Charleston, West Va. We had some ministers there who were not good, but things have greatly improved. We have had a number of Hampton graduates there who have sown good seed that can be seen springing up — Dr. Merchant and H. B. Rice (both of '77), and G. B. Howard. The churches now will not tolerate immorality in their members. They bring those who are bad to trial and excommunicate them. That's the only way we are going to work it out among us."

*   *   *   *

The hour had come for the last words of the Conference. Mr. Frissell expressed the School's satisfaction in seeing so large an attendance of its graduates. "Nothing would have pleased General Armstrong more than to see you here. One of his great ideas was that of keeping in touch with the graduates. Some have said that colored people don't stand up for each other. We know that Hampton's graduates have stood for each other and for the School. One of the last thoughts of the General's while he was with us was to bring the graduates still more into co-operation. You know of Miss Cleaveland's work as Graduates' Correspondent and of the Bureau of Distribution of Reading Matter, and how the General and I have visited your schools. He had planned more such work. Mr. Turner,[10] our Assistant Chaplain, was appointed by the General as head of the 'Missionary Department' to go and see more of you and your people, and we hope to have more graduates going out as Mr. Brandom has gone. You have heard what a reformation has been wrought in Smithfield Co. where there is an organization of Hampton graduates for temperance work, etc., largely the result of the efforts of Mrs. Della Hayden ('77) and Miss Martha Doles ('82) and Miss Maggie Stevens ('86). We must push such work. In the North I speak of the graduates' work as many sided — tell how you not only teach books but housekeeping, farming, etc., object lessons to your people. I am glad of what some of you said about sticking to one place. It is well to teach and preach, but most of all Hampton graduates should show the people how to live. Then you can help Hampton by sending us good material for the shops, to learn trades and so become useful. You know how close to the General's heart that work always was. In his last illness he sent a boy to see how the saw mill was getting on, whether the raft had come in. I feel unfit for this responsibility that has come to me, but I feel that I am not alone in it. It rests also on you. We have friends here from whom we want to hear: Dr. Rice of the American Tract Society, under which some of you have been colporteurs. It is doing good work. The only way to keep out bad reading is to send in good. And Dr. Strieby an old veteran of the American Missionary Association and a trustee of this School from the beginning."

Mr. Washington: "We graduates are always sure when we come into contact with A.M.A. people, of meeting men and women with whom we can co-operate and who will help us."

Dr. Strieby spoke as follows:

"It is just sixty years ago since I became an Abolitionist. That meant abuse, mobs, stoning, in those days. It is thirty years since I entered the American Missionary Association. I have listened with great interest to you this afternoon. I don't believe that in the history of mankind there has been another instance of such progress as has been made by the Negroes of the United States since they were emancipated, in which time they have increased from four to eight millions. But now, with hundreds of others, I am concerned about them, to help them make the full success that we will make because God is with us. Race prejudice exists in the North as well as the South. There is almost no place there where a colored man can learn a trade. The mass of your race and the mass of mine will be simply hard laborers, but if you are all simply that you will not rise as you ought to. Your reports have been more encouraging than I had expected. There are hindrances and discouragements. Some are claiming that colored men are being supplanted also as coachmen, restaurant waiters, etc., because they haven't the energy and quickness of the whites. If true, it is a discouraging fact. But what will you do about it?

"You have got to cultivate energy as well as to learn trades. Hampton is doing a work looking far forward. It may be that industrial effort is your great work but it is not all; there is moral power also in your Sunday School and other work. Make yourselves the men and women you need to be and God will take care of the results."

Rev. Mr. Turner Asst. Chaplain said, "Your discussions have been right along the line of my work among and with the graduates. In my two trips to visit your schools and homes, I have seen hopeful signs and also special needs.

"1st. It is a good thing that the great majority of colored people have country life, and are in agricultural work. It is a more healthful, hopeful life than that of cities. The smallness of wages, on the other hand is discouraging. Some receive only $100 or $80 a year; half in old clothes.

"2nd. There is great willingness to make sacrifices to keep the children in school. I have known of parents going without breakfast so the child could take the food to school for his dinner. I saw a Hampton graduate who carried on three churches for $39 a year, though he had an opportunity to make more.

"3d. I saw thrifty economy, and a desire to accumulate property. It is the office of the Missionary Department to help you in all this work for your people."

Rev. Dr. Rice, a Southerner by birth said; "I have vivid recollections of slavery time. As I compare this time with that I am satisfied that there has been great progress in morality. The race is naturally religious — as Paul said of the Athenians 'too religious' in a sense — too emotional. They need to learn that religion touches all sides of life — as at Hampton. When I was a little boy our old cook, Aunt Fanny, would make me a little cake or pie if I would read the Bible to her. I wished she knew how to read so I could go play. President Winston says the race has learned to read and write. That certainly is progress. Of course it makes us a new anxiety, just as it makes me anxious to know what my boy shall read now that he has learned how. The American Tract Society is trying to send good literature into the South to meet this need. It is required by our constitution to be strictly undenominational, such as any Christian church could not object to. We hope to employ more Hampton graduates as colporteurs to do this good work for their people. We need men of integrity, competent to keep accounts. Personally, as missionary secretary of the Tract Society, I am anxious to do something for the colored race. I owe a great deal to them and I watch their progress with anxiety. The problem is not yet worked out. There are encouragements and you have had helpful advantages, but if there is one thing I believe it is that no race can work out your problem except your own race, with the help of God. There is one thing more I want to add; after this visit and this Conference, I shall give a more hopeful picture of your people than I ever have before."

Specially requested, Miss Hyde,[11] head teacher of Hampton, spoke a few words of encouragement and advice and gave this cheering testimony:

"You spoke of there being improvement. I know that is so. I notice it every year as the new students come to enter the night school. There is great improvement. The girls show it in more refinement, and better preparation; so do the young men. I see a great difference too in the children that come to the Whittier.[12] It is certainly a hopeful sign. I agree with you that better teachers must be sent out. This year the Senior class is small because it has been more carefully weeded out than ever. I hope the preparation will be better and better. Five months school terms are of course too short, but only try to do your best in the time you can get. We have made a special study this year in the training class from the Whittier to see how much can be done in five months. We sent some of the work to the World's Fair. It is surprising to see how much can be done even in five months with careful and wise work. As to our sending out Middlers, it is a great benefit to them, and they have been trained in teaching. Some stay out more than a year. But if you graduates will stick to your places, we can't send Middlers to those. We will try to send out better teachers every year. Help us by sending in good material."

* * * *

Mr. Washington then spoke as follows:

"I never felt so proud of being a Hampton graduate, never felt so sure that Hampton is doing the right work in the right way. I don't believe there could have been a similar meeting in any other state in the Union where we could hear such reports. We need to have this work reinforced and multiplied in the far South. I have had the privilege of attending many Teachers' Meetings, and have been, for eight or ten years, president of the Teachers' Association of Alabama, and have attended those in adjoining states. As I hear your reports

346

of progress by solid facts, I am more and more convinced that this is just the work we want in the far South.

"If I could call back the years of my life and choose between an education for my life work at Harvard or Yale, and an education at Hampton, I should choose Hampton.

"We want this work in the far South. As I compare the reports I have heard in different meetings and conferences there with those we have had here to-day, you don't know how far ahead you are of the states far South; for some questions that we are fighting you have passed, some you hardly know about. If every state in the Union had a Hampton Institute we'd have a different state of affairs. It is reported that in a famous lawsuit, where Daniel Webster and Rufus Choate were on different sides, after Choate by a long argument had tried to prove that the patent on a certain machine was rightly held by his client, Mr. Webster just pointed to the machine — which was set up but wouldn't work — and said only, 'Gentlemen, look at it — look at it — look at it!' — and he won his case. We've got to come to this point in our efforts for civilization — when our white friends need not depend on their imagination to be convinced that the Negro can be civilized, moral, educated, useful, but when every man who doubts can be pointed to a living manifestation to exemplify the fact; then, the Negro Problem will have passed away.

"No one can pass from here without being a better man, a better woman, because of the sweet, strong influences gathered on these grounds. I hope we shall have an Armstrong Memorial meeting to rededicate ourselves every year to the work he would have us do."

At Mr. Washington's request an explanation of the Dixie Training School and the opportunity it gives our graduate girls to become trained nurses, was made by Miss Bacon.[13] Her beautiful verses in tribute to General Armstrong, which were printed in our June number, were effectively read by Mrs. Harris Barrett. The benediction was pronounced by Dr. Rice and the Conference adjourned.

Southern Workman, 22 (July 1893), 115-22.

[1] Blanche Kelso Bruce.
[2] John Wheeler Harding.
[3] Augustus Field Beard?
[4] Sunday school.
[5] George Tayloe Winston (1852-1932) was president of the University of North Carolina from 1891 to 1896. He was president of the University of Texas from

1896 to 1899, and then served as president of the North Carolina College of Agriculture and Mechanical Arts (now North Carolina State University, Raleigh).

[6] Michael E. Strieby.

[7] William Augustus Rice (1850-1926) was an 1873 graduate of Auburn Theological Seminary and held pastorates in New York, Michigan, and New Jersey. From 1890 to 1897 he was secretary of the American Tract Society.

[8] The American Tract Society, founded in 1825, was an interdenominational Protestant publishing and missionary organization. In the late nineteenth century the society concentrated on reaching Catholic immigrants as well as rural blacks.

[9] Robert Russa Moton (1867-1940), successor to BTW as principal of Tuskegee Institute, was the son of former Virginia plantation slaves. He graduated from Hampton in 1890. During BTW's career at Tuskegee, Moton was commandant of the Hampton cadets and a close adviser of Hollis Burke Frissell. He was also BTW's protégé, and traveled with him on speaking tours, sponsored by the Southern Education Board and the Slater Fund, to promote education and economic advancement of rural southern blacks. Shortly before BTW's death, with his encouragement, Moton founded the Virginia Cooperative Association to aid in the self-improvement of rural and small-town blacks. He envisioned an eventual nationwide organization. He became principal of Tuskegee Institute in 1915. In 1919 he became president of the National Negro Business League and was the leading spokesman for the Tuskegee approach to black progress and race relations in the two decades prior to his retirement in 1935. He was never the powerful leader or boss that BTW was. His most important book, *What the Negro Thinks* (1929), is a restatement of the Tuskegee formula to meet the demands of a better-educated and race-conscious black middle class. In that work Moton decried racial discrimination in law and legislation, transportation, education, and housing, and advocated a civil equality of races who in social life should remain "ethnologically distinct." "As for amalgamation," Moton said, "very few expect it; still fewer want it; no one advocates it; and only a constantly diminishing minority practice it, and that surreptitiously."

Moton brought to the Tuskegee approach the tone of the Progressive era. He was an advocate of the government commission as an instrument for solving racial problems "by conference and adjustment rather than by legislation in the heat of agitation that rarely if ever expresses the wisest thought or the best sentiment on either side...." He helped found the Commission on Interracial Cooperation and was in and out of federal agencies as a representative of black Americans. Woodrow Wilson sent him to France in 1918 to make a survey of opinion about the Army among black soldiers. Later he headed a committee of black leaders working with the Hoover presidential commission on the Mississippi River flood disaster in 1927. Moton was a member of the National Advisory Commission on Education, the commission to study education in Liberia, and chairman (1930) of the U.S. Commission on Education in Haiti. He also contributed to the literature of exposure, compiling an annual report of national lynching statistics that was widely circulated. The restrictive immigration legislation of the 1920s signaled to Moton that blacks had been found more satisfactory than immigrants in American industry. This, he surmised, was so because the black man, while "he refuses to be less than an American," at the same time "is adaptable and in the face of resistance is rather given to compromise." In essence, Moton's approach to race relations was compromise. While the "ultimate goal of equal opportunity with all other Americans" should be preserved, blacks, through the interracial commission, would be willing to bargain for a less than ideal modus vivendi.

Moton participated widely in black institutional life. He moved Tuskegee toward the model of the standard American college in the 1920s by beginning a junior college program, eventually expanded to a four-year college curriculum. He was a director of the Dunbar National Bank in New York City and of the Tuskegee Institute Savings Bank. In 1924 he helped found the National Negro Finance Corporation, headquartered in Durham, N.C., and served as its president. He was on the board of trustees of a number of black educational institutions, including Fisk University and the People's Village School at Mt. Meigs, Ala. He was chairman of the National League on Urban Conditions among Negroes, a forerunner of the National Urban League. In 1930 he received the Harmon Award in Race Relations, and in 1932, the Spingarn Medal. He wrote an autobiography in 1920, *Finding a Way Out*. (Moton, *What the Negro Thinks,* 241, 263-64.)

[10] Herbert Barclay Turner (1852-1927), a Congregational minister educated at Amherst and Union Theological Seminary, became assistant chaplain at Hampton Institute in 1892, succeeding Hollis Burke Frissell as chaplain when Frissell became principal in 1893.

[11] Elizabeth Hyde.

[12] Whittier School, the demonstration school at Hampton Institute.

[13] Alice M. Bacon of the staff of Hampton Institute later wrote *The Negro and the Atlanta Exposition* (John F. Slater Fund Occasional Papers, No. 7, Baltimore, 1896).

To Collis Potter Huntington

[Tuskegee, Ala.] June 1 [189]3

Dear Sir: There have been only a few times in the history of this institution when I have had to ask of any one what I now ask of you. We have obligations due to various persons in not very large amounts that ag[g]regate $1200. These amounts are troublesome and I do not want to attempt to carry them through the summer in their present shape. Is it possible for you to lend us this amount with interest to be returned in 4 months at the rate of $300 per month. As I shall be in the North collecting money during the summer I can easily return $300 each month.

I can give you my personal note for the debt. Yours truly

Booker T. Washington

ALpS Con. 106 BTW Papers DLC.

349

To Julius B. Ramsey[1]

[Tuskegee, Ala.] June 2nd [189]3

Dear Sir: According to promise I now write to say that we shall be glad to give you the position as Commandant in this institution for the coming school year. The duties of this position include the care of the young men in all respects, the drilling of companies, boys' study-hour, inspection of rooms, general discipli[ne] etc.

We can pay you for this work $30 per month and board for t[he] first year. Board will include room lights, fuel etc. all expen[ses] except travelling. We should like for you to be here by next September. Yours truly,

Booker T. Washington

TLpS   Con. 106   BTW Papers   DLC.

¹ Julius B. Ramsey was a graduate of Hampton Institute, class of 1893. General Armstrong recommended Allen Washington, another senior, but Robert R. Moton recommended Ramsey instead, and Hampton employed Allen Washington as Moton's assistant. Moton said of Ramsey that he was the "Senior Captain" of the cadets, that he had spent three years in the school's pastors' class, and that he was also a good painter. "They are both good drill-masters having had special instruction from Army officers during this and other terms," wrote Moton. (Moton to BTW, Mar. 24, 1893, Con. 105, BTW Papers, DLC.) Ramsey became "Major Ramsey" as commandant of cadets at Tuskegee for many years beginning in 1893. He taught military science and was also in principal charge of discipline of the men students, inspecting their dormitories and marching them to meals and classes as well as conducting military drill.

"I planned," Ramsey later said, "to take a profession — the exact one not decided upon — intended to go to Oberlin when I was asked to come to Tuskegee. And for several years after coming I would say 'this would be my last year.' " He saw it as his responsibility to develop "obedience, politeness, reliability, promptness, cleanliness in person and in surroundings, physical endurance, physical development, respect for authority, and respect for their fellows." ("Hampton at Tuskegee," undated typescript, 1915, Con. 959, BTW Papers, DLC; J. E. Davis, "Hampton at Tuskegee," *Southern Workman,* 44 [Oct. 1915], 531-32. The typescript was an early draft of the article and contained matter later eliminated.)

From Charles Winston Thompson

Tuskegee Ala. June 6th, 1893

Dear Sir: I have the pleasure to inform you that you have been accepted by the Mutual Life Ins. Co.

I have your Policies in hand and will deliver them to you th[e] first opportunity. Kindly call at the Bank the first time you come down Town. Yours Truly,

C. W. Thompson

TLS Con. 6 BTW Papers ATT. Original destroyed.

To Robert Wesley Taylor

[Tuskegee, Ala.] June 9th [189]3

Dear Taylor: This letter may be somewhat of a surprise to you, but I hope you can see your way clear to accede to our request. After deliberating for a good deal of time over the matter, we have determined to put some one of our graduates in the field in the North to collect money for the school; interest and instruct the people about our work, and we have settled on the conclusion that we can get no better person to represent us than yourself.

To accept this position may be somewhat of a disappointment to yourself at present, but I hope that for the good of the race you will be willing to do so. It will give you an experience in coming in contact with the best people of the country that will be of very great value to you in whatever you undertake. If you think you could accept we should like for you to be ready to start North the first of September. I shall write you later about the work and salary. We shall want you to spend your time in speaking before churches, Sunday Schools etc., seeing individuals and the like. We all feel that you can be successful in this work.

Please give me an immediate answer. Your friend,

Booker T. Washington

TLpS Con. 106 BTW Papers DLC.

351

To William Burns Paterson

[Tuskegee, Ala.] June 12 [189]3

Dear Sir: I said that I would write again regarding yours of May 8. I thought when I received your letter and still think that you will make a mistake if you have nothing to do with the Association.[1] In all I think we have held 11 meetings. At 10 of them there was nothing that was unpleasant to you. Is it fair to judge all the future by one meeting[2] in view of the past?

I do not believe that any one can do the best work in the State who fails to keep himself identified with such institutions. Yours truly

Booker T. Washington

ALpS Con. 106 BTW Papers DLC.

[1] Alabama State Teachers' Association.
[2] See the letter from J. D. Bibb, July 5, 1892, above.

From Robert Wesley Taylor

Pensacola, Fla., June 14– '93

Dear Friend: Your letter of recent date was the greatest surprise imaginable.

I have thoroughly considered the offer made to me and have decided to off-set my ideas of going to school next term, so as to comply with your request. As you know, Alma-Mater means nourishing Mother.

From an intellectual stand-point I consider Tuskegee my mother — so I am perfectly willing to act in the capacity of a child.

You may inform me at your earliest convenience of the full particulars and I shall endeavor to be ready to answer whenever you call.

Kindly inform me as to whether or not we will go to Chicago before the Fair closes as I am very anxious to go. If not I intend going before September. Your friend

R. W. Taylor

ALS Con. 6 BTW Papers ATT. Original destroyed.

From Portia Marshall Washington

Tuskegee, Ala., July 9th 1893

Dear papa. You dont know how glad I was to receve your letter and was glad to have you tell me about Boston on the 4th of July. but we had a delightful time   we got up in the morning happy as birds and I did my work   then we went to breakfast   after breakfast I washed dishes then I came up stairs and sewed   then I went down stairs and practised   by that time it was dinner time   after dinner I washed dinner dishes   then I came up stairs and played with Baker's ball untill mamma said I could g[o] over to see Emma   I went over their and I helped Emma wash her dishes. I played with Emma and Gracie[1] and Theodore & Horace.[2] we shot some fire crackers. then I went home and did work   then it was supper time   after supper I washed dishes. we had all ready fixed up our porch with drapery and flags the evening when I came home from Emma's. we had a concert out on the porch   I played a peice on the pano   Baker spoke a peice   this was it   Id rather be a marshall and ride a prancing horse and take lead with my fine steed and where a badge of course. after the concert I went with the rest of people down on the croquet ground and played. We shot fire crackers and roman cannons and sky rockets. I wish you could have been here. Papa you want me to tell you a the fourth of Jyly. ~~In 1620 a few years after Capt. Smiths visit to England.~~ A little more than one hundred years ago. The king of England did not govern theas colonies well and so the people became dissatisfied and on the fourth of July in 1776, declared what is know as the declaration of Independence that they woud not be governed by England any lounger. War with Eng. followed and Genarel Washington (thats you) one of the greatest and best men commanded our armys   the war lasted nearly seven years   we were fine. Then they joined them selves together and called their selves the United States. I must close now for I am tired   Your loveing daughter

Portia

P.S. All send love. Pappa I think you owe me 65 cts.

P.

ALS   Con. 17   BTW Papers   DLC.

¹ Gracie Penney, seven-year-old daughter of Edgar J. Penney, Tuskegee's chaplain.

² Horace Penney, nine-year-old son of Edgar J. Penney.

From Jabez Lamar Monroe Curry

Asheville, No. Ca. 10 July 93

Dear Sir— Your recollection of the increased appropriation is accepted as final and we shall expect such results in Normal and Industrial work as to justify the enlargement. So much of what is done in some of the Schools along these lines is so superficial and unsatisfactory, except in individual cases, that I sometimes fear the Slater money is failing to do the good it ought.

We want to publish a monograph giving the history of negro education in the South from 1861 to 1893, and it is necessary to have papers from each State showing what has been done by the State, by denominations, by individuals. The material thus collected will be edited or classified and arranged into a single paper. Dr Cravath of Fisk in May published an article in a Tenn. Nashville, paper, which is just what I seek. It was historical, giving verifiable facts and not speculations and opinions. I want you to prepare me such a paper, concise and clear, or get some one to do it by the first of September or October. I have the promise of such papers from Va. No. Ca. Geo. Miss. and La. It is very probable that you have already in possession most of the data. Yours truly

J. L. M. Curry

ALS   Con. 6   BTW Papers   ATT.   Original destroyed.

To Henry Demarest Lloyd

Tuskegee, Ala., July 29 1893

Dear Sir: Your letter of July 15 notifying me that you will expect me to speak Sept 2 — on "The Progress of the Negroes As Free Laborers" is received. In reply would say that I shall be present to perform the duty. Yours truly

Booker T. Washington

ALS   Henry D. Lloyd Papers   WHi.

From Lottie Virginia Young

Tuskegee Ala. Aug. 3– 1893

Dear Mr. Washington: I came home from the Farm Tuesday P.M. I left my work as far as possible in as good shape as I could. I *hope* I discharged my duty towards the young men respecting their rooms, and their appearance and manners in the dining room. The Sundays were allways pleasantly spent. I had prayer meeting in the morning — Sunday School in the P.M. and prayers at night. I also read sermons and Mrs. H. B. Stowe's work[1] for them.

I was sorry that a bath tub was seen on the young men's piazza when you brought Rev. Mr. Stokes down on last evening. They have been spoken to so often and have been demerited and charged for it many times, but S. P. Fort[2] bathed and left the tub where he knew he should not have done. So I sent in a fine for him to Mr. J. B. Washington. The Students had a "Tuesday evening Literary Club" and that I think added largely towards making the Farm seem School like. Your friend

Lottie V. Young

ALS   Con. 105   BTW Papers   DLC.

[1] Harriet Beecher Stowe, *Uncle Tom's Cabin* (1852).

[2] Simon Peter Fort of Forest, Miss., attended Tuskegee Institute from 1891 to 1894. He did not graduate.

To Grindall Reynolds[1]

[Tuskegee, Ala.] Aug. 11th, '93

My dear Sir: Learning sometime ago from Mrs. Frothingham and others that the late Rev. Frederick Frothingham,[2] of Milton, Mass., left a bequest of $20,000 to the American Unitarian Association with the provision that the income from this amount be used by the Association for the education of the colored people, I hereby make the request that the interest on this legacy, or a fair proportion of it be given to the Tuskegee Normal and Industrial Institute.[3] These are my reasons for making the request:

1st, From the founding of this institution, until his death — as Mrs. Frothingham will testify — Mr. Frothingham was an annual contributor to this institution and always approved in the highest terms of the work that it is doing.

2nd, The Tuskegee Institute is entirely free from sectarian control or influence. It is broad and liberal in all its teaching, seeking to make strong helpful Christian men and women rather than Baptists or Methodists. Two of its trustees, — Rev. Geo. Leonard Chaney and Rev. C. F. Dole[4] are of the Unitarian denomination.

3rd, This institution is located right in the heart of the South, among and in touch with the masses most needing help.

4th, This institution is educating not little children, — thus confining its influence to one community, but men and women, who, in turn, scatter all through the South each in turn making another centre of light.

5th, Tuskegee already has a plant in the way of buildings, shops, industries, real-estate &c. that is valued at $180,000 and a constituency in the form of an annual attendance of about 600 new students from 14 States, and can thus make this money accomplish more direct good than a school without such a foundation.

6th, The annual expense of carrying on this institution is now about $60,000 each year, and $45,000 of this amount I am compelled to raise very largely by personal effort each year in an almost a "from door to door" canvass.

Much of my time and strength that should be spent in making the work of the school more valuable are taken in securing the needed income. With help from the Frothingham Fund my burden would be greatly lightened and more good accomplished.

Our trustees, I am sure, would be willing to be guided by any restrictions of your association as to the use of the money should we receive it. Yours respectfully,

[Booker T. Washington]

TLp Con. 106 BTW Papers DLC.

¹ Grindall Reynolds (1822-94), a Massachusetts clergyman, was secretary of the American Unitarian Association beginning in 1881.

² Frederick Frothingham (1825-91) was ordained a Unitarian minister in 1856 after graduating from Harvard Divinity School. A Garrisonian abolitionist, he served the American Anti-Slavery Society as an orator and writer. He was a Unitarian pastor in Milton, Mass., from the 1870s until his death.

³ The American Unitarian Association voted unanimously to approve BTW's request and for many years gave Tuskegee the annual interest of the fund.

⁴ Charles Fletcher Dole (1845-1927) was a Congregational minister, educator, and pacifist. He taught Greek for one year at the University of Vermont (1873) and for two years was a pastor in Portland, Me. For forty years he served the First Congregational (Unitarian) Society in Jamaica Plain, Mass. His son, James Drummond Dole, was a wealthy pineapple grower in Hawaii. Charles Dole was a trustee of Tuskegee from 1893 to 1916 and was also a supporter of Hampton. A prolific writer, he was the author of numerous books and pamphlets. He also wrote for the *Atlantic Monthly* and other magazines.

From Wilson H. Reynolds[1]

Vicksburg, Miss., Aug. 14, 1893

Dear Sir: As I have been recently elected President of Alcorn A & M College,[2] I seek certain information. *First* — The Executive Committee of that College is in search of a *first class* agriculturalist: one having both the science and art; one who knows the philosophy, the *how* one does and *why*. Will you please recommend such a person, whom you feel would meet the requirements and would enter our employ? The salary is $900. per year; yet while I have no authority to say it, should he prove fully proficient the first year, the Board may increase the salary. This suggestion of increase is wholly my own and has no foundation in the Board. So important is that feature of the school, I have led myself to think this. Let the one recommended base his prospects on $900.

(2) Again: Will you please let me know just how you regulate your *literary* and *industrial* classes so as to keep them from coming in conflict, and yet do the greatest possible good? (3) I would also like to know the basis upon which you grade your school. What two (or three) branches do you use as a gauge? Please be very *explicit* in answer to questions 2 & 3.

Kindly accept the thanks of a co-laborer for whatever you may do in this matter. Please find stamp. Yours for progress,

W. H. Reynolds

P.S. Colored Prof. of Agriculture desired.

ALS   Con. 105   BTW Papers   DLC.

¹ Wilson H. Reynolds, previously a teacher in the Vicksburg public schools, served as president of Alcorn A & M College for four months before his death late in 1893.

² Alcorn A & M College was founded at West Side, Miss., in 1871 through the efforts of James Lusk Alcorn, a Reconstruction governor of Mississippi. The state purchased the property of Oakland College, a Presbyterian school founded in 1830, to provide a campus for the black school. In 1878 it became the first land-grant college for blacks. Under the Morrill Land-Grant Act it received three-fifths of the 210,000 acres secured by Mississippi from the federal domain. The first president of Alcorn was Hiram R. Revels, former U.S. senator from Mississippi, who served the college from 1871 to 1882.

To Wilson H. Reynolds

[Tuskegee, Ala.] 8/21st/'93

My dear Sir: I am sorry to have kept you waiting so long, but I have been [tur]ning the matter over in my mind to see if I could hit upon a stable person to recommend for your Agricultural department. I [am] free to say that I cannot think of a man who comes up to what you want in every respect. The person I have in mind, whom I [thi]nk will suit you best is Mr. Henry C. Ferguson of Hempstead, [Tex]as. He was in charge of the Agricultural work in connection with this institution for three or four years, and gave satisfaction in his work.

You, as I understand from your letter, want a person who is equally as good in the science as in the practice. Mr. Ferguson is much better in practical work than he is in the science. When it comes to practical work, I think he has few superiors. Still I do not mean to say that he is unable to teach the science of Agriculture. He is a man of a great deal of common sense and push, and would, I think, make your farm a good object lesson for the students. You would find that, once in a while his grammar would be a little out of gear, and now and then he would mis-spell words. He is a man, who I think, would grow in the position, and in the course of a few years, would give satisfaction in all respects. I think, if I were entering into such a work as yours, I should choose this man.

In answer to your second question as to how we regulate our literary and industrial classes. In our regular day school we have seven classes. These are: A, B, and C, Preparatory, Junior, B Middle, A Middle and Senior. Several of these are sub-divided into divisions. We arrange the schedule so that a certain number of these classes or divisions work on each of the 5 school days each week, and divide them so as to make as nearly as possible an equal number of students work on one day. For example, on Mondays the Seniors and A Middlers work, Tuesdays the B Middlers and two divisions of the Junior class work. In addition to this the whole school is divided into two divisions, one of which works every Saturday. Thus you see that each of our students is in the class room four days and works one day out of each week, and every other Saturday. This, we think is much better than having the students work only a few hours out of each day. We have found that a great deal is lost by attempting to have a student work on the farm one or two hours each day. By the time he changes his clothes and goes to work, finds out what he is to do, a good proportion of the time is lost.

For some time we have admitted a limited number of students [to] our Night school. These are a class who come to us with no [mon]ey whatever to pay a portion of their board. We allow these [to] work on the farm or at some other industry the whole year, and [al]low them a small amount of money which is retained in the hands of our Treasurer to be used in payment of their board bills the following year when they enter the day school. So far as the industries are concerned, and especially in the matter of trades, these we find make better progress than those in the day school who only work one day in the week and every other Saturday. The enclosed circular will explain to you a little more in detail how [we] deal with our Night students.

As to your third question. We make mathematics and grammar the basis on which our classes are organized. Our regular literary work begins with the Junior class, and in order to be admitted to that class, the student must pass an examination in arithmetic through common fractions, and must understand the first principles of grammar. It is

359

true that we examine them for admission into the Junior class in geography, history etc. but if they are well up in grammar and arithmetic, they are seldom kept back on account of the other studies. If I can be of any further service to you at any time, I shall be glad.

If at any time you are in need of persons to take charge of your trade departments, I think we can serve you. Yours truly,

Booker T. Washington

TLpS   Con. 106   BTW Papers   DLC.

To Robert Charles Bedford

Tuskegee, Ala., Aug 22 1893

Dear Mr. Bedford: The first time you go into Chicago I hope you will find time to see Mr. Lloyd & Dr. Roy[1] and explain my failure to fill my engagements. I regret it very much and fear they will not appreciate my situation or the condition of the South. It is hard for those away from here to understand matters. The situation is constantly changing and no one knows what the next day may bring. Montgomery merchants sent out word a few days ago to all their customers that they would only sell for cash hereafter and that they would not accept checks but must have the currency. The merchants make this demand when at the same time the banks refuse to pay out currency even to those who have money on deposit. The Bank of Tuskegee will not cash a check of any kind on any body. But for Mr. Campbell's cashing our checks I do not see what we would do.

We have always been able to get our supplies on 30, 60, and 90 days time, but now to have to open school on a cash basis is going to be very hard for us. Under these circumstances I do not think I should be absent when school opens.

We can use all the names you can send. Yours truly

Booker T. Washington

ALS   Henry D. Lloyd Papers   WHi.

[1] Joseph Edwin Roy.

An Article in *The Congregationalist*

[Tuskegee, Ala., Aug. 31, 1893]

The South and Lynch Law

I have not the slightest sympathy with any one who commits, or attempts to commit, an outrage upon the person of a woman, and when the truth of such a crime is ascertained I believe that death in a lawful manner should follow. The epidemic of lynching of my people that has prevailed in the South for some time and seems to be extending into the West should convince all that the Southern problem cannot be solved by a mere wave of the hand, a flourish of trumpets, the giving of a few hundreds of dollars or the placing of a schoolhouse and church here and there.

Within the last year the States that permit lynchings have been told by the Northern press and a portion of the Southern press and Southern governors that the lynchings prevent immigration, keep out capital, that the home seeker reasons that if the criminal law is disregarded so will be the civil law, that if these outrages go on foreign nations will regard the States that permit them as half-civilized, that the lynchings and burnings, which are often witnessed by numbers of young and tender children, do the race that inflicts these punishments many times more harm by blunting its moral sense than the race or individual against whom they are directed. All this has been said and more, and still the evil does not cease. To begin with, colored men were lynched here and there for assault on the persons of white women, then the evil grew till well-nigh every such attempt or assault was followed by unlawful death. The lynching habit has gotten to the point till now cases are reported where white men lynch black men for rape, attempted rape, murder, attempted murder, incendiarism, stealing and for murdering black men, and for the same class of offenses we now and then hear of white men lynching white men and black men lynching black men.

With all this the outlook is not discouraging for the negro. We have passed through a series of outbreaks. Ku Klux, White Liners League, schoolhouse burnings, murder of negro leaders with no suspicion of crime against them, are, I think, matters of the past. As a rule, now there are specific criminal charges (in too many cases insufficiently proved) against the persons lynched. Why do I say the outlook is not discouraging? We have grown to the point where there is almost no community in the South where a negro school cannot be planted and permitted to grow and flourish, and often by the aid and encouragement of the Southern whites, and there is practically no Southern community where the black man is not free to purchase property and accumulate wealth.

But what is the remedy for lynching? Christian education for the white man and the black man. Does the country understand to what an extent there is a lack of this, in the broadest sense, in the South? If the broken necks of the poor negroes can be made to serve to call the attention of the country to this lack some good end will have been reached. When one leaves the cities and larger towns it will be seen that the white man's opportunity for education is but little, if any, better than that of the blacks. In Massachusetts, last year, each child of the legal school age had spent upon him about $24, each one in Alabama about eighty-nine cents. In Massachusetts the State provides a schoolhouse in every community. The State of Alabama has, as yet, been able only to provide schoolhouses in a few of the larger cities. I question whether a single decent schoolhouse can be found today in the rural districts of Alabama built from the public fund.

The average school term is about three and a half months in Alabama, while in New England it is about ten months. The average length of time that an individual spends in school in the South is less than two and a half years, while in New England it is seven and a half years. Massachusetts employs 111 superintendents who give their time in overseeing the schools. Alabama has hundreds of schools in the country districts that have not been visited by a superintendent within the last ten years for the reason that the State has but a mere pittance to pay these superintendents. Nearly every city, town and village in New England has its public library, reading-room and Y.M.C.A. Alabama has not a single public library in the usual sense, open to all classes of her citizens. The white and colored people who live in the country districts seldom have a lecture and, as a rule, preaching but once a month. The Christian academies scattered all through the North to which the poor can send their children with small cost and often free of charge are wanting in the South. It is true that in the cities and the towns there are good high schools and often colleges, but the poor white people in the country are not able to pay the high rate of charges at these private institutions, neither are they able to send their children to the State universities, where the cost is a great deal despite free tuition. What I have said of Alabama applies with equal force to the other Gulf States. A few days ago in a criminal trial in Birmingham, in which a large number of illiterate white people from a back county were involved, the United States attorney had to secure an interpreter, so that the language spoken by these people might be understood.

United States Senator Pugh of Alabama says that an educational qualification to vote will disfranchise forty per cent. of the white people of Alabama. When we add to this amount eighty-five per cent. of the colored vote is it any wonder that crime exists? The meager advantages for education do not mean that the South is not trying to elevate the masses. Alabama, I know, is making a great effort and is taxing property about as heavily for education as the North does, but you "can't get blood out of a turnip."

The time has come, it seems to me, for Northern men, Southern men, black men, white men to blot out their prejudices and look matters squarely in the face as they are. The whole country was responsible for slavery. Thirty years ago the Southern white man and the black man started life anew on almost equal footing — the black man with empty hands and the whites nearly so. To organize a free school system and educate the children of the whites as well as the children of those whom the State had but yesterday recognized as slaves, and at the same time to place the whole industrial system on a new footing, was a task the magnitude of which has not been sufficiently understood. To give to the South the light which will be the only permanent cure for crime among blacks and whites individuals and religious organizations in the North and West have done nobly. But when the true condition of the masses of the South is realized, so far as education is concerned, I believe more will be done. When one reads of a single individual in the North spending $1,000,000 in building a private residence, and reflects that this is almost twice as much as the million and a half of people in Alabama will have to spend for the education of all their children this year, it makes one wonder if the real need for Christian education in the South is known.

With the masses of the white people and the colored people in the country and towns well educated, the black man owning stores, operating factories, owning bank stock, lending white people money, manufacturing goods that the white man needs, interlacing his business interests with those of the white man, there will be no more lynching in the South than in the North. Let a black man have $500,000 in a bank in the South, every officer and director of the bank will take special care to see that this black man is not driven from the town or unlawfully punished.

In the town of Tuskegee and vicinity I regard the race question as practically settled. Not long ago parties living at a distance from Tuskegee made two attempts to lynch colored men confined in the Tuskegee jail for rape on a white woman; each time the mob was prevented from carrying out its intentions by the strong public sentiment in the town. The black men were given a fair and legal trial, condemned and executed in a lawful manner — the only instance of the kind in Alabama since the war. Explanation: both the white and colored people in Tuskegee have excellent opportunity for that kind of education that teaches that, "And as ye would that men should do to you, do ye also to them likewise."

The Congregationalist, 78 (Aug. 31, 1893), 282-83. Reprinted in *Southern Workman,* 22 (Nov. 1893), 172.

An Account of a Speech before the Labor Congress, Chicago[1]

[Chicago, Ill., Sept. 2, 1893]

. . . . .

The other feature of yesterday was that the morning session of the Labor Congress was given to a discussion of the industrial problem as it affects the negro.

The venerable Fred Douglass presided and the first paper was by Booker T. Washington, president of the Tuskegee Industrial Institute, Alabama, on "Progress of Negroes and Free Laborers." He described the evils of the mortgage system, which as it is practiced in the South, is but another form of slavery, and which could not exist but for the ignorance of the negro. There was but one remedy for ignorant labor, he said, and that was intelligent labor. The crop lien system has fastened its fangs on all forms of business affecting the white-man as well as the black man. Farmers who are compelled to raise their crops under this mortgage system are charged an interest on the goods that ranges from 25 to 50 per cent. Mr. Washington said:

SHYLOCK'S POUND OF FLESH

"It is safe to say that of the colored farmers of the black belt of the South three-fourths are to-day in debt for supplies to raise last year's crop; and it is safe to say four-fifths are in debt for supplies furnished to make the present crop, and these four-fifths live in small one-room cabins. This system affects the black man not only industrially but morally as well. Recently a money-lender living near Tuskegee expressed the situation very accurately when he said: 'When the crop is being made the negroes get all they can out of me, and after it is made I get all I can out of them.' During slavery the negroes reasoned something like this: 'My body belongs to my master, and taking the master's chickens to feed master's body is not stealing.' And some are inclined to apply this kind of logic to the mortgage system, and it is not hard for you to judge some of the results of this kind of reasoning. This system has grown until these liens are not only put on the crop, but on cows, mules, hogs, wagons, chickens, etc."

President Washington, to show what the negro would do if he but had the opportunity, told the story of the Tuskegee Institute. Twelve years [ago] the land where the institute now stands was an abandoned cotton plantation. Mr. Washington, with his fellow workers, went there with nothing but the determination to start an industrial school. They sent out word of their plan and pupils flocked in. To supply food the students cultivated the farm, to get building materials they started a sawmill, a brick yard, carpenter's department, blacksmithing, tinsmithing, masonry, and kindred trades. Within these twelve years these students have erected almost wholly with their own hands twenty-four buildings and created property worth $185,000 free of debt. The students are now cultivating 500 acres of land, have manufactured this season over half a million bricks, built any number of wagons and buggies, manufactured a steam engine and a number of other things. The printing for white and colored of that whole county is done in the institute printing office. Within the last few weeks they have been compelled to refuse admission to 300 worthy young men and women for lack of room and means. There is an insatiable enthusiasm throughout the South among the colored young people for manual training.

.   .   .   .

Chicago *Inter Ocean*, Sept. 3, 1893, 13.

¹ This speech was part of a program of several days of a labor congress in connection with the World's Columbian Exposition in Chicago. BTW was followed by Ida B. Wells, who said that the white South did not want the black man to leave, "for the black man is the wealth-producing factor of the South." She complained that black workers were not allowed to join labor organizations. A southern representative of the American Federation of Labor, George E. McNeill, said that the labor movement "knew no color," and that the "labor unions of the world were always open to the black man." Henry Demarest Lloyd, who was largely responsible for inviting BTW, said the black man was not only a victim of the mortgage system but also of the scrip system, which forced him to buy goods at a store owned by the employer, at monopoly prices. Henry George, whose Single Tax Congress was also meeting at the Chicago fair at this time, spoke on "Labor and Taxation." (*Ibid.*)

To the Faculty Committee on the Course of Study

[Tuskegee, Ala., Sept. 15, 1893]

The programme of the day school is in bad shape, and the students are losing every day, to say nothing of the confusion and irritation, and I am therefore, compelled to ask the Committee on Course of Study, to take the matter in hand at once, and make out a reliable and wise programme. In doing this I am especially anxious that the committee arrange the course with reference to the time of day when heavy studies can best be taken; also with reference to the fitness of teachers to do a certain grade of work and to teach particular branches.

Also make allowance for possible divisions of classes into sections. Also arrange the programme so that the studies laid down in the catalogue can be covered.

As some of the academic teachers teach in Phelps Hall care must be exercised to see that the teachers can do their duty in both places.

The accompanying list contains the names of the teachers with *about* the amount of work that each can be called on to do. This I have given careful study, and I believe the programme can be arranged to cover the studies down against each teacher.

It is the policy of the school to give each teacher just as far as possible, a special branch to teach and I wish this carried out as nearly as possible. A teacher can do the best work when he has but one or two branches.

Mr. Young has a plan for a schedule which I think the Committee will find valuable.

I beg of the committee to give at once this matter IMMEDIATE, but careful attention as the school has now been in session two weeks at an expense of $2500 with the programme not right. Yours truly,

B. T. Washington

TLpS Con. 106 BTW Papers DLC.

To Susan B. Bransford[1]

[Tuskegee, Ala.] Sept. 30th, 1893

Miss Bransford: I am very anxious to have you take Miss Burke's[2] place in the matter of looking after the missionary work done by the girls. This would include looking after the missionary society which I think meets twice a month and the outside work being done by the society.

The greater portion of your salary this year, in case you take this work will be paid by the Woman's Home Mission[ary] Association, and you would have to correspond with them at least once a month letting them know of the missionary work etc. Your salary this year, would be $30. per month and board. In addition to this, in case you take this work, your travelling expenses would be paid, that is the expenses incurred in coming from your home to the school. If you will take this work and will make out a bill for your expenses from your home to the school this year, the money will be sen[t]. Yours,

[Booker T. Washington]

TLp Con. 106 BTW Papers DLC.

[1] Susan B. Bransford in 1892-93 was assistant matron of Alabama Hall and

teacher in night school. From 1893 to 1895 she was Lady Principal and teacher of household economy.

2 Wilhelmina C. Burke, a Hampton graduate, was matron of Alabama Hall in 1892-93.

To Hollis Burke Frissell

Tuskegee, Ala., Oct. 2, 93

Dear Mr. Frissell: Our teachers and students have just given $558 towards this year's expenses of the school. Several of the teachers gave $50 others $25, $10 &c. I spoke to them of each one's doing his best in every way in view of the hard financial year and with out suggestion from me the subscriptions were started. Yours truly

Booker T. Washington

ALS   BTW Folder   ViHaI.

To Hallie Quinn Brown

Tuskegee, Ala., Oct. 31, 1893

Miss Brown: It is due you and the interests of the school that I speak plainly to you regarding several matters. The trouble Sunday regarding the girl that was taken to town for treatment by your order   the unbecoming language used in Alabama Hall in the hearing of students in connection with this trouble is not the main cause of this communication but is merely incide[n]tal.

After giving the matter careful consideration in connection with several of our oldest and most experienced teachers I am convinced and those consulted agree with me, that there is a want of confidence and respect for you and your work as Lady Principal that is at the foundation of much if not all the existing trouble. The position that you hold demands a person who is a leader in educational principles and practice, who can command the confidence and respect of all the teachers in all matters of education. This confidence can only be secured and held by hard patient research, investigation and study not only during school months but during vacation. When the teachers have seen by your failure to make out a programme at the beginning of the term and your failure in several other directions to come up to the standard of a leader and example for other teachers, many of whom are constantly studying in season and out of season to make themselves qualified for their work, they have come to lose that respect for and confidence in you that should exist in a person holding your position. This is the reason of the unbecoming squabbles that too often take place. Knowing this to be true, I could not be honest with you and loyal to the institution without saying so frankly.

To be still more frank it is just to you to say that I have been seriously considering with some of the trustees and others whether it would not be best for the interest of the institution to ask for your resignation. But feeling that it is not impossible for you to overcome the difficulties referred to, this step has not been taken. But this is done with the understanding that from now till the end of the term these personal and disgraceful wrangles especially in the presence and in the hearing of students must cease. And also with the further understanding that you must exhibit a thorough acquaintance with all branches of your work instead of the seeming superficiality that is now too often exhibited and thus command the confidence and respect of all.

The cooperation and good will of all the teachers, as does not now seem to be the case, are especially needed in the case of one occupying your position.

These squabbles lower the tone of the whole school and compromise all the teachers and breed an atmosphere of coarseness and commonness that injures the whole institution for all time.

In regard to the trouble that took place Sunday about sending the girl to town, you certainly went beyond your bounds in sending the girl to another than our resident Physician. If there was anything in the case requiring the attention of another physician you should have reported it to the principal or the one acting in his stead. Dr. Dillon erred also in not giving you an explanation of her actions for not treating the girl Sunday. This explanation I have requested her to make to you and which she says she would have made to you in your room had she been permitted. It is a very serious matter to spend the money of other people in the way that we do at this institution.

The interest[s] of the institution are at all times to be placed first. This consideration often makes it my duty to take action that is far from pleasant when considered from a personal standpoint; but duty to the institution and fidelity to its supporters as well as my own sense of what is right are considerations which I can not disregard.

Booker T. Washington

HLS   Con. 103   BTW Papers   DLC.

From William Sidney Pittman

[Tuskegee, Ala.] Oct. 31, 1893

Dear Sir, Not being in the Chapel last night on account of "drawing," I heard that my name was read out 3 times for talking in the dining Room. I must say Mr Washington that it is a mistake in some of the Moniters. Since my name was read out last week 4 time I have been trying to do better in the way of quietness in the dining room. As to my knowledge I know that I havn't talked at least once since I heard my name so many times last week.

Mr Washington I know if you would look into the matter and examine closely you would yourself think "how in the world can the same name be here so many times & dont do any better surely they dont mean to stay here or it must be the moniters that is not doing their duty."

It seems to me that the monitor just get the same names every time if they cant get any new ones. But that is not right. And another thing is that I dont like for my name to get so common in the Chapel simply because they have the power. Mr Washington I know they are not doing me justice & I wish you would see them privately & give them a talk & examine it closely. I am here for the right thing and not for the wrong. Respectfully,

W. S. Pittman

ALS   Con. 6   BTW Papers   ATT.   Original destroyed.

From Booker Taliaferro Washington, Jr.

Tuskegee, Ala., Nov. 10, 1893

Dear Papa: I hope you will excuse my lead pencil.

We are all well.

Please hurry and come home. We miss you   Please get mamma some curtains.

Mamma Portia and Davison send love. Your little boy,

Baker Washington

ALS   Con. 6   BTW   Papers   ATT.   Original destroyed. BTW Jr. was 6½ years old at the time of the letter. Although the handwriting is definitely that of a child, its clear cursive style indicates he was well tutored in handwriting.

A News Item from the Atlanta *Journal*

[Atlanta, Ga., Nov. 15, 1893]

A Negro Talks Sense[1]

The eyes of the delegates to the Christian workers convention were opened by a colored man this morning.

He gave a plain and simple but a very intelligent account of a great work being done among the colored people — an account that was worth more than a cart load of the gush some of the delegates have been getting off on the negro question about which they know as much as a "hog knows about holiday."

After the devotional exercises, conducted by Rev. Thomas Hunter, of New Brunswick, Canada, Booker T. Washington, a young colored man, was introduced as the president of the Tuskegee Normal and Industrial institute.

He made a brief, but telling, talk about the work being done at this institute.

Down in the Black Belt

He began by saying that if it was necessary to save members of the Anglo-Saxon race, which was on its feet, how much more necessary was it to save and put on its feet the other and less favored race.

371

He laid particular stress on the fact that this was a work done down in the black belt of Alabama by his own people.

It was carried on there where the colored people outnumbered the whites three to one, and great good was being done.

An Abandoned Cotton Plantation

The work was started twelve years ago on an abandoned cotton plantation with one teacher and thirty scholars.

Now there were forty-one teachers and officers and 600 students.

The place covers 1,900 acres of land and has nineteen industrial institutions in which work is carried on in wood, leather, machinery, agriculture, and other such branches.

The property at present is worth nearly $200,000 and no mortgages upon it. The annual expenses of the place run up to nearly $65,000 a year.

A few students were found able to pay $8 a month, but many others who couldn't pay were allowed to work one-half of their board.

An Object Lesson It Is

Five hundred acres of land are cultivated on the farm which is made an object lesson to the students.

No industry, said the speaker, is needed more among the colored people of the south than that of agriculture.

All the buildings on the place with the exception of the larger ones were erected by the students.

A three story brick building was now being erected by the students, all the brick being made in the brick yard of the institute. The students were doing the work on this building, even to the painting and finishing.

The Dignity of Labor

The speaker grew eloquent in saying one of the aims at the institute was to emphasize the dignity of labor.

There was a sentiment not alone among the colored people that manual work was a disgrace and it was the work of the teachers to expel this idea for an education that did not teach the hands to work with the brain was a very sorry education.

The state of Alabama, he said, was doing all it could which was very little, as the colored children drew but 78 cents from the public fund, while the white children drew but a few more cents.

He said that the colored people, if they had learned anything from slavery had learned to work hard.

The trouble about them at this time was that they still knew how to work hard, but didn't know what to do with the results. This institute is aiming to teach them how to apply the results of their hard labor.

. . . . .

Atlanta *Journal,* Nov. 15, 1893, 1. The article continued with other highlights of the morning session.

¹ This is a report of the speech to which Washington referred in *Up from Slavery* as "Two Thousand Miles for a Five Minute Speech." (See above, 1:323-24.) He believed that this was the prelude to his Atlanta Compromise address. No full text of the speech has been located.

The Atlanta *Journal* did not give as favorable treatment to other black participants in the Christian Workers' Convention. Headlines on Nov. 13 read: "Drawing the Color Line / Some 'Uppity' Darkeys Have Wounded Feelings / With Their Noses in the Air They Leave the Convention." "That the great Christian convention is still running," commented the *Journal,* "is doubtless a sore disappointment to a half a dozen or more presumptuous latter day darkeys. They left it in high dudgeon today, doubtless believing that their departure would result in disrupting the convention, but it didn't. One section of the gallery has been set apart for the colored people. This morning one of them walked in among the white people and settled himself for a good time. A policeman sought the colored individual and made him move into the side reserved for his race. When this was done a squad of negroes headed by a mulatto woman who had been listening to hints of the social equality from the northern speakers turned up their noses and left the convention in a body. The convention is still running, however, and will meet again this afternoon and tomorrow." (Atlanta *Journal,* Nov. 13, 1893, 1.)

From Anna Garlin Spencer[1]

Providence. R.I. Nov 19th 1893

Dear Mr. Washington, Please do not forget that you are pledged to Bell St. Chapel, Providence R.I. on Sunday afternoon at 3 oclk Dec. 10th 1893. You are expected to fill the whole time of the discourse & it is desired that you give as exhaustive a statement as 40 to 45 minutes will allow of "The Negro in America; his condition and prospects." You have all freedom to put your emphasis where you please. I enclose a calendar for Nov. which will give you some indication of the scope of the series in which you are asked to take part. The calendar for Dec. will soon be printed, with your name opposite Dec. 10th. My hope is to show, with you for the Afric-American and Alice Fletcher[2] for the American-Indian our duty toward the races we have oppressed. I shall hope to entertain you, a part of the time at least, in my home. Mr. Calloway said we might have the pleasure of listening to your quartette of singers on the occasion of your address. I shall be most happy to welcome them, with yourself, to my platform-pulpit. You will come to a cordial free & broad minded people, & I think have an excellent audience. You will receive a fee of $25.00 personally & a collection can be taken for the school in addition. I trust nothing will occur to mar our plans. Yours sincerely

Anna Garlin Spencer

ALS   Con. 6   BTW Papers   ATT.   Original destroyed.

[1] Anna Carpenter Garlin Spencer (1851-1931), a leading proponent of religious liberalism and the social gospel, was born in Attleboro, Mass., and educated in Providence, R.I. She taught in the Providence schools, wrote for a daily newspaper, and did considerable public speaking before her marriage in 1878 to William Henry Spencer, a Unitarian minister eleven years her senior. The marriage probably encouraged her drift toward liberal religion. She had withdrawn from the Union Congregational Church of Providence in 1876 on doctrinal grounds. She often preached in her husband's churches throughout New England. In 1891 she became minister of the Bell Street Chapel, a liberal, nondenominational ethical group endowed in 1888 by James Eddy, a local philanthropist. Her ordination attracted much attention, for she was the first woman minister in the state. Many of her sermons dealt with controversial social problems of the day. In 1902 she moved from the Bell Street Chapel to New York City, where she joined the New York Society for Ethical Culture, becoming its associate director in 1904. Differences with its director, Felix Adler, however, led to her retirement around 1912, after which she held academic posts at Meadville Theological Seminary, the University of Chicago, and Teachers College, Columbia University. By speech and pen she served many social causes, including child-labor reform, child welfare, prohibition, women's rights, woman suffrage, and peace.

[2] Alice Cunningham Fletcher (1838-1923), an ethnologist and Indian reformer, was an employee of the Peabody Museum of Archaeology and Ethnology at Harvard with a particular interest in American Indian archaeology when she met "Bright Eyes" (Susette La Flesche Tibbles), then touring the eastern states in behalf of Indian reform. Miss Fletcher decided to study Omaha Indian life at first hand. Her strenuous efforts to protect Indian lands and rights won her a following among them. She used this to help persuade them to accept the Dawes Severalty Act of 1887. She believed, as did other white reformers, that the Dawes Act would serve the Indians' interests by promoting economic individualism. With James R. Murie, a Pawnee graduate of Hampton Institute, she wrote *The Hako: A Pawnee Ceremony* (1904). She was the author of many articles in anthropological and folklore journals. She was active in the cause of Hampton Institute

and the Training School for Indian Youth at Carlisle, Pa., and in the Lake Mohonk Indian Conferences.

From Portia Marshall Washington

Tuskegee, Ala., Nov 19th 1893

Dear Papa   It was mamma's requst that I should write you a letter, so I thought I would write it. Mamma all the orther children send their love and miss you. We are very sorry that you have to go a way so much. Baker & Davidson are well and happy. I have a few head a[ches] one made me feel very badly all though I did not tell mamma because Ada is sick and I knew it would be to much for her if I were to get sick. But I am glad to say that Ada is much better than she was when you were here. Papa I like Mr Johnson[1] for arithmetic very much, he does not have us use any thing [but] our mind. we dont work on the board. We are reviewing what we have been over while Mr Hamilton[2] was here. Papa I try to make people love me but one habit I try and out grow is being slow   it is pretty hard because the hardest scolding I ever got from mamma was because I did not get the children's room cleaned up fast a nough that night   I said I'm not going to try to pleas mamma she's to hard to suit but a book I read gave me better thoughts. some times feel as if I have no friend in the world and I just cry and mamma will say "Portia what are you crying a bout?" but I never tell her. I all ways tell you my thoughts be cause I think you will like to hear them. . . . is still up here. Baker is just a bout the same. Davidson is learning a lesson from Ma. this is it, when he asks Ma. for everything she has she is not going to give it to him. Its a pretty hard lesson to him. Pappa please excuse the blots at the top of the page because I did not know they were there untill I had finnished the first page. Good evening I must go and get ready for supper. yours.

Portia Washington

Gossip with Pa.

P.S. Pappa, I wrote a letter to Schovell,[3] Albert's[4] little brother. Pappa I am going to ask you to please send me a nice useful present for mamma Xmass. did not let mamma see the part about the present. She'll be there soon.

ALS   Con. 17   BTW Papers   DLC.

[1] John Q. Johnson.
[2] Presumably Robert Hannibal Hamilton.
[3] Scovill Johnston.
[4] George Washington Albert Johnston.

From Emily Howland

Sherwood N.Y. Nov. 24. 1893

Dear friend   I enclose herewith a draft for fifty dollars payable to your order. You know where to apply it to do the most in the conduct of your great & growing institution. If not needed for the hospital or the new hall for girls (is it not?) then I should like it to pay the tuition of an ambitious girl. I say "girl" not because I would discriminate against boys, but because girls are discriminated against in this world, and more than that, in the nature of things they are, and always will be the home-keepers and makers, so they should have the first chance for knowledge.

I do not get your little paper the "Southern Letter" any more, so I cannot keep posted about you, so well as formerly. I was impressed and instructed by your article in the last Hampton "Southern Workman."[1] It is as remarkable as it is admirable that you can discuss that literally *burning* subject in the calm, dispassionate manner that you do. I should think one would need to be anchored above this horrid swirl we call our civilization, some time before he could discover his own judgement, filtered clear from emotion. I give little credence to any of those charges, many of them are doubtless wholly manufactured, others are "founded on fact," and a small portion true. This is another phase of Ku Kluxism, it works rather better than that did, it fixes on its victim charges of a crime of which mankind has a horror, and sacrifices him before he can rebut any charges. It will pass. I believe, now that the indignation of the world is being focussed upon it, it is declining. For a time one rarely looked in a paper without being shocked with horrid details of lynching. You are a terse, vigorous writer, it is a loss that you cannot write more. The impossible cannot be done, however, and you reach the limits of the possible now, in keeping up with the developments of your work, I know.

With kind regards to Mrs. W. and Misses Hawley[2] & Brown[3] if they are still in the institution   I am   Cordially

Emily Howland

Is Mrs. Fisher[4] the night watch living? I should like to be remembered to her too.

ALS   Con. 6   BTW Papers   ATT.   Original destroyed.

[1] BTW's article "The South and Lynch Law," which originally appeared in *The Congregationalist*, Aug. 31, 1893, above.

[2] Anna C. Hawley.

[3] Hallie Quinn Brown.

[4] Mrs. Fisher was apparently a longtime employee of Tuskegee Institute who was the night watch for the girls' dormitory, Alabama Hall. BTW fired her in January 1894 when she refused to follow his orders regarding the use of a watchman's punch clock. (See BTW to Mrs. Fisher, Jan. 19 and 24, 1894, below.)

To the Editor of the Indianapolis *Freeman*

Tuskegee, Ala. [Nov. 25, 1893]

Editor Freeman: If those who compose the Turner Convention[1] shall show themselves able to hide themselves behind a great cause, it will succeed; otherwise, fail. Men cannot exhibit themselves and do the best thing for a great cause at the same time.

What should the Convention advise? Let the colored people settle quietly down and get money and property and acquire character and education. Let there be twenty black men in any Southern town worth $1,000,000 and there will be no race question in that town. This talk of any appreciable number of our people going to Africa is the merest nonsense, and it is surprising that it has engaged the attention of serious minded people for a minute. It does no good, but on the other hand does a great deal of harm among the more ignorant of our people, especially in the far South, where some are led to feel that there is a power in the government or somewhere that can move them to Africa or to the West as it sees fit; hence instead of settling down and accumulating property they live from hand to mouth, always expecting to go somewhere. They are much like the Adventists who are always expecting the world to be destroyed, and are continually getting rid of their property with the expectation of going to heaven. The Negroes make too little preparation to live here on earth. Let the Convention emphasize the fact that we are to work out our own salvation as other races have, not by mere talk and speech-making, but by earnest work, over-coming prejudice and acquiring the elements of civilization.

The question as to who shall be Chairman of the Convention is a very minor one and should be settled in five minutes. It will be a disgrace if a half day is spent in wrangling as to who shall be the Chairman.

[Booker T. Washington]

Indianapolis *Freeman*, Nov. 25, 1893, 3. The article appeared with the headline "AFRICAN TALK — Mere Nonsense — Chairmanship a Minor Question."

[1] Bishop Henry McNeal Turner (see above, 2:342) of the A.M.E. Church called for a national convention of blacks to discuss the deteriorating racial conditions in America and to promote his idea of emigration to Africa. He believed that there was no "manhood future in this country for the Negro, and that his future existence, to say nothing of his future happiness, will depend upon his nationalization." The Indianapolis *Freeman* polled black leaders on their feeling regarding the convention and the idea of emigration, and published thirty-nine replies, including the one by BTW. Only two favored emigration outright, and twenty-two rejected the idea. The remainder opposed mass exodus but gave qualified support to emigration. Ida B. Wells and P. B. S. Pinchback, for example, said they were in favor of emigration for those who wanted to go.

The convention was held in Cincinnati with 800 delegates and many local black citizens present. Turner's ringing appeal for black self-determination and black nationalism was well received. Yet most of the voting delegates were opposed to emigration. The convention ultimately polarized around Turner's belief that the black man had little chance for advancement or justice in America and the belief of Albion W. Tourgée, one of the white delegates present, who believed that, if black people would appeal to the white man's sense of outrage, eventually public opinion would swing in favor of black civil rights and advancement. The convention adjourned without taking a clear stand on emigration, since Turner saw that the battle was lost and kept the issue from a direct vote of the delegates. (Redkey, *Black Exodus*, 183-93.)

BELL STREET CHAPEL.

SEASON OF 1893-'94.

SUNDAY SERVICES 3 P. M.

· · · ALL SEATS FREE · · ·

You and your Friends are cordially Invited

TO ATTEND A SERIES OF DISCOURSES UPON

Human Growth,

Illustrated along the lines of Political, Racial, Educational, Philanthropic, Scientific and Religious Evolution.

The Series will begin the first Sunday in November and continue through April, and a monthly announcement of topics and speakers will be made.

Calendar for December:

EVOLUTION OF RACES AND TYPES OF HUMANITY.

Dec. 3d. RACIAL DEVELOPMENT AND ITS PROBLEMS IN MODERN LIFE.—MRS. SPENCER.

Dec. 10th. THE NEGRO IN AMERICA: HIS CONDITIONS AND PROSPECTS.—MR. BOOKER T. WASHINGTON, Principal of the Tuskegee Normal School, Tuskegee, Alabama. (Accompanied by a Quartette of men-singers, young colored students in the School, who will give the songs of the slave and freedman.)

Dec. 17th. AMERICA'S DEBT TO AND DUTY TOWARD THE NATIONS.—WILLIAM LLOYD GARRISON, of Boston.

Dec. 24th. CHRISTIAN CIVILIZATION, THE PRODUCT OF MIXED RACES AND A COMPOSITE RELIGION.—MRS. SPENCER.

Dec. 31st. THE AMERICAN INDIAN: HIS WRONGS, HIS RIGHTS AND HIS CAPACITIES.—MISS ALICE C. FLETCHER, (Fellow of Harvard College. Department of Archaeology and Ethnology; and Special U. S. Government Commissioner to Divide the lands of Indians in Severalty.)

SUNDAY SCHOOL at 1.30. Adult Class led by Mrs. SPENCER studying Gizycki's Ethical Philosophy. All are welcome.

OFFICERS OF THE SOCIETY:

REV. ANNA GARLIN SPENCER, President and Resident Minister, 387 Broadway.
MR. ALFRED WILSON, Secretary, 99 Tell St.
MR. CHARLES MULCHAHEY, Treasurer, 45 Burrows St.

PD   Con. 7   BTW Papers   ATT.   Original destroyed.

To Julia Strudwick Tutwiler

[Tuskegee, Ala.] 12-27-1893

Dear Madam: I hope you will pardon the delay in replying to your kind letter of December 11th. At the time it came I was absent and have now been home but a few hours.

I am very much interested in what you say regarding the two girls,[1] and on your recommendation shall be willing to allow them to come here, and give them the chance that you outline. I presume, from what you say, that it is their wish to come this session. In case they wish to do so it will be well for them to come as early as possible in January as we are likely to be unusually crowded very soon.

We have an excellent man,[2] a graduate of the New England Conservatory of music, in charge of our instrumental music department. I am very sure that the younger girl would receive excellent training under him in music.

I thank you very much for what you were kind enough to say of my address in Chicago. I wish very much that you could have heard or read the whole address. Newspaper reports, at best, I find, are very unsatisfactory. Enclosed I send you a marked copy of the Congregationalist containing an article by me on the [subject] of "The South and Lynch-Law," which I thought you might like to read, tho I do not know whether you will agree with all the conclusions.

In regard to the establishment of a Colored Theological Institute for the training of Presbyterian ministers under the Southern Presbyterian Church, near this institution, I would say that I am quite sure that such a plan will meet with no objection on the part of any one connected with this institution; and on the other hand I am sure that it would be welcomed and encouraged in every way possible. I have long thought that one of the weak points in connection with the work being done at Tuskaloosa, is that few of the men there receive any literary training. Here these men could receive literary training without additional cost to them, and can, of course, go ahead with their Theological Training in about the same way they do at Tuskaloosa. I know something of the institution established in Nashville by the Episcopalian Church in connection with Fisk University, and I am quite sure that a similar plan can be easily followed out here. Should you think it wise I should at the proper time make such a proposition to the Southern Presbyterian Church. The candidates for the ministry would be allowed to live in their own hall under the care of the Instructor in Theology, and of course these instructors would be men of our own race or of the white race, as the Presbyterian Church thought best. In case you write an article for the Christian Observer on this subject, I should like very much to see it.

You may already know that Rev. Mr. Morton lives in Tuskegee and has charge of the Presbyterian Church here in connection with other Missionary work. He is a very close friend of this institution and gives us a great deal of help in one way or another, and I am sure if the Theological Institute were established here, it would have a warm and helpful friend in Mr. Morton. Very truly yours,

B. T. Washington

TLpSr Con. 113 BTW Papers DLC.

[1] Lula and Bellina Moore, daughters of a black woman employed by Julia S. Tutwiler. At Miss Tutwiler's request, BTW admitted them to Tuskegee on scholarships. (See Tutwiler to BTW, Jan. 11, 1891, Con. 4, BTW Papers, ATT. Original destroyed.)

[2] Charles A. White taught instrumental music at Tuskegee from 1893 to 1895.

To Julius B. Ramsey

[Tuskegee, Ala.] 12-30th-[189]3

Captain Ramsey: I was very much surprised the other day when a committee I appointed to examine into the efficiency of the fire department in connection with the school, reported that there was no such organization of the kind on the grounds. You will remember that just before I left for the North I told you that the organization of this department was one of your duties. I am very much surprised that you have neglected this matter. I wish you would, next week, organize a fire company among the young men and see that this company is drilled at least once a month, oftener would be better.

I also wish you, in connection with Miss Bransford, would see that the girls are made properly acquainted with the fire escapes and the methods of escaping in case of fire.

B. T. Washington

TLpS Con. 113 BTW Papers DLC.

To John Henry Washington

[Tuskegee, Ala.] Jan. 5th, 1894

Mr. J. H. Washington: Please let me know as soon as possible where we can get some tisonite seed.[1]

I wish you would see that the tin or sheet iron under the stoves where coal is used is put far enough out in front of the stoves so that in case the coals should fall out of the stove it will not catch on fire with the floor.

I also wish you would let me know how much it will cost to put watchman's clocks in Ala. Hall so that the building can be more carefully looked after at night.

I call your attention to the importance of seeing that the repairs on the place that have been begun are finished as early as possible. I have in mind now the new palings that were put on the fence surrounding Cassidy Hall sometime ago. You will notice that these palings have never been painted, and do not present a very good appearance. This is the kind of thing that Dr. Curry found fault with when he was here.

I think that the rooms in Mr. Young's house can be cut down from their present size. The hall might remain the same.

If you will make out a schedule of the way in which you wish the teachers to go to Auburn I will see that they go accordingly.

I have spoken to all of the heads of Departments whom you reported to me that your orders are to be strictly followed. If there is no immediate improvement I mean to see that your orders are strictly carried out by the Heads of Departments. There is no other way to do business but to see that this is done.

B. T. W.

TLpI Con. 113 BTW Papers DLC.

[1] Teosinte, an annual grass similar to maize, used primarily as a forage crop.

To John Henry Washington

[Tuskegee, Ala.] January 6th, 1894

Mr. J. H. Washington: I wish you would see that hitching posts are put up at all places where horses stand so that the horses will not have to be hitched to the trees.

The fire hose in Alabama Hall needs to be placed in a better position than it now is. If it has not already been done, it is very important that the lady teachers who room in Alabama Hall be instructed as to the use of this hose.

I wish you would let me know whether or not the inventory ordered sometime ago, has been completed.

There is some work needed to be done in the attic of Phelps Hall under the direction of Mr. Penney.

B. T. Washington

TLpS   Con. 113   BTW Papers   DLC.

To Emily Howland

Tuskegee, Ala., Jan. 12, 94

Dear Miss Howland: A few days ago I sent you a receipt for the money you sent which has proven most helpful to us. We shall be very glad to use the money in the way you suggest. There are thousands in this region who seem to have nothing on which to live from day to day, still they manage to keep soul and body together, but many of them suffer severely. In many cases *every thing* in the way of food has been taken from them for debt. Many are learning lessons of economy out of these hard times that are going to be of great value to them in the years to come. On New Years day they had their first Emancipation Celebration in this region and about 3000 it seems to me marched through the town and came to the school where I spoke to them and I tried to impress the importance of thrift, economy and the value of a home upon them.

Several copies of the little paper "Fraternity" came to us and I find it valuable.

383

Mrs. Washington desires to be remembered to you. I wish you could enjoy with us the beautiful weather which we are now having. I fear it will not last long. Enclosed I send you a peach bloom from a tree on our farm. Yours truly

Booker T. Washington

ALS   Emily Howland Papers   NN-Sc.

From Emily Howland

Sherwood N.Y. Jan. 15. 1894

Dear friend   Your letter of the 12th and the stem of pretty peach blossoms came to hand this evening.

The poverty this year is appalling. I have hoped with you that the sufferers might, some of them learn to save whenever the time of abundance should come, but many will not. As this is of the first importance, it will be worth all the suffering it costs to those who take the lesson to heart. I am glad that you speak to the people of the importance of learning to forecast in the day of plenty for the future.

That march of the 3000 must have been imposing. I thought while reading it, that but for the moral influence of your institution and of your own character such a procession might have ended disastrously. It always astonishes me that people recognize nothing but force as a ruling power; men are especially given to telling how gov'ts rest on force, when decrying women's ability for citizenship. They seem unaware that but for the power within the right-minded that makes for righteousness a large part of the most orderly communities would be in anarchy, & it would require an immense military force to preserve a semblance of the true order that this moral force secures. I enclose herewith a div'd of the N.Y. Cent. & H.R.R. for $55.00 made payable to your order. It seems to me it will do more good there than any where else that I can put it. Fifty for tuition of some one of your girls and the five remaining for the relief of the poor. I should like one dollar of it given to the "One Cent Club." They can credit me with the no. of contributions it would cover. Place it all with them if you think best, it is for you to decide.

Remember me to Mrs. W, Mrs Fisher — all who recall me as I do them pleasantly.

I should like to send the Christian Register & Our Dumb Animals to some teacher who would like to receive them. Can you give me a name? Cordially your friend

Emily Howland

I rejoice to see in the Register that Tuskegee will have a handsome sum from a bequest left by Rev. F. Frothingham. I was somewhat acquainted with him. An excellent man.

ALS   Con. 7   BTW Papers   ATT.   Original destroyed.

From Ellen Collins

New York. Jany. 16/94

My dear Mr. Washington, We were very glad to have your letter, and to know that you are better. I wonder if it would be at all annoying to you, if I were to offer just here a little advice. You recognize the largeness of your work. Though you are most efficiently supported, you cannot but see that all such schemes (or designs I should say) call for one central person. You are student of physiology enough to know that the human body will not wear like iron, & perhaps your race is hardly as tough as ours yet. So will you not consider carefully the need of confining your work to what is already in hand? There is no question that many doors would open, but should you go in? or your wife?

Excuse this long disquisition & let me turn to another topic.

Mr. Frissell made a remark to us a little while ago, that seemed to me had light in it. He said when Genl Armstrong began his work the Negroes had no money; now they are estimated to hold a great amount of property, & there was reason in thinking that if a family had not yet shown any ability to gather up something, it was so far unfavorable to them. Therefore the requirement of some money from each scholar on entering seemed likely to be a fair method of drawing into schools the better & more promising of those who aim at becoming pupils.

Now for your water. I am concerned. Have you had time to examine into the condition of the stream and its banks? I remember that in the village of Pullman near Chicago, the founders believed that they had proved that water that was allowed to stand in reservoirs for a length of time became purified. I only want to say that if by such a plan, or any other, you have reason to believe you can correct a recognized evil, we will be very glad to send you $300. or $400. to do the necessary work.

Has Portia received a little book I sent her called "Capn. Polly?" We sent with it the volume containing the U.S. Constitution, the Declaration of Independence that I showed you. Please thank your wife for her letter. I will write to her soon. Truly yrs

Ellen Collins

ALS Con. 9 BTW Papers ATT. Original destroyed.

To Mrs. Fisher

[Tuskegee, Ala.] Jan. 19/1894

Mrs. Fisher: Capt. Ramsey tells me that up to the present you have not used the Watchman's Clock in the way he instructed you to do. I write to say that we must insist that you perform this duty. In putting the clock into Alabama Hall, we do not do so for the reason that we do not trust you, in fact I would just as soon trust you without the clock as any person we could employ; but the school is very large and, Alabama Hall has been enlarged to the extent that we do not feel that we could run any risks that could safely be avoided regarding the safety of the girls. I shall give you a few more days to decide regarding whether or not you will use the clock, and if you finally decide that you can not use it, then we shall have to make other arrangements in regard to getting some one to look after the Hall at night. You have done very well up to the present time, and we should not like to have you leave, and I see no reason why you should do so. The rules of the school must be carried out.

Booker T. Washington

TLpS Con. 113 BTW Papers DLC.

To Mrs. Fisher

[Tuskegee, Ala.] January 24th, 1894

Mrs. Fisher: Maj. Ramsey reports to me that you have altogether failed to carry out orders in regard to the use of the Watchman's clock placed in the kitchen. I feel quite sure that you have been given ample opportunity to make up your mind as to what you intended to do, and I am sure that there is no excuse for your not carrying out the orders of the school. The excuse you give, that it has not been done in the past, has little force in it. The mere fact that a thing has been done in a certain way in the past does not mean that it will be that way always. I explained to you the fact that the school is constantly growing larger; that Ala. Hall has been considerably enlarged and we cannot afford to run any risk with the lives of so many girls in danger of being lost in case of fire, and we cannot afford to let them go unprotected. You have been connected with the school for a long while and, as a rule, have given satisfaction in your work; but it is not possible for any person to remain here and absolutely refuse to carry out orders, no matter how long they may have been here or how well they have done their work. It is my duty to put someone else in Alabama Hall who will carry out orders given, and I see nothing to do but ask you to give up the position which you are now holding so that someone else can be put in charge of the Hall. Mr. Logan will make settlement with you if you will call on him.

B. T. Washington

TLpS Con. 113 BTW Papers DLC.

From John Henry Washington

Tuskegee, Ala. Jany. 24th 1894

Mr. B. T. Washington Below you will find the names of teachers that have drawn books, from the industrial library and the number of books drawn by each:

Mr. M. T. Driver[1]	5
" Lewis Adams	1
" Augustus Williams[2]	1
" J. M. Greene	1
" W. V. Chambliss	2
Miss E. S. Adams[3]	2
" F. C. McKinney[4]	1

Respectfully

J H Washington

P. S. The enclosed list are not all the books but, the books of most value, there 51 in all.

J. H. W.

ALS Con. 109 BTW Papers DLC.

[1] Matthew T. Driver was born in Arkansas in 1863. He graduated from Hampton in 1888 and joined the Tuskegee faculty that same year. He taught wheelwrighting in the industrial department and taught Sunday school on the Tuskegee campus and in the town of Tuskegee. In 1899 he became a business agent for the school. He married Virginia L. Adams, daughter of Lewis Adams and a member of Tuskegee's first graduating class.

[2] Augustus Williams was in charge of the sawmill from 1893 to 1895.

[3] Eliza S. Adams, an ex-student of Hampton Institute, was an instructor in plain sewing and millinery from 1893 to 1896. In 1892-93 she was in charge of the sales room.

[4] Fannie C. McKinney was in charge of the laundry from 1893 to 1896.

From Cornelius Nathaniel Dorsette

Montgomery, Ala. 1/27th 1894

Dear Prof Washington   Yours to hand and in reply — Mrs Fisher came direct to me about the matter and I simply told her that I could say nothing & she must simply abide by the rules & direction of the school and that I could do nothing whatever in the case. She spoke of the clock arrangments & firmly say she could not & would not do the punching. I fully agree with you as to the risk and danger of fire, I have often while listening at the fire bell here, said to myself what would we do if that was Tuskegee. By the way have you any Babcock Extinguishers? They are splendid in the beginning of small fires. Miss

White[1] & her whole force of Teachers want to attend the Conference. Cant she be cared for on the grounds? She is afraid of burdening you & asks about hotels & I told her the school would be too glad to care for her & teachers. Will you write her?

How are the horses paning out? Hastily yours

Dorsette

P.S. Cant you urge Prof Chavis of Bennett[2] to be prsent at the Conference he will learn much of our race & do him good to see your work.

ALS Con. 7 BTW Papers ATT. Original destroyed.

[1] Alice L. White was principal of a black girls' industrial school in Montgomery.
[2] Bennett College, Greensboro, N.C.

To Charles W. Greene

[Tuskegee, Ala.] Jan. 30th [1894]

Mr. C. W. Greene: From receipt of this note I wish you would see that all chickens belonging to the school are kept up in the lot, and not allowed to run about in the lot or elsewhere, on the farm. I wish you would consult with Mr. J. H. Washington and have the turkeys put away in some lot so that they will not injure the farm as they are doing. Please also notify Mr. Logan that his turkeys are injuring the farm and we wish he would make arrangements to keep them off.

B. T Washington

HLpSr Con. 113 BTW Papers DLC.

To William Eugene Hutt[1]

[Tuskegee, Ala.] Feb. 3rd, 1894

Mr. Hutt: I do not think that you are doing yourself justice here and I hope you will excuse me if I speak to you rather plainly. I very much hope that you will be able to remain here until the end of the year with credit to yourself and profit to the school. The main trouble is that you do not push ahead; you wait too much for somebody to direct and lead you. You ought to see, it seems to me, the difference between your work and that of Mr. Taylor,[2] who has had about the same course of training as yourself. Mr. Taylor is constantly leading in his work, working in season and out of season. Instead of having some one to lead him he is constantly making suggestions as to what should be done. As a sample of your work: Yesterday morning the Council planned some special work that we wished you to do in connection with Mr. Taylor, and Mr. Taylor has also previously asked you to report to him in the afternoon in order to get out some special work. Yesterday I found that you had gone off the place without notifying Mr. J. H. Washington or myself, notwithstanding you had promised to go into the blacksmith shop every afternoon and give instruction. You also promised to go into the Blacksmith shop every Saturday and take some of the boys. As it is, Friday and Saturday of this week are thrown away so far as giving instruction to industrial students is concerned.

You may think that I speak to you very plainly; but it is a good deal better to speak to you this way now than wait until the end of the term and say to you that we do not wish your services longer. I hope very much that we can keep you in the employ of the school, and shall do so if you prove worthy, but certainly if you do not, you cannot expect to be re-employed next term. You have ability, and you should certainly put into practice the line of work that you came here to do. By this time in the term you should have made a great deal of advancement in practical work in the shop and in mechanical drawing. Dr. Curry and Dr Gilman[3] of Johns Hopkins University, will be here about the latter part of this month to make an inspection of our industrial system, and I do hope that between now and that time you will put your department in shape to be inspected, but in order for you to do yourself justice it is going to require hard and constant work on your part, and you will have to apply yourself in a way that you have never done before.

Booker T. Washington

TLpS Con. 113 BTW Papers DLC.

[1] William Eugene Hutt was instructor of mechanical drawing and ironworking

from 1892 to 1894. He then became band and orchestra instructor and worked in the treasurer's office as a clerk until 1896.

² Robert R. Taylor, a graduate of Massachusetts Institute of Technology, came to Tuskegee in 1892 after several years' experience with an architectural firm in Cleveland, Ohio. He remained at the school throughout BTW's career, as teacher of architectural and mechanical drawing, the architect of most of the campus buildings, and later as director of mechanical industries.

³ Daniel Coit Gilman (1831-1908) was president of the University of Wisconsin (1867-72), the University of California (1872-75), the Johns Hopkins University (1875-1908). He became in 1882 one of the original trustees of the John F. Slater Fund and succeeded Rutherford B. Hayes in 1893 as its president. He was a trustee of the Peabody Education Fund after 1893 and a founding member of the General Education Board in 1902. From his position on these foundations he fostered Tuskegee's development and occasionally criticized its methods sharply.

From Royal J. Perry

Weldon, N.C., Feby 7th 1894

Dear Sir   You will hardly remember me as your schoolmate twenty years ago at the Hampton Normal School; but seeing an article in the Raleigh Gazette, about the work you are doing for our race, it made my heart feel glad and I resolved to write you a letter. To say that I am proud would be a poor way of putting it. When I read about the work your school was doing with you as the guiding spirit I thought of the Booker Washington of twenty years ago as a student at Hampton. And remembering your sturdy qualities, your devotion to your studies, and your wonderful skill as a mathematician — (for you know you excelled in Algebra) I fain would say that I am disappointed in the man.

But it was in the debates before our societies that I remember you best. I never shall forget the fleecing you gave our side on one of those occasions — you litterally took the school by storm. Well! well! those days will never come again, may God speed you in your good work and crown all your efforts with success. Write to me and send me a Catalogue of your School. Your Old Schoolmate

Royal J. Perry

ALS Con. 6 BTW Papers ATT. Original destroyed. Written on stationery of R. J. Perry, tonsorial artist.

From Smith W. Easley, Jr.,[1] C. C. Wimbish,[2] and Henry A. Rucker[3]

Atlanta, Ga. Feb'y 9th 1894

Dear Sir: The managers of the Cotton States International Exposition to be held in Atlanta Ga beginning Sept 1st and closing Nov 30th, 1895 has decided to erect a building to be exclusively devoted to the exhibiting of the product of the colored people from all part of America.

The Exposition Company has also decided to appoint three colored men from each of the Southern States South of the Ohio River as commissioners of said Exposition.

We therefore respectfully request that you accept as one from the State of Alabama, if so please advise us at once when you will be further advised by Hon. Clark Howell[4] editor of the Atlanta, Ga. Constitution and also by the Director General of the exposition Company.

Trusting that the above will merit your most favorable consideration and we will be gratefully yours   Very respectfully

Smith W. Easley Jr
C. C. Wimbish
H. A. Rucker

ALS   Con. 6   BTW Papers   ATT.   Original destroyed.

[1] Smith W. Easley, Jr., was a black Republican political leader of Atlanta. From 1888 to 1892 he was one of the leaders in an unsuccessful campaign to elect blacks to the city council.

[2] Christopher C. Wimbish was federal surveyor of customs in Atlanta, Ga. He was a black man born in Georgia.

[3] Henry A. Rucker, born in 1855, was one of the ablest of the southern black officeholders of the McKinley-Roosevelt era. Born in Georgia, he attended Atlanta University, earning his tuition by teaching public school during vacation periods. He attended Republican conventions in 1880 and in 1896, where he was a supporter of William McKinley for the presidential nomination. President McKinley in 1897 appointed him collector of internal revenue for the state of Georgia, a position for which Atlanta Democrats and businessmen supported him. He served so well that, though a McKinley-Hanna man, he was reappointed by President Theodore Roosevelt. In 1906, when the National Negro Business League met in Atlanta,

Rucker persuaded Atlanta businessmen and political leaders to relax the segregation laws for the occasion. Though somewhat more militant than BTW, Rucker was loyal to the Tuskegean. His removal from office in 1910 was not the result of any failure to perform well the duties of his office, but was part of a campaign of President Taft to remove blacks from federal offices in the South.

⁴ Clark Howell (1863-1936), eldest son of Evan Park Howell, after graduating from the University of Georgia, joined his father's newspaper, the Atlanta *Constitution*, in 1884, then in its heyday under Henry W. Grady's managing editorship. Howell spent five years in the Georgia House of Representatives, the last year (1890-91) as speaker. He was a Democratic national committeeman from 1892 to 1924. He was president of the Georgia Senate from 1900 to 1906, resigning to run unsuccessfully for the governorship against Hoke Smith and Tom Watson. Considering himself an enlightened conservative, Howell generally opposed racial demagoguery, though with occasional lapses. In the twenties he endorsed Al Smith and opposed the Ku Klux Klan. His active campaigning for Franklin D. Roosevelt was rewarded by chairmanship of the National Aviation Commission. Howell was friendly to BTW, but at the time of the dinner at the White House and several other times when BTW sought to go beyond the Atlanta Compromise racial formula, Howell sharply criticized him.

To Julius B. Ramsey

[Tuskegee, Ala.] 3/5/1894

Major Ramsey: Sometime last week I asked Mr. Calloway to make an inspection of all the boys' dormitories, and report to me. The enclosed is his report, which you will see. By it you will see that many of the rooms need to be brought up, and I have asked him to assist you in this matter during the coming week. I realize that one of the great troubles is want of hay and straw, and I have told Mr. Calloway to order sufficient hay and straw for the beds. The general appearance of all the rooms on the place needs to be improved greatly. The work that you have before you can only be accomplished by hard effort, but I think you can do this work before the close of the term.

Please return Mr. Calloway's report as soon as you read it.

[Booker T. Washington]

TLp   Con. 113   BTW Papers   DLC.

From John Henry Washington

[Tuskegee, Ala.] March 9th, 1894

Mr. B. T. Washington: After noticing for several days I found out whose chickens they are that still stay around on the grounds, doing damage to whatever is planted.

Mr. J. B. Washington's and Mr. J. N. Calloway's chickens are out and stay, nearly all the time, on the rye. Mr. Penney keep his up, as a rule, until 3 o'clock and then turn them out, some days there are out all day, as was the case last week. Mr. Young's are out quite often; also Mr. Logan's turkeys still come over into Mr. Greene's[1] onion patch occasionally. There are a few chickens out that no one will own. Mr. Greene and I have asked different ones about them and cannot find the owner. I will have some of the boys to catch them, and I will send them to the Teachers Home to be used. Mr. Hamilton's and my chickens, I will state, have not been put up, but they do not come on the school grounds on account of the fence. We have taught them more than two years ago to roam in the woods back of our place, which they do now.

I think it well for you to give diffinite orders regarding these chickens before you leave.

J. H. Washington

TLS Con. 109 BTW Papers DLC.

[1] Charles W. Greene or James M. Greene.

To Hollis Burke Frissell

New York March 28th 1894

Dear Dr. Frissell: I see that a report to the effect that we are going to introduce Latin into our course of study at Tuskegee, has gotten out. Just before the Conference the matter was discussed in one of the teacher's meetings, there was only one teacher who cared anything about it. After the Conference the subject was taken up again in the next meeting, and it was decided that it would be a great mistake for Tuskegee to depart in any way from its original methods and ideas, and we would not put Latin into the course, whatever improvements we make, are likely to be in the line of the Sciences and Industries, not in the introduction of languages.

There is no general desire of the students or teachers at Tuskegee, for Latin, the teacher who advocated it, was in favor of giving it to one or two of the brightest students, for one or two years.

I put you in possession of these facts, thinking you might be asked about the matter. Mrs. Barrows[1] has been much troubled about the matter and I have written her to the same effect. Yours truly,

Booker T. Washington

TLS   BTW Folder   ViHaI.

[1] Isabel Hayes Chapin (Mrs. Samuel J.) Barrows (1845-1913) was a supporter of BTW and a benefactor of the Kowaliga school. She was an emancipated and sophisticated woman of broad reform interests, including women's prison reform. She attended the Lake Mohonk conferences on the Indian, the Negro, and international arbitration. After her first husband, a Congregational minister, died, she married Samuel J. Barrows and with him became a Unitarian. She served as stenographic secretary to Secretary of State William Seward and to congressional committees. She helped her husband in editing the *Christian Register*. She also for a time was on the faculty of the medical school of Howard University, having done advanced study in medicine at the University of Vienna.

From Hollis Burke Frissell

[Hampton, Va.] March 30/94

My dear Mr. Washington: Your favor of the 28th is at hand. I know that Mrs. Barrows felt a little troubled from some thing she heard at Tuskegee in regard to the matter of the introduction of Latin, and I am very glad to know from you that her fear is entirely unfounded. I meant to have spoken to you about it, but it escaped my mind.

I had a talk with President Gilman of Johns Hopkins in regard to school matters, and he spoke very favorably of your work, and gave me to understand there was not likely to be any special change in it this year, and that the Slater people had no intention of starting an institution[;] certain propositions were made to them by some Southern community offering to do so themselves. I had an interesting talk with him and shall be glad to see you when I can to give you the more full particulars. I think this trip South opened his eyes to a good many matters.

I expect to be North about the middle of the month and hope I may have a chance to see you. Very truly yours,

[H. B. Frissell]

TLp Frissell Letterbooks ViHaI. Addressed to BTW at the Grand Union Hotel, New York.

To Frederick Douglass

New York, Apr. 2 1894

Dear Mr. Douglass: Enclosed I send a note of acknowledgement for Mrs. Carpenter.[1] A formal receipt will be sent you by our treasurer. You can not realize how very grateful we are for your interest and help. The grand and unselfish way in which you are giving your self to the cause of our race is a rebuke to many who live only for self. I am very grateful to you for kindly presiding at the meeting where I gave my little talk Friday night. Have put a note in the "Age" this week regarding the gift from Mrs. Carpenter. Yours Sincerely

Booker T. Washington

ALS Microfilm Reel 3 Frederick Douglass Papers DLC. Written on stationery of the Grand Union Hotel.

[1] Mary (Mrs. Russell Lant) Carpenter was a longtime friend of Frederick Douglass. She donated $242.75 to Tuskegee in 1894. (Warren Logan to Douglass, Apr. 5, 1894, Microfilm Reel 3, Frederick Douglass Papers, DLC.)

From Frank Bell

Pratt Mines, Ala., April the 4 1894

My dear teacher   I will take much pesure in writing you a few linds To let you know that I am well. But not doing So well and I hope that this letter will find you well and doing the Seame.

Mr. Washton I am very glade to say that I am expence time I think as much off one mumit I thought off one dollar   So Mr Washton if you will get me out off this please I will in shower you that I have expence time not four my sake but the sake off my Mother father sisters and brothers. Mr. Washton That truble I got in thour Shooles boys got me inter that But my mother cold not get me in now mour truble This have lount me a leson to not to fued with bade boys. I get a student from school ever weeke and that makes me feald good. I want to go to school one mour time if you will get me out   I want to inproved my self out. My father wants me to go back to school whene I get out this truble   Mr. Washton Will you let me come back   if sou let me know in you letter. And tell all off my school mats that I say the beter make good off the time I will get out some time. If life laskeed

Mr. Washton I am puting all off my trust me him and the Loard. So will come to a clouse four this time   But you moust write and tell me all the news   So good by from you truley frind

Frank Bell

and give all my love to the teachers four me that some day that I will see thim again. Writ sone

ALS   Con. 107   BTW Papers   DLC.

An Account of a Speech in Washington, D.C.

Washington, D.C., April 7 [1894]

A Negro Who Has Sense

Frederick Douglass, John M. Langston, John R. Lynch, Blanche K. Bruce and the other colored men of national reputation living in and around Washington have very little to do with the mass of the colored citizens here, except in a business way or by making speeches or addresses to them. With their families and friends, these leaders of their race form a society of their own as exclusive as the most fashionable white society, and socially have almost as little to do with their brethren as though they were entirely white instead of almost so, as most of them are. The other colored people do not feel identified with them, and, although they are in a way proud of their prominence, they are not fond of them personally. They do not feel as though they were being helped very much by these leaders in any direction.

Even when these great men condescend to make speeches or addresses to them they are almost always on political lines and without practical suggestions for the betterment of the race. Even as to politics, these orators devote themselves chiefly to bewailing their wrongs rather than suggesting remedies, and they have little or nothing to say in the way of practical advice as to the ordinary affairs of life. Intelligent colored men have frequently said to me that they wished Mr. Douglass, for example, would be a little less eloquent over their political wrongs in order to be a good deal more practical in his advice to them as to their every-day duties. Mr. Douglass (still for example) has by prudence and frugality accumulated a small fortune, estimated by some of his race at as much as a quarter of a million dollars, but if he has ever publicly given his people a single leaf out of his business experience my informants, who have followed his public utterances pretty closely, have not heard of it.

A PRACTICAL NEGRO EDUCATOR

With this in mind it was very interesting to me to see Frederick Douglass presiding and John M. Langston and others of the colored leaders sitting by at a meeting the other night in the hall of the Colored Young Men's Christian Association here in town, when Booker T. Washington, the head of the Tuskegee Normal and Industrial Institute for Negroes, at Tuskegee, Ala., delivered the most sensible and practical talk on how his race should work out its material salvation which I ever heard or read. Booker Washington has been called "General Armstrong's Timothy," because the heroic and saintly founder of Hampton Institute regarded him as the very flower of his work, and as such selected him from all the other graduates of Hampton to take charge of Tuskegee Institute, when it was founded, 12 years ago. Washington is undoubtedly a remarkable man intellectually, in several different ways; but nothing in him, not even his executive ability, marked as it is, is so extraordinary as his development of common sense. This was so evident in his talk the other night that he carried his audience with him from beginning to end, and even men like Douglass and Langston were forced to applaud utterances which, where they did not run counter to what they themselves had said, put them to the blush by contrast.

Washington indulged in no flights of rhetoric, but his cold facts, with homely but striking illustrations, were more convincing than eloquence. "It is all very well," he said, "to bewail our wrongs. I feel them as keenly as anyone else. But I think we have had quite enough talk about them, and that the thing to do now is to try to get our rights."

This was not to be done by making stump speeches, or even running for Congress, although, as he said, with that humor which kept his audience laughing half the time, "the misfortune of being elected to Congress is liable to happen to the best of men."

VALUE OF FINANCIAL FREEDOM

But the thing to do was to achieve financial freedom, and this would give the full use of the political freedom which now in the nature of things in the great majority of cases at the South could be but a name. "If you live in somebody else's house, wear somebody else's clothes, and eat somebody else's food, you can hardly expect to cast your own vote," he said. "You are an industrial slave, even if you are a political freedman. What you want is to own your house, your clothes, your tools and be able to provide your own food, and then you will be independent and will get all the rights, political and otherwise, that you are entitled to."

"The prejudice," he said, "against us negroes is not on account of our color, but because of the badge of slavery — the slavery we used to be in and the industrial slavery we are in now. When I was at Hampton I had charge for a time of the Indians there, and once I was sent to Washington in charge of an Indian whom I was to deliver at the Interior Department and take a receipt for him, so that he might be shipped West, just as if he were a bill of goods. We started up on the Norfolk boat, and when supper was announced we went down to the dining room. The Indian was a little ahead of me, and he walked right in and sat down at the table without anybody saying anything to him. But when I reached the door they stopped me and told me that I must wait until everybody else got through, and yet that Indian was a good deal darker than I am. But his people had never been in slavery, and my people had been and were, and that was the difference." It was of no use to fret about the fact of inferiority or kick against it. The only thing to do was to face it and then try to change it.

The negroes must get property and so make themselves influential in the community in which they live. "We amount to nothing because we haven't got anything and can do comparatively nothing," he said. "I was talking the other day with a Southern railroad man and he said: 'The railroads have no prejudice against color. There is no sentiment in business and we are all for business. But, from a business point of view, you colored people don't amount to anything. You don't furnish us enough freight, and so we don't give you any special consideration; but just put you off in the Jim Crow Car.'" Washington said that he had no doubt this was so and that it would be so if the negroes were white instead of black.

No Color in Business

"There is no color," he said, "in business, as there is no sentiment. From a business point of view one white man shows consideration to another, only because that other has something that he wants to get. He shows no consideration to a white man, who has nothing to give him. He treats poor whites and poor blacks exactly alike. Suppose," he said, "there is a colored man in Montgomery, Ala., who furnishes one of the railroads with freight yielding $10,000 a year, do you think his wife or children will have to ride in the Jim Crow car? Not much. If necessary, the road will put on a special car for them rather than lose that freight. And suppose there are ten colored business men in any of the small towns in the South, whose aggregate deposits in the leading bank of the town amount to $100,000, and suppose those depositors heard that some colored man was going to be lynched one night and suppose they went to the president of the bank and said, 'If that man is lynched to-night we will draw out our deposits to-morrow morning,' do you think that lynching would occur that night? No; it wouldn't, nor any other night. The president and directors of that bank don't propose to have it weakened and perhaps ruined simply to gratify the thirst of a mob for blood.

"If you are a negro," he said, "and you go to work to make something, say it's bricks, as you make good bricks and sell them as low as anybody else or a little lower, the white men will buy your bricks just as quickly as they will buy any other bricks. You never heard of anybody refusing to buy a good thing at a low price because the man that offered it was black, and you never will. Now, suppose you sell bricks to a white man to build a house and you take a mortgage on the house for part of the purchase money and you can foreclose that mortgage at any time, do you think that when you go to the polls to vote you will find that white man there trying to keep you away? You know you won't.

Can Come In as Stockholders

"There is a colored man in Montgomery," he continued, "who owns houses and lots and stands well as a business man. Two of the prominent white business [men] met him on the street the other day, talked with him for a little while and then went on. One of the white men was overheard to say to the other, as they walked along, 'Do you know it's as much as I can do to keep from calling that fellow "Mister." ' And there is an old colored man near Tuskegee, born a slave and kept a slave after the war by the cursed mortgage system, who got a gleam of hope at one of the conferences for practical progress we have held at Tuskegee and made up his mind that he would be free, indeed, before he went to his grave, and so, having no time of his own except at night, worked by moonlight, planting his cotton and picking it, on a bit of rented land, harnessing himself up to the plow and getting a boy to steady it, because he didn't own even a mule, and saving and investing his money, so that now he owns stock in the Tuskegee Bank and just a day or two before I came away he showed me an invitation he had received from the president of the bank inviting him to a meeting of the stockholders. The white people," said Washington, dryly, "haven't quite got to the point of inviting us to their prayer meetings, but they do invite us to their stockholders' meetings when we happen to own some stock."

The Way to Industrial Freedom

Of course, industrial education, which he defined as all the education a man or a woman could get, provided in getting it he or she learned to apply it practically, was the way to industrial freedom which Mr. Washington pointed out. Learn all you can, but learn to do something or your learning will be worthless. An educated man standing around with his hands in his pockets isn't a bit better, he said, than an uneducated man standing around with his hands in his pockets. At Tuskegee he educates on this line, training his pupils to make practical application of all they learn, and to work, even if they have to work for nothing at first. All the work of the place, which now comprehends nearly 2000 acres, 650 being under cultivation, and has a score of buildings, is done by the boys and girls, of whom there are 650 in all, under 40 instructors. The boys are taught incidentally nearly a score of trades, while the girls are taught the art of housekeeping and the woman's work of a farm or plantation in all its branches. The buildings have been planned and erected by the pupils, under the direction of the instructors. The whole growth of the institution from the poor shanty on hired ground, with an old church building, in which the start was made by Mr. Washington, and one or two other teachers and 30 students 12 years ago, until now, when the property of the institute is valued at $200,000 and is absolutely free from debt, has been possible only because every dollar contributed to it has been made two dollars by the work of the pupils themselves. And its graduates are proving by their practical success that the education they got at Tuskegee was just what it purported to be. It is not strange that Mr. Washington's work has won him the confidence and support of the best men and women, North and South, who are interested in the solution of what is called the negro problem, which, as Mr. Washington pointed out, is simply a phase of the common human problem of material success.

Philadelphia *Record*, Apr. 8, 1894, 12. The newspaper account was written by Henry McFarland.

From David Clarke John[1]

South Atlanta, Ga., Apr 16, 1894

Dear Bro.; Though late, I write to express my gratification with the work of your convention. I am also pleased with a citation of brave words from you in the Constitution of yesterday. I believe you are on the right track and bid you godspeed in your work. I am trying to dignify labor here, for I find some of our best students look upon it very much as the Southern white people do, and so long as they maintain this attitude toward the source of all wealth they are doomed to poverty.

Again, I believe it is better to discuss means of improvement in our essays and orations, rather than rehearse our wrongs; which irritate and embitter, but rarely inspire nobler and higher aspirations. I believe that it is best for the Negro to cultivate friendly relations, even with the whites of the South. Alienation and vindictiveness will only prolong the contest, while magnanimity, honesty, industry and thrift must gradually overcome unjust prejudices and unreasonable discriminations against the colored race. Money, intelligence and morality will float any one who possesses them, black or white.

But, my brother, there are so many intelligent and good colored men who do not take your view of the case, who never speak in public but to rehearse wrongs and inveigh against the white race as a whole, they are really alienating the young from those who alone can help them. How do you account for this? Can you suggest anything that will bring about a better state of things? Very Respectfully Yours,

D. C. John

ALS Con. 107 BTW Papers DLC.

¹ David Clarke John was president of Clark University in Atlanta, teacher of "Mental, Moral and Political Science," and editor of *The Corona,* a magazine published in Milwaukee.

From Jabez Lamar Monroe Curry

Washington, D.C., April 17, 1894

Confidential.

My dear Sir: To aid you in your arduous work and because of the pecuniary stringency of the times, our Board has decided to increase your appropriation, so as to make it, for the next year, $5000. All appropriations by the Fund, as you know, are annual and imply no promise of future continuance. This is especially true of the additional $1000.

Your past work is the promise and assurance, as we believe, of still better work in the future, along normal and industrial lines. The announcement is made thus early that you may make your arrangements accordingly.

Now I desire to make a proposition, which is strictly *confidential*, and I am sure you will receive it kindly, knowing that it comes from those who have shown, in marked degree, their friendship for the Institution and its president. In our visits to Tuskegee we saw much to admire and to commend as is evidenced by the increased appropriation. Candor however constrains us to say that there was something in the general appearance that awakened criticism. An air of untidiness, bordering on a want of neatness, was sometimes visible in the school rooms and about the premises. There seemed to be wanting the eye, the taste, the supervision, of some one who had a quick apprehension of what was untidy and the power to enforce an improvement. The contrast betwixt your school and some others, in the respect indicated, was very noticeable. Prompted solely by a desire to aid you in your laudable ambition, the Board is willing to make a *temporary* appropriation of a few hundred dollars to enable you to employ some competent and trained woman[1] to give her attention to household improvement. It was suggested in the Board that Miss Giles[2] at Spelman could probably recommend such a person.

I am sure you will receive this suggestion in the spirit of friendship which has prompted it. Please let me know whether you think favorably of the proposition and are willing to undertake to find such an one as I have indicated. Yours very truly,

J. L. M. Curry

TLS Con. 861 BTW Papers DLC.

[1] BTW employed Alice J. Kaine, a white woman from Milwaukee, Wis. (BTW to Alice J. Kaine, Sept. 5, 1894, below.)

[2] Harriet E. Giles (1833-1909) was principal of Spelman Seminary (later College) for black women in Atlanta. Born in Salem, Mass., and educated in that state, Miss Giles, with her lifelong friend and companion Sophia Packard, helped organize the Women's American Baptist Home Mission Society in 1877. During a trip to the South to study educational conditions there, the two women were struck by the need for a school for black women. When the society declined to support this project, Misses Giles and Packard raised the money themselves, opening a school in 1881 with eleven pupils, in the Rev. Frank Quarles's Friendship Baptist Church in Atlanta. John D. Rockefeller and the Slater and Peabody funds gave financial aid. In 1884 the school was named Spelman Seminary in honor of Mrs. Rockefeller's mother, Laura Buel Spelman. Sophia Packard died in 1891, and Harriet Giles continued as sole principal until her death. (Read, *The Story of Spelman College.*)

To David Clarke John

My dear Sir: I have your kind favor of the 15th, and in reply would say that I thank you heartily for your encouraging words; and if you will give me permission, I should like very much to use a portion of your letter in a paper which we publish at this institution. I am quite sure that the words will accomplish good in many ways.

It seems to me that the only way to turn the tide of thought of the masses of colored people forward, instead of backward, is through the constant reminding of the young men and women in our institutions of learning, what is the best course to pursue. Thus far I fear we have been inclined to dwell too much on the past; to magnify our wrongs instead of our advantages. I confess that up until a few years ago it never occur[r]ed to me that one could accomplish more by dwelling on the bright side instead of the dark side, and that almost nothing was to be accomplished by continually reminding our race of the wrongs perpetrated upon them. I think the time has come when all of us must look at the matter squarely and charitably, and lay aside sectional and race prejudices. I believe that if we can send out from our educational institutions a stream of young men and young women every year who will constantly hold up before our people the great advantages that they have thrown open to them, especially along the industrial lines in the South that within a decade a marvelous change can be made in the condition of the masses of people.

Sometime I hope to see you personally and go over this matter with you more satisfactorily. Yours very truly,

[Booker T. Washington]

TLp Con. 113 BTW Papers DLC.

From Lucy M. Washburn[1]

My Dear Friend: We were glad to receive your letter two days ago — to be assured that you had made a safe journey and found all well at home and that you look upon your experience here with pleasure. We are as gratified as you. I felt all along that it was worth an effort to bring you into touch with the University people. I wanted their thought enlarged and quickened as to the need, work, and results at the South — I wanted them to know *you*. And you have won them, as I knew you would. It is acquaintance that is needed, where people have open minds and hearts, as here. President Schurman[2] said warmly to Mr. Lord that he had learned much from you. (On another subject, he once said he wanted his epitaph to be "This man died learning.") Prof. Willcox[3] spoke to his Sociology class, just taking up the race questions in this country, of your "admirable presentation of the subject." Prof. Jenks[4] expressed his personal satisfaction and assured me he had heard only favorable comments. Prof. Burr[5] said to me, "None of these young people will ever look on the subject in the same light as before." And the students do show an interest. Many have spoken to me, and a literary club among the Sage College girls asked me to tell them more about it all, as I had just come from my trip South; they gathered about a third of the girls last evening in the Sage parlors, to listen very intently and linger to express their interest.

One case among the professors comes nearer home than you could have expected. Do you remember the young professor from Auburn whom we met on the car? I had talked with him before, and knew that life in Alabama had changed his Northern to strong Southern views. I saw him out that evening, and a day or two later he stopped me to say, "That was a very fair and sensible address the other night — the most so I ever heard. I went to hear him as a Southern man; and barring one or two little things there was nothing from which any fair-minded Southerner, however radical, could dissent. I mean to write to Dr. Brown[6] what a fair and sensible speech it was!"

My dear friend, I do not hesitate to tell you these things that please me so, for I know that the same good sense which has enabled you to see questions broadly and truly has kept you from being personally spoiled by success; and I want you to have the comfort of knowing when you do good. As for our family, they have taken you right into their heart and thought. It was a peculiar pleasure for me to bring you and my Uncle together. Though in so short a time you could know but little of his beautiful life, you could but recognize his spirit. To know him has been so large a part of my own education. I felt it must be worth something to you to be brought into contact with him. And on his part, so heavily do humanity's burdens weigh on him, that I knew, as proved true, that it would brighten him more than almost anything else to realize in you the outcome of one of the struggles for better things in which he had worked with all his heart.

I have myself read the Northrup book since you returned it. It was that state of things that made my Father count not his life dear, and nerved my Mother to give up him who was more to her than life. And how it comforted her to see Hampton! For it was not the mere release from outward bondage that my Father and Mother cared for, but the fuller life of the spirit. It is indeed a long "distance that you have traveled" that may give you courage for what remains to be traversed. And I often think that you can afford to go without some sympathy from the people around you, when you have such eager watchers among spirits gone before.

Mr. Lord wishes me to urge you to visit us when you come to Rochester in June. Do try to come. All will welcome you warmly; and you know California is a long way off — it may be a long time, if ever, before I have another opportunity to see you.

I enclose the full names you asked for of addresses for the Southern Letter. There are more professors who heard you more than once, if you wish to lengthen the list.

I wish I knew how soon your term closes for the summer. Please send me a postal stating this if you have no time to write more. With regards to your wife (I hope you give my messages to her and others.) Cordially yours —

Lucy M. Washburn

Had you been a day later, it w'd have been hard to gather audiences — there came on a storm with *two feet* of snow!

ALS Con. 109 BTW Papers DLC.

[1] Lucy M. Washburn was a teacher at Hampton when BTW was a student there. After several years at Hampton, she went to San Francisco, where she taught in a state normal school. She lost her position through politics in 1900, but soon secured another position in San Jose. BTW considered her "one of the best teachers in the country," and urged Hollis B. Frissell to employ her again at Hampton. (BTW to Frissell, Dec. 31, 1900, BTW Folder, ViHaI.)

[2] Jacob Gould Schurman (1854-1942) was Sage Professor of Philosophy at Cornell from 1886 to 1892 and president of Cornell from 1892 to 1920. The

author of several books, he was also a distinguished public servant, serving on the first Philippine commission (1899), as minister to Greece and Montenegro (1912-15), and on special missions in China (1921-25) and Germany (1925-30).

³ Walter Francis Willcox (1861-1964) was professor of economics and statistics at Cornell from 1891 to 1931. He was chief statistician of the 1900 census and was president of the American Economic Association in 1915.

⁴ Jeremiah Whipple Jenks (1856-1929) was professor of political economy at Cornell from 1891 to 1912. A scholar of prodigious energy, he concentrated on the accumulation of data rather than economic theory.

⁵ George Lincoln Burr (1857-1938), a native of New York, graduated from Cornell University in 1881. He served for many years as secretary to President Andrew D. White. In 1888 he was appointed to the Cornell faculty, and from 1892 to 1922 held the chair of medieval history. He was a specialist in the history of superstition and witchcraft. He also served as librarian of the Andrew D. White Library. In 1896 he was a historical expert appointee to help settle the boundary dispute between Venezuela and British Guiana. He was associate editor of the *American Historical Review* from 1905 to 1916 and president of the American Historical Association in 1916-17. Though he himself published little, much of his work went into the writings of friends and colleagues, one of whom even raided his lecture notes to produce a textbook of distinction.

⁶ William LeRoy Broun, president of Alabama Polytechnic Institute at Auburn.

An Article in the *A.M.E. Church Review*

[Tuskegee, Ala., April 1894]

TAKING ADVANTAGE OF OUR DISADVANTAGES

Four years ago a Jew, only a few months from Europe, passed through the town of Tuskegee, Ala., on foot, with all his earthly possessions in a cheap and much-worn satchel which was swung across his shoulder. This Jew, by accident, stopped over night, sixteen miles from Tuskegee, at a common country settlement in the midst of the cotton-raising district. Looking about the next morning with an eye to business, this Jew soon decided to remain for awhile in this community, and he soon found some one to hire him for a few dollars per month. Soon he began renting land to sub-let to others; then followed the opening of a store, and the development and accumulation have gone on to the extent that to-day this Jew does a business of $50,000 a year. He owns hundreds of acres of land; contracts the cotton from all the plantations in that neighborhood; and there is not a man, woman nor child within five miles who does not pay tribute to this

Jew. His note or check is honored at any bank, and his credit with wholesale merchants is almost without limit.

What this Jew has done, the blackest Negro in the United States can do in Alabama. "What," says one, "do you mean to say that a black man in the Black belt of Alabama has the same opportunity for business development as a Jew or a white man?"[1] Yes; this is just what I mean to say. I make this assertion with knowledge not based on hearsay, but upon what I have actually come in contact with during the last twelve years in the heart of the South. Of course the black man, like the Jew or white man, should be careful as to the kind of business he selects, as he, like the white man, can succeed in one branch of business better than in another. When it comes to business, pure and simple, stripped of all sentiment, I am constantly surprised to see how little prejudice is exhibited. There are always those who are ready to take advantage of the ignorant. I am not at all unmindful of the fact that the South is full of those (just as it is true of most parts of our country), who are ready to take advantage of the ignorant and unfortunate of any race.

We have made a mistake, I fear sometimes, in not constantly keeping in sight our advantages. We have had any number of conventions and organizations, whose objects were to redress some grievance. This is right and proper; but with a race as with an individual, it will begin to make progress backward if it is continually dwelling on the dark side; is continually grumbling and finding fault; is continually finding a way *not* to succeed instead of finding a way *to* succeed. It requires a man with no special gift in brain power to find fault with an individual, organization or state of things. After all, what we want — and it is what America honors — is the man who can teach his fellows how to overcome obstacles; how to "find a way or make one."

While I write I am not unmindful of the fact that we in the South are surrounded by prejudice, deprived of a share in government, in most cases, and are too often shot down and lynched, and denied our just rights on public carriers. It is my firm conviction that every right of which we are now deprived can be secured through business development, coupled with education and character. Suppose in any town in the South there were ten colored men worth a half million dollars each, how much Negro oppression would be practiced in that town? Suppose in Montgomery, Ala., there were ten colored men whose freight bills amounted to $10,000 a year each. Not one of the competing railroads between Montgomery and New York, would dare thrust one of these colored men into a "jim crow" car. No man, North or South, black or white, is respected until he gets something that somebody else wants, something of culture, influence or of material wealth. When two individuals stick close to each other, one has something that the other wants. Two nations or races are good friends in proportion as the one has something by way of trade, the other wants. It is surprising to see how quickly sentiment and prejudice will disappear under the influence of hard cash. No street railway in the South will pay if the patronage of the Negro is withdrawn. If the city street cars discriminate, the Negro stops riding as was the case in Atlanta a few months ago. Seeing that the Negro's nickel is necessary to keep the street railway corporation alive, the same white man who refuses to ride in the same steam railway coach when the Negro is perhaps sitting fifty feet from him, will get out of the steam car and sit right beside the same Negro, though black and dirty he may be; the law of necessity makes this respectable, and the time is not far distant for this law to make it respectable for the white and black man to ride in the same railway coach. My advice to the Negro is: Get dollars! get dollars!! and spend them wisely and effectively.

In a recent speech in Washington, Prof. Hugh Brown used this illustration: A certain ship had been lost at sea for many days. Suddenly a sail was sighted, and when the two vessels came into signaling distance, the unfortunate vessel signaled — "water, water." The answer was signaled back — "cast down your buckets where you are." Again the lost vessel signaled — "we want water; we die of thirst." "Cast down your buckets where you are," was signaled back a third and then a fourth time, and finally the captain of the unfortunate vessel obeyed, and the bucket came up full of pure, fresh, sparkling water from the Amazon river.[2] In our effort and anxiety to secure every right that is ours at once, I fear we are often inclined to overlook the opportunities that are right about us. We fail to cast down our buckets where we are, thinking that relief is far away. In the first place, a man who does not try to make friends with those among whom he lives, is a fool.

As I said in the beginning the colored man's present great opportunity in the South is in the matter of business, and success here is going to constitute the foundation for success and relief along other lines. We need first an industrial or business foundation. No one, not even in the North, cares much about the rights of a hungry man. We of the Negro race are too hungry and too empty-handed to exert much of an influence. In business, what are our opportunities? The Southern white has not advanced to the point yet where he will invite a Negro to his *prayer-meeting,* but has advanced to the point where he will invite him to the *stock-holders meetings,* as I can prove by numerous examples. If a colored man wants to borrow money on his note or get his note discounted, in no city in the South does the color of the face enter in. It is simply a question of reliability. The black man in this regard is given absolutely the same showing that the white man is given. Any colored man with common sense, a reasonable education and business ability, can take $1,000 in cash and go into any Southern community, and in five years be worth $5,000. He does not meet with that stern, relentless competition that he does when he butts up against the Northern Yankee. The black man can sooner conquer Southern prejudice than Northern competition. There are one thousand places in the South where a colored man can take $600 and open a brick yard, and in a few years grow independent, and when the colored man sells $10,000 worth of bricks to a white man and gets a mortgage on his house, this white man will not drive that Negro away from the polls when he sees him going up to vote, nor will the railroad, over which he ships $25,000 worth of bricks a year, put him into the smoking car.

Land is cheap all over the South; cheaper now than it will ever be again.

Another great advantage that the Negro has in the South, and one that I fear he does not value high enough, is in the matter of trades or skilled labor. Here again, there is almost no color-line drawn. While I write, within a few yards of me, is a large printing office in charge of a colored man with two Southern white printers under him who work by the side of dozens of colored printers, without a word of objection.

In conclusion, let us stop spending so much of our strength in whining, complaining, fault-finding, but let us go forward conquering and to conquer. If the acquisition of property, education, morality, refinement and religion do not, in God's own time, bring us every political and civil right, then Nature is false, God is false, the teachings of Christ are false, everything is false.

Have we made any progress? Let the reading of the two subjoined business notices answer.

(Newspaper notice, December 2, 1843.)

PUBLIC SALE OF VERY VALUABLE NEGROES AND STOCK

"The subscriber will offer for sale at his residence, on the 20th of December next, if a fair day, or the next fair day, 45 or 50 very valuable young negroes, consisting of men, women, boys and girls. At the same time he will offer for sale his entire stock of blood horses, together with some farm stock. Sale to commence at 10 o'clock A.M."

SELMA, ALABAMA

(Newspaper notice, February 7, 1894.)

"At a public auction yesterday, a large tract of land at Cahaba, Ala., which was formerly the State Capital of Alabama, and on which the capital building once stood, was sold to a colored man by the name of John Smith. Years ago this tract of land contained not only the capital building, but a large number of the most aristocratic and wealthy families in Alabama resided there, and many evidences of their former wealth and prosperity are to be seen in Cahaba to-day.

"The fact that the former capital of Alabama, with the many valuable town lots and other improvements that were made in former years, have passed into the hands of a colored man, marks quite a change in the history of the State."

Booker T. Washington

A.M.E. Church Review, 10 (Apr. 1894), 478-83. A shorter version appeared in the *Christian Register,* 73 (July 12, 1894), 437-38.

¹ BTW's characterization of Jews as being in a separate category from the white race incurred the wrath of Isaac M. Wise, editor of the *American Israelite.* BTW needed "a lesson in primary ethnology," Wise wrote. "All Jewish Americans are Caucasians and when the Rev. Prof. uses such an expression as 'a Jew or a white man' he commits a scientific blunder." Wise suggested that BTW harbored "the secret malice that invariably marks a servile nature seeking to assume a feeling of equality with something higher, which it does not possess." (*American Israelite,* 41 [July 26, 1894], 4.)

² Hugh Mason Browne used this metaphor in a Thanksgiving service at the Lincoln Memorial Church in Washington in 1893. Washington used it again in a speech in Montgomery on Jan. 1, 1895 (see below). He also used it in the Atlanta Compromise address, Sept. 18, 1895 (see below).

To John Wesslay Hoffman¹

[Tuskegee, Ala.] Apr. 31 [May 1?], 1894

My dear Sir: I write according to promise.

Until late I have been trying to persuade Mr. J. D. McCall, who has had charge of our scientific work for sometime, to transfer to the department of mathematics in lieu of the sciences, but he has not as yet consented to make the transfer. Of course I could make the change without his consent, but with a teacher who has been here for sometime and who is faithful in doing the best he can, I dislike to make a change that is not agreeable to Mr. McCall.

We are pushing more and more our scientific work, and it has now gotten to the point where it is entirely too much for any one person to do acceptably. I have just had a talk with Mr. McCall about this, and he agrees with me thoroughly on this point. As matters now stand it seems to me best for you to come here and take charge of a part of our scientific work. In connection with this there is one class in composition and another on rhetoric, which we should want you to have charge of for next year.

The science work which we should like to have you take charge of, especially for the next year, would be an elementary course in nature study that would tend to prepare the students who are in the lower classes for the study of the higher sciences the study of insects with the view of finding those that are injurious to plants, and finding remedies to check their ravages; Agricultural bacteriology; Dairy chemistry, veterinary science; and perhaps we shall want you to take charge of agricultural chemistry, but of this latter I am not quite sure. It is my plan to give you plenty of room to demonstrate everything in connection with the scientific work before mentioned, and to make a close connection between the industrial and scientific work, doing as much individual work with the students as you can find time for.

In connection with what I have said, you will not find Mr. McCall a disagreeable person with whom to work. He is a very pleasant man, and wants only to do what he can for the furtherance of the work.

I think what I have attempted to outline would be a good entrance wedge for you, and I believe that within a few years you will have on foot a scientific work that will be a credit to the whole race.

Your plan of spending the Summer at the University of Wisconsin is admirable. You could not find a better place for this work. I am under engagement to speak at the Summer Assembly at Madison on the 2nd of August, and in case you accept the position I shall be glad to see you there.

I am sure that this letter outlines what neither you or myself would wish, but I do think that in the end you would not regret coming to us. We have a large number of students who are enthusiastic over the scientific and industrial work. We also have plenty of land, and I think by the beginning of next term, we shall have plenty of room for the development of this department.

As to the salary we cannot offer you anything tempting or generous. It has been our policy from the very first to secure those teachers who would come for the work's sake more than for the amount of money to be received. To begin with we can give you a salary of $48. per month and board, — board to include all expenses except traveling expenses. You will find here a congenial and pleasant set of teachers, and I am sure your life, in every way, will be pleasant and satisfactory.

It may be, however, necessary to make some slight change in the outline of your work, but in the main, I think it will remain as it is.

Please let me have an early reply. Yours very truly,

[Booker T. Washington]

TLp   Con. 113   BTW Papers   DLC.

¹ John Wesslay Hoffman wrote BTW that he needed a salary of at least $50 per month plus board since he was making $60 in his present position. He was willing, however, to take a cut in pay to be able to go to Tuskegee. He told BTW that he would make his science lessons practical "so that the students can put them into practical every day life." Hoffman wanted his scientific work to be "felt by many farmers in the State of Ala and the adjacent states." He wanted to build a science department "that will be a credit to the Race and to the entire South." (Hoffman to BTW, May 3, 1894, Con. 107, BTW Papers, DLC.) Hoffman taught agricultural chemistry and biology at Tuskegee Institute from 1894 to 1896. He later taught in other black schools at Orangeburg, S.C., and Prairie View, Tex., and helped to introduce cotton-growing in British West Africa.

From Thomas Junius Calloway

Washington, D.C., May 2 1894

Dear Mr. Washington, Your favor of 30th ult. is just received. I find myself unable to express my appreciation for the very high compliment you pay me and the friendly interest you have taken, especially at a time when your own work must be very taxing.

The presidency of Alcorn I shall accept if offered, not so much because of my confidence in myself but rather because of my faith in the work and I have long since reached the conclusion that there is no disgrace to fail in a good cause. Personally I should enjoy I think the work at Tuskegee better, because the responsibilities on me would not be so great and I should not have to worry or be solicitous of the future. But in as much as Alcorn presents a larger field and for reasons before stated I shall accept without a moments hesitation if it is offered.

In regard to Prof. Greener's[1] family I have ascertained that Mrs. Greener is a native of this city — being a Miss Fleet before marriage. She is colored and never passed for anything else while here. It is understood here however that she associates only with whites in New York. They are poor and in very straightened circumstances.

Before receiving your telegram I had just been considering whether I might not advantageously devote the Summer to the writing of "The Story of Tuskegee," and I had just mapped out a plan which consisted of the nine chapters which I enclose. The first chapter I should endeavor to make as careful a picture of plantation life as I could, describing the various customs and regulations which have contributed to give to the slaves such habits as are now shown in the ex-slaves. Under emancipation I should describe the wars their effects reproduction and missionary work in general as it sought to help the ex-slaves. Chapter three would be devoted to a biography of yourself — Your home in Virginia, your life at Hampton and a brief description of Hampton — Mrs. Olivia Davidson Washington and such other points as would suggest themselves. The other chapters will suggest their own line of treatment. This work might result in a book of three or four hundred pages, and I thought it would perhaps be well to submit the publishing of it to some New York Pubs. Co. and arrange to have such number as the school should want printed in a special binding and paper as you might cho[o]se, the others for them to print in their usual binding for the trade. One reason I thought for doing the work this summer was the reason that while here and in easy reach of the great libraries and near Hampton and your home I could gather the material for those chapters with perhaps more care that when I should actually be in the harness at Tuskegee. Of course before I should consider the work complete I should submit it for revision to all connected with Tuskegee whose interest and relations justified it. In its preparation I should spend some time at Tuskegee, and enter into correspondence with teachers, ex-teachers, graduates, students and ex-students, but principally upon you would I rely for material.

Should the position at Alcorn come I am afraid I shall have to abandon the plan, and I have outlined it here so that should any of the ideas be worth anything you would have them before they were crowded out by other matters. I shall not only accept your welcome to spend two or three weeks at Tuskegee but I could hardly nerve myself to accept such a responsibility did I not feel I could rely on you for counsel and assistance at all times. My only ambition will be to get Alcorn in to the Tuskegee idea of education.

With kindest regards from Mrs. Calloway, Mrs. Nolen and myself, I remain, Very sincerely.

Thos. J. Calloway

P.S. News has just reached me that William E. Matthews died this afternoon after an illness of three weeks.

T. J. C.

ALS Con. 107 BTW Papers DLC. Calloway's letterhead showed that he was manager of "The Colored Teachers' Agency" established to aid black teachers in finding employment.

[1] Richard Theodore Greener.

To Frank R. Simon[1]

[Tuskegee, Ala.] May 3rd, 1894

Mr. Simon: In connection with your employment for the coming school year, I deem it well to speak with you rather frankly and plainly about several points in connection with your work.

You have ability, and in a great many respects do well in your department, but there are several defects which prevent your department from producing the best results.

In the end I am quite sure it will be more just and helpful to you to speak plainly about these defects than to let them go on unnoticed.

In the first place, I do not think you have enough disposition to learn from others; that is, you give one the impression that you know everything about your work. This is always a failing. The persons who know the most are always those who are anxious to learn, and who are willing to be taught even by a mere child. Every teacher here should be willing to get all he can that will tend to improve his department. This information can often be gotten by asking questions and by accepting advice in the right spirit.

Another criticism is that you do not stay close enough to your work. It does not present a very business-like appearance to see a teacher all dressed up with the appearance that he is afraid he will soil his collar or cuffs, especially a teacher of Blacksmithing. If you were to go into the blacksmithing department of Cornell University, you would find the professor of that department with a pair of overalls and find him very near the students, giving ACTUAL instruction. You must bear in mind that our shop cannot be run on the same principles that a shop in the city is run upon, that is, merely for making money.

You want to cultivate more patience and forbearance. There are several instances where you have made mistakes in teaching and dealing with the students and which would have been better had you acknowledged your error, and then you would have held their respect.

In regard to the order and looks of your shop, Mr. J. H. Washington reports to me that you have put your shop in excellent condition, and if you will keep it so hereafter, there will be no criticism in this respect.

One other point: there is entirely too much iron wasted. I mean iron that could be worked up. You will find that there are thousands of pounds of irons on the place that should be worked up.

When we had the man from Montgomery, he was always very careful to use the scraps. Since he left we have been going backward in this respect.

I hope you will see that I mean these criticisms only for your own good. If I do not hear from you to the contrary I shall understand that you are going to keep your same department next September.

[Booker T. Washington]

TLp   Con. 113   BTW Papers   DLC.

[1] Frank R. Simon was an instructor of blacksmithing at Tuskegee from 1892 to 1895.

To W. B. Murdock[1]

[Tuskegee, Ala.] May 9– 1894

Dear Sir: Your kind favor of May 2nd, asking if I could be induced to accept the position of President of Alcorn College is received.

I am pleased to know that you should think of me in this connection, and of course feel complimented in the highest degree, but I think it best to say in the beginning that I do not think I could be induced to give up my present position. The salary you name is much larger than I am at present receiving but I prefer to remain for the reason that I think for some years to come I can do MORE GOOD here than elsewhere, and for the further reason that there are a number of individuals throughout the North who have given and are giving rather large sums of money to this work, based on [their] faith in my devotion to this work, and it would be very disappointing to them as well as to the officers of the State of Alabama for me to leave here. There are also several important problems in connection with this institution that are now in process of being worked out that would, I fear, fail were I to leave. I trust you will not think me egotistic when I add that this institution is very largely my own creation, and you can realize how I would feel to leave it.

I am deeply interested in the success of Alcorn College, and at the request of Dr. J. L. M. Curry, and Commissioner W. T. Harris, I wrote recommending Thos. J. Calloway, of 1732 V St., N.W., Washington, D.C. for the position. I know the man thoroughly, and I believe him the best qualified man in the country for this position. In the usual sense he may not be considered an educator, but he knows how to use men and means in a way to produce the best educational results. He has great executive ability: sees right through things and sees them in all their relations. He also understands the South, its needs and the relations of the races. I believe that industrial education is to be the salvation of our people. Book education alone increases their wants, without increasing their ability to supply these wants. It is my opinion that if Alcorn College could be brought to the point where more attention could be given to the industrial side, it would result in much more good for the masses of our people. Most of the institutions with which I am acquainted fail to make their industrial work a success for the reason that it seems that they do not know how to divide the time between the literary and industrial work. If Mr. Calloway is appointed to the position, I feel quite sure that I can give him such help as will enable him to overcome this difficulty. He believes thoroughly in the industrial work, and would push that side in connection with the literary work.

I have taken the pains to write you thus at length because of my interest in the subject.

If after or before you have elected a president I can be of the least service in promoting the industrial work, please do not hesitate to call on me.

If you have not seen it, I should like to send you a copy of the Review of Reviews, which contains a full account of the work of this school. Respectfully yours,

Booker T. Washington

TLpS Con. 113 BTW Papers DLC.

[1] W. B. Murdock was a trustee of Alcorn A & M and a cotton planter with plantations in Madison Parish, La., and in Claiborne County, Miss., near Alcorn A & M College. He asked BTW to take the job as president at a salary of $2,000 plus housing. (Murdock to BTW, May 2, 1894, Con. 108, BTW Papers, DLC.)

From Griffin Anderson Allen[1]

Tuskegee, Ala. May 9, 94

Dear Sir; I write to tell you I have been to Maj. Ramsey three times and he said he would go to see you this P.M.

I thought I would explain everything to you. I was straitening the things in my trunk one P.M., when I came across several cigaretts which I was saving untill I left school. I decided that I would give up the use of tobacco altogether and on that day I vowed that I would not put another taste in my mouth. I had to go and see Maj. Ramsey about being absent from class and he happened to smell it on my hands. I told him what I was doing with it, but he didn't seem to notice it.

I didn't have any tobacco in my pockets and I didn't try to hide that I had in my trunk; because I didn't know (as I had never heard any one say,) it was wrong or against the rules to have it in my possesion.

If you will please excus me this time it will never be the case again.

In regards to the impertinence. If I have been impertinent to any one I don't know it, but if I have I am willing to beg their pardon.

Waiting to hear from you at your earliest convenience. I remain,

Griffin A. Allen

ALS Con. 107 BTW Papers DLC.

¹ Griffin Anderson Allen, of Girard, Russell County, Ala., was in the B middle class in 1893-94 and 1894-95, and in the A middle class in 1895-96.

To Julius B. Ramsey

[Tuskegee, Ala.] May 11th, 1894

Major Ramsey: I call your attention to the following extracts from the report of the committee appointed to investigate the condition of the boys' rooms:

"Everywhere, the windows need washing. We found closets filled with old shoes, and even dirty socks. Bed-bugs are everywhere. Blankets are used to lengthen beds. Many bed-steads are broken, three in one room at the barn. Seven whiskey bottles were found in one room."

The committee also says that the bath room also needs to be opened, sunned and aired, and otherwise disinfected.

They also call attention to the fact that it is necessary that the students dust their rooms just as regularly as they are swept.

Please give these matters immediate attention, especially the broken beds, and the matter of bed bugs.

[Booker T. Washington]

TLp Con. 113 BTW Papers DLC.

Griffin Anderson Allen to the Tuskegee Faculty

Tuskegee, Ala. May 14th '94

The Faculty, Your punishment for my charge was just. I acknowledge that I have done wrong. Although if I had to have known it was against the rules of this institution to have tobacco in my trunk or any where near me, I would have thrown it away sooner, but I will assure you that it will never be the case again.

I have now realized what a warning or suspension is and how low and degrading it is. Now I wish to call you[r] attention to the temptations of one like me. I am liable to fall into bad company and go from bad to worse, but if I stay here and gain more knowledge and training, I am will not be so easily tempted to do wrong.

If you will allow me to enter school again you will not have any more trouble with me at all. If you don't allow me to enter school; allow me to work untill the end of the term.

Waiting to hear from you at your earliest convenience for I am in a great suspense.

G. A. Allen

ALS   Con. 107   BTW Papers   DLC.

From Nathaniel Southgate Shaler[1]

Cambridge, Mass., May 15 [1894]

Dear Sir; I have your letter of May 12th.

I regret to say that at present there are no colored men in this school. There are however, two or three in the College. I shall have inquiries made concerning them and ask the Dean to send you word.

Although I am a southern born man, and of a slave holding family I feel a very keen interest in advancing the cause which you have in hand. I shall be very glad at any time to do anything I can to aid you. Yours very truly,

N. S. Shaler

TLS   Con. 108   BTW Papers   DLC.

[1] Nathaniel Southgate Shaler (1841-1906) was a prominent geologist, lecturer, and author who wrote prolifically on the natural sciences. He taught at Harvard

for almost forty years. In 1891 he also became dean of the Lawrence Scientific School, a position he held until his death. On May 16 Shaler wrote to BTW giving him the names and addresses of three black students at Harvard: William Monroe Trotter, William Taylor Burwell Williams, and Napoleon Bonaparte Marshall. Shaler described Trotter as "a *decidedly* able person." (Shaler to BTW, May 16, 1894, Con. 108, BTW Papers, DLC.)

An Account of Testimony before the House Committee on Appropriations[1]

[Washington, D.C., ca. May 15, 1894]

. . . . .

When Bishop Grant sat down only six or seven minutes of the time were left to the last speaker. Booker Washington, unlike the others, was small of stature and not prepossessing in appearance, but his ability was immediately recognized. He rose with an envelope in his hand, and glanced from time to time at some notes which he had penciled on it. He attracted attention at once by the statement that for fifteen years he had eschewed all participation in politics or political gatherings, and had advised his people to do the same. He had devoted his energies during that time to educating his own people, especially in the practical and industrial pursuits of life. He had urged the negro to acquire property, own his land, drive his own mule hitched to his own wagon, milk his own cow, raise his own crop and keep out of debt, and that when he acquired a home he became fit for a conservative citizen. He told them that the way to secure their political rights was to obtain something which the white people wanted, to wit, property. Let the negro fit himself to be one of the units that make up the conservative body of the government and then all his legal and political rights would be accorded him. The progress of his people, in all the walks and pursuits of life, had been remarkable. The white people of the South did not fully realize what was going on, and the white people in the North and the rest of the world had no idea of it. In conclusion, he told them that, for the first time in fifteen years, he had left his school, and come on telegraphic summons, at his own expense, without any previous conference with any of the Exposition Company, to take advantage of this opportunity, and he earnestly asked for Congressional aid, in order that his race might have the chance to give an account of its stewardship.

. . . .

Walter G. Cooper, *The Cotton States and International Exposition and South, Illustrated* (Atlanta, 1896), 24.

[1] BTW was one of three black men who were asked to accompany a group of about twenty-five prominent white southerners in their appearance before the House Committee on Appropriations on behalf of the Cotton States and International Exposition. For more than two hours the committee listened to the delegation. Most of the time was taken up by the exposition president Charles A. Collier. Joseph G. Cannon of Illinois, the "watchdog of the treasury," was chairman of the committee. When Collier had made a detailed statement of the value of the exposition to the South and to the country as a whole, "Uncle Joe" Cannon interrupted him. "Mr. Collier, you say this is a cotton exposition?" he asked. "Yes, sir." "How many states grow cotton?" "Ten or twelve." "Do you mean to say that the whole nation should spend its money for something that benefits only a few states?" L. F. Livingston, the congressman from Atlanta who sponsored the bill, jumped to his feet and saved the day. "Mr. Chairman," he said, "this exposition is for the benefit of all those who grow cotton and all those who wear cotton." This witty response apparently won over "Uncle Joe," who made no further objection. (Garrett, *Atlanta and Environs*, II, 319.) After all the whites had spoken, attention focused on the three black delegates who had been hastily summoned to appear and who only had fifteen minutes together with the delegation before the hearings began. The first two black speakers, both bishops of the A.M.E. Church, were Wesley J. Gaines of Georgia and Abram L. Grant of Texas. Bishop Gaines argued that the exposition would give blacks the opportunity to exhibit the progress the race had made, a chance that was denied at the Columbian Exposition at Chicago the year before. Grant took a similar position and also appealed to the southerners on the committee by pointing out that Negroes and whites understood each other in the South. Both Gaines and Grant were of large stature, each being over six feet tall. When BTW rose to speak he seemed of slight build by comparison. After the hearing BTW stayed on in Washington for several days lobbying on behalf of the exposition. Washington recalled several years later that this was the first time he had shaken hands with Speaker Thomas B. Reed. When the bill reached the floor it was championed by another black man, South Carolina congressman George W. Murray. Congress passed a $200,000 appropriation for the exposition. (Cooper, *The Cotton States and International Exposition*, 23-25; Harlan, *BTW*, 205-7.)

To John Randolph Lewis[1]

Tuskegee, Ala. May 19th, 1894

Dear Sir: The following is a bill of my actual expenses in connection with my trip to Washington, a few days ago.[2]

Railroad fare from Tuskegee to Chehaw,   ·50
   "   "   "   Chehaw to Atlanta, $ 4.50
   "   "   "   Atlanta to Washington, $17.50

Returning
   From Atlanta to Chehaw, $ 4.50
   " Chehaw to Tuskegee,   ·50
     Meals, lodging etc., $ 3.00

                   Total, $30.50

Yours truly,

              Booker T. Washington

TLS   Con. 7   BTW Papers   ATT.   Original destroyed.

¹ John Randolph Lewis (1834-1900) was born in Erie County, Pa. A dental surgeon, though he did not practice his profession, Lewis joined the Union Army and rose to the rank of colonel before being mustered out in 1864 after loss of his left arm in the Battle of the Wilderness. He became a general in the Veterans Reserve Corps, then reentered the Army for three years. He served as Georgia state school commissioner from 1870 to 1872, organizing the state school system from almost nothing. After a number of years as a merchant in Des Moines and Buffalo, he returned to Atlanta, where he went into the mercantile business as head of the Atlantic Rubber Company. He was secretary of the Atlanta Cotton Exposition in 1880-81 and of the Cotton States and International Exposition in 1895. He was postmaster of Atlanta from 1889 to 1893.

² This refers to BTW's trip to lobby on behalf of the Cotton States and International Exposition appropriation bill. (See An Account of Testimony . . . , May 15, 1894, above.) In his testimony before the congressional committee BTW remarked that he had come to Washington at his own expense. He was, however, apparently reimbursed for his efforts at a later date.

To Ednah Dow Littlehale Cheney

Tuskegee, Ala. May 19, 94

My dear Mrs. Cheney: I was away in the county when your letter came hence the delay in answering it. I am very grateful for the money you send for the school.

Now in regard to your Association coming South this fall.

1 I do most earnestly want you to come to Tuskegee and all of us will give the ladies a hearty welcome.

2 We should want you to inspect the school and hold 2 or 3 meetings that could be attended by the public and our teachers and

students. We should also want to take you into the county where you could see something of the life of the women on the plantations.

3 The main interest in the meetings would be manifested by the colored citizens and by some of the white men. The Southern women — I mean those near us would hardly attend the meetings.

[4] It would be best to hold the meetings in our chapel. Both the white and colored people are in the habit of coming to the school for all kinds of meetings. There would be no race trouble here — there could be entire freedom of discussion. This vicinity is very liberal. In addition to the colored men and women you would have some of the best white men.

5 We could easily accommodate a dozen or more ladies on the school grounds and would like to do so. There is also a hotel in the town.

6 Mrs. Washington has had for some time an organization among the women in this county which meets every week and is accomplishing great good. It would be especially encouraging to this body to have your Association come here.

There are at least a half dozen white ladies from the North teaching in this part of the South who would be glad to meet you here.

Please send any circulars that will give information.

If I can be of more service please do not hesitate to use me. Yours Sincerely

Booker T. Washington

The public meetings here could be well reported in the leading Southern daily papers in this section. They are quite friendly to us. I hope to call to see you in June.

B. T. W.

ALS   New England Hospital Papers   Sophia Smith Collection   MNS.

To Edgar James Penney

[Tuskegee, Ala.] May 22nd, 1894

Mr. Penney: Hereafter I shall consider it a part of your duty to keep a lookout as to the attendance of teachers on the various exercises of the school, especially the morning preaching service and the opening exercise in the chapel in the morning, and I suggest that where you find teachers getting into the habit of absenting themselves from these exercises, that you speak to them, and if they persist in absenting themselves, I wish you would report them to me. I, of course, do not mean to say that teachers are to be put under the same surveillance as the students, but we bear in mind that we conduct a religious institution, and in every thing, teachers must set the proper example.

Booker T. Washington

TLpS   Con. 113   BTW Papers   DLC.

From James Knox Powers[1]

Florence, Ala. 5-23-1894

Prof. Washington, I sincerely trust that you will yet see your way clear to support the School Amendments.

I would not be in favor of the *proviso* as to a possible division of the funds along *racial* lines,[2] as in original proposition. But, it is in the bill, and as a whole the amendment will help Alabama Education, rather than hinder it.

Let me ask your attention to this point. Some very prominent people no longer hold this *proviso* to be *unconstitutional.* If so, the *proviso* only, and *legislation* putting it in force would be so declared, and we would still have the principle of local taxation without the objectionable fixture. This should commend itself to your judgment.

Again, I feel sure that the moral effect of all teachers and believers in *public* education standing together on this will be *immense.*

The white people of Alabama have in the past dealt fairly with your people. They can safely trust their interests in this matter. Very truly yours

Jas. K. Powers

ALS   Con. 108   BTW Papers   DLC.

[1] James Knox Powers (1851-1913) was president of the state normal school at Florence, Ala., from 1888 to 1897. A graduate of the University of Alabama, he served as superintendent of education of Lauderdale County during 1885-86. He was a founder and president of the Alabama Educational Association. From 1897 to 1901 he served as president of the University of Alabama. Subsequently he

was an agent of a Richmond publishing company. In 1911 he returned to the presidency of Florence.

[2] The Hundley amendment was sponsored in the legislative session of 1892-93 by Oscar R. Hundley, a state senator from Madison County and an agrarian reformer. By a joint resolution of both houses the proposal to empower school districts to levy local taxes was submitted to the voters in the 1894 election. One of the amendment's provisos was "that the money collected from persons of the white race may by law be applied exclusively to the education of children of the white race; and the money collected from persons of the colored race, may by law be applied exclusively to the education of the children of the colored race." Powers led the campaign for the amendment, with support from Superintendent John G. Harris and J. L. M. Curry, but it was defeated overwhelmingly by the voters. (*Acts of the General Assembly of Alabama, 1892-93,* 1215-17.)

Proceedings of the Second Hampton Negro Conference

[Hampton, Va., May 25, 1894]

Fifty graduates and twenty other students gathered in Whitin Chapel of Virginia Hall on the day following Commencement in response to the School's invitation sent sometime before, to consider various questions of practical importance to their race and to the success of their work as teachers and leaders among their people. Ten classes were represented and five states, seventeen counties of Virginia, also Maryland, North and South Carolina, Alabama and Florida. All had been and most are still teachers. Many had come at some personal sacrifice and effort, influenced both by interest in the subject of the conference and by loyalty to Hampton. The just graduated class of '94 was invited to sit with the conference, and listened with lively interest to the suggestions which they will soon have occasion to act upon. There were present also Mr. and Mrs. Henry E. Pellew of Washington; Mr. Pellew is Secretary of the Episcopal Church "Commission for church work among the Colored People of the South" — Rev. H. B. Tunnell, Dean of King Hall, a divinity school in Washington founded by that Commission; Prof. Peabody[1] of Harvard, Mr. Geo. Foster Peabody of New York, Mr. Calloway,[2] a graduate of Fisk, and others including of course the teachers and officers of Hampton.

The morning session opened with prayer, at ten o'clock. Then Dr. Frissell presiding, made an introductory statement of the origin and object of the conference, which was convened as last year, by the last invitation of the General, to see how much better work for the people can be done by Hampton and its graduates. Dr. Frissell then called on Mr. Booker T. Washington — Class of '75, principal of the Tuskegee School, Alabama, to put the first question — one of his own proposing — before the conference.

1. Are the white people of the South opposed to the purchase of land by the Negro?

Mr. Washington: "A recent number — I think the April number of the magazine published by the Baptist Home Missionary Society, says that the white people of the South oppose the buying and owning of land by the colored people. I want to ask you if you found that statement warranted by your observation in Alabama. Mr. Logan and I are convinced it is inaccurate. It is not true in that state. Of course with some there is a disposition to hold on to the land; not to sell it all; but where a white man can buy a colored man can. I believe the statement quoted is true in some parts of Louisiana, but in Georgia, Alabama, and Mississippi, I believe it is not true."

Mr. Thomas C. Walker, class of '83, a successful lawyer in Gloucester Co. Virginia: "It is not true in Virginia in my experience. The whites own a great deal of land and they want money. If a colored man has got money and wants land he can get it. I can back up this statement from the court records of Gloucester. At the close of the war the Negroes did not own one hundred acres of land in Gloucester Co.; now, they own ten thousand. This is equally true for Middlesex Co., Essex, King and Queen; all the way up the Rappahannock river they are buying up land. I never found a white man refusing to sell it to a colored man because of his color; I have seen them refuse to sell it because of his want of money to pay for it."

Mr. Wm. J. Claytor, of '90, in charge of agricultural work and training in the State Colored Normal and Industrial Institute, Tallahassee, Florida — "I have known no such case in middle Florida. I am not acquainted with the west, east, and south section of the state. In middle Florida the great trouble is that much of the land is owned by the capitalists in great tracts, and they will only sell it in large quantities. They say, How many acres do you want? If you say ten, they say no, but you can have so many hundreds. And they hold it at a greater valuation than it is worth. But it is just the same to a white purchaser as to a colored. There was a case right adjoining our school farm, where twenty acres were bought for $25 an acre."

Rev. Charles A. Boston, of '73 — Taught fourteen years, now a Baptist preacher, owns a house and lot in Roanoke city, lives in Towano,³ James City Co. "With some exception, there is no trouble; the better class of whites have no objections to sell land to the colored. The Chesapeake and Ohio Railroad Company has bought up all the land it could get and its agents are out now buying from here to Roanoke. That makes it difficult for the colored people to buy, but equally so for the white people."

Dr. Frissell: "Is there any opposite testimony?"

Mr. Geo. W. Brandom, '82: employed by the Missionary Department of the school to visit graduates and others, throughout the state. "My work takes me through all the counties of the state. The only exception I have seen to the general willingness testified to, is in the small towns and cities, where the whites don't want colored people to buy in certain localities."

Mr. Washington: "Is it the same in Boston, Massachusetts?"

Mr. Brandom, "Yes."

Mr. Warren Logan, '77: Treasurer of the Tuskegee School, Alabama. "In Tuskegee Mr. Washington owns good lots in the heart of the city."

Mr. Calloway: Graduate of Fisk University, about to enter into the service of Tuskegee in its Northern campaign for raising funds; — "I saw a deed of land in the city of Nashville one of whose conditions was that the land deeded should never be sold to a Negro; but the seller was a Northern man."

Dr. Frissell: "It seems to be the general experience of the conference (no other report of opposition having been secured by inquiry) that there is little opposition to the owning of land by the colored people, except in certain localities in some cities. Let us pass to the next question."

[2.] How much are the Negroes getting hold of land?

The last census is said to be disappointing in this particular.

Mr. Harris Barrett, '85, resident of the town of Hampton where he owns a house and lot; employed as book keeper in the Treasurer's office of the School; Secretary and Treasurer of the Colored People's Building and Loan Association in town, — "I am gratified to see how the colored people are getting hold of the land around here. Whole sections of the town are owned by them, and they are holding on to it well. It is the one aim of most of them to get a lot. Rev. Mr. Spiller's people own $20,000 worth. To be sure they owe a great deal on it yet. It is a very hopeful sign I think."

Mr. Walker, Gloucester. "Twenty per cent. of the land in Gloucester County is owned by the colored people — not all have finished paying and taken their deeds yet."

Mr. Wm. Reid, '77, practicing law with much success in Portsmouth, Va. "Efforts are made all the time to prove this or that from the census; but all such statements in regard to the comparative purchase of land, based on the census must be simply theory. In order to know whether there has been any gain or the contrary from 1880 to 1890 in the colored people's ownership of land, we should need to know just what they owned in 1880. But then no separate lists were kept of their holdings and purchases. So it is impossible to accurately tell what the difference is. But from 1890 the records have been separated, so that we shall know by the next census. So the present statement that there has been no progress is only theory."

Miss Margaret Stevens, '86, a teacher ever since graduation, in Southampton Co. "Where I live about ten per cent. of the colored people own land."

Dr. Frissell: "Is there anything to show that the colored people are losing their desire for land?"

Miss Catherine Fields, '78, resident in the town of Hampton where she owns three lots with houses on them, and where she has taught ever since graduating. "A Richmond paper recently warned the white people of the state that the colored people are getting possession of a large proportion of the land."

Mr. F. D. Banks, '76, resident in the town of Hampton where he owns his home: employed as head book keeper in the School Treasurer's office.

"I believe that the colored people are caring more than ever to own land. In Roanoke, I have a friend, a graduate of this school, who said when he went there that he meant to own land in every section of the town. One section was laid off in it, called Peach and Honey; — Just for colored people. My friend owns twenty lots in the town in different sections, one in Peach and Honey. He said nobody should be able to come into Roanoke without passing through his land, and he has accomplished that ambition. He owns land worth $80,000. His own house is not in Peach and Honey, but within a hundred and fifty yards from the principal hotel."

A visitor asked if colored women often own land. Dr. Frissell replied that many of our own graduates do. [The summary of the records of twenty classes ('72-'90) — in the book XXII Years' Work of Hampton Institute shows the amount of property reported by young women (chiefly in land, houses and live stock) is $31,115 making an average of $111.12 to each of the 280 in those classes.][4]

Miss Maggie Stevens: "I do," [most of the other graduate young women present might have echoed her response.]

Capt. Robert R. Moton, '90, Disciplinarian of the School: "The only foundation for the assertion as to decrease of land purchased, is that many at first bought too much land, and now have learned to buy smaller amounts; once they thought they must buy seven hundred or a thousand acres; now they buy from fifty to a hundred, which is better for them."

Mr. Claytor; "I know a woman in Florida who is successfully running a truck farm left her by her husband." [One of our own graduates present with her sister manages her father's farm while he runs a brick yard.]

Mr. Warren Logan of Tuskegee, asked Mr. Walker of Gloucester "What is the mode of making land sales to colored people?"

Mr. Walker: "The same as to white. If the purchaser can pay cash, he gets his deed at once; if he pays only part down, he gives his note and the granter makes a deed conveying title and the purchaser gives him a deed of trust. Sometimes he just takes a note from the buyer and as the note is paid states on the receipt what the money is for."

Mr. Barrett remarked that "there is one other way. If the purchaser wants to pay in installments the deed is given reserving the grantor's right to take it back if all is not paid in four, six or eight months, as the agreement may specify, the grantee then forfeiting all that has been paid, which is considered to go for rent of the land."

Dr. Frissell then proposed the next question for consideration.

3. Are the young people moving away from the land, to any extent — leaving the country for the cities, North and elsewhere?

Mr. George E. Stephens, Class of '74, principal of the Colored High School in Lynchburg, Va. "Yes, that is true. With those near us, the reason is the desire for better school advantages. The schools in Lynchburg run nine or ten months; in the country districts, five or less. Then Lynchburg is a great tobacco centre and they come to find employment in the tobacco factories. There is less employment now than four or five years ago, and now they go North from Lynchburg, rather than return to the country. Many are demoralized."

Dr. Frissell: "Will Mr. Walker tell the conference of the emigration I understand he has noticed."

Mr. Walker: "I referred more to Essex, King and Queen Counties, and others in that section. In Gloucester they stay at home more. From March to June, any time, going down the Rappahannock as I often do, from Fredericksburg to the mouth of the river I see a great many on the steamboats, going to take the steamer North for the summer, till the middle of November. The trouble is they don't bring back any money with them to speak of. They go with a carpet bag and come back with a carpet bag, and with little money. I never got a sensible reason from one of them for it. They don't go for money and come back to buy land. But they get attached to city life. They are not planting themselves in the earth, they are leaving the homes their fathers paid for and are getting none of their own. I don't know how we can remedy it. How can we stop those folks from going North and make them plant themselves in the earth?"

Mr. Thomas B. Patterson: '90 — in charge of agricultural work and training in the Calhoun School, (Miss Dillingham[5] and Miss Thorne's[6]) Calhoun, Ala. "There is a tendency around Calhoun, in the young men and women, to leave the farms. They don't have money enough to think of going North — that's one good thing in their favor — but in some ways the southern cities are as bad for them as the northern ones. The chief reason for their leaving the country I think is that their parents don't know how to till the soil to advantage themselves and so don't teach their children to, and they don't see what could be gotten from the soil."

Rev. Charles Boston: "It is not so in the central part of Virginia as Mr. Walker reports about Fredericksburg, still some go North because they can't make a living on the farms. In southwestern Virginia the colored people don't own as much land. In James City Co. most of them own land. You may go clear from Chickahominy Church to New Zion — five miles — and not find a white land owner. But they don't till it properly, only raise a little corn. The young people can't make money off it, so they go North; not to stay, but some send money back to help their parents. We've got to learn how to farm. Then farming is so much like work! [laughter] But people who don't own land, and women who haven't men to work it — widows and young girls — see they can't make much off the pea patch, and they go North."

Mr. John W. Lemon, '90 — teacher, farmer and land owner in Gloucester Co.: "I think this has much to do with it. In slavery, white men thought it not gentlemanly to work; the colored people haven't grown out of that idea."

Mr. Stephens of Lynchburg: "It is generally admitted that there is a disposition on the part of white young men to shun manual labor, and it is natural for the colored to take the same view. I lately saw an editorial in a white paper urging young white men to enter mechanical trades."

Dr. Frissell: "The same tendency to drift into the cities is seen in the North among the white people."

Mr. B. T. Washington of Tuskegee: "Notwithstanding this tendency in the South, ninety per cent of the colored people there are outside the large cities. That is stated in the Home Missionary Magazine of which I spoke."

Mr. Brandom: "All over Virginia, there is this tendency, and the young man who comes back from the city to buy land in the country is an exception to the rule."

Mr. Boston T. Parsons: '87 — Teacher in Norfolk Co; "I don't think the majority of our people go to the cities; a large number are going, but the large majority are in the country, stay at home."

Mr. Brandom: "I referred to the young people; young men and young women."

Jeffries '94 — home in Charlotte Co.: "In my part of the state a good many go North, but all return, buy farms and live on them."

Mr. Banks: "I know two families in Southampton Co. In one there are five boys; smart fellows; one has gone into a factory in New Jersey, one to New York city, one has a barber shop in Norfolk, one only is at home. The other family has four boys: one is employed on a steamer running from Norfolk to New York; one in a city store, one in Philadelphia, the fourth is at home off and on. Both fathers own good peanut farms, one of seventy-five the other a hundred acres."

Dr. Frissell: "Mr. Hoffman, now living in Hampton, has collected and published in the *Forum* and in pamphlet form, the vital and criminal statistics of several large cities, New York, Boston, Philadelphia, etc.; showing that the colored people there are doing very poorly; the proportion of criminals compared to that among the whites is ten to one; showing that the effect of this emigration to the cities is bad. Let us have some information as to this point."

4. How are the Negroes doing in the cities?

Mr. George Stephens: "In Lynchburg the effect is bad. The criminal class is made up of the younger people. Before the chain gang was recently abolished, I've often noticed as many as twenty young colored men in it at one time; some of them had been in the schools. I rarely have seen a grey haired or elderly man in it, one born before the war."

Mr. George Foster Peabody: "It is a general fact that the majority of criminals all over the world are young men between seventeen and thirty."

Mr. Stephens: "I don't know about that, but the question is as to the drift of the younger element of our race. It is in the wrong direction. In the streets the disorderly characters are young people. They are not settled and so are easily drawn astray. If they were employed in some useful work this wouldn't be so largely true. They have no useful employment. If an odd job comes in their way they take it, but if not they are satisfied."

Ques. — "How about the death rate?" "Yes, they live in the worst parts of the city, so the death rate is high. The best of the colored population don't die any faster than the whites, but among the poorest class are unsanitary conditions of living and no proper medical attendance."

Rev. Mr. Tunnell, Dean of King Hall, Washington, D.C. "As to the tendency of colored young men to go North and to return, my experience is that most who go to the large cities seldom or never want to return South. This is true of those who come to Washington. Howard University is itself doing a great deal to populate the city. The colored population of Washington numbers eighty thousand and is increasing. Howard University is doing a great deal to attract young people there, and they don't get out again; the city is a tremendous magnet. On the second point, as to how the colored people are doing in the cities, my experience in Boston and other places is that the influence of city life upon the colored population is constantly, steadily deleterious, harmful. What has been said of Lynchburg is precisely the case in Boston and New York; the death rate is very great, and the criminal statistics alarming. A Philadelphia judge lately, with the kindest intention, called the attention of the country to this state of things, and it comes from what has been said. Some go North to get away from injustice — from southern lynch law, etc. In the North they find they can't compete with the white mechanics and the trades unions, and from lack of employment go down to starvation, crime and death, or the penitentiary."

Mr. Benjamin Boulding, '88 — principal of the public school in Nottoway Co.: "The criminal statistics show the disproportion that has been stated — as you can read in those published by the *Smithsonian*. But this also is true of Washington. A policeman there is promoted on the largest number of arrests made, instead of because he can show that he has kept his district most peaceable so that he has had to make fewest arrests, as is the method of promotion in Chicago. The consequence is that he arrests small boys — those whom he can arrest most easily, who can make the least resistance, for very small offences. I've seen a policeman in Washington arrest four small colored boys at once for shooting at sparrows with flippers."

Mr. Henry E. Pellew of Washington, Sec'y of the Episcopal Commission for church work among the colored people. At Dr. Frissell's request, Mr. Pellew spoke on the subject as follows:

"As to the first point, the census shows a tendency of the colored population to drift from north-east to south-east. As to the cause and effect of the drift of the population to the cities, the question is complex. I have been president of a Farmer's League Club. The question has often been argued and we have not been able to fix upon the sufficient answer. The question is complex, and involved with other questions which have not been touched to-day in your discussion. The only point you have touched on to-day is the unwillingness of the young people to stay at home with their ignorant fathers on bad farms. If they are ambitious and intelligent this is natural. One of the main objects of this Institution is to teach them to make the country home what it should be; not a miserable cabin with no windows, and with a mud chimney. It can't be possible that young people will not be tempted to leave such homes to seek better opportunities. One of the first things to do is to improve the home, to induce the young people to stay in it, and teach them how to make farming profitable. The same tendency exactly is seen among the white people of the North.

"My advice is that all who can obtain country homes should do so and make them pleasant, and keep some of the family at home; if others go off to earn money, give them a home to which they look back with pleasure and which they will wish to reproduce for themselves.

"As to the second question — how the colored people are doing in the cities: — in Washington there is a curious mixture of the white and colored population. Some of the best property in Washington is owned by colored people. Within the last fortnight, some of it belonging to a colored family of thirteen was sold at $6.50 a square foot. In some of the most important streets, beautiful palaces stand beside frame buildings owned by colored men who won't sell but for their price. There is absolutely no prejudice against colored people's owning land in Washington. I would advise every colored person who can to own a home and hold it. A renter gets into difficulties; a great deal higher rent is asked of colored renters too.

"As to the third question — as to mortality in the cities, that is a question which has been thoroughly considered by the Sanitary League in Washington. It is very important that there should be such a league in every town, and in connection with it a Town Improvement Society. The statistics collected by Dr. Billings, published within the last few weeks, show that the mortality is largely among the young children under five; and that the actual average mortality is exactly double that of the whites, in the whole population. This probably arises from the more unsanitary condition of their dwellings, and is so far remediable and likely to be improved shortly.

"As to the fourth point the drift is unquestionably to the cities. It is rather unfortunate, but is intelligent and natural; and is the same at present in every country in the world. When the census previous to the last was taken the population of the cities was twenty-eight or thirty per cent. of the whole population of the country. Now it is fifty per cent. and in the next decade will probably exceed this. This tendency is unfortunate, but has some advantages. The question is how to regulate it. We American citizens [Mr. Pellew is an American citizen by choice, an Englishmen by birth] have only to hear of difficulties to find a remedy for them."

Miss Eliza Bolling, '81, of Farmville, Cumberland Co. has taught most of the time since graduating, there and in the Tuskegee School, Ala.; manages with her sister, their father's farm while he runs a brickyard. "The young people do leave home on account of having no chance of work in the country that will bring in money. If there were enough industrial schools to teach them all farming so they could farm profitably it would make a great difference. They don't mean to settle permanently in the cities, but they have nothing else to do often. Some stay and get land; some go and return and buy land. But it is hard to make enough to buy land by working on a farm. You can find very few who have bought their farms except by other ways than farming. Willie Taylor's father and my father did, but most have got their money to buy land in other ways than farming. I can't blame young women for going, for it is hard for them to work in the field."

Dr. Frissell then proposed the next question:

5. How can we obviate this tendency to leave the country and drift to the cities?

What can we do to make the home attractive, and improve agricultural industry? What can teachers do about it?

Mr. Booker Washington: "I think in seeking a remedy for this, we must bear in mind that the colored man is a very social animal, in every sense of the word. Then, as Mr. Stephens said, a great many go for school advantages. I don't believe that you can find a case where if there is a ten months school in a country district, there is a tendency to leave it. Prolong your school terms in the country districts from four or five months to nine or ten. Anchor the people to the land and they'll stay there. In a county of Alabama, four years ago only there was on what had been a large plantation, a community living in small cabins, and raising cotton only. There was a tendency among the young people to drift to Montgomery. Now there is a great improvement; the people have a church and a Sunday school, and they take newspapers, have a building and loan association and other societies; a social atmosphere, that gives the young people a centre of attraction, something pleasant to look forward to, and they are satisfied to stay at home and become prosperous on their land. And all the change has been brought about through the influence of a good industrial school established among them. The second remedy I would suggest is to put brain into agricultural work. I have lived in the country myself, and if I had to follow an old mule round year after year, I'd get out of it; but if I could get up on a cultivator and make three furrows at once as I rode over the field and drop the grain into them, and when it was up sit on a reaper under an umbrella, I'd like farming. We've got to put brain into agricultural pursuits not merely give the sweat of our brows without any profit."

Dr. Frissell: "We're trying more and more to send out good farmers from Hampton. I believe that that is the hope of the colored race. Will Mr. Goodrich please speak a word to us. He lectures to our students in our department of agriculture. He may be of help to some of you. I should be glad if you would send to him for suggestions at any time. I am glad to introduce to you Mr. Goodrich."

Mr. Charles L. Goodrich, from Stockbridge, Mass. in charge of agricultural and horticultural training at Hampton. "I am trying to do what I can. I hope to get out among the farmers. From what I have seen and heard it seems to me that many of the farmers of the South don't know how to farm to the best advantage, as to preparation of the soil, the planting, fertilizing and cultivating of the crops. The work I am trying to do in the School is to teach the boys as much as possible of the mechanical production of the soil, then of rotation of crops, the proper use of fertilizers, the care of the crop, and the knowledge of the plant itself. Some knowledge of chemistry is needed, and can readily be acquired; you can know nitrogen and phosphates as well as you can know bread and butter. We are having lectures and talks in the class room and illustrations by actual demonstration on the farm."

Dr. Frissell: "Can we have a Farmer's Conference here some time."

Mr. Thos. B. Patterson, '90, in charge of agricultural work and training in the Calhoun School, Ala. — "In Calhoun we found the people very ignorant in these ways, and we started a monthly County Farmers' Conference. The people say they never had so much benefit. Any man who teaches a country school will have no trouble about getting up a Farmer's Conference; the people are anxious to learn. We have taken up in our conference, first the question of home life and influence. A great number about us still live in one room cabins — one man who has actually twenty-five children lives with all of them in two rooms. The next thing we discussed was diversified crops instead of only cotton; now they are improving in this respect, raising half corn also hogs and chickens. Yet to-day there isn't a farmer in Lowndes Co. who has meal enough to carry his family through the rest of the year; so they will have to pay from twenty to twenty-five per cent profit for corn they might have raised. The white man says, "aught's an aught, figure's a figure — you've got the paper, and I've got the cotton." I've found that one great reason the farmer doesn't cultivate his land better there is because he doesn't own it, so he has no interest in it, and fears too that his improvements will make his rent higher."

The morning session now adjourned.

After a pleasant social noon hour, lunching together in the Recreation Hall at the School, the members of the Conference assembled at two o'clock for an afternoon session. The first question discussed was:

6. How can we bring up the character of the public schools?

At the request of Dr. Frissell, Miss Hyde,[7] our head teacher, introduced the discussion of the subject.

"General Armstrong's idea as we know was that one of Hampton's first objects is the education of teachers for the country schools. We feel more strongly than ever that this is one of the first objects before us. That is why we are now offering to our graduates an advanced normal course; which doesn't mean Latin, but advanced training along the same line you have been studying here. My recent trip through the South convinced me of the importance of this. I visited a great many schools, and found too many teachers using words and signs instead of objects; the children talking and reading about things instead of looking at the thing first. There were too few objects used. Some said it was hard work to obtain them, but often they might have got all they needed by going out doors. They had eyes but they saw not. I have brought here some objects that we use in our own classes, for the purpose of showing you how easy and simple a matter it is to provide yourselves with them. We feel we haven't yet done enough of this. We are trying to unify the manual training and academic work. We feel that unless nearly every study is helped by the eye and hand it doesn't amount to much. For example, here are little pumps made by students of the class in physics — they will work. Here are various measurers, made by the Seniors from patterns procured from the tin-shop. I found the children — and our own classes, talking about gills, pints and quarts, without a clear idea of those measures; a child that handles these measures, fills one from another, day after day — doesn't have to study the table from the book. Some of the teachers in the country say they can't get tin measures — or can't afford to. We are going to have all our Seniors make such as these to take back with them. You see they are made of manilla card board and so fastened that they can be taken apart and laid out flat in a trunk. Of course

439

they won't hold water, but you can fill them with sand and they are vastly better than nothing. Then we make the dry measure in the same way; and make up bundles of different weight, pounds, etc., in packages of many different substances of different bulks. Then here is a large card board on which are fastened a collection of specimens of vegetable products of the place — made by the students themselves. Here is a putty map made by a student — like a sand map, but more lasting. Here are foot-rules, and tape measures, made by the middlers to take out with them when they go to teach. Here are our different kinds of models made by the students in the physiology class to show the manner and effect of expanding and contracting the lungs. A great many things like them can easily be devised and made by teachers and students.

"Now I want to ask you if anything can be done by our graduate teachers to send us a more thoroughly prepared class of students. What is in the way of it and how can it be done? We find very often that the application paper — made out by the pupil but endorsed by the teacher — claims better preparation than his examination proves him to have."

Dr. Frissell: "The question is How can we all make our work more thorough. One of General's last words to the school was, 'Do what you can do well, and do it as well as you can.' That is what has made the school a success thus far, and we must do all we can to live up to it."

Mr. Wm. J. Claytor, '90, now teacher in Wake Co., N.C. for two years in charge of farm work and training in State Normal and Industrial School in Tallahassee, Fla. "One great difficulty in the way is that the school terms are so short; and the teachers are so often changed. Many stay in one place only a year; then a new teacher comes, sets the pupil back to the beginning of the book and changes the method. The reason for the changes of teacher is that the salaries are so scant. When the legislature provides ten months and better salaries, and a good teacher stays in the same school for years, improvement can be made."

Dr. Frissell: "In Alabama, in many places, the people have lengthened the school terms themselves. If General Armstrong had waited for the government to establish this school, it never would have been established. He went at it without encouragement. You can't wait for government to make the improvements, make it yourselves. The question is How can you do it?"

Mr. Wm. B. Weaver — Middle class of '75 — Principal of the very successful Gloucester Normal and Industrial School founded by himself: "Hampton's second son," as he well calls it. "One trouble is teachers push the children on into the Fifth Reader before they can read the Third. They don't grade their schools right. If Hampton would send on a graded program, or schedule, it would be a great help to their work.

"As to securing longer terms, the people can do it, one way or another by going to work, making some sacrifices. We have succeeded in doing it in Gloucester County. When I was teaching a county school there, we lengthened the term almost every year, and added to the county school building; and the people are doing it still. Superintendent and school officers will agree to an improvement when they see it accomplished, but if you wait for them to begin, you will never have it."

Dr. Frissell: "I want to bear testimony to the successful work Mr. Weaver has done in Gloucester by going at it without waiting for others to begin, and also the work brother Spiller has done here at Hampton to increase the people's interest in educating their children."

Mr. John W. Lemon — '77: "Last winter, we got up meetings and entertainments in Gloucester and Mathews Cos. to get up interest in education. We feel if we can get them interested in educating themselves, and see that if the Negroes must be educated, they must see to it themselves, it will be a great thing done."

Rev. Mr. Spiller — pastor of First Baptist Church in the town of Hampton: "I have been much impressed with what Miss Hyde has said. I wish I could say all I feel on that point. One thing that has injured our public school system in some parts of the state is politics. That has caused perpetual changing of teachers. But it is not the case in this county, and not anywhere in the state as it was some years ago. Another reason for teachers' lack of success, they hold off from the people sometimes, don't visit the parents enough. We must labor to interest the parents and the people generally, for the time is coming when we must do more to help ourselves in educating our children or they will not be educated."

Mr. Whit T. Williams, '76 — one of the original "Hampton Student Singers," teaching ever since his graduation, resident of Norfolk, where he owns a home: "So far as lengthening the school term is concerned, that can be done whenever it is desirable. This is the truck gathering season, when the children must unavoidably be taken out of school. Our boards in Norfolk Co. run the schools till the trucking season opens — except in one district where they run six months. In one place I taught, the people always lengthened the terms themselves a month or six weeks.

"I have never found trouble in working up an interest, at the Brown's Hill School, for instance, the people raised $50 for patent desks. The Board generally have only just enough money for a short term. Now in Norfolk county there is no money in the Treasury. School boards will assist when they can. I am not teaching just now, but I am interested in the schools and believe in Miss Hyde's talk, and Mr. Weaver's suggestion of a schedule from Hampton."

Mr. Washington: "In Alabama the first thing our teachers have to do is to get a school house; the state only gives what it can for the salary. The average school term is three and a half months, for country and city. We try to make a specialty of having our teachers from Tuskegee settle down and stay in one place. The first two or three years the teacher has a hard time to get the confidence of the people. They have been deceived so often — by teachers, preachers, politicians, everybody — that they are suspicious. But after two or three years, it is not hard to get the people to give something to extend the school term, two, three or four months. A few days before I came here, in one community a teacher told me the people had paid $670 to extend the school term. A few years ago they had no school house; now they have a school running eight months, with three or four teachers. Something like that can be done in every community in the South. I know some teachers who get their students together out of school hours to raise cotton to help do this. One school raised two bales, that equals $70 — or two or three months school. The state appropriation for education is very small; the children increase faster than the money increases. We shall have no school at all after awhile unless we help ourselves. The people are glad to do it."

Mr. Weaver, "It is a good way to begin collecting at the beginning of the term. I want to urge on the Conference the idea that has been suggested of having a meeting of the Superintendents of the state to consider these things."

Dr. Frissell: "I will do all I can to bring it about; will go myself to see State Superintendent Massey.[8] We are to have a summer 'Institute' here from July 12th to August 8th. Remember you are all children of Hampton, children of the General; pushing ahead, not satisfied with the past."

Rev. Chas. Boston: "I believe there is a great deal in a teacher staying in a place. The way to get the people to lengthen the term is to make the teaching so good the children will like to come to school. Our school terms in Norfolk County have been lengthened by the people's contributions."

Mr. Charles Vanison, '77, long in charge of the School's Hemenway farm and now successfully working a farm of his own near Hampton: "I know a teacher — a Hampton graduate, who has been teaching near me for two years and has so won the love of the children and respect of the parents that that teacher is wanted as long as he will stay."

Dr. Frissell: "How many here have taught in one place two years? How many four? How many six?" Almost all hands were raised on the first inquiry — and a good many on the last.

Miss Nellie Evans, '85; a teacher in the same school in Gloucester County, her home, ever since graduating, first as assistant of another Hampton graduate, and afterwards as principal: "I think more can be accomplished through staying in one place than just lengthening the term. The trustees in our county keep us in one school as long as they can, and give the teachers from the County preference, so we can be more with the people and do more."

Mr. Andrew Bassett, '76, teaching near Hampton; also a lawyer; owns a farm: "I taught two terms in Sussex County, and was then transferred to this county. The school board here is making efforts to do all it can for the schools; it would run them all ten months if it could. It makes no difference as to politics, we're all democrats, republicans and readjusters as it may be. The only reason a teacher is kept is because they can't find a better one. When the people are attached to a teacher, the Superintendent will keep him. When we only had five or six months, I'd go to the Superintendent and ask him, 'Can you cut my pay down and run one month more?' So we'd run on to six, seven or eight months. In Chesapeake District they ran the school eight months. Some teachers put themselves in opposition to the trustees because of politics. It is foolish in them."

Dr. Frissell then put the next question.

[7.] How far can we carry out the idea of Industrial and Agricultural education in public schools?

"I hope that the time will come when there will be some such instruction in every public school. Mr. Walker tells me that the school law of Virginia at present forbids it, that they require the carrying out of a regular schedule. How is that?"

Mr. Geo. Stephens: "Something of it might be done. In the first place it needs knowledge in the teacher. If he has knowledge of it he can introduce it to some extent, for the idea is being advocated by some of the state officers. The teacher must urge it on the Superintendent, he will urge it on the state officers, they on the legislature, and so the way will be opened. The most important of the trade teaching at Hampton will be lost unless we can get it into our public schools. Our Superintendent in Lynchburg is favorable to it. Teachers should take some educational journal and keep posted on advanced educational methods. The educational journals and papers are favorable to industrial education for industrial training is what every American boy needs — to know how to win his bread. All we teachers have to do is to unite in the effort. A teacher from Hampton might go round to different schools and be paid to give lessons in this line."

Mr. Washington: "I heard a colored teacher tell what he had accomplished in Louisville where there are the best colored public schools in the South, but there was no industrial training. He introduced sewing — both for girls and boys — the Superintendent saw and was struck by it, and now it is in all the colored schools in the city, in every building and every room."

Mrs. Annie J. Cooper of Washington, author of "A Voice from the South by a Black Woman of the South," a woman of culture, and ability and of experience as a teacher: "I believe in industrial education with all my heart. We can't all be professional people. We must have a back bone to the race. It was once doubted if a Negro had a soul. After it was found that he had a soul, there was still question whether he had brain. A little time ago, a descendant of Calhoun said that if Calhoun had known what he knew about the Negro's brain power, there would not have been the war. There is a crisis ahead in the labor question. The foreign element is unstable, and restive, ready for strikes, and as a rule impatient of control. The people of this country will inevitably look around for a stable working class. When the time comes for the need to be appreciated and satisfied, the Negro must be ready to satisfy it; there will be no prejudice against the colored man as a worker.

"In slavery days, the white man taught the colored man trades to make a better tool of him and make himself richer. Now the old Negro master mechanics are dying out and those white men who have the skill are closing the doors against all, colored or white who are outside the ring. If our young men are to have trades they must get them in industrial schools. If I were a boy I'd get to Europe some how and see if I couldn't get hold of some special superiority at a trade, and come back and teach it to all the colored boys I could get hold of."

Dr. Frissell: "I hope we may establish here and elsewhere agricultural conferences. Can't we at least cultivate the grounds around our school buildings? Miss Fields, could you not fix up the school grounds as I saw you had the inside of your room. How about that Mr. Spiller?"

Mr. Harris Barrett: "When I went to school in the country, my teacher used to make us work a flower garden."

Dr. Frissell: "I remember how I was impressed by Mr. Weaver in Gloucester with a paint brush in his hand, painting his own school house. It is a good lesson for the children, and good to make them help."

Mr. John W. Lemon, '77, Gloucester: "Simply speaking to my girls about neatness, I found had great effect. The larger girls have a committee to dust, etc. every recess; the boys to sweep the yard. Every fall I carry an axe and have the bushes cleared away."

Elder Spiller: "For twenty-two years I have been a preacher, but I am also a teacher, a carpenter, a painter and a whitewasher. I have to pray forgiveness for the sins of my school yard. I have very little time, but I try to improve. I have my scholars pick up papers, etc. I'll say this, you can tell a Hampton Normal School student anywhere, teacher or scholar for their neatness and attention to such things."

Dr. Frissell announced the next question:

[8.] How can Hampton be more helpful to its graduates — for instance, can it be helpful in teaching them more about business?

Mr. Thos. Patterson, '90, Calhoun, Alabama: "That is one way. I think the greatest efforts should be put into trades. Our people must be really skilled to compete with white mechanics."

Mr. Wm. M. Reid, '77, Portsmouth; "The more I see of people the more I see the utter lack of business knowledge. They need instruction in keeping accounts; to know the difference between the debit and credit. It is a difficult matter to find a man who doesn't belong to some society. In the societies very much money is collected and much is lost, not from dishonesty of purpose, but from ignorance of accounts. This school can't give its students too much knowledge of book keeping."

Mr. Thos. C. Walker, '83, Gloucester C. H. "Skilled labor is the solution to the question. When we started the Gloucester High School, we wanted to give it to a colored man in the county, but we couldn't find a skilled man nearer than Norfolk and gave it to a white man. Now a Hampton boy is putting up the new buildings and doing it just right."

Miss Mamie Grooms, '77, Baltimore, Md., of long successful experience in country and city schools: "I think it is of great importance that our people be taught carefulness. An instance of the too common want of this came under my observation lately. I had occasion to have some printing done. It was a nice job and I wanted to give it to a colored printer who I knew did some good artistic work. He kept my letter a week without answering it. I went to his place and inquired about it. He said he had been waiting to call to see me about it. I told him there was no need of that; he might have just written. He said 'I don't do that kind of work' — there was some engraving to be done. I said why didn't you tell me; you have put back my work and made me lose confidence in you as a business man. I shan't be likely to send you any more work or advise others to. He said, 'It wouldn't pay me to learn to do that kind of work. I would be old before I learned it.' Well, I said, I think you make a great mistake. If I were in your place I'd want to fit myself to do all in my line in the best way and attend promptly to every opportunity. I think that business training is of great importance to our people."

Miss Catherine Fields of Hampton; "I know an old man in Hampton who is not a skilled mechanic, but he is never without employment; the white people are after him all the while to work for them. I met him late one evening, after six, and I said to him 'Where are you going now — not going to work at this hour are you?' He said he had been piling lumber, and he saw a storm was coming on, and he thought it ought to be covered so the builders would have no trouble with it the next day — and he was going to see about it. That is the secret of his being always wanted. He's the first man at his work and the last to leave it; and he takes an interest in it just as if it were his own; doesn't grudge extra time or extra work now and then. That's what we all want to learn."

Dr. Frissell: "We are trying to push the idea of business training here, and the trades. If any of you know some young people who ought to have trades, send them to us. Don't send us indifferent material, boys their teachers and parents want to get rid of. Picked material is what we ought to have. Talk up Hampton to the people. Some of the children in a graduate's school I visited didn't know about Hampton. That can't be so in many I'm sure; but I hope you will all in this way try to help Hampton's work for your people."

· · · · [9]

Southern Workman, 23 (July 1894), 122-27.

[1] Francis Greenwood Peabody, professor of philosophy at Harvard.
[2] Thomas J. Calloway.
[3] Toano.
[4] Brackets here and elsewhere in this document appeared in the original.
[5] Mabel Wilhelmina Dillingham.
[6] Charlotte R. Thorn.
[7] Elizabeth Hyde.
[8] John E. Massey.
[9] Francis Greenwood Peabody and Edwin D. Mead made short addresses at the end of the conference.

From Richard Theodore Greener

New York City, May 26, 1894

My dear Prof. Thanks for your kind note just rec'd. I am glad you like the article, which is very incomplete, many passages cut out to suit the small space, and it is besides, full of misprints. I had no chance to correct the proof, and my hurried chirography puzzled the printer. I have never been idle, in this line, although I have not had my say over my own signature. I am doing my work in my own way, since there is no chance for me to do it in the way I should prefer for the race. Of course, I am aware, while scoring the white people for their ignorance of the Negro's past, that the Negro himself for the most part is equally ignorant of it. He needs to know it, to hold his head up higher, for after all it is something to have traditions behind you.

I have many facts, to illustrate all the points I make, which I may incorporate with the article into a lecture, or a pamphlet, or into a volume of my speeches, and addresses, which I hope sometime to publish.

I am devoting myself now to literary work, what I always should have done, and, perhaps, it may be found in time, that my pen has not been idle nor my influence lost, because for a time I had disappeared beneath the waters. I never was in better health or spirits for real work, and there is much to be done. Neither the white nor the Black Problem will be settled in our day.

I always keep the run of you, through the papers, and your little journal, which comes regularly, and feel proud naturally of your work. How great an advance since my visit of 1884! You can always depend on me to sustain you by words or counsel, inadequate as they may be. If my two years work in So. Car. can give as it does occasionally glimpses of some good done there what must yours be for Alabama and the South, fifty years from now? Have you paid much attention to the land question, the getting hold of the *public lands* in the state? My dream is to hold the South, ultimately to dominate it: but I know well the only way to do that is to get possession of the soil. But I suppose all such questions were debated at your conference. But I have never forgotten the trips we took to Selma, Marion &c., and the amount of land I then saw unoccupied, apparently. You know how hard it is to gain an entrance into any leading journal, when one speaks hotly. Therefore, I should feel indebted if you, or any one else would write to Mr. Hale,[1] the more the better, and thank *him* for the bravery he shows, in allowing me to say what I could scarcely have said elsewhere. This is due to Mr. Hale, because when I wrote to him on other lines, showing what ought to be done, he cordially said write such an article for me, I will publish it. Yours &c.

R. T. G.

Another thought, while I think of it. Any additional facts, touching on the points I have made should be brought out in the colored press. I have much data myself, and am anxious to gain additional ones. An article I wrote some 12 years ago, started a dozen other articles, and I have been amused sometimes to see it reproduced almost entire. That is all right. All published thought is the property of the world, and is best of service, when used quoted, and spread abroad. Have you never thought of enlarging your paper, and making it a vehicle of news, for the race as well as Tuskegee? It is worth considering. Hastily,

G.

ALI Con. 107 BTW Papers DLC.

[1] Edward Everett Hale.

To Halle Tanner Dillon Johnson

[Tuskegee, Ala.] June 12, 94

Dr. Johnson: I have made careful inquiry and investigation and I find it to be the invariable rule of our Treasurer to deduct from the wages of teachers when ever they have 2 or more continuous weeks of sickness. This being the rule he had no authority to make an exception in your case, there are several cases where teachers have been more or less on the sick list for some time but when ever they have been sick for 2 *weeks at a time* deduction has been made. This much as to the other side.

In view of the professionally high character of your services, your faithfulness, the extra work performed in many ways without compensation, and still further in view of the fact of your being hired by the year I shall ask Mr. Logan to deduct for but one month only during the time that you were sick. Yours Res.

Booker T. Washington

ALpS Con. 113 BTW Papers DLC.

From William Jenkins

Washington July 1, 1894

Dear Mr. Washington: Unless all indications are deceptive, I am sure that you could spend a few very profitable weeks here in Washington. The Southern men seem bent on proving to the country that they are the Negro's best friends. The Atlanta Exposition is to have a Col'd. Commissioner. I nominate you for the position on the first ballot. The Washington Post champions the idea.[1] Senator Walsh[2] is saying many good things about the Negro.

You might not care to be a Comsr. But I feel sure that you are the best fitted of any man in the South for organizing the Col'd. Exhibit. Then again you would have an opportunity to make a world wide reputation second not even to Fred. Douglas.

I would advise that you come here ostensibly for the purpose of looking out for a slice of that Freedman Bureau pie in the meantime I can assist you in getting an airing through the press here which airing would be of immense help to you & the cause you represent. "All things come to those who wait" is an old saying; but in these times of rivalry and competition the hustler gets there every time.

Enclosed clipping is from Sunday Post. An inquiry was sent to the Treas. last week as to how much of the Freed'm fund remains. The parties that recd the Home money were comparatively unknown. How much advantage you would have in this respt!! Your Friend

Jenkins

ALS Con. 6 BTW Papers ATT. Original destroyed.

[1] In an editorial, "Give the Colored Folks a Chance," the Washington *Post* said: "The suggestion that some representative colored man be placed upon the board of commissioners of the Atlanta Exposition should encounter no opposition. As many colored men as may be needed to look after the interests of the race on this great occasion should be assigned to duty as a matter of course." Blacks in the South had made phenomenal progress since the Civil War, it said, and a comprehensive exhibit would cast instructive light on the race problems yet remaining. (Washington *Post*, June 26, 1894, 4.)

[2] Patrick Walsh (1840-99) was U.S. senator from Georgia by appointment in 1894-95.

An Announcement in the Indianapolis *Freeman*

[Tuskegee, Ala., July 7, 1894]

THE NEGRO CHAUTAUQUA

Last year the Independent published an article from the pen of Prof. Nathan B. Young, Tuskegee, Ala., headed "A Chautauqua for

Negroes." This was certainly a pleasant surprise to many colored preachers, lawyers, physicians and other brain workers throughout the South, who had long looked for just such an opportunity — an opportunity to carry their wives and children to some respectable place where both pleasure and instruction could be secured. Beginning August 21 and continuing till August 31 there will be another "Chautauqua for Negroes," and it is to be hoped that every colored man who can possibly do so will take advantage of this rare opportunity and bring his family and friends to what is known as the Tuskegee Summer Assembly. The program is replete with lectures by persons, men and women, of known and singular ability. The preacher who comes will have an opportunity to add to his stock of theological information facts of the highest order; the school teacher cannot go away without having been benefitted by the many presentations of the best and latest methods of school governments, including all branches of pedagogy; the housewife, the loving mother, will learn many new things which she never knew could be put into practice in that most sacred place on earth, the home.

In addition to these many pleasures and opportunities, there will be an abundance of opportuntiies for amusement, research and study.

For particulars regarding rates, etc., address, Booker T. Washington, Tuskegee Institute, Tuskegee, Ala.

Indianapolis *Freeman,* July 7, 1894, 3.

From George Washington Murray[1]

Washington D.C. July 7, 1894

Dear Friend: I have been intending, or planning to write you since my return from your magnificent institution, in whose praise I am very loud at all times and in all places.

I am now preparing a bill appropriating all the money belonging to the estates of deceased colored soldiers — amounting to about four hundred thousand dollars to establish and maintain in different sections of our country three or four institutions model[ed] upon the plan of yours for the literary and industrial training of colored youths.

I intend making yours one of them.

I want you to furnish me with all the information possible, both as to the plan of your institution and the results obtained. I want it to use in my speech before congress in advocacy [of] my bill.

Please forward my cut at the earliest possible moment to Mr. J. J. Washington   Beaufort S.C.

Tender my kindest regards to the madame. I am very truly yours

Geo. W. Murray

ALS Con. 7 BTW Papers ATT. Original destroyed. In another hand is the note: "Ans. Cut was retd to the Freeman."

[1] George Washington Murray (1853-1926) was born a slave at Rembert, Sumter County, S.C. Orphaned after the Civil War, he secured an education and taught school for fifteen years. He attended the University of South Carolina from 1874 to 1876. He was defeated for the South Carolina House of Representatives in 1884. In 1888 he became chairman of the Republican party in Sumter County. For two years, 1890-92, he was inspector of customs for the port of Charleston. Closely associated with the Colored Farmers' Alliance, he rose from the ranks to defeat two veteran politicians, one of whom was Robert Smalls, for the congressional nomination in 1892. He then went on to win the congressional seat on a free silver platform. In 1894 he lost the election to William Elliott, but he successfully contested it and regained his seat early in 1896, only to lose it again in the elections of 1896 and 1898. He returned to Sumter County as a farmer and real-estate dealer. Convicted of forgery in 1904 or 1905, he fled to Chicago, where he remained until his death. He was often referred to as "the Republican Black Eagle." (Tindall, *South Carolina Negroes*, 56-58.)

From Thomas McCants Stewart, Jr.[1]

Tuskegee, Ala. July 11th 1894

Dear Prof. Washington: Conserning the trouble which I have lately had, I feel as if it is no more than simply my duty as doing justic to myself that I may obtain justic and not only that but because it is my duty to let you know of such that happens to me while here. However I feel safe in saying that should you have been here we would have gotton justic and everything been done in a just way. But the faculty has ered in many ways — which I shall try to the best of my ability to do. Where the trouble first started was from a pan of water which was put over the door for another boy and Mr. Penny while slipping around caught it — that is came in the door, and the water fell on him, thus;

You know that we room in Washington Cottage just above the hospital — there are two rooms which the boy[s] are permitted to use — the boys here are all like brothers and often play between the two rooms — different sorts of tricks — so on July the 4th — Wed. night one of the boys in the other room whose name is Pullin[2] put a man [pan?] of water over the door to catch any one of us that would come in there — as often we do for water (freash) after bell at night before bed, so do they come to us when they have none. Henry E. Johnson[3] who rooms here in Marshall's[4] place for the summer went to the next room and opening the door to go in the pan of water fell on him. He took it as a joke as it was intended and on the following Saturday night I and Henry put a pan of water over our door to catch Pullin who has gone to town and would not be back until late. Before he came K. D. Williams[5] who rooms in the other room came to our door we told him not to come in but he came and knock the first pan down so we put up another one and *about* five minutes after Mr. Williams left the room some one was down at the gate calling   no one heard except Gilchrist[6] who said that he said he was coming up — we did not know that it was Mr Penny because he neaver stands down stairs and calls at the gate so that was no ans. and no one heard him coming up stairs until he pushed the door open and the water and pan fell down on him. He did not knock and slipped up stairs to see who was up with the lamp burning low (as it was after last bell and Chris had just gotten in from locking the office) (Saturday night) and Chris was bathing. Had Mr. Penny knocked or walked up stairs we might have heard him and told him to wait as we told K. D. Williams at first but *no* he wanted to slip around and catch who was up. When he come in and turned the light up we explained and begged pardon and expressed our sorrow for him in many ways and did all in our power to show and tell him how the matter was but he would not grant pardon or believe that we put it there for the other fellow and went out Sunday morn. putting out the report that we put a pan of water up over the door for him. He got the report well circulated so as to be ready on Mon. afternoon to carry his point as to having me expelled as he said *before hand I should be.*

Monday morn. Mr Penny came and took me from the printing office and told me that he was going to move me from Washington Cottage leaving Chris there and putting no one in my place just simply moving me because he wanted to do something to make it unpleasent for me. He gave me my choice between two rooms one in No. 11 — a durty broken cottage out in the field — with Alger Bryant[7] and a room with another boy in a nother cottage quite as bad. I told him that I did not like the room or the boys and that please get me a room where Chris and I could move togather   he refused to do so saying that if I did not get out of Washington Cottage ere 7 o clock that day my things would be in the hall   so I then emphaticaly refuse to move unless he move me to Phelp Hall he said he would not. As I understand it and have alway understood it not only from *you* but from my *farther* we were always to room to gather while here and that we were to keep this room here in Washington Cottage or move to Phelp Hall both of us always rooming to gather always. Upon those grounds I did not move.

Now he (Mr Penny) goes to the faculty with his tale all mad up determined to have me expelled (with the assisants of Mr Young) he makes matters just as bad as he possibly can, tells the faculty I do not respect him; and that the room does not like him — makes matters just as bad as he possibly can. The faculty does not hear the boys of the rooms neither do they hear me or investigate the matter at all, have not eaven had up before a committe and no one in their knows about it except those I've personaly gone and seen. The faculty takes what *he says* to be true and expells me warns Johnson, gives Chris a repremand and thus it is. Prof. Washington honestly the thing has not been given justic and I wish you would attend to it at once. Those people that personaly have investigated it say it is a shame.

Mr. Penny has not liked me and that is why or one of the main reasons why I did not want to stay this summer. I can get on with every one else all right. When Mr Calloway[8] had the boys I did not have any trouble. I am sorry that this has accured for I am quite anxious to finish my trade and also have a course in music next year. I did enjoy my work very much and Mr Mann has alway encouraged me. I went to see Mr. J. H. Washington about work as Mr Mann as a plenty for me. But he was sick. Shall see him as soon as he gets up and try to get work as a journey-man until you come or this is settled. For Mr Washington after this is investigated, truly, investigated if you say that I should be expelled Johnson warned and Chris repromanded I am willing to take such for I think that you will deal justly with it. Mr Penny said many thing which we can *prove* are not true conserning the water   the fact is that justic has not been given. I've been to every teacher on the faculty and they say that they have not power to do any thing. You see you are away and there is realy no head to any thing at all.

Hopeing to hear from you at an early date. I am as ever   Yours truly

McCants Stewart

ALS   Con. 7   BTW Papers   ATT.   Original destroyed.

¹ Thomas McCants Stewart, Jr., son of the famous black lawyer and minister, entered the Tuskegee B middle class in 1892. His father sent him to Tuskegee with full knowledge of his son's unruly and intractable nature: "He has *always* given trouble. . . . Mac is dominated by the Harris blood and influence, I am sure that what you say of the grandmother is true. Mac has never learned to *obey* — even *me*." (Stewart to BTW, July 16, 1894, Con. 7, BTW Papers, ATT. Original destroyed.) Stewart Sr. urged BTW to handle Mac firmly: "I feel *sure* that you would deal with Mac as with your own son. Just be sure that his body keeps *warm*, and feet *dry*; and the coarser the clothing the better in the end for him, I think. He would like nothing better than to pose as 'the dude' of his neighborhood." (Stewart to BTW, Sept. 27, 1894, Con. 108, BTW Papers, DLC.) After graduating from Tuskegee in 1896, Stewart attended law school at the University of Minnesota, where he was business manager of the *Twin City American*. He graduated in 1901 and moved to Oregon.

² Charles Pullin of Atlanta was in the junior class in 1893-94. He did not graduate.

³ Henry Edwin Johnson of Brunswick, Ga., was a junior in 1893-94. He was in the A middle class in 1897-98 and apparently did not graduate.

⁴ Probably Charles Lives Marshall of Henderson, Ky., in the A middle class in 1893-94. He graduated in 1895. He taught shoemaking at Wiley University for a year, and became principal and instructor of shoemaking at Christiansburg Industrial Institute.

⁵ King David Williams of Rome, Ga., was in the D class of the night school in 1893-94. He did not graduate.

⁶ Gilchrist Stewart (Chris), son of Thomas McCants Stewart, entered Tuskegee Institute in the B middle class in 1892 and graduated in dairying in 1895. He studied dairy science at the University of Wisconsin and taught at South Dakota Agricultural College and at Ontario Agricultural College at Guelph, Ont. Later he moved to New York City, where he became a lawyer and took an active part in race affairs. John E. Milholland, president of the Constitutional League, employed Stewart as an organizer and attorney. In 1906 Joseph B. Foraker employed him to investigate the Brownsville affray, and Stewart was one of the earliest persons to reach what is now the generally accepted conclusion, that the two black regiments dismissed from the Army for alleged rioting were innocent.

Stewart occasionally relayed information regarding race matters in New York to BTW and his chief New York contact, Charles W. Anderson. His affiliations and ideas were more militant than those of Washington's lieutenants, however, and he moved to the side of Washington's critics. An early activist in the NAACP, Stewart headed the New York Vigilance Committee, which investigated cases of discrimination against blacks in greater New York. In 1911 the committee's success in winning several cases involving discrimination in an amusement park and a New York theater was instrumental in shaping the NAACP's aggressive legal work on behalf of black citizens. (Kellogg, *NAACP*, 39, 121-24.)

[7] Algie Bryant of Union Springs, Ala., was in the B class of the night school in 1893-94.

[8] James Nathan Calloway.

From Margaret James Murray Washington

Tuskegee Ala   July 19 1894

Have been ill two weeks. Why not write me.

Maggie J Washington

HWSr   Con. 7   BTW Papers   ATT.   Original destroyed.

An Announcement in the Indianapolis *Freeman*

[Tuskegee, Ala., July 21, 1894]

TUSKEGEE SUMMER ASSEMBLY

There are hundreds of ministers and other brain workers in the South who, with their wives and friends, would gladly go away during the summer for a few months of rest, recreation and study, but heretofore, they have had no place to go. The Tuskegee Institute has decided to supply this need.

Phelps Hall, the large new building recently completed, has large cool rooms, a wide veranda all around it, and is in every way suited for the purpose.

The Assembly will convene Tuesday, August 21st, and will close Friday, August 31st. Lectures by persons of known ability will be given each day on the following subjects: Theology — E. J. Penney, A.M., Dean, "The proper observance of the Sabbath"; "Relation between Religion and Politics." The Family — Marriage, Divorce,

Polygamy; "What is the true basis of Church Union?" "A Layman's advice to the Ministry." Ministry — "The relation between Morals and Religion"; "The Uses and Abuses of Property"; "The Negro Ministry, its rise and progress"; "The Negro Ministry, its present needs."

Methods of School Work — Prof Nathan B. Young, A.M., Dean. Twelve lectures will be delivered upon the following subjects considered from a pedagogical standpoint. These lectures, in a large measure, will be simply suggestive; not exhaustive. The latest methods of teaching these subjects will be given and that, too, in such a way that the teacher will be able to follow them in practice or in study. To this end each lecturer will supply his class with the bibliography (or list of authorities) of his subjects: "A System of Physical Culture"; "Advantages of Musical Education"; "Nature study through Language study"; "How to make History Interesting"; "University Extension"; "Fractions taught Objectively"; "Shall we write Vertically?" "The economy of Blackboards and Charts"; "Literature for Grammar and Primary Grades"; "Correlation of Studies." Matters pertaining to school economy, etc., will be discussed incidentally. The plan is to make the meeting not only a school of methods, but also a school for study and review.

Domestic Economy — Mrs. Warren Logan, Dean: "Domestic Culture"; "Woman's work for Woman"; "Fruit, Fresh and Preserves"; "Health: Children's claims on Parents"; "Breads and Pastries"; "Substitute for Saloons: Music in the home."

EXPENSES

Including board, room, furniture, light and lectures will be $3.00 per week in advance. Those who wish to board elsewhere and attend the lectures, will be charged $1.00 per week. The social and recreative features will not be overlooked. Besides the music furnished by an orchestra, there will be entertainments of various kinds at night. There will be abundant opportunity for such innocent games as croquet, lawn tennis, for drives in the country, etc.

LOCATION

Tuskegee Institute is located near the center of Alabama, in one of the most cultivated towns in the South, and can be easily reached by railroad. It is one mile from the center of the town, on a farm on high land, with large groves near by. No whisky is sold in the county, and the location is quiet and retired, just the place for rest. Tuskegee has always been noted for healthfulness, and the nights in Tuskegee in August are always cool and pleasant. Tuskegee is forty miles east of Montgomery, and five miles from Chehaw Station on the Western railroad, with which it is connected by the Tuskegee railroad.

NEED OF REST

Many ministers, teachers and other brain workers, feel that they cannot afford to take a rest. Experience shows that any one who gives himself one or two weeks of rest and change of scenery, can do much better work because of it. It is especially urged that churches provide the means for their minister to attend the "Tuskegee Assembly."

BILL OF FARE

Everything possible will be done to provide a good and tempting bill of fare for each meal. Among the lecturers will be all or a portion of such well known persons as these: Rev. R. M. Cheeks,[1] B.D., Rev. R. T. Pollard, Rev. W. J. Larkin, Rev. J. W. E. Bowen, Rev. E. J. Penney, A.M., N. B. Young, A.M., J. Q. Johnson,[2] A.B., Mrs. Hallie Dillon Johnson, M.D., Mrs. Booker T. Washington, A.B., Prof. J. D. McCall, A.B., Rev. H. B. Peterson,[3] B.D. Those who expect to come should write at once and engage rooms. Address: Booker T. Washington, Tuskegee, Ala.

Indianapolis *Freeman,* July 21, 1894, 1.

[1] Pastor of St. John's A.M.E. Church, Montgomery.

[2] John Quincy Johnson, born in 1870, graduated from Fisk University in 1890. He later studied at Princeton Theological Seminary and Hartford Theological Seminary, where he secured a B.D. degree. He taught mathematics at Tuskegee in 1893-94. In 1894 he married Dr. Halle Tanner Dillon. He left Tuskegee in 1894 to become president of Allen University and dean of its theological school for a year. From 1895 to 1898 he was an A.M.E. minister in Montgomery, and later held pastorates in Birmingham (1898-1900), Nashville (1900-1903), and Princeton, N.J.

[3] Butler H. Peterson, as assistant in Phelps Hall Bible School. On the staff of Tuskegee from 1893 to 1903, he taught at various times Bible history, sacred geography, mathematics, and mental and moral science.

From William Edward Burghardt Du Bois[1]

Gt. Barrington, Mass., 27 July '94

President Washington, Sir! May I ask if you have a vacancy for a teacher in your institution next year? I am a Fisk and Harvard man (A.B. & A.M.) & have just returned from two years abroad as scholar of the John F. Slater trustees. My specialty is history and social science but I can teach German, philosophy, natural science classics &c. You[r] wife knows of me, and I refer by permission to

President Gilman, Johns Hopkins Univ., Baltimore

Secretary Harvard Univ.,

    5 University Hall, Cambridge

President   Fisk Univ. Nashville

Rev. C. C. Painter of Indian Rights Association.

President Calloway of Alcorn

I can procure letters from any and all of these. Respectfully yours,

W. E. B. Du Bois

ALS Con. 103 BTW Papers DLC. Reprinted by permission of Shirley Graham Du Bois and the University of Massachusetts Press from *The Correspondence of W. E. B. Du Bois*, Vol. I, © Copyright 1973.

[1] William Edward Burghardt Du Bois (1868-1963) was BTW's principal critic and rival. The two men had sharply different backgrounds, though their formative years in the late nineteenth century affected the outlook of both. Du Bois was born free, of free parents, in Great Barrington, Mass. He attended Fisk at the same time as Margaret Murray Washington, and then Harvard University, where he secured a Ph.D. in history after two years of study in German universities with the aid of the John F. Slater Fund. His letter published here began a flirtation of almost a decade with a possible position at Tuskegee. Almost a month after Du Bois wrote, BTW sent him a telegram offering a position in mathematics, but Du Bois had by then accepted a position at Wilberforce. (Du Bois, *Autobiography*, 185.) In 1896, at the suggestion of his Harvard adviser Albert Bushnell Hart, Du Bois sent another feeler. BTW this time replied more promptly, but Du Bois delayed a decision. (*Ibid.*, 192-93.) Hart was anxious for the two men to establish an alliance (Hart to BTW, June 5, 1899, Con. 155, BTW Papers, DLC), but Du Bois went instead to Atlanta University, where he expected a more scholarly atmosphere and freedom from BTW's dominant personality. BTW renewed his invitation in 1899-1900, offering Du Bois a position as director of research. He promised to leave Du Bois "free to use your time as you decide would be most desirable" (BTW to Du Bois, Oct. 26, 1899, Con. 282a, BTW Papers, DLC), but Du Bois feared that he would be exploited as BTW's ghostwriter. He resisted

the persuasions of BTW, William H. Baldwin, Jr., and others, and remained at Atlanta. (Du Bois to BTW, Apr. 10, 1900, Con. 170, BTW Papers, DLC.)

Du Bois was meanwhile drifting further and further from the Tuskegean in his thought on racial affairs. After the Atlanta Compromise address he had sent BTW a congratulatory telegram and had written favorably of his racial strategy in the New York *Age.* His review of *Up from Slavery* six years later showed more skepticism of a black leader whom the whites so universally approved, and one who emphasized the duties and shortcomings of blacks rather than their rights. In his collection of essays published in early 1903, *The Souls of Black Folk,* Du Bois devoted a chapter to BTW. He criticized industrial training on the Tuskegee model as inadequate for the education of a great people, and BTW's accommodationism as too compromising to serve black advancement. The essay's chief importance was that, for the first time, it gave the opposition to BTW a coherent philosophy. Du Bois stated his case moderately enough, and actually taught summer school at Tuskegee in 1903, but in that summer occurred an event which was a turning point in the relationship of the two men.

After the so-called Boston Riot in 1903, Du Bois publicly praised the courage of its leader, William Monroe Trotter, while disapproving of the action. To BTW this ambiguity was intolerable, and he put down Du Bois, who stayed at Trotter's house by a prior arrangement after the riot, as a conspirator with Trotter. A final effort by BTW to prevent the division of blacks into two opposing factions was the secret conference of about forty black leaders, including Du Bois, at Carnegie Hall for three days in January 1904. BTW himself doomed the conference by packing it with his supporters, and the resulting Committee of Twelve for the Advancement of the Negro Race was abortive as a focus of racial leadership. In 1905 Du Bois founded the Niagara Movement, a militant protest and civil-rights group of black intellectuals and professional men. It sought to attack white racial discriminations, but much of its energy also went into denouncing BTW. BTW for his part did all he could to render the Niagara Movement ineffective, and he was to a large degree successful. In 1909, however, white liberals and radicals outraged by the growing racial violence and injustice joined with the Niagara Movement blacks to form the National Association for the Advancement of Colored People.

At Atlanta University for more than a decade, Du Bois had tried through the annual Atlanta University Studies of the Sociology of Race to bring the power of social science and reason to the solution of American race problems. Seeing a worsening of the racial crisis rather than improvement, Du Bois turned to propaganda. He moved to New York as editor of *Crisis,* the magazine of the NAACP. It immediately became and remained throughout his editorship of more than two decades the leading black periodical, the chief voice of black protest and also a force for black cultural identity. Du Bois himself wrote many novels, stories, and poetry. He also sponsored many other black writers and artists, making *Crisis* a vehicle of the New Negro. As BTW declined in physical vigor after about 1910, he was less a target of Du Bois. In the 1930s, when the Great Depression brought new miseries to the black communities and seemed to Du Bois to call for new remedies, he broke with the white liberal leadership of the NAACP, resigned as editor of *Crisis,* and moved to the left.

In the 1940s and 1950s, Du Bois endorsed black communal movements in the ghettos in what seemed to be an echo of BTW's sponsorship of Mound Bayou, an all-black town. He believed that in the Soviet Union a model of egalitarianism and cultural pluralism was developing that might be applied to all multi-ethnic societies. His championship of the Soviet Union became increasingly difficult. In his last years he joined the Communist party and transferred his citizenship to Ghana, where the Nkrumah regime promised to sponsor his *Encyclopedia Africana* and his lifelong interest in Pan-Africanism. This major prophet of black liberation died a few days before an event he had not anticipated. Many Americans heard of his death for the first time while attending Martin Luther King's epochal March on Washington in 1963. (See Broderick, *Du Bois;* Rudwick, *Du Bois.*)

A Resolution of the Executive Committee of the Cotton States and International Exposition Company

Atlanta, Ga. [Aug. 24] 1894

x   x   x

Mr. Amorous[1] moved the following resolution:

"Resolved, that the action of President Collier,[2] Directors Howell[3] and Evans,[4] in guaranteeing to the Conference Committee of the House of Representatives, 25,000 square feet of space and as much more as may be needed for an exhibit by the Colored People of the United States, free of all expense for entrance fees and rent for exhibits, be and the same is hereby ratified; and that the original agreement be spread upon the Minutes." Adopted.

The following is the original:

Washington, D.C., Aug., 14/94

Hon. Joseph D. Sayres,[5]

Chairman House Committee, in Conference on Civil Sundry Bill.

Sir: The Cotton States & International Exposition Company hereby agrees that said Company will provide upon their grounds, a suitable building, to contain not less than 25,000 square feet of space, and as much more as may be needed for an exhibit by the Colored people of the United States. Said space so provided to be used exclusively by said race in education, art, mining, agriculture, and all other pursuits and industries; said exhibit to be made at the time and under the rules and regulations governing all other exhibitors.

In witness whereof the said Exposition Company hereunto attaches its signature by its President.

(signed) The Cotton States & International Exposition Company,

By C. A. Collier, Prest.,

Evan P. Howell, Director,

Clement A. Evans, Director,

In the presence of: Jno. B. Gordon,[6]

United States Senator

x   x   x

The above is a true extract from the Minutes of the Meeting of the Executive Committee, held August 24, 1894, at the Office of the Prest.,

J. R. Lewis Secy.

TLS Con. 108 BTW Papers DLC. Written on stationery of the Cotton States and International Exposition Company.

[1] Martin F. Amorous (b. 1858) was general manager of the Atlanta Lumber Company in 1885. He was an Atlanta city councilman from 1887 to 1891 and again in 1903-4.

[2] Charles A. Collier (1848-1900) was vice-president and manager of the Capital City Bank in Atlanta. He had been president of the Piedmont Exposition in Atlanta in 1887, and its success led to his choice as president of the Cotton States and International Exposition in 1895. He was elected mayor of Atlanta for 1897-98.

[3] Evan Park Howell (1839-1905), after serving as a Confederate captain, moved to Atlanta as a newspaper reporter, lawyer, and politician. In 1876 he bought an interest in the Atlanta *Constitution* and became its editor, a position he held until 1897. He employed the more famous Henry W. Grady as managing editor. From 1903 to 1905 he was mayor of Atlanta.

[4] Clement Anselm Evans (1833-1911), a Confederate general who became a Methodist clergyman after the Civil War. He also dealt in real estate in Augusta, Ga. He became active in the United Confederate Veterans in 1889 and became commander-in-chief of that group in 1908. He wrote extensively on Confederate military history. He was chairman of the Committee on the Colored Exhibit at the Atlanta Exposition.

[5] Joseph Draper Sayers (1841-1929) was a member of the U.S. House of Representatives from Texas (1885-99). He was governor of Texas from 1899 to 1903.

[6] John Brown Gordon (1832-1904), after service as a general in the Confederate Army, became Grand Dragon of the Ku Klux Klan in Georgia. He was elected U.S. senator in 1873 and resigned in 1880 to promote the Georgia Pacific Railroad. He was elected governor of Georgia in 1886, and served again in the U.S. Senate from 1891 to 1897.

To Julius B. Ramsey

[Tuskegee, Ala.] August 28th, 1894

Major Ramsey: It is very important that you organize at the opening of school a well-equipped fire department among the students and teachers. This department should have drills at least once a month, oftener if possible.

I wish you to see that fire buckets are kept at all times in their proper places in all the large buildings on the place. See that the hose etc. are kept in order; that the students and teachers receive instruction in the use of the trap-doors; see that these trap-doors are in working order at all times. Also see that the fireaxes etc. are kept in the proper place at all times. In giving fire drills I wish you would see that the companies are instructed that in case a building is on fire, the buildings near it are carefully protected. Men should be instructed to go on the roofs of the buildings and cover them with wet blankets or use the fire buckets so that no more than one building may be reached by the fire. See that the ladders etc. are kept ready for use at all times.

This is a very important matter, and I think I have already stated to you that the fire department was not at all satisfactory last year, and I hope you will make it what it should be this year from the very beginning.

General instruction as to what to do in case of fire should be given in the chapel at all times, or as often as possible.

· · · ·

[Booker T. Washington]

TLpf   Con. 113   BTW Papers   DLC.

To George W. Scott[1]

[Tuskegee, Ala.] September 3rd, 1894

Mr. G. W. Scott: This is to notify you that you are suspended from the position of Steward for neglect of duty till such time this week as the Council can act on your case. In the meantime you can turn over the Boarding department work to Mr. Diggs,[2] and the Commissary to Mr. J. N. Calloway.

In my mind you are plainly neglecting the work for which you were hired. The idea in getting you was to secure a specialist in the preparation and serving of the food, and one who would give special and personal attention to this work.

You are neglecting your duty in these respects:

You do not spend enough time in the kitchen to see that the food is properly cooked and served. For example, Saturday morning you did not go into the kitchen at all before the food had been served. Sunday at dinner, the same thing was true. On both of these occasions I was in the kitchen. These are but samples of the neglect. You do not see regularly that the food is rightly apportioned among the tables, and that the dishes and the food present the proper appearance before going into the dining room. All this, as well as other important matters, is left to irresponsible persons.

The kitchen and the room adjoining it are almost never clean. Both this morning and Saturday there was no attempt made to clean the room joining the kitchen before the meal began. Old brooms, dirty dish-rags, and many other things are left thrown about without regard to system or cleanliness. The cooks themselves usually present an untidy appearance.

An examination shows that the school is losing much every day because of the fact that the meal is not well sifted — a large proportion of it now goes into the slop because of the fact that no one is giving personal attention to the sifting of the meal; and you know you have been spoken to more than once in regard to the same kind of waste in connection with the greens.

I repeat that your position demands some one who will make an intelligent and thorough study of the preparation and serving of foods, study how to get much out of little, how to vary the preparation of the same kind of food from day to day, so that students will not feel that they have the same thing all the time. This can only be done by a study of books, papers and other sources of information. The position demands some one who will plan ahead, and feel a personal responsibility for the whole food question.

In taking this action, I am not unmindful of your condition, and your responsibility as the head of a family, and how much loss and inconvenience it will be for you to be compelled to seek new work at this season, but at the same time I owe a duty to the students and supporters of the school which I cannot escape. It is plain to me that you do not understand what is expected of you in connection with the boarding department, or knowing it, do not do your duty.

If you desire it I shall be glad to have you make a statement before the Council.

In this connection, I am glad to recognize the satisfaction that you have given in connection with the commissary accounts, but too large a proportion of the money received by this institution, passes through the kitchen to have that part of the work neglected as heretofore. Yours truly,

Booker T. Washington

TLpS Con. 113 BTW Papers DLC.

[1] George W. Scott was steward in charge of the Tuskegee Institute commissary from 1893 to 1895.

[2] Charles L. Diggs was a steward at Tuskegee in 1892-93, in charge of the Teachers' Home from 1893 to 1895, and in charge of the supply department in 1895-96.

To John Henry Washington

[Tuskegee, Ala.] Sept 4 '94

Mr. J. H. Washington, Supt. of Ind. Not later than this week I wish you to go over the whole subject of the wages of students and recommend whatever reduction you think should take place. I wish a reduction of not less than one-third to be made. Small boys whose work can be of almost no service need special attention.

Booker T. Washington

ALpS Con. 113 BTW Papers DLC.

To Alice J. Kaine[1]

[Tuskegee, Ala.] Sept. 5th, 1894

Dear Madam: Replying to yours of August 22nd, would say that we wish to employ some woman who can assist us in improving our Household Departments. We wish a person who can stay with us long enough to get each department in the best possible condition. We wish one who understands the science of household economy in the broadest sense, who will be frank in all her criticisms, and have the executive ability to have matters properly adjusted.

It is my idea to have the one employed take each department in turn, and remain in it long enough to make whatever improvements are necessary, all, of course, to be done in connection with the teacher directly in charge, who, I am sure, will be willing to co-operate in the right spirit.

During the time that this school has been in existence, we have overlooked in almost every department, because of our rapid growth, many of the conveniences, attractions and comforts, and I might add, much in the way of neatness and tidiness indoors and outdoors, that help constitute an education. We wish also that the matter of preparing and serving the food be given special attention. We want to know how to serve the cheapest food consistent with health at the smallest possible cost.

In our class rooms there are pictures, maps and other school apparatus and furniture, but in many cases you will find them out of place and out of harmony. The grounds immediately surrounding the various buildings need to be put in a more attractive condition. My own impression is that it will require three months for the right person to do this work as it should be done.

We have in all our departments, literary and industrial, over 500 students and 50 instructors, all of whom are colored people. In case you come to us, you will be the only white person on the grounds for any length of time. You can easily see that the work I have attempted to outline requires a person of superior bearing and executive ability and moral strength. A weak person in such a position, would be worse than none.

If, with this information, you would like to undertake the work I shall be very glad to correspond with you further in regard to salary etc. I might add here that the money to pay for this work comes to us from a special source.

I should like to have you answer my letter as early as possible, as it may be that I shall be called North for a short while soon and want to get matters straight as soon as possible. Should you decide to come, we would want you to come at once. It will be of a special advantage to have some one who has worked among the colored people and who has no special feeling against them, but on the other hand is in sympathy with such a work as ours.

The enclosed report will give you further information regarding our work. Yours very truly,

[Booker T. Washington]

TLp Con. 113 BTW Papers DLC.

¹ Alice J. (Mrs. J. L.) Kaine was a white home-economics expert from Milwaukee, Wis., and secretary of the Wisconsin Industrial School for Girls. The Slater Fund, through J. L. M. Curry, suggested that BTW hire someone to help improve the tidiness of the school, and BTW hired Mrs. Kaine for this task during several months each year from 1894 to 1896. (See Curry to BTW, Apr. 17, 1894, above.) She worked primarily with the girls' household departments, but her suggestions for improving Tuskegee's appearance ranged over the entire campus. Her salary, paid by a special grant from the Slater Fund, was $80 per month and board, more than twice the salary of the average woman teacher. BTW allowed her broad powers to make changes, and some of the teachers complained that "her word was *law*." Since much of BTW's financial support was tied to tours of inspection by various individuals and groups, BTW pragmatically accepted many of Mrs. Kaine's suggestions to improve the appearance of the campus. (Harlan, *BTW*, 274-75.)

From Alice J. Kaine

Milwaukee Wis   Sept 12th 1894

Dear Sir   Yours of Sept 5th is at hand. I have taken time to very carefully consider the demands of your institution which seem to be many and to need an *all round* person.

The Science of Household Economy has scarcely been formulated and as yet has no limitations but I think I understand in a general way what you want done. I also realize that it is impossible for you or for me to say that I or any one will be equally successful in all departments.

I can only say this in answer to the prescribed qualifications for the woman you seek. My time is my own and I can not plead guilty to any suspicion from my friends of being a weak woman. I believe I can in a large measure put your departments in proper shape. If I cannot I shall at once abandon the effort.

I have never worked among the colored people but in trips South have always attended their Schools and Churches and when Dr Hartzell[1] was in New Orleans he and his wife gave me open sesame to their work there. It has been one of my hobbies — that is all. I am warmly in sympathy with them and their struggles and believe they have struck the key note to success in taking up the industries.

With this explanation, if you think I am the one to take charge of your institution I shall be glad to hear further from you, and if other things are satisfactory will enter with enthusiasm into your plans.

I must however, add that I fear it would be to my disadvantage and yours to come to you this early in the year. The change from this sharp lake air to the extreme South is always enervating and I should like to retain all ability as possible. Miss Clarke, who lectures on cooking in the South, warns me that the middle of October is full early for so marked a change. But what is your own opinion and what is the latest convenient date to you for my coming — provided always of course that I do come. My trips South have never been at this season of the year therefore I cannot know just how much the change may mean.

I have taken more time for my reply than I have wished to but a hasty decision could not be made in what seems an important matter.

I have given myself the pleasure of sending you a report of our School. It appeals to my pride because I had the entire management of the *make up* in printing and pictures as it was intended for the Worlds Fair.

It would please me, if your trip North should lie in my direction, to have you call upon me whether I enter upon your work or not. I am interested in what seems to be the only practical Southern effort. Believe me   Sincerely Yours

Mrs J. L. Kaine

ALS Con. 108 BTW Papers DLC.

[1] Joseph Crane Hartzell.

To Jabez Lamar Monroe Curry

[Tuskegee, Ala.] September 21st, 1894

My dear Sir: Though I have not written to you about it for some months, I have not forgotten or laid aside our plan to secure a competent woman to improve the condition of our institution in the way suggested by you and Dr. Gilman. I have been almost constantly on the lookout for the proper person.

I know you will agree with me that a weak person in such a position would be worse than no one. I applied to Miss Giles, of Spellman Seminary as you suggested, but she was only able to name one person, and that person could not accept. I then applied to Miss Richards,[1] who has charge of the Household Department of the Massachusetts Institute of Technology, and through her I have been able to secure a Mrs. J. L. Kaine who is at present secretary of the Wisconsin Industrial School for Girls. I have taken a great deal of pains to acquaint Mrs. Kaine with our needs, and have also been equally careful in getting information that would lead me to determine whether or not Mrs. Kaine has the ability and disposition to do the work which we want done. I am now satisfied that she is the proper person.

In your first letter you did not state the amount that the Slater Fund Trustees would be willing to pay for this work, and consequently I am unable to make a definite agreement with Mrs. Kaine before hearing from you on this point. From the information I now possess, I think she cannot be gotten for less than $75. or $80. per month, board and traveling expenses. Of course we can provide the board. If you would kindly give me the amount of the proposed appropriation, I would know better how to act, at the same time securing her for just as small a salary possible. I think she would have to remain with us three months in order to put the institution in the condition that it should be.

While in Massachusetts this summer, I had conversation with Mr. F. L. Olmstead,[2] of Brookline, Mass., the landscape gardener who laid out the World's Fair Grounds and the Central Park grounds, and he told me that he had an engagement that would bring him to Mr. Vanderbilt's estate at Asheville[3] sometime during October or November, and that he would gladly come to Tuskegee to help us lay out our grounds providing we pay his traveling expenses from Asheville to Tuskegee and return.[4]

Our institution is now in an encouraging condition.

Enclosed I send you a copy of my recent annual report which may interest you. Yours respectfully,

Booker T. Washington

TLpS Con. 113 BTW Papers DLC.

[1] Ellen Henrietta Swallow Richards (1842-1911), a pioneer home economist, graduated from Vassar in 1870 and secured permission to study at Massachusetts Institute of Technology. She received a B.S. in sanitary chemistry in 1873 and was for many years the only woman graduate of M.I.T. She taught there after her graduation and sought the application of chemistry to improving the environment, better opportunities for women in science, and professionalization of home economics. She organized in 1899 the American Home Economics Association, of which she was the first president.

[2] Frederick Law Olmsted (1822-1903), America's most distinguished landscape architect, was also the author of a brilliant series of travel books on the South on the eve of the Civil War. Through his park designs he sought to save in an urbanizing nation what he felt to be the virtues of rural and small-town life.

[3] George W. Vanderbilt's home, "Biltmore," was surrounded by a large wooded and agricultural estate designed by Olmsted.

[4] It is not clear whether Olmsted did in fact visit Tuskegee, for 1894 was the last year that he was active professionally.

To John Henry Washington

[Tuskegee, Ala.] Sept. 21st, 1894

Mr. J. H. Washington: I wish you would issue from your office an order to all teachers who have the paying of students under their charge, to make a reduction of 20% for all work done by students.

B. T. Washington

TLpS Con. 113 BTW Papers DLC.

To Daniel Coit Gilman

[Tuskegee, Ala.] Sept. 22nd, 1894

Dear Sir: Hon. Jno G. Harris, the present State Superintendent of Education of Alabama, gives up his present work this Fall by reason of the expiration of his term of office, after having held it for four years.

Maj. Harris is especially interested in the work of the colored people of the South, and has shown his interest in the most practical and unselfish way throughout his whole term of office, as well as before becoming an officer in Alabama. Maj. Harris understands the needs and condition of the colored people in the South, perhaps better than any white man in Alabama.

He is very anxious — and the colored people are equally anxious to have him do so — to continue his work for the colored people after his term of office expires, and this can be done in a most effectual manner by lectures, teachers' institutes, speeches before religious gatherings, and by a series of lectures in the various institutions of the State.

No one who knows the influence that Maj. Harris has among the colored people, and his gift for such work, would doubt the far-reaching effect of such service.

The point of this letter is to ask if the Slater Fund Board would like to assist in paying the expenses that would be incurred in connection with this work. Major Harris would be willing to work for a reasonable salary. Yours very truly,

Booker T. Washington

TLpSr Con. 113 BTW Papers DLC. In a letter of the same date, BTW asked John D. Rockefeller to assist in paying Harris's expenses. (Con. 113, BTW Papers, DLC.)

To Robert Hannibal Hamilton

[Tuskegee, Ala.] September 23rd, 1894

Mr. Hamilton: Friday the Council went carefully over the whole matter of music in connection with the school. It is but fair to say that the music last year under you was not what we had hoped that it would be. In the first place you remember that there was a promise made last year that there would be a large musical chorus organized to sing before public gatherings. This plan was not carried out.

And then we are of the opinion that there is not enough effort made to raise the quality and tone of the singing. By this, we do not mean to have you discard the plantation songs, but improve the singing of them as well as the other songs.

No unprejudiced judge can fail to see that the music, during the last three or four years, has failed to keep pace with the growth of the school in other respects. It is with music as with anything else — it must either go backward or forward. The proper results can only be accomplished by constant planning for the work of the musical department. Of course I am not criticising in any way, the present year's work, as there has not been time to judge of it; I am only mentioning that we hope this year's work will show better results than last.

It has also been suggested that you train four instead of three young men for the Northern trip, so that in case one would drop out for any reason, there would be no trouble in filling his place. There has been a good deal of adverse criticism on our quartette's singing by competent judges. I very much hope that the quartette for the present year will be gotten in better condition than it is.

You should make it a strong point of getting hold of new songs. I wish you would try to get hold of some of the peculiar songs that are sung in Louisiana while the people are boiling syrup; also some of the rice plantation songs of South Carolina as well as of the Mississippi bottom songs. A few of the Mississippi steamboat songs will do well. I think, by making a constant effort among the new students, we can get hold of many new songs of this character.

Hereafter please see that the choir begins singing, or the orchestra begins playing when the girl heading the line enters the chapel door; let this be the rule at all exercises.

There is still some trouble about the distribution of papers or books. I wish you would see that they are evenly distributed all over the chapel and gallery.

The Council suggests that it would be a good plan to have the three young men take voice culture until they get ready to go North with the quartette. The Council suggests that it would be a good plan and quite an addition to the singing in the chapel if you would let Prof. White play the piano, and you stand up before the whole school and beat time, leading them in the way that is usually done where there are large bodies singing.

B. T. Washington

TLpSr   Con. 113   BTW Papers   DLC.

From Hollis Burke Frissell

Boston, Sept. 23d 1894

My dear Mr Washington   I wrote you some time since asking about the gentle man of whom you kindly wrote me earlier in the season in Nashua whom you thought I ought to look up. I directed to the Crawford House and probably you did not receive. In my letter I spoke of a criticism that I heard of thro Mr M. K. Jesup on the lack of tidiness of things at Tuskegee. I have always taken it for granted that one of the best evidences of my friendship would be the reporting to you any criticism unfavorable to the school. I should certainly consider any such suggestion from you in regard to Hampton in that light. I think we came near losing the Fayerweather legacy from lack of care in the matter of cleanliness. Mr Huntington has been very severe in his criticism on us along that line.

Your picture and that of the school has appeared at every meeting of our summer campaign and every where the story of your school has been told. I write thus because I am anxious that no words of mine should ever seem unkindly. I expect to be in Hampton next week. Sincerely Yours

H. B. Frissell

ALS   Con. 107   BTW Papers   DLC.

From the Tuskegee Institute Senior Class

Tuskegee, Ala. Sept. 24, 1894

To the Executive Council: We the members of the Senior class, not wishing to step beyond the law or limits of the same ask to know the social priviledges granted to the members of this class.

In other years Senior young men have been allowed to call at Alabama Hall and Senior young women have been allowed to receive calls at Alabama Hall once a week, Senior young women have been allowed to attend church accompanied by the Senior young men once a month or if the case was such that they could not attend church they were allowed the pleasure of taking an evening walk.

It has also been the priviledge of Senior yo[ung] women to go to the city shopping in comp[any] with other young women of the class and not compelled to go with the crowd accompanied by some teacher as is the case at present.

Now in view of these facts we the members of the present Senior class ask that these priviledges be allowed us. Very respectfully,

Senior Class

HL Con. 108 BTW Papers DLC. Missing letters have been supplied in brackets where a corner of the document is torn.

From Thomas McCants Stewart

New York, Sept. 24th., 1894

My Dear Professor: I appreciate very much your thought of me *in re Student* with Chris'[1] letter. It is very readable. Indeed, it is above the average. The boy shows great humor as well as considerable serious thought — not so much in what is said as in what is suggested.

What are *we* going to do with Chris after this year? I am inclined to adhere to my original plan to let him grow up *in* and *with* the South. I see very little hope for the *Negro* out of it. *There* he can make a table for himself (lands, banks, business enterprises etc.), and eat from it. Here the best of us live on the crumbs that fall from the rich man's table. I write you now about Chris as we both must prepare to deal with an important question next May, when I hope that Chris will graduate with the valedictory.

Do give us a chance to get at your hand when you are North next time.

Enthusiastic expressions from me to the household. Yours truly,

T. McCants Stewart

ALS Con. 108 BTW Papers DLC.

¹ Gilchrist Stewart.

From Jabez Lamar Monroe Curry

Asheville No. Ca 25 Sep. 94

My dear Sir— Your interesting letter of 21st & Report have been received. I am glad you have found a competent Superintendent of Household. In a few months, one of your own Faculty might be trained thoroughly for the work. Tact, taste, energy, industry, capacity, administrative ability, an eye for neatness and beauty, &c. may be found in some one you can retain & who can be substituted when your present employee leaves. Of course, the Slater help for this purpose is temporary. Such work as we seek to promote should be a part of the organic life of every institution. I think we can give you $400.

I like your landscape gardening idea your place is susceptible of much improvement. With plans & specific directions given, in a few years, with your boys you could convert the Institute into a beauty. It is impossible to estimate what an educatory influence in morals, and aesthetics, such an object lesson has.

With best wishes for the best year you ever had and sincere regards. I am Yours truly

J. L. M. Curry

ALS Con. 104 BTW Papers DLC.

A Speech before the National Unitarian Association

Saratoga, N.Y. September 26, 1894

A few days ago it was my privilege to investigate the condition of my people in Alabama where there are 30,000 colored people, and but 6,000 whites; where no colored public school has been in session this year longer than three months, and no colored teacher paid more than $15. per month for his services, and yet, in the midst of this darkness, this intellectual and moral night, what did I find?

Some years ago a poor boy from this community found his way to the Tuskegee Institute where he was trained in head, hand and heart. Returning to his home by his manly bearing and earnest heart, he so impressed himself upon a Southern white man who once was the owner of his father and mother, as well as scores of other slaves, that this ex-slave-holder deeded a number of acres of land on which this young man could erect a comfortable and commodious school house, and today there stands on a portion of this same plantation, where, a few years ago could be heard the crack of the overseer's whip, and the yelp of the blood hound, a well built school house of three rooms that would do credit to any community. How was it built? By the hands of this young teacher, by the small cash contributions of the colored people, by the gift of a day's labor this week and another the next week, by the gift of a pound of nails by this white man and a few shingles by another, and the financial assistance of this ex-slave-holder.

And then, as I turned to the three teachers, all of whom had been my pupils at Tuskegee, I said "what is your pay for this work?" One said, "I am working this year for my board, in order to get the work on its feet." Another was receiving $10. per month. And during the three years that the principal and founder of this school had labored there, he had not received more than $150 in cash; preferring to make this sacrifice that the school house might be built and the session extended from three to eight months.

My friends, were I to speak an hour, I could give you no better idea of the potency of the work at Tuskegee. Who will dare say that the $50. a year given by some Northern friend or organization for the education of the young man who started this school, has not been paid in the highest and best sense?

Then add to the direct influence of this school, the stimulus and guidance given the masses in the direction of buying land, saving money, replacing the one-room cabins, ceasing mortgage crops[,] a higher standard of morals and religion; and what, in missionary work in this or in any other country begins to compare with it for good or will give better results for money invested.

This case is only one of many that I could describe. When these communities have been lifted out of darkness into light, out of degradation into civilization, you may label their regeneration Methodism, I care not, label it Presbyterianism, I care not, or a Bapitist belief, I care not, or even Unitarianism, call the transformation what you will, I care not, I know what it is: it is American Christian manhood, something above creed or denominational labels.

Some have thought that the problem could be settled by merely going from plantation to plantation, or community to community and organizing churches. It cant. The Negro is not unlike any other race. I do not know how you find it here, but in the South my experience [is] that it is a mighty hard thing to make a Christian of a hungry man. By daily contact with the masses of my people in the South, I find that no matter how long they belong to the church, and get happy and shout in church as they like to do, if they go home hungry at night from the meeting and dont find anything to eat, they are tempted to find something before morning. I simply mean to say by this that we cannot expect permanent progress unless, while we are giving intellectual and religious training, the industrial life is improved at the same time.

As a race, our people have a great deal of feeling. I believe that we can feel more in five minutes than a white man can in a day. You can beat us thinking, but we can beat you feeling. We feel our religion, and when a black man becomes converted, and does not jump and shout, we say he has the white man's religion. The emotional side of our nature leads us to like to live in the next world. Analyze the average Negro sermon in the South, and three-fourths of it consists of an imaginary description of Heaven. Our people like to talk about heavenly mansions, and at the same time are content to live in one-room cabins in this world. They like to talk about golden slippers, and too often go barefooted here. They are fond of singing about living on milk and honey in Heaven, and living on cornbread and peas in this world. They are fond of singing the old song, which says "You may have all de world, but give me Jesus." In our school work at Tuskegee, and at the Negro Conference, we teach that the way to have the most of Jesus, and to have him in a substantial way, is to mix in some land, cotton and corn and a good bank account; and we find, by actual experience, that the man who has Jesus in this way has a religion that you can count on seven days in the week.

The problem as to the relation of the races in the South, has never, I confess, seriously troubled me. I should be ashamed of my education if I loved a northern white man more than a southern white man, or a black American more than a white American. To me, a man is simply a man and a brother "for a' that and a' that." It seems to me that the time has come for the Southerner to forget that he was the conquered and the Northerner the conquerer; for the Negro to forget that he was the enslaved, and the white man the enslaver, and all unite with hand and heart for the righting of the great wrong of slavery.

That there is friction, no one should deny. When the black man can raise better and more corn than the white man, the white man will come to the Negro for corn. When the Negro can manufacture a better wagon than the white man, the white man will come to the Negro. When a black man has $50,000 invested in a southern bank, there is no danger of that black man's being driven out of the town, not even on election day. When the black man can print as good books as the white man, the black man will supply the white man with books. (Printing Tuskegee News.)

Let a colored man spend $10,000 a year in hauling freight on a rail road where there are competing lines: do you think the rail roads will put this man and his family into a Jim Crow car? Not at all. Rather than lose his patronage they will put on a Pullman Palace Car for him. The American dollar has not an ounce of sentiment in it.

As a race we have made some mistakes in the past. We began at the wrong end. We have spent time and money trying to go to Congress that would have been better spent in becoming the leading real estate dealer or carpenter in our town. We have spent time and money in making stump speeches and attending political conventions that could have been better spent in starting a truck garden or dairy farm, and thus laid a foundation on which we could stand and demand political rights.

The work at Tuskegee is your work, not mine; it is the nation's work, not the South's. For the work at [the] Tuskegee School, these are exceedingly hard and trying days in a financial sense, but we are not discouraged. When I left Tuskegee the other day I left seven hundred as worthy and earnest students as can be found in this country, hard at work, erecting their own buildings, raising, to a large extent, their own food, at work in wood, iron, tin, leather, and the millinery and sewing room, and printing office, each one doing what he can to help himself, paying for their own board in cash and labor. But with all that they can do, they cannot provide the $50. per year which it costs to teach each one.

Ten days ago we were compelled to give notice to the effect that for lack of room and means, that not another student could be admitted, and now the saddest duty that we have to perform is to say "no" to the scores who are constantly applying.

My friends, these students are not seeking an education that they may use it in furthering selfish ends; but that they may use it in helping some one walk who has never walked before, in helping some one see who has never had the opportunity of seeing.

TM Con. 955 BTW Papers DLC. There are occasional minor corrections in BTW's hand.

To Hollis Burke Frissell

New York, Sept 29 1894

My dear Dr. Frissell: Both of your letters have just reached me. The one dated Sept 3 was not forwarded to me from the Crawford House till a few days ago. Please feel *perfectly* free to speak to me at any time on any subject connected with Tuskegee. It is only by such information that we can find our weak points. I think Mr. Jesup misunderstood a little Dr. Curry's criticism. It was not so much untidiness as want of taste and lack of attention to little points that go to impress one favorably, but however that may be I am sure the criticism was just. At first I did not think so, but since I have made a close study of the matter I am satisfied that it was a good criticism and is going to do us good. We have just secured a first class white woman from Wis. who is proficient in the whole subject of house hold economy to go

479

to Tuskegee for 3 months and help us improve along the lines named. The Slater Fund people bear the expense. Dr. Curry and I have talked the subject over very frankly.

I very much wish that you could go to Tuskegee oftener. You could help us greatly in many matters by an annual visit.

The name of the man in Exeter, N.H. is Mr. Isaac Shute.

Richard Potts of Notasulga Ala. is a good honest hard working fellow but he has little education, but is doing good.

I think Simmons[1] will do well. He has some opposition from the teacher whom he is trying to succeed. I told him when he got his local fight settled I should help him all I could.

Are you to be in N.Y. soon? We need money badly. You may be able to give me some suggestions. I shall be here for 10 days or more. Can you send me any names?

Hope matters at Hampton are going well. Yours Sincerely

Booker T. Washington

ALS BTW Folder ViHaI. Written on stationery of the Grand Union Hotel.

[1] Daniel Simmons, a graduate of Hampton Institute in 1894.

From Charles A. Collier and John Randolph Lewis

Atlanta, Ga. Oct. 16th. 1894

Dear Sir: By authority of the Directory of the COTTON STATES AND INTERNATIONAL EXPOSITION COMPANY, Mr. B. T. Washington, of Tuskegee Alabama has been appointed Chief Commissioner for the State of [Alabama] and Messrs

> C. N. Dorsett,　　　Montgomery, Ala.
> Rev. W. R. Pettiford, Birmingham, Ala.
> H. A. Loveless,　　　Montgomery, Ala.
> Prof. W. H. Council, Normal, Ala.

have been appointed Auxiliary Commissioners for the State of Alabama, to take charge of the work of collecting, forwarding, and installing the exhibits of the colored people of Alabama at the COTTON STATES AND INTERNATIONAL EXPOSITION.

The above will comprise a State Board, to convene at the call of the Chief Commissioner to formulate plans and inaugurate all the machinery required for the purpose, under the direction of a *Central Board* to be composed of the Chief Commissioners of all the States, who will meet in Atlanta and formulate the general plans, and issue such instructions and information as may be necessary.

Trusting that you will fully appreciate the importance of this work, and will enter into it with the energy and enthusiasm it demands, Very respectfully,

C. A. Collier   President

J. R. Lewis   Secretary

TLS   Con. 112   BTW Papers   DLC.

An Address at the Funeral of Mabel Wilhelmina Dillingham

[Augusta, Me., ca. Oct. 17, 1894][1]

The Starting of the Calhoun School

It was some four years ago, I think, that I was on a visit to the Hampton Institute. I had told the students there something about the condition of my people in the black belt of the South. Miss Dillingham and Miss Thorn came to me the next day, stating that they had made up their minds to spend the remainder of their lives in the South in work for the uplifting of my race. They wanted me to help them, if possible, to find the place where the people were most in need, and where they could accomplish the greatest good. Very soon after my return to Tuskegee I set about looking up such a place, and my mind was very soon attracted to Lowndes Co., Alabama, because I remembered that of all the counties in the state, that county perhaps had the largest proportion of colored people.

I very soon decided that this county was the best place and that Calhoun would perhaps be the most suitable spot for the location of the school they proposed to found. I wrote to them, and very soon came back enthusiastic and grateful replies, saying that they were ready, they were willing and they were thankful for the opportunity.

A few months elapsed and Miss Dillingham and Miss Thorn came to Alabama. I remember distinctly the day that we went together to Calhoun. I remember that it had been raining, it seems to me for a week, and it rained harder and harder. Reaching Calhoun, we waited in a little cabin there for the rain to stop. It did not stop. Finally Miss Dillingham suggested that we provide ourselves in the best way we could against the wet weather and go out and select the spot where they would put their first building. I remember distinctly my feelings, and how gloomy, how dismal and how poverty stricken it seemed; how everything seemed to present the worst appearance possible. I wondered if she would not falter, if she would not grow discouraged. I remember I said to her at the close of the day: "I am glad that you have come here on such a day. I am glad that you have an opportunity of seeing things in just this condition, because if after this you can keep your courage, can still make up your mind that you want to come here, I think that everything will be all right." She did not seem the least daunted, not the least discouraged, and the place was selected. I see her now as she stood with an umbrella over her head and with the mud up to her ankles, while we decided upon the exact spot and measured off the ground where the first building was to be.

I can also remember the impression that the coming of these two young women made upon the people, especially upon the black mothers and fathers, those people into whose lives had never come a ray of light or hope. They could not understand it. They could not realize how it was that somebody was enough interested in their condition, in their life, to come there on such a day as that desiring to give life itself for their uplifting. I remember, too, how they were looked upon with suspicion by the white people in that neighborhood. I remember it was thought these white teachers had not come there with the best motives, and it was suspected that after all something would be wrong by reason of the coming of these women into that community.

But now how changed is all that! Three years have passed away, and how changed is the life! Go to Calhoun and look into the countenances of those black men and black women who were bound down by slavery, who were fettered not only in body, but in morals and mind. Go there to-day and see their countenances beaming with hope and light, feeling that they and their children have something to live for, something to look forward to. See their dress changed. See their houses changed, inside and out. See their religious and moral life wonderfully changed. Then go and look into the faces of the white people. When they see northern men and northern women getting off at that little station to day, they do not look upon them with suspicion. They greet them with kindness, they greet them with confidence. This simple, loving, unselfish life that Miss Dillingham lived in that community a little more than two years has had the effect to change completely the ideas and the bearing of most of their white neighbors. If you could have been there a few days ago and could have seen how kind, how loving was their interest; how they came to the school building and asked if there was anything that they could do. "Is there anything we can do to lighten this burden? If there is, let us know that we may do it, without money, without price." What a change! For we must remember that this is the "black belt" of Alabama, where only a few years ago it was a crime, punishable with death, to teach a black boy or girl a letter in a book. What a change this life has wrought in that community! Let us pray that this death added to this life may indeed bring the white man and the black man together in love and in hope for the uplifting of my race. As I look over the last few years, I see that we have had many precious sacrifices. We have had precious gifts laid upon the altar of love for my race. I remember Gen. Armstrong and Gen. Marshall, and now Miss Dillingham. I remember some months ago when my wife and myself had been on a short visit to Calhoun, and we looked into Miss Dillingham's face and followed her through the work there, after we got off of the ground, my wife said to me: "It seems almost sad that that young, bright, beautiful woman should be growing so serious because of her deep interest and love for this work." But when I think of her work and her life, her services for my race, I believe that if a few years before she was called of God to Alabama she could have seen just what was going to take place, and if she could have had the opportunity of placing the services that she was to perform there in Calhoun over against a long life of ease in society, I believe that she would have deliberately preferred to live this short useful life that she did there and put in motion this work which is going to last. You cannot realize, my friends, the lasting influence of this work. It is going on. The colored people of the South are going to see to it that they do their part. And those of us who loved her and those of us who admired her — what is our duty for the future? I believe we can show our love and admiration for her in no better way than by giving of our services, of our means, seeing that the work that she started and lived for and died for, goes on as she had planned.

Southern Workman, 23 (Nov. 1894), 188-89.

[1] Miss Dillingham died at Calhoun, Ala., on Oct. 14, 1894, and was buried in Maine.

To Ednah Dow Littlehale Cheney

Tuskegee, Ala. Nov. 3 / 94

My dear Mrs. Cheney: Your kind letter is received. A telegram also came from Mrs. Howe.[1] We are delighted to know that so many delegates are coming to Tuskegee.[2] You will I think find it best to leave Atlanta at 5:35 A.M.* — pretty early — this will land you at Tuskegee at 10:30. We shall meet you at the depot and as I wrote before we want all to come direct to the school as we ar[e] plan[n]ing to entertain all here.

Mrs. Washington is planning to have a meeting of [the] Club Friday after noon at 2. Yours Sincerely

Booker T. Washington

* We prefer that you come on this train.

ALS   Ednah Dow Cheney Papers   MB.

[1] Julia Ward Howe (1819-1910) was active in the abolitionist, peace, and woman-suffrage movements. She was also a poet and essayist of distinction and composer of "The Battle Hymn of the Republic."

[2] It may have been at this time that Julia Ward Howe and six feminist companions visited Atlanta University and Tuskegee Institute. Mrs. Howe later recounted the experience. Arriving at night, they revived their spirits in the balmy air on the long ride from the Chehaw station. "Mr. Booker T. Washington stood ready to usher us into a pleasant sitting room, with such an open fire as one sees only in the land of 'far wood.'" The cooking class served a supper it had prepared. Then they went to the chapel, where the students greeted them with the Chautauqua salute and spirituals, and some of the visitors spoke. Next day they visited classes. "We had found daintiness, order, thrift, and industry, and moreover, good English, good manners, and good taste." (Lecture, "Atlanta University and Tuskegee, Largely Reminiscent," Nov. 1898, Folder 19, Julia Ward Howe Papers, DLC.)

From Mary A. Elliott

Columbus Ohio   Nov 12th 1894

Dear Brother   I received your letter   have just returned from Athens Ohio, and found it waiting for me. I am glad to hear that you are all well. I have been thinking of my dear little boys and all of you, so much of late. We can Still hear from the School through the little papers which gives us great comfort. I suppose Baker, and Davidson have grown considerable since I saw them last. They have already grown out of dresse's into pants since that time; I know more a bout little Portia's size   I hope that she is having her health   We heard some time back through the little papers that Mrs Washington was not having her health so well. But we also heard that she was convalescent again and was glad to hear it. I oftimes think that it is wonderful, dear brother how that you manage to keep your health and stay up on your feet and do the amount of work that you do with out giving down some time. You must understand the laws of governing physical health and obey them, or perhaps *Strong Will Power,* has something to do with it, I know not which   Thanksgiving and Holidays will soon be here again. How time is flying   soon be three years since I was with you all. Kiss all the children and Mrs Washington also for me   Aunt Mary

Dear Brother, you can never know how much that mother and I appreciate your kindness in sending us the Hernando letter which gave us such a plain understanding as pen picture of the graves   I can understand a bout them better then ever before, although Dear Olivia had tr[i]ed to make evry thing plain to me years ago, she it was that designed the epitaphs for the head Stones did evry thing that was done, dear girl. That is one time that I prepared to go to her side to help her but Mother was taken Sudenly Ill. The shock was more than she could stand. Lizzie had ondly been dead a little over three months When Josie died or was killed by the CuKlucks (I dont know how to spell it) and he was mother's baby boy, and our youngest brother   he was the prettiest child that mother ever had. Oh! Booker those were dark days, of sorrow that I wish none may ever have to pass through any thing like them and it was many weeks before mother could realize any thing. She hovered between life and death part of the time, and I sit by her bedside most of the time, and she has since that time disliked to hear of any of us going South to live. She use to say that the ondly think that she would like to visit the South for would be to see these graves.

Dear Brother, how considerate of you to think of these graves. I know that you spoke of them to me some time ago. I feel that it is my duty to help bare the expenses, and I will do so willingly if you will let me know how to send it to you or to the one that dose the work. I will send it to you if you let me know How much it will cost. May the Blessings of Heaven ever abide with you   Your Sister.

Mary A. Elliott

P.S. If you want me to send the Hernando letter back plase to drop me a card

M. A. E.

This leaves us all well. Times are dull in our City yet. But think buisness will be better soon.

ALS   Con. 107   BTW Papers   DLC.

From Margaret James Murray Washington

[Tuskegee, Ala., Dec. 9, 1894][1]

My Dear Booker. It has been a whole week since I have written you. And it has been a longer time since you wrote me. Are you angry or are you having so much to do that you can not find time to write.

The week has passed so rapidly that I have not realized its passing.

Things are running on well. We are having just such a fall as we had the first year Dillon was here. The weather and all are alike. There is now another boy just as low as he can be. He was taken in the night Friday night and since the first has been sick unto death. The doctors pronounce Brain conjestion. I think the students, the younger ones are very much frightened and Mr. Logan has never thought to try to make them see it all in its true light. I spoke to Mr. Penny this morning and he mentioned it in his sermon.

Mrs. Penney is still in bed. I really feel that she is miserable and

486

her life is just ebbing slowly away. I feel sorry for her but she profits by nothing that is said to her.

Mrs. Young is now quite sick and Mr. Chambliss is still confined to bed. I feel afraid for him.

Baker went horse back riding with John[2] yesterday. He fell from the horse and was badly frightened but not hurt at all. He is perfectly happy at the Training School now. Grace and the J. H. children also go.

Dave recites to me two or three times a day. He is getting on so nicely.

Mrs. Kanie[3] has been trying to get the water closet near Alabama Hall removed further down the hill she has not succeeded. You know how contrary Mr. J. H. Dr. Washington also, sees that she should have this attended to immediately.

People are now criticising Miss Robinson[4] for having little Charlie Pitts[5] come to her room. I should judge him to be at least sixteen. It is said to day that she has been in bed and that he has been there twice. I think she should be told that no one young man nor boy can be treated in this familiar way but Mr. Logan is a big coward and would never speak to her, and he would say that Mr. Calloway is pressuring if he should do it. And of course it will be left for you. ThanksGiving Day she kissed this boy and Mr. Penney instead of speaking to her said "I am going to tell Mr. Washington.["]

The Emerson[6] moves on. Not all attend but we have a pleasant time — now and then we have a little fruit.

I am having a good full meeting now, if only I had a little more time to give to it.

The friend in New Mexico sent you a buggy robe. It is made with the hand and is very warm although it does not look so well. There was no letter with it.

The Conference is over. Mr. McMillain was left here but the people did not want him. They say he is too stupid and slow.

Two or three young men have lately entered the Bible Training School — one very bright man came in last week. Mr. Harding[7] influenced him in coming here.

The Prayer meeting on Friday night, for the work students is not in good order. Last week I counted more than twenty in the hall. They study their lessons, talk and the whole thing is demoralizing.

I spoke to Mr. Logan. He spoke to Mr. Penney and thats the last of it.

I hope that you will write me soon. I wrote Miss Haven[8] not long since.

Maggie

ALS Con. 17 BTW Papers DLC.

[1] The dating was suggested by Warren Logan's mention on Dec. 8 of the deaths of students and the mention above of the sermon that morning. (See BTW to Warren Logan, Dec. 12, 1894, below.)

[2] Probably John H. Washington, Jr.

[3] Alice J. Kaine.

[4] Jennie Robinson was instructor in vocal and physical culture for the 1894-95 academic year only.

[5] Charles Nathaniel Pitts of Macon, Ga., attended Tuskegee from 1894 to 1897. He did not graduate.

[6] The Emerson Club, a faculty group devoted to the study of the works of Ralph Waldo Emerson, whose exhortation to be "up and doing" in the life work of self-improvement was an important element in Tuskegee's educational philosophy.

[7] John Wheeler Harding?

[8] Probably Miss E. A. Haven of Portsmouth, N.H., who, along with her sister Charlotte M. Haven, were occasional donors to Tuskegee. Charlotte Haven was apparently deceased by the time of this letter. (See E. A. Haven to BTW, Feb. 7, 1894, Con. 109, BTW Papers, DLC.)

To Warren Logan

Crawford House, Boston, 12/12/1894

Dear Mr. Logan: I have yours of the 8th regarding the feeling among the students over the recent deaths at the school.

In the end, I find that people usually take the common sense view of things, and I think the students and their parents will do that in this case; but of course there are a great many things to be borne with while people are settling down to the common sense view.

So far as I can learn, none of these students — or certainly no more than two — have died of the same disease. It is to be noted that there is an unusual amount of sickness all over the country, especially in schools, this year. A good many public schools in New England have been closed on account of dyptheria. A girls' college in connection with Princeton University was closed recently for this same purpose, and there have been a good many cases of typhoid fever at Yale and Wesleyan Universities. I think the death-rate in the healthiest part of our country is 25 or 30 per 1,000; and when it is considered that at Tuskegee we have almost continually a population of at least 1,000 persons, it will be seen that we are considerably below the average death-rate. I believe that there are few communities in the whole country whose death-rate is so low as ours.

However, we want to be sure that everything about the school that relates to its sanitary condition, is right. I am going to take steps this week to secure a Sanitary Engineer to go to Tuskegee and make thorough examination of our surroundings.

I wish you would ask Dr. Washington [to] write me something regarding the history of the cases that have resulted fatally; that is, what the diseases were in each case, how long the students were sick, where their rooms were &c.

Mr. Hoffman,[1] I notice, has made some criticism to my brother regarding the condition of our water. He says it needs filtering. I dont see the need, however, of filtering water that comes from a pure spring.

Every precaution should be taken to see that the students' food is at all times cooked done.

I wish you would also speak to the students about the careless habit that a great many of them have of going out at night in their night clothes, very often without shoes, to the well or water-closets. Of course all this is very dangerous.

It is now my purpose to leave here on the night of the 23rd of December, and I shall perhaps reach Tuskegee on the 25th or 26th. Yours truly,

Booker T. Washington

Prof. Hincks has just died at Atlanta of fever and another teacher is sick. Miss Thorn has had to leave Calhoun on acct of sickness.

TLS Con. 9 BTW Papers ATT. Original destroyed.

[1] John Wesslay Hoffman.

To Hollis Burke Frissell

Boston, 12/12/1894

Dear Dr. Frissell: I am very anxious to secure a good, strong woman, I mean *strong* in every sense of the word to come to Boston or go to

Pratt Institute and take a thorough course in the preparation and serving of food with the end in view of going to Tuskegee to take charge of our students' food department. They have recently established a new course at Pratt Institute, and if we can secure the right woman, I think it best for her to go there.

The course has for its object the preparation of women for service in institutions where there are a large number of people to be cared for. Can you put me in communication with a Hampton woman who would fill the bill? We shall be willing to pay her expenses while she is North taking the course, and can take it out of her salary later on. It is an excellent chance for the right woman I think.

I shall be here until the 23rd.

Enclosed I send you a notice regarding the meeting we are to hold in Trinity Church, next Sunday evening. Yours very truly,

Booker T. Washington

TLS BTW Folder ViHaI.

From William Calvin Oates[1]

Montgomery, Ala. Decr 12th, 1894

My dear Sir. I am thinking of keeping house. My wife & myself have about arranged to do so & write you to inquire if you can recommend to me two girls — one a good cook and the other a Chambermaid who also knows how to sew on a machine &c. I would like to have two intelligent girls trained in your School & would prefer them goodlooking and of light color or if dark good looking, nice intelligent girls who would room together in my house.

If you have any such whom you can commend please state at what price they will serve or have them to write me upon the subject themselves. There are numbers here I could get & at very low wages but I want nice girls who are intelligent & know how to do their work. Very respectfully

Wm C Oates

ALS Con. 7 BTW Papers ATT. Original destroyed. Docketed in Warren Logan's hand: "Ans No girls to send."

¹ William Calvin Oates (1835-1910) was born of poor parents in Pike County (now Bullock County), Ala. He studied law in Eufaula and was admitted to the bar in 1858. A Confederate war hero who lost an arm in battle near Petersburg, Va., Oates became an active Democratic politician, serving in the Alabama House of Representatives beginning in 1870. He was elected to Congress in 1880, serving seven terms. In 1894 he was elected governor of Alabama for one term in a colorful campaign against the agrarian Reuben F. Kolb. He ran for the U.S. Senate unsuccessfully as a Gold Democrat in 1897. During the Spanish-American War he commanded troops at Camp Meade, Pa., and later returned to law practice in Montgomery. Oates opposed the grandfather clause. He favored suffrage qualifications that would reduce the size of the electorate, but thought they should be the same for both races. In 1901 he was a member of the state constitutional convention and of its committee on suffrage and elections. He fought eloquently but unsuccessfully for a racially nondiscriminatory standard of suffrage. A champion of Tuskegee and BTW, Oates represented the paternalism of the upper-class white southerner.

From Margaret James Murray Washington

Tuskegee, Ala. Dec. 13. '94

My Dearest Booker: I meant to have written you yesterday but I am so blue these days that I do not feel inclined to write to any one. Some way or rather this fall, I have felt so unwell and so unhappy that I have been little or no account to myself or to any one.

I tried to throw off this feeling last night by meeting all of the girls at half past eight in the Chapel.

There is a good deal of unrest here among the girls. Many of them are really unhappy. They walk around and abuse the teachers and the school and many of them are trying to get home.

Kate Foster¹ said to me, "The girls have no [one] to go to for any thing. They go either to Mr. Young or to you. If they go to Miss Bransford she tosses her head in the air and passes right on. Often she shuts the door right in the face of the girls and we do not go to her. Any girl on the place who feels inclined can demerit the girls and Miss Bransford takes them in & the warning is given often without even an investigation." This much I positively know. Two weeks ago Miss McKinney² had the girls giving them her Laundry rules. They, the girls, were disorderly — one girl in the crowd took a good many names for coughing. She afterwards handed the names to Miss Kaine with this request.

"Please hand this note to Miss Bransford.["] It was night, Mrs. Kaine did not know the girl, but she passed the note containing the names to Miss Bransford, not even suspecting that it was what it was.

Miss Bransford took the names into the Council as having come from Mrs. Kaine and the warnings were given. Mr. Calloway is the only one who felt that it was an abominable piece of cowardice on the part of Miss Bransford. The Council claimed that the names were the worst kind of girls, this was true but I firmly believe that this whole business was unjust to some of the girls.

Miss Bransford in her dealing with the Senior girls tries to keep this thing before them — "You are under me and you shall be kept as low as possible.["] And very few of them ever speak to her except they are absolutely obliged to do so. I feel sorry that we have never been able to get a good woman who will understand that these girls need more than some body to go around and read out rules to them. Mr. Young told me to day that he had a hundred students to have a warning now. I am just disgusted with the whole thing here.

I had to laugh when you said that all of us are afraid of these women. I feel that Miss Robinson is a bad woman but we have her and it seems to me that since she has settled a little it is best to keep her until the end of the year. Mrs. Kaine certainly gave it to her. Miss Chapman[3] is a fast young woman but I do not think that she should be kept unless she changes. She does harm I am sure as far as these boys are concerned and little good as far as all are concerned. She is made wrong.

You remember that I spoke to you of the manner of spending money here for entertainments. Mr. Calloway tried to get the Council to look into this but they preferred to leave it to Miss Bransford. Mrs. Kaine criticised this severely and then the teachers who are capable of thinking of such things also criticised. And it seems to me that now before Xmas you should say how much shall be spent here for these social gatherings. It is a shame to have boys here with some body to pay their board and pay seventy five cents or one dollar for a social.

The children are doing very nicely. Baker is getting on well in school and Dave gets four lessons a day from me. He comes to the Office in the morning and I hear him at night also. We all read together now and have the prayer also. I have not kept up with Portia and her Arithmetic. I think she is studying now for she has little else to do. She has begun to study History now.

I hope that you will not work too hard. It seems hard to have you away so much and yet I will not complain. What about the presents? Do not buy too much. Mrs. Young and Mrs. Penney are still confined to bed. Mr. Chambliss also. Write soon.

Maggie

ALS Con. 17 BTW Papers DLC.

[1] Katie Louise Foster of Spartanburg, S.C., entered Tuskegee in 1893. She graduated in 1896 and became a laundress and trained nurse.

[2] Fannie C. McKinney.

[3] Leonora Love Chapman Kenniebrew taught rhetoric and English in 1894-95. From 1895 to 1899, she was Lady Principal. She married Dr. Alonzo Homer Kenniebrew, Tuskegee's resident physician, in 1899 and continued to teach at Tuskegee until 1901.

To Emily Howland

Tuskegee, Ala. Dec. 27, 94

Dear Miss Howland: I did not reach home from Boston till day before yesterday and was very glad to find your letter of Dec. 14.[1] You can not realize how very much your money and words help and encourage us.

As you say we do need the chapel very much but I think it best to go slow and not go in debt for it, and then we want to be sure of putting up one that will serve for all time.

Mary Blandon,[2] the girl, whose school house burned, graduated last May and she is [a] very fine girl. Her parents were able to raise her better than most of our girls, still she is just as willing as any to give herself to the work of helping others even at the cost of great personal discomfort. She is still teaching in her bed room and keeps up a brave spirit. You will see a letter from her published in the Dec. Southern Letter. She is in a cotton raising region where the masses of the colored people are held in practical slavery by the mortgage system.

If you want more information I shall be glad to write you.

We are having now some *very* cold weather and I "shiver" for the poor people.

Our school work is in good condition.

Mrs. Washington desires to be remembered to you. Yours truly

Booker T. Washington

ALS   Emily Howland Papers   NN-Sc.

[1] Miss Howland sent BTW a draft for $136, bringing her total contribution to the school to $500 in 1894. (Howland to BTW, Dec. 14, 1894, Con. 700, BTW Papers, DLC.)

[2] Mary Willa Blandon Lockhart taught at Cowles, Ala., in 1894-95, then married B. H. Lockhart and lived in Columbus, Ga., as a housekeeper and dressmaker, and as a teacher at Price Normal and Industrial School.

To Elizabeth J. Scott[1]

[Tuskegee, Ala.] Dec. 28th, 1894

Mrs. Scott: I am informed by Mrs. Kaine that you do not co-operate with her in the proper spirit in relation to the changes and improvements to be made in your department. I am very sorry to hear of this. I have stated more than once that Mrs. Kaine's suggestions and orders are to be carried out, and I can certainly make no exception in your case; in fact, I am sorry that you take my time in compelling me to repeat an order which has already been given more than once. Mrs. Kaine is not here for the purpose of begging teachers to do what she asks, nor should it be required to repeat an order. I hope you will look at this matter calmly, and when you have thought it over, I think you will find that it is best for you as well as for the school to obey Mrs. Kaine and carry out her suggestions in the proper spirit. The school will be satisfied with nothing less than this.

I hope the matter will not come to my attention again. Yours truly,

[Booker T. Washington]

TLp   Con. 113   BTW Papers   DLC.

[1] Elizabeth J. Scott was in charge of the diet kitchen in 1894-95 and of the teachers' laundry in 1895-96.

An Agreement to Form a Building
and Loan Association

[Tuskegee, Ala., ca. 1894-95]

We, the undersigned, hereby express a desire to unite in the formation of a Building & Loan Association and upon the due incorporation of said association and the adopting of by-laws, we severally agree to take the number of shares of stock in said association set opposite our respective names. The entrance fee will be 25 cts a share and dues 30¢ per share each mo.

NAME	SHARES
Booker T. Washington	25
Warren Logan	25
J. D. McCall	20
R. H. Hamilton	15
Wm. Jenkins	25
J. B. Washington	10
W. E. Hutt	20
Mack Williams	15
C. W. Greene	20
J. M. Greene	20
G. W. A. Johnson	15
A. J. Wilborn	10
Thos. A. Harris	10
J. A. Roy	20
J. N. Calloway	20
F. R. Simon	20
Thos L Mann	15
J. H. Washington	15
J. C. Green	15
M. T. Driver	10
M. Gaston Daniels	10

HDS Con. 8 BTW Papers ATT. Original destroyed. The statement is in Warren Logan's hand.

A Newspaper Report of an Emancipation Day[1] Address

Montgomery, Ala. [Jan. 1, 1895]

This is the fifth or sixth time we have celebrated the greatest of all great days to the Negro, and I can say without fear of contradiction that every year doubles its interest. The address was delivered by that scholarly and deep thinking gentleman, Prof. B. T. Washington of the Normal school at Tuskegee. The address was as usually delivered by the speaker plain and instructive. The speaker told how a vessel out at sea had thrown up its signal for help from another vessel not far off, saying help, save us or we perish for water, and the captain of the other vessel's reply was, cast down your buckets where you are, and finally after several attempts to get help, and every time hearing the same command, cast down your buckets where you are, decided to try, and in so doing the buckets were drawn up with clear, cool, sparkling water from the mouth of the Amazon. Right here the speaker impresses us to cast down our buckets in the same like manner, and they would come up as merchants, manufacturers, scientific and men of all skillful advantages. The speaker tried to impress his hearers to apply their time and money in giving their children an industrial education through which medium we as a race will gradually grow stronger and independent.

Indianapolis *Freeman,* Jan. 26, 1895, 6.

[1] Emancipation Day, a holiday widely celebrated by black people in the nineteenth century, was Jan. 1, the day the Emancipation Proclamation went into effect in 1863.

From Francis J. Grimké

Washington, D.C., Jan. 6th. 1895

Dear Prof. Washington: Your letter was quite a surprise to me. I had no idea that Dr. Blyden[1] was thinking of leaving Africa for work in this country. He is a man of great abilities, of great learning, and of rare scholarship: in some respects the most distinguished representative of our race now living. As to his character, I cannot speak so positively. Like yourself, I have heard whispers which tended to cast a doubt upon his moral soundness, but whether they are well founded or not, I cannot say; or whether they have reference to what occurred, or is alleged to have occurred, twenty-five or thirty years ago, in Africa, or to something that may have occurred in more recent years, I do not know. I know nothing personally, against his character, though, as I have said, these whispers against him I have heard.

I read with the greatest interest your last Report to the Trustees, and would be obliged to you if you would send me a few copies for distribution.

Hoping that you are well, and with kindest regards for yourself and Mrs. Washington, and with best wishes for your continued success in the great work in which you are engaged, I am as ever, Your sincere friend,

Francis J. Grimké

TLS Con. 8 BTW Papers ATT. Original destroyed.

[1] Edward Wilmot Blyden (1832-1912) was born a free black in the Danish West Indies. He came to the United States in 1850 to study at Rutgers Theological College but was refused admittance because of his color. The New York Colonization Society heard of his plight and sent him to Liberia to be educated by Presbyterian missionaries. As a teacher and clergyman Blyden became Liberia's major spokesman in the United States and Europe, encouraging blacks to emigrate to West Africa. Blyden toured the United States in 1889, sponsored by the American Colonization Society, to urge support of the Butler bill to aid emigration to Africa.

BTW and Blyden met in Washington, D.C., in 1890 through their mutual friend Francis J. Grimké. Their views on race pride and self-help were similar. They differed sharply, however, regarding African emigration. In 1894 Blyden wrote to BTW and expressed agreement with the Tuskegean's philosophy of eschewing politics in favor of industrial education. He admitted to BTW that any general exodus of black Americans remained in the distant future. BTW publicly praised Blyden as an outstanding intellectual. Blyden's nationalistic views, however, included the notion that mulattoes could play no important role in fostering nationalism; only pure blacks could lead the way. This viewpoint was a common one in the West Indies. The idea strained Blyden's relationship with most black American leaders. Blyden's position of cooperation with European powers persisted in spite of strong opposition on the part of the other African leaders to the increasing European imperialism in Africa in the late nineteenth century. After BTW's dinner at the White House in 1901, Blyden decided he was a race amalgamator like other mulattoes and turned against him. He once sought to interest southern whites in a school for blacks to compete with Tuskegee. He fell into disrepute as a Liberian leader and died poor and isolated from power. Black leaders in America and Africa continued to praise Blyden because of his lifelong advocacy of black unity and race pride. (See Lynch, *Edward Wilmot Blyden,* and Redkey, *Black Exodus.*)

From Alice J. Kaine

Tuskegee, Ala. Jan. 8 — 1895

Mr Washington   In presenting a resumé of work accomplished up to date and plan of future work, I should like to state that the first three or four weeks after coming were employed in bringing about, what I would term a better moral atmosphere.

The work that I came to do could not well be undertaken until a better state of quiet and order maintained.

The halls are now comparatively quiet. The students about the grounds are more orderly and much more quiet. The girls and boys enter the dining hall in silence and remain so until after Grace has been sung. Study hour is better worth the name and students themselves begin to appreciate the favorable change. All work in the industrial departments is carried on quietly and a degree of application is possible which did not exist before.

While the work for which I came is being carried on, I still divide it with this less tangible but larger undertaking as I believe the latter to be the foundation of all character building and particularly a necessity here where the students as a whole, come from homes void of discipline and where the home life in a high sense is wholly unknown. Very Sincerely

Mrs J. L. Kaine

ALS Con. 8 BTW Papers ATT. Original destroyed. Attached was a two-page list of furnishings and repairs completed and planned.

From A. W. Parker[1]

Brooklyn, Jan. 8th, 1895

Dear Sir: It is strange to me that people of such eminent good sense as has been shown in the management of Tuskegee, should have persistently held to the idea of making a model cottage on such lines and in such proportion as to be utterly out of reach of the people for whose use it was designed. If at the outset, you had asked me to put up a building for the older girls I might have then considered as I am willing to now consider, the matter irrespective of making it a model poor man's cottage — that is to say, if you had abandoned the idea of the model, the first building of which you sent me a sketch would be suitable and proper and satisfactory to me; but if you have started out to make a model cottage it should be so. You and I well know that one in a hundred, probably one in five hundred leaving the school would be able to put up more than a two room cottage with a leanto for a kitchen. My idea was and is to take this limitation, perhaps enlarge on it in some degree, and build something that students may look at and endeavor to copy. It is preposterous to suppose that they can to any extent use even this last proposed cottage for a model. You do not give me the probable cost but I imagine it is not less than from four to five hundred Dollars, and who is there in your school now who can spend even four hundred Dollars on a house?

I understand the annoyance resulting from my repeated rejections of your plans and I see too the feeling which your people naturally would have to have everything inside the school-grounds nice in proportion as well as appearance, therefore, I suggest one of two things, either let us entirely abandon the idea of a model and build a cottage for the graduating class where they can have practical experience in house-keeping or else let us have what we started to have, model cottages — and make them so; that is, to put up something that the students may possibly be able to copy. A row of three or four or five model cottages would not be disfiguring and would be an object lesson for the men, but if this is impracticable, let us go back to the first idea and build a two story cottage. Yours truly,

A W Parker

TLS Con. 8 BTW Papers ATT. Original destroyed.

[1] A. W. Parker was an attorney, about fifty-four years old in 1895. He resided in Hempstead, Long Island.

To A. W. Parker

[Tuskegee, Ala.] Jan. 15th, 1895

My dear Sir: Yours of Jan. 8th has been received, and has been fully considered by our Executive Council. The last plan sent you, I examined very carefully, and had two objects in view: one was that we should put up a model cottage that would serve as a permanent object-lesson for our students, — I mean one that would not only answer the present purpose, but would answer the same purpose ten or twenty years from now. It is a fact that as the colored people receive education, they grow in ability, and we felt that it would not be best to put up a house that would not serve our purpose a good way into the future.

And then too, we felt that while not a large number of our students at present, could build a house exactly like the one called for by the plan sent you, we thought it well to have one that they could imitate as nearly as possible. In other words, we wanted to have an ideal toward which they could aspire. I know at least a half dozen of our graduates who have already built houses not very much different from the one described in the plan sent you. Of course, I dont mean to say that they have built these houses, paying cash for them at once, but they have built them by making monthly or quarterly payments.

Our Executive Council are of the opinion, — and I agree with them — that it will not be the best thing to put up a number of houses on the school grounds that are any smaller than the one called for by the plan sent you. As between putting up a number of smaller houses, and the two-story house called for by the first set of drawings sent you, I think it better to erect the latter where we can have all the girls together, and teach the principles of house-keeping.

When I sent the last set of drawings, I felt rather sure that I had hit your idea of what was wanted. I think, after you have the opportunity of seeing the work that will be done on the two-story building, you will feel that no great mistake has been made in having that instead of the number of smaller houses.

Mr. Logan, our treasurer, makes the suggestion that there are a number of small houses near the school of the kind in question that our students are constantly coming in contact with, and that by reason of this contact, they will be led to try to build houses somewhat on that order.

I hope very much that I make myself clear in the matter. We all appreciate in the highest degree your generosity and interest in this matter, and we have only been seeking to do the best thing for all concerned. We are more than grateful for what you are doing. Yours very truly,

Booker T. Washington

TLpS Con. 113 BTW Papers DLC.

From A. W. Parker

Brooklyn, Jan 17th 1895

Dear Sir— This is a case of "making haste slowly." I think perhaps it has not been all time wasted in studying up this matter and I sincerely hope that your people have reached the wisest thing in abandoning the cabin or cottage plan and in place of it put up the neat 2 story structure that will effectually make a *housekeeping school* for the older girls.

I enclose my check for $500. and hope now that nothing will prevent or delay you in advancing this plan of teaching. If it is well carried out I expect only the best results. Yours very truly

A. W. Parker

ALS Con. 8 BTW Papers ATT. Original destroyed.

From Timothy Thomas Fortune

New York, Jan. 18 1895

Dear Professor Please accept my thanks for your favor of the 14th instant, enclosing Professor Blyden's letter to you. We will use the Blyden letter in The Age, despite the fact that Blyden is a big rascal in several directions and has been barred out of Liberia. Yours truly

T. Thomas Fortune

ALS Con. 8 BTW Papers ATT. Original destroyed.

An Interview in the Chicago *Inter Ocean*

[Chicago, Jan. 26, 1895]

ELEVATING THE RACE

WORK OF THE TUSKEGEE INDUSTRIAL INSTITUTE FOR NEGROES

METHODS OF INSTRUCTION

STUDENTS TAUGHT TRADES AND MADE SELF-RELIANT

Booker T. Washington, the Principal, Tells of the Success
of the Institution

Mr. Booker T. Washington, principal of the Tuskegee Normal and Industrial Institute for Negroes, at Tuskegee, Ala., has been in the city this week, and went to Madison, Wis., yesterday. Mr. Washington visited the University of Chicago Thursday and addressed the students, and next week he will speak at the Armour Institute. He will be in Chicago tomorrow, and address three meetings in different churches, morning, afternoon, and evening. The afternoon meeting will be in Plymouth Congregational Church, with Dr. Gunsaulus[1] presiding, and such men as Bishop Fallows,[2] Jenkin Lloyd Jones,[3] Professor Graham Taylor,[4] Professor Edward W. Bemis,[5] and John C. Grant[6] present to speak with him.

Mr. Washington is a negro who, having educated himself, is now devoting all his energy and talent to helping other negro boys and girls to a practical education. He went to Hampton Institute with 50 cents in his pocket, worked his way through the course there, and when the Governor of Alabama wrote to General Armstrong to recommend a man to start a similar institution in that State Armstrong sent Booker T. Washington.

That was thirteen years ago. Alabama made an annual appropriation of $2,000 for a negro industrial school, and Mr. Washington began his school in a small negro church at Tuskegee, one teacher and thirty students.

Today the school has 1,810 acres of fine farm land under diversified cultivation, property, including lands, buildings, and stock, valued at $200,000, nearly 800 students, and forty-eight instructors. In connection with the ordinary educational work there are twenty-three industries in operation at the school, and every student, boy or girl, must spend a part of each day in working at some trade and earning a part of his board by work.

MUST LEARN A TRADE

Mr. Washington has modeled much of his work on his own experience in working his way through college, and allows no student at Tuskegee to pay all his way. He must work and learn a trade while he is also acquiring an education.

Mr. Washington says: "The colored people throughout the South are beginning to demand industrial education in a way that they have never done before. All of our industrial departments have been full and many students refused for lack of room. We have had to refuse the applications of more than 200 girls for admission this year, because we cannot find the room for them. We have 325 girls now, and they are as eager as the boys for industrial training. They are taught sewing, laundry work, housework, dressmaking, and nursing. Our training school for nurses promises to open a good field for colored women. We have about 450 boys and could have many more if we had the room for them. At present we are renting cottages outside the grounds to accommodate some of the boys until they can complete a new dormitory they are building. We do not hire outside help to put up our buildings.

"The money spent on them is only for material and the support of the boys who do the work while they are learning their trades. They make the brick and lay them. They get out the timber and manufacture the lumber which goes to the carpenter shop and from there into the building. We have no dealings with contractors or outside builders. We do all this work as a part of the practical teaching in an industrial education.

"The boys are now at work on a new three-story brick dormitory. When that is completed and we can get the money to carry on the work we must add another large dormitory for the girls. We are now building a model home cottage for the use of the advanced class of girls, where they are to live and have entire charge, learning how to become thorough housekeepers and understand the economies of a household.

AT THE MODEL HOME COTTAGE

"This might seem unnecessary to those who do not understand the condition of the great mass of negroes whose homes have always been in one-room cabins. But that old life is the greatest embarrassment to the progress of the race. We are leading our young people to aspire to better homes and how to secure them. We must also teach the girls how to take care of such homes, and they take great interest in the work at the model home cottage."

"Has Governor Oates shown any interest in your work?"

"Yes. The Governor visited Tuskegee soon after his inauguration last fall and he seemed well pleased and much interested in the work we are doing. He realizes the necessity for industrial education among the negroes and I believe he will do all in his power to help along the work. But Alabama felt the hard times very much, and the State Legislature will not be able to help us much this year. We feel that we have the good will of this administration as we had of the last, for Governor Jones was always very friendly to Tuskegee and the work we are engaged in there."

"Will you hold your annual negro conference at Tuskegee this year?"

"It will be held next month, beginning Feb. 20. We expect to enlarge it, and have representative farmers from Georgia, Louisiana, and Mississippi. Heretofore it has been confined to the negroes of the black belt of Alabama, but in our discussion of diversified farming we want to enlarge the field and bring farmers from other States to give their experiences. We expect to have some of the negro sugar-cane raisers of Louisiana at the conference to tell our people how to make that a successful crop. We have been experimenting with sugar cane at the school farm, and last year made seventy-five barrels of syrup from the crop.

TO MAKE THEM SELF-RELIANT

"We want to teach the negroes of the black belt of Alabama how to get away from cotton raising, for there is no money in the crop. We are teaching them to raise corn and potatoes and beans, to produce pork, and in fact raise first what will feed them rather than depend upon an outside market. It has too long been the rule in the South to raise only cotton and buy all food products. We are getting away from that old idea, and we hope that the cane growers of Louisiana will give our conference some practical suggestions regarding growing cane in Alabama. We do not want to go into the sugar business, but teach our people to raise their own sugar cane and produce their own syrup instead of buying it."

"How is your school supported?"

"The State of Alabama contributes $2,000 a year. We get several thousand dollars more from the Peabody and Slater funds. The students pay a part of their expenses with labor, but it costs us $50 a year for the educational work and the tuition is free. This money is contributed by those who are interested in educating the negroes. Our teachers are paid salaries that average less than $400 a year. They are all very earnest workers, and many of them could command much higher pay elsewhere, but they appreciate the work we are doing, and all of them being negroes — there is not a white man or woman connected with the institution — they feel that they owe this duty to the race and do their share to lift it to a higher level. Much of my success I owe to the loyalty and industry of my corps of teachers, who are working just as earnestly as I am to teach the negroes how to take care of themselves and be independent by knowing how to work at some trade as wage-earners. Industrial education will do more than all else to emancipate the negro from the helplessness of ignorant and unskilled labor."

Mr. Washington is making his first visit to the West, and is much satisfied with the interest he finds here in his race and his work to elevate and liberate that race from the ignorance that was the natural inheritance from slavery.

Chicago *Inter Ocean,* Jan. 26, 1895, 9.

[1] Frank Wakeley Gunsaulus (1856-1921) was pastor of the Plymouth Congregational Church from 1887 to 1899. His sermon on the need for a technical school that would offer poor boys a chance to become rich inspired Philip D. Armour to found Armour Institute in 1893, with Gunsaulus as president, though he had no technical training. Gunsaulus was a prolific writer of verse and novels as well as devotional works. After leaving Plymouth Church, he was pastor of the Independent Central Church of Chicago for the last twenty years of his life.

[2] Samuel Fallows (1835-1922), bishop of the Reformed Episcopal Church in Chicago. Born in England, he migrated to the United States in 1848 and graduated from the University of Wisconsin in 1859. He entered the Methodist ministry and became a Union Army chaplain and then an infantry officer, breveted a brigadier general at the end of the war. He was Wisconsin state superintendent of education 1870-74. In 1875 he joined the Reformed Episcopal Church and became rector of St. Paul's Church in Chicago. He was an active prohibitionist and founded the People's Institute in Chicago.

[3] Jenkin Lloyd Jones (1843-1918) was a Unitarian clergyman and editor who fought in the Civil War but became a staunch opponent of war. After graduation from Meadville Theological Seminary in 1870, he served as a Unitarian minister

in the Midwest and West. He published a series of Sunday-school lessons that stressed the evolution of man and the unity of world religions. In 1885 he became minister of All Souls Church in Chicago and was active in the World's Parliament of Religions at the Columbian Exposition in 1893. He edited a religious weekly, *Unity,* from 1880 until 1918. Jones was an early activist in the Chicago branch of the NAACP. He was a supporter of BTW, and tried to moderate the NAACP's outspoken demands for civil rights, which he believed to be too radical. He sailed to Europe on the Ford Peace Ship Expedition in December 1915, and opposed U.S. participation in World War I. Among his publications were *A Search for an Infidel* (1901) and *Love and Loyalty* (1907).

[4] Graham Taylor (1851-1938) graduated from Rutgers and attended the Reformed Theological Seminary in New Brunswick, N.J. In 1873 he was ordained in the Dutch Reformed Church. He became professor of theology at Hartford Theological Seminary in 1888 and professor of social economy at the Chicago Theological Seminary in 1892. There he founded the Chicago Commons Social Settlement and was president of the Chicago School of Civics and Philanthropy. Active in the social gospel movement, he wrote *Religion in Social Action* (1913).

[5] Edward Webster Bemis (1860-1930) was for many years beginning in 1892 professor of political economy at the University of Chicago. Born in Springfield, Mass., he graduated from Amherst and received a Ph.D. at Johns Hopkins in 1885. He wrote works on cooperatives, labor unions, and local government.

[6] John Cowles Grant (1848-1914), principal of the Harvard School in Chicago from 1880 to 1914, was a trustee of Tuskegee Institute from 1895 until his death. He put BTW in contact with a number of wealthy men in Chicago.

From Timothy Thomas Fortune

Charleston, S.C., Feb. 8, 1895

Dear Friend: Your note of the 4th instant was received. I have been here ten days hustling for the Sun,[1] and shall go to Jacksonville, Fla., for ten days on the 13th instant.

You can't afford to pin to Dr. Blyden. He is utterly unreliable and withal a propagandist of the blacks against the mulattoes of the race. Such a man is dangerous anywhere, and I have sent an editorial note to the Age cordially to remain in Africa, as we have no need of him here. Yours truly

T. Thomas Fortune

ALS   Con. 8   BTW Papers   ATT.   Original destroyed.

[1] The New York *Sun,* for which Fortune regularly reported on black affairs.

To Irene Bond[1]

[Tuskegee, Ala.] Feb. 9th, 1895

Mrs. Bond: I have thoroughly considered your attitude in regard to taking part in the inspection of the girls' rooms. Whatever I said to you last year or at any other time in reference to your being excused from night work had reference to work that would interfere with your being with your children. Ever since you have been here I have always considered that in view of the fact that you were kept away from your children during the day that exception in your case ought to be made in every way possible so as to allow you to be with them after the day's work was done. I cannot see that asking you to spend ten or fifteen minutes in taking your turn every three weeks in inspecting seven or eight girls' rooms is in any way breaking faith with you. I have always tried to be reasonable and considerate with all teachers, and expect that they in turn will be the same way with the school. It appears to me that you desire more now to take advantage of a technicality in what I said to you than to get rid of the duty of inspecting.

Ever since the beginning of this school, we have made it a point to try to secure teachers who would be willing to work wherever and whenever duty called, and in this respect I feel that we have been unusually successful. This school is supported almost wholly by people who make sacrifices of personal conveniences in order that they may give to us, and I cannot feel that it is right to allow a teacher to refuse, without adequate reasons to give a small sacrifice of her time to work that has the good of the girls in view, while at the same time our Northern friends and others are doing all they can to support the school in the belief that each teacher is willing to perform her duty in the same spirit that they give the money. We have a large number of girls whose mothers have entrusted them to our care [and it] seems to me that you should count it a privilege to go into their rooms once in a while and get acquainted with them and help them in a way that will impress them all through their lives. Such work should not be counted a task.

In view of the circumstances, I cannot make any change in what I have said to you in connection with performing this duty. There will be no change in this decision.

Booker T. Washington

TLpS Con. 113 BTW Papers DLC.

¹ Instructor in dressmaking from 1892 to 1895.

A Sunday Evening Talk

Tuskegee, Ala., Feb. 10th, 1895

UNIMPROVED OPPORTUNITIES

There are several things I shall say to you to-night, which may not sound very agreeable or encouraging to many of you, yet you will agree with me that they are facts that cannot be denied.

We have got to recognize, in the first place, that our condition is, in a large measure, different from that of the white race by whom we are surrounded; that our capacity is in a large measure, different from theirs. I know we like to say the opposite. It sounds very well in compositions, does very well for rhetoric and makes a splendid essay for us to make the opposite assertion. It sounds very well in a newspaper article sometimes; but when we come down to the hard fact of the matter, we must acknowledge that our condition and our capacity are not equal to those of the white people with whom we come in daily contact. Of course, that doesn't sound very well. To say that we are equal to the whites, is to say that slavery was no disadvantage to us. That is the logic of it. It is saying that slavery was not a disadvantage, but an advantage, in that we were able to remain in slavery for nearly two hundred and fifty years, and then come out with a capacity equal to that of any other race. To illustrate — suppose a person is confined in a sick room, deprived of the faculties, use of his body and senses, and then he comes out and is placed by the side of a man who has been healthy in body and mind — is the condition of those two persons equal? Are they equal in capacity? Is the young animal of a week old, though he has all the elements that his mother has — as strong as she? With proper development it will, sometime in the future, be as strong, but it is unreasonable to say that it is now as strong as its mother. And so, I think, this is all we can say of ourselves — with proper development our condition and capacity will be the same as any other race's.

Now, this difference in condition and capacity, demands certain difference in education, a certain difference in training. True, we have a great many disadvantages, still we have the opportunity of learning at this stage of our growth and education, a great deal from the mistakes of the white race. The white race has been two or three thousand years getting to the point where it has learned that it has made a mistake in confining education to the head, and not coupling that education on to matter — not dove-tailing mind into matter. The white race has only learned that within the last dozen years. All that has been done in the way of industrial education has come about within the last dozen years. I say the white race has been three thousand years discovering this error, while, within the last twenty-five years, we are born right into this thing, where we can take advantage of all mistakes that the white race has been making during all this time. In this we have a great advantage.

Our children have educational advantages that thousands of white children never did have. Take the President of the United States; the smallest boy on the grounds has four or five times the chances he had in the way of education. Tell a white man forty or fifty years old about Kindergartens — about learning the alphabet without going through the old humdrum method, and he will tell you he knew nothing about such a thing. Here our children are born into this thing. They have an opportunity to take advantage of all the mistakes the white race has been so long learning, and which they have learned at such a cost of labor.

In the first place, our condition is not the same as that of other people, because, as a race, as I have often said, we are hungry. I was talking with President Calloway, of Alcorn, a few days ago, regarding the condition of things as they exist in the Mississippi bottoms and throughout the State of Louisiana, and he says that the colored people in those sections are hungry. I have had letters only this week from South Carolina and other States, and the one general piece of news they contain, is that the colored people are hungry. Of course, that does not sound well. It would not be very appropriate for a Fourth of July oration, to say that our people are hungry. Of course, we may not be feeling the pangs of hunger, and have clothing and get along very well, but there is still hunger among the masses. They are hungry in that they are without food, clothing, shelter, bank account — without the things that constitute the foundation of life. If you will agree with me that we are hungry as a race, that is, we are without the material necessities that any race must have before it can rise very far; if you agree with me in that, then isn't it most sensible in giving all our time and strength toward supplying the things that we most stand in need of?

Understand me, I am not now, nor have I ever been, opposed to any man or woman getting all the education they can. It does not matter where they get it or how they get it; what are they going to do with it, is the question. What we need to do for the next fifty or one hundred years, is to apply that education in the direction of conquering the forces of nature — to conquering matter. In other words, the power of that education, whether it be much or little, the whole strength of it should be applied during the next fifty or hundred years, in the direction of filling up our stomachs — I mean in that larger and wider sense, in supplying food, shelter, raiment — something that we can lay by for a rainy day.

In Scotland, where higher education has been within the reach of the people for many years, and where the people have reached a high degree of civilization, it is all right for the young people to give their time and attention to the study of metaphysics, law and the other professions. Of course, I don't mean to say that we should not have lawyers, metaphysicians and other professional men after a while, but I do mean to say that the efforts of a large majority of us should be devoted to securing the more material necessities of life.

THE OBJECT OF INDUSTRIAL EDUCATION

When you speak to the average person about labor, industrial work, especially, he gets the idea at once that you are opposed to his head's being educated — that you simply want to put him to work. Anybody who knows anything about industrial education, knows that it teaches a person just the opposite — how not to work. It teaches him to make water work for him, to make air, steam and all the forces of nature work for him. That is what is meant by industrial education.

Now, for a few illustrations: Yesterday I was over in the creamery, and was greatly interested in the process of separating the cream. The only energy that was spent was in turning a crank. The apparatus had been so constructed as to utilize the natural forces, and with the exception of the crank movement, it can be said that that process of separation was brought about by the force of nature. Now, compare the old method of butter-making with the new. Before, you had to go through a long process of drudgery before the cream could be separated from the milk, and then another process of drudgery before the milk could be turned into butter, and even then after churning three or four hours at a time, you got only a spoonful of butter. Now, what we mean by giving you an industrial education is to teach you how to put brains into your work, so that, if your work is butter-making, you can simply stand and turn a crank and produce butter. Now, that is what some people call teaching.

If you are studying chemistry be sure to get all you can out of the course here, and then go to a higher school some where else. Become as proficient in the science as you can. When you have done all this, don't be content to sit down and wait for the world to honor you because you know a great deal about chemistry — you will be disappointed — but if you want to make the best use of your knowledge of chemistry, come here in the South and use it in making this poor land rich, and in making good butter where we have had poor butter before. In this way you will find that your knowledge of chemistry will cause others to honor you.

During the past twenty-five or thirty years, we have let some golden opportunities slip from us, and I fear we have not had enough plain talk right on these lines that I am mentioning to you now. If you ever have the opportunity to go into any of the large cities of the North, you will see some striking examples of this kind of thing. I remember that the first time I went North — and it hasn't been so many years ago — it was not an uncommon thing for one to see the barber shops in the hands of colored men. I know colored men who could have gotten comfortably rich. You cannot find to-day in the city of New York or Boston, a first-class barber shop in the hands of a colored man. Something is wrong — that opportunity is gone. Coming home, you go to Montgomery, Memphis or New Orleans, and you will find that the barber shops are gradually slipping from the hands of the colored men, and they are going back on these dark streets and opening little holes. These opportunities have slipped from us largely because we have not learned to dignify labor. The colored man puts a little dirty chair and a pair of razors into a dirtier looking hole, while the white man opens up his shop on one of the principal streets or in connection with some fashionable hotel, fits it up in fine style, with carpets, fine mirrors, etc., and calls that a tonsorial parlor. The proprietor sets up at his desk and keeps the books and takes in the cash. He thus transforms what we call a drudgery into a paying business.

And still another. You remember that only a few years ago and one of the best paying positions that a very large number of colored men were doing, was that of whitewashing. A few years ago it would not have been hard to see colored men around Boston, Philadelphia and Washington, carrying a whitewash tub and a long pole into somebody's house to whitewash the walls. They very often not only whitewashed the walls, but the carpets and pictures as well. You go into the North to-day, and you will find a very few colored men whitewashing. White men learned that they could dignify that work, and so began to study the work in schools. They became acquainted with the chemistry composing the various ingredients, learned decorating and frescoing, and now they call themselves House Decorators. Now, that's gone, to come no more perhaps. Now, that these men have elevated this work and added more intelligent skill to it, do you suppose that any one is going to allow some old man with a pole and a bucket to come into his house?

And then there is the matter of cooks. You know that all over the South we have held, and hold now, to a large extent, the matter of cooking in our hands. Wherever there is any cooking to be done, a colored man or woman does it. But, while we have something of a monopoly of this work, it is a fact that even this is gradually slipping away. People do not always want to eat fried meat, and bread that is made almost wholly of water and salt. They get tired of that, and they want a person to cook for them who will put brains into the work. To meet this demand, white people have transformed what formerly was the menial occupation of cooking, into a profession — they have gone to school and studied how to elevate the work, and if we judge by the almost total absence of colored cooks in the North, we are led to believe that they have learned how. And even here in the South they have gradually disappeared, and unless they get a hustle on themselves, they are going to be completely left. In the North they have disappeared because they have not kept pace with the most improved methods of cooking, and because they have not realized that the world is moving rapidly in the march of civilization. A few days ago when in Chicago, I noticed in one of the fashionable restaurants a fine looking man, well dressed, who seemed to be the proprietor. I asked who he was, and was told that he was the "chef," as he is called — the head cook. Of course I was surprised to see a man dressed in such a stylish manner and presenting such an air of culture, filling the position of chief cook in a restaurant, but I remembered then, more forcibly than ever, that cooking had been transformed into a profession — into dignified labor.

And still another opportunity is going, and we laugh when we mention it. When we think of what we could have done to elevate it in the same way that white persons have elevated it, we realize that after all it was an opportunity, and that opportunity was that of bootblacking. Of course, here in the South we have that to a large extent, because the competition is not quite so sharp as in the North. You go into Montgomery and want to get your shoes blacked. Very soon you will meet a boy with a box thrown over his shoulders. When he begins to polish your shoes you will very likely see that he uses a very much worn shoe brush, or worse still, a scrubbing brush, and unless you watch him very closely, the chances are he will polish your shoes with stove polish. But you go into any Northern city, and you will find that such a boot-black as you meet in Montgomery doesn't stand any chance of making a living. White boys, and even men, have opened shops which they have fitted up with carpets, pictures, looking glasses, large comfortable chairs, and very often their brushes are run by electricity. They have the latest newspapers always within reach, and so they make money and get rich. The proprietor of such an establishment is not called a boot-black; he is called the proprietor of such and such a "Shoe-blacking Emporium." Now that's gone to come no more. Now there are many colored men perhaps who understand a great deal about electricity, but where is the colored man who would apply that knowledge of electricity to running brushes in a boot-black stand?

In the South, it is a common thing that when a person gets sick, they always notify the old mammy nurse. But a few days ago I saw an advertisement in an Atlanta paper for a number of persons desiring to become trained nurses. We have had a monopoly of the nursing business for the last fifteen years, and the common opinion up to a short time ago was that no body could nurse but one of these old mammies, but that idea is becoming dissipated. In the North when a person gets sick, he does not think of sending for any one but a professional nurse, one who has received a diploma from some nurse training school or a certificate of proficiency from some reputable institution.

I hope you have understood me in what I have been trying to say of these little things. They all tend to show that if we are to keep peace [pace?] with the progress of civilization, we must pay attention to the small things as well as the larger and more important things in life. They go to prove that we have got to put brains into what we do, and if education means anything at all, it means putting brains into the common affairs of life, and making something of them, and that is what we are seeking to tell to the world through this institution's work.

There are so many opportunities all about us where we can use our education. In all of these matters we place ourselves in demand. You very rarely see a man who knows all about house building, who knows how to draw plans, to test the strength of materials that enter into the making of a first-class house, out of a job. Did you ever see such a man idle? Did you ever see that man writing letters applying for work at this place and that place? People are wanted all over the world who can do work well. Men and women are wanted who understand the preparation and supplying food — I don't mean in the small and menial sense, but who know all about it. Even here is a great opportunity. A few days ago I came in contact with a woman who has spent several years in this country and in Europe studying the subject of food economics in all its details. I learn that this person is in constant demand by institutions of learning and other establishments where the preparation and purveying of food are an important feature. She spends a few months at various institutions. She is wanted everywhere because she has applied her education to one of the most important necessities of life.

And so you will find it all through life, especially for the next fifty or one hundred years, that those persons who are going to be constantly in demand, constantly sought after, are those who make the best use of their opportunities, who work unceasingly to become proficient in whatever they attempt to do. Always be sure that you have something out [of] which you can make a living, and then you will not only make yourself independent, but will be in a better position to help your fellow men.

I have spoken about these matters because I consider them the foundation of our future success along all lines. We often hear of a man who has moral character; a man cannot have moral character unless he has something to wear and something to eat three hundred and sixty five days in the year. He can't have any religion either. You will find that at the bottom of much crime, is the fact that criminals have not had the common necessities of life supplied them. They must have some of the comforts and conveniences — certainly the necessities of life supplied them before they can be morally what they ought to be, or religiously what they ought to be.

Tuskegee Student, 9[?] (Feb. 21, 1895), 1; (Feb. 28, 1895), 3; (Mar. 7, 1895), 3. Stenographically reported by Frank E. Saffold.

From Marshall Gaston Daniels

[Tuskegee, Ala.] Feb'y 10, 1895

Dear Sir: I drop you this note in consequence of your actions toward me to-night in the Chapel. For you to treat me with such roughness when I attempt to do the best I can in my work here, is a little more than I care to stand. You asked for a certain song and I thought it my duty to furnish it. The manner in which you checked my efforts was not proper, before the people. Most of the plantation songs we sing are in books, they have been put in books for convenience. I did no more tonight in looking in the book for the song than Mr. Hamilton has done and not once have I heard him spoken to *in the Chapel* as you spoke to me tonight. I think I deserve fair treatment. If you don't want songs sung from the book any more I shall cease having them sung. I think it best to have them sung by persons promiscuously, anyhow.

Mr. Washington, I regret that there was an occasion for this note, but if there is one thing I do not like it is to be treated with any amount of sarcasm in public. Respectfully

M. Gaston Daniels

ALS Con. 110 BTW Papers DLC.

From Timothy Thomas Fortune

Charleston, Feb 13 [1895]

Dear Prof. Washington: Yours of the 7th and 11th are received, and give me the usual pleasure. As to the first, *I am extremely gratified that you endorse the sentiments contained in the Editorial on "Calamity Howlers."* I propose to use your good sentiments editorially, and I am going to keep up the fight along that line.

I would be glad to visit Tuskegee on the 20th but I can't. I am due in Florida about that time and shall leave for Jacksonville tomorrow afternoon. Yes, I could get a good article out of the matter for the Sun and [a] great deal of information I could use otherwise. I brake the record by having three signed articles in the Sunday Sun of the 10th inst., all from Charleston.

My health is good and I am in good working trim. Yours truly

T. Thomas Fortune

ALS   Con. 8   BTW Papers   ATT.   Original destroyed.

From Irving Garland Penn[1]

Lynchburg, Va. Feb. 14, 1895

My Dear Friend: Your favor of the 5th reached me on my return home Monday and I have your telegram also of this morning. As to both I am thankful and write to say a few things and to yet get your help. 1st, I have accepted the office of Chief of the Negro Dept. for $75 per month upon the Express conditions that I should only do such work as they would do in corresponding with the State Boards, etc. I send you President Collier's letter. He makes a distinction between the duties of Chief etc. and that of Secretary of Central Board. I send his letter and also that of General Lewis. I agree to do what Pres. Collier makes the duty of Chief for $75. As you see, the Central Board is to provide for the other yet. Note in Lewis' letter that Crogman[2] promised to write Chief Commissioners etc. Has he written you yet on this subject. You evidently know that the work enumerated in the subjects of Collier's letter which he claims is the duty of the

Secretary of Central Board — these are the things that should be begun. If Crogman has written you as indicated, I will ask you to write Gen'l Lewis and hurry up Crogman. He (Crogman) is miserably slow. I want everything fixed by my arrival in Atlanta on the 1st of March. You say in telegram, "Matters in good shape here." Write me fully as to what you mean. That is if matters as to me and everything concerned are in good shape. I asked for $125. per month and everything furnished. The thing stands like this: for chiefship Negro Dept. I get $75. Stationery, postage necessary furnished as relates to that work. The $50 per month as Secretary Central Board, office and appurtances for that office is yet to be provided for by Central Board concerning which, Crogman promises to write all Chiefs. *You see the situation.* Write me fully how matters stand and do what you can in pushing Crogman to the front as to writing to Com's of Central Board. An early reply at length would be appreciated. In the meantime I am hustling organizing the District, W.Va., Md., Ken., etc. etc. Yours faithfully

I. Garland Penn

HLS Con. 112 BTW Papers DLC.

¹ Irving (Irvine) Garland Penn was principal of a black public school in Lynchburg, Va. Born in 1867 in New Glasgow, Va., he had a high school education. In 1886 he was a correspondent for the Richmond *Planet,* the Knoxville *Negro World,* and the New York *Age.* He was the author of *The Afro-American Press and Its Editors* (1891) and *The College of Life* (1902), an encyclopedia. After serving as head of the Negro exhibits at the Cotton States and International Exposition in 1895, he remained in Atlanta for sixteen years as the secretary for blacks of the Epworth League of the Methodist Episcopal Church. He then became secretary of the Freedmen's Aid and Southern Education Society of the Methodist Episcopal Church, residing in Cincinnati.

² William Henry Crogman (1841-1931) was professor of Greek and Latin at Clark University in Atlanta from 1876 to 1903 and was its president from 1903 to 1921. Born on the island of St. Martin's, British West Indies, he went to sea at fourteen. He attended Pierce Academy in Massachusetts from 1868 to 1870. He was an English instructor at Claflin University, Orangeburg, S.C., from 1870 to 1873, then took the classical course at Atlanta University, graduating in 1876. At the Atlanta Exposition in 1895 he was a commissioner from Georgia for the Negro Building.

A prolific writer and speaker on racial themes, Crogman in the 1880s was an outspoken critic of segregation and discrimination. By the turn of the century he was more oriented toward BTW's conservative philosophy. In 1897 he helped to found the American Negro Academy, and later became its president. After the Atlanta Riot in 1906, BTW praised him as one of the courageous black leaders who stayed on the scene.

To Samuel Laing Williams[1]

[Tuskegee, Ala.] Feb. 15th, 1895

Dear Mr. Williams: This is to invite you to deliver our Commencement Address, which occurs one day during the latter half of May. I could name the definite date in this letter, but there is some probability of our changing the date, but it will occur in any case some time during the last half of May.

In extending this invitation I appreciate your interest in the South, as well as your knowledge of both races, and I am sure that you can deliver an address that will be of help to all who may hear it.

Our Commencements are attended in very large numbers by the common, hard working colored people, and by, usually, 50 to 100 white people, mainly from the town of Tuskegee and vicinity.

If you accept, I am sorry to say that we could not promise now to do more than pay your expenses, as you know this has been a very hard year with all institutions. I wish very much that we could compensate you for your time and the valuable services which I am sure you will render. Hoping to hear from you soon, I am   Yours truly,

Booker T. Washington

TLpS   Con. 113   BTW Papers   DLC.

[1] Samuel Laing Williams was one of BTW's most active and loyal supporters in Chicago. Born in Georgia, he moved to Chicago in the mid-1880s after graduation from the University of Michigan and from the Columbian Law School in Washington in 1885. He was admitted to the bar and briefly shared a law office with Ferdinand L. Barnett, later one of BTW's bitterest critics. In 1887 he married Fannie Barrier, whose speeches and newspaper articles on racial topics, and particularly in defense of BTW and Tuskegee, made her a more prominent figure in the Chicago black community than her husband. In 1887 Williams organized the Prudence Crandall Club, a Chicago literary society of elite membership. He delivered the commencement address at Tuskegee in 1895. In 1904 he was the ghostwriter of one of BTW's least satisfactory books, a biography of Frederick Douglass.

Williams was more than a supporter of BTW. He was also a personal friend, and hundreds of his letters are in the BTW Papers. His friendship caused him to go to greater lengths for BTW than most of the other Bookerites. He spied on the activities of Chicagoans in the Niagara Movement, and served as BTW's go-between in subsidizing and influencing the Chicago black newspapers. These activities hurt Williams when he sought a political career. In 1904 he was prevented by more militant Chicago blacks from becoming head of the Republican Negro Bureau in Chicago. When BTW tried to reward his loyalty by securing for him a high federal office, he was repeatedly blocked by the anti-BTW faction, which had influence with leading white Illinois Republicans. Finally in 1908, after years of effort, BTW secured for Williams an appointment as an assistant U.S. attorney. He was discharged a year later, but BTW arranged for his reinstatement. In 1912, however, he was discharged permanently, on a claim that he lacked energy and practicality. Allan H. Spear found in Williams's career a certain ambiguity. While Williams loyally supported BTW and sought rewards through him, Williams was not an accommodationist in his public utterances, and in his private social life he sought the company of those who were most critical of BTW. By 1913 he was active in the Chicago branch of the NAACP, and did legal work on some of its civil-rights cases. This drift toward greater militancy continued after BTW's death, and until Williams's death in 1921. (See Spear, *Black Chicago*, 66-69.)

To Irene Bond

[Tuskegee, Ala.] Feb. 16, 95

Mrs. Bond: Your communications have been considered. With your present feelings toward the official head of the institution I can not see how you can be of that service to the institution that a teacher should be and am surprised that you even thought of remaining in your present condition of mind. You say in so many words that you have no confidence in the institution yet you are willing to use it as a convenience for the time being.

As above stated it seems to me that with your present feelings it will be best for all concerned for you not to be connected with the institution. Respectfully,

Booker T. Washington

ALpS Con. 113 BTW Papers DLC.

To Nathan B. Young

[Tuskegee, Ala.] February 18th, 1895

Mr. Young: At the next meeting of the Faculty, there is a question to come up as to whether or not certain students have been allowed to leave their study-hour to attend the Latin and other outside classes in violation of the vote of the teachers sometime before you went away. I do not know whether or not this has been done, but a number of the teachers express themselves as being very sure that such is the case. I have always followed this plan in regard to [the decisions]: I am very careful as to what matters are permitted to come before the teachers for their vote or decision. After they have voted upon a question, I am always very careful to see that their vote and decision are respected. In this way, I have been able to avoid much friction. In your various teachers' meetings, you have the absolute right to say whether this or that question is proper to come before the teachers for their vote or decision, and in this way, you will find that many very unpleasant things can easily be avoided and disposed of for good and all. But when the vote is taken, care should always be exercised to see that the rule thus made is always carried out.

I think it would be better for you to mention this matter yourself in the next Faculty meeting.

Booker T. Washington

TLpS Con. 113 BTW Papers DLC.

From Frederick Douglass

Cedar Hill   Anacostia D.C. Febry 19 1895

Dear Mr Booker T. Washington. The Bearer of this paper, Mr Smith of Chicago has shown to me an invention which may be made of in-calcu[l]able value in the preservation of the food products of the South and which may be made the means of placing the colored people of the South in comparative independence of the oppressive conditions that tend to keep them paupers. I would advise you to look into the claims of Mr Smiths invention and make it useful to your great and leading educational institution. Yours truly

Frederick Douglass

ALS Con. 110 BTW Papers DLC.

An Account of the Tuskegee Negro Conference

[Tuskegee, Ala., Feb. 20-21, 1895]

One dazzling sheet of snow spread unbroken from horizon to horizon, all the way from Richmond to Atlanta, as Hampton's delegates to the Tuskegee Conference journeyed southward over the Piedmont Air Line on February 18th. Its melting fringes, trailing through the woods and across the prairies of Alabama, made their swampy roads even more formidable than they usually are at this season of the year to the farmers expected at the Conference; but to hold it a few weeks later would interfere with their spring plowing and planting.

We had the pleasure of finding Miss Anna L. Dawes[1] on our train from Atlanta, and of meeting also Mr. Wm. H. Baldwin, Jr.[2] vice-president of the Southern Railway, in which the Piedmont Air has been merged; both on their way to the Conference.

The little "narrow gauge" from Chehaw station took us through woods sadly changed from the magnolia scented glades my memory called for, but there was no chill in the welcome that waited for us, from Mr. Washington and the twenty other Hamptonians on his staff, and their associates. The union of other institutions with Hampton in Tuskegee's good work, is seen not only in its school rooms and workshops but in a number of its happy homes, including that of its Principal, whose wife is a Fisk graduate, and that in which the Doctor[3] and I were very hospitably and pleasantly entertained during our stay by Mr. and Mrs. Jas. Green. We could hardly help calling Mrs. Green, Sarah Peake[4] as of old. Her good husband, a representative of North Carolina, we heard instructing a bright class in the theory of masonry which they are putting into practice under his superintendence, on the rising walls of Tuskegee's new Science Building.

Our early arrival, on the morning of the day before the Conference gave us the opportunity of a preliminary look through the workshops and other buildings with Mr. Washington's escort, but its interesting details must be postponed to another letter, for which they can furnish ample material. Armstrong Hall, a view of which he kindly lends for our cover page this month, is the oldest of many new features which have been added to the institution since my last visit in 1892. It was completed in that year for the young men's use and named in honor of the General. Next to it stands Porter Hall, answering to our Academic, the oldest building on the place. In the Assembly Room of the latter, from whose wall look down the faces of General Armstrong, Abby May and Hampton's daughter, Mrs. Olivia Davidson Washington, who laid down her life for Tuskegee, the Conference was held for the fourth year on Wednesday, February 20th.

In spite of the terrible condition of the roads and "slews" which one old farmer declared "only strong faith in a-mighty providence could fotch any mule through," between five and six hundred earnest men and women from a dozen counties in the state succeeded in reaching the Conference; some driving as many as forty miles, some walking from ten to twenty. Over a hundred of the number were women. Seventy-five were teachers and twenty nine were ministers — but the majority of these were or had been farmers as well. For the first time a few farmers were present from other states: Louisiana, Mississippi, Georgia and the Carolinas. To meet with them had come, President John, of Clark University, Atlanta, Prof. Dodge, of Berea College, Prof. Silsby, of Talladega, Rev. Dr. Satterfield, of Scotia Seminary, N.C., Rev. Pitt Dillingham and Miss Showers of the Calhoun School, Rev. A. T. Burnell, of the Burrill School, Selma, Ala., Prof. Harris, of Fisk, Miss White and Miss Beard, of the Montgomery Industrial School, Miss Tapley and other lady teachers of Spelman Seminary, Atlanta, Mr. Ferguson,[5] of Alcorn College, Miss., Rev. Geo. L. Chaney, of Richmond, Virginia, Rev. Mr. Bedford, of Rockton, Ill., Mrs. Steele, of Chattanooga,[6] Miss Anna L. Dawes and Mr. W. H. Baldwin, Jr. of Boston, as before mentioned, Dr. Frissell and the other representatives of Hampton. Towards the end of the Conference, a few of the School's Southern friends dropped in: notably, Rev. Mr. Morton, of Tuskegee and Mr. R. O. Simpson,[7] a planter from Selma who made one of the most effective speeches of the occasion.

Mr. Washington gave the key note of the Conference in his opening speech. "These meetings are called to confer upon the evils we can remedy ourselves. It seems to me, that as we do this we shall find other troubles also disappearing. Till I was eleven years old, I believed with all my heart that nobody but a Baptist ever got to heaven. That idea wasn't argued out of me, but it got out gradually as I came in contact with good Methodists and other good people. I was the creature of circumstances. So is many a Southern white man or woman who honestly believes that a black man or black woman can never be capable of education and citizenship. We may spend our time in cursing them for it, but that isn't going to change their mind. But let a graduate go out from this or some other school, settle near them, live a good life, keep a clean house, with a yard full of flowers, raise forty bushels of corn instead of twenty to an acre; and by and by the white neighbor is going to notice it, and stop by the gate to look at the flowers and talk about the crop; and gradually he will conclude there are exceptions, and after a while find other exceptions, and find common ground of interest, and in this way our problem will gradually work itself out. We have been depending too much on the power of the mouth instead of object lessons. Now let us all speak simply and to the point, and above all practice what we preach."

Mr. Logan Green, a shrewd faced farmer of Macon Co., thought "There is no need of complaining so much. Eight years ago I never had a meat-skin [to grease the griddle]. To-day I own eighty acres, all paid for. I got rich too fast once and lost everything. I told God that if he'd forgive me that once I'd do better and I have did it. I work from Monday till Saturday. One Scripture some don't like to hear: Six days thou shalt work. They plant ten acres of cotton and that's not enough to keep 'em busy six days. The mortgage system is your own fault. You don't mortgage for just what you need but you buy brass pins and Jew's-harps. I don't want nobody's foot on my neck. I don't go to the store and say, 'Please give me a *little* coffee, please give me a little flour.' I don't want a *little,* I want a heap and I pay for it. My land's my own; the birds on it are mine, the snakes on it are mine. Don't sit round saying you'll trust God. God aint goin' to hoe for you. Trust God and go to work."

The Committee appointed to guide the discussions of the Conference presented a set of "Declarations" which were severally considered and unanimously adopted, as follows:

"I. Four sessions of the Tuskegee Negro Conference have made clear their wisdom. They give the masses a day in school under most inspiring influences. Education, property, character, and how to cure the evils that lie in our power to remedy, are the subjects discussed."

Many hearty testimonies were given to the value of the Conferences. One who was unable to be present sent a letter reporting that seven in Selma have bought their homes and now raise their own meat, some up to nine hundred pounds a year — one woman raised four hundred pounds of pork and three hundred chickens since the last

Conference. In another neighborhood fifteen men had bought and paid for land. Mr. Green of Macon Co. declared that the Conferences have "even done the cows good." Rev. Mr. Jeter,[8] a very intelligent preacher and farmer, who has been present at all the Conferences, and himself owner of 420 acres in the same county, said the people about him had bought over two thousand acres as the result of the Conferences. A presiding elder reported in his circuit of three or four hundred miles the people buying land in groups; others are talking of it. Over a hundred were thus reported as securing homes; and raising their own food; others found difficulty in obtaining small holdings, and one told of having had his corn crop seized for debt, while another pathetically asked the Conference to petition the moneyed men to let their tenants raise more food and less cotton. A North Carolina farmer gave an interesting account of Mrs. Steele's benevolent enterprise of securing a large plantation for subdivision, and a Mississippi farmer told of a similar operation of his own, for his neighbors' benefit.

The second "declaration" was as follows:

"II. The seriousness of our condition lies in that, in the States where the colored people are most numerous, at least 90 per cent. of them are in the country, they are difficult to reach, and but little is being done for them. Their industrial, educational and moral condition is slowly improving, but among the masses, there is still a great amount of poverty and ignorance and much need of moral and religious training."

Varying reports were given on this point from different localities, and it was extremely interesting to see that while in some sections, as one frankly acknowledged, "Morals are down twenty degrees below zero," the isothermal line of higher moral temperature follows the track of the good school teacher. "Around the schools it's a little Paradise," said one, "but beyond the edge of their influence, nothing gets the devils out until the river rises." "Many of our people are suffering, hardly know how to get bread." "Plenty don't have food enough to eat," said others. There was hopefulness as well as pathos in the very frankness of the confessions, which were well summed up by one honest faced minister who could speak for Mississippi and Louisiana as well as Alabama: "We hate to face the truth, but it's no use to dodge it. We're not what we ought to be, we're sadly wanting; but we're not so bad as we used to be twenty years ago, and we're going to be better."

The third Declaration turned from the evils to the remedies:

"III. We urge all to buy land and to cultivate it thoroughly; to raise more food supplies; to build houses with more than one room; to tax ourselves to build better school houses and to extend the term to at least six months; to give more attention to the character and welfare of our leaders, especially preachers and teachers; to keep out of debt; to avoid law-suits; to treat our women better; and that conferences similar in aim to this one be held in every community where practicable."

The sentiment of the Conference was very unanimous and hearty in favor of this declaration.

"Buying land makes better citizens," said a man who had walked ten miles to the Conference. "It makes a man more truthfuller," said Mr. Liggon,[9] whose intelligent old face is a familiar one at the Conference, and who is himself a large land owner, and a bank depositor. "To own property is to own character; when a man who owns land gives his word he knows he can't run away." A farmer from "Big Hungry" wanted his neighbors to own land as well as himself; "for if my pocket is full and my neighbor's is too, I can sleep comfortably." "As soon as a man and a woman buy their home, they hedge themselves round with little homeside law. You size up a man according to his home," said another. "I'm a good sized little man myself. My house has four rooms, one for my boys, one for my girls, one for me and my wife, and one for any teachers that may come. We own about a hundred acres." A brave man from "Warrior Stand" said, "I've got twelve children, ten boys. I've always had to work hard and never could learn nothing. I own 270 acres, a five-plow farm, and haven't bought a grain of corn since I went to farming. I raise my own meat. I raise a plenty, eats a plenty and never does somethin' for nothin'." "What do you think of the one-room cabin?" asked Mr. Washington. "I think we've been free long enough to get out of the ashes." Rev. Mr. Jeter urged the men to be kind to their wives: "My wife is the smartest woman in the world, and when I die I want her to go by my side to heaven."

On inquiry, the very interesting fact was brought out that out of fifteen school districts reported from, in twelve the public school term of three months has been lengthened to from five to nine months by contributions of the people themselves. The grinding crop-mortgage system had been so thoroughly discussed in former conferences that there was little more to say about it. "A system of death and hell," said Mr. Liggon; another added, "And the 'waive note' takes what the mortgage leaves; the mortgage takes the crop and the waive note sits at the table a sopping out the plate." Many have pulled out from its clutches by following the suggestions of the Conference, and several have been successful in holding similar ones in their neighborhood.

"IV. More can be accomplished by going forward than by complaining. With all our disadvantages, nowhere is there afforded us such business opportunities as are afforded in the South. Self-respect will bring us many rights now denied us. Crime among us decreases as property increases."

A Hampton graduate who is in charge of the blacksmith shop at the Tuskegee School testified, "In the North I inquired for a place for a colored mechanic and found none. In Atlanta white and colored mechanics work side by side, and a black man can be first man at the forge. Southern people have sentiment for the black men; Northerners are all for business." As to foreign emigration, it was rather curtly dismissed. "Last week," said one, "a man came here and carried a great crowd off to Mexico. I said, I don't go away just as the light begins to shine." Mr. Liggon added sententiously, "A fool in Africa is no better than a fool in America."

"V. Where the people are reached by this and similar conferences and their earnest efforts, their improvement is marked, they are less in debt, have better houses and schools, and, in spite of the very hard times, have more home supplies. We believe these conferences afford one of the quickest and most economical ways of reaching large numbers of the people, and of helping them to help themselves."

So much had been said, "and so well said" on this closing point earlier in the day that it was passed without further discussion, except that one man wished to testify: "This Conference has did me good before I came. I has lived in every kind of house the brethren has been talking 'bout, but I has always moved for improvement. I has tenants of my own now, and I likes them to raise cotton for me, but I raises corn for Lucy and the baby."

A few years ago a young man, after graduating from Tuskegee, went to teach in a county district school near Selma. His good work so attracted the attention of a neighboring planter that he invited him to open a school on his plantation, furnished the school-house and land and has ever since contributed to the work. He came in at the end of the Conference, and at Mr. Washington's invitation spoke as follows:

"I was the son of a slaveholder and have been one of those merchants who take mortgages and money from Negro tenants. But I have been much interested in the race ever since I became a Christian, ten years ago. The Negro has improved since freedom. Colored teachers and ministers are better than they used to be. The advice given by these Conferences will do great good. The colored people ought to make up their minds to live here; the white people should make up their minds to live in peace with them and do away with race prejudices. The problem of the two races is a great problem; we should study it. I believe that the Negro will be an important factor in the development of America, in its religious, moral and material development. There are many places where white men can't live and black men can and are needed to develop the land. This School is a great blessing to the race and to the state. The influence of its graduates is good. I am convinced that there is not the same prejudice in either race that there has been; it is dying out; they will be more friendly in future. It has done me good to be here. I shall take more interest in the School and in the colored people than ever before."

The Women's Conference

On Wednesday afternoon a separate Conference was held for the women, in Phelps Hall, presided over by Mrs. Logan, the wife of Tuskegee's treasurer. The subjects of dress and care of home and children were considered. There was naturally less freedom of utterance than in the other Conference, but some touching experiences were brought out, especially in regard to the difficulty of lessening the hours of field work exacted sometimes by merciless creditors, sometimes by husbands who did not hesitate to force their authority with a stick. One woman, while her ten children were growing up, had had to work all day in the cotton field leaving the baby rolled up in a shawl on the bed, coming home only to nurse it, and then would sometimes spend half the night running the sewing machine to keep the family in clothes. A sewing machine is as apt to surprise you in a one room cabin as in an Indian tepee. Some excellent advice on domestic matters

527

was given to the women by several of the Tuskegee teachers, and some suggestions on health matters by Doctor Waldron.

THE TEACHERS' CONFERENCE

On Thursday a conference was held in Phelps Hall, by the seventy teachers who stayed over a day for the purpose. Less unique and picturesque than the farmers' meeting, it was no less promising of good results. Dr. Frissell presided, and, on his suggestion, the morning was occupied by delegates from the various schools and colleges represented, in briefly sketching their special characteristics. Those of Calhoun and Mt. Meigs I will keep for another letter, as we had the pleasure afterwards of visiting them. The rest are so generally known that they need no description here. It was especially interesting to see the evidence of unity in variety, the oneness of purpose and the harmony of spirit in the different workers. Mr. Simpson again came in for a few moments at the close and gave an interesting account of the plantation school, with further friendly words.

The questions discussed in the afternoon were, How can we dignify the common duties of life, and fit our pupils for its realities; How can the schools influence to the greatest extent their graduates, and how can race prejudice be overcome.

Upon the first topic, Mr. Washington said, "I don't want to give the impression that I don't believe in the highest brainwork, but I believe in turning it to use in the real duties of life. Men go through college and never get it into their heads that their best use of geometry is to make good roads and that the best use of their chemistry is to make good butter. I believe in teaching the people to apply what they know to elevating and ennobling the common things of life; teach the farmer who has been raising ten bushels of corn to the acre, how with less labor to raise forty; then his education means something. Ninety per cent. of our people — and of all people — have got to earn their living along these common ways. Teach them to put brains into them before they slip away from us into more skilled hands." Mr. Ferguson, a Hampton graduate now at the head of agricultural work and instruction in Alcorn College, Miss., made the excellent point that a thorough mechanical or business training is itself intellectual training. Dr. Satterfield of Scotia Seminary, and others spoke briefly and in harmony with this point.

As to the importance of influencing our graduates, Prof. Harris spoke feelingly of Fisk's homelike influence and hold on its alumni, and Mr. Washington made touching allusion to Hampton's relation to Tuskegee, and the inspiration from the visits of General Marshall and General Armstrong.

The subject of race prejudice brought out some interesting and hearty testimony to kindness received from white neighbors, and some frank admission of prejudice existing on the other side. Prof. Chavis, of Bennett Methodist College, N.C., said manfully, "Let us strive only to grow into true manhood and womanhood and God will take care of the rest," and this well summed up the general expression of sentiment on the subject.

The Atlanta Exposition was mentioned. No time remained for discussion of the subject and none was needed. Mr. Washington strongly recommended a general representation of the schools in it. Miss Bannister, editor of *The Future State*, the equivalent of "Public Opinion" for the colored press, spoke a few earnest words for industrial education. Miss Anna L. Dawes made an impressive speech on the value of the smaller schools, and the Conference adjourned.

Southern Workman, 24 (Mar. 1895), 36-38. Helen Wilhelmina Ludlow wrote this account. Another colorful account is in the Montgomery *Advertiser*, Feb. 21, 1895, 7.

[1] Anna Laurens Dawes (1851-1938) of Pittsfield, Mass., was the daughter of Henry Laurens Dawes, author of the Dawes Act of 1887. She was active in Indian reform work and was a longtime secretary to her father. She was also active in the American Missionary Association and in prison reform. A journalist and author, she wrote a biography of Charles Sumner (1892).

[2] William Henry Baldwin, Jr. (1863-1905) was born in Boston of abolitionist ancestors. His father, William Henry Baldwin, was the founder of the Boston Young Men's Christian Union (1852) and an active supporter of numerous humanitarian causes, including support of Negro education and Tuskegee Institute. Baldwin Jr. was educated at Harvard, graduating in the class of 1885. In 1886, at the age of twenty-three, he went to work for Charles Francis Adams, president of the Union Pacific Railroad, and rose rapidly in the railroad management hierarchy. Adams believed in business leadership by a socially responsible elite, and Baldwin was to be in the vanguard of that movement. In 1894, after numerous positions with the Union Pacific and other lines, he became second vice-president of the Southern Railway and then vice-president and general manager. From 1896 until his death in early 1905 he was president of the Long Island Railroad. Baldwin was active in many reform and humanitarian causes, including membership on the Southern Education Board, the first chairmanship of the General Education Board (1902-4), and chairmanship of New York's Committee of Fifteen. BTW asked Baldwin to become a trustee of Tuskegee in 1894, but Baldwin did not accept the position until 1895, and only after he had thoroughly inspected the school, going so far as to break open bread in the Tuskegee kitchens to see how well it was cooked.

Baldwin quickly became BTW's closest contact with the northern philanthropists and his most consistent friend on the Southern Education Board. The two men developed a warm friendship. BTW was greatly impressed with Baldwin's brisk business manner and his executive qualities. Baldwin espoused BTW's conservative philosophy and his public utterances were in full agreement with BTW. On occasion Baldwin went beyond BTW's accommodationism in his attempt to placate the white South, and his public utterances had a decidedly racist tone. Speaking in 1899 at the Conference for Christian Education in the South at Capon Springs, W.Va., Baldwin said that the Negro "will willingly fill the more menial positions, and do the heavy work at less wages" than whites. He urged blacks to "avoid social questions; leave politics alone; continue to be patient; live moral lives; live simply; learn to work . . . know that it is a crime for any teacher, white or black to educate the negro for positions which are not open to him. . . ." (*Southern Workman,* 27 [Aug. 1899], 285-87.) As Baldwin's private correspondence reveals, while he played the role of the brusque captain of industry, he believed that his practical advice would advance racial peace and justice. He had an obsessive fear that northern interference would lead to race war. At the time of BTW's Atlanta address in 1895 Baldwin was so worried over BTW's reception that he could not bring himself to attend the speech; instead he paced nervously outside the Negro Building. For dramatic effect, BTW used this incident in both of his autobiographies. (See above, 1:72, 329.) Baldwin was instrumental in getting Andrew Carnegie to give Tuskegee $600,000 worth of U.S. Steel bonds in 1903. Of this sum, $150,000 was put in trust for BTW's personal use. In 1904 Baldwin was stricken with a brain tumor that made him an invalid and claimed his life in January 1905.

[3] Martha Mercelia Waldron.

[4] Sarah F. Peake (Mrs. James Matthew) Greene.

[5] Henry Clay Ferguson (see above, 2:233-34). Ferguson died at Farm, W.Va., on Oct. 5, 1895, at the age of thirty-six. Thomas J. Calloway, president of Alcorn A & M College in Mississippi, notified BTW of Ferguson's death, stating: "His death was not altogether unexpected for the doctor seemed unable to locate his trouble." (Calloway to BTW, Oct. 5, 1895, Con. 110, BTW Papers, DLC.)

[6] Probably Mrs. A. S. Steele of Chattanooga, a donor to Hampton and Tuskegee.

[7] Randall O. Simpson, born in Belleville, Ala., in 1842, was a white champion of black education in Alabama. He began school at an academy near his home but interrupted his studies to fight for the Confederacy in the Civil War. Returning home penniless, he began planting and soon prospered. Because he settled near Furman, Wilcox County, in the Black Belt, Simpson depended mainly on black laborers. One of the young black men who lived nearby once borrowed some money from Simpson to attend school, and Simpson forgot the debt until the man, William Junior Edwards, an 1893 graduate of Tuskegee, returned the money. Impressed with what education had done for Edwards, Simpson persuaded him to start a school on his land, and it opened with twenty-five pupils in 1893. The school was called Snow Hill Normal and Industrial Institute, and Simpson kept a firm hand on it, donating the campus, serving as president of the board of trustees, and helping financially whenever there was a shortage of money. Later he began another such school in Wilcox County. BTW noted that Simpson had been "outspoken and strong in his stand in favor of the colored man receiving justice in the courts and in favor of his being permitted to vote, wherever he satisfied the demands of the

state constitution." Simpson was a trustee of Tuskegee from 1897 until after BTW's death in 1915. (BTW's biographical sketch of Simpson, Feb. 24, 1905, Con. 307, BTW Papers, DLC.)

[8] Purim Jeter, who had fifteen children in an eight-room house. (Montgomery *Advertiser*, Feb. 21, 1895, 7.)

[9] Willis Ligon.

To William Jenkins

[Tuskegee, Ala.] February 25th., 1895

Mr. Jenkins: I regret to have to remind you again that it is the policy of this institution for its academic teachers to be present in the chapel every morning at the morning prayers.

We cannot permit any exceptions to be made.

Booker T. Washington

TLS Con. 111 BTW Papers DLC. Jenkins replied on BTW's memo: "If you will give me some place to prepare my lessons instead of my bedroom I shall be only too glad to comply with your order, as it is I have nowhere save the recitation room and that is open to me at the time indicated in your order."

To Nathan B. Young

[Tuskegee, Ala.] Feb. 25th, 1895

Mr. Young: Before making it compulsory that each teacher must attend the morning exercises, I wish to try this plan: I wish you would report to me in writing at the end of each week, the names of any academic teachers who have failed to attend the morning exercises.

Booker T. Washington

TLpS Con. 113 BTW Papers DLC.

From Nathan B. Young

Tuskegee, Ala. Feb'y 25, 1895

Mr. Washington, In reply to your note regarding the attendance of academic teachers upon morning devotionals, I would say that Rev. Penny, Miss Samuels, and myself are the only ones who attend *regularly.*

Next in order of attendance are Miss Lane,[1] Miss Beula Thompson,[2] Mr. Hoffman, and Mr. McCall. *All* the rest are very sporadic in their attendance. Mr. Jenkins *never comes.*

In this matter we are an exception to the rule of schools devoted to the education of the Negro youth. I *do not think* that it ought to be optional with the teacher as to whether or not he will attend this exercise especially. If a teacher does not see that it is an imperative duty to begin the day with pray[er] *with his students,* I think that they ought to be compelled to attend. It is very unfortunate in my opinion that so many of our teachers seem to regard the matter so lightly. I therefore recommend that you send an order to each of the academic teachers making attendance upon morning devotions compulsory.

This may be "heroic treatment," but I deem it to be a case requiring firm measures. We can not afford to be too much unlike other institutions engaged in a similar work. I firmly believe that we ought not to *require* the performance of any *religious* duty on [the] part of the students, which is not required of the teachers also. Our non-sectarianism ought not to be so straight as to make us non-religious, un-Christian. At present the tendency seems strongly set in that direction, to say the least.

Pardon this long note, but I now feel, and have always felt, that we are entirely too lax along these lines, for that reason our spiritual life is always at "low ebb." Revivals and conversions which pervade other Christian schools never touch us to any considerable extent. There is something wrong somewhere. Water will never rise higher than its source, nor will the spiritual and religious life of a school rise higher than that of the teachers. A Christian school necessitates Christian teachers, who will willingly attend all of the stated religious services, if not prevented by *unavoidable* duties elsewhere. Respectfully,

Nathan B. Young

ALS Con. 113 BTW Papers DLC.

[1] Elizabeth E. Lane taught English at Tuskegee from 1893 to 1899.

[2] Beulah Thompson Davis was librarian and night-school teacher from 1892 until she married during the 1895-96 school year.

From Matthew T. Driver, Harry E. Thomas,[1] and James Nathan Calloway

Tuskegee, Ala., Feb 25 1895

We the committee appointed to examine into the writing of an immoral letter by J. A. Porterfield to Annie Simmons report the young man guilty of immorality and recommend his expulsion from the school. There being some doubt as to the guilt of the young lady we recommend for her that she be publicly reprimanded and denied all society for the remainder of the year.

M. T. Driver
H. E. Thomas
J N Calloway

ALS Con. 110 BTW Papers DLC.

[1] Harry E. Thomas was, for many years beginning in 1894, in charge of plumbing and machine work at Tuskegee Institute.

To James B. Washington

[Tuskegee, Ala.] Feb. 27th, 1895

Mr. J. B. Washington: You have been connected with the office now five or six years, and should know how to perform, at least common duties around the office. If you do not know it is your own fault. I entrusted to you the mailing of the Advertisers which were purchased at quite an outlay,[1] and I find that the whole expenses and work in connection with this work, are to a large extent, thrown away by reason of the fact that the papers were not properly wrapped. I did not suppose it was necessary to go into each detail and tell you how to wrap these papers. They have been wrapped, I find, with no idea of making the marked article conspicuous, and at least half of the persons to whom the papers will go will not see the article owing to your carelessness.

533

It seems to me just that a part of the expense connected with purchasing these papers should be charged to your personal account.

Booker T. Washington

TLpS Con. 113 BTW Papers DLC.

¹ Probably the account of the Tuskegee Negro Conference in the Montgomery *Advertiser,* Feb. 21, 1895, 7.

To the Colored Citizens of Alabama

[Tuskegee, Ala., Feb. 28, 1895]

Greetings: The directors of the Atlanta Cotton States and International Exposition have provided a large, convenient and attractive building, known as the Negro Building, to be used exclusively for an exhibition of the progress of the colored people of this country. The colored citizens of Alabama should take advantage of this rare opportunity.

The Exposition opens September 18th and continues until December 31st, 1895, so there is not a day to be lost; what is to be done should be begun at once.

The main exhibit will have to come from the various schools in the State of Alabama. It will soon be time for many of the schools to close, hence the importance of beginning without delay.

Let the schools prepare special exhibits of class-room and industrial work.

We want the farmers and mechanics of Alabama to make a special effort to do themselves credit at this Exposition, which is going to be attended by thousands of visitors from all parts of the world.

The main departments from which we want exhibits, can be embraced under the following heads:

A. Mineral and Forestry.
B. Agriculture, Food and its accessories.
  Machinery and appliances.
C. Horticulture, Viticulture, Pomology, Floriculture, etc.
D. Machinery.
E. Manufacturers.

F. Fine Arts, Painting, Sculpture and decoration.

Liberal arts, Education, Literature, Music and the Drama.

G. Live Stock, Domestic and Wild Animals, Fish, Fisheries and Fish Culture.

For list of premiums or for further information, address Chief Commissioner or any of the Assistant Commissioners.

Booker T. Washington

Chief Commissioner for Alabama

Tuskegee, Ala.

ASSISTANT COMMISSIONERS

C. N. Dorsett, Montgomery,	Ala.
Rev. W. R. Pettiford, D.D., Birmingham,	"
Rev. R. T. Pollard, Montgomery,	"
Sidney E. Murphy, Eufaula,	"
Henry A. Loveless, Montgomery,	"
W. H. Council, Normal,	"

Tuskegee Student, 9[?] (Feb. 28, 1895), 2.

To William Jenkins

[Tuskegee, Ala.] Feb. 29 [Mar. 1], 95

Mr. Jenkins: I have received your note[1] which I consider one of the few disrespectful communications that I have received during my connection with this institution as its official head.

I have neither time nor inclination to debate the matter with you of your attending devotional exercises and even if there were a disposition to debate the matter or for the school to change its policy, the attitude assumed in your communication leaves, the school, but one course to pursue.

I have stated plainly the wish and policy of the school to you, it now remains for you to make your choice.

Booker T. Washington

ALpS Con. 113 BTW Papers DLC.

[1] See BTW to Jenkins, Feb. 25, 1895, above.

Washington's Account at the Tuskegee Institute Commissary[1]

[Mar. 1–Dec. 30, 1895]

B. T. Washington

[March 1895]

			Dr	
March	1st	3℔ Lard 23¢ Mar 2 — 3℔ Grits 9¢	32	
	2	18℔ Flour 36¢ 1 pk meal 20¢	56	
		1℔ Butter 20¢ 1℔ B. powder 25¢	45	
		½℔ Tea 20¢ 1 box Jelatine 15¢	35	
		1 box Pearline[2] 5¢ 4℔ Gr. Sugar 22¢	27	
	3	3℔ Beef 18¢ Mar 5 — 3℔ Lard 23¢	41	
	5	3℔ O.Meal 15¢ ½℔ Butter 10¢	25	
	7	Salt 5¢ 2½℔ Beef 15¢	20	
	10	½℔ Beef 3¢ 18℔ Flour 36¢	39	
	9	3℔ Gr Sugar 17¢ 3℔ Lard 21¢	38	
		3℔ Rice 15¢ 1℔ Butter 20¢	35	
		1 box Jelatine 15¢ 3℔ Grits 9¢	24	
		1 box Pearline 5¢ 1℔ Coffee 25¢	30	
	12	1 pckg Matches 10¢ 1℔ Butter 30¢	40	
		3 C corn 36¢ 3 C Tomatoes 25¢	61	
		7℔ prunes 70¢ 1 box Cocoa 25¢	95	
		3℔ Beef 18¢ 3℔ Gr. Sugar 17¢	35	
		¼℔ Steak 2¢ 18℔ Flour 36¢	38	
	13	30℔ Gr. Sugar 1.65 — 6 Doz Eggs 90¢	2.55	
	14	1℔ B. powder 25¢ 18℔ Flour 35¢	60	
	15	19℔ Salt 19¢ 1 Gal Syrup 40¢	59	
		2¼℔ Ham 28¢ Mar 16 — 1℔ Coffee 25¢	53	
		3℔ Gr Sugar 17¢ 3℔ O.Meal 15¢	32	
		6 bars Soap 25¢ 3℔ Rice 15¢	40	
		18℔ Gr Sugar 99¢ Mar 17 — 1℔ Beef 6¢	1.05	
	16	1 pk meal 20¢ 1 pk. Salt 15	35	
		onions 5¢ Mar 18 — 1 box polish 5¢	10	
	19	1 pk. S. potatoes 15¢ 3℔ Lard 21¢	36	
		4℔ Beef 24¢ Mar 20 — 1℔ Dairy Butter 30¢	54	
	24	2℔ Beef 12¢ Mar 25 — 3℔ Grits 9¢	21	
		3℔ OMeal 15¢ 18℔ Flour 45¢	60	
		1 box Pearline 5¢ ½ pk. W. potatoes 20¢	25	
		½ pk S. potatoes 8¢ 6 bars Soap 25¢	33	
		3℔ Lard 21¢ Mar 25 — 3℔ Steak 18¢	39	
	27	2℔ Beef 12¢ Onions 5¢	17	
		3℔ Gr. Sugar 18¢ March 29 — 1 S. bone	23	
	29	1 C. Tomatoes 10¢ 3℔ Lard 21¢	31	
		3℔ Gr Sugar 17¢ 1℔ pork 8¢	25	
	30	2℔ prunes 20¢ 1℔ D Butter 30¢	50	
		3℔ Grits 9¢ 3℔ Hominy 9¢	18	
		3℔ Rice 15¢ 1 Gal Syrup [50¢]	50 [65]	
		½ pk W potatoes 20¢ 1 pk meal 20¢	40	
		18℔ Flour 45¢ 1℔ Sugar 6¢	51	
		1 box Pearline 5¢ 3℔ O.Meal 15¢	20	
		Salt 5¢ 1℔ Coffee 25¢	30	17.88 [19.88]

April 1895

April	1st	¼# cheese 5¢ 1# Beef 6¢	11
		3# Gr Sugar 17¢ 1 can corn 12¢	29
	3	3# Lard 21¢ ½# B. powder 13¢	34
		1# Beef 6¢ 1# Butter 20¢	26
		2 Doz Eggs 20¢ Apr 6 — 4# Gr Sugar 22¢	42
	6	3# Rice 15¢ 3# Grits 9¢	24
		1 pckg Matches 10¢ 6 bars Soap 25¢	35
		1 box Pearline 5¢ 1# Butter 20¢	25
		1 Doz Eggs 10¢ 16# Flour 40¢	50
		3# Lard 21¢ ½# Steak 3¢	24
	9	2# Gr Sugar 11¢ ½# Butter 10¢	21
		3 Doz eggs 30¢ 6 Mackerel 60¢	90
		½# B. powder 13¢ 17# Flour 43¢	56
	10	1 pk meal 20¢ ½ pk peas 13¢	33
	11	2# Beef 12¢ 1# Butter 25¢	37
		1# Lard 7¢ 3# Grits 9¢ 4 qts Beans 40¢	56
	13	3# Gr. Sugar 17¢ 18# Flour 45¢	62
		1 Gal Syrup 50¢ 3# Lard 21¢	71
		3# Hominy 9¢ 1 Sack Salt 5¢	14
		¼# B. powder 9¢ 2# Beef 12¢	21
	15	3# Gr. Sugar 17¢ 5# Salt 5¢	22
	18	2# Macaroni 18¢ ½# Butter 10¢	28
		1# pork 8¢ 2# Beef 12¢ 1 box polish 5¢	25
		1 box Pearline 5¢ Apr 19 — ¾# Butter 15¢	20
	19	1# Steak 6¢ Apr. 20th 17# Flour 34¢	54
	20	1 pk meal 20¢ 4# Gr Sugar 22¢	42
		1 box Pearline 5¢ 5 bars Soap 25¢	30
		3# Grits 9¢ 3 Doz Eggs 30¢	39
		3# C Hominey 9¢ 4# Starch 20¢	29
		3# Lard 21¢ 1# D. Butter 25¢	46
		1# Coffee 25¢ 2½# Beef 15¢	40
	24	1# Lard 7¢ to Fisher 25¢	32
	26	3 Doz Eggs 30¢ Apr 27 — 1# D Butter 25¢	55
	27	½# Butter 10¢ 1 pk. meal 20¢	30
		3# Rice 15¢ ½# B. powder 13¢	28
		18# Flour 45¢ 2 Doz Eggs 20¢	65
		6# Gr Sugar 33¢ 2# Grits 6¢	39
		3# Hominey 9¢ nutmegs 5¢	14
	30	1# Steak 6¢ 2# Roast 12¢	18	14.17

May 1895

May	1st	1# Butter 23¢ 3 Doz Eggs 30¢	53
	2	2# pork 16¢ May 3 — 1 qt Berries 10¢	26
	3	to mdse 1.50 May 4 — 6# Gr Sugar 33¢	1.83
	4	18# Flour 45¢ 3# Lard 21¢	66
		1# Butter 25¢ ½# C butter 10¢	35
		3 Doz Eggs 30¢ 5 bars G. Soap 25	55
	6	1 box Pearline 5¢ 5# Starch 25¢	30
	5	1 pk G. peas 25¢ 3# Beef 18¢	43
	8	2# Coffee 50¢ May 10 ½# Spice 10¢	60
	10	1# Lard 8¢ 2# Steak 12¢	20
	9	2# Butter 40¢ 6# Gr. Sugar 33¢	73
	10	2¾# Ham 34¢ May 11 — 18# Flour 45¢	79

537

11	1 pk meal 20¢ 3℔ Lard 23¢	43
	5℔ Gr Sugar 28¢ 3℔ Rice 15¢	43
	3 qts Beans 25¢ 3 qts peas 15¢	40
	1℔ Butter 25¢ 3℔ Grits 9¢	34
	6 bars Soap 25¢ ½℔ Soda 5¢	30
	1 box polish 5¢ May 15 — 2 Doz Eggs 20¢	25
15	3℔ O.meal 15¢ 1℔ D Butter 25¢	40
18	1 pckg C. Starch 10¢ 1 pk. meal 20¢	30
	18℔ Flour 45¢ 1 Gal Syrup 40¢	85
	1℔ Butter 25¢ 3℔ Sugar Gr. 17¢	42
	1℔ B. powder 25¢ 3℔ Grits 9¢	34
	1 box Pearline 5¢ 6 box matches 5¢	10
	6℔ Butter 1.20 — 1℔ citron 18	1.38
	1℔ Raisins 8¢ 1℔ Currants 8¢	16
	½℔ Cinnamon 10¢ ¼℔ Cloves 5¢	15
	Spice 5¢ Lemon Ex 40¢	45
	1 bot Vanilla 55¢ 5 Doz Eggs 50¢	1.05
	Gr Sugar 47¢ May 17 — 18℔ Flour 45¢	92
17	3℔ Lard 23¢ May 19 — 2℔ Beef 12¢	35
20	2 Doz Eggs 20¢ 11℔ Gr Sugar 60	80
	10℔ Salt 10¢ May 21 — 2℔ Lard 15¢	25
23	6 bars Soap 25¢ 1 box Pearline 5¢	30
25	3℔ Gr Sugar 17¢ 17℔ Flour 51¢	68
	3℔ Lard 23¢ 3℔ grits 9¢	32
	1 pk meal 20¢ 2℔ Coffee 50¢	70
	1℔ B. powder 25¢ May 26 — 1℔ Beef 6¢	31
26	3 Doz Eggs 30¢ 2℔ Butter 50¢	80
28	4℔ Ice 5¢ 1℔ Beef 6¢	11
	2 Doz Eggs 20¢ 5℔ gr. sugar 30¢	50
30	27℔ Ice 34¢ 6℔ Gr. Sugar 36¢	70
	25℔ Ice 31¢ 3℔ Salt 3¢	34
29	5℔ gr Sugar 30¢ 1 pckg matches 10¢	40
	2℔ D Butter 50¢ Vinegar 3¢	53 22.99

[June 1895]

June 1	18℔ Flour 54 2℔ Lard 14	68
	pepper 05 ½℔ Soda 05	10
4	2 Doz. Eggs 25 1 pk. meal 20	45
	½℔ B. Powder 13 7℔ Gr. Sugar 42	55
8	18℔ Flour 54 1 pk. meal 20	74
	3℔ Lard 23 5℔ Sugar 30	53
	1 [6?] Bars soap 25 1℔ D. Butter 25	50
	1 Box Pearline 05 June 9 — 5℔ sa't 05	10
	1 gal. Syrup 50 June 10 — 3℔ Grits 09	59
	1℔ D. Butter 25 7℔ Sugar 42 4℔ starch 20	87
12	18℔ Flour 54 2℔ Lard 14	68
	½℔ B. Powder 13 (13) 1℔ Butter 25	38
	2 Doz. Eggs 20 1 qt. vinegar 05	25
15	2 Doz. Eggs 20 1℔ Butter 25	45
	3℔ Gr. Sugar 18 1℔ Pepper 20	38
	2℔ Lard 14 Bluing 05	19
16	1½℔ Coffee 38 June 18 — Salt 05	43
	15℔ Gr. Sugar 90 J 22 — 1 pk. meal 20	1.10
	17℔ Flour 51¢ 12℔ Gr. Sugar 72¢	1.23
	1℔ Lard	08

24	2 Doz. Eggs 20¢ 6 Bars soap 25	45	
	1 Box Pearline 05¢ June 27 — 10℔ Gr Sugar 60¢	65	
29	½ Doz. Eggs 05¢ ½℔ Butter 10	15	
	½℔ B. Powder 13¢ Pearline 05¢	18	
30	½℔ Beef	03	11.74

[July 1895]

July	2	6½℔ Gr. Sugar 39¢ (7-6) 2℔ Lard 16	55	
		10℔ Flour 35¢ 2 Doz. eggs 20	55	
		1 pk. meal 20¢ 1 Box Pearline 05¢	25	
	10	½℔ Beef 03¢ (7-11) Soap 25¢ eggs 05	33	
	13	15℔ Flour 53¢ 3℔ Sugar 18	73	
		2℔ Lard 15¢ ½ gal Syrup 20¢	35	
	14	½℔ Beef 03¢ (7-15) 2℔ Starch 10¢	13	
		½ Doz. Eggs 05¢ (7-16) 10℔ Salt 15	20	
	18	1¼℔ Flour 05¢ (7-19) 1 gal vinegar 20¢	25	
		1 Box Pearline 05¢ st[o]ve polish 05¢	10	
	20	7℔ Sugar 42¢ 10℔ Flour 35¢	77	
		3℔ Lard 23¢ (7-22) 10℔ Sugar 60	83	
	23	10℔ Gr. Sugar 60¢	60	
	25	1 gal. vinegar 20¢ 6½℔ Sugar 39¢	59	
		1 pk. meal 20¢ (7-26) 1 qt. vinegar 05	25	
	27	1 gal vinegar 20¢ 5℔ Sugar 30¢	50	
	29	3℔ Gr. Sugar 18¢ 1 Box Pearline 05¢	23	
		6 Bars Soap 25¢	25	7.46

[August 1895]

Aug	2	10℔ Gr. Sugar 60¢ ½℔ Soda 05¢	65	
		½ gal. vinegar 10¢ (8-3) 2℔ Lard 16	26	
		10℔ Flour 35¢ 10℔ Gr. Sugar 60	95	
	4	1℔ B. Powder 20¢ 6 Bars soap 30¢	50	
		5℔ Lard 40¢ (8-5) 1℔ Bacon 08¢	48	
		6 Bars G. Soap 30 1 Pkg. Pearline 05	35	
	9	1½℔ Beef 09¢ (8-10) 10℔ Flour 35¢	44	
		2℔ Lard 16¢ (8-13) 1 pk. meal 20¢	36	
	14	Spices 20¢ 1½ gal vinegar 30¢ 2℔ Lard 16	66	
	16	25℔ Gr. Sugar 1.50 (8-17) 4℔ Bacon 32	1.82	
		18℔ Flour 63¢ 3℔ Lard 24¢	87	
		1 Box Pearline 05¢ 1 B. Powder 10¢	15	
	20	Mdse 50¢ (8-21) 1 B. Powder 10¢	60	
		2℔ Lard	16	
	22	6 Bars Soap 25¢ 1 Pkg. Pearline 05¢	30	
	20	2½℔ Beef 15¢	15	
	24	22℔ Gr. Sugar 1.32 16℔ Flour 56	1.88	
		1℔ Lard 08¢ 2½℔ Starch 13¢	21	
	26	2 Boxes Bluing 05¢ Pearline 05	10	
	27	1 gal Syrup 40¢ Salt 05¢	45	
		2℔ Lard 16¢ ½ Doz. nutmegs 05¢	21	
	30	3℔ Beef 16¢ 1℔ Lard 08	24	
		1 Pkg. Pearline 05¢	05	
	31	3℔ Rice 15¢ 30℔ Flour 75¢	90	
		B. Powder 10¢ 3℔ Lard 24¢	34	
		4℔ Bacon 32¢ Soap 25¢	57	
		Pearline 05¢	05	10.70 [13.70]

[September 1895]

Sept	3	3# Beef 18¢ (9-4) 18# Flour 45¢	63	
		½ pk W. Potatoes 13¢ 2# Lard 16¢	29	
		1# Coffee 25¢ 6 Chickens 1.00	1.25	
	5	1½ pk. W. Potatoes 13 1½# Fish 12	25	
	7	1 pk. meal 20¢ 3# Lard 24	44	
		Soda 05¢ ½# B. Powder 13	18	
		Pearline 05¢ ½# Butter 10¢	15	
		3# Lard 21¢ 1# D. Butter 25¢	46	
		18# Flour 42¢ 3# Beef 18¢	60	
	12	2# Steak 12¢	12	
	12	Jno. Harris	1.00	
		5# Ice 10¢	10	
	14	Mds 75¢	75	
	17	4½# Salt 5¢ pkg. pearline 5¢	10	
		2# Flour 10	10	
	21	18# flour 38 1# Steak 06	54 [44]	
		1 bar pearline [5], 6 bars Soap 30 1# Lard 8	38 [43]	
	24	2# Starch 10cts		
	25	Onions 10 cts	20	
	26	1 doz. Eggs 10 cts 1# Fish 8 cts	18	
	28	18# Flour 30 1# B. Powder 25	55	
		3½# Beef 15 1 doz. eggs 15	30	
		6 bars soap 30 1 Gal oil 15	45	
		1 Gal Oil 15	15	
	30	1 pk apples	20	8.37 [9.37]

[October 1895]

Oct.	1	2# Beef	[12]	
	3	2# Lard 15 ½ pk meal 10	25	
		½ Soda 05	05	
	4	2 Sticks Stove polish 10	10	
	5	1 pkg matches 05 2# Lard 15	20	
		16# Flour 32 2# Salt 03 1 doz Eggs 20	55	
		1 pk. Apples 20	20	
	8	3# Beef 18 1# Soda 10	18 [28]	
	10	1 doz eggs 20 1 pk meal 20	40	
		1 pk. W potatoes 20	20	
		1# Butter 25 Onions 20	45	
	16	½ pk meal 10 (18) Groceries for Stafford 125	1.35	
	22	3# Steak 18 (24) 1# Butter 25 2# Lard 16	59	
	24	2 cans corn 33 2½# cheese 32 2# Liver 12	77	
		2# Bacon 16 (25) Pumpkin 10	26	
	25	Beef 20 matches 5 Sugar 18 Soap 25	68	
	26	1 pk apples 35	35	
		1 pk meal 20 2# Lard 14	14 [34]	
		1 pumpkin 05	05	6.82 [6.77]

[November 1895]

Nov	1	2# Lard 16 18# Flour 54	70
		½ pk apples 20 matches 20	40
		1 box blueing 05 Vanilla 25	30
		2# Beef 12 1 qt onions 05	17

2	7℔ Sugar 42 3℔ Rice 15	57	
	1 pk apples 35 nutmegs 05	40	
	1 pkges matches 10 2℔ Beef 12	22	
	6 chickens 70 1 pk potatoes 15	85	
4	½ pk W. potatoes 20	20	
	3℔ Starch 15 ½ pk apples 20	35	
5	5 Bars Soap 25	25	
8	2℔ Bacon 13	13	
9	13℔ Flour 47 4℔ Sugar 24	71	
11	5℔ Bacon 33 ½ pk apples 20	53	
12	½ pk W potatoes 20 1 can To[matoes?] 25	45	
13	5℔ Bacon 26 1 can corn 11	37	
	½℔ Butter 13 ⅓ doz eggs 06	19	
15	3℔ Rice 18 6℔ Sugar 36	44 [54]	
	1 pk meal 15 ½℔ butter 10	25	
16	2℔ pork 14 3℔ Lard 24	38	
	2℔ Steak 14 6℔ Sugar 42	56	
	5 bars Soap 25 1℔ Soda 10	35	
22	1℔ B powder 25 4℔ Rice 20	45	
24	1 gal vingar 20 1 gal Syr 30	50	
	40℔ flour 120 1℔ cheese 12	1.30 [1.32]	
	2℔ beef 12 2℔ Beef 12	24	
25	1 doz onions 10 2℔ Bacon 14	24	
	½℔ Mustard 15 1 pk meal 15	30	
26	1 pk potatoes 15 3℔ Lard 21	36	
	2℔ Pork 14 ½ pk apples 20	34	
29	1℔ Butter 20 1⅔ Turnips 05	25	
	2℔ Sugar 13 ½℔ Cheese 18	31	
	3℔ Rice 18 5℔ Roast 18	36	
	Mds.	90	13.07 [14.32]

[December 1895]

Dec	2	18℔ flour 54 ½ pk potatoes 20	74	
		macaroni 13 1℔ Steak 06	19	
	3	½ pk. potatoes 08 3℔ Sugar 18	26	
		3℔ Salt 05 ½ pk apples 20	25	
		1℔ Liver 06 4½℔ cabbage 18	24	
	5	1 pk meal 15 1 doz. apples 10	25	
	6	18℔ flour 54 1℔ cheese 15	69	
		6℔ Sugar 42 1 pk W potatoes 30	72	
		⅓℔ Ginger 10 3℔ Rice 15	25	
		5 bars Soap 25 1½ doz. onions 15	40	
		3℔ bacon 21 1 pk. potatoes 35	56	
		3℔ Lard 35 1 pk. peas 90	1.15 [1.25]	
		1 qt. meal 05 ½ pk. meal 8	13	
	12	2℔ Roast 12 1 pkg. matches 10	22	
	14	18℔ flour 54 5℔ Roast 30	84	
		6℔ Sugar 42 4 cabbage 16	58	
		1 pkg. potatoes 30	30	
		Syrup 10 cts 3℔ Rice 15	25	
	16	5℔ Lard 30 3℔ crackers 30	60	
	17	1 pk W potatoes 45 ½ Gal. Syrup 20	65	
		½ bu. potatoes 15 2℔ honey 06	21	
		2℔ Lard 12 1 pk apples 45	57	
		1℔ pork and 3 pt [?] 37	37	

18	3℔ Roast 18 2℔ Steak 12		30
	1 pk. meal 15 3℔ Mincemeat 36		51
	1 doz. eggs 20 1 pk apples 45		65
	2℔ Steak 12 2℔ Macaroni 18		30
	2℔ Steak 12 1℔ cheese 15		27
	3℔ Lard 21		21
27	½℔ hops 20 cts potatoes 15		35
28	1 doz eggs 20 1 pk. apples 15		35
	25℔ flour 60 2℔ Lard 14		74
	2℔ coffee 50 2℔ Starch 15		65
	3℔ Rice 09 1℔ butter 12		21
	1℔ butter 20 Roast 12 cts Steak 27 cts		59
30	1℔ butter 20	20	[15.85]

HD Con. 1003   BTW Papers DLC. Corrections of errors of addition or omission appear in brackets. The original is a ledger book of 254 pages about 8½″ x 14″. BTW's accounts are on pp. 190-98. Weekly totals and sums carried over onto another page have been omitted, and only monthly totals are included.

[1] George W. Scott was in charge of the commissary in the 1894-95 school year. In the following year Y. E. McKinney and John M. Flournoy each served part of the year. It is impossible to determine who served first, but the document shows a change occurred on June 1 and another on Sept. 17, 1895.

[2] A nationally advertised powdered laundry soap manufactured in New York beginning about 1880.

To Nathan B. Young

[Tuskegee, Ala., Mar. 5, 1895]

Mr. Young: Hereafter Porter Hall, including the steps, halls and recitation rooms is to be scrubbed every other day, and the chapel twice a week. The unfrosted windows are to be cleaned every week. The paint is to be carefully wiped off or washed once a week, especially the paint on the doors around the knobs.

Mr. Calloway will explain the details of this work to you if you will see him. This same thing applies to the recitation rooms in Armstrong Hall and Slab Hall.

Booker T. Washington

TLpS Con. 113   BTW Papers DLC.

To Susan B. Bransford

[Tuskegee, Ala.] Mar 7, 95

Miss Bransford: Lydia Robinson[1] claims that she is wrongfully accused of making noise and consequently is being wrongfully punished. I do not write about this as I know that many of the students claim that they are wrongfully punished when it is not true.

What I speak of is this: This girl claims that she has been refused by you any opportunity to make a statement of her case. She says that you refuse to hear any statement from her and "shut the door" in her face. If this last statement of this girl is true, she should be treated differently. Of course I do not say that any of the girls statements are true. But in case her latter statement is true care should be taken to see that girls are not treated in this way. The most humble and the worst girl should be given a chance to make a statement of any side of her case. I never refuse any student even though I *know* the student is guilty, the opportunity to sit down in my office and make a statement of his side of any case. In no other way can we hold the respect and confidence of the students.

Booker T. Washington

ALpS Con. 113 BTW Papers DLC.

[1] Lydia Corrie Robinson of Greensboro, Ala., who graduated in 1897 and became a teacher in the Troy (Ala.) Industrial Academy. In 1900 she completed a postgraduate course at Tuskegee. She worked as a dressmaker and milliner in Decatur, Ala.

To the Faculty Committee on the Atlanta Exposition Exhibit

[Tuskegee, Ala.] March 14th, 1895

Messrs. J. H. Washington, Taylor & Young: You are hereby appointed a Committee on the school's exhibit for the Atlanta Exposition, and

I wish you would meet regularly every Thursday at 2 o'clock (beginning to-day) in my office to consider matters connected with the exhibit.

B. T. Washington

TLpSr   Con. 113   BTW Papers   DLC.

To Jennie Robinson

[Tuskegee, Ala.] April 1, 95

Miss Robinson: Information comes to me to the effect that you go into Prof. White's room to see him un-accompanied. In case it is necessary for you to go to see Mr. White or to go on the same floor where he is during his sickness, I wish you would not go without being accompanied by some lady teacher.

Booker T. Washington

ALpS   Con. 113   BTW Papers   DLC.

From J[ohn] J. Benson[1]

[Tallassee, Ala.] April the 2 95

Dear Sir. you May be Surprised to get a letter from me. But I Will Write you a few lines any Way. We are having Some nice Weather now for farm Work. for the first time Since crismas. We have had our county Stained With 2 horrible crims lately   the White caps[2] Whiped 6 or 7 colord Men last Spring. there Was a Mr. Swinel Who was a Witness a gainst them   they order him to leave his home So they Would get rid of the testimony that he would give. he did not go So they come to his house on the 23 night of March taken him out and kill him   he was a good young man. On the morning of the 24 Tallassee lost one of her best men   he has ben imployd by the company a long time and was getting along better than any other colord man in that place. a White man came to his house and Shot him ded on the Spot   you may know him. Grant Birney.[3]

you Said you Would come over hear   I Will be Sure to look for you and as many others Wants to come   Please let me know about What time you can come   yours truly

J. J. Benson

ALS Con. 9 BTW Papers ATT. Original destroyed.

[1] Probably John Benson, listed in the 1880 census as a thirty-year-old literate black farmer living in Elmore County near Tallassee.

[2] Whitecaps were a sort of informal Ku Klux Klan. Bands of masked, armed white men in the rural South in the 1890s and later used violence and threats to drive blacks from economic competition or the polls. Whitecaps were particularly prevalent in Mississippi but also appeared in surrounding states. (See Holmes, "Whitecapping: Agrarian Violence in Mississippi, 1902-1906.")

[3] Grant Burney, an employee of the Tallassee Falls Manufacturing Company, reported to a Mr. Hutchinson that James Lee, a delivery man, had eaten oysters from a package he was carrying to Hutchinson. Lee went to Burney's house and demanded that he retract the statement. When Burney refused, Lee shot and killed him and then fled. Though citizens of the town offered a $100 reward, which the governor matched, apparently Lee was never apprehended. (Montgomery *Advertiser*, Mar. 27, 1895, 3.)

From A. M. De Vaughn[1]

Pensacola, Fla. Apr. 6, 1895

Dear Sir: I've been frequently asked whether the negroes should attend the Atlanta Exposition, and ride in Second class cars, and there will be a meeting to discuss the matter as to whether they should or not, at which place and time I am to show why they *should*.

There are some strong reasons shown why they should not, and for this and other reasons I should like to have your strongest private views in the case.

Inclosed find stamp for an immediate reply to Yours Obt'ly

A. M. DeVaughn

ALS Con. 9 BTW Papers ATT. Original destroyed.

[1] A. M. De Vaughn, born about 1849, was a black schoolteacher in Pensacola, Fla.

From Wilbur Olin Atwater[1]

Middletown, Conn. April 17th, 1895

Dear Sir: I enclose herewith an authorization from the Secretary of Agriculture to yourself to make a series of investigations on food supply and consumption in the State of Alabama and especially at Tuskegee,[2] and a communication from the Director of the Office of Experiment Stations advising you of the authorization. The expectation is that the investigation will be conducted in accordance with the conversations which have taken place between yourself, Director True,[3] Mr. Woods[4] and myself. It is expected that you will be able to make dietary studies of typical negro families of different occupations, but more especially representative of farm or plantation life. The chemical analyses for these studies will be completed at Auburn by Prof. Ross,[5] although the preparation of the samples will doubtless have to be made at Tuskegee.

Mr. H. Monmouth Smith, who has been with us for several years and has more recently assisted in the introduction of dietary studies at Knoxville and La Fayette, will be at Tuskegee very soon if he has not already arrived. He will be able to explain to you the way in which we have been in the habit of conducting these studies. He does not, however, go to Tuskegee to direct the work. The immediate charge of this investigation is left in your own hands, but you are aware of the importance that it be conducted in the same manner at Tuskegee as elsewhere in order that the results may be comparable. For this purpose you will naturally utilize Mr. Smith's information so far as practicable. We think that you will find him to be an agreeable young man and well informed in these lines.

May I ask you to report your progress from time to time, the more frequently and fully the better?

We expect most valuable and interesting results from your work and wish you the best success. Respectfully,

W. O. Atwater
Special Agent in Charge of
Nutrition Investigations

TLS Con. 9 BTW Papers ATT. Original destroyed. Written on stationery of the U.S. Department of Agriculture, Office of Experiment Stations.

[1] Wilbur Olin Atwater (1844-1907), a pioneer in agricultural chemistry, was professor of chemistry at Wesleyan University from 1873 until his death. It was largely through his lobbying efforts that Congress passed the Hatch Act in 1887, providing that every state should receive $15,000 a year to maintain at least one agricultural experiment station. With Professor E. B. Rosa, a physicist at Wesleyan, he built the Atwater-Rosa calorimeter, testing the heat value of foods, out of which he developed the calorie charts still in use. In 1888 Atwater became founder and chief of the Office of Experiment Stations, U.S. Department of Agriculture, in addition to his professional duties. He served in this post until 1893. He was the author of several hundred scientific papers, most of them on the physiology of metabolism.

[2] This study was reported in Wilbur O. Atwater and Charles D. Woods, *Dietary Studies with Reference to the Food of the Negro in Alabama in 1895 and 1896: Conducted with the Cooperation of the Tuskegee Normal and Industrial Institute and the Agricultural and Mechanical College of Alabama* (Washington, 1897). The 67-page report was *Bulletin No. 38* of the Office of Experiment Stations, U.S. Department of Agriculture.

[3] Alfred Charles True (1853-1929), son of a Wesleyan University professor, was himself for four years an instructor there in Latin and Greek. He joined the staff of Wilbur O. Atwater's Office of Experiment Stations in 1888. He became its director in 1893. He later led the implementation of the Smith-Lever Act of 1914, a program of instruction of farmers through county agents and agricultural demonstration projects.

[4] Charles D. Woods.

[5] Bennett Battle Ross (b. 1865) received A.B. and M.S. degrees from Auburn and was assistant chemist there from 1881 to 1887. He was professor of chemistry at the University of Louisiana from 1887 to 1893. Returning to Alabama, he was state chemist and also served on the board of directors of the Bank of Auburn and of the Opelika cotton mill.

To Hollis Burke Frissell

Tuskegee, Ala. April 20, 1895

Dear Dr. Frissell: You have perhaps heard of the death of Mr. Robt. H. Hamilton of this institution, while engaged in work in the North for the school.[1] He died, as Gen. Armstrong used to say, with his boots on, right in the midst of his work. For twenty years Mr. Hamilton has given his time and talent unselfishly to the work of Hampton and Tuskegee, and has thought little about providing for his family. His death leaves a wife and four small children with no provision for the future. We are making an effort to provide his family with a small but comfortable home near Tuskegee, and I thought that in view of the circumstances, you might feel it a privilege to contribute a small mite toward the purchase of this home. Our teachers have made a generous contribution, and Mr. C. P. Huntington, of New York, has given $50. Yours very truly,

Booker T. Washington

TLS   BTW Folder   ViHaI.

¹ Robert Hannibal Hamilton died at Dobb's Ferry, N.Y., on Mar. 27, 1895, and was buried at Tuskegee. In the 1894-95 Tuskegee catalog he was described as: "One to whom we delighted to refer as one of God's chosen vessels for the uplifting of his race, and a power for good wherever his lot was cast."

From Hollis Burke Frissell

Hampton, Va. Apr. 23, 1895

Dear Mr. Washington: Your letter of April 20th in regard to making provision for Mr. Hamilton's family, is at hand. I shall be glad to see that the matter is brought up here, and we can perhaps do something to help. His death is indeed a great loss. Very truly yours,

H. B. Frissell

TLpS   Frissell Letterbooks   ViHaI.

A Sunday Evening Talk

[Tuskegee, Ala.] April 28th 1895

THE WORK TO BE DONE BY TUSKEGEE GRADUATES

What I shall say to-night will be directed mainly to the members of the graduating class and the others that are to follow.

I think the thing for us to do is to keep constantly in mind the work that is right about us, the work that we are responsible for doing, and the work that is constantly calling us every hour of our life; and we cannot escape the responsibility of throwing ourselves into the thickest part of the fight, and making ourselves felt.

I believe that the majority of students who come here and graduate should work in what is known as the "Black Belt" of the South, and I am glad that the majority of our graduates have done so thus far, and are working in one way or another for the elevation of those about us. You will hear many students especially those who are in the higher classes, say that they intend to practice medicine, study law or something else when they graduate, but the majority, after all, will be found in these fields of work that lie about in the "Black Belt" of the South where our best talent and other influences are needed.

What is the thing to do? It is not necessary for me to describe the conditions that exist in Mississippi, Louisiana, South Carolina and other Southern States. You know what the condition is. But how can you make your life most felt in improving the condition of the masses of these people? In the first place you want to get a nucleus for your work, a starting point, and I believe that the best you can do is to take the public school for this nucleus, notwithstanding it does not last more than two or three months during the year. By doing this, you accomplish two things: you get a small financial start, and then you secure the confidence of the people in the community, which is a thing not to be lost sight of.

And then after you have done that, the next thing for you [to] do is to try to secure the co-operation and encouragement of the ministers in these various districts, and you will find that in doing this, you will have an influence with this minister. Because a minister is ignorant or immoral, I don't believe you gain anything by attempting to get rid of him. I don't believe you gain anything by that kind of procedure. You gain more by helping him with his faults, trying to help him become more intelligent, and in that way instead of having to spend your force in fighting somebody, you spend it in making a friend that is going to be of some value to you and the people in the community. This is the method which many foreign missionaries are adopting. Instead of the missionaries going to Japan, Africa and other heathen countries fighting the religious customs of the natives, they are going to take hold of their religion and get out of it whatever is good upon which they can build a stronger and better religion. As a rule the minister is a good representative of the people, and if you undertake the task of getting rid of the minister you may have to get rid of the people. You must educate them to appreciate better things, and in many cases you will find that you can inspire them and so build them up to the point where you can make them of mutual use.

Today I visited one of the churches in town, and was really surprised to hear the sermon that was preached by the minister. There were no grammatical errors in it, and it would have done credit to any minister. Now I suppose that this man's education in a large measure was obtained in our Bible Training School, where in two or three years he has been made all over again. This is an illustration of what you can do by attempting to improve the minister, and if you go to work earnestly, you will very often succeed.

Next you need a school house. You cannot teach school in log cabins without doors, windows, lights, floor or apparatus. You need a school house, and if you are in earnest the people will help you. But you must make the start yourself. It is easy to get people to help when they see the foundation for the building being laid. People are more willing to give to something that they can see with their own eyes than to anything else. That is something tangible, something that they are not afraid is going to run away with their money. You ask them to give money toward something that is not so tangible, and unless you have been among them for a long time and have gained their confidence, they are doubtful of your honesty, and will very often refuse you point-blank. Remember you must have a school house at all hazards. I need not attempt to enumerate the ways in which you can get the money for that building. I remember one case especially, that of Abner Jackson[1] who graduated some years ago and went down in Henry County, and began his work with one of the three-month public schools. He needed a school house, and went among both white and colored people, and got subscriptions of from five to ten dollars, and then he had festivals, fairs, and got the people to give cakes and chickens, just as we did here, and thus very soon Jackson replaced an old log cabin with a spacious and comfortable school house. The same thing can be said of many other of our graduates, and I hope that many of you will go out and do the same thing.

Then of course, after getting up the school house, the thing to do is to extend the school term. You cannot get the people to pay money toward the education of their children, buy books, become interested in the school, until you get to the point where the school term is going to last longer than three or four months.

Begin by inducing the people to supplement the school term as long as they can, and if you remain in one community year after year the people will supplement the term until you have a good six, seven or eight months school. Do as Mr. Michael[2] is doing at Mt. Meigs. He has planted a certain acreage in cotton, and with the help of the students, has been able to raise three and four bales of cotton which he sells and thus continues the school. That can be done in most any county in the State.

Now you have got to make up your minds that you are going to have a hard time. You cannot get hold of large salaries at first. If you can get your board and some clothes for the first year you are being pretty well paid; but you will find after you have been in one of these communities and succeeded in lengthening the school term your pay will increase in proportion as you get the people to the point where they are able to pay you more.

After this you want to begin thinking about putting into that community a model home of your own, a home that is going to be a model for those people, a house containing four rooms if you are able to have that many, and then get a model farm, some thing that they can look at, take pattern after.

And then there is no reason why in all of these communities and this applies to the young women mainly — you can organize the women who congregate around the stores and street corners, and you can talk to them about things that concern their home life, and you will be surprised to see the encouragement that will come to you, and the changes that will take place.

And then I hope that as far as possible each graduate or student who goes out to teach in these communities will have some kind of organization where you can advise the people, and talk simply to them. Don't use any big words and high flowing sentences. Don't go out to show your education; talk to them in plain, simple words. Simply have the people sit down and talk to them in a plain common-sense way. Find out their condition. Tell them how to stop mortgaging their crops; how to quit living in an old one-room log cabin. Another good thing to do is to have them bring specimens of their products to these conferences, clubs, societies, or whatever you may call them. Have the man who has raised the largest hogs, best vegetable, etc., bring them to these meetings, and let them serve as object-lessons to the others. That is the way the people in the Northwest have done, and that is the way the people in New England and the West are doing to-day; they are holding farmers' conferences to which the farmers bring specimens of their products, and others seeing them have done the same thing.

You must keep in mind that the time to get hold of the people is in the fall when they have money. You know that the average farmer in all of these cotton-raising districts have their money, as a rule, during Oct., November, and December, and it is then you must induce them to save their money for after that they usually have none.

Now, in conclusion, you must go out with the determination to do this kind of work. Do not become discouraged. You must have a missionary spirit. You must remember that whatever has been done in any country, has been done because somebody was brave enough to go out and be the leader. Take the great State of Oregon as an example. Why, that State owes its very existence to-day to the self-sacrifice, to the life, as it were, of Rev. Mr. Whitman[3] who went out there when there was nothing but the bare wilderness, when he had to do his own cooking, and nearly starve to death in order that he might settle that country and open a way for civilization! When we think of persons who are going to Japan and Africa of other races, as well as our race, suffering by reason of the heat, insects, reptiles and fever, when we think of their being willing to go out into these various fields, should not we be inspired with the same spirit, go out and give ourselves, bodies, talents and whatever education we have, to helping those who are groping in darkness right around us? Three-fourths of the young men and women who are being educated in these Southern schools, are being educated at a terrible price. Their education being bought with the lives of such men as Gen. Armstrong, Mr. Hamilton and other men of that kind, who have been willing to lay down their lives in order that somebody might have a chance. Begin in an humble simple way and work to build up institutions that will put the people on their feet. It is that kind of life that tells. Go out and be a center, a life giving power as it were to the whole community when an opportunity [comes] to give life where there is no life, hope where there is no hope, power where there is no power.

That is what you are being educated for, and that is what money that comes to us year after year is used for — in order that you may be filled with this missionary spirit, this self-sacrificing spirit. Those who give to us do so because they want to see you go out into these communities and give your lives, talents and education and everything else to the upbuilding of these people.

Are you willing to do that?

Tuskegee Student, 9 (May 3, 1895), 1, 3.

[1] Abner Beecher Jackson, a graduate of Tuskegee in 1890, became the principal of the Jackson Enterprise School in Newville, Ala.

[2] John Henry Michael, who graduated from Tuskegee in 1892, was superintendent of industries at Mt. Meigs Colored Institute, Waugh, Ala., from 1892 to 1895, when he went to a similar position in the Slater Industrial Academy in Winston-Salem, N.C.

[3] Marcus Whitman (1802-47).

From Daniel Coit Gilman

Baltimore, Md. May 9, 1895

Dear Sir: In a recent conversation with one of the Trustees of the Slater Fund, Mr. William E. Dodge, he spoke to me of two matters pertaining to the welfare of the colored race of the South, and suggested that I should write to you in regard to them. The first is the tendency of the Negroes to borrow money on their land and other property, often at exorbitant rates, and usually by mortgaging their property to foreigners. Second, the tendency, in some parts of the country, to revert to uncivilized and almost barbarous methods of life, or at least to ignorant and superstitious religious practices.

We raise the question whether a well-chosen colored man, of intelligence and tact, might not get at the facts by visiting certain regions and gathering information which cannot be brought out by any of the usual processes of statistical inquiry.

Will you regard this letter as confidential, and let me know what your impressions may be? Yours truly

D C Gilman

TLS Con. 9 BTW Papers ATT. Original destroyed.

A Sunday Evening Talk

Tuskegee, Ala., May 12th, 1895

GROWTH

I want especially to urge to-night, upon those who finish their course of study here this year, and upon all of the students who are to go home or elsewhere for their vacation, the importance and necessity of trying to continually grow. That is going to be one of the hardest things that you are going to have to contend with. It is going to be very hard for some of you to grow, and, as I have often said, a person cannot stand still; he is either growing better or is growing worse, he is either getting hold of more knowledge, or is becoming more ignorant. Some of you are going to find it a pretty hard task to go forward. Many of you will find everything tending downward instead of upward. You will have temptations to wrong-doing instead of right-doing. Evils will beset you on every hand, both in conversation and in the temptation to read that which you ought not to read; and so, you will have to make a special effort to keep yourselves from going downward instead of upward.

Many people who are inclined to help in the work of education, often become discouraged that the Indians, after becoming educated, often go back to their tribes and resume the old customs and habits which they had before they were educated. But people very often overlook the tremendous sentiment and opposition to education that exist among the Indian tribes. The educated Indian returns to the reservation, where he is surrounded constantly by people who believe in the old customs, who scorn civilization, and the tendency downward is so great, that unless he has great force of character, he will soon go back to the blanket. Perhaps, in a less degree, the same thing is largely true of those who graduate from these Southern institutions. You go into the cities as well as into the country, and there is something that will pull you downward. There is nothing so discouraging to teachers and others, as to come in contact with young men and women on whom much time and money have been spent, who are going downward instead of upward. These young men and women, who are soon to graduate, are going downward or upward, beginning with the day they leave this institution.

In the first place, in order to keep yourselves growing, you want to have the right kind of aspiration. You want to be very sure they are none but the highest. You want to be very sure that you make no effort in the direction of that which is not noble and true. Be sure that your foundation floor is strong, and then if you keep in the right way, you will begin to grow — you will grow upward and not downward. And then make up your minds, once for all, that you are not going to pick out for your associates persons who are not going to make you better — that whether you are popular or unpopular, you are going to be at all times with those people who are going to make you better men and women, instead of worse — those who are going to make you better in your conversation. Be sure that you come in contact with the best there is in the world in whatever you read. Be sure that you get the best newspapers, the best books, and thus come in contact with the best thought and sentiment in whatever you read. No matter where you are located, be very sure that at least once a week, you come in close communion with the other world through the medium of good reading. Do not be satisfied to take anything that is second or third class. If you cannot hear the best conversation, if you cannot hear the best lectures and sermons, you can, as I said, through the medium of the public prints, at least once a week, come in contact with the best our civilization affords.

And then, you want to be very sure that what ever your specialty is, whether school teaching, agriculture or mechanical work, no matter what it is, you want to be very sure that you are growing in the line of that specialty. You want to be sure that you are a stronger man this week than you were last week in that line of work, and then you want to be sure that you are worth more, as time passes, to persons who employ you.

Aside from the mere financial and material gain that comes to a person, it pays one, from a moral standpoint, to grow in whatever he is doing. A person who does not feel that he has ambition — that animal spirit, as I might perhaps call it, that spirit of satisfaction that is a result of the feeling that he is growing better, that he is better prepared for the work to-day than he was yesterday, I say he who does not feel that, is more likely to yield to temptation than one who does. When you find a person who is thus satisfied with his work, you can see his work leaping forward, as it were; you can see him grow day by day, and you can see in his face that he is more a master of his work than he was some time before. He is always open to suggestions or criticism, and is consequently always growing in value to the persons who employ him. I say that such a person is not as likely to yield to temptation as those that I have described.

And then you want to be constantly measuring yourself by yourself. You are very often told to measure yourself by others, but there is the great trouble; we are likely to measure ourselves by persons who have had a great many more advantages than we have — persons who are too far above us. If you measure yourself by yourself, you can judge whether or not you are progressing. Any man can tell whether or not his work is better systematized this year than it was last year. You can very easily tell whether your mind is growing broader and whether you are growing upward instead of downward. Consequently, stop and take your moorings; find out where you are whenever you find yourself going downward and backward in any way; mentally, physically, morally. Stop and think, and if you find yourself going backward, make another leap forward, and say: "With God's help, I am going to make another start and go upward, not downward."

Tuskegee Student, 9 (June 26, 1895), 1.

From John Wesslay Hoffman

Tuskegee, Ala., May 24th 1895

Dear Sir: Your note is before me requesting a report of the work that has been done on the "Food Investigation." I cannot give in detail any thing like a full account of the Investigation as yet. Up to date we have examined into the Dietery of seven families located within a radius of eight miles of the Institution. You are aware of the fact that the Govment is very anxious to know of the kind of Food the masses of people are eating and in the station here to find out the food used by the Negroes when left alone to provide for themselves. Our work is thus we go out every day and visit certain families to find out the amount of food use[d] by them, the kind used and the number of persons at each meal.

We then take a sample of the food especially the corn meal for the purpose of making an analysis of the same.

At the end of this investigation in June I am to make a full report to you of the work covering the analysis of the food the amount used etc and the same to be transmitted by you to the Govment Dept. through Dr. Atwater.

A most interesting line of facts will be develope[d] in our work which is this the Govt. Dept. will see that the masses are not eating food that will build up strong men and women mentally and morally. As their food[s] are deficient in Proteins or food for muscle and brain and in place they use a great deal of *fat* and Carbohydrate necessary for energy and heat.

We are now studying the Dietary of two families on Russell's Plantation about eight miles from here. The work with these families will close on Monday afternoon of next week.

We are now just beginning a line of work in our Institution that will give prominence to our School not only in this country but Europe — as this line of work was first started in Germany a few years ago.

I forgot to state that Mr. Smith the Govts Special Agent is in Auburn making a careful analysis of samples of the various kinds of food collected here viz: cow peas, corn meal, Flour, butter, native beef, mutton, pork and chickens. We have not the facilities here for making such analysis. I am, Yours very truly

J. W. Hoffman

ALS   Con. 9   BTW Papers   ATT.   Original destroyed.

From John Orman Turner[1]

Montgomery, June 1st 1895

My Dear Sir: The rush was so great in leaving your place, that I did not have time to thank you and your brother and all your teachers and pupils for their marked interest in my visit and for their repeated acts of kindness during the day. It will afford me extreme pleasure to speak a good word in behalf of you and your noble Institution in my visits over the state. While my entire life has been devoted to the cause of education, I must confess our people over the state do not realize the wonders you are performing and can never appreciate fully your worth to the state and your *race* throughout the Nation, unless they visit your College. I am glad your school is located in Ala. You

557

are to-day in a position to do more good than any man in Ala or perhapse in the South. I bid you God's speed. May your last days be your best. Whatever I can do to aid you as Supt. of Education to promote your College or the interest of your people — I shall only be too glad to do so. Again thanking you for your repeated acts of kindness — while in Tuskegee. I am Very truly your friend

Jno. O. Turner

ALS Con. 863 BTW Papers DLC.

[1] John Orman Turner (b. 1850) was the Alabama state superintendent of education from 1894 to 1898. Previously he had been principal of a high school and president of Ashville College (now Samford University). A warm supporter of BTW and of Tuskegee methods, Turner seems to have been a sincere promoter of black as well as white education within the limits set by Alabama politics and racial restrictions. A Democrat until 1896, he opposed Bryanism. He also opposed ratification of the Alabama constitution of 1901, which disfranchised most of the black voters. He supported Theodore Roosevelt and unsuccessfully sought a federal office through BTW's help. "Nothing was too good for the Democrats to say of me when I sang their song," he wrote BTW. (Turner to BTW, Nov. 18, 1902, Con. 243, BTW Papers, DLC.)

A News Item from the Tuskegee *News*

[Tuskegee, Ala., June 13, 1895]

A SHAMEFUL EPISODE!

Last Saturday night about 10 o'clock the residents of Tuskegee were startled by a wild hubbub in the N.E. end of the city — a furious barking of dogs was accompanied by other sounds of a more startling nature. Suddenly four or five pistol shots rang out on the air, followed by agonized screams of women, and a man's voice shrieking in pain. It was terrible to listen to: "Help! Help! My God, they have killed him — Oh they have killed him!" These words shrieked over and over soon drew a crowd of men and boys to the residence of Mr. John Alexander where it was found that Mr. Alexander had been accidently shot and was supposed fatally wounded by a mob of masked men who had entered his premises in pursuit of Tom Harris,[1] a notorious mulatto man, negro lawyer and rather a seditious character, who had against Mr. Alexander's orders taken refuge within his gates from a

558

pursuing mob. Tom Harris is a very ambitious and rather an idle negro man, extremely unpopular with his own race on account of his airs of superiority, and having little influence with them. So far as known he has never been guilty of any crime whatever, but his impudent utterances and insolent bearing have made him very obnoxious to the white people, and once before now he has had to leave the city on a prolonged stay. He purchased some years ago a very comfortable home for his family — the Hayden residence in the immediate vicinity of Mr. Alexander's home, and there his family reside. His wife is considered a model colored woman, she is industrious, virtuous and thoroughly orderly in every respect and has endeavored to raise her large family of children with propriety. His eldest son Wylie, is a well known young yellow man who has a butcher's shop here. Some two or three weeks ago a yankee preacher named Kelly appeared in this county. He put up with respectable citizens at Cross Keys and was told that he might preach to negroes but that in this part of the country social equality was not tolerated. He conducted himself accordingly there, but coming to Tuskegee he was entertained at Tom Harris' house, and it is said walked the streets between two of Harris' daughters, holding an umberlla over them. It is also stated that he preached social equality, and from the pulpit denounced certain citizens of this place, calling no names but making such pointed remarks that there could be no doubt of his meaning, and that Tom Harris had given him the dots. A meeting of citizens was called in which all rash suggestions were voted down, but it was resolved that a committee of citizens should go to the house of Tom Harris and order the yankee to leave our city within 6 hours. This was accordingly done. It was well and good, and the matter should have ended there. But Saturday night a letter was sent to Tom Harris saying that his life was demanded, this letter was taken home by Wiley at a late hour (probably from the Post-office) and the negro could scarcely have had time to have escaped after receiving it before the arrival of the mob at his house. Instead however, of immediately retreating from the neighborhood he took the letter over to Mr. Alexander's and calling from the front gate requested to see him. Mr. Alexander was at the time seated on his front gallery with his daughters. He stepped into the road and Tom Harris told him of the letter and asked his advice, directly looking down the moonlit road [ex]claimed, "There they are now, coming to kill me!" and rushed into Mr. Alexander's front yard. Mr. Alexander seeing the approach of several masked men recognized the danger to his family and rushed into the yard attempting to run Tom Harris out, at the same time calling to the men not to shoot for fear they might kill or frighten his daughters. The mob however, not to be deterred from their purpose rushed into the yard and one of them putting his pistol within a foot of Harris fired meaning of course to kill him. The negro squatted in time to avert the shot which struck Mr. Alexander (who was immediately back of him trying to evict him from the premises,) hitting him in the throat, the ball ranging toward the spinal column where it lodged. Other shots followed in immediate succession and Tom Harris was wounded in the leg and fell as he was running down the road, and it is said the bone was shattered. The screams of pain were from the wounded negro who called loudly for help, but no attention was given him excepting by his family who gathered around him, though in the crowd that rushed to the scene were several medical men who proceeded to render Mr. Alexander all the assistance in their power. It was thought at first that Mr. Alexander was mortally wounded. He is said to have borne himself with wonderful coolness and nerve, and though probing for the ball was unsuccessful he has rallied, to the surprise of all, and bids fair to recover. If he does it will be due in large measure to the devoted attention he has received from our medical men, who, as well as every other citizen of this community, feel the greatest sympathy for him in his suffering and for his family in their anxiety and distress. Failing to get any white doctor to attend his father Wylie Harris took him over to the Normal School that night, where however he was not received, for Booker T. Washington the president of the Negro school has ever conducted himself and his school in the most prudent and conservative manner, and learning that a mob was in pursuit of Harris he told him that he could not be admitted there. What has become of Harris we do not know. That he is painfully wounded is certain, and after the vindictive demonstration to which he has lately been subjected it is scarcely probable that he will ever again attempt to make his residence in this city. The lawless action of these masked men cannot be too severely condemned. [In] The first place Harris [has] done nothing to make him amenable to law. Personal dislike and a vindictive feeling of animosity give no excuse for any attempt on a man's life be he white or black. In the second place the unlawful entering of the premises, of Mr. Alexander and shooting him, an entirely innocent person, even though

it [is] claimed that hurt to him was not intentional, was a most unprecedented outrage, and we call upon the Sheriff of Macon County
to do his duty in this matter. If he will, we believe that he can.

Tuskegee *News,* June 13, 1895, 3.

[1] Thomas A. Harris was born a slave in Macon County and served as the body
servant of a Confederate officer. After the Civil War for many years he took an
active part in Republican politics in Tuskegee, an experience that may have
kindled a desire to be an attorney. Harris attended Tuskegee for the school year
1883-84. In 1890 he passed the state bar examination in Montgomery. A former
governor, a general, and a state attorney general approved his examination, pronouncing him "an intelligent and well-behaved negro." After practicing briefly in
Birmingham, Harris returned to Tuskegee to practice law and to live with his
large family.

After the incident described in this document, Washington secretly helped
Harris to escape his pursuers and to get medical help from Dr. C. N. Dorsette of
Montgomery. Harris stayed in Selma and in Okolona, Miss., until his broken
leg healed. Concluding that the whites of Tuskegee did not want him to practice
law, he moved on to Lafayette and Anniston, Ala.

On BTW's part in the Harris episode, see Harlan and Daniel, "A Dark and
Stormy Night in the Life of Booker T. Washington"; Harlan, *BTW,* 171-75.

From Portia Marshall Washington

Aberdeen, Miss. June 17. 1895

My Dear Father We arrived here last Thursday. I like this place
very much. It is very pretty. The people are very pleasant and nice.
There are a great many little girls here. Most of them near my age.
Alice[1] and Roscoe[2] are my cousin's they are very nice Roscoe will
come to Tuskegee to school next term. He is very full of fun. I practice my music lessons an hour every day, by the clock.

Aunt Laura's[3] store is a nice little distance from here. Nearly every
day we go up to her store. Dave always has a bag of some thing with
him evey day, which is as you know a great pleasure to him.

Alice told me tell her Uncle Booker Howdy which I will in her
name.

Several ladies have just left. I played a great many pieces for them
and they played for me.

Well papa dear have you thought any more about me going north
I have for my part decided to go.

Aunt Wille arrived here to day, she is a very sweet lady and when I first saw her I fell in love with her.

Good bye dear papa. I must go to dinner. Your loving

Portia

ALS Con. 863 BTW Papers DLC.

[1] Alice Simmons, daughter of one of Margaret Washington's sisters.
[2] Roscoe Conkling Simmons, Alice's brother.
[3] Laura Murray Donaldson, sister of Margaret Washington.

From Margaret James Murray Washington

Aberdeen Miss 6-21-'95

My Dear Booker. I meant to have written you yesterday but I did not. I had promised to speak at the Methodist church last night and all day yesterday I felt so nervous. However I got through and so many of the people, men and women, spoke to me afterwards. I spoke of the Importance of Organization for Young People. I hinted that there ought to be some public place where the young men might drop in and look over a paper a magazine &c and to day I hear the back room of one of the Colored stores is being fixed up for this purpose. I find the people so kindly disposed. The people are very fond of Laula[1] and she is just working herself down.

I have not been to Macon as yet. I first [thought] I should go to-morrow but I do not feel very well. My stomache and[2] have given me trouble ever since I came out here.

The water has a peculiar effect upon me. The children keep well and are still carried away with this town. Dave eats all of the time. None of them want to come back, but I think now that after the first week in July I will go back. I do not think that I can come to Boston. Laula is kept at the store all day and I should be afraid to leave them and then too I have so little inclination to do any thing. I will perhaps feel better after awhile.

I think it will be better for us to take the children's room next year. It is a large room, and we need a large room. I do not feel at home studying in the Library and if we take this room I can then have in it my desk which I miss so much and some of my books which are now in the Library. I think matting will be nicer for the floor. We can have some pretty rugs and pretty curtains and bring up the furniture from down stairs. And too you will be right at the bath room. Will you not like this better? Tell me. I mean to give Baker and Davidson the room Mrs Kaine had and then I can better see after them.

I had a nice letter from Mrs. McCall to day. She seems very happy over her new life.

I had to laugh at your sarcasm in reference to Fiskites. We are a poor set I guess. I wish you had time to go through the school oftener and things I am sure would be different.

I am going to write Miss Chapman soon.

Miss Jackson will be back soon. I am truly sorry. I certainly hope she will not be in the Office another year. I have not heard from Mrs. Kaine for quite awhile. I mean to write to day or tomorrow. Are you still intending to have the Assembly? I hope not. It will work you so hard. I have been practising a great deal since I came over here. Some days I practice two hours. Portia keeps her practice and Baker and Dave each have two Reading Lessons a day.

Baker wrote to Smith yesterday. It took him three hours to write four lines and then he would not send it. Write me as often as you can.

Maggie

ALS   Con. 113   BTW Papers   DLC.

¹ Laura Murray Donaldson.
² Word omitted in original.

To Warren Logan

Crawford House   Boston, 7-5-1895

Dear Mr. Logan: It will be necessary for the school to rent the house which I think you control, that was built by Calloway in Greenwood. I want to get this for the music teacher, Mr. Chas. G. Harris,¹ who will take Mr. Hamilton's place.

I have yours of the 2nd, and note what you say regarding the $100. from the Government. I am glad the matter of signing cheques has been permanently arranged. I wrote you some days ago about the $3,000.

I want to impress upon you the importance of seeing that the Dizer Fund[2] is very carefully looked after. It is Mr. Dizer's intention to make another donation in the fall, and I think he will add to it every year if he sees that it is being administered in a business-like manner. It will be far better to foreclose one or two mortgages than to lose the use of this fund which we will do if collections are not made. Just as far as possible, I hope you will also see that houses erected wholly or in part by this money, are put up in a creditable manner. It is now the plan of Mr. and Mrs. Dizer to go to Tuskegee in February largely with the view of seeing as many of these houses as possible. I am glad to hear that matters are going well.

I wish you would confer with Mr. Calloway and Mr. J. H. Washington at once, and see what is best to do regarding sending the cattle to Marshall Farm. Mr. Calloway says that we are at too great expense in keeping the cattle at the school; that they can be kept at no expense at the Marshall Farm. Yours truly,

Booker T. Washington

TLS Con. 9 BTW Papers ATT. Original destroyed.

[1] Charles G. Harris taught vocal music and choir at Tuskegee from 1895 to 1902.

[2] The Dizer Fund, established by Silas C. Dizer of Boston about 1892, granted $1,500 to the trustees of Tuskegee Institute for revolving loans to black farmers to help them buy or build homes. Tuskegee graduates and students had preference. The borrowers paid 8 percent interest. The purpose of the fund was to set examples of a "model Christian home" among the tenant shacks of the Black Belt. (Boston *Evening Transcript,* Dec. 22, 1894, 16.)

By 1895, when the Dizer Fund had been increased to $3,000, Warren Logan reported to BTW that a balance of $749.10 remained and that this amount had been pledged. Fourteen persons had been aided by the fund, seven of them in Tuskegee, two in Montgomery, and the others elsewhere in Alabama. (Logan to BTW, July 10, 1895, Con. 862, BTW Papers, DLC.)

To Emily Howland

Crawford House Boston, July 9 1895

Dear Miss Howland: I have been thinking a good deal to day about your question as to how you could best help us in case you decided to give the amount of a scholarship. Besides the permanent scholarship there is one other thing I want to put before you and you can decide between them. For more than a year I have been making an effort to fit up at Tuskegee a first class machine shop and the students have put up an excellent building for this purpose. A firm in New York that is interested in the school has agreed to let us have a first class out fit, including all kinds of iron working tools and machinery for $1300. The regular price of these tools &c is not less than $2000. We also have a first class colored machinist to take charge of this department, but I fear he will grow discouraged if we are not able soon to fit up his department so that he can do good work. There are so many students that are anxious to learn this trade. I want to push this work because young colored men who learn this trade are in demand in the South and if colored men are not fitted to fill the places foreigners will soon take the places. The additional $300 I think I could raise.

With this need supplied we would have a plant that would enable us to turn out for years a number of first class machinists every year.

I hope you will excuse the liberty I take in putting the matter before you.

Even with the few tools that he has our teacher has done jobs for white people that they themselves could not do. Yours truly

Booker T. Washington

ALS   Emily Howland Papers   NN-Sc.

From George Washington Lovejoy

Mobile, Ala. July 17th 1895

My Dear Mr. Washington: I received your letter of the 13 instant. You may be sure that if an injustice is don[e] the Tuskegee Normal and Industrial Institute and such injustice comes to my knowledge, the school will always be protected at my hands.

I watched these complaints with considerable interest. They will prove to be no more than a gust of wind. The heaviest of it has already blown over.

I have not heard of any papers attacking you and your action in the Harris matter,[1] except the Richmond Plannet and the Press news printed in Mobile by Mr. A. N. Johnson.[2]

Mr. Johnson mad[e] his onsault because he saw that Mitchael[3] had done so.

The great majority of the would be Negro leaders, are not them selves great characters and have not the power to beget the confidence of the masses, so they show their greatness in trying to tare dow[n] the reputations of other men. The people soon see them in their true colores though. I sent Mr. Logan the two papers which were printed here that said any thing about you or the Harris matter. I had a letter from Dr. S. S. H. Washington, concerning the Harris trouble, which I thought made some defense for the school authorities and so I had it printed in Johnsons paper. I dont think Johnson cares to say anything more a bout the matter. He knows that I am standing ready to defend the school. I showed Johnson your letter, but did not let him have it for print. Still I think it would knock him right out if it were given to the public. The school has a number of friends here, who cannot be turned by small blows unfounded.

The thinking people believe that Johnson acted rashly and used but very little judgement.

No paper has said so far as I know, that any white citizens had waited upon you, in regards to the schools intertain white citizens from the North.

Mr. John W. Jones[4] of Montgomery told me that such a committee had waited upon you, and that one of the teachers of the school had given him that information; but he did not remember who that teacher was.

You will remember that all successful business interprises headed by colored men, have their enimies, and too among our own race. I have nothing of which to complain in regards to myself and business.

I shall call the Alabama committee togather one day next week in the city of Montgomery to select persons as required by the commission issued by Chief Penn.

Well you are tiard of reading I will not say more. From your Friend

Geo. W. Lovejoy

ALS Con. 862 BTW Papers DLC.

[1] The Thomas A. Harris near lynching in June. (See A News Item, June 13, 1895, above.)

[2] A. N. Johnson went to Mobile in 1891 as editor of the *State Republican*. In 1894 he founded the Mobile *Weekly Press,* which he edited for many years. In 1896 he rented a hearse and became an undertaker in addition to his editing. He advertised "Finest White and Black Funeral Cars in the City, First Class Carriages for Weddings and Balls." He was active in the National Negro Business League after 1900. He was a member of the Republican state committee and was a delegate to the Republican national conventions in 1896, 1900, and 1904. In 1904 he was the "last Negro in Ala. nominated for Congress on the Regular Republican ticket." (Johnson to BTW, Dec. 6, 1904, Con. 22, BTW Papers, DLC.)

[3] John Mitchell, Jr. (1863-1929), was born a slave in Henrico County, Va. As a youth he was a carriage boy to a wealthy white lawyer who had been his owner. Mitchell attended Richmond Normal High School from 1876 to 1881. In 1884, after two years as a correspondent for the New York *Freeman,* he became editor of the Richmond *Planet* and held that position until his death. An outspoken opponent of all forms of racial discrimination, he supported BTW's ideas of self-help and business enterprise. Mitchell's editorial on June 22, 1895, suggested that Harris should have been given asylum on the Tuskegee campus and that "we shall await to hear the explanation of Prof. Washington with reference to his refusal to admit a wounded man."

[4] Presumably the same John W. Jones who wrote to BTW in 1899 warning him that John C. Leftwich was organizing a district farmers' conference, a preliminary to attracting the region's black farmers from the Tuskegee Negro Conference to Montgomery. He urged BTW to withhold from Leftwich the free federal seed packages that he usually distributed at the Tuskegee Negro Conference. (Jones to BTW, Jan. 30, 1899, Con. 156, BTW Papers, DLC.)

From Irving Garland Penn

Atlanta, Ga. Aug. 12, 1895

My Dear Friend: I quote from the minutes of the Com. on Negro Exhibit certain action taken by them on my recommendation. "Mr. Oglesby[1] moved that this committee recommend that Mr. Booker T. Washington, or some suitable colored man be selected to represent the colored Race in the opening ceremonies of the Exposition."

I shall push the thing. I think, though, that Gen. Lewis is privately in favor of a man here. You can imagine who that is. I shall see each member of the committee on ceremonies and ceremonial days individually. Forward this letter promptly to your Madam I send in your care. Hope you are well. When am I to see you? Yours faithfully,

I. Garland Penn
Chief Negro Dept.

HLS Con. 863 BTW Papers DLC. "Dictated."

¹ J. G. Oglesby was one of the five members of the Committee on the Colored Exhibit. He was a white wholesale grocer in Atlanta.

From Irving Garland Penn

Atlanta, Ga. Aug 19th 1895

My Dear Friend: Your favor of the 17th is to hand. I am working on the matter for all it is worth. The latest dodge is by President Collier suggesting that we have a separate dedicatory exercise of the Negro Building and asking me to consider the same. I shall insist upon your name on the principal programme and shall either get you or a point blank refusal, then it *may be* that I will take to the dedication business. I am using for all it is worth your help to them at Washington, and the magnificent exhibit you are making here. I have many interesting things to tell when I see you. I have kept your Exhibit before the world and truth to say it has aroused considerable jealousy. I will talk with you. They cant down me. I am putting your Exhibit to the front because it is something and there is something behind it. In your next let me know exactly what date you will be here and over what road you are coming. It is possible that I may have to be in Virginia for a day or so during the first week in September. I send you a number of tags and clips for shipping. Good work at Wetumpka. I am very glad to see it. Governor Bullock a very good friend of the Committee on Ceremonies and Ceremonial Days is in New York. I have written him urging that he write to President Collier in your interest. Faithfully yours

I. Garland Penn
Chief Negro Dept.

HLS Con. 863 BTW Papers DLC. "Dictated."

From Irving Garland Penn

Atlanta Ga   Aug 23 1895

Congratulations   You are the Orator   see Constitution[1] and letter
sent

I Garland Penn

HWSr   Con. 863   BTW Papers   DLC.   Addressed to Crawford House, Boston.

[1] The Atlanta *Constitution* announced that "A Colored Orator Has Been Invited to Participate in the Opening." The article presented the rationale of the
exposition board of directors. They stated that from its inception the exposition
sought "to include in all features the interests of the negroes." BTW was chosen
because of his "strong personality" and "his eloquence and ability." BTW's lobbying effort in May 1894 also impressed the board. C. A. Evans, chairman of the
Committee on the Negro Exhibit, said "I was in Washington at the time the committee went on in behalf of the appropriation, and I saw the good work done by
Booker Washington. I heard his speech, which was clear, forceful and logical. He
is an able man, and his speech on that occasion struck us all as being one of the
best we had heard for a long while." (Atlanta *Constitution,* Aug. 23, 1895, 9.)

From Irving Garland Penn

Atlanta, Ga. Aug 23/1895

My Dear Friend: Accept congratulations and I feel congratulated my
self over the success of our fight. We have verily fought a *good fight*.
You are the man. I will stand by my friends everytime. For four days
I have zealously worked with every member of the committee and
many members of the Board that things might come allright. I am
as happy as ever you dared be. It is a surprizing recognition and one
deservedly bestowed. I want to see you to give you a hearty shake of
the hand. For my part you know I am all smiles. I have written Jesse
Lawson[1] of the Colored American by this mail to give you good notice
in next weeks issue of the Colored American[2] and have written to the
Chicago people to send your cut to Washington. I have also written

the Chicago Appeal to use your cut since they are going to get out a special edition on next week. Lets hear from you. Yours faithfully

I. Garland Penn
Chief Negro Dept.

ALS Con. 863 BTW Papers DLC.

¹ Jesse Lawson was born in Charles County, Maryland, in 1856 and was a graduate of Howard University and Howard Law School. He was employed at the Bureau of Pensions in Washington, D.C., from 1882 to 1926, rising from janitor to legal examiner. In 1884 he was a delegate to the Republican national convention. He was counsel for John M. Langston in his contest for seating in the House of Representatives in 1889. Lawson was also a sociologist and was founder and president of the National Sociological Society. He was editor of the Washington *Colored American* from 1893 to 1897, and served as one of the national commissioners of the Atlanta Exposition in 1895. As chairman of the legal committee of the Afro-American Council, he worked closely with BTW in court cases involving the grandfather clause and segregated transportation.

² See A News Item, Aug. 31, 1895, below.

From Charles A. Collier

Atlanta, Ga. August, 24th, 1895

Dear sir: I have the honor to notify you that [at] a Meeting of the Board of Directors of the Cotton States & International Exposition held on Thursday, August, 22nd., it was voted to direct the President to extend an invitation to you to participate in the Opening Exercises of the Exposition on the Opening Day, as one of the Speakers, especially to present the Negro Exhibit, and directing that a part of the Auditorium be set apart for the use of the Colored People.

I most cordially extend the invitation, and trust that you will consent to accept the duty and serve on that day, in furtherance of the intentions and plans of the Exposition Management to make the Colored Exhibit a grand success.

The indications are ample to show the Exhibit will be worthy of the occasion. Hoping to have a prompt reply, Very truly yours,

C. A. Collier

TLS Con. 862 BTW Papers DLC.

An Invitation

[Atlanta, Ga., ca. Aug. 24, 1895]

[*Seal*]

The Board of Directors
requests the honour of the presence of
Prest. B. T. Washington
at the
Opening Ceremonies
of the
Cotton States and International Exposition,
Wednesday, September the eighteenth, 1895.
Atlanta, Georgia.

PD   Con. 863   BTW Papers   DLC.

An Admission Card

[Atlanta, Ga., ca. Aug. 24, 1895]

Complimentary

[*Seal*]   Opening Ceremonies
of the
Cotton States and International Exposition,
Wednesday, September the eighteenth, 1895,
Atlanta, Georgia.
Admit *Prest. B. T. Washington.*

C. A. Collier
President & Director General

PDSr   Con. 862   BTW Papers   DLC.

571

A News Item from the Washington *Colored American*

[Washington, D.C., Aug. 31, 1895]

RACE RECOGNITION

The Cotton States and International Exposition Company has shown a disposition all along to treat the colored brother with that consideration which his worth deserves. It has given him just what he has been asking for since emancipation, namely, an opportunity to show what he is capable of doing. The South has taken a long stride ahead of the North in recognizing the Negro in the formalities of opening day at the exposition. Prof. Booker T. Washington of the Tuskegee Institute has been selected by the Board of Control to speak in the regular exercises on opening day. That is ahead of anything that was done for us either at the Centennial in Philadelphia, in 1876, or at the great Columbian Exposition in Chicago, in 1893. At the other expositions, above referred to, Congress made large appropriations for their maintenance, but it all went to the white man, for his glory and his advancement. The Atlanta Exposition people had to raise their own funds, and they have done more for the Negro out of their private funds than has been done by the Nation out of the money of tax payers.

Hereafter in counting the true friends of the Negro, we must not forget to mention the names of Collier, Lewis, Kontz and Alex Smith, the faithful officers of the Exposition Company.

The Exposition will open on the 18th of September, and every colored woman, man and child who can possibly get there ought to go, if for no other reason than to hold up the hands of Prof. Washington, as the children of Israel held up the arms of Moses while he fought the battles of the Lord.

Washington *Colored American,* Aug. 31, 1895, 4.

To Charles A. Collier

Tuskegee, Ala. Sept. 3, 1895

Dear Sir: I am in receipt of your valued communication informing me that your Board of Directors have requested you to invite me to deliver an address in connection with the opening exercises of the Exposition, September 18th. Allow me to say in reply that I appreciate the honor of this invitation, not so much in a personal sense, but in the recognition of the race.

In accepting the invitation I beg to assure you and your Board of Directors that the colored people of this country will not forget the generosity with which, as a race, they have been treated at every stage of the progress of the Exposition.

It will be my aim to make my remarks of service to the Exposition — especially the colored department — and to both races in the South.

Thanking you for the honor, I am, Yours respectfully,

[Booker T. Washington]

TL Copy   Con. 863   BTW Papers   DLC.

From Julius Sterling Morton[1]

Washington, D.C. September 5, 1895

Dear Sir: You are hereby authorized to make investigations on the nutritive value and economy of human foods in the State of Alabama, which shall include dietary studies and statistics of food supply and consumption of negroes, in accordance with directions to be given you by Prof. W. O. Atwater, Special Agent of this Department in charge of nutrition investigations, for which you will be paid a sum not to exceed $250, all work to be completed and reported in form for publication not later than June 30, 1896, to be paid for out of the funds appropriated for nutrition investigations for the fiscal year ending June 30, 1896, and payment to be made in two instalments at the discretion of the Director of the Office of Experiment Stations. Respectfully,

J. Sterling Morton
Secretary

TLS Con. 863 BTW Papers DLC. Written on stationery of the U.S. Department of Agriculture.

[1] Julius Sterling Morton (1832-1902) was Secretary of Agriculture under President Grover Cleveland. Though he had founded Arbor Day in Nebraska in the 1870s, as an advocate of governmental economy Secretary Morton halted during his term the free distribution of seeds by congressmen to farmers.

To Emily Howland

Tuskegee, Ala. Sept 6, 95

Dear Miss Howland: I thank you very much for your note regarding the Atlanta speaking. It was a great surprise to me as it has been to the colored people in general to receive such an invitation. No one had dared dream that the Directors would invite a colored man to deliver an address in connection with the main programme and from the same stand as the white speakers. Had your letter not come I should not have been led to emphasize the dignity of labor so much as I now have in mind to do.

While the appointment brings an honor to the race, to me personally it brings a serious responsibility. We are expecting the machinery in a few days, though some of the larger pieces are delayed — more time being required to get them ready. You will have a letter soon from Mrs. Washington.

We plan as soon as we can make proper conveniences to put some of our girls into the dairy to learn that industry. In some parts of Europe many girls earn their living at this industry. We decided yesterday to give a larger number of girls the opportunity to learn printing and tailoring.

We shall hope to see you at Tuskegee before the winter closes. Yours Sincerely

Booker T. Washington

ALS   Emily Howland Papers   NN-Sc.

From Robert Charles Bedford

Rockton Ill   Sep 6 1895

Dear Prof   I send a few names this morning. The item about Mohonk Col[1] has appeared in Outlook and Inter Ocean so far. Have not seen other papers yet. I think of you as opening of school draws near also Exposition. Hope you may be at your best on that great day.[2] You have my prayers and sympathy. I know God will be with you and help you. I saw Mrs Mary Holmes of Shopiere Wis yesterday. She is

83 years old. She assured me she had the school mentioned in her will. The sum will not be large.

Will send frequent lists of names. Yours

R C Bedford

ALS Con. 862 BTW Papers DLC.

¹ Attached to the letter was a clipping: "Mr. Albert K. Smiley, proprietor of the Lake Mohawk Mountain House, invited Booker T. Washington to speak to his guests the evening of Aug. 26. The result was a collection of $1,100 for Tuskegee, the largest ever taken by Mr. Washington."

² Bedford wrote BTW again the next day: "I think the matter of your speaking at the opening of the Exposition is one of the greatest land marks in the history of freedom. It will receive universal comment on both sides [of] the sea." (Bedford to BTW, Sept. 7, 1895, Con. 862, BTW Papers, DLC.)

From Irving Garland Penn

Atlanta, Ga. Sept. 9th 1895

My Dear Friend: Your favors to hand and contents noted. I have sent out a letter in this mail to leading newspapers seeking to correct the impression that you speak on the Opening of the Negro Building. Our Colored people are not used to a big thing like this and hence they have got the thing twisted, and yet, I sent to those very papers — such as Freeman and Colored American myself and gave them to know of the recognition, asking them to use your Cut etc. I send you clippings bearing both on the Negro Exhibit and yourself. Some I have marked with blue pencil (V) thus — for your special and most careful reading. They are suggestive. Return the clippings when you have done. Concerning points that you may refer to. At your request permit me to say that first — These white people ought to be commended for their concessions to the Negro, and yet be made to know that they could not get along without him, for instance, it was Negro influence that secured the National Application. Thus it might be shown that the races are in the South to help each other etc. The officers in general and particularly Collier, Lewis and Committee on Negro Exhibit, should be liberally complimented. The Committee on Negro Exhibit is (see pamphlet sent by this mail). I should think you might refer only to the general character of the Exhibit and not single out any except as you may feel disposed. If any are singled out, better refer to Negro inventions. "See Inventive Age" "I send by this mail." An impression as to why we make our exhibit, and what we expect from it is very necessary. "See thoughts marked in paper of July 28th, sent you by this mail." Plead for kind treatment of the Negro and little friction during the Exposition etc. I will mail you on Wednesday a Copy of the article I have prepared for the Constitution which will give you the Exposition side of this exhibit and also the Negro side of it. By reading it over it may be suggestive. It is the article which will appear on the 18th. Send me three or four photos of yourself. The last one sent me has gone to the World. The one I now have the Constitution will use. Send me four or five. I will need them as I am called upon. You should have some one here *at once* to look after the Alabama State exhibit. It should be *going up. How many Carpenters can you send up here if needed?* Reply to these later queries at once. I am run down almost. Yours truly

> I. Garland Penn
> Chief Negro Dept.

HLS Con. 863 BTW Papers DLC. "Dictated."

From Irving Garland Penn

Atlanta, Ga. Sept. 9 1895

Prof. B. T. Washington: Your favor to hand of the 6th. I have turned in with my approval the application for $50.00 and have asked about it this morning. The people at the main office have just simply not gotten to it. They will reach it to day. I have urged them. It will be forthcoming.

On matter of invitation of persons in Atlanta and Georgia will talk with Lewis on his return to morrow and act. Hurriedly Yours.

> I. Garland Penn

Hope you will have something definite concerning our personal matter upon which we may talk when we see each other. I am anxious about it. I can go for other Expositions but dont think now I care to, certainly not for this money. Yrs

> Penn

The Colored Military of Atlanta will be in regular line to escort you and Chief Negro Dept and Commissioners who may be in the city. We are trying to do the thing *up brown.*

ALS Con. 863 BTW Papers DLC.

From Gustavus Richard Glenn[1]

Atlanta, Ga., Sept 10th, 1895

My Dear Sir: I desire to recommend to our Legislature some changes in regard to the industrial education of the negroes in Georgia. I should be very glad to have from you any statement which in your judgment will be helpful to me in this matter. We are doing next to nothing in the way of industrial education for the Negro Race, and I believe that we should revise our whole system, as it affects him. So, I will thank you very much for any plans that you have operated successfully in your school. Asking your prompt attention, I am Yours very truly,

G. R. Glenn
State School Commissioner

TLS Con. 862 BTW Papers DLC.

[1] Gustavus Richard Glenn (1848-1939), born in Jackson County, Ga., was president of Columbus Female College in Georgia from 1875 until its destruction by fire in 1884. He was a professor at Wesleyan College, Macon, Ga., 1884-94, Georgia state school commissioner 1895-1903, and president of North Georgia Agricultural College in Dahlonega for many years after 1904. He was one of the most progressive of the southern state school commissioners, writing and speaking eloquently in support of better schooling for both races. He met increasing frustration and opposition from legislators in his efforts to increase school expenditures.

From William Henry Baldwin, Jr.

Atlanta. September 17, 1895

Dear Sir: I have your note of the 14th with reference to Harper's Weekly article.[1] I am not at all ashamed of it. I am convinced that the work you are doing at Tuskegee is exactly right, and that it is doing a large amount of good for the colored people as well as for the whole south. I shall hope to see you when you are here in Atlanta, and I am delighted to know that you are to represent the colored people in the address at the opening of the Exposition. Yours truly,

W H Baldwin Jr

TLSr Con. 862 BTW Papers DLC. Written on stationery of the Southern Railway Company, Washington, D.C.

[1] *Harper's Weekly,* 39 (Sept. 14, 1895), 876-79. The article, by John Gilmer Speed, entitled "The Tuskegee Plan," was a favorable account of the work of Tuskegee, including twenty illustrations of students at work and other scenes. The article mentioned Baldwin as a trustee of the school.

The Manuscript Version of the Atlanta Exposition Address

[Atlanta, Ga.] September 18, 1895

Mr. President and Gen[t]lemen of the Board of Directors:[1]

One ~~haf~~ half[2] of the population of the South is of the Negro race. No enterprise seeking the ~~civil~~ material, civil or moral welfare of this section can disregard this element of our population and reach the highest success. I but convey to you, ~~the sentiment~~ Mr. President ~~and gentleman of the Board~~ and Directors, the sentiment of the masses of my race, when I say that in no way has the value and man hood of my race,[3] been more fittingly and generously recognized than by the managers of this magnificent exposition at every stage of its progress. It is a recognition which will do more to cement the friendship of the two race[s] than any occur[r]ence since the dawn of our freedom.

Not only this but the opportunity here afforded will awaken among us a new era of industrial progress. Ignorant and inexperienced it is not strange that in the first years of our new life we began at the top instead of the bottom, that a seat in congress or the State legislature was ~~most~~ more sought than real estate or industrial skill, that the poli[ti]cal convention, or stump speaking had more attractions than starting a dai[r]y farm or truck garden.

A ship lost at sea for many days suddenly sighted a friendly vessell. From the mast of the unfortunate vessell was seen the signal: "Water." "Water — we die of thirst." The answer from the friendly vessell at once came back, "cast down your bucket where you are." A second time the signal, "water water, send us water" ran up from the distressed vessel and was answered "Cast down your bucket where you are" and a third and fourth signal for water was answered "cast down your bucket where you are." The captain of the distressed vessell at last heeding the injunction cast down his bucket and came up full of fresh sparkling water from the mouth of the Amazon River. To those of my race who seek to depend on bettering their condition in a foreign land, or feel the importance who underestimate the importance of cultivating friendly relations with the Southern white man who is their next door neighbor, I would say cast down your bucket where you are. Cast it down making friends in every manly way of the people of all races by whom we are surrounded. Cast it down in agriculture, in mechanics, in commerce, in domestic service and in the professions, and in this connection it is well to bear in mind that whatever other sins the South may be called upon to bear, that when it comes

Not away from Race.[4]

to business pure and simple, it is in the South that the Negro is given a man's chance in the business[5] world and in nothing is this exposition more eloquent than in emphasizing this chance. Our greatest danger is, that in the great leap from slavery to freedom we may over look the fact that the masses of us are to live by the production of our hands and fail to keep in mind that we shall prosper in proportion as we learn to dignify and glorify common labor and put brains and skill into the common occupations of life — No race can prosper till it learns that there is as much dignity in tilling a field as in writing a poem. shall prosper in proportion as we learn to draw the line between the superficial and the substantial, the ornamental gew gaws of life and the useful. No race can prosper till it learns that there is as much dignity in tilling a field as in writing a poem. It is at the bottom of life we must begin at and not at the top. We should not permit our grie[va]nces to over shadow our opportunities.

To those of the white race who look to the incoming of those of foreign birth and strange tongue and habits for the prosperity of the South, were I permitted, I would repeat what I say to my own race: "Cast down your bucket where you are." Cast it down among these

8,000,000 Negroes whose habits you know, whose loyalty[6] and love you have tested in days when to have proved treacher[o]us meant the ruin of your fire sides. Cast down your bucket among these people who have[7] tilled your fields, cleared your fore[s]ts, builded your Rail roads and your cities and ~~made possible~~ brought forth treasures from the bowels of the earth — and helped you make possible this magnificent representation of the progress of the South. Casting down your bucket among my people, helping and encouraging them as you are doing on these grounds, and to education of head, hand and heart, you will find that they will buy your surplus land make blossom the waste places in your fields, and run your factories. While doing this you can be sure in the future as you have been in the past, that you and your families will be surrounded by the most patient, humble[8] and faithful and law abiding ~~people~~ and unresentful people that the world has ~~ever~~ seen. As we have proved our loyalty to you in the past, in nursing your children, watching by the sick bed ~~side~~ of your mothers and fathers and often following them with tear dim[m]ed eyes to their graves, so in the future ~~we shall~~ in our humble way we shall stand by you, ~~ready if need linking our interests to yours be to lay down our lives if need be in~~ with a devotion that no for[e]igner can appr[o]ach ~~linking our interests to yours~~, ready to lay down our lives if need be in defense of yours, interlacing our industrial, commercial ~~life moral religious~~ civil ~~with yours~~ and r[e]ligious life with yours in a way that shall make the interests of both races one. In all things that are purely social we can be as separ[a]te as the fingers yet one as the hand in all that pertains to our mutual interests.[9] If any where there are efforts tending to curtail the fullest growth of the Negro, let these efforts be turned into stimulating, encouraging, and making the Negro the most useful and intelligent citizen and effort or means so invested will pay a thousand per cent interest. These efforts will be twice blessed — ~~it will &c.~~ "Blessing him that gives and him that takes."

There is no escape through law of man or God, from the inevitable:

> "The laws of changeless justice bind
> Oppressor with oppressed
> And close as sin [and] suffering joined
> We march to fate abreast."

Many many millions of hands[10] will aid you pulling the load upwards or they will pull against you the load downwards. We shall constitute one half[11] of the ignorance and crime of the South or one half[12] its intelligence and progress; we shall contribute one half[13] to the business and industrial prosperity of the South, or we shall prove a veritable body of death, stagnating depressing, retarding every effort to advance the body politic.

———

Here in the heart of Georgia, ~~the home~~ where Sherman and ——— fought and where lived Tombs and Stevens, and ~~Grady and~~ Brown and Grady — the example of fair play to the Negro has been set that all the world should copy.[14]

———

My friends: In the name of my race As you witness[15] our humble effort at an exhibition of our progress you must not expect over much, starting 30 years ago with ownership here and there ~~of~~ in a few quilts, and punkins and chickens (gathered from various[16] sources,) remember the path that has led us from these to the ~~production~~ invention and production of agricultural implements, buggies steam engines, news papers, books, statuary, carving, paintings, the ma[na]gement of drug stores and banks, has not been trodden without contact with thorns and thistles.

~~Thanks for help out of your little and~~ While we take just pride in ~~the in the success the~~ what we exhibit as a result of our own independent efforts, we do not for a moment forget that our part in this exhibition would fall far short ~~but for the (A.M.A. Slater)~~ of your expectations but for the constant help that has come to our educational life not only from the Southern States ~~themselves,~~ but especially from Northern philanthropists who have made their gifts a constant stream of blessing and encouragement. The wisest among my race understand that the agitation of questions of social equal[it]y is the extremest folly and ~~The wisest among my race understand~~ that progress in the enjoyment of all the privileges that will come to us, must be the result of severe and constant struggle, rather than of artificial forcing. No race that has anything to contribute to the markets of the world is long in any degree ost[r]asized. It is important and right that all the privileges of law be ours, but it is vastly more impor[ta]nt that we be prepared for the exercise of these privileges. The op[p]ortunity to earn a dollar in a factory ~~is worth in~~ just now is worth infinitely more than the opportunity to spend a dollar in an opera House.

In conclusion, may I repeat that nothing in thirty years has given us more hope and encouragement and nothing has drawn us so near to you of the white race as the opportunity offered by this exposition, and here bending as it were over the altar that represents the results of the struggles of your race and mine, both starting practically em[p]ty handed 3 decades ago, I pledge to you effort[17] to work out the great and intricate problem which God in his has laid at the doors of the South, you shall have at all times the patient, sympathetic help of [my] race, only let this be constantly in mind, that while from in these buildings[18] and on these grounds, the products of field, of forest, of mine, of factory, letters and arts, much good will come to us, yet far above and beyond these material benefits, will be that higher good, that let us pray God will come, in a blotting out of sectional differences, and racial animosities[19] and suspicions, in a determination to administer absolute justice, in a willing obedience among all classes to the mandates of law. This, coupled with our material prosperity, will bring into our beloved South a new heaven and a new earth.

AMf President's Office ATT. The autograph version presented here, by courtesy of Dr. Luther H. Foster, seems to be the most authentic, and the deleted passages seem to suggest something of BTW's thinking as he prepared the address. A typescript of the address and an early pamphlet printing of it are in Con. 955, BTW Papers, DLC. It has, of course, been widely reprinted in documentary publications. It appeared in full in both of BTW's autobiographies. (See above, 1:73-76, 330-34.)

[1] A comparison of this autograph version and the standard printed version in *Up from Slavery* shows some discrepancies or modifications. In the standard version, "and Citizens" was added here.

[2] Changed to "one-third" in the standard version.

[3] In the standard version, "my race" was changed to "the American Negro."

[4] Apparently this phrase was intended as a subhead or a note to himself.

[5] In the standard version, "commercial."

[6] In the standard version, "fidelity."

[7] In the standard version, BTW significantly added here "without strikes and labour wars."

[8] The word "humble" was omitted in the standard version.

[9] In the standard version, "all that pertains to our mutual interests" was changed to "all things essential to mutual progress." He then added another sentence to begin a new paragraph: "There is no defense or security for any of us except in the highest intelligence and development of all."

BTW may have borrowed the phrase "separate as the fingers" from a speech of Rutherford B. Hayes at the twelfth anniversary of Hampton Institute, May 20, 1880. Ex-President Hayes said: "We would not undertake to violate the laws of nature, we do not wish to change the purpose of God in making these differences of nature. We are willing to have these elements of our population separate as the fingers are, but we require to see them united for every good work, for national defense, one, as the hand. And that good work Hampton is doing." In May 1880 BTW was a teacher at Hampton Institute. (See Sinkler, *The Racial Attitudes of American Presidents,* 168.) In 1885 BTW used a similar expression in a letter to the Montgomery *Advertiser* urging equal railroad accommodations. He wrote: "We can be as separate as the fingers, yet one as the hand for maintaining the right." (See above, 2:273.)

[10] The standard version reads: "Nearly sixteen millions of hands."

[11] In the standard version, "one-third and more."

[12] In the standard version, "one-third."

[13] In the standard version, "one-third."

[14] None of this paragraph appears in the standard version. The names of Robert Toombs and Alexander H. Stephens are misspelled.

[15] In place of this opening passage of the paragraph, the standard version reads: "Gentlemen of the Exposition, as we present to you. . . .'"

[16] In the standard version, the more coy word "miscellaneous."

[17] In the standard version, "to you effort" was changed to "that in your effort."

[18] In the standard version the phrase reads: "from representations in these buildings."

[19] The autograph version ends here on its tenth page. Probably an eleventh page has been lost. The remainder of the document is taken from the standard version.

The Standard Printed Version of the Atlanta Exposition Address[1]

[Atlanta, Ga., Sept. 18, 1895]

Mr. President and Gentlemen of the Board of Directors and Citizens: One-third of the population of the South is of the Negro race. No enterprise seeking the material, civil, or moral welfare of this section can disregard this element of our population and reach the highest success. I but convey to you, Mr. President and Directors, the sentiment of the masses of my race when I say that in no way have the value and manhood of the American Negro been more fittingly and generously recognized than by the managers of this magnificent Exposition at every stage of its progress. It is a recognition that will do more to cement the friendship of the two races than any occurrence since the dawn of our freedom.

Not only this, but the opportunity here afforded will awaken among us a new era of industrial progress. Ignorant and inexperienced, it is not strange that in the first years of our new life we began at the top instead of at the bottom; that a seat in Congress or the state legislature was more sought than real estate or industrial skill; that the political convention or stump speaking had more attractions than starting a dairy farm or truck garden.

A ship lost at sea for many days suddenly sighted a friendly vessel. From the mast of the unfortunate vessel was seen a signal, "Water, water; we die of thirst!" The answer from the friendly vessel at once came back, "Cast down your bucket where you are." A second time the signal, "Water, water; send us water!" ran up from the distressed vessel, and was answered, "Cast down your bucket where you are." And a third and fourth signal for water was answered, "Cast down your bucket where you are." The captain of the distressed vessel, at last heeding the injunction, cast down his bucket, and it came up full of fresh, sparkling water from the mouth of the Amazon River. To those of my race who depend on bettering their condition in a foreign land or who underestimate the importance of cultivating friendly relations with the Southern white man, who is their next-door neighbour, I would say: "Cast down your bucket where you are" — cast it down in making friends in every manly way of the people of all races by whom we are surrounded.

Cast it down in agriculture, mechanics, in commerce, in domestic service, and in the professions. And in this connection it is well to bear in mind that whatever other sins the South may be called to bear, when it comes to business, pure and simple, it is in the South that the Negro is given a man's chance in the commercial world, and in nothing is this Exposition more eloquent than in emphasizing this chance. Our greatest danger is that in the great leap from slavery to freedom we may overlook the fact that the masses of us are to live by the productions of our hands, and fail to keep in mind that we shall prosper in proportion as we learn to dignify and glorify common labour, and put brains and skill into the common occupations of life; shall prosper in proportion as we learn to draw the line between the superficial and the substantial, the ornamental gewgaws of life and the useful. No race can prosper till it learns that there is as much dignity in tilling a field as in writing a poem. It is at the bottom of life we must begin, and not at the top. Nor should we permit our grievances to overshadow our opportunities.

To those of the white race who look to the incoming of those of foreign birth and strange tongue and habits for the prosperity of the South, were I permitted I would repeat what I say to my own race,

"Cast down your bucket where you are." Cast it down among the eight millions of Negroes whose habits you know, whose fidelity and love you have tested in days when to have proved treacherous meant the ruin of your firesides. Cast down your bucket among these people who have, without strikes and labour wars, tilled your fields, cleared your forests, builded your railroads and cities, and brought forth treasures from the bowels of the earth, and helped make possible this magnificent representation of the progress of the South. Casting down your bucket among my people, helping and encouraging them as you are doing on these grounds, and to education of head, hand, and heart, you will find that they will buy your surplus land, make blossom the waste places in your fields, and run your factories. While doing this, you can be sure in the future, as in the past, that you and your families will be surrounded by the most patient, faithful, law-abiding, and unresentful people that the world has seen. As we have proved our loyalty to you in the past, in nursing your children, watching by the sick-bed of your mothers and fathers, and often following them with tear-dimmed eyes to their graves, so in the future, in our humble way, we shall stand by you with a devotion that no foreigner can approach, ready to lay down our lives, if need be, in defense of yours, interlacing our industrial, commercial, civil, and religious life with yours in a way that shall make the interests of both races one. In all things that are purely social we can be as separate as the fingers, yet one as the hand in all things essential to mutual progress.

There is no defense or security for any of us except in the highest intelligence and development of all. If anywhere there are efforts tending to curtail the fullest growth of the Negro, let these efforts be turned into stimulating, encouraging, and making him the most useful and intelligent citizen. Effort or means so invested will pay a thousand per cent interest. These efforts will be twice blessed — "blessing him that gives and him that takes."

There is no escape through law of man or God from the inevitable: —

> "The laws of changeless justice bind
> Oppressor with oppressed;
> And close as sin and suffering joined
> We march to fate abreast."

Nearly sixteen millions of hands will aid you in pulling the load upward, or they will pull against you the load downward. We shall constitute one-third and more of the ignorance and crime of the South, or one-third its intelligence and progress; we shall contribute one-third to the business and industrial prosperity of the South, or we shall prove a veritable body of death, stagnating, depressing, retarding every effort to advance the body politic.

Gentlemen of the Exposition, as we present to you our humble effort at an exhibition of our progress, you must not expect overmuch. Starting thirty years ago with ownership here and there in a few quilts and pumpkins and chickens (gathered from miscellaneous sources), remember the path that has led from these to the inventions and production of agricultural implements, buggies, steam-engines, newspapers, books, statuary, carving, paintings, the management of drug stores and banks, has not been trodden without contact with thorns and thistles. While we take pride in what we exhibit as a result of our independent efforts, we do not for a moment forget that our part in this exhibition would fall far short of your expectations but for the constant help that has come to our educational life, not only from the Southern states, but especially from Northern philanthropists, who have made their gifts a constant stream of blessing and encouragement.

The wisest among my race understand that the agitation of questions of social equality is the extremest folly, and that progress in the enjoyment of all the privileges that will come to us must be the result of severe and constant struggle rather than of artificial forcing. No race that has anything to contribute to the markets of the world is long in any degree ostracized. It is important and right that all privileges of the law be ours, but it is vastly more important that we be prepared for the exercise of these privileges. The opportunity to earn a dollar in a factory just now is worth infinitely more than the opportunity to spend a dollar in an opera-house.

In conclusion, may I repeat that nothing in thirty years has given us more hope and encouragement, and drawn us so near to you of the white race, as this opportunity offered by the Exposition; and here bending, as it were, over the altar that represents the results of the struggles of your race and mine, both starting practically empty-handed three decades ago, I pledge that in your effort to work out the great and intricate problem which God has laid at the doors of the South, you shall have at all times the patient, sympathetic help of my race; only let this be constantly in mind, that, while from representations in these buildings of the product of field, of forest, of mine, of factory, letters, and art, much good will come, yet far above and beyond material benefits will be that higher good, that, let us pray God, will come, in a blotting out of sectional differences and racial animosities and suspicions, in a determination to administer absolute justice, in a willing obedience among all classes to the mandates of law. This, coupled with our material prosperity, will bring into our beloved South a new heaven and a new earth.

Up from Slavery, above, 1:330-34.

[1] An account of the delivery and reception of the speech is in Harlan, *BTW*, 214-21.

ADDENDUM

To Darwin W. Esmond[1]

Malden W.Va. Sept. 13th 1879

Mr. Esmond: I learn through Miss Mary Mackie that I am indebted to you for your kindness in securing law-books for me.

My greatest difficulty since I began the study of law[2] has been the want of books.

The books that you secured for me will be very valuable helps to me, and I feel very grateful to you for your kindness.

I have been receiving instruction this summer from a white lawyer,[3] but not very regularly.

I expect to go to Hampton in two weeks, where I shall teach this year. I think I shall have a very good oportunity to study there. I think. Any help that you can give me there will be gladly received. The advice that you wrote to me a year or two ago has been very va[l]uable to me.

With many thanks, I am   Yours truly

B. T. Washington

ALS   In possession of M. A. Harris, New York City.

[1] Darwin W. Esmond (ca. 1846–ca. 1922) was a lawyer in Newburgh, N.Y.

[2] On BTW's study of the law, see above, 1:26, 391. While a student at Hampton Institute he expressed to Nathalie Lord, one of his teachers, his desire to be a lawyer. She arranged for him to study law under a teacher who had had legal training. (Lord, "Booker Washington's School Days," 257-58.)

[3] Romeo Hoyt Freer (1845-1913) was born in Trumbull County, Ohio. He attended Oberlin for one year. In 1861 he volunteered in the Union Army and served until the end of the Civil War. Settling in Charleston, W.Va., he taught school for two years, read law, and was admitted to the bar in 1868. An eloquent

public speaker, he took an active part in local Republican politics. BTW may have heard him speak at a celebration of the ratification of the Fifteenth Amendment in Charleston by the black people of Kanawha County in the spring of 1870. (Charleston *West Virginia Journal,* May 18, 1870, 2.) In 1868-70 he was prosecuting attorney for Fayette and Boone counties, and assistant prosecutor for Kanawha County. In 1870-72 he was prosecuting attorney for Kanawha County. In the election of 1872 Freer was a member of the Kanawha County Republican Executive Committee. His work for the Grant ticket won him appointment in 1872 as U.S. consul in Nicaragua for four years. Returning to Charleston, he formed a partnership with H. C. McWhorter, later a state supreme court justice, and forged ahead as a criminal lawyer. He was counsel for Rufus Estep and John Dawson, accused of murder, who were taken from jail and lynched in 1876 after Freer pleaded unsuccessfully for a change of venue. Moving to Harrisville in 1882, he held a succession of offices there, legislator, county prosecutor, circuit judge, congressman, state attorney general, and finally, from 1901 to 1913, postmaster of Harrisville. A brigadier general in the National Guard, a leader in the G.A.R., and an intense Republican, he took part in every campaign for forty years.

Ex-Governor William A. MacCorkle later recalled of BTW's study under Romeo Freer: "Freer was a Republican lawyer at Charleston, and Washington did not study law in his office as was currently reported. Freer loaned him books and examined him on the law which he had studied during the week at his home." (MacCorkle, *Recollections of Fifty Years,* 569-70.)

BIBLIOGRAPHY

THIS BIBLIOGRAPHY gives fuller information on works cited in the annotations and endnotes. It is not intended to be comprehensive of works on the subjects dealt with in the volume or of works consulted in the process of annotation.

Alabama. *Acts of the General Assembly of Alabama, Passed by the Session of 1892-93.* Montgomery, 1893.

——. *Biennial Report of the Superintendent of Education of the State of Alabama for the Scholastic Years Ending September 30, 1894.* Montgomery: Brown Printing Co., 1894.

Alabama State Teachers' Association. *Minutes of the Eleventh Annual Session, Held at Birmingham, Ala., June 8th, 9th, and 10th, 1892.* Tuskegee: Normal School Press, 1893.

Aler, F. Vernon. *Aler's History of Martinsburg and Berkeley County West Virginia.* Hagerstown, Md.: Mail Publishing Co., 1888.

Bond, Horace Mann. *Negro Education in Alabama: A Study in Cotton and Steel.* New York: Octagon Books, 1969.

Broderick, Francis L. *W. E. B. Du Bois: Negro Leadership in a Time of Crisis.* Stanford: Stanford University Press, 1959.

Burgess, Larry E. "We'll Discuss It at Mohonk," *Quaker History,* 60 (Spring 1971), 14-28.

Cooper, Walter G. *The Cotton States and International Exposition and South, Illustrated.* Atlanta: Illustrator Co., 1896.

Dabney, Charles W. *Universal Education in the South.* 2 vols. Chapel Hill: University of North Carolina Press, 1936.

Daniel, Pete. *The Shadow of Slavery: Peonage in the South, 1901-1969.* Urbana: University of Illinois Press, 1972.

Du Bois, William Edward Burghardt. *The Autobiography of W. E. B. Du Bois: A Soliloquy on Viewing My Life from the Last Decade of Its First Century.* New York: International Publishers, 1968.

Garrett, Franklin M. *Atlanta and Environs: A Chronicle of Its People and Events.* 2 vols. Athens: University of Georgia Press, 1969.

Harlan, Louis R. *Booker T. Washington: The Making of a Black Leader, 1856-1901.* New York: Oxford University Press, 1972.

————. "The Secret Life of Booker T. Washington," *Journal of Southern History,* 37 (Aug. 1971), 393-416.

————, and Pete Daniel. "A Dark and Stormy Night in the Life of Booker T. Washington," University of Maryland *Graduate School Chronicle,* 3 (Feb. 1970), 4-7; reprinted in *Negro History Bulletin,* 33 (Nov. 1970), 159-61.

Holmes, William F. "Whitecapping: Agrarian Violence in Mississippi, 1902-1906," *Journal of Southern History,* 35 (May 1969), 165-84.

Kellogg, Charles Flint. *NAACP: A History of the National Association for the Advancement of Colored People, 1909-1920.* Baltimore: Johns Hopkins Press, 1967.

Lord, Nathalie. "Booker Washington's School Days at Hampton," *Southern Workman,* 31 (May 1902), 255-59.

Lynch, Hollis Ralph. *Edward Wilmot Blyden: Pan-Negro Patriot, 1832-1912.* New York: Oxford University Press, 1970.

MacCorkle, William Alexander. *The Recollections of Fifty Years of West Virginia.* New York: G. P. Putnam's Sons, 1928.

Meier, August. *Negro Thought in America, 1880-1915: Racial Ideologies in the Age of Booker T. Washington.* Ann Arbor: University of Michigan Press, 1963.

Moton, Robert Russa. *What the Negro Thinks.* Garden City, N.Y.: Doubleday, Doran, & Co., Inc., 1929.

Read, Florence Matilda. *The Story of Spelman College.* Princeton: Princeton University Press, 1961.

Redkey, Edwin S. *Black Exodus: Black Nationalist and Back-to-Africa Movements, 1890-1910.* New Haven: Yale University Press, 1969.

Rose, Willie Lee. *Rehearsal for Reconstruction: The Port Royal Experiment.* Indianapolis: Bobbs-Merrill Co., Inc., 1964.

Rudwick, Elliott M. *W. E. B. Du Bois: A Study in Minority Group Leadership.* Philadelphia: University of Pennsylvania Press, 1960.

Sinkler, George. *The Racial Attitudes of American Presidents: From Abraham Lincoln to Theodore Roosevelt.* Garden City, N.Y.: Doubleday & Co., Inc., 1971.

Spear, Allan H. *Black Chicago: The Making of a Negro Ghetto, 1890-1920.* Chicago: University of Chicago Press, 1967.

Sweat, Edward F. "Francis L. Cardoza: Profile of Integrity in Reconstruction Politics," *Journal of Negro History,* 46 (Oct. 1961), 217-32.

Tindall, George B. *South Carolina Negroes, 1877-1900.* Columbia: University of South Carolina Press, 1952.

Trayser, Donald G. *Barnstable: Three Centuries of a Cape Cod Town.* Hyannis, Mass.: F. B. and F. P. Goss, 1939.

Wharton, Vernon Lane. *The Negro in Mississippi, 1865-1890.* Chapel Hill: University of North Carolina Press, 1947.

Women's National Indian Association, Annual Report. Philadelphia: J. A. Wilbur Printing House, 1891.

INDEX

(1902-6); Turner, John Orman
(1894-98)
Albert, Aristide E. P., 119, *120
Alcorn, James Lusk, 358
Alcorn Agricultural and Mechanical
College (Miss.), 177, 357, *358, 522,
528, 530; BTW declines offer of
presidency, 418-19; Thomas J. Callo-
way on presidency, 415-16
Alcott, Louisa May, 48
Alexander, John, 558-60
Alexander, Robert, 306
Alger, Cyrus, 194
Allain, Theophile Tarence, *96-97, 155-
56
Allain, Theophile Tarence, Jr., 96, *97
Allen, Griffin Anderson, 419, *420, 421
Allen, Julia Crudine. *See* May, Julia
Crudine Allen
Allen University (S.C.), 256, 458
All Souls Church (Chicago), 506
A.M.E. Church Review, 113, 166, 219
American Anti-Slavery Society, 67, 68
American Baptist Foreign Missionary
Society, 4
American Board of Commissioners for
Foreign Missions, 42
American Economic Association, 408
American Federation of Labor, 366
American Freedmen's Union Commis-
sion, 43
American Historical Association, 408
American Historical Review, 408
American Home Economics Association,
470
American Hospital for Seamen (Hono-
lulu), 212
American Israelite, 412
American Missionary, 69
American Missionary Association, 43,
53, 78, 118, 279, 325, 581; BTW
evaluates, 158, 280; officers and
members of, 43, 69, 168, 221, 296-97,
344, 529; officers visit Tuskegee In-
stitute, 220
American Negro Academy: members
of, 108, 517
American Tract Society, 334, 342, 344,
*348
American Unitarian Association, 51,
356, 357

Amherst College (Mass.): alumni of,
168, 349, 506
Amorous, Martin, 461, *462
Anderson, Charles W., 455
Anderson, W. C., 336
Anderson School, 55
Andover Theological Seminary (Mass.),
73; alumni of, 42, 53
Anthony, Susan Brownell, 23
Anti-Caste, 33, *34
Anti-lynching campaign. *See* Lynching
Anti-Semitism: BTW accused of, 412.
See also Jews
Apache Indians: education of, 127-28;
prisoners at Mt. Vernon Barracks,
Ala., 128, 133
Arena, 46
Armistead, John M., 11, *12
Armour, Philip Danforth, 505
Armour Institute (Chicago), 502, 505
Armstrong, Mary Alice Ford (Mrs.
Samuel Chapman), 61, 336
Armstrong, Samuel Chapman, 34, 40,
133, 212, 277-78, 304, 332, 343, 344,
347, 350, 385, 398, 428, 439, 440,
483, 522, 547, 552; at Lake Mohonk
Negro Conference, 60, 61; attitudes
of whites toward, 319, 320-21; BTW
on significance of, 322-24; BTW
praises, 199-201; BTW speaks at
memorial service of, 317-21; endorses
T. Thomas Fortune as minister to
Haiti, 153-54; favors Hawaiian annexation, 290; health of, 54, 195, 201,
290; influence on black education,
317-24; influence on Tuskegee Institute, 313, 317-21, 529; last visit to
Tuskegee, 290, 291-94, 295, 303;
letters from, 12-13, 216, 290; letters
to, 4, 5, 10-11, 21-22, 36-37, 62-63,
65, 126, 127, 151-52, 219-21, 312-13;
offers to help Tuskegee, 290; recognition by delegates of Tuskegee Negro
Conference, 298; recommends BTW,
10-11, 174; second marriage of, 61;
speaks at Tuskegee Negro Conference,
295, 296
Armstrong Hall, 542
"As separate as the fingers," 580, 585;
origin of phrase, 582-83. *See also*
Atlanta Exposition address